THE POLITICS OF JUDICIAL CO-OPERATION IN THE EU

The European legal order is largely based on judicial co-operation between the European Court of Justice and the national courts. In this book, three case studies on Sunday trading, on equal treatment of men and women and on good faith in contract law reveal that national courts and national litigants are mainly pursuing national interests by means of European law. The European Court of Justice seeks European solutions by delimiting the scope of the European legal order, by transforming the subjective rights of market citizens into political rights of union citizens, and by developing European remedies to enforce European rights. Micklitz contributes to the debate on the role and function of the preliminary reference procedure in the making of EU law, and does so on the basis of concrete examples. He offers an original analysis of the limits of the European legal order, and of the role and function of subjective rights and European remedies.

HANS-W. MICKLITZ is Jean Monnet Professor of Private and European Economic Law at the University of Bamberg, and Head of the Institute of European and Consumer Law (VIEW) in Berlin. He was a Fellow of the European University Institute, Florence, Italy, and visiting Professor at the University of Michigan, Ann Arbor, and at Somerville College, University of Oxford. He has published very widely in the areas of European and consumer law.

THE POLITICS OF JUDICIAL CO-OPERATION IN THE EU

Sunday Trading, Equal Treatment and Good Faith

HANS-W. MICKLITZ
University of Bamberg

CAMBRIDGE
UNIVERSITY PRESS

CAMBRIDGE UNIVERSITY PRESS
Cambridge, New York, Melbourne, Madrid, Cape Town, Singapore, São Paulo

Cambridge University Press
The Edinburgh Building, Cambridge CB2 2RU, UK

Published in the United States of America by Cambridge University Press, New York

www.cambridge.org
Information on this title: www.cambridge.org/9780521825160

First published 2005

Printed in the United Kingdom at the University Press, Cambridge

A catalogue record for this book is available from the British Library

ISBN-13 978-0-521-82516-0 hardback
ISBN-10 0-521-82516-4 hardback

In memoriam Ch. R. and H.-J. M.

CONTENTS

FIGURES

TABLES

PREFACE AND ACKNOWLEDGMENTS

While I have attempted in this book to consider, as a whole, the co-operation between the English courts and the European courts, it is nevertheless clear that there are limits to the scope of the research that I have undertaken. My views of the English law will always remain those of a German lawyer who was not educated in the common law system and who is not fully familiar with all its nuances and implications. The reader, it is hoped, will accept my apologies for missing those nuances but will nevertheless benefit from an outsider's view of the English legal system.

The project could not have been undertaken without the help and support of many people. I would like to thank first and foremost Stephen Weatherill, Professor of Law at the University of Oxford, for his invitation to join Somerville College. I would also like to thank the following persons for their substantial input into my research: Paul Gurowich of the Office of Fair Trading; Francis F. B. Reynolds, Professor of Law at the University of Oxford; Lord Hoffmann; Harriet Hall, legal adviser at the National Consumer Council; Arthur Hugh Vaughan QC, barrister; Michael Beloff QC, barrister; Lord Goff of Chieveley; Stuart Isaacs QC, barrister; Tony Askham, solicitor; Eileen Brennan, legal adviser at the Consumers' Association; Advocate-General Walter van Gerven; Paul Diamond, solicitor; Pauline Matthews of the Equal Opportunities Commission; Brian Bercusson, Professor of Law at the University of Manchester; and the anonymous referees who read the manuscript of this book. I also thank Andrea Wechsler for her time, energy and ideas in assisting me to reconstruct the Sunday trading litigation.

Last but not least, I would like to thank the Volkswagen Foundation which made the execution of the project possible, and Professor Dr Hagen Hof for his help and advice whenever it was needed.

TABLE OF CASES

TABLE OF TREATIES

TABLE OF EC DIRECTIVES

TABLE OF STATUTES

TABLE OF STATUTORY INSTRUMENTS

ABBREVIATIONS

AC	*Appeal Cases*
ALJR	*Australian Law Journal Reports*
All ER	*All England Law Reports*
AuR	*Arbeit und Recht*
BGB	*Bürgerliches Gesetzbuch*
BLR	*Building Law Reports*
CJ	Chief Justice
CLC	*Commercial Law Cases*
CMLR	*Common Market Law Reports*
ConLR	*Construction Law Reports*
Const LJ	*Construction Law Journal*
CPD	Common Pleas Division
DTI	Department of Trade and Industry
ECJ	European Court of Justice
ECR	*European Court Reports*
EGLR	*Estates Gazette Law Reports*
EHRR	*European Human Rights Reports*
EMLR	*Entertainment and Media Law Reports*
EOC	Equal Opportunities Commission
EuZW	*Europäische Zeitschrift für Wirtschaftsrecht*
FLR	*Family Law Reports*
FSR	*Fleet Street Reports*
ICR	*Industrial Cases Reports*
IRLR	*Industrial Relations Law Reports*
IStR	*Internationales Steuerrecht*
JZ	*Juristenzeitung*
KB	*King's Bench*
KritV	*Kritische Vierteljahresschrift für Gesetzgebung und Rechtswissenschaft*
KSSC	Keep Sunday Special Campaign
LC	Lord Chancellor

LGR	*Local Government Reports*
LJ	Lord Justice
LJJ	Lord Justices
MP	Member of Parliament
MR	Master of the Rolls
NGO	non-governmental organisation
NJW	*Neue Juristische Wochenschrift*
OFT	Office of Fair Trading
OJ	*Official Journal of the European Communities*
QB	*Queen's Bench*
QC	Queen's Counsel
RabelsZ	*Rabels Zeitschrift für ausländisches und internationales Privatrecht*
RIW	*Recht der Internationalen Wirtschaft*
RUC	Royal Ulster Constabulary
SC	*Session Cases*
SI	Statutory Instrument
SJ	*Solicitors' Journal*
SLT	*Scots Law Times*
TLR	*Times Law Reports*
Tr LR	*Trading Law Reports*
UCTA	Unfair Contract Terms Act 1977
UTCCR	Unfair Terms in Consumer Contract Regulations
VR	*Victoria Reports*
VuR	*Verbraucher und Recht*
WLR	*Weekly Law Reports*
ZEuP	*Zeitschrift für Europäisches Privatrecht*
ZEuS	*Zeitschrift für Europarechtliche Studien*
ZGR	*Zeitschrift für Unternehmens- und Gesellschaftsrecht*

1

Judicial activism and legal politics

The purpose of this book

In legal literature, only a handful of books and articles endure for more than a relatively short period of time. Most are overtaken by the ever-growing volume of more recent literature, and are forgotten. In the area of law of interest to us here, two publications in particular deserve to be remembered. The first is Eric Stein's article, 'Lawyers, Judges and the Making of a Transnational Constitution', published in the *American Journal of International Law* in 1981. The second is Joel F. Handler's book, *Social Movements and the Legal System: A Theory of Law Reform and Social Change*, published in 1978. I had the privilege of meeting Professor Stein while I was a visiting professor at Michigan Law School. I took the opportunity of discussing with him the unique role of the European Court of Justice (ECJ) in transforming an international treaty system into a constitutional framework. I never met Professor Handler, but his book remains an impressive analysis of the use of rights and remedies in the US courts to establish civil rights, to establish environmental protection and to improve consumer protection.

These two publications formed the basis for my habilitation on an 'International Product Safety Law', in which I attempted to set out a theory on an 'International Constitution for the Trade in Dangerous Products'. Here, I tested the judge-made EU constitution as a basis for action in the international arena. However, a stumbling block in my reasoning quickly became apparent: the fragile legitimacy of an international order in which lawyers and judges step beyond the boundaries of market freedoms and engage in matters of social policy and social change. Fritz W. Scharpf's article, 'Joint Decision Trap: Lessons from German Federation and European Integration', published in *Public Administration* in 1988, foretold the now all-too-apparent struggle between law and politics in the future constitution of Europe.

Since then, my academic interests have revolved around three issues:[1] the judge-made EU legal order; the role and function of social movements in using the ECJ for social change; and (though to a lesser extent) the legitimacy and accountability of the ECJ's leading role in European integration (I say 'to a lesser extent' because political scientists do not devote enough attention to the role of law,[2] or, should I say, to the rule of law?). If politics prevail over law, the outcome could well be that the European Union (or, legally speaking, the European Community) would 'face a rapid process of dilution and would soon be transformed into one of the many international organisations which rub along more or less effectively according to the changing interests of the contracting states'.[3] I will not hide my admiration for the wisdom of judges and their sense of 'realism and passion' in building the EU legal order,[4] while I equally admit the moral right, even the necessity, to raise the question of legitimacy.

The scenario for judicial activism and legal politics

The preliminary reference procedure under Article 234 (ex Article 177) of the EC Treaty brings together (1) national courts and the ECJ, (2) the social movements in the Member States and the EU as legal players and (3) issues of the legitimacy of judge-made law. Therefore, it goes without saying that the preliminary reference procedure lies at the heart of my academic interests. While there is a rich literature on the preliminary reference procedure, I sought in vain for the answers to three questions:

(1) What is the role and function of individual and/or collective litigants in achieving market freedoms and/or in implementing social change in, for example, sex discrimination, environmental protection and consumer protection? The relative lack of research

[1] 'Principles of Social Justice in European Private Law' (1999/2000) 19 *Yearbook of European Law* 167.

[2] Cf. K. Armstrong, 'Legal Integration: Theorizing the Legal Dimension of European Integration' (1998) 36 *Journal of Common Market Studies* 155.

[3] Here, I am slightly twisting the wording of Mancini and Keeling's eminent analysis of the ECJ's politics. In analysing *Costa* v. *ENEL* and *van Gend en Loos*, they demonstrate that the ECJ's intention was to shield the European Community against precisely such a danger. See G. F. Mancini and D. T. Keeling, 'Language, Culture and Politics in the Life of the European Court of Justice' (1995) 1 *Columbia Journal of European Law* 397.

[4] Again, these are words used by Mancini and Keeling.

in this area may be due to the more state-focused perspective of the literature on European law, in contrast to the position in the United States where litigation is a substantial and legitimate element in implementing economic and social rights.[5] This is what I term the 'Joel Handler-type of question', or, in other words, the role and importance of organised law-enforcement in the EU.

(2) The Article 234 preliminary reference procedure has been used to establish the European legal order, mainly in order to guarantee the operation of the *common market*. Key issues here include the use of market freedoms, and the use of negative rights, to remove statutory barriers to trade and to remove outmoded and outdated manifestations of national decision-making in order to achieve market integration.[6] However, it is by no means clear to what extent the Article 234 preliminary reference procedure is equally apt to realise the *internal market*, a concept which goes beyond mere market freedoms and strives for the implementation of a market in which social policy has a place.[7] Positive rights in the hands of private individuals or public interest groups are necessary in order to ensure the implementation of, for example, equal treatment, environmental protection and consumer protection, and in order to enforce market regulation. If these rights exist, and if the courts are willing to enforce them, then the legitimacy issue becomes a central issue. The position is even more complex with regard to the role and function of Article 234 in private law issues: can the preliminary reference procedure be equally used to establish a European private legal order? Analysis of the role and function of the Article 234 preliminary reference procedure is therefore needed at three levels: at the level of the common market; at the level of the internal market; and at the level of the European private legal order.

(3) The Article 234 preliminary reference procedure is initiated by litigants in the national courts of the Member States. We know that the courts of the Member States make use of the procedure to

[5] See H.-W. Micklitz and N. Reich (eds.), *Public Interest Litigation in European Courts* (Baden-Baden, 1996).

[6] S. Weatherill, 'Pre-emption, Harmonization and the Distribution of Competences to Regulate the Internal Market' in S. Barnard and J. Scott (eds.), *The Law of the Single European Market* (Oxford, 2002), 42.

[7] See C. Kilpatrick, T. Novitz and P. Skidmore, *The Future of Remedies in Europe* (Oxford, 2000).

varying degrees. However, we do not know *why* the courts of certain Member States bring certain issues before the ECJ. This forms the third question. This third question is based on the hypothesis that each and every Member State makes a unique contribution to the building of the European legal order by means of the preliminary reference procedure.

Limitations on and pre-conditions to this study

My analysis starts from the premise that the Article 234 preliminary reference procedure is the key to building a European legal order. However, the analysis will include a consideration of judicial co-operation between the national courts of the Member States and the ECJ, of how and why rights and remedies are used by individual and collective litigants, and, last but not least, of whether and to what extent the solutions found by the courts are legally and politically 'legitimated'. Therefore, an analysis of the interplay between judicial co-operation, organised law-enforcement and legal-political legitimacy will need to consider the questions not just of pure market freedoms, but also of the 'Europeanisation' of social policies and national private legal orders. And, if possible, the question of the contribution of the Member States will have to be assessed. All these questions boil down to the question simply of how far the law reaches, and/or whether the issue is more correctly one of politics. Ideally, the book can be read as a contribution to the European integration process, or, more ambitiously, to European constitution-building from the bottom up.

I will not be able, however, to provide answers to all the questions raised. I hope, though, to be able to shed light on unresolved issues. In order for the analysis to be constrained to manageable proportions, I will first set the book in the context of a stream of research in order to make clear the current state-of-the-art and the sorts of gap that may be filled by the analysis undertaken here. Therefore, I will set out the basics of the European legal order, and the importance and reach of direct effect and supremacy in the common market, the internal market and the European private legal order. Against this background, it will then be possible to fit the analysis into the current state of research on judicial co-operation, organised law-enforcement and the legal-political legitimacy of the judge-made legal order. The 'common market', the 'internal market' and the 'European private legal order' are terms which will have to be dissected in order to establish precisely what they mean. The overall idea is to link the common market to the notion of 'freedom', the internal market to the notion of 'equality' and the European private legal order to the notion of 'justice'. Again, these are broad categories and deserve even greater attention.[8] For the purposes of this book, however, I will not enter into a legal-philosophical debate, but rather will use these terms in a pragmatic way.

The issues then remaining are more technical in nature, though they are nevertheless of considerable importance to the analysis undertaken here. I will need to demonstrate why I have selected the United Kingdom in order to establish the hypothesis of a genuine national input into the Article 234 preliminary reference procedure. Last but not least, I will need to explain why I have chosen the Sunday trading, equal treatment and good faith issues as my field of research, and the methodology I have used. This is particularly necessary as the book relies heavily on case studies as an appropriate research method to provide answers to the theoretical issues on which the whole book rests. Once I have explained the reasons for my choices, I hope this will stimulate the reader to read the three case studies and the conclusions at the end of the book in order to decide for himself whether I have provided answers to these issues.

The basics of the European legal order

An overview

The European legal order rests on the doctrines of direct effect[9] and supremacy.[10] The Single European Act transformed the 'common market' into the 'internal market', thereby shifting the focus from market freedoms to the integration of social policies. The process is reflected in the ECJ's notion of the European legal order, which is now understood as a 'constitutional charter'.[11] Table 1.1 highlights the ongoing European integration process and the legal-political difficulties which result from the growing intrusion of EC law into the arena of social policy and private law matters. The table highlights why particular fields of research were chosen: the Sunday trading cases are a striking

[8] Most recently J. Rawls, *Justice as Fairness* (Cambridge, 2001).

[9] Judgment of 5 February 1963, Case 26/62, *van Gend en Loos* [1963] ECR 1.

[10] Judgment of 15 July 1964, Case 6/64, *Costa* v. *ENEL* [1964] ECR 1251.

[11] Judgment of 25 February 1988, Case 249/83, *Les Verts-Parti Ecologiste* v. *Parlement* [1988] ECR 1017.

Table 1.1 *The European integration programme and its legal-political difficulties*

	Common market	Internal market	Private legal order
	Market freedoms	Social policies	Consumer protection
	Arts. 28 and 48	Art. 141 and the equality Directives	Art. 153 and the Directives on consumer protection
			Part of social policy and part of private legal order
Supremacy	+/+ (plus/plus)[a]	+/− (plus/minus)	−/− (minus/minus)
	Stable	Unstable	Under attack
Horizontal direct effect	Horizontal effect of Art. 48	Horizontal effect of Art. 141	Horizontal effect of Art. 153 (?)
	No horizontal effect of Art. 28	No horizontal effect of the equality Directives	No horizontal effect of the consumer protection Directives
Vertical direct effect	Vertical direct effect of Art. 28	Vertical direct effect of Directives	Vertical direct effect of Directives
Statutory liability	Claim for compensation if Art. 28 is violated (*Brasserie du Pêcheur*)	Claim for compensation in case of non- or incomplete implementation (*Francovich*)	Claim for compensation in case of non- or incomplete implementation (*Dillenkofer*)

[a] + means 'strong'; double ++ means 'very strong'; − means 'weak'; and −/− means 'very weak'.

example of the realisation of market freedoms; the equal treatment cases are the prime example of the reach of EU social policy in labour law; and the good faith cases are the prime example of private law being affected by European law.

The vertical/horizontal dimension of the European legal order

The two constituent elements of the European legal order, direct effect and supremacy, were developed in the early 1960s at a time when the ECJ was establishing the European legal order for a *common market*. The focus therefore was on the market freedoms, in particular on removing barriers to trade which discriminated against imports. The prime example of such a case was *Van Gend en Loos.*[12] Private parties were given the right to invoke Article 28 (ex Article 30) against a Member State's legislation in order to remove unlawful barriers to trade. These rights may be considered as negative rights, as they are designed to eliminate barriers to trade and to enlarge market freedoms. *Costa* v. *ENEL*[13] expressly established what was implicit in *Van Gend en Loos*, that is, the supremacy of EC law over national law. For more than two decades, the ECJ developed the European legal order by granting direct effect to various Articles of the EC Treaty, mainly those designed to establish the common market. Typically, the parties to this type of litigation were private individuals suing their own Member State. This type of case involved the *vertical* effect of EC law.

The decisive step forward, the true shift away from a market-focused European legal order, came with the adoption of the Single European Act. The Single European Act transformed the *common market* into the *internal market*, thereby focusing on the necessary integration of social policies. This process is reflected in the ECJ's notion of the European legal order, which is now understood as a 'constitutional charter'.[14] The implicit message here is that the internal market can be completed only by establishing social standards for EU citizens. Social policies therefore became part of the EC Treaty, indirectly in Article 95 (ex Article 100a) and directly in integrating health and safety at work as well as environmental protection. Consumer protection followed suit in the Maastricht Treaty (Article 153 (ex Article 129a)). This does not, however, mean that the original Treaty of Rome and

[12] Judgment of 5 February 1963, Case 26/62, *van Gend en Loos* [1963] ECR 1.
[13] Judgment of 15 July 1964, Case 6/64, *Costa* v. *ENEL* [1964] ECR 1251.
[14] Judgment of 25 February 1988, Case 249/83, *Les Verts-Parti Ecologiste* v. *Parlement* [1988] ECR 1017.

the secondary law adopted under the unanimity rule of Article 94 (ex Article 100) have been restricted to realising the market freedoms alone. The two equality Directives, Directives 75/117/EEC and 76/207/EEC, as well as early consumer protection Directives on product liability (Directive 85/374/EEC) and doorstep selling (Directive 85/577/EEC) provide evidence of an emerging European legal order under which sex discrimination could not be permitted to remain and in which the consumer was beginning to be shaped into the powerful figure that he would eventually become in the internal market.

The traditional means of giving shape to social policy objectives, as laid down in the EC Treaty, is by the adoption of Directives. Directives are addressed to the Member States, and therefore substantive rights can *prima facie* only emerge once the Directives are implemented in national law. The two constituent elements, direct effect and supremacy, could not be applied 'as is' to the early social elements of the common market nor to the more ambitious elements of the internal market. However, as early as 1974, the ECJ held in *van Duyn*[15] that, in certain circumstances, provisions of Directives not yet implemented in national law may be relied on by private individuals. The ECJ went on to grant vertical direct effect[16] to a number of Directives. However, it declined to grant horizontal direct effect to Directives. That is why the 'constitutional charter' remains incomplete, despite the efforts of Advocate-General Lenz in *Faccini Dori*[17] to justify the granting of horizontal direct effect to Directive 85/577/EEC on doorstep selling. The famous *Francovich* doctrine,[18] as confirmed in *Dillenkofer*,[19] and the EU conformist interpretation of national law,[20] were meant to compensate for any remaining deficiencies caused by the lack of horizontal enforcement of Directives. The ECJ used the same type of thinking to close the gap resulting from the lack of direct effect of Article 28.

[15] Judgment of 4 December 1974, Case 41/74, *Van Duyn* v. *Home Office* [1974] ECR 1337.

[16] Judgment of 26 February 1986, Case 152/84, *Marshall* v. *Southampton and South West Hampshire Area Health Authority* [1986] ECR 723 (*Marshall I*); Judgment of 14 July 1994, Case C-91/92, *Faccini Dori* [1994] ECR I-3342.

[17] Advocate-General Lenz' conclusions, 9 February 1994, Case C-91/92, *Faccini Dori* [1994] ECR I-3342, paras. 67–73.

[18] Judgment of 19 November 1991, Cases C-6 and 9/90, *Francovich and Bonifaci* v. *Italy* [1991] ECR I-5357.

[19] Judgment of 8 October 1996, Case C-178/94, *Dillenkofer* [1996] ECR I-4845.

[20] Judgment of 13 November 1990, Case C-106/89, *Marleasing* v. *La Comercial Internacional de Alimentacion* [1990] ECR I-4135.

In *Brasserie du Pêcheur*,[21] the ECJ recognised the Member State's liability to compensate private parties for damage resulting from the non-application of Article 28.

At first, it was only the *vertical* direct effect of primary and secondary EC law that was in issue. It was not until the early 1980s that the question of *horizontal* direct effect was considered. In 1981, in *Jenkins*,[22] the ECJ held that Article 141 (ex Article 119) is equally applicable in contractual relations between an employer and an employee. However, the judgment was seen by many to be limited to the area of labour law. The situation changed, however, in 1995 when, in *Bosman*,[23] the ECJ granted horizontal direct effect to Article 39 (ex Article 48). Since then, the debate over horizontal direct effect of Treaty provisions has intensified. The revised Article 153 (ex Article 129), granting a right to information, introduced in the Treaty of Amsterdam, is said to have horizontal direct effect.[24] Thus, it seems that the history of horizontal direct effect, whether of Treaty provisions or of Directives, has only just begun.

The supremacy of EC law in the area of trade is relatively well established. However, *Keck*[25] has demonstrated that there are limits to a European legal order built on direct effect and supremacy, and, today, a more sophisticated approach to the rights and responsibilities of the Member States, the market participants and the European Community is required.[26] This is particularly true with regard to supremacy in the field of social policy. The creation of social policy is a part of the core activities of the nation state. Without competence for social policy, the legitimacy of the nation state itself is challenged.[27] That is

[21] Judgment of 5 March 1996, Case 46/93, *Brasserie du Pêcheur* [1996] ECR I-1029.

[22] Judgment of 31 March 1981, Case 96/80, *Jenkins* v. *Kingsgate (Clothing Productions) Ltd* [1981] ECR 911.

[23] Judgment of 15 December 1995, Case 415/93, *Bosman* [1995] ECR I-4921.

[24] N. Reich, 'Verbraucherpolitik und Verbraucherschutz im Vertrag von Amsterdam' (1999) VuR 1 at 6.

[25] Judgment of 24 November 1993, Case C-267 and 268/91, *Keck and Mithouard* [1993] ECR I-6097.

[26] M. Maduro, *We the Court: The European Court of Justice and the European Economic Constitution* (Oxford, 1998).

[27] C. Joerges, 'Legitimationsprobleme des europäischen Wirtschaftsrechts und der Vertrag von Maastricht' in G. Brüggemeier (ed.), *Verfassungen für ein ziviles Europa* (Baden-Baden, 1993), 91; C. Joerges, 'The Europeanisation of Private Law as a Rationalisation Process and as a Contest of Legal Disciplines – An Analysis of the Directive on Unfair Contract Terms in Consumer Contracts' (1995) 3 *European Review of Private Law* 175. For a German article, see C. Joerges, 'Die Europäisierung des Privatrechts als

why the internal market project has taken the EU a long way beyond the boundaries of a mere market order. The ongoing resistance of the Member States to the ECJ's reading of Article 141 and the two equality Directives is evidence of the delicacy of EU labour law – a law which does not sit well with many national legal traditions and cultures.

There is, however, a further dimension inherent in the internal market project which has long remained hidden within the broader understanding of 'social policy', and the potential of which for conflict in the furtherance of European integration, of the building of a European legal order, based on direct effect and supremacy, becomes ever clearer. This dimension is the ever-growing number of EC private law rules,[28] with consumer protection rules being the prime example.[29] The question now therefore is whether and how a European private legal order, based on direct effect and supremacy, may be made compatible with the rules governing the legal order on market freedoms and the legal charter on social policies. EC intervention goes to the heart of a nation state's cultural and historical identity, to the very existence and availability of a genuine national private legal order.[30] The implications of the emerging European private law seem to overarch the set of principles governing social policy. EC rules do not involve Member States alone, with their responsibility for the social protection of their citizens. European private law now affects the contractual relations between private parties, and thus a European construction of contract law is now emerging.[31] Directive 93/13/EEC, on unfair terms in consumer contracts, lies at the heart of this conflict.

Rationalisierungsprozeß und als Streit der Disziplinen – Eine Analyse der Richtlinie über mißbräuchliche Klauseln in Verbraucherverträgen' (1995) ZEuP 181. However, cf. J. Basedow, 'A Common Law Contract Law for the Common Market' (1997) 33 *Common Market Law Review* 1169.

[28] There is a growing amount of research on European private law: see e.g. S. Grundmann, *Europäisches Schuldvertragsrecht* (Berlin, 1999); and S. Grundmann and J. Stuyck (eds.), *An Academic Green Paper on European Contract Law* (The Hague, London and New York, 2002).

[29] K. Tonner, 'Die Rolle des Verbraucherrechts bei der Entwicklung eines europäischen Zivilrechts' (1996) JZ 533.

[30] F. Wieacker, 'Foundation of European Legal Cultures' (1990) 38 *American Journal of Comparative Law* 1; H. Collins, 'European Private Law and the Cultural Identity of States' (1995) 3 *European Review of Private Law* 353; P. Legrand, 'European Legal Systems Are Not Converging' (1996) 45 *International and Comparative Law Quarterly* 52.

[31] S. Whittaker, 'Unfair Contract Terms, Public Services and the Construction of a European Conception of Contract' (2000) 116 *Law Quarterly Review* 95; M. Storme, 'Harmonisation of the Law on (Substantive) Validity of Contracts (Illegality and Im-

Conclusion to this part

Because the common market, the internal market and the private legal order all follow different legal patterns, and because they need to meet different legal challenges, each area must be investigated separately in order to provide a solid basis for comparison.

The three pillars of the European legal order: judicial co-operation, organised law-enforcement, and political legitimacy

The establishment of a European legal order by the ECJ is based on three major premises: (1) successful co-operation between the national courts and the European courts in the Article 234 preliminary reference procedure;[32] (2) organised law-enforcement in respect of the market participants;[33] and (3) the legal and political acceptance of the leading role of the ECJ in European integration.[34] The purpose of the analysis which follows is to set the book in the context of the current theoretical debate over the feasibility and legitimacy of a judge-made EC law, thereby demonstrating where and how the above three premises may need to be supplemented and/or reshaped.

Judicial co-operation

Joseph Weiler succeeded Eric Stein at Michigan Law School. Weiler concentrated his academic interests on the role and function of the ECJ in the integration process.[35] Judicial co-operation here is understood

morality)' in J. Basedow, K. Hopt and H. Kötz (eds.), *Festschrift für Ulrich Drobnig* (Tübingen, 1998), 195.

[32] See, in particular, M. A. Dauses, *Das Vorabentscheidungsverfahren nach Artikel 177 EG-Vertrag* (2nd edn, Munich, 1995); J. H. H. Weiler, 'The European Court of Justice and Its Interlocutors' (1994) 26 *Comparative Political Studies* 510; J. H. H. Weiler, 'Journey to an Unknown Destination: A Retrospective and Prospective of the European Court of Justice in the Arena of Political Integration' (1993) 31 *Journal of Common Market Studies* 417; A.-M. Burley and W. Mattli, 'Europe before the Court: A Political Theory of Legal Integration' (1993) 1 *International Organization* 41.

[33] H.-W. Micklitz, 'Organisierte Rechtsdurchsetzung im Binnenmarkt' (1992) KritV 172.

[34] J. H. H. Weiler, 'The Transformation of Europe' (1991) 100 *Yale Law Journal* 2403; G. Hirsch, 'Europäischer Gerichtshof und Bundesverfassungsgericht-Kooperation oder Konfrontation' (1996) NJW 2457.

[35] Weiler, 'The European Court of Justice', 510; Weiler, 'Journey to an Unknown Destination', 417.

by, among others, Slaughter, Stone Sweet and Weiler[36] as co-operation between the ECJ and the national constitutional courts. The focus is on constitution-building, and on the broad principles of direct effect and supremacy, most notably in the aftermath of the German Constitutional Court's *Maastricht* decision. The subject-matter necessarily is trade law.[37] While the courts may disagree on the reach and importance of direct effect and supremacy, co-operation will always be based on the common interests of the courts, both national and European, in European integration.

More recently, however, a new school of thought has arisen, which has been taking a closer look at the role of national courts in the co-operation process. Since the mid-1990s, researchers have been seeking answers to the questions of why judicial *dialogue* occurs, and, more narrowly, why national courts participate and why they refer cases to the ECJ. What is at the heart of this research is not so much judicial co-operation *per se* in the process of European integration, but rather the way in which national courts and the ECJ communicate, and why they communicate. That is, it is *dialogue* rather than *co-operation* which is at the heart of this recent research. The dialogue which is initiated by national courts is seen very much as driven by self-interest. Mattli and Slaughter[38] have identified three strands of national judicial interest in the dialogue with the ECJ: (1) judicial review; (2) judicial competition; and (3) the promotion of interests. Alter[39] identifies competition between the lower and higher courts in the Member States as the motor of co-operation. Both approaches are neo-functionalist in that the national courts are regarded as using the reference procedure for their own – national – purposes. The change from co-operation to dialogue, from a joint interest to a self-interest, is bound to a change in perspective. These findings result from subject-related research, in which the broad constitutional perspective of European integration is of less interest.

36 A.-M. Slaughter, A. Stone Sweet and J. H. H. Weiler (eds.), *The European Court and National Courts - Doctrine and Jurisprudence: Legal Change in Its Social Context* (Oxford, 1997).

37 See Maduro, *We the Court*.

38 W. Mattli and A.-M. Slaughter, 'Constructing the European Community Legal System from the Ground Up: The Role of Individual Litigants and National Courts' (Robert Schuman Centre, European University Institute, 1996), 56.

39 K. J. Alter, 'The European Court's Political Power' (1996) 19 *Western European Politics* 458.

This recent research has encouraged a growing debate over co-operation/dialogue. This has led to a study of judicial co-operation in context.[40] Sciarra[41] and Kilpatrick[42] both start from the idea that any hypothesis which focuses on the relationship between national courts and the ECJ will fall short of getting to grips with the true complexity of the communication process inherent in the Article 234 procedure. Both of these commentators integrate into their analyses those parties who have legal standing in the ECJ, such as the litigant and the national governments. However, they do not stop at a formal analysis of the parties who are integrated into the reference procedure. They look far beyond, and focus their attention on all those institutions and persons who stand behind litigants, such as expert witnesses, lawyers and national legislators. This theoretical concept is able to include new actors if there is a need, and/or to attribute different roles to the same institutional players. Therefore, public interest groups are not necessarily composed only of non-governmental organisations; even national courts may behave as public interest groups.[43] Kilpatrick refers to the discourse between the 'communities of the courts'; she offers a most useful analysis of the style of communication that governs the community of the courts. She identifies three types of communication: (1) same issue repetition; (2) same issue, same court repetition; and (3) persuasive repetition. Again, this sounds rather instrumental, that is, functionalist. Both dialogue and discourse research focus on particular subject-matters of EC law; in the case at hand, both Sciarra and Kilpatrick deal with European labour law, more particularly gender equality.

[40] I. Maher, 'Community Law in the National Legal Order' (1998) 36 *Journal of Common Market Studies* 237, underlines the link between existing law and social processes. Co-operation in context requires a particular social, economic and political background which unites national and European courts. Where no such context exists, co-operation might fail.

[41] S. Sciarra, 'Integration Through Courts: Article 177 as a Pre-Federal Device' in S. Sciarra (ed.), *Labour Law in the Courts: National Judges and the European Court of Justice* (Oxford, 2001), 1.

[42] C. Kilpatrick, 'Gender Equality: A Fundamental Dialogue' in S. Sciarra (ed.), *Labour Law in the Courts: National Judges and the European Court of Justice* (Oxford, 2001), 31, focusing on the interplay between German litigants, German courts and the ECJ; the same author has also considered the position of the UK in 'Community or Communities of Courts in European Integration? Sex Equality Dialogues between UK Courts and the ECJ' (1998) 4 *European Law Journal* 121.

[43] Kilpatrick, 'Gender Equality' in Sciarra (ed.), *Labour Law in the Courts*, 31 at 65.

This survey of the existing research into judicial co-operation/dialogue/discourse demonstrates the interrelationship between, on the one hand, the EU constitution, and, on the other hand, European labour law. Putting the emphasis on the national courts, and on all those who stand behind the national litigants, necessarily implies a shift away from the European integration process as such, towards differentiating between the subject-matters which are brought before the ECJ under the Article 234 procedure. Labour law and labour law litigation before the ECJ constitute a promising field of research, as the ECJ has taken a prominent role in this area of law. There seems to be a time lag of nearly two decades between the adoption of secondary community law and the emergence of a reasonable flow of European litigation. Therefore, it is not surprising that the initiative undertaken by the Max-Planck-Institut to consider the role of the Article 234 procedure in the field of European private law did not produce any startling results.[44] The rapporteurs were asked to analyse the reference procedures either in particular areas of civil law or in particular countries. Only the reports submitted by Hakenberg[45] and Hess[46] raised issues of more general concern, though without dwelling on the idea of co-operation dialogue or discourse in European private law. The reports are mostly legalistic in nature, and demonstrate that the reference procedure in traditional civil law matters is very much focused on the legal issues behind the reference procedure, thereby setting aside theories already developed on judicial co-operation.

The difficulty in the current stream of research seems to be that each discipline of law views the reference procedure only in the context of its own subject-matter. Constitutional lawyers discuss direct effect and supremacy; labour law lawyers discuss the influence on national labour law; and civil law lawyers discuss legal doctrine, that is, the disintegrative effects of EC litigation on national civil law. This may sound somewhat overstated, but it highlights where the true difficulties lie. I would suggest that constitutional lawyers alone look at the European legal order as a whole, whereas labour law and civil law lawyers look mainly

[44] The articles are published in the RabelsZ, vol. 2, issue 3, April/July 2002. They resulted from the Symposium zum 75 jährigen Bestehen des Max-Planck-Instituts für ausländisches und internationales Privatrecht in Hamburg, 17–18 September 2001, under the heading of 'Europäische Gerichtsbarkeit, Erfahrungen und Reformdiskussion im Lichte des europäischen Privatrechts'.

[45] W. Hakenberg, 'Vorabentscheidungsverfahren und europäisches Privatrecht – Erfahrungen aus europäischer Sicht' (2002) 66 RabelsZ 367.

[46] B. Hess, 'Rechtsfragen des Vorabentscheidungsverfahrens' (2002) 66 RabelsZ 470.

at their own areas of interest, that is, respectively, national labour law and civil law. The former perspective is horizontal, the latter vertical.

Organised law-enforcement

The most ambitious theoretical concept sets aside the interests behind individual and collective litigation and looks instead at the *democratic character* of the preliminary reference procedure. From such a perspective, the ECJ has paved the way for an ordinary citizen to base his or her claim on his or her rights under Community law against governmental authorities, especially at the national level. When any such right is infringed, he or she may invoke that right before a national court, which in turn may (or, if its judgment is subject to appeal, must) refer the matter to the ECJ under the preliminary reference procedure.[47] Such a reading highlights the interplay between direct effect (that is, substantive rights under the Treaty) and supremacy (that is, EC law prevails over national law) and the judicial co-operation between the referring court and the ECJ. The Article 234 procedure is democratic in that it provides the only opportunity for EU citizens to raise their voice in the European legal-political order. They have no direct access to the law-making procedure, which is governed by the Member States and the EU. Petersmann argues, with regard to the constitutionalism of international organisations, that the rights-based approach of the ECJ confirms that individuals are the best guardians and promoters of rule-oriented international co-operation.[48] The linkage between the democratic character and individual rights in courts highlights an understanding whereby legal-judicial incentives are needed to overcome political apathy and ignorance in the Member States.[49] While the ECJ rejects the horizontal direct effect of Directives, it puts more and more emphasis on the availability of remedies,[50] most recently in *Courage*.[51] The 'invention' of the European right to claim damages from the

47 Mancini and Keeling, 'Language, Culture and Politics', 397.

48 E.-U. Petersmann, 'Constitutionalism and International Organizations' (1997) 17 *Northwestern Journal of International Law and Business* 398.

49 Regarding the democratic character of judicial review in the US constitution, see E. V. Rostow, 'The Democratic Character of Judicial Review' (1952) 66 *Harvard Law Review* 193; for a view of the European context, see Burley and Mattli, 'Europe before the Court', 41.

50 For a criticism of the availability of remedies, see G. F. Mancini and D. T. Keeling, 'Democracy and the European Court of Justice' (1994) 57 *Modern Law Review* 175.

51 Judgment of 20 September 2001, Case 453/99, *Courage Ltd* v. *Crehan* [2001] ECR I-6297.

Member States for a violation of primary and secondary EC law pays tribute to the idea of the Article 234 procedure as the democratic element in the judge-made legal order.

Other research, which looks into the reasons why private litigants initiate the Article 234 procedure, can be categorised according to whether the research uses a qualitative or a quantitative approach. Both approaches, however, share the notion that judicial co-operation is litigant-driven. Stone Sweet, Brunell and Sandholtz[52] base their analysis on a quantitative, statistical breakdown of Article 234 references. They argue that individuals or groups who would benefit from supranational rules or from co-ordination in certain policy areas are the principal driving force behind European integration and the push to replace national law and practice with European law and practice in a self-sustaining logic of institutionalisation leading to a growth in activity in that policy area.[53] Such an approach is certainly helpful in identifying areas of conflict in Member States, where EC law challenges long-standing traditions and cultures, and/or where the lower courts might invoke the Article 234 procedure in order to prevent the case being referred or appealed to a higher national court. Quantitative research, however, must necessarily remain somewhat superficial, in that the methodology is not apt to explain fully the reasons behind the litigation.

Qualitative research on organised law-enforcement has been undertaken mainly in the field of labour law. *Labour Law in the Courts*, edited by Sciarra, brings together a number of research projects on the role and function of the Article 234 procedure as it is used in labour law. Of principal interest here is the research undertaken by Kilpatrick. She compared German and UK litigation before the ECJ in gender equality cases (though her choice of subject area, gender equality, necessarily makes her findings difficult to apply to other areas of social policy). She argues that the degree to which gender equality cases reach the ECJ depends on both the 'legal structuring' and the 'institutional alchemy'.[54]

[52] A. Stone Sweet, T. L. Brunell and W. Sandholtz, 'European Integration and Supranational Governance' (1997) 4 *Journal of European Public Policy* 297; A. Stone Sweet and W. Sandholtz (eds.), *European Integration and Supranational Governance* (Oxford, 1998), 92.

[53] See also A. Stone Sweet and T. L. Brunell, 'The European Court and the National Courts: A Statistical Analysis of Preliminary References' (1998) 92 *American Political Science Review* 63.

[54] Kilpatrick, 'Community or Communities of Courts', 121 at 131 and 133.

'Legal structuring' refers to the existing national legal structures in which gender equality cases are dealt with (which are assumed to be compliant with EC law), the way in which these rules are applied by national courts, and the existence of professional legal actors such as the Equal Opportunities Commission in the UK. 'Institutional alchemy' refers to the socio-economic environment in which litigation emerges as a possible option for action. Kilpatrick's findings strongly underpin the need to integrate into a theory of judicial co-operation the actors and all those who stand behind the actors, such as expert witnesses, lawyers and academics. However, Sciarra rightly points to the lack of a consistent theory on organised law-enforcement. In her view, actor self-interest lies behind a number of research projects, although this is never made explicit.[55] Litigants demonstrated an under-estimation of the role of the ECJ in equal treatment litigation. This turned into an over-estimation of the role of the ECJ once litigants discovered the potential of EC law. When those expectations were not met, the litigants rejected the value of EC law altogether. The explanation for this may be found in the lack of professionalism in certain public interest groups.

Challenging the legal and political legitimacy of a judge-made European legal order

The principal proponent in the debate over the fragile legitimacy of the judge-made European legal order is Scharpf. His book, *Governing in Europe: Effective and Democratic?*, published in 1999, is his principal critique.[56] The central hypothesis of the book is that the 'dual and inter-related processes of economic globalization and European integration' have led to a 'weakening of political legitimacy in Western Europe'.[57] He describes the scenario of the judge-made legal order in the following terms: 'By judicial fiat . . . the freedom to sell and to consume had achieved constitutional protection against the political judgment of democratically legitimized legislatures.'[58] Inherent in such a scenario is the conviction that the European legal order is not democratically legitimated, and that the Single European Act as well as the subsequent

[55] Sciarra, 'Integration Through Courts' in Sciarra (ed.), *Labour Law in the Courts*, 1.

[56] F. W. Scharpf, *Governing in Europe: Effective and Democratic?* (Oxford, 1999); see O. Gerstenberg's review, 'The New Europe: Part of the Problem – Or Part of the Solution to the Problem' (2002) 22 *Oxford Journal of Legal Studies* 565.

[57] Scharpf, *Governing in Europe*, 2. [58] *Ibid.*, 56.

amendments to the Treaty of Rome made at Maastricht and Amsterdam, which were designed to cure the market-driven legal order *politically*, did not outweigh the *legal-judicial* framework set up by the ECJ.

What does all this mean for judicial co-operation? In terms of constitution-building, the critique made by Scharpf aims at reducing the power of the (EC) judiciary and at increasing the power of the (national) executives and legislatures. Thus the legitimacy issue inevitably leads to a conflict between 'law' and 'politics'. 'Law' in this context is equated to fostering market freedoms in the EU by direct effect and supremacy, whereas 'politics' is meant to maintain and defend national democratically legitimated social policies against the intrusion of EC market freedoms. These findings seem to contradict overtly the steadily increasing importance of politics in the EU and the increasing importance of (judge-made) law. The two most recent Treaty amendments have strengthened the importance of politics. Since its 'November revolution'[59] in 1993, the ECJ is no longer willing to be or no longer – legitimately – capable of being the motor of European integration through law. As the legitimacy issue becomes increasingly important, the conflict between law and politics will deepen.

Scharpf seeks an explanation in the failure of (national) democratic politics to halt the one-sided expansion of market freedoms into areas of social welfare. He finds an explanation in the distinction between 'input' and 'output' legitimacy.[60] From the input perspective, political choices are legitimate 'if and because they can be derived from the authentic preferences of the members of a community'. From the output perspective, by contrast, political choices are legitimate 'if and because they effectively promote the common welfare of the constituency in question'.[61] Democratic self-determination requires that the choices made by a given political system be driven by the authentic preferences of the citizens. This suggests a chain of accountability linking those governing to those governed. This is input legitimacy, or *government by the people*. Here, the enduring debate over the EU's democratic deficit finds its focus. But democratic self-determination demands that those exercising political power are able to achieve a high degree of effectiveness in meeting the expectations of the

[59] N. Reich, 'The November Revolution of the European Court: Keck, Meng and Audi Revisited' (1994) 31 *Common Market Law Review* 459.

[60] Alter, 'The European Court's Political Power', 458, offers, as an additional element to the rule of law, that judges cannot be politically disciplined.

[61] Scharpf, *Governing in Europe*, 6 and 10.

governed. The democratic process, for Scharpf, is an empty ritual without such effectiveness. This is output legitimacy, or *government for the people*. Scharpf argues that too little attention is paid to the inadequacies of states when judged from the perspective of output legitimacy.

When considered in our context of judicial co-operation, input legitimacy would require a more open, transparent and democratic election of judges, an option which should be debated. Output legitimacy, according to Scharpf, requires a 'pre-existing collective identity', a 'Europe-wide policy discourse' and a 'Europe-wide institutional infrastructure that could assure political accountability to a European constituency'.[62] This sounds very much like the rationale of the German Constitutional Court's *Maastricht* decision, in which the Court denied the existence of a European people.[63] In Scharpf's perspective, output legitimacy might result from the newly developing 'Open Method of Co-ordination',[64] in which politics prevail over law and in which there is no room for the ECJ to intervene. The reactions of the EC Commission to the European Parliament's strong plea for a European Civil Code seem to strengthen Scharpf's argument. The Commission is very much looking towards new forms of legal integration above and beyond the adoption of a fully fledged European Civil Code.[65] However, these forms increase 'competence creep' and may produce even greater dissatisfaction and lack of transparency.[66]

Seen from a legal perspective, the EU could become a supranational organisation embedded in a loose legal framework. While it is clear that Scharpf is not discussing the Article 234 preliminary reference procedure, it follows from his analysis that the mechanism of

[62] *Ibid.*, 8.

[63] *Bundesverfassungsgericht*, Judgment of 12 October 1993, Entscheidungssammlung des Bundesverfassungsgerichtes, 89, 155, based on the reading given to it by J. H. H. Weiler, U. R. Haltern and F. C. Meyer, 'European Democracy and Its Critique' (1995) 18 *Western European Politics* 4.

[64] The 'Open Method of Co-ordination' is commonly described as a four-stage process: first, EU ministers agree on policy goals in the policy area concerned; secondly, the guidelines are translated by the Member States into national and regional policies with specific targets; thirdly, the ministers agree on benchmarks and indicators in order to measure and compare best practice within the EU and worldwide; fourthly, through evaluation and monitoring, Member States' performance is assessed relative to each other and to their declared goals.

[65] For a full account of recent developments, see S. Grundmann and J. Stuyck (eds.), *An Academic Green Paper on European Contract Law* (London, 2002).

[66] S. Weatherill, 'Competence Creep and Competence Control' (2004) 23 *Yearbook of European Law*, forthcoming.

the preliminary preference procedure would have to be reconsidered, because it is diagnosed as being the 'evil' responsible for direct effect and supremacy and for the dominating principle of market freedoms which prevail over social policies. The question remains of whether the European Community could survive without the 'law' tying it together. At a much more concrete level, the findings that I set out below will demonstrate that Scharpf's initial premise is flawed, that is, that the ECJ has demonstrated its commitment to a European legal order beyond the issue of market freedoms.

Legal-judicial responses to close the legitimacy gap

Commentators did not overlook the issue of the fragile legitimacy of the judge-made European legal order, which became clearer the more the integration process advanced. Commentators looked to the case law of the ECJ in order to defend the supremacy of the European legal order while maintaining the role of politics.

In a direct response to Scharpf's distinction between input and output legitimacy, Menon and Weatherill[67] argue, in light of EU trade law, that assuming either state-level legitimacy or European-level legitimacy as the necessary and appropriate basis for assessing the European Union is doubly flawed – they assume one or the other instead of accepting the contributions of both, and they tend to assume input legitimacy as a sufficient basis. Drawing on the work of Maduro, they start from the premise that national policies have two major failings: on the one hand, they cannot control decisions which are made outside their borders, and, on the other hand, national polities exclude from participation many interests which are affected by their decisions.[68]

In contrast to Scharpf's findings, the European legal order, and more particularly the ECJ, are said to have compensated for these deficiencies.[69] ECJ decisions on trade law are said to integrate out-of-state trading interests and in-state consumer interests into the national

[67] A. Menon and S. Weatherill, 'Legitimacy, Accountability, and Delegation in the European Union' in A. Arnull and D. Wincott (eds.), *Accountability and Legitimacy in the European Union* (Oxford, 2002), 113 at 128.

[68] M. P. Maduro, 'Europe and the Constitution: What If This Is As Good As It Gets?' in J. H. H. Weiler and M. Wind (eds.), *European Constitutionalism Beyond the State* (Cambridge, 2003), 74.

[69] Menon and Weatherill, 'Legitimacy, Accountability, and Delegation' in Arnull and Wincott (eds.), *Accountability and Legitimacy*, 123.

system. Therefore, the ECJ's case law asserts the democratic potential of supranational law in curing the shortcomings of state-level decisions taken in a transnational economy. The horizons of political, administrative and legal actors within the Member States are widened. While Menon and Weatherill's analysis fits well into Scharpf's framework of analysis, as it focuses on the interrelation between the ECJ, the Member States and the EU as law-makers, it is of no direct help in legitimating judicial co-operation between national courts and the ECJ. Their findings will have to be tested outside the area of EU trade law in the judicial co-operation between national courts and the ECJ.

Menon and Weatherill touch upon what has been at the core of Joerges' research for more than two decades, that is, the role of the law and the role of the judiciary and its legitimacy in European governance. Joerges started his analysis in the field of the law and economics of competition, in the so-called *Entdeckungsverfahren Wettbewerb*, that is, the competition-led discovery procedure.[70] He understands the comitology established within the 'new approach to technical harmonisation and standards' as an *Entdeckungsverfahren Praxis*, that is, as a discovery procedure *praxis* in which the Member States, the Commission and other parties interested in rule-making co-operate within a loose legal framework.[71] The research undertaken was a blueprint for his contribution to the constitutional debate on the European Community, more particularly to the debate on the concept of 'deliberative supranationalism'.[72] His most recent contribution has been his interpretation of European private law as *Entdeckungsverfahren Rechtsprechung* (that is, a discovery procedure for the judiciary).[73] This research centres around the question of whether and to what extent the law

[70] C. Joerges, 'Wettbewerbsschutz und Vertragsgerechtigkeit in den Beziehungen zwischen Automobil herstellern und -händlern: Über die Aufgaben richterlicher Rechtspolitik in "Relationierungsverträgen"' in C. Broda, E. Deutsch, H.-L. Schreiber and H.-J. Vogel (eds.), *Festschrift für Rudolf Wassermann* (Neuwied, 1985), 697. By 'competition-led discovery procedure', I am referring to the process or procedure by which one can determine, or discover, in the case at issue, the rules governing competition, etc.

[71] C. Joerges and E. Vos (eds.), *EU Committees: Social Regulation, Law and Politics* (Oxford, 1999).

[72] C. Joerges, 'Deliberative Supranationalism – Two Defences' (2002) 8 *European Law Journal* 133.

[73] C. Joerges, 'Zur Legitimität der Europäisierung des Privatrechts, Überlegungen zu einem Recht-Fertigungs-Recht für das Mehrebenensystem der EU' in C. Joerges and G. Teubner (eds.), *Rechtsverfassungsrecht – Recht-Fertigung zwischen Privatrechtsdogmatik und Gesellschaftstheorie*, Internationale Studien zur Privatrechtstheorie vol. 4 (Baden-Baden, 2003).

and the judiciary are able to govern the discovery procedure. If the judiciary oversteps the boundaries of market freedoms, it may lose its legitimacy. In Joerges' concept, direct effect and supremacy are rather fragile instruments to be used for implementing social policies in the EU. These instruments are not rejected, but are subservient to three all important *constitutional* principles: accessibility, transparency and accountability. It is for the ECJ then to give shape to these principles and to ensure that they are enforced. Just like Menon and Weatherill, Joerges points to the participatory element in the ECJ's case law. *Centros*[74] and *Überseering*[75] are therefore not simply two further steps in opening up markets, but rather offer the opportunity to EU citizens to engage in a dialogue with the Member States.

Joerges' findings are of direct importance to the analysis of judicial co-operation. In his understanding, judicial co-operation between national courts and the ECJ is just another variant of a discovery procedure for the judiciary. Its general character allows one to draw preliminary conclusions regarding the legitimacy of judicial co-operation. Judicial co-operation may be considered settled as long as the ECJ refrains from defining material standards and instead develops ground rules for the correct procedure to be followed. This book will not be able to test whether direct effect and supremacy survive in the ever more integrated EU. However, Joerges' emphasis on the legal principles which govern the discovery procedure allows us to revisit the 'subterranean cracks'[76] of the pre-*Keck* trade law in order to elaborate on what political rights EU citizens are given in the development of market freedoms and beyond.

However, there is a lacuna in both concepts, that is, in Joerges' concept on the one hand and in Menon and Weatherill's on the other. Joerges presupposes a legal understanding of political *rights*, whereas Menon and Weatherill rely on *interests* instead of rights. Reich[77] offers a perspective which aims to close that gap. His perspective has two elements. First, he derives from the recent amendments to the Treaty

[74] Judgment of 9 March 1993, Case 212/97, *Centros* [1999] ECR I-1459.

[75] Judgment of 5 November 2002, Case 208/00, *Überseering* [2002] ECR I-9919.

[76] Weiler, 'The Constitution of the Common Market Place' in P. Craig and G. de Búrca, *The Evolution of EU Law* (Oxford, 1999), 369.

[77] N. Reich, Bürgerrechte in der Europäischen Union: Subjektive Rechte von Unionsangehörigen und Drittstaatsangehörigen unter besonderer Berücksichtigung der Rechtslage nach der Rechtsprechung des EuGH und dem Vertrag von Amsterdam (Baden-Baden, 1999).

of Maastricht and the Treaty of Amsterdam a transformation from the 'EU market citizen' to the 'Union citizen'. This tallies with Joerges' understanding of EU rights as political rights. Union rights, however, are understood as subjective rights established by the ECJ. Union citizens make their voices heard through safeguarding their individual rights. Constitution-building, in Reich's terms, depends on the individual enforcement of subjective rights. A paternalistic attitude on the part of the ECJ when considering in-state consumer interests and the out-of-state interests of traders is insufficient for this purpose. Individuals may only play an active part if their interests can be conceptualised as subjective rights.

At this point, what is missing from the legal research is an analysis of the interplay between the EU *rights* and the EU *remedies* needed to meet the legitimacy challenge. The ECJ 'invented' the preliminary injunction in *Factortame* and *Zuckerfabrik Süderditmarschen*[78] and state liability in *Francovich* and *Brasserie du Pêcheur*. In *Courage* and *Sánchez*,[79] the ECJ made clear that it is willing to develop a common European concept of liability irrespective of the addressee, be it the state or a company. Only van Gerven[80] appears to have recognised the true character of an emerging European tort law. *Marshall I*[81] and *Marshall II*,[82] and more recently *Cofidis*,[83] demonstrate that a third remedy, 'sanctions', is being developed. The ECJ is evidently focusing more and more on providing 'European remedies' to enforce European rights. The use of these European remedies may prove to be a powerful means of making the European legal order effective. *Sánchez*,[84] however, is evidence that the Member States are not willing to let the ECJ continue unrestrained. To permit the ECJ to continue unrestrained could, in theory, increase

[78] Judgment of 21 February 1991, Cases C-143/88 and C-92/89, *Zuckerfabrik Süderdithmarschen* [1991] ECR I-415.

[79] At least this is *my* understanding of the true character of *Sánchez*.

[80] W. van Gerven, 'Bridging the Unbridgeable – Community and National Tort Laws after Francovich and Brasserie' (1996) 45 *International and Comparative Law Quarterly* 507; reprinted as W. van Gerven, 'Bridging the Unbridgeable – Community and National Tort Laws after Francovich and Brasserie' in H.-W. Micklitz and N. Reich (eds.), *Public Interest Litigation before European Courts* (Baden-Baden, 1996), 57.

[81] Judgment of 26 February 1986, Case 152/84, *Marshall* v. *Southampton and South West Hampshire Area Health Authority* [1986] ECR 723 (*Marshall I*).

[82] Case C-271/91, *Marshall* v. *Southampton and South West Hampshire Area Health Authority* (*Marshall II*) [1993] ECR I-4367.

[83] Case C-473/00, *Cofidis SA* v. *Fredout* [2002] ECR I-875.

[84] Council Decision, 19 December 2002, OJ 2003 No. C26, 4 February 2003, 2.

the legitimacy of the European legal order in areas beyond the market freedoms; nevertheless, it may ultimately lead to failure if the Member States refuse to accept the ECJ's rulings. As the ECJ is quite reluctant to apply the principles in concrete cases,[85] it seems as if Alter's distinction between broad legal principles and their non-application might help the ECJ to escape the legitimacy trap.

The political legitimacy of judicial co-operation in EU trade, labour and private law

To move this judicial strategy from the abstract to the concrete requires us to consider how it applies to the three major fields which lie at the heart of this book: EU trade law, EU labour law and EU private law. Here, it is not the legitimacy of judicial co-operation in constitution-building which must be analysed but the legitimacy of judicial co-operation in areas of real conflict. This necessitates a change in our perspective, to the substance of EC law in action. We need, therefore, by way of background, to look briefly at the substantive law in these three areas before our analysis can be continued.

EU trade law is *negative* law, that is, the litigation deals with the reach of the market freedoms, or, to put it another way, the litigation considers to what extent Member States may legitimately establish and maintain barriers to trade by means of administrative-economic law. In trade law, market freedoms clash with outdated manifestations of 'protectionism' pursued by Member States. In order to be permitted to remain in place, such protectionist rules must be justified by the Member States. The Sunday trading rules are a prime example of the conflict between market freedoms and protectionism. The ECJ's answer to the conflict between market freedoms and protectionism was the *Keck* case. The legitimacy debate is enshrined in the conflict between EC market freedoms, on the one hand, and the Member States' autonomy in maintaining justifiable market restrictions, on the other. In stepping back from *Dassonville*[86] and *Cassis de Dijon*,[87] the ECJ has

[85] In the aftermath of *Francovich*, see Judgment of 10 July 1997, Case 373/95, *Federica Maso* [1997] ECR I-4051; Judgment of 10 July 1997, Case C-94 and 95/95, *Bonifaci* [1997] ECR I-3969; Judgment of 10 July 1997, Case C-261/95, *Palmisani* [1997] ECR I-4025.

[86] Judgment of 11 July 1974, Case 8/74, *Dassonville* [1974] ECR 837.

[87] Judgment of 20 February 1979, Case C-120/78, *Rewe-Zentrale AG* v. *Bundesmonopolverwaltung für Branntwein* [1979] ECR 649.

built a bridge between law and politics. One may read *Keck* as a message addressed to the Member States as well as to the litigants to resolve certain types of trade law conflicts in the political arena rather than by using the law. The Sunday trading cases may easily have been the start of such a shift from law to politics.

By contrast, EU labour law and EU private law (mainly manifested as consumer law) are *positive* law. The EU sets rules at the European level to define a European standard of protection for workers and consumers. These European rules are not meant to wholly replace congruent national rules. Usually, the European rules are enacted to resolve particular problems which the Member States believe can be better dealt with at the European level (an approach which is sometimes and well described as 'pointillist'). No matter how limited these EU rules are in extent, in every preliminary reference these EU labour and private law rules will clash with national labour and private law rules. The difficulty for the ECJ is that it has to use the *incomplete* set of EU rules as a yardstick against which to judge the *complete* national legal order. Conflicts between the EU rules and the national legal orders are therefore inevitable. Any judgments of the ECJ will therefore inevitably cause friction between the ECJ and the national courts. In theory, comparative law could help to close the gaps in the EU labour and private law systems. In practice, national courts and the ECJ interact on the fragile basis of a piecemeal EC law and a coherent, consistent and complete national law.

Therefore, as Sciarra correctly says, 'diversification of national labour law systems, owing to historical reasons and to the role played by organised labour over the decades, especially in the transition to democratic regimes, adds to the uncertainty on how to build a supranational architecture'.[88] The results of such a clash are potentially harmful to the authority of the ECJ's rulings,[89] and the legitimacy of co-operation would thereby be endangered. The solution to this loss of legitimacy might be to step back from the over-ambitious aim of establishing an EC law on, for example, equal treatment and instead to define procedural ground rules in line with Joerges' theory. Hitherto, the fragile

[88] Sciarra, 'Integration Through Courts' in Sciarra (ed.), *Labour Law in the Courts*, 1.

[89] S. Sciarra, 'Dynamic Integration of National and Community Sources: the Case of Night-Work for Women' in T. K. Hervey and D. O'Keeffe (eds.), *Sex Equality Law in the European Union* (Chichester, 1996), 99; S. Sciarra, 'Job Centre: An Illustrative Example of Strategic Litigation' in S. Sciarra (ed.), *Labour Law in the Courts: National Judges and the European Court of Justice* (Oxford, 2001), 241.

basis of EU labour law has favoured a procedural conception under which claims for justice are difficult to settle.

The situation is even more difficult in European consumer law. The relevant Directives rest on national legal orders, though this is not made explicit. The Directives could be neither implemented nor enforced without a complex set of national private law rules, which have often been developed over centuries. In such a case, the legal and political acceptability of direct effect and supremacy will need to be reconsidered; this at least is the message conveyed by legal doctrine.[90] The disintegrative effects of preliminary rulings in, among other areas, consumer law have stimulated great debate.[91] This is all the more so because of the lack of even rudimentary rules of a European private law. National courts might be inclined to defend the national legal orders against disintegrative effects by simply refraining from referring relevant cases to the ECJ.[92] The result will then be an emerging body of case law which is not in accord with the rules of Community law.[93] If national courts do not change their attitude, if in practice they really do refuse to co-operate with the ECJ, then the legitimacy of judicial co-operation will be truly endangered. It may well be too early to conclude that the national courts have terminated their co-operation in private law matters, but legal doctrine overwhelmingly points to a reluctance by national courts to refer relevant private law issues to the ECJ.[94]

Conclusion to this part

These findings are of great relevance for the design of my research. First, political legitimacy in judicial co-operation is subject-related: it

[90] The debate is centring around Directive 93/13/EEC on unfair terms in consumer contracts: see W.-H. Roth, 'Generalklauseln im Europäischen Privatrecht' in J. Basedow, K. Hopt and H. Kötz (eds.), *Festschrift für Ulrich Drobnig* (Tübingen, 1998), 135; M. Franzen, *Privatrechtsangleichung durch die Europäische Gemeinschaft* (Berlin, 1999), 556.

[91] C. Joerges, 'Legislative Folgen legislativer Harmonisierung: ein komplexes Problem und ein unscheinbares Exempel' in H. Schulte-Nölke and R. Schulze (eds.), *Europäische Rechtsangleichung und nationale Privatrechte* (Baden-Baden, 1999), 205.

[92] This is the general message of all the contributions made at the Max-Planck symposium referred to in note 44 above; L. Niglia, 'The Non-Europeanisation of Private Law' (2001) 4 *European Review of Private Law* 575, rightly points to the ignorance of academics.

[93] S. Weatherill and P. Beaumont, *EU Law* (3rd edn, London, 1999), 347.

[94] This is the predominant undertone in all presentations made at the Max-Planck symposium referred to in note 44 above.

depends to a large extent on the availability of a body of EC law. In the field of trade law, the ECJ has built up a set of rules and principles which provide guidance for resolving conflicts between EU trade law and Member States' laws and regulations which have the effect of restricting the freedom of trade. Such a complex set of rules cannot be found in EU labour law, even though EU labour is much more firmly established than EU private law. Secondly, judicial co-operation is entirely bound up with the preparedness of national courts to use the preliminary reference procedure. It presupposes that national courts view the ECJ as an appropriate body to resolve conflicts between EC law and national law. Thirdly, where a reference is made, a ruling by the ECJ, even one in line with well-established EC legal standards, might nevertheless be rejected or ignored by the national courts because the decision has disintegrative effects. Therefore, particular emphasis must be put on the way in which national courts react to ECJ judgments. National courts are requested to send the implementing judgment to the ECJ. Although a database is maintained,[95] it is nevertheless rather difficult to obtain implementing decisions in the fields of research undertaken here.

Judicial co-operation, organised law-enforcement and political legitimacy; and the common market, the internal market and the private legal order

EU judge-made law is based on judicial co-operation, organised law-enforcement and political legitimacy. The discussion so far provides answers on two levels: first, on constitution-building, and, secondly, on market-building (that is, social-policy-building), in both cases by means of judge-made law. However, what is still missing from our analysis is a clarification of the three categories of the common market, the internal market and the private legal order, and of the relationship between the values of freedom, equality and justice respectively enshrined in those three categories. Clarification reaches beyond a mere stocktaking of research. This relationship is built on an *a priori* set of assumptions, which guide this book. This becomes all the more evident when the categories of the common market, the internal market and the private legal order are related to the three pillars of the judge-made law, that is, judicial co-operation, organised law-enforcement and legal and political legitimacy. Table 1.2 sets out the development of a working hypothesis.

[95] Hakenberg, 'Vorabentscheidungsverfahren', 367 n. 28.

Table 1.2 *The relationship between the European legal order, judicial cooperation and organised law-enforcement, and freedom, equality and justice*

Article 234	Freedom	Equality	Justice
European legal order	Common market Market freedoms Art. 28 freedom to trade	Internal market Social policies Art. 141 and Directives 75/117 and 76/207	Private legal order Consumer protection Art. 153 and Directive 93/13
Judicial cooperation	Well established, but *Keck*	Relatively well established, but resistance from the higher courts against lower courts	Higher courts tend to control access to ECJ, but growing self-confidence of the lower courts
Organised law-enforcement	Traders, consumers and workers as free-riders	Trade unions, women's organisations and the Equal Opportunities Commission	Public agencies and consumer organisations, individual consumers in test cases
Legal and political acceptability/ legitimacy	Widely confirmed and granted	Shaky, Treaty of Maastricht, *Barber* protocol	Widely in-existent, action-plan of the Commission on European private law
	Market freedoms guaranteed	Equality = equal access	Justice = access to justice (*Zugangsgerechtigkeit*)

The categories: market freedoms, equality and justice

The common market involves the establishment of market *freedoms*, the internal market requires *equality* in the labour market and probably social *justice* in European private law.[96] This needs explanation.

There is common agreement that the starting-point of the European legal order has been and remains the establishment of a European market. The four freedoms, mainly related to trade and services, may be categorised as *negative rights*. Such a classification comes from constitutional theory, and has its origin in the first generation of cases in which individual freedoms were asserted against an intrusive nation state.[97] Market freedoms are certainly not the essence of constitutional theory, but they lie at the heart of the European economic constitution.[98] The literature on European law uses different synonyms, but the message remains the same: EU market citizens invoke the market freedoms to eliminate national barriers to trade resulting from national administrative-economic law.

The next two categories, equality and justice, are associated with *positive rights*, that is, with positive integration and market regulation.[99] Both categories share the characteristic that EU citizens do not defend individual freedoms against an intrusive nation state but rather claim rights from the state in order to protect him- or herself against undue economic or social risks. This is the social welfare dimension in constitutional theory. It has already been noted that the Single European Act integrated social policy objectives into the EC Treaty, which were to be concretised by secondary Community law, usually in the form of Directives. Two questions arise: first, do the Articles of the Treaty, if necessary taken together with the implementing Directives, grant

[96] With regard to equal treatment, see G. More, 'The Principle of Equal Treatment: From Market Unifier to Fundamental Right?' in P. Craig and G. de Búrca, *The Evolution of EU Law* (Oxford, 1999), 517; with regard to contract law, see Micklitz, 'Social Justice', 167.

[97] For the distinction between negative and positive rights in the context of the European legal order, see A. Cassese, A. Clapham and J. H. H. Weiler (eds.), *Human Rights and the European Community*, vol. I, *A Critical Overview*; vol. II, *Human Rights and the European Community: Methods of Protection*; vol. III, *Human Rights and the European Community: The Substantive Law* (Baden-Baden, 1991).

[98] See H.-W. Micklitz and S. Weatherill, *European Economic Law* (Basingstoke, 1997).

[99] For a basic understanding, see H.-W. Micklitz, 'Consumer Rights' in A. Cassese, A. Clapham and J. H. H. Weiler (eds.), *Human Rights and the European Community*, vol. III, *Human Rights and the European Community: The Substantive Law* (Baden-Baden, 1991), 53.

individual rights to EU citizens, and, secondly, what is the substance of these rights?

Social policies are associated with equal treatment issues. This is where EC law in general and the ECJ in particular are at their best. It will have to be shown – and indeed it has already been shown – that EC law as interpreted by the ECJ does not go beyond guaranteeing equal treatment in a formal sense. The concept behind the principle is one of equality between men and women in *obtaining access to the European labour market*. EC law is reluctant to set out the conditions under which this access is guaranteed. In essence, my hypothesis is that EC labour law cannot grant 'justice' to European citizens, justice being understood here as distributive or substantive justice.

Distributive and substantive justice, however, form the core of private consumer law.[100] The standards set in the Directives on consumer law are meant to provide minimum protection throughout the Community against economic risks and against risks to health and safety. This is nothing less than distributive justice at a minimum level.[101] As there is no relevant European private legal order beyond that established in the consumer law Directives, and as the consumer law Directives establish pattern of justice, the research starts from the premise that the ECJ will need to develop a European understanding of 'justice'. There may be certain overlaps between the three areas of research: the completion of the internal market touches upon market freedoms, and the setting up of equal treatment standards in the labour market concerns social justice as well. The focus, however, is on freedoms in the common market, equality in the internal market and justice in the European private legal order.

A hypothesis on the relationship between (1) the three pillars for the establishment of a European legal order and (2) freedom, equality and justice

Market freedoms can easily be developed within the three pillars system (judicial co-operation, organised law-enforcement and political legitimacy). The European legal order fosters market integration.

[100] For a full account, see N. Reich and H.-W. Micklitz, *Europäisches Verbraucherrecht* (4th edn, Baden-Baden, 2003).

[101] On minimum levels of justice, see J. Stuyck, 'Patterns of Justice in the European Constitutional Charter: Minimum Harmonization in the Field of Consumer Law' in L. Krämer, H.-W. Micklitz and K. Tonner (eds.), *Law and Diffuse Interests in the European Legal Order: Liber Amicorum Norbert Reich* (Baden-Baden, 1997), 279.

Judicial co-operation is well established, although *Keck* has resulted in uncertainties on the exact scope of Article 28 (ex Article 30). This is all the more so as the ECJ has not yet clarified the relationship between Article 28 (ex Article 30) post-*Keck* and Article 95 (ex Article 100a) post-*Tobacco*.[102] The key litigants here are mostly traders and their representative organisations. Consumers and their representative organisations, although given legal standing in the ECJ's case law, have so far been 'free-riders'. One may wonder whether the market freedoms are running into a deadlock and whether the ECJ is able and competent to overcome legitimacy gaps which result from the impact of a market-driven order. *The hypothesis is that the ECJ, in narrowing down the scope of Article 28 (ex Article 30), is entering into an open procedure which allows EU citizens to make their voice heard in order to obtain market freedoms.*

The situation is much more complex with regard to 'equality'. Article 141 (ex Article 119) and Directives 75/117/EEC and 76/207/EEC have set up a relatively complex European legal framework for dealing with equal treatment issues. While there have been conflicts between the higher and the lower courts and between the judiciary and the national legislator, it seems as if judicial co-operation works to the mutual benefit of the courts at both ends. The driving forces behind equal treatment litigation are trade unions and women's organisations who choose test cases to refer to the ECJ. For the most part, German and UK national courts have collaborated with the ECJ to establish European labour law. The ECJ grants equal access to men and women; Member States and national courts remain competent for 'distributive justice'. Despite the so-called *Barber* Protocol, the legal-political legitimacy of judicial co-operation remains fragile. There is irritation on all sides, for the litigants who no longer know what to expect from EC law and the ECJ, for national courts which no longer know where the borderline between EC law and national law is, and, last but not least, for the ECJ in its relationship with the national and European legislatures. *The hypothesis is that the ECJ, in co-operation with the national courts, has elaborated the outlines of an emerging European labour law which might serve as a precedent for other fields of social policy.*

The last area to be analysed, the European private legal order and more specifically private consumer law, lags far behind the legal and judicial development of the other two areas. There is no comparable

[102] Judgment of 8 June 2000, Case 376/98, *Germany* v. *Parliament and Council* [2002] ECR I-8419.

case law at hand which would allow for a preliminary assessment of judicial co-operation, organised law-enforcement and legal-political legitimacy. The number of Article 234 (ex Article 177) references is still very small; this is even more so with regard to Directive 93/13/EEC, on which the research rests.[103] Judicial co-operation is still in its infancy here. National courts must be willing and able to overcome the tight grip which is exercised on them by the higher courts in the Member States. National courts, however, may gain self-confidence over time, and they may break the grip of the higher courts.[104] *Schulte*[105] is certainly a good example of a bold lower court unwilling to accept the authority of the German Supreme Court in implementing *Heininger.*[106] The role of litigants in private consumer law is far from being clear. EC law, more particularly Article 153 (ex Article 129) in combination with the consumer law Directives, provide that a collective application may be made for an injunction as the minimum effective legal protection.[107] For the time being, there is no clear commitment by consumer organisations to use the Article 234 (ex Article 177) reference procedure for the furtherance of European consumer law. The legal-political legitimacy of judicial co-operation, in particular the supremacy of EC law over national private law, is extremely fragile, if not non-existent. A lot will depend on the future of the Commission's action plan on European private law. If there is a growing commitment not only in the academic world but also in the legal-political environment in the Member States to elaborate if not a European Civil Code then at least European principles as an alternative to national law, then the legitimacy of judicial co-operation in the area of consumer law will increase. In sum, the hypothesis states that the prospective development of European consumer law might resemble and/or benefit from the experience in European labour law. *Therefore, the key to legitimacy must be sought in a new pattern of justice, not distributive justice but access to justice in private law (Zugangsgerechtigkeit).*

[103] For a full account of implementation and interpretation, see H.-W. Micklitz, '§13 Missbräuchliche Vertragsklauseln' in Reich and Micklitz, *Europäisches Verbraucherrecht.*

[104] See L. Gormley, 'References for a Preliminary Ruling: Art. 234 from the United Kingdom Viewpoint' (2002) 66 RabelsZ 459.

[105] Conclusions of Advocate-General Léger of 28 September 2004, Case C-350/03, *Schulte*, not yet reported.

[106] Judgment of 13 December 2001, Case 481/99, *Heininger* [2001] ECR I-9945.

[107] Micklitz, '§ 30 Kollektiver Rechtsschutz' in Reich and Micklitz, *Europäisches Verbraucherrecht*, 1160, at 11.

The choice of the UK as a subject for study

The United Kingdom, the European legal order and the private law challenge

Under the theoretical framework presented here, twenty-five legal orders would have to be analysed in order to determine their relationship with the European legal order, and *vice versa*, as evidenced in the Article 234 preliminary reference procedure. However, this book aims to be no more than a start to the research in this area, and is limited to the UK. There are good reasons why the UK constitutes an appropriate testing ground, and there are equally good reasons for assuming that the UK courts have an identifiable linguistic and cultural identity.[108] However, what does this identity look like?

The legal traditions of the UK courts

The UK courts have greatly contributed to the development of EU market freedoms and EU labour law, and will no doubt make a similar contribution to the European private legal order. Although statistics demonstrate the willingness of the UK courts to make use of the ECJ, the relatively low number of references does not allow for downgrading the role of the UK courts in the judge-made European law.[109] Of more importance for our purpose is the quality of the references and the judicial infrastructure which lies behind the references.[110] This can only be determined by a study of concrete cases. UK references are notable in all three fields of interest here.

Factortame[111] represents a conflict in the area of market freedoms, not only as regards supremacy in the UK legal order but also as

[108] Sciarra, 'Integration Through Courts' in Sciarra (ed.), *Labour Law in the Courts*, 1, comes to the conclusion that the national courts tend to maintain their cultural identity; however, she does not explain what sort of cultural identity she is talking of. C. J. Wallace, 'Community Sex Discrimination in National Courts: A Legal Cultural Comparison' in J. Shaw (ed.), *Social Policy in an Evolving EU* (Hart Publishing, 2000), 119 at 120, identifies a culture of enthusiasm with which national courts approach the possibility of dialogue with the ECJ.

[109] See Gormley, 'References for a Preliminary Ruling', 459; for a criticism of the usefulness of preliminary proceedings, see J. Golub, 'The Politics of Judicial Discretion: Rethinking the Interaction between National and the European Courts' (1996) 19 *Western European Politics* 360.

[110] See C. Lenz and G. Will, 'The Preliminary Ruling Procedure and the United Kingdom' (1996) 19 *Fordham International Law Journal* 865.

[111] Case C-213/89, *R.* v. *Secretary for State of Transport, ex parte Factortame* [1991] ECR I-3905; see L. Smith, 'Fischereipolitik, EG-Recht und britische Justiz' (1992) EuZW 308.

regards the institution of a new remedy, the preliminary injunction. The particular characteristic of the UK legal order relevant to *Factortame* is how the UK legal order deals with supremacy; in the case at hand, this led the House of Lords to act like a Supreme Court in that it held the Merchant Shipping Act 1988 to be inapplicable. *Factortame* must be seen as an incentive to UK traders to have their cases referred to the ECJ in order to remove national barriers to trade. In the field of EU labour law, UK courts have made considerable use of the preliminary reference procedure to clarify the substance of equal treatment and to define the rights and remedies required to implement EC law.[112] For a German lawyer, the most striking characteristic of the UK courts is their insistence on the availability of appropriate remedies.[113]

The common law has been subject to extensive analysis, at first in relation to continental (civil law) private law, but more recently in relation to EC law.[114] Nowhere do different legal cultures and traditions clash so violently as do the civil law legal order and the common law. Lord Goff puts this well:

> [A] few years ago, we [the UK] received an informal approach from an Eastern European country that it might for the future adopt English commercial law. This flattering proposal, however, ran up against two insuperable objections – the first was that nobody knew precisely what English commercial law consisted of, and the second was that nobody knew where to find it.[115]

This may be less of a problem as regards private consumer law, owing to the considerable amount of codification that has been done in this area, and thus there will be less uncertainty as to what constitutes the law.[116] However, UK consumer law, as in the other Member States, rests

[112] See Kilpatrick, 'Community or Communities of Courts', 121; Lord Mummery, 'The Community Law Impact on Employment Cases' in M. Andenas and F. Jacobs (eds.), *European Community Law in the English Courts* (Oxford, 1998), 191.

[113] See Mancini and Keeling, 'Language, Culture and Politics', 397; T. Koopmans, 'The Birth of European Law at the Crossroads of Legal Traditions' (1991) 39 *American Journal of Comparative Law* 493 at 503, refers to judicial review.

[114] See G. Radbruch, *Der Geist des Englischen Rechts* (Göttingen, 1956), 13: 'Es ist die Eigenart englischen Rechtssinnes, dass er nicht auf ein ideales Recht, auf eine überpositive Gerechtigkeit gerichtet ist, vielmehr auf das geltende englische Recht (the law of the land), einschließlich all seiner historischen Absonderlichkeiten.'

[115] Lord Goff, 'The Future of the Common Law' (1997) 46 *International and Comparative Law Quarterly* 745.

[116] G. Howells and S. Weatherill, *Consumer Protection Law* (Dartmouth, 1995).

on private law, and therefore civil law lawyers all over Europe will continue to remain puzzled by it. It is not so much the difference between codified and uncodified law but the difference in legal methodology which is striking.

Characteristics of legal methodology

Two issues arise whenever one attempts to define the differences between the civil law and the common law: first, the use of case law in preference to legal principles; and, secondly, the use of purposive interpretation.[117] Civil law lawyers reason *downwards* from abstract principles embodied in a code, whereas common law lawyers reason *upwards* from the facts, moving gradually from case to case. Civil law lawyers are searching for the *Zweck im Recht*, the purpose and objective behind the legal ruling, if the wording of the rule to be applied, its position in the broader framework of the code in which the rule is embedded or the history of the rule do not provide guidance. Common law lawyers view purposive interpretation as an alien element.[118] Again, I would like to quote Lord Goff, who, in brilliantly summing up the differences, *sotto voce* claims the stylistic superiority in the area of judge-made law:[119]

> Continental lawyers love to proclaim some great principle, and then knock it into shape afterwards. Instead, the boring English want to find out first whether and, if so, how these great ideas are going to work in practice. This is not at all popular with the propagators of the great ideas.

The careful reasoning of English judges is admirable, as is their focus on the wording of the rule in question, the elaboration of the meaning of the rule, and their careful explanation of the application of the

[117] Lord Goff, 'The Future of the Common Law' (1997) 46 *International and Comparative Law Quarterly* 745; B. S. Markesinis, 'Learning from Europe and Learning in Europe' in B. S. Markesinis (ed.), *The Gradual Convergence: Foreign Ideas, Foreign Influences and English Law on the Eve of the 21st Century* (Oxford, 1994), 1; Koopmans, 'The Birth of European Law', 493 at 503.

[118] See, *inter alia*, Bingham J in *Customs and Excise Commissioners* v. *ApS Samex* [1983] 1 All ER 1042 at 1056.

[119] Lord Goff, 'The Future of the Common Law' (1997) 46 *International and Comparative Law Quarterly* 745 at 753; see also R. Goode, 'Insularity or Leadership? The Role of the United Kingdom in the Harmonisation of Commercial Law' (2001) 50 *International and Comparative Law Quarterly* 751, quoting Lord Wilberforce: 'The elegance, style and analytical powers of the British legal community have survived the decline of the British Empire intact.'

rule to the particular facts of the case.[120] It is this peculiarly British pragmatism in looking at where the problem lies and at how to find an answer in the case law and/or in the rules which is so startling to a civil law lawyer who is fixated on rules.[121]

Conclusion to this part

All these differences between the civil law system and the common law system are well known, and these differences largely determine the interaction between civil law and common law lawyers. These differences are readily apparent in European law, and more particularly in the ECJ, but their coming together in European law may eventually pave the way for the development of a common European legal culture. Whether the two legal cultures are converging or not, European law as it stands today combines elements of both.[122] The civil law legal methodology may be found in the strong emphasis on purposive interpretation, the common law methodology in the case law approach. It is apparent, however, that any assessment of the future of European law will reveal the difficulties which result from the different styles of reasoning. What therefore could the contribution be of the UK courts to the making of the European legal order? I would argue, being modest and ambitious at the same time, that there is a message behind the common law style of judge-made law: let us not forget what the law is – and let us be cautious in opening the floodgates for politics intruding into law. However, where the law is clear, it must be enforced effectively, through appropriate rights and remedies.

The selection of the case studies and the methodology

The reasons for choosing the particular fields of research

There are a number of reasons justifying the choice of the Sunday trading litigation as a case study, even though the Sunday trading issue is well known in the UK and even though it has been subject to

[120] Markesinis, 'Learning from Europe and Learning in Europe' in Markesinis (ed.), *The Gradual Convergence*, 1.

[121] H.-W. Micklitz, T. Roethe and S. Weatherill (eds.), *Federalism and Responsibility* (London, 1994).

[122] See Markesinis, 'Learning from Europe' in Markesinis (ed.), *The Gradual Convergence*, 1 at 31.

extensive legal-political analysis,[123] not only in the UK but also in other Member States.[124] First, it is a good example of the reach of market freedoms in the European legal order. Weiler had Sunday trading in mind when he referred to the 'subterranean cracks'[125] in the ECJ's pre-*Keck* case law on market freedoms. Ideally, a study of the Sunday trading cases may serve as a starting-point in undermining the ECJ's preparedness, as diagnosed by Joerges and Weatherill, to view the market freedoms as political as well as legal rights (political in so far as such rights allow the citizens of a Member State to require their governments to justify their actions).[126] Thus the Sunday trading cases define the demarcation line between the law and politics. Secondly, the Sunday trading litigation has made EC law popular in the UK (a hitherto unprecedented effect). Each Member State has had its own *Cassis de Dijon* experience. For Germany, it needed *Cassis de Dijon* to make people realise that there existed something like a 'European law'; for the UK, it was the Sunday trading cases that enhanced the role and importance of EC law.

I have referred a number of times in the introduction to EU labour law, and more particularly to the EU rules governing equal treatment. Equal treatment of men and women, although already established (in a rudimentary manner) in the Treaty of Rome, might be understood as being paradigmatic for the Single European Act in its striving for a 'European market with a human face'. Equal treatment belongs to the field of social policy.[127] The advantage of choosing equal treatment from among the other possible choices lies in its relatively dense European regulation, which permits us to study equal treatment as a subject in its own right. However, there is a second reason, which is

123 M. Jarvis, 'The Sunday Trading Episode: In Defence of the Euro-Defence' (1995) 44 *International and Comparative Law Quarterly* 451; M. Maduro, 'Never on a Sunday – What Has (EU) Law Got To Do With It' in S. Sciarra (ed.), *Labour Law in the Courts: National Judges and the European Court of Justice* (Oxford, 2001), 273.

124 E. Schalla, *Das Sonntagsverkaufsverbot in England und Wales: unter Berücksichtigung europäischen und deutschen Rechts* (Cologne, 1995).

125 Weiler, 'The Constitution of the Common Market Place: Text and Context in the Evolution of the Free Movement of Goods' in P. Craig and G. de Búrca, *The Evolution of EU Law* (London, 1999), 369.

126 C. Joerges, 'On the Legitimacy of Europeanising Private Law: Consideration on a Justice-Making Law for the EU Multi-Level System' (2003) 7.3 *Electronic Journal of Comparative Law*, Part III.3.

127 More, 'The Principle of Equal Treatment' in Craig and de Búrca, *The Evolution of EU Law*, 517.

directly related to the importance equal treatment litigation has gained in the UK. In an early stage of my research, I compiled a list of all UK references coming under the broad heading of social policy. Equal treatment constituted by far the most important category of such references over a period of more than twenty years. In their relationship with the German courts, the UK courts have contributed considerably to shaping a true European understanding of equal treatment, an understanding which has not found common support as the ECJ equalises equal treatment of men and women with providing equal access to the labour market.

The European private legal order does not (yet) exist. Therefore, litigation in this field overarches the concept of the internal market. Most of the Directives in this area deal with consumer law. The most prominent Directive, other than Directive 99/44/EC on consumer sales, is undoubtedly Directive 93/13/EEC on unfair terms in consumer contracts. The adoption of Directive 93/13/EEC shocked private lawyers, academics and judges throughout the European Community. They came to realise that a whole new body of European private law had arisen in the field of consumer protection. The rules and principles of this body of law affect traditional private law matters. This is particularly so with regard to the concept of 'good faith', a concept which is designed to deal with unfairness in consumer contracts. This concept, although alien to the common law, has attracted particular attention in the UK, first in the academic world and more recently in the English courts. It is therefore a proper subject of study here, where the two legal cultures, the common law legal culture and the civil law legal culture, are most directly opposed to each other. The UK understanding of good faith may contribute to a European understanding of good faith, just as happened in the area of equal treatment, and, moreover, may also contribute to a European understanding of 'justice'. A study of good faith litigation brings to light the fact that even the 'constitutional charter' might be insufficient to build a European private legal order that enshrines justice.[128] It highlights the difficulties the European

[128] On the social welfare dimension of good faith, see R. Brownsword, G. Howells and T. Wilhelmsson, 'Between Market and Welfare: Some Reflections on Article 3 of the EC Directive on Unfair Terms in Consumer Contracts' in C. Willett (ed.), *Aspects of Fairness in Contract* (London, 1996), 25; E. McKendrick, 'Good Faith: A Matter of Principle?' in A. Forte (ed.), *Good Faith in Contract and Property Law* (Oxford, 1999), 39.

Community faces in developing a European Civil Code, in whatever form, whether as a fully fledged and binding legal document, or as non-binding optional legal principles.

Qualitative and quantitative research: the reconstruction of the cases

Qualitative research seems to be best suited to analysing the role of the preliminary reference procedure in the making of the European legal order through its three pillars (judicial co-operation, organised law-enforcement and legal-political legitimacy). Qualitative research allows for an in-depth analysis in the form of three case studies, one each on Sunday trading, equal treatment and good faith. This is a good way of avoiding focusing too narrowly on co-operation in its strict sense, and instead focusing on what Sciarra terms 'judicial discourse', in which the actors behind the litigation are included in the analysis.

The idea then was to *reconstruct* the three series of cases to the fullest extent possible,[129] that is, in their national and European legal contexts and in their social-political contexts. This is what Kilpatrick had in mind when she referred to the policy dependence of 'legal structuring' and 'institutional alchemy'.[130] It means in essence that the legal material had to be as complete as possible, including the judgments of the courts and the comments of academics, in order to define the arguments of the parties in the litigation, to give shape to the role of solicitors and barristers in the cases and to take a hard look at how national judges, the Advocates-General and the ECJ shape their arguments. However, reconstruction of the cases means more than simply collecting and evaluating documents.

'Reconstruction' is a term borrowed from qualitative sociological methodology. As used here, the term refers to more than a mere compilation of empirical data for a case study; in addition, it seeks to decipher the structure of meaning in the ongoing process of argumentation which shapes a case. This type of legal-sociological analysis includes the interpretation of laws, Directives, documents, interviews with the parties concerned, and the results of discourse and bargaining processes in written or oral form. Thus, a chain of arguments can

[129] For a similar approach Micklitz, see Roethe and Weatherill, *Federalism and Responsibility*.

[130] See the text at note 54 above.

be discerned and considered in its national and European contexts. Its diachronic emergence should also become apparent. The result of this reconstruction should enable us to discern the latent structures of meaning which are part of the process of decision-making.

The reconstruction of the three case studies follows the same order and the same method. The reconstructions set out the history of each case from the beginning, starting with the factual legal-political background to the litigation, the way in which the case first reached the national courts, the arguments brought forward and the efforts made to bring the case to the ECJ, the handling of the case before the ECJ, its reception in the national and/or European academic environment, and whether and to what extent the ECJ's ruling was or was not implemented by the national courts.

While the concept behind the reconstruction of each of the three cases is the same, in the event it became impossible to stick too rigidly to a common structure. The reconstruction of the Sunday trading cases stuck most closely to the original idea of the reconstruction. The Sunday trading cases were one single coherent stream of litigation which could be readily analysed. It combines the two basic elements of market freedoms and the rights and remedies available and was well suited to the application in practice of these two elements. The equal treatment litigation turned out to be different. A single case did not suffice to provide a full picture of what lay behind the equal treatment rules. Therefore, and in order to do justice to its development in the UK, the equal treatment litigation has been reconstructed over a period of more than twenty years. That said, however, the basic approach to the reconstruction remained the same. Just as in the Sunday trading cases, equal treatment is reconstructed in the interplay of its legal substance and its use of rights and remedies. Good faith was different again. While the 'legal structuring' and the 'institutional alchemy' of equal treatment stand on their own, the legal concept of good faith can be understood only in its broader private law context. Directive 93/13/EEC and its implementation in the UK has to be placed in the framework of the common law. A reconstruction of the good faith litigation in the UK and in the ECJ can only be undertaken against that background. Again, the rights and remedies in enforcing good faith are fully considered.

Despite these necessary differences in approach to the reconstruction of the three case studies, the case studies must and should be seen as a whole; taken together they will shed light on the making of the European legal order in its three dimensions (market freedoms, social policies and private law) by way of judicial co-operation and through organised law-enforcement. This book reaches beyond existing research in the depth of its analysis owing to the chosen methodology and by submitting three divergent policy fields to the same scrutiny.

How to read this book

Four chapters follow this introduction; a chapter is dedicated to each of the three case studies, and each stands in its own right. The final chapter is meant to bring together the three case studies and to give clearer shape to the possibilities and limits of the three premises that have contributed to the making of the European legal order (judicial co-operation, organised law-enforcement and legal-political legitimacy).

A summary of the findings of this book

The main findings are as follows:

(1) On judicial co-operation: national courts do not behave like the European courts. Communication between the national courts and the ECJ is flawed. The national courts seek solutions to their national problems. They have a *vertical* perspective of the ECJ as being a Supreme Court, able and competent to decide the case, where this is necessary. The ECJ provides an answer by reading and interpreting EC rules. It considers the referred question from a *horizontal* perspective: the answer to the referred question must be equally satisfactory for all twenty-five Member States and must fit into twenty-five legal orders.

(2) On organised law-enforcement: public interest groups misunderstand the possibilities and the limits of EC law in establishing social standards in the European legal order. They too behave like national legal players, looking only at national concerns. Public interest groups lack a European perspective; most of all they lack the necessary professional skills to engage in European litigation. A professionalisation of public interest groups might contribute to closing the legitimacy gap in social policies. Public interest groups are in a position to engage in international co-operation and to

introduce into the preliminary reference procedure a truly European dimension.

(3) On political legitimacy: the ECJ has developed three strategies to close the legitimacy gap: delimiting the scope of the European legal order; transforming the subjective rights of market citizens into the political rights of Union citizens; and developing European remedies to enforce European rights.

2

The reconstruction of the Sunday trading cases

Article 28: a weapon to win the Sunday trading war?

The Shops Act 1950 dates back to a proposal by the Royal Commission on Shopping Hours. The Commission had been established after the Second World War to consider, amend and consolidate the existing regulations on shopping hours. The Shops Act 1950 constituted a consolidatiom measure which was intended to consolidate all the Acts which had been passed since 1890 relating to shopping hours. Material to the Sunday trading litigation is section 47 of the Shops Act 1950. Twenty years after its enactment, section 47 became the focus of concern to certain retailers in the UK. Section 47 provided as follows:

> Every shop shall, save as otherwise provided by this Part of this Act, be closed for the serving of customers on Sunday.

From 1970 onwards, traders realised the extent to which they could increase their profit by trading on Sundays. Consequently, they launched a campaign in Parliament advocating the total deregulation of shopping hours. When this campaign failed, they resorted to more radical means by simply opening their shops on Sundays regardless of section 47. This deliberate flouting of the law was a challenge to local authorities (who were responsible in the UK for enforcing this particular law). The 'war'[1] lasted for more than a decade, with various other warriors more or less successfully entering the battlefield. Victory or defeat in the Sunday trading war became dependent on the outcome of the battle in the European courts. This victory, in turn, depended on whether Article 28 (ex Article 30) of the EC Treaty was a suitable weapon for the Sunday traders to use to defeat their opponents, the

[1] Martial language was used by the parties to describe the litigation, especially by Arthur Hugh Vaughan QC, counsel for the retailers, in an interview on 23 June 1999 and by Tony Askham, solicitor of Bond Pearce (formerly Hepherd, Winstanley and Pugh) for the retailers, in an interview on 26 July 1999.

local authorities. As it turned out, Article 28 was *not* such a suitable weapon. The position of the local authorities was much stronger than commentators had expected. Their arguments were based on an established national legal system, constitutional principles, established principles of EC law and a developing EC law system, which combined to prevent Article 28 (ex Article 30) from striking down section 47 of the 1950 Act. Yet, even though the local authorities won the Euro-law battle, the use of Article 28 (ex Article 30) had long-term effects which were finally determinative of the Sunday traders' victory in the overall war. Attacks and counter-attacks, offensives and defences, as well as the combatants in the Sunday trading war, will now be reconstructed.

The Sunday traders' role in the Sunday trading saga

The Sunday traders

Most of the Sunday traders involved in the Sunday trading saga were furniture stores, DIY[2] stores, home improvement stores and garden centres, above all B&Q plc.[3] Other stores in the forefront of the Sunday trading litigation included Texas Homecare Ltd, Wickes Building Supplies Ltd, Payless DIY Ltd and W. H. Smith Do-It-All Ltd. Also involved in reported cases in the Sunday trading litigation were RMC Homecare (South) Ltd, Anders Ltd, Paul Madley Ltd, Midland Enterprises (Special Events) Ltd and Charles Robertson (Developments) Ltd. Towards the end of the Sunday trading litigation, in the early 1990s, these furniture and DIY stores were joined by all the major supermarket operators in the UK. From the very beginning in the 1970s, the motive for the Sunday traders in attacking section 47 was the growing market for DIY and gardening products due to a change in consumer habits and the development of a new breed of customers.

The Sunday traders as 'repeat players'

The most important advantage the Sunday traders had was their enormous financial resources which they could employ in an expensive legal and political campaign. There was also 'safety in numbers', in that

[2] That is, 'do-it-yourself'.

[3] B&Q is the UK's leading home improvement retailer and garden centre, and, since a merger in December 1998, has been the largest DIY retailer in Europe. With 289 stores, B&Q holds a 19 per cent share (1998/99) of the UK market.

there was no single DIY store fighting against the Sunday trading prohibition. There were many such traders trading unlawfully on Sundays. These traders could, according to Galanter's typology of parties, appropriately be classified as 'repeat players'. A 'repeat player' is defined as:

> a unit which has had and anticipates repeated litigation, which has low stakes in the outcome of any one case, and which has the resources to pursue its long-run interests.[4]

Applying this definition to the Sunday traders, it can readily be seen, first, that the outcome of any single court case would not significantly alter their overall strategy to legalise Sunday trading. Secondly, large DIY and furniture stores have the resources to pursue their long-term interests, even at the expense of their short-term interests. This can be illustrated, for example, by the fact that criminal prosecution and the imposition of fines proved unsuccessful in deterring offenders in several cases. The traders considered the fines to be 'peanuts'.[5] Thus, it seems as if the Sunday traders, as repeat players, were in a very favourable position to win the Sunday trading war.

The overall strategy

The Sunday traders' long-term litigation strategy may be described as the 'exploitation'[6] of European Community law – more specifically Article 28 (ex Article 30) – to achieve their economic ends, that is, Sunday opening. From the outset, political and legal campaigns were tightly interwoven. From 1979, the Sunday traders' focus was on lobbying Parliament in order to achieve the total deregulation of Sunday trading. However, from 1986 onwards, when the Shops Bill 1986 was defeated on second reading – thus rendering a political solution in the near future very unlikely – the Sunday traders' focus shifted to their legal campaign.

Illegal Sunday opening was already occurring in the early 1980s, that is, before the defeat of the Shops Bill 1986 in Parliament. The first Sunday trading cases were litigated when the Sunday traders were prosecuted by the local authorities concerned. Yet, at that time, the

[4] M. Galanter, 'Why the "Haves" Come Out Ahead: Speculations on the Limits of Legal Change' (1974) 9 *Law and Society Review* 95 at 98.

[5] Tony Askham, solicitor for the retailers, in an interview on 26 July 1999.

[6] This terminology was used by Arthur Hugh Vaughan QC in an interview on 23 June 1999.

'European defence' had not yet been invented, and the Sunday traders tried to defend themselves using the so-called 'motor accessories defence'.

The 'motor accessories defence'

Schedule 5 to the 1950 Act permitted a variety of products to be sold despite the general Sunday trading prohibition. Schedule 5 contained a list of transactions for the purposes of which a shop may be opened in England and Wales for the serving of customers on Sunday. There had already been a number of cases before the Sunday trading war began in which Schedule 5 and its predecessor had been the focus of litigation.[7] These cases are evidence of early attempts to stretch the interpretation of the Shops Act 1950 to its limits in order to be able to trade on Sunday. Yet, it was not until the late 1970s that the 'motor accessories defence' became popular among Sunday traders.

Material to the motor accessories defence was paragraph 1(h) of Schedule 5. This allowed for the sale of 'aircraft, motor, or cycle supplies or accessories'. In light of this provision, the argument of the Sunday traders was that, as a matter of fact, all of the items which had been sold at their shops were capable of being motor accessories. In *Hadley* v. *Texas Homecare Ltd*,[8] eight appeals were heard together in the Queen's Bench Division. In each case, the prosecutor was the local authority responsible for the enforcement of the provisions of Part IV of the 1950 Act. The items involved in those cases ranged from abrasive pads, brush cleaners, ceramic tiles and roofing felt to radiators, to name only a few. The question before the court was whether in selling such items the defendants were selling motor accessories. Both Mann J and Watkins LJ rejected the contention that any of the items in those cases was a motor accessory as 'perverse'.[9] The question was merely whether an object *was* in fact a motor accessory, not whether it could be *used* as a motor accessory.

[7] In *Wardale* v. *Binns* [1946] 2 All ER 101, the question was whether the sale of a loaf was the sale of a 'meal or refreshment'. The court held that it was. The relevant provision at issue in this case was later re-enacted as Schedule 5, para. 1(b), to the Shops Act 1950. In *Warley Caravans* v. *Wakelin* (1968) 66 LGR 534; (1968) 112 SJ 330, the question was whether touring caravans were 'motor accessories'. Parker CJ held that they were not. In *Hudson* v. *Marshall* (1976) 75 LGR 13, a T-shirt emblazoned with a 'Bugs Bunny' motif was held to be within the exception in Schedule 5, para. 1(l) which permits the sale of 'souvenirs' in holiday resorts on a Sunday.

[8] (1988) 152 JP 268.

[9] *Hadley* v. *Texas Homecare Ltd* (1988) 152 JP 268.

This judgment was rendered on 21 December 1987, that is, after the defeat of the Shops Bill 1986 in Parliament. The judgment demonstrated that the judges were not prepared to bring about a relaxation of the Sunday trading law by judicial activism. The decision can be taken as a warning that the judiciary was not prepared to help retailers to trade on Sundays contrary to Parliament's intention. However, this warning had no significant effect on the Sunday traders' strategy, since the only consequence of being found guilty in those criminal prosecutions was the imposition of low fines, which the traders paid without much ado.

The financial considerations of the Sunday traders

One of the underlying reasons for the continuing breach of the Sunday trading ban was the low level of fines imposed by section 59 of the 1950 Act.[10] In *Rochdale* v. *Anders*, Caulfield J stated in relation to the financial considerations of the Sunday traders:

> [P]rosecuting him [Anders] does no good. He pays the fines and continues to open his premises in breach of the 1950 Act.[11]

In addition, the profitability of Sunday trading was always in the traders' mind. Eventually, however, these financial considerations had to be weighed against legal considerations, which became more and more significant the longer the Sunday trading war lasted. The strategy of the 'haves' in terms of power, wealth and status was substantially undermined by local authorities instituting civil proceedings for injunctions. Yet, it was not until the ECJ decision in *Torfaen*[12] that local authorities sought injunctions on a large scale. This was due to the fact that even the local authorities at first believed in the force of the 'European defence'.

The rise of the 'European defence'

The 'European defence' was first raised by John Evans, solicitor of Stephens and Scown, in *Charles Robertson (Developments) Ltd* v. *Caradon District Council*.[13] John Evans was the first British lawyer to

[10] The maximum fine being £1,000 (later increased to £2,500 by the Criminal Justice Act 1991).

[11] *Rochdale Borough Council* v. *Anders* [1988] 3 All ER 490 at 491.

[12] Case C-145/88, *Torfaen Borough Council* v. *B&Q plc* [1989] ECR 3851; [1990] CMLR 337.

[13] [1988] 1 CMLR 293.

raise the Article 28 (ex Article 30) defence in national courts, first before the Liskeard Justices and then on appeal before the Bodmin Crown Court. He was also the first solicitor in the Sunday trading litigation who successfully sought a reference to the ECJ in order to obtain a ruling on Article 28 (ex Article 30) and the Sunday trading restrictions. Robertson had been convicted of trading on a Sunday in goods which, under the Shops Act 1950, were not permitted to be sold on a Sunday. The goods included a substantial quantity of items imported from EEC countries. It was argued that, if the appellant was not free to sell these goods on a Sunday, it would necessarily reduce the quantity of goods it imported from other Member States. Therefore, the Shops Act 1950 was said to be in conflict with Article 28 (ex Article 30). Mr Evans further argued that, because section 47 of the Shops Act conflicted with Article 28 (ex Article 30), it was the Treaty which should prevail, so that the prohibition in the Shops Act was of no effect. Thus, as part of their case, the appellant raised a question of EEC law and asked the Crown Court to refer that question to the ECJ. Judge Jonathan Clarke stated the referred questions in the following terms:

> Do the provisions of Part IV of the Shops Act 1950 conflict with the provisions of [Article 28 (ex Article 30)] of the Treaty of Rome? If the answer is yes, then are the provisions of the Act saved by any part of [Article 28 (ex Article 30)] of the Treaty, particularly on the grounds of public morality or public policy or by the so-called rule of reason?[14]

It is clear from these questions that the court and the parties proceeded on the basis of established Community law, that is, a mechanical application of the *Dassonville*[15] formula. The only other authority cited in support of the trader's argument was *Blesgen*.[16] There was not as yet any attempt to develop a sophisticated argument around Article 28 (ex Article 30) or to single out different lines of case law so as to develop the case law in any particular direction. Nevertheless, Judge Jonathan Clarke considered the *Dassonville* formula 'clear enough'[17] for there to be force in the appellant's argument that the Shops Act on its face did conflict with the provisions of Article 28 (ex Article 30). In any event, he felt that he should refer the point to the ECJ; he was

[14] *Ibid.* [15] Judgment of 11 July 1974, Case 8/74, *Dassonville* [1974] ECR 837.
[16] Case C-75/81, *Belgium* v. *Blesgen* [1982] ECR 1211; [1983] 1 CMLR 431.
[17] *Charles Robertson (Developments) Ltd* v. *Caradon District Council* [1988] 1 CMLR 293 at 295.

also seemingly attracted by the respondent's 'pragmatic view that this point [was] likely to be referred to [the ECJ] sooner or later'.[18] The lawyers representing B&Q heard of this argument, and did not hesitate to adopt and refine it for use in their own litigation.

The European aspects of the traders' strategy

The European defence arose at the right moment for the Sunday traders. The overall strategy seemed to have run into deadlock. After the failure of legislative reform in Parliament, and after the national courts demonstrated their unwillingness to accept the 'motor accessories defence', the campaigners lost forty stores, which were injuncted. This was the low point of the traders' campaign. The European defence was a glimmer of hope to revitalise the campaign and to take it into new territory. The use of the European defence can be traced back to the ingenuity of Arthur Hugh Vaughan QC, the barrister representing B&Q, and his determination to take advantage of – or arguably to 'exploit' – European Community law in order to win the Sunday trading litigation. *En masse*, the Sunday traders now relied on the European defence, and argued that section 47 of the Shops Act 1950 was in breach of Article 28 (ex Article 30) of the Treaty of Rome, thus raising issues of European law and making a preliminary reference to the ECJ under Article 234 (ex Article 177) necessary.

For a correct understanding of the European defence, it is necessary to draw a distinction between the preliminary reference under Article 234 (ex Article 177) *as such* and the issues of substantive law involved in the Sunday trading litigation. The attainment of both the short-term interests of the Sunday traders as well as their long-term interests were dependent on the question of a reference under Article 234 (ex Article 177) as such and the ruling by the ECJ as to the compatibility of the Shops Act 1950 with Article 28 (ex Article 30).

The use of Article 234 as a tactical ploy

Article 234 (ex Article 177) did not serve the purpose merely of obtaining a ruling from the ECJ on an issue necessary to render a judgment in a case nor of clarifying the law on Article 28 (ex Article 30). Resort to Article 234 (ex Article 177) by the Sunday traders was intended to delay proceedings in the national courts. It is well known that a reference to the ECJ leads to the proceedings being stayed in the national

[18] *Ibid.*

courts for about eighteen months. As long as final judgment in any particular case was not rendered or an interim injunction not granted, the Sunday traders could simply continue to open their shops on Sundays. The longer the delay, the more opportunities for the traders to make profits on Sundays. Thus the short-term interests of the Sunday traders could be secured. This aspect of the European defence exemplifies the instrumental use of Article 234 (ex Article 177) in national proceedings.

The Sunday traders, however, had to overcome the threshold Lord Denning set in *Bulmer* v. *Bollinger*[19] for referring a case to the ECJ. As Judge Jonathan Clarke had put it in *Charles Robertson (Developments) Ltd* v. *Caradon District Council*:[20]

> Is it necessary for this Court to refer that question to Luxembourg? I have been greatly helped by the guidelines given by the then Master of the Rolls Lord Denning in *Bulmer* v. *Bollinger*. It is clear to me that, even where (as is the position in this case) a European point of law or interpretation falls to be decided, English courts should not shy away from deciding themselves, and should not readily refer a point to the European Court with all the delay and expense thereby involved, even though (as is the situation in the instant case) the respondents take a pragmatic view that this point is likely to be referred to Luxembourg sooner or later and therefore it would be quicker and more expedient and certainly less expensive for it to be referred by this court today rather than by another court at another time. I still have to be satisfied that a point 'necessary for decision' has arisen in the terms of [Article 234 (ex Article 177)].

Judge Jonathan Clarke did not devote much attention to an analysis of Article 28 (ex Article 30) and the corresponding jurisprudence. It took him only a couple of sentences to state that 'it is necessary to have a definite ruling on these matters involving, as they do, not only the

[19] *H. P. Bulmer Ltd* v. *J. Bollinger SA (No. 2)* [1974] Ch 401; [1974] 3 WLR 202; [1974] 2 All ER 1226; [1974] 2 CMLR 91; see also the dense analysis of Lord Denning's judgment by C. Lenz and G. Will, 'The Preliminary Ruling Procedure and the United Kingdom' (1996) 19 *Fordham International Law Journal* 844 at 853–60, who underline the influence of Bingham J in *Customs and Exercise Commissioners* v. *ApS Samex* [1983] 1 All ER 1042 at 1055 on the attitude of High Court judges. However, in 1993, Lord Denning's criteria were famously revisited by Bingham MR in *R.* v. *International Stock Exchange of the United Kingdom and the Republic of Ireland, ex parte Else (1982) Ltd* [1993] QB 534 at 545D–F; see L. Gormley, 'References for a Preliminary Ruling: Art. 234 from the United Kingdom Viewpoint' (2002) 66 RabelsZ 459.

[20] *Charles Robertson (Developments) Ltd* v. *Caradon District Council* [1988] CMLR 293 at 295.

interpretation of the Treaty but the validity of the Act of the country said to be in conflict'.[21] Following Lord Denning, the national court has to take a second step, which, in Judge Jonathan Clarke's words, can be stated thus: 'Should we in any event exercise our discretion?'[22] Instead of specifying the criteria upon which he should make his decision, Judge Jonathan Clarke seemed to be much more influenced by the fact that he had the mutual consent of the parties to refer the case to the ECJ.

This approach, however, was not always accepted in other courts. In *Wychavon District Council* v. *Midland Enterprises*,[23] Millett J did not consider Lord Denning's guidelines, but instead entered into a thorough analysis of whether the actual facts provided evidence that the Shops Act affected intra-Community trade. Millett J relied explicitly on *Jan van der Haar*[24] in order to establish the responsibility of the national courts to investigate whether the Shops Act was in itself likely to hinder, directly or indirectly, actually or potentially, trade between the Member States.[25] He found forceful arguments to shape the role and the responsibility of the national courts:

> Accordingly, in the present case it is for the national court to decide whether the statutory discrimination between fresh produce and manufactured products competing therewith puts imported goods at a disadvantage. It is for the national courts to investigate the facts and to decide whether the statute is capable of having adverse effect on the volume of imported goods. *Whatever* the answer the European Court may give to the interpretation of [Article 28 (ex Article 30)], there is no evidence before me which enables me to hold that any of the provisions of the Shops Act have such an effect.[26]

While Millett J is correct in defining the role of the national courts, he went too far in his defence of independence. 'Whatever' the ECJ decides, suggests some hostility towards the ECJ and even more so to EC law. Millett J, however, went on correctly to examine Article 234 (ex Article 177) and the right of the national courts to refer the case to the ECJ 'if the national court considers that a decision on the question is

[21] *Ibid.*, para. 12. [22] *Ibid.*, judgment, para. 15.
[23] [1988] 1 CMLR 397.
[24] Joined Cases 177–178/82, *Jan van der Haar* [1984] ECR 1797; [1985] 2 CMLR 566.
[25] Millett J quotes Joined Cases 177–178/82, *Jan van der Haar* [1984] ECR 1797; [1985] 2 CMLR 566, para. 22.
[26] *Ibid.*, para. 35 (emphasis added).

necessary to enable it to give judgment'.[27] No reference is made to Lord Denning here. Following his robust line of argument, Millett J rejected the need to invoke Article 234 (ex Article 177) in the case at issue:

> The absence of any evidence of any causal connection between the provisions of the Shops Act and any possible discrimination against imported goods makes it impossible to formulate any relevant question the determination of which would enable the Court to decide the case in favour of the defendants.[28]

The real concern of Millett J seems to be that the defendants have been trying to misuse European law:

> I am satisfied that the defendant's real concern is to obtain a two year delay so that they may continue to trade in infringement of the criminal law and at very great profit to themselves in the hope that the answers to these theoretical questions can be long delayed.[29]

However, it was not important merely to have the particular proceedings stayed in which a reference could be obtained. It was also of the utmost importance for the Sunday traders to bring proceedings in any court in any area in England and Wales to a standstill. This enabled them to open their stores throughout the country and not only in the areas of jurisdiction of particular councils. Thus it was the strategy of the Sunday traders to ensure references from a magistrates' court, a Crown Court and the High Court. According to Tony Askham, solicitor for B&Q, the legal team of the Sunday traders deliberately approached 'pragmatic'[30] local authorities where it was likely that they would agree to a joint reference. In every case in which there was a chance to obtain agreement to a reference, Tony Askham consulted the local authorities and, in proceedings in magistrates' courts, also the legally qualified clerk of the court in order to convince them of the force of the European defence and the need to make a reference. The Sunday traders were willing to indemnify the local authorities with their costs, and, perhaps even more importantly, the Sunday traders made it clear that they would accept the result of a judgment of the ECJ. This strategy proved successful.

The Sunday traders obtained a reference in High Court proceedings in *Rochdale* v. *Anders*,[31] a reference from the Shrewsbury Crown

[27] *Ibid.*, para. 37. [28] *Ibid.* [29] *Ibid.*, para. 42.

[30] Tony Askham, solicitor for the retailers, in an interview on 26 July 1999.

[31] *Rochdale Borough Council* v. *Anders* [1988] 3 All ER 490 at 491.

Court and a reference from the Cwmbran Magistrates' Court. All in all, the Sunday traders obtained more references than required to enter the European stage. The Sunday traders did not attempt to obtain a reference from the Court of Appeal, as they were sceptical of the willingness of the Court of Appeal to agree to this. It should be noted that, in the late 1980s, it was unusual for lay magistrates to refer cases to the ECJ. It was the Cwmbran Magistrates' Court's reference that was eventually selected for decision by the ECJ in the now famous *Torfaen* judgment.

Delaying proceedings in the national courts

The effectiveness of using Article 234 (ex Article 177) in this way was dependent on, first, how the ECJ dealt with multiple references on the same point of law, and, secondly, on how judges in national courts dealt with cases when a case was pending before the ECJ. While the *Torfaen* and *Stoke-on-Trent*[32] cases were pending before the ECJ, the President of the ECJ deferred the hearing of references in similar cases in accordance with Article 55(2) of the ECJ's Rules of Procedure. It is the ECJ's general practice to defer cases on the same point, and to hear one case, such as *Torfaen*, as a test case. After the test case has been decided, the ECJ will sometimes take the informal course of writing to the referring court in all the other cases pending on the same point, informing them of the ruling in the test case, and inquiring whether they still wish to have their cases heard. In the event, once the ECJ had made its decision in *Torfaen* on 23 November 1989,[33] all the other references made by the English courts at approximately the same time as *Torfaen* were withdrawn. Nevertheless, as a delaying tactic, the traders' strategy worked. For example, in *Derry City Council* v. *Hampden Homecare plc*,[34] the reference was originally made in 1988, but it was not until 17 September 1991 that the reference was withdrawn. Thus, the proceedings in the national court had been successfully delayed for some three years.

[32] Case C-169/91, *Stoke-on-Trent City Council* v. *B&Q plc* [1992] ECR I-6635 at 6657 and 6693.

[33] Case C-118/88, *Suffolk Coastal District Council* v. *Notcutts Garden Centres Ltd*, removed 10 May 1990; Case C-134/88, *Mansfield District Council* v. *Payless DIY Ltd*, removed 17 January 1990; Case C-232/88, *Derry City Council* v. *Hampden Homecare plc*, removed 17 September 1991.

[34] Case C-232/88, *Derry City Council* v. *Hampden Homecare plc*, removed 17 September 1991.

Magistrates' courts have a power to adjourn cases before them under section 10 of the Magistrates' Courts Act 1980. This discretion is not, however, unfettered. Diamond argues that to adjourn cases *sine die* pending a determination by the ECJ of a similar case may well amount to a 'refusal of jurisdiction'.[35] It is, however, suggested that adjournment was fully justified in the circumstances. Alternatively, the courts could have referred the case to the ECJ. In terms of delay, that would have had the same effect as adjournment of the case. A further alternative would have been to try the case. Such a course would, however, have required the magistrates to decide issues of Community law. It is no surprise, therefore, that, in most cases, the magistrates exercised their discretion under section 10 of the Magistrates' Courts Act 1980 and adjourned the cases before them, pending judgment in the ECJ. Considering that adjournment is considerably cheaper for the parties than a referral to the ECJ, and at the same time it had the same delaying effect as a referral, the magistrates' willingness to adjourn *sine die* was perfectly in tune with the Sunday traders' short-term interests: the latter continued trading in contravention of the 1950 Act until a final ruling on the compatibility of the Shops Act with Article 28 (ex Article 30) had been obtained.

The European defence: issues of substantive law

The European defence provided the possibility of obtaining a ruling from the ECJ holding the Shops Act 1950 to be in breach of Article 28 (ex Article 30). Such a ruling would have been in tune with both the long-term and the short-term interests of the Sunday traders. In the long run, incompatibility of the Shops Act with Article 28 (ex Article 30) would have necessitated an amendment to or a repeal of the Shops Act and might have promoted the Sunday traders' general interest in complete deregulation. In addition to the promotion of this general interest, a resort to the European defence was considered necessary for the outcome in each particular case.

In criminal proceedings, the question of the imposition of fines under section 59 of the Shops Act 1950 depended on the success of the European defence. In *Torfaen*, for instance, B&Q argued that Article 28 (ex Article 30) had direct effect, and that a person could not be convicted on the basis of a national law which was incompatible with directly effective Community law. In civil proceedings, the defence

[35] I. P. Diamond, 'The Shops Act and the EEC Treaty' (1989) 153 JP 51 at 53.

would have prevented the courts from granting an injunction against Sunday traders. It should, however, be noted that, before the decision in *Torfaen*, civil proceedings for injunctions were very rare since even the local authorities saw the force of the European defence. Nevertheless, successful resort to Article 28 (ex Article 30) would have legitimated Sunday trading in the particular area concerned for the time being. For an evaluation of the force of the European defence, a digression into the EC legal background as it existed in 1988 is necessary.

The EC law background in 1988

Understanding the interrelationship between Article 28 (ex Article 30) and Article 30 (ex Article 36), as well as the subsequent case law defining, refining and creating exceptions to Article 28 (ex Article 30), is essential to an understanding of the Sunday trading litigation. It should be noted at the outset that the litigants had to present arguments which justified a preliminary reference in the cases concerned, particularly considering the power of the national courts to decline to make a reference if they regarded the matter as *acte claire*.

Article 28 (ex Article 30) provides as follows:

> Quantitative restrictions on imports and all measures having equivalent effect shall be prohibited between Member States.

Article 28 (ex Article 30) is concerned with the free movement of goods, and should be seen as a step along the road to the creation of a fully functioning common market. 'Quantitative restrictions' in Article 28 (ex Article 30) are measures designed to prohibit or limit exports or imports of particular classes of goods by reference to their number, weight, value or other quantitative criteria. 'Measures having equivalent effect', which are of particular importance in the Sunday trading cases, have proved more difficult to define. To offer guidance as to the meaning and scope of such measures, the Commission passed Directive 70/50/EEC,[36] which on the face of it applied only to the removal of restrictions during the transitional period.[37] Measures which can constitute measures having equivalent effect to quantitative restrictions are specified in Article 2 of the Directive. However, in the case of *Procureur du Roi* v. *Dassonville*,[38] the ECJ set out its own definition

[36] Directive 70/50/EEC of 22 December 1969, OJ 1969 No. L13, 18 January 1969, 29.

[37] Which for the original Member States ended in 1969.

[38] Case 8/74, *Dassonville* [1974] ECR 837; [1974] 2 CMLR 436, para. 5.

of such measures, which is usually referred to now as the '*Dassonville* formula'. The formula provides as follows:

> All trading rules enacted by Member States which are capable of hindering, directly or indirectly, actually or potentially, intra-Community trade are to be considered as measures having an effect equivalent to quantitative restrictions.

The significance of this definition for the purposes of the Sunday traders lies in the fact that it does not require a measure to be discriminatory in order for it to be caught by Article 28 (ex Article 30). Thus it paved the way for the distinction between 'distinctly applicable' (that is, discriminatory) and 'indistinctly applicable' (that is, non-discriminatory) measures in the case of *Cassis de Dijon*. Directive 70/50/EEC[39] had already distinguished between distinctly applicable measures[40] and indistinctly applicable measures.[41] According to the non-binding guidelines in Directive 70/50/EEC,[42] distinctly applicable measures appear to be acceptable provided they comply with the principle of proportionality. Following this approach, *Cassis de Dijon* is authority for the proposition that certain measures, though caught by the *Dassonville* formula, will not infringe Article 28 (ex Article 30) in so far as they may be recognised

> as being necessary in order to satisfy mandatory requirements relating in particular to the effectiveness of fiscal supervision, the protection of public health, the fairness of commercial transactions and the defence of the consumer.[43]

Prior to *Cassis de Dijon*, it was assumed that any measure, whether distinctly or indistinctly applicable, falling within the *Dassonville* formula would infringe Article 28 (ex Article 30) unless justified under Article 30 (ex Article 36).[44] Article 30 (ex Article 36) allows Member States legitimately to limit the freedom of movement of goods and thus to derogate from principles comprised in Article 28 (ex Article 30). It

[39] Directive 70/50/EEC of 22 December 1969, OJ 1969 No. L13, 29.
[40] *Ibid.*, Art. 2. [41] *Ibid.*, Art. 3. [42] *Ibid.* [43] Para. 8.
[44] Art. 30 (ex Art. 36): 'The provisions of [Art. 28 (ex Art. 30)] to 34 shall not preclude prohibitions or restrictions on imports, exports or goods in transit justified on grounds of public morality, public policy or public security; the protection of health and life of humans, animals or plants; the protection of national treasures possessing artistic, historic and commercial property. Such prohibitions or restrictions shall not, however, constitute a means of arbitrary discrimination or a disguised restriction on trade between Member States.'

is important to note that, even though the grounds in Article 30 (ex Article 36) appear extensive they have been narrowly construed by the Court. First, there are specific grounds for derogation, that is, 'public morality, public policy or public security; the protection of health and life of humans, animals or plants; the protection of national treasures possessing artistic, historic or archaeological value; or the protection of industrial and commercial property'. Secondly, in order to qualify as a derogation under Article 30 (ex Article 36), the prohibition must not 'constitute a means of arbitrary discrimination or a disguised restriction on trade between Member States'. At the time of the Sunday trading litigation, distinctly applicable measures had to meet these two conditions in order to be saved from the prohibition under Article 28 (ex Article 30).

However, following *Cassis de Dijon*, it was clear – and it still is clear – that, in cases of indistinctly applicable measures, in addition to Article 30 (ex Article 36), courts are free to apply the 'rule of reason' laid down in *Dassonville.*[45] Thus, regardless of Article 30 (ex Article 36), a further exception to Article 28 (ex Article 30) for indistinctly applicable measures had been created by *Cassis de Dijon*. The significance of this decision for the Sunday traders was – as will be seen – the fact that the mandatory requirements under *Cassis de Dijon* were non-exhaustive and considerably wider than the categories under Article 30 (ex Article 36). This was apparent in *Cinéthèque SA* v. *Fédération Nationale des Cinémas Francais*, in which the ECJ held that the French rule was *prima facie* within Article 28 (ex Article 30) but justifiable on *Cassis de Dijon* principles. The ECJ seemed to extend the *Cassis de Dijon* list of mandatory requirements by adding a further ground for objective justification, that is, the encouragement of the creation of cinematographic works.[46] This decision illustrates the essential problem of whether 'equal-burden' rules should be held to be outside Article 28 (ex Article 30) or whether they should be deemed to be incompatible with Article 28 (ex Article 30) unless saved by one of the mandatory requirements.

For a better understanding of the 'equal-burden' rules, further elaboration on the nature of trading rules is necessary, in order then to be able to correctly classify the Sunday trading legislation. As noted by Weatherill and Beaumont,[47] a distinction can be drawn between

[45] Para. 6. [46] Para. 23.
[47] S. Weatherill and P. Beaumont (eds.), *EC Law* (2nd edn, London, 1995), 532.

'equal-burden rules' and 'dual-burden rules'. This distinction is based on the impact of the rules in question. Dual-burden rules are those rules which the decision in *Cassis de Dijon* rendered incompatible with Article 28 (ex Article 30) unless justifiable under the heading of mandatory requirement. As the label 'dual-burden' indicates, such rules have the effect of imposing a 'second' burden or, alternatively, an 'additional' burden on imported goods. First, the goods must comply with the relevant trade rules in their country of origin. Secondly, those rules labelled 'dual-burden rules' require the compliance by imported goods with certain requirements, concerning for example the content of the goods, despite the fact that those goods already comply with the relevant trade rules of their state of origin. The imposition of an *additional* burden on imported goods puts those goods at a disadvantage and, thus, amounts to a measure having equivalent effect to quantitative restrictions within Article 28 (ex Article 30). On the other hand, equal-burden rules are those rules applying indistinctly to all goods, whether imported or domestic, which are designed to regulate trade in some way but which burden imports no more than they do domestic products. Such rules are not designed to be protectionist as such, or to regulate patterns of cross-border trade. Rather, they are designed to regulate the national market. Nevertheless, they may have an effect on the overall volume of trade, even though that effect is unrelated to the fact that the goods may or may not have crossed a national border.

In light of this definition, a preliminary question arising in the Sunday trading cases was whether the Sunday trading prohibition amounted to a dual-burden rule or an equal-burden rule. Considering that the Shops Act 1950 was not designed to restrict trade in imported goods more than in domestic goods, considering, equally, that the Act was a measure intended to regulate the domestic market as such rather than intra-Community trade, and considering that a common market does not require regulatory uniformity in relation to shop opening hours, it seems to follow that the rules at issue should properly be classified as equal-burden rules.

On the assumption that the Sunday trading prohibition is correctly classified as an equal-burden rule, the essential question which followed was whether – by analogy to the dual-burden rules – the effect of *Cassis de Dijon* was to render the Sunday trading prohibition – and thus equal-burden rules in general – incompatible with Article 28 (ex Article 30). In this respect, the decision in *Cinéthèque* can be taken to indicate such a development. *Cinéthèque* concerned a French law banning the sale or hire of videos or films for a year following release of the film. The rule applied to both domestic and imported videos alike, and was therefore an equal-burden rule. The ECJ held that the rule, designed to encourage the creation of cinematographic works, was justified on *Cassis de Dijon* principles and did not infringe Article 28 (ex Article 30). It should be noted that the ECJ held the rules to fall *prima facie* within Article 28 (ex Article 30). In the immediate aftermath of this decision, the central issue in the Sunday trading cases therefore became the proper limits of Article 28 (ex Article 30) and how the case law could be taken advantage of by the Sunday traders.

The Sunday traders' construction of Article 28 in *Torfaen*

In the *Torfaen* proceedings before the ECJ, it was argued for the Sunday traders that section 47 of the Shops Act 1950 amounted to a measure having an equivalent effect to a quantitative restriction on imports within the meaning of Article 28 (ex Article 30) and the *Dassonville* formula. B&Q adduced evidence that there was a significant loss of turnover resulting from the closure of their shops on Sundays. If overall sales were reduced, it was argued, imports from the European Community would consequently be reduced. Considering that 15 per cent of goods sold by DIY stores (that is, more than £40 million worth of goods per year) were imported directly from the Member States of the Community, the Shops Act 1950 was also significantly restricting the value of imports from such Member States. Hence, section 47 amounted to a measure having an equivalent effect to quantitative restrictions. In essence, it was submitted therefore that section 47 was *prima facie* contrary to Article 28 (ex Article 30).

It was further contended by the Sunday traders that section 47 would not come within the exceptions to Article 28 (ex Article 30): neither Article 30 (ex Article 36) nor the category of 'mandatory requirement' established in the *Cassis de Dijon* case could be relied on. In relation to Article 30 (ex Article 36), the line of reasoning consisted essentially of three submissions. First, it was argued that section 47 could not be justified under any of the exempted categories, since Article 30 (ex Article 36) had to be construed strictly. Secondly, even if the challenged rule came within one of the exempted categories, it would constitute a 'means of arbitrary discrimination or a disguised restriction on trade between Member States'.[48] Finally, if the rule passed even the latter test, it would be caught by the proportionality test. As regards the *Cassis de*

[48] Art. 30 (ex Art. 36).

Dijon exception, it was submitted that section 47 was not 'necessary in order to satisfy mandatory requirements'.

It is well established by the ECJ's jurisdiction that both Article 30 (ex Article 36) and the *Cassis de Dijon* doctrine are subject to the proportionality test. The significance of the proportionality test is that it constitutes the final hurdle which a measure must pass before it can be held to come within one of the exceptions to Article 28 (ex Article 30). In the case of the Sunday trading litigation, it was therefore capable of being determinative of whether or not the Sunday trading prohibition could be upheld. As to the proportionality requirement, it was argued that, as a result of the anomalies of the Act, the prohibition on Sunday trading could not be regarded as reasonable. The anomalies were generally attributed to Schedule 5 to the 1950 Act which provided for exceptions to the prohibition contained in section 47. The Auld Committee in its 1983 report[49] listed a series of these anomalies including:

> the fact that a razor blade could be sold for the purposes of cutting corns, but not for shaving; and that a pornographic magazine could lawfully be sold at any shop, but that a Bible could only be sold from a bookstall at a designated airport or railway or bus station.[50]

In addition, the fact that none of the provisions in issue applied to Scotland[51] was taken to render the Act disproportionate. In effect, there was no bar to Sunday trading in Scotland, apart from section 67.[52] Two riders to this argument should be noted. First, due to its distinct history and traditions, Scotland has its own legal system. Secondly, similar provisions to that of the Shops Act 1950 apply to Northern Ireland,[53] where there is no legal tradition distinct from that of England and Wales. These riders undermine the force of the proportionality argument to some extent.

The reasoning of B&Q can be summarised as follows. Section 47 of the Shops Act 1950 is a trading rule. As such, it amounts to a measure having an effect equivalent to a quantitative restriction on imports, since it indirectly, but actually, hinders intra-Community trade.

[49] Cmnd 9376, Report of the Committee of Inquiry, *The Shops Act: Late-Night and Sunday Opening* (London, 1984).

[50] P. Oliver, 'Sunday Trading and Article 30 of the Treaty of Rome' (1991) 20 *Industrial Law Journal* 298 at 299.

[51] Shops Act 1950, section 66.

[52] Relating to the business of hairdressing and barbering in Scotland.

[53] Shops Act (Northern Ireland) 1946.

Section 47 is therefore *prima facie* within Article 28 (ex Article 30), and is neither justifiable under Article 30 (ex Article 36) nor necessary and proportionate to satisfy mandatory requirements. Even though the ruling of the ECJ in *Torfaen* did not follow this reasoning, it was regarded as a victory by the Sunday traders.

A purposive interpretation of the ruling in *Torfaen*

In essence, in *Torfaen* the ECJ held that:

> [Article 28 (ex Article 30)] of the Treaty must be interpreted as meaning that the prohibition which it lays down does not apply to national rules prohibiting retailers from opening their premises on Sunday where the restrictive effects on Community trade which may result therefrom do not exceed the effects intrinsic to rules of that kind.[54]

The ECJ went on to state that:

> The question of whether the effects of specific national rules do in fact remain within that limit is a question of fact to be determined by the national court.[55]

This ruling was immediately subject to different interpretations by the parties, by academics and (most importantly) by the national courts. The Sunday traders' initial reaction was that they had lost their case. This was an unsatisfactory outcome for the Sunday traders for the following reason. The Sunday traders had undertaken to abide by the decision in *Torfaen*, that is, they had undertaken to plead guilty in criminal proceedings or to accept the closure of their shops on Sundays should they lose in *Torfaen*. This would have meant the end of the Sunday trading war. After more detailed consideration of the judgment, however, Arthur Hugh Vaughan QC realised that it offered scope for argument in national courts and that it was capable of constituting a 'tremendous victory'[56] for the Sunday traders. The Sunday traders came to the view that the outcome of the Sunday trading litigation depended on the national court's decision on the proportionality issue. As a result, the traders' first shifted the focus of their argument onto the issue of proportionality, while, secondly, directing their resources

[54] Case C-145/88, *Torfaen Borough Council* v. *B&Q plc* [1989] ECR 3851 at 3889, para. 17.

[55] *Ibid.*, para. 16.

[56] Arthur Hugh Vaughan QC, in his first statement after the *Torfaen* decision.

towards proving that section 47 was disproportionate. At the same time, the local authorities shifted the emphasis of their activities from prosecuting the Sunday traders to seeking injunctions against them, since they were convinced that *Torfaen* constituted the death-knell for the European defence.

Legal considerations affecting the Sunday traders' strategy

Section 71(1) of the Shops Act 1950 obliged local authorities to enforce the provisions of the Act. In light of the futility of criminal proceedings, the local authorities were obliged to institute civil proceedings in order to obtain injunctions against the Sunday traders and thus to secure observance of the Act.

It is a civil contempt of court to disobey a judgment or order of the court requiring an individual or corporate body to abstain from doing a specified act. Under Order 45, rule 5(1), of the Rules of the Supreme Court, a judgment or order against a corporate body may be enforced by an order of committal against the directors or other officers of the corporation. The court may give leave for the issue of a writ of sequestration against the property of the corporation or of any of its directors or officers; the corporation itself cannot be committed, but it can be fined. For the Sunday traders, this meant that breach of an injunction would carry not only financial but also serious legal consequences. This, together with the hope of obtaining favourable rulings in national courts following the decision in *Torfaen*, as well as possibly a further ruling from the ECJ, led the Sunday traders to ask for cross-undertakings in damages from the local authorities. This is the usual practice in private law proceedings, yet the legal position in public law was contentious and thus taken advantage of by the Sunday traders.

Cross-undertakings in damages were a serious threat to the local authorities' budgets, since there was still the possibility of losing the Sunday trading war. Therefore, until the decision of the House of Lords in *Kirklees Metropolitan Borough Council* v. *Wickes Building Supplies Ltd*,[57] most local authorities refrained from seeking injunctions for fear of the requirement to give cross-undertakings in damages. The decision of the House of Lords in *Kirklees* made it considerably easier for local authorities to apply for injunctions. It was held that an injunction could be granted without the need for local authorities to give a cross-undertaking in damages.

[57] [1992] 3 All ER 717, reversing the decision of the Court of Appeal, [1991] 4 All ER 240; for a further discussion, see pp. 79–83 below.

Parallel to the cross-undertaking battle in the national courts, the Sunday traders continued to use the European defence in national courts while now concentrating on the issue of proportionality.

Interpreting *Torfaen* in the national courts

The Sunday traders argued that, in effect, the ECJ had decided that section 47 of the Shops Act 1950 was incompatible with Community law, subject to the doctrine of proportionality.[58] Considering that, even before the ruling of the ECJ, B&Q had argued that, due to the anomalies of the Act, the prohibition on Sunday trading could *not* be regarded as proportionate, it was no surprise that the judgment in *Torfaen* was eventually considered to be a victory by the traders.

In order to prove that the 1950 Act was indeed disproportionate, a 'troupe of experts'[59] and witnesses such as shop-workers willing to work on Sundays toured the country giving evidence in the Sunday traders' favour. The leading expert for the Sunday traders was Terry Burke, an academic economist with the Polytechnic of Central London, who was an expert on Sunday trading. Together with Tony Askham, of Hepherd, Winstanley and Pugh,[60] solicitors, who acted for a number of the retailers, and David Ramsden, Controller of Retailing for B&Q plc, he even visited the then twelve Member States of the European Community in order to conduct a survey of EC Sunday trading rules. The result of this survey was a comparative review of shop-opening regulations across the European Community and an analysis of current court cases.[61]

However, the subsequent *Torfaen* decisions in the English courts and the ECJ thwarted the reasoning of the Sunday traders. It was held in the national courts that section 47 did no more than was necessary to achieve its inherent objective, that is, the preservation of the traditional English and Welsh Sunday as a non-trading day, and any effect which it had on Community trade could not exceed that which was intrinsic in rules of that kind.[62] Even more importantly, the decisions

[58] *Kirklees Metropolitan Borough Council* v. *Wickes Building Supplies Ltd* [1993] AC 227, submissions by Andrew Collins QC and Paul Lasok for the defendants.

[59] [1990] 3 CMLR 31 at 44. [60] Now Bond Pearce, solicitors.

[61] T. Askham, T. Burke and D. Ramsden (eds.), *Current EC Legal Development Series, EC Sunday Trading Rules* (London, 1990). There has never been a second edition, as only 189 copies were sold.

[62] For a more detailed discussion of the application of the proportionality test in national courts, see pp. 130–51 below.

of the ECJ in *Conforama*[63] and *Marchandise*[64] constituted a potential threat to the traders' success in national courts, even though those cases were concerned with Sunday employment rather than Sunday trading. These developments required the Sunday traders, first, to rethink their Euro-wide collaboration, and, secondly, to reconsider their interpretation of the *Torfaen* decision.

The failure of the European collaboration

An essential element of B&Q's strategy was to co-ordinate its moves with those taking place in other Member States. Arthur Hugh Vaughan QC, counsel for the Sunday traders, is known to have been consulted by his French counterparts in the *Conforama* proceedings. Equally, Tony Askham, solicitor for a number of the Sunday traders, seems to have been in contact with lawyers throughout Europe. However, despite this, it would be going too far to talk about Euro-wide networking or concerted litigation. Nevertheless, it can be seen that the lawyers built on the submissions of their colleagues in earlier cases and adapted their reasoning depending on the success or failure of those submissions. It can equally be seen how the outcome of the application of the proportionality test in the national courts in England and Wales influenced the approach of the defendants in *Conforama* and *Marchandise*. After it had become evident that in the majority of cases the national courts would not hold the rules at issue to be disproportionate, the Sunday traders decided that the way forward would be to request the ECJ to determine issue of proportionality. The ECJ was therefore provided with all the facts relevant to the issue of proportionality. However, this strategy of undermining the authority of the national courts did not prove successful since in *Conforama* the ECJ held, as regards the legislation at issue:

> [T]he restrictive effects on trade which may stem from such rules do not *seem* disproportionate to the aim pursued . . . [I]t must therefore be held that the prohibition contained in [Article 28 (ex Article 30)] of the Treaty, properly construed, does not apply to national legislation prohibiting the employment of staff on Sundays.[65]

[63] Case C-312/89, *Union Departmentale des Syndicats CGT de l'Aisne* v. *Sidef Conforama* [1991] ECR I-997.
[64] Case C-332/89, *Ministère Public* v. *Marchandise* [1991] ECR I-1027.
[65] Case C-312/89, *Union Departmentale des Syndicats CGT de l'Aisne* v. *Sidef Conforama* [1991] ECR I-997 at 1025, paras. 12–13 (emphasis added).

If this decision on the prohibition of the employment of staff on Sundays is taken to be authoritative also on the issue of the prohibition of Sunday trading, then it must be taken to indicate the failure of the Euro-wide collaboration of the Sunday trades. By analogy to Sunday employment, it may then be argued that the restrictive effects on trade which might arise from the Sunday trading prohibition were not proportionate to the aim pursued. This would be the end of the Sunday traders' case. Certainly, it would be too far-fetched to maintain that *Conforama* and *Marchandise* constitute a *precedent* for the Sunday trading litigation. A decision on Sunday employment does not constitute a direct ECJ ruling on Sunday trading. However, even if the decision cannot be treated as a direct precedent, it might nevertheless be seen as capable of closing the door to further references by Sunday traders on the issue of the prohibition of Sunday trading. In *Da Costa*,[66] it had been held that, in cases in which the questions of interpretation posed were 'identical'[67] with those already settled and 'no new factor [had] been presented to the Court',[68] the national court should follow the previous judgment. This is considered to be the first ruling leading to the establishment of an *acte claire* doctrine in Community law. It is arguable that the question of trading on Sundays is materially identical with the question of employment of workers on Sundays.

As a consequence, with the failure of the Euro-wide litigation strategy and the *acte claire* doctrine in mind, counsel for the Sunday traders began to deny any connection between the proceedings in *Torfaen* and those in *Conforama* and *Marchandise*. Following the decisions in *Conforama* and *Marchandise*, there was obviously a need to undermine the significance of the latter decisions if the Sunday traders wanted to win their case. This is even more so as the Sunday traders found themselves again before the ECJ, this time being much more the object than the subject of concern.

The lost initiative: the national courts go to Luxembourg

The Sunday traders had unleashed a legal avalanche; now they were in danger of themselves being buried as the English courts considered the implications of *Torfaen* from their own perspective and referred Sunday trading to the ECJ to resolve the issue of how to handle the proportionality test. Three cases were referred to Luxembourg, from

[66] Case C-28–30/62, *Da Costa* [1963] ECR 31. [67] *Ibid.* [68] *Ibid.*

the magistrates' court, the High Court and the House of Lords: *Reading Borough Council* v. *Payless DIY Ltd*[69] was referred by the Reading Magistrates' Court; *Stoke-on-Trent City Council* v. *B&Q plc*[70] was referred by the House of Lords; and *Rochdale Borough Council* v. *Anders*[71] was referred by the Queen's Bench Division of the High Court. The Sunday traders did their best to tackle the new issue, but it seemed as if the European defence – not the campaign as such – had lost its impetus. The arguments brought forward on behalf of the Sunday traders sounded half-hearted. They seemed to have known that the legal battle based on Article 28 (ex Article 30) was already lost before the ECJ handed down its final decision.

The Sunday traders' defence in *Stoke-on-Trent* ran as follows. The *Torfaen* judgment was not affected by the judgments in *Conforama* and *Marchandise*. Rather, the latter judgments as a whole were taken as an approval of the judgment in *Torfaen*. It was submitted that the use of the word 'seem' in paragraph 12 of the *Torfaen* judgment indicated that – as stated in *Torfaen* – the proportionality issue was a question of fact to be determined by the national courts. Thus it was clear that the ECJ had not itself determined the issue of proportionality. The cases were further distinguished on the grounds of differences in legislation, factual evidence and the approach of the parties. However, if the ECJ wished to decide on the issue of proportionality, it was submitted that those rules were disproportionate since the objective of section 47 could not 'possibly have sufficient importance to outweigh a reduction in intra-Community trade of around one billion ECUs per annum'.[72] The anomalies of the legislation itself as well as its sporadic enforcement would undermine any objectivity inherent in those rules.

The primary submission of B&Q was, however, that the ECJ's approach in *Torfaen* had been correct, that is, that Sunday trading rules such as those in the Shops Act 1950 amounted to measures having equivalent effect to quantitative restrictions on trade within the meaning of Article 28 (ex Article 30), and that proportionality was a question of fact to be determined by the national courts. The ruling in *Stoke-on-Trent*, however, thwarted this reasoning and put an end to the European defence.

[69] Case C-169/91, *Stoke-on-Trent City Council* v. *B&Q plc* [1992] ECR I-6635; [1993] 1 CMLR 426.

[70] *Ibid.*

[71] Case C-306/88, *Rochdale Metropolitan Borough Council* v. *Anders* [1992] ECR I-6457.

[72] Case C-169/91, *Stoke-on-Trent City Council* v. *B&Q plc* [1992] ECR I-6635 at 6642.

A victory in the Sunday trading war despite a defeat in Europe

The constant adaptation by the Sunday traders of their arguments demonstrates that Article 28 (ex Article 30) was merely a vehicle for the Sunday traders to obtain their long-term goal of trading lawfully on Sundays. What they needed in those circumstances was time, as well as a court ruling stating the incompatibility of national legislation with Article 28 (ex Article 30). Their plan was simple: if they could not obtain their policy goal on a national level, they would try to obtain it on a European level, and *vice versa*. The implementation of this plan can be described as follows. After having been defeated in the national proceedings,[73] the Sunday traders raised the European defence, hoping for a favourable ruling by the ECJ. However, their apparent victory in *Torfaen* was in effect nullified by the reluctance of the national courts to disapply primary legislation. Having been unsuccessful in the national courts, the Sunday traders once again relied on the ECJ decisions in *Conforama* and *Marchandise*, hoping that the ECJ would decide the issue of proportionality in their favour. Their hopes having been dashed by the ruling of the ECJ in *Torfaen*, the Sunday traders again sought to rely on the national courts and requested the ECJ in *Stoke-on-Trent* to state that proportionality was a question of fact for the national courts. Again, this plan failed when the ECJ decided the issue of proportionality itself and the House of Lords then made it expressly clear that it would be 'undesirable'[74] for their Lordships to make any further comment on the issue of proportionality. Yet, in the meantime, the existing legislative regime had been brought into such disrepute by the Sunday traders' campaign that the time was ripe for the matter to be resolved in Parliament.

Even though the Sunday traders had lost the Euro-law battle, this did not constitute the end of their campaign. Their desperate search for a means to achieve lawful Sunday trading can be seen, for example, in the line of cases in which the Shops Act was contested on the basis of sex discrimination. It was argued in this line of cases that the effect of the Sunday trading ban was to discriminate against women since the majority of workers on Sunday would be women. However, the

[73] When they attempted to use the 'motor accessory defence' in *Hadley* v. *Texas Homecare Ltd* (1988) 152 JP 268 and *Stoke-on-Trent City Council* v. *B&Q (Retail) Ltd* [1984] AC 754; [1984] 2 WLR 929; [1984] 2 All ER 332.

[74] *Stoke-on-Trent City Council* v. *B&Q plc* [1993] 2 All ER 297 *per* Lord Goff.

most important of these cases was withdrawn in the Court of Appeal when the ban on Sunday trading was eventually lifted by Parliament. In addition to the legal campaign, the Sunday traders had never given up their political campaign.

The Euro-law battle had provided the Sunday traders with the time they needed to undertake a political campaign. When the judgment in *Stoke-on-Trent* was delivered by the ECJ, the Sunday traders were only four or five months short of obtaining a political solution. While the Euro-law battle was still ongoing, the political campaigner of the Sunday traders, David Ramsden, Controller of Retailing for B&Q plc, had succeeded in getting their political message across to the public, the media, the shop-workers' unions and the politicians. Monthly polls proved that 62–5 per cent of the population favoured some form of relaxation of the Sunday trading restrictions. Shortly after the decision in *Stoke-on-Trent*, the Sunday traders succeeded in getting the shop-workers' unions, the Labour Party (the principal opposition party in Parliament at that time), consumers and retailers as a whole on board. The shop-workers' unions agreed to support legislative reform when the Sunday traders guaranteed higher rates of pay for Sunday workers. The Labour Party took their cue from the shop-workers' unions. Consumers had in general always been supportive of the campaign for

Table 2.1 *Criminal and civil references to the ECJ in the Sunday trading litigation*

	Criminal jurisdiction	Civil jurisdiction
Highest level	House of Lords No references	House of Lords Kirklees Stole-on-Trent
	Court of Appeal (Criminal Division) No references	Court of Appeal (Civil Division) Kirklees
	Crown Court Shrewsbury Wellingborough	High Court Kirklees Peterborough Rochdale Stoke-on-Trent
Lowest level	Magistrates' Court Reading Torfaen	County Court No references

Sunday opening, and the retail sector relied on the increased turnover brought by more flexible opening hours. Thus the time was ripe for the law to be changed, and the Sunday Trading Act 1994 was passed in Parliament. It is to the credit of the Sunday traders that they achieved political change and ensured the enactment of a law which was enforceable. More importantly, however, it is also to the credit of the Sunday traders that they dispelled the fears of English practitioners in using European law.

The local authorities

The dilemma

Following the Sunday traders' blatant breach of the Shops Act 1950, the local authorities' position can be aptly characterised as a dilemma. The Shops Act itself imposed on them a statutory duty to enforce the Act. If the local authorities decided not to enforce the Act, they could have been held liable for breach of statutory duty. If, however, they made efforts to enforce the Act, they were in danger of having to give cross-undertakings in damages as long as final judgment of the ECJ on the issue of Sunday trading was pending. Thus, the question of whether to enforce or not to enforce the Act involved serious financial considerations for the local authorities.

The underlying interest of the local authorities in the interpretation of Article 28 (ex Article 30) by the ECJ must therefore be described as follows. The incompatibility of the Shops Act 1950 with Article 28 (ex Article 30) would have relieved the local authorities of their statutory duty to enforce the Act. A finding of compatibility of the 1950 Act with Article 28 (ex Article 30) would equally have clarified the local authorities' position and confirmed the legality of their enforcement measures. The significance of this clarification for those local authorities in whose areas the law was being broken can be seen in the professional planning of their strategy and their close co-operation with each other.

Professional planning and co-operation

Using Galanter's classification and typology of parties,[75] one might be tempted to classify the local authorities as 'one-shotters',[76] having only occasional recourse to the courts. In fact, the co-ordination shown

[75] See the text at note 4 above.

[76] M. Galanter, 'Why the "Haves" Come Out Ahead: Speculations on the Limits of Legal Change' (1974) 9 *Law and Society Review* 95 at 97.

by the local authorities can in no way be compared to the level of professional planning shown by the Sunday traders. Nevertheless, the role of certain local authorities and the co-ordination of their policies should not be under-estimated.

The determination to enforce the Sunday trading rules differed considerably from one authority to another. Some local authorities such as Rochdale Borough Council either were reluctant to take action or only sporadically enforced the law. Others, however, such as Stoke-on-Trent City Council and Torfaen Borough Council proved determined to uphold the rule of law. As early as 1984, Stoke-on-Trent City Council sought an injunction against B&Q,[77] who had traded in contravention of the Shops Act 1950. It is possible to detect a pattern according to which Labour councils,[78] in particular those in Wales, were inclined to enforce the Shops Act, possibly in order to obtain increased pay for Sunday workers, whereas Conservative councils,[79] particularly in the south of England, took a rather more lax attitude to the question of enforcement of the Shops Act 1950. Thus, those councils, or to be more precise their legal departments, which took the lead had considerable legal experience of dealing with this issue before their cases were referred to the ECJ.

The co-operation between the local authorities was manifest on two levels. In general, the local authorities exchanged views on and their experience of the enforcement of the Shops Act 1950 in a conference held in London in December 1989 under the title 'Successful Enforcement Strategies on Sunday Trading'. More specifically, however, almost all of the local authorities were represented by the same legal team, namely, Stuart Isaacs QC and Neil Calver.[80] It should, however, be noted that the impetus for co-ordination did not come from the local authorities themselves but from Stuart Isaacs. It was Isaacs who wanted to keep a tight grip on the cases so as to ensure a consistent approach by the local authorities and in order to prevent a situation arising in which lawyers inexperienced in European law appeared in court

77 *Stoke-on-Trent City Council* v. *B&Q (Retail) Ltd* [1984] AC 754; [1984] 2 WLR 929; [1984] 2 All ER 332.

78 That is, councils which were under the political control of the Labour Party, the political party in the UK most traditionally associated with the trade unions.

79 That is, councils under the political control of the Conservative Party, the political party in the UK most closely associated with the interests of business.

80 Other barristers occasionally acted for the local authorities, for example Sharma, Straker, Newman, Jack, Reich, Patten, Beloff and Sauvain.

for the local authorities. As a result, the legal approach of the local authorities – including their submissions to the ECJ – were consistent, and were essentially Isaacs' interpretation of Community law.

In conclusion, it can safely be stated that the legal team of the local authorities, being engaged in much similar litigation over time, developed such a coherent strategy and such expertise that the local authorities could more aptly be classified as 'repeat players'. A closer look at the local authorities' dilemma will demonstrate that this co-operation and professional planning proved to be useful, and to some extent successful.

The local authorities' statutory duty to enforce the 1950 Act

The main reason for the local authorities taking action against traders opening their shops in contravention of the Shops Act 1950 was their statutory duty under section 71(1)[81] of the Act to enforce the provisions of the Act. Section 71(1) obliges local authorities to institute such proceedings 'as may be necessary' to secure the observance of the Act. Therefore, if criminal proceedings against Sunday traders prove futile, section 71(1) impliedly compelled the local authorities to use their powers under section 222 of the Local Government Act 1972 to institute civil proceedings in their own name. However, civil proceedings remained the last resort for local authorities to secure observance of the Shops Act 1950. Particularly in light of the Court of Appeal's ruling in *Kirklees*,[82] and after the increase of fines in the Criminal Justice Act 1991, criminal proceedings continued until the reform of the Sunday trading laws in 1994. The significance of this compliance with their statutory duty becomes obvious when analysing the liability of the local authorities for breach of statutory duty.

The liability of the local authorities for breach of statutory duty

Non-compliance by the local authorities with their statutory duty under section 71(1) of the Shops Act 1950 could have been challenged

[81] Section 71(1) provides: 'It shall be the *duty* of every local authority to enforce within their district the provisions of this Act and of the orders made under those provisions, and for that purpose to institute and carry on such proceedings in respect of contraventions of the said provisions and such orders as aforesaid *as may be necessary* to secure observance thereof.' Emphasis added.

[82] [1991] 3 WLR 985.

in two ways: first, by means of judicial review; and, secondly, by an action for breach of statutory duty.

In theory, depending on the nature of the duty and the identity of the complainant, it would have been possible to challenge a failure by the local authorities to enforce the provisions of the Shops Act by means of an action for judicial review. In 1977, a new procedure for applying for judicial review was introduced by the Rules of the Supreme Court (Amendment No. 3) 1977.[83] The effect of the changes was substantially to reduce the procedural requirements imposed upon an applicant for judicial review; this procedure was later enshrined in section 31 of the Supreme Court Act 1981. Following the introduction of Order 53 of the Rules of the Supreme Court, private law as well as public law remedies became available to an applicant seeking judicial review of administrative action. Judicial review remedies therefore now fall into two groups. On the one hand, there are the 'prerogative orders',[84] that is, *certiorari*,[85] prohibition[86] and *mandamus*;[87] on the other hand, there are the 'private law' remedies of declaration,[88] injunction and damages. Failure to comply with the duty under section 71(1) of the Shops Act would most likely have led to an order for *mandamus* being sought by an applicant – possibly also with a request for damages. *Mandamus* is a prerogative order from the High Court instructing the inferior body or authority concerned to perform a specified public duty relating to its responsibilities. Following the introduction of Order 53, rule 7, in 1977, it became possible for an applicant for judicial review to add a claim for damages.[89] However, an applicant who wished to add a

[83] SI 1977 No. 1955.

[84] Prerogative orders are orders issued by the High Court for the supervision of bodies such as local authorities exercising judicial or quasi-judicial functions.

[85] From the Latin meaning 'to be informed', *certiorari* is a remedy whereby the High Court orders that decisions of inferior courts, tribunals and administrative bodies be brought before it in order to quash them if they are found either to be *ultra vires* or to have been based on an error of law.

[86] Prohibition is a remedy in which the High Court orders an ecclesiastical or inferior court, tribunal or administrative authority not to carry out an *ultra vires* act.

[87] From the Latin, meaning 'we command'.

[88] A declaration is a discretionary remedy involving a finding by the High Court as to a person's legal status, rights or obligations.

[89] Order 53, rule 7, provides: 'On an application for judicial review the court may ... award damages to the applicant if the court is satisfied that, if the claim had been made in proceedings for damages begun by the applicant at the time of making his application for judicial review, he could have been awarded damages.'

claim for damage to his application would have had to show that such a remedy would have been available in an action started by writ.[90]

Yet, an application for judicial review might not have been as attractive to the complainant as an action for breach of statutory duty. Judicial review is discretionary, as are the remedies therefor, and the court might have decided that the Sunday trading cases were not appropriate cases for the granting of *mandamus*, either because some other more suitable remedies existed, or because the duty was worded in such broad, vague terms that supervision of its performance would have been impossible. Hence, an action for breach of statutory duty might have been more likely to be brought by certain applicants, for instance shopowners, who did not pursue wider political interests which required them to seek an order of *mandamus*.

While the tort of breach of statutory duty has been recognised for many years by the courts, it is not necessarily the case that every such breach will give rise to a right to damages. An action for breach of statutory duty will lie only if the statute can be interpreted as giving rise to individual rights of action in respect of the particular plaintiff and in respect of the sort of injury or damage suffered by the plaintiff.[91] Faced with this requirement, it therefore seems unlikely that a plaintiff would have been able to establish a right to damages in an action brought against a local authority in relation to its failure to enforce the Sunday trading prohibition. These observations are corroborated by the decision of the High Court in *R.* v. *Braintree District Council, ex parte Willingham*.[92]

Precedent on the statutory duty under section 71

The decision in *ex parte Willingham* constitutes a precedent which neatly demonstrates the pressure under which the local authorities found themselves. In essence, following this decision, the local authorities were under a duty to enforce the Shops Act regardless of whether enforcement would carry serious consequences such as the giving of cross-undertakings in damages.

[90] A writ of summons is a writ by which an action is commenced in the High Court. A writ must be used when the action is one in tort, as would have been the case in a tort action for breach of statutory duty.

[91] The most recent consideration of the relevant case law by the House of Lords arose in *X (Minors)* v. *Bedfordshire County Council* [1995] 3 WLR 152.

[92] (1982) 81 LGR 70.

In *ex parte Willingham*, three members of the local chamber of commerce were granted leave to seek judicial review to challenge the local authority's failure to enforce the provisions of the Shops Act. The facts of this case were as follows. Certain persons began to operate a Sunday market within the district of the respondent council. The market operators purported to run the market as a club within the meaning of section 65(1)(b)[93] of the Shops Act, thus permitting the sale on Sundays of goods which could otherwise not be lawfully sold pursuant to section 47 of the Act. The respondent proffered information against a number of persons operating the market, alleging breaches of section 47 of the Act. However, in April 1981, the respondent council withdrew from the court proceedings after having received petitions from shopkeepers and from the stallholders of the Sunday market on the grounds, first, that legal action was an expensive course to pursue, and, secondly, that the operation of the Sunday market had attracted much public support. The policy committee of the respondent council considered that there was an element of doubt as to whether or not the council had an overriding duty to prosecute in every case in which the Sunday trading laws appeared to be infringed and that there was a probability that the court would hold that what was being done at the Sunday market was legal and that the council could legitimately refuse to institute litigation the outcome of which was uncertain. Consequently, three members of the local chamber of commerce applied for judicial review of the council's decision and for an order of *mandamus* requiring the council to perform its statutory duty under section 71(1) of the Shops Act 1950.

The court held that the council did not have a general discretion to decide whether or not to take steps to enforce the Shops Act 1950, nor to decide whether it would be too expensive or otherwise undesirable to institute proceedings. The only scope for discretion was whether any particular proceedings were necessary in order to secure observance of the Act. Hence, it was the council's duty under section 71 of the Act to enforce the Act within their district, and for that purpose they had a duty to institute and continue such proceedings in respect of alleged contraventions as might be necessary to secure observance of the Act.

It should be noted that *ex parte Willingham* was decided on 19 May 1982, that is, before the European defence was first resorted to by the

[93] By section 56(1) provides: 'Nothing in this Part of this Act shall prevent ...(b) the sale, dispatch or delivery of goods to a club for the purposes of the club ...'

Sunday traders. It is, however, suggested that, by analogy to this decision, the use of the European defence would not have altered the duty of local authorities to enforce the provisions of the 1950 Act. In fact, there are striking similarities between the situation in *ex parte Willingham* and that which subsequently arose in light of the European defence.

In *ex parte Willingham*, Donaldson LJ stated:

> Here, the council are faced with a new type of trading, which may or may not be legal. They have been advised by counsel that it probably is not. They know that there are at least two other cases in which the courts have held similar schemes to be a sham. They will not be able as a matter of law to determine this because it requires an investigation of the act. Somebody has to go to do the investigation.[94]

Despite this uncertainty, a mandatory order requiring the council to perform its duty under section 71 of the Act was granted. By analogy, the fact that an authoritative decision from the ECJ concerning the compatibility of the Shops Act 1950 with Article 28 (ex Article 30) was still pending in the Sunday trading cases would not have relieved the local authorities from their duty to enforce the provisions of the Act. And this is exactly where the pressure on the local authorities stems from.

Narrowing the scope of Article 28 to counter the European defence

The local authorities' quest for legal certainty becomes evident when analysing the submission of Torfaen Borough Council to the ECJ. Counsel for the local authority, Stuart Isaacs QC, submitted to the ECJ that the relevant legislative provisions of the Shops Act 1950 were *prima facie* outside Article 28 (ex Article 30). He concentrated on persuading the ECJ that they were not 'trading rules' as defined in *Dassonville* but rules in the nature of a 'police power'[95] indistinctly applicable to both domestic and imported products. As such, they were concerned with the general regulation of social or commercial life rather than with trade. According to Isaacs,[96] the legal team of the local authorities was convinced – and in retrospect still is – that section 47 was not a trading rule. The legal team, including Isaacs, was therefore taken aback when the ECJ interrupted the submissions of the local

[94] R. v. *Braintree District Council, ex parte Willingham* (1982) 81 LGR 70 at 79.
[95] Case C-145/88, *Torfaen Borough Council* v. *B&Q plc* [1989] ECR 3851 at 3855.
[96] Interview, 24 July 1999.

authorities questioning the interpretation of section 47 as a police power. It should be noted that it was very unusual at that time for the ECJ to interrupt submissions. The interruption was due to the fact that – as can be seen in its judgment in *Torfaen* – the ECJ was not convinced by this interpretation of section 47 but considered it to be a trading rule. It is, however, beyond doubt that the interpretation of section 47 as a police power that was indistinctly applicable would have been the easiest way for the ECJ to put an end to the Sunday trading saga.

Further, the council denied there was any reduction in imports in absolute terms. It was submitted that B&Q had failed to adduce factual evidence relating to the alleged effect of a reduction in B&Q's imports on the pattern of imports into the UK generally. In any event, the reduction of imports in question did not amount to a 'sufficient'[97] quantitative restriction. It is suggested that this approach comes close to the subjection of Article 28 (ex Article 30) to a '*de minimis* rule'.

The relevant legislative provisions being *prima facie* outside Article 28 (ex Article 30), there was no need to justify them either under the *Cassis de Dijon* doctrine or under Article 30 (ex Article 36). If, however, they had to be regarded as falling within Article 28 (ex Article 30), they were, first, necessary in order to satisfy mandatory requirements relating to the improvement of working conditions, the protection of the health and welfare of workers and the protection of public health. Secondly, they were saved by the categories of 'protection of health and life of humans', of 'public policy' and of 'public morality' in Article 30 (ex Article 36) and did not constitute a 'means of arbitrary discrimination or a disguised restriction on trade between Member States'. For historical reasons, the provisions would not fail the proportionality test, if its application should be necessary.

The subsequent ruling of the ECJ, no matter how 'terse and unhelpful'[98] it can be said to have been, was considered at first to have been a victory for the local authorities. In order to capitalise on this apparent success, it was necessary for the local authorities to shift their focus onto the issue of proportionality. When the ECJ judgment in *Torfaen* was subsequently applied in the national courts, in most cases the Shops Act was held to be proportionate. Further support for the local authorities' position came from the ECJ judgments in *Conforama* and *Marchandise*.

[97] Case C-145/88, *Torfaen Borough Council* v. *B&Q plc* [1989] ECR 3851 at 3855.
[98] A. Arnull, 'What Shall We Do on Sunday?' (1991) 16 *European Law Review* 112.

The rulings in *Conforama* and *Marchandise* as weapons in the national courts

The decisions in *Conforama*[99] and *Marchandise*[100] were welcomed by the local authorities as support for the view that Article 28 (ex Article 30) did not apply to section 47. It is necessary to illustrate briefly how those decisions were interpreted by the local authorities. The first influential decision in the English courts after the two judgments in the ECJ on 28 February 1991 was the Court of Appeal decision in *Kirklees Metropolitan Borough Council* v. *Wickes Building Supplies Ltd*[101] on 30 April 1991. In *Kirklees*, the proceedings had been brought by two councils under section 22 of the Local Government Act 1972, and an application had been made for interlocutory injunctions to restrain Sunday traders from using their shop premises for trade on Sundays in breach of section 47 of the Shops Act 1950. According to Dillon LJ, delivering judgment, Stuart Isaacs QC, counsel for the local authorities, submitted that:

> by its decisions in the *Conforama* and *Marchandise* cases the [ECJ] has tacitly rejected the view expressed in paragraph 16 of the judgment in the *Torfaen* case. It follows therefore, he says, that the application of [Article 28 (ex Article 30)] was a matter of Community law for the [ECJ] and that the decision in the *Conforama* and *Marchandise* cases upholding the French and Belgian Sunday trading laws necessarily involves that [Article 28 (ex Article 30)] does not apply to section 47.[102]

It was argued for the local authorities that this interpretation was in accordance with Hoffmann J's decision in *Stoke-on-Trent City Council* v. *B&Q plc*,[103] and that, consequently, Wickes and B&Q did not have a European defence to the claim against them. The reason why counsel for the local authorities relied on this line of reasoning is to be found in the fact that this interpretation provided the necessary certainty in relation to the local authorities' duty under section 71(1). According to this interpretation, Article 28 (ex Article 30) would not apply to section 47, thus rendering any enforcement measures taken by local authorities lawful. Yet, *Conforama* and *Marchandise* were not considered by the

99 Case C-312/89, *Union Departmentale des Syndicats CGT de l'Aisne* v. *Sidef Conforama* [1991] ECR I-997.

100 Case C-332/89, *Ministère Public* v. *Marchandise* [1991] ECR 1027.

101 [1991] 3 WLR 985.

102 [1991] 3 WLR 985 at 991.

103 [1990] 3 CMLR 897.

national courts to provide the legal certainty that the local authorities were striving for.

The local authorities' continuing uncertainties over Article 28

In the Court of Appeal in *Kirklees*,[104] Dillon LJ rejected Stuart Isaacs' submission insofar as he held that there was nothing on the face of the judgments in *Conforama* and *Marchandise* to suggest that the court had resiled from the view expressed in paragraph 16 of the *Torfaen* judgment. There was no explanation of why the actual decisions in *Conforama* and *Marchandise* were worded differently from the decision in the *Torfaen* case. It therefore followed, according to Dillon LJ, that the proper interpretation of the decision in *Torfaen* in light of the decisions in *Conforama* and *Marchandise* could only be determined by a further reference to the ECJ. Such a reference would have entailed, first, the risk for the local authorities of an adverse judgment, and, secondly, the risk of their actions taken against Sunday traders being unlawful. This course of action was therefore rejected by the local authorities.

The weight of judicial authority seemed to be against the local authorities. For, when the above-mentioned submissions were being made in the Court of Appeal, Hoffmann J's decision was already the subject of a 'leapfrog' appeal to the House of Lords. It should also be noted that this reasoning was subsequently weakened when, on 20 May 1991, in *Stoke-on-Trent*,[105] the House of Lords referred certain questions to the ECJ. Therefore, in *Kirklees*,[106] as in the Court of Appeal, the submissions of the local authority in the House of Lords were not accepted by their Lordships. Lord Goff, delivering judgment on 25 June 1992, held that the arguments of the local authorities were not sufficiently powerful to rule out the necessity of a reference under Article 234 (ex Article 177). However, on the facts of the case and in light of the reference of the House of Lords in *Stoke-on-Trent*,[107] a reference was not considered to be necessary. Yet, even though a reference was not considered necessary, the effect of the judgment was to increase the

[104] [1991] 3 WLR 985.
[105] *Stoke-on-Trent City Council* v. *B&Q plc* [1993] 2 All ER 297.
[106] *Kirklees Metropolitan Borough Council* v. *Wickes Building Supplies Ltd* [1992] 3 WLR 170 at 186.
[107] *Stoke-on-Trent City Council* v. *B&Q plc* [1993] 2 All ER 297.

local authorities' uncertainties as to the consequences of the exercise by the local authorities of their duty under section 71(1).

To summarise, the attempts of the local authorities in the national courts to argue that *Conforama* and *Marchandise* had been disposed of in such a way as to demonstrate that the Shops Act was valid and had thus settled the law on Article 28 (ex Article 30) were unsuccessful.

The requirement to give cross-undertakings in damages: a death-knell for the local authorities?

The significance of the Court of Appeal decision in *Kirklees*[108] should not be confined merely to the rejection of the local authorities' submission. The finding that the local authorities should have been required to give cross-undertakings in damages at first instance as a condition of the grant of the interlocutory injunctions was also a significant decision. Mervyn Davies J had previously ruled in the High Court[109] that the Kirklees Metropolitan Borough Council may be granted the interlocutory order *without* giving cross-undertakings in damages. The decision set a precedent for the whole country and had been followed more than 100 times. Mervyn Davies J found the justification in *Hoffmann La Roche* v. *Secretary of State for Trade and Industry.*[110] Here, the House of Lords had released the Crown from signing a cross-undertaking, at least when the Crown was enforcing the law in the public interest. Mervyn Davies J saw no reason to differentiate between the Crown and the local authorities to whom the enforcement of the Shops Act had been entrusted. The judgment was immediately challenged by the Sunday traders – whose whole strategy was to keep the shops open on Sunday, whatever the status of the law, was jeopardised. The decision of the Court of Appeal in *Kirklees* was therefore of the utmost importance for both sides. The Court of Appeal established that the protection of the Sunday traders' putative right to trade on Sundays, and thus the full effectiveness of Community law, should be achieved by requiring cross-undertakings in damages. European law, again, served as a means to increase economic freedoms.

The reasoning runs as follows. If there were no cross-undertakings in damages, and if the Sunday traders could establish the incompatibility of section 47 with Article 28 (ex Article 30), the traders would

108 [1991] 3 WLR 985.

109 *Kirklees Metropolitan Borough Council* v. *Wickes Building Supplies Ltd* [1990] 2 CMLR 501.

110 [1975] AC 295.

have been adversely affected by having been prevented by injunctions from Sunday trading pending a final decision in *Stoke-on-Trent* with no compensation. First, this would run against the unrestricted retroactive effect required by *Simmenthal.* Secondly, it would run counter to the decision in *Factortame I*, in the sense that a rule which prohibited absolutely the grant of interim relief would contradict the principle of effectiveness of Community law. For a comprehensive understanding of why it was the duty of the national court to protect the putative right to Sunday trading and for an understanding of the Court of Appeal's line of reasoning in *Kirklees*, it is necessary to elaborate on the ECJ's case law as it stood at that time.

The EC legal background to the Court of Appeal ruling in *Kirklees*

With the passing of the European Communities Act 1972,[111] more specifically by virtue of section 2(1) of that Act, the European Community Treaties were incorporated into UK law. Thenceforth, all Community law became directly applicable, and 'any rights or obligations created by the Treaty [were] to be given legal effect in England without more ado'.[112] Yet, what is more significant in relation to the Sunday trading cases is the direct effect of Treaty Articles as well as the principle of supremacy of Community law.

The concept of the direct effect of provisions of the Treaty was developed by the ECJ in *Van Gend en Loos* v. *Nederlandse Administratie der Belastingen.*[113] The ECJ held that, provided it is, first, unconditional and unqualified, and, secondly, sufficiently precise and clear, a Treaty Article may be invoked directly in the national courts. The latter requirement will not be satisfied if it leaves substantial discretion to the Member States. The ECJ's underlying reason can be stated as follows: the objective of the EC Treaty was to benefit not merely the Member States in the newly created Community legal order but also their nationals. Consequently, citizens should be able to enforce provisions of EC law directly before their national courts. The ECJ has subsequently found a large number of Treaty provisions to be directly effective. All

[111] Note in particular section 2(1), which provides for the direct application of Community law.

[112] *H. P. Bulmer Ltd* v. *J. Bollinger SA (No. 2)* [1974] Ch 401; [1974] 3 WLR 202; [1974] 2 All ER 1226; [1974] 2 CMLR 91 *per* Lord Denning MR.

[113] Judgment of 5 February 1963, Case 26/62, *van Gend en Loos* [1963] ECR 1.

the basic principles relating to free movement of goods may now be invoked by individuals before their national courts. In *Iannelli & Volpi SpA* v. *Ditta Paolo Meroni*,[114] the court held, concerning the prohibition in Article 28 (ex Article 30):

> The prohibition of quantitative restrictions and measures having equivalent effect laid down in [Article 28 (ex Article 30)] of the Treaty is mandatory and explicit and its implementation does not require any subsequent intervention of the Member States or Community institutions. The prohibition therefore has direct effect and creates individual rights which national courts must protect.[115]

For the purpose of the Sunday traders, this principle of the direct effect of Article 28 (ex Article 30) had to be, and indeed was, explicitly relied on in the submissions of B&Q[116] before the ECJ. The immediate effect of a finding of direct effect is the question of priorities between directly effective international law and domestic law.

The first statement of the principle of supremacy of EC law is also to be found in the case of *Van Gend en Loos*. The ECJ reasoned that, if the long-term Treaty goals such as a common market and an 'ever closer union'[117] were to be achieved, there was a need for a uniform application and interpretation of Community law in each Member State and thus a need for the principle of supremacy of Community law over national law. This principle was clearly affirmed by the Court in *Costa* v. *ENEL*.[118] In that case, the ECJ did not merely state the principle as such but also elaborated on the implications for a provision of national law which was in conflict with a provision of EC law.

The implications of this were neatly put in the ECJ's decision in *Simmenthal*. For present purposes, it is sufficient to concentrate on the aspect of unrestricted retroactive effect of Community law, since the Shops Act 1950 came into effect before the coming into force of Article 28 (ex Article 30).[119] It was held that, in accordance with the principle of the precedence of Community law, Community provisions, by

[114] Case 74/76, *Iannelli & Volpi SpA* v. *Ditta Paolo Meroni* [1977] ECR 595; [1977] ECR 557; [1977] 2 CMLR 688.
[115] *Ibid.*, para. 13.
[116] Submission of B&Q plc, p. 2, para. 4.
[117] EC Treaty, preamble.
[118] Judgment of 15 July 1964, Case 6/64, *Costa* v. *ENEL* [1994] ECR 1251.
[119] The EC Treaty came into effect on 1 January 1958.

virtue of their entry into force, rendered 'automatically inapplicable any conflicting provision of current national law'.[120] The ECJ went on to say that:

> [E]very national court must ... *set aside* any provision of national law which may conflict with it, whether *prior* or subsequent to the Community rule ... A national court which is called upon ... to apply provisions of Community law is under a duty to give full effect to those provisions, if necessary *refusing of its own motion to apply any conflicting provision of national legislation.*[121]

In view of the direct effectiveness of Article 28 (ex Article 30), a national court would have been under a duty to set aside section 47 of the Shops Act, or alternatively to refuse to apply it, if it considered it to be in conflict with Article 28 (ex Article 30). The difficulty, however, was that whether or not a national law is to be regarded as incompatible with Community law depended on the court's interpretation of the judgments in *Torfaen* as well as *Conforama* and *Marchandise.*

In light of the uncertainty surrounding the compatibility of section 47 with Community law, there is a further issue which needs exploration, namely, the question of interim relief. Section 2(4) of the European Communities Act 1972 provides that:

> any enactment passed or to be passed ... shall be construed and have effect subject to the foregoing provisions of this section.

The proper construction of this provision was considered by the House of Lords in *Factortame*. In brief, the House of Lords sought a preliminary ruling as to whether under Community law the English courts were under an obligation to grant interim relief to the applicants pending the outcome of the Court's ruling on substantive questions of EC law. Further, the question was submitted of whether in such a case the English courts were given the power to do so. Following the judgment of the ECJ, the national courts are required to ensure the full effectiveness of Community law. It was held by the ECJ that:

> The full effectiveness of Community law would be ... impaired if a rule of national law could prevent a court seised of a dispute governed by Community law from granting interim relief in order to ensure the full

120 Case C-106/77, *Amministrazine delle Finanze dello Stato* v. *Simmenthal SpA* [1978] ECR 629 at 643, para. 17.

121 *Ibid*., paras. 21 and 24 (emphasis added).

> effectiveness of the judgment to be given on the existence of the rights claimed under Community law. It follows that a court which in those circumstances would grant interim relief, if it were not for a rule of national law, is obliged to set aside that rule.[122]

On the basis of *Simmenthal* and *Factortame*, it was the duty of the national courts to protect the putative right to trade on Sundays. If the Sunday traders were correct that section 47 was incompatible with Article 28 (ex Article 30) and was thereby overridden, they would have a right to open their stores for Sunday trading, and it would be the duty of the national courts to protect that right. According to the Court of Appeal in *Kirklees*, this protection could be achieved by requiring the local authorities to give cross-undertakings in damages.

The local authorities' dilemma between statutory duties and budget constraints

The local authorities therefore found themselves in a dilemma between, on the one hand, their statutory duty to enforce the Act, and, on the other hand, the requirement to give cross-undertakings in damages which amounted to a serious threat to their budgets. Thus, in the wake of the *Kirklees* decision, most of the interlocutory injunctions which had already been obtained by local authorities were discharged for fear of the potential liability for damages resulting from an adverse judgment of the ECJ. The underlying reason was illustrated during debates in Parliament as follows:

> Recently, the City of Hull council . . . was faced with a demand in the court for a cross-undertaking for £2 million . . . Not surprisingly, the authority could not risk local taxpayers' money and was forced to give way.[123]

In effect, the situation can therefore be described as one of total deregulation, since even if there were rules they could not be enforced under section 71(1) of the Shops Act 1950. This situation lasted for more than one year until, on 25 June 1992, the House of Lords reversed the decision in *Kirklees*.[124]

[122] Case C-213/89, *R.* v. *Secretary of State for Transport, ex parte Factortame Ltd* [1990] ECR I-2433 at 2474, para. 21.
[123] Official Reports 5th series, Parliamentary Debates, House of Lords, vol. 534, col. 520, 17 January 1992, *per* Viscount Brentford.
[124] [1993] AC 227; [1992] 3 WLR 170; [1992] 3 All ER 717.

Relief came too late for the local authorities

There are two reasons for the length of time it took for the case to be decided by the House of Lords. First, it seems as if the appeal from the Court of Appeal to the House of Lords was more difficult than expected. In theory, an appeal lies from any judgment or order of the Court of Appeal to the House of Lords, provided that leave to appeal is obtained from either court.[125] An application for leave to appeal is made first to the Court of Appeal, normally immediately after judgment. This is what was done by the local authority in *Kirklees*.[126] However, this application to the Court of Appeal for leave was unsuccessful. Consequently, a petition for leave was made directly to the House of Lords, within one month from the date of the order to be appealed.[127] Petitions to the House of Lords for leave are heard by an appeal committee of three Law Lords. In *Kirklees*, the members of the appeal committee were Lord Bridge of Harwich, Lord Ackner and Lord Browne-Wilkinson. In their decision, their Lordships were not unanimous on whether leave should be given, and thus the petition was referred for an oral hearing by the committee.[128] It was only after the oral hearing that their Lordships recognised the importance of the granting of leave. This may have been due to the fact that none of the three Law Lords specialised in EC law at that time, and thus they underestimated the European dimension of the litigation. Neither Lord Ackner, as a criminal and commercial lawyer, nor Lord Browne-Wilkinson, as a trust lawyer, can be said to have had a truly European outlook at the time of the Sunday trading litigation. Nevertheless, the fact that eventually even the Attorney-General applied for and was granted leave to intervene in the proceedings in the House of Lords in order to represent the interests of the Crown underlined the significance of the appeal.[129]

A second explanation for the delay between the judgment in the Court of Appeal and the judgment in the House of Lords seems to have been the decision in *Francovich*.[130] It seems as if their Lordships

[125] Appellate Jurisdiction Act 1876, section 3; Administration of Justice (Appeals) Act 1934, section 1.

[126] [1991] 3 WLR 985.

[127] House of Lords Practice Directions applicable to civil appeals, July 1994 edition, Direction 2.

[128] *Ibid.*, Direction 4. [129] Stuart Isaacs QC, in an interview on 24 July 1999.

[130] Judgment of 19 November 1991, Cases C-6 and 9/90, *Francovich and Bonifaci* v. *Italy* [1991] ECR I-5357.

took their time to carefully consider the impact of *Francovich* on the facts in *Kirklees*. Judgment in *Francovich* was rendered in November 1991. In *Francovich*, the ECJ held that:

> Community law lays down a principle according to which a Member State is obliged to make good the damage to individuals caused by a breach of Community law for which it is responsible.

The *Francovich* decision left many questions as to the scope and shape of the Community damages remedy to be clarified by subsequent case law. It should be noted that it was not until the decision in *Brasserie du Pêcheur/Factortame III*[131] on 5 March 1996 that it was explicitly recognised that the principle of state liability should not be confined to a failure to implement EC Directives. It was held that it should also attach to other failures to comply with Community law, notably Treaty provisions such as Article 28 (ex Article 30). Nevertheless, considering the novelty of the *Francovich* principle in 1991 and the unclear implications for Member States, it is not surprising that the House of Lords took its time to consider the effect of the ruling in *Francovich* on the Court of Appeal's decision in *Kirklees*.[132] Indeed, the ruling in *Francovich* seemed to work in favour of the local authorities. The underlying reason becomes clear when considering the judgment of the House of Lords in *Kirklees*.

In *Kirklees*, the House of Lords held that a requirement that the plaintiffs should give an undertaking had no justification in Community law, since any obligation to make good any damage suffered by the defendants in the event of section 47 being found to be in breach of Article 28 (ex Article 30) would fall upon the UK government. Lord Goff cited the judgment in *Francovich*, and went on to analyse the significance of that ruling for the case before him. He argued that, since the obligation – if there was one – on the UK to make good any damage suffered by the companies would arise irrespective of any cross-undertaking in damages given by the council, 'such an undertaking would be superfluous'.[133] In addition, he emphasised the fact that requiring a cross-undertaking in damages from the council would run counter to the essence of the ruling in *Francovich*, as it was the

[131] Cases C-46 and 48/93, *Brasserie du Pêcheur SA* v. *Germany* and *R.* v. *Secretary of State for Transport, ex parte Factortame Ltd* [1996] ECR I-1029.
[132] [1991] 3 WLR 985. [133] [1992] 3 WLR 170 at 189.

Member State which was liable in such circumstances rather than the council:

> [I]t is the Government which would, on the hypothesis that section 47 was invalid because inconsistent with [Article 28 (ex Article 30)], have failed to take the necessary steps to ensure that section 47 was amended or repealed as necessary. If so, it would be wrong that the council, because it has performed its statutory duty under the national law to enforce section 47, was to find itself under a liability in damages as a result of performing that duty.[134]

In consequence, the House of Lords allowed the appeal by Kirklees Metropolitan Borough Council, holding that requiring the council to give a cross-undertaking in damages had no justification in Community law. The result, however, seems to have depended largely on the presumed outcome of the *Stoke-on-Trent* case. Lord Goff did not consider that much weight could be attached to the respondent's argument that section 47 was inconsistent with Article 28 (ex Article 30). In a stronger case, the House of Lords might well consider the need to grant a cross-undertaking in damage. Therefore, the first case in which the *Francovich* defence arose in the English courts turned against the possible beneficiaries.

This ruling came as a relief to the local authorities. However, too much time had already passed, and it was foreseeable that the judgment in *Stoke-on-Trent* would soon be rendered. It was therefore hardly surprising that most of the local authorities were hesitant to take further action until the ECJ had given a final ruling on the Sunday trading litigation in *Stoke-on-Trent.* Again, the key to success for the local authorities seemed to be the argument that *Conforama* and *Marchandise* had settled the law on Article 28 (ex Article 30).

The rulings in *Conforama* and *Marchandise* as weapons on the European level

On a European level, in *Stoke-on-Trent,* counsel for the local authorities – unlike B&Q – submitted that section 47 of the Shops Act 1950 was 'materially indistinguishable'[135] from the employee protection measures at issue in *Conforama* and *Marchandise.* Section 47

[134] *Ibid.*

[135] Case C-169/91, *Stoke-on-Trent City Council* v. *B&Q plc* [1992] ECR I-6635; [1993] 1 CMLR 426.

was not designed to control trade between Member States and – applying to domestic and imported products alike – did not render the marketing of imported products more onerous than the marketing of domestic products. The prohibition contained in Article 28 (ex Article 30) did not apply to national rules such as section 47 of the 1950 Act, that is, national rules such as those in issue in the proceedings were *prima facie* outside Article 28 (ex Article 30). However, since this submission had already failed on a national level, counsel for the local authorities was keen to establish a safeguard in case this submission should fail on a European level as well.

Twisting the law for the sake of legal certainty

If section 47 was held to be incompatible with Article 28 (ex Article 30), then, by analogy to the ECJ's justification of the employee protection measures and its ruling that the restrictive effects which those measures might have on trade were proportionate to the aim pursued, the national court would not be required to apply the criteria set out in Article 3 of Directive 70/50/EEC.[136] The local authorities' reasoning went as follows, Directive 70/50/EEC provided for a *balancing test* as well as a *necessity test* in order to save provisions which might *prima facie* be caught by Article 28 (ex Article 30). Referring to the ECJ's case law in relation to Article 28 (ex Article 30) and the Treaty itself as well as paragraphs 15 and 16 of the *Torfaen* ruling, it was argued that the application of the proportionality principle was satisfied by the application of the necessity test, and therefore no balancing test need be made.

This line of reasoning amounts to a deliberate twisting of Community law and might even be characterised as contrary to established Community law. The underlying reason is that the necessity test seemed to promise an outcome favourable to the local authority while there was at least a slight possibility that the ECJ would hold that the Shops Act would not satisfy the balancing test. It is for this reason that the local authority concentrated on the necessity test, even if this required the stretching of the law to its ultimate boundaries. The significance of the application of the necessity test alone, in contrast to the balancing test, will now be illustrated.

First, the necessity test requires that the measure at issue is subjected to a test of whether the particular measure is necessary to obtain the

[136] Directive 70/50/EEC of 22 December 1969, OJ 1969 No. L13, 29.

desired objective or whether the same objective could be attained by other means which were less of a hindrance to trade. In the context of the Sunday trading cases, the application of the necessity test involved the question of whether the prohibition of Sunday trading was necessary to ensure that working and non-working hours are so arranged as to accord with national or regional socio-cultural characteristics. The insistence of the local authority on the application of the necessity test as the sole test is to be understood in light of the previous decision in *Torfaen*. In *Torfaen*, it had already been held – by analogy to the decision in *Oebel*[137] – that the national rules at issue constituted a legitimate part of economic and social policy, consistent with the objectives of public interest pursued by the Treaty. It was argued that the proportionality of section 47 was therefore 'immediately apparent',[138] and that no evidence had to be adduced to establish that the restrictive effect of the rules in issue did not exceed the effects intrinsic to rules of that kind. Thus, the sole application of the necessity test seemed to promise an outcome favourable to the local authority.

Secondly, the balancing test is generally understood as a test of whether the restrictive effects on the free movement of goods are out of proportion to their purpose. In relation to the Sunday trading cases, the application of this test would have involved a balancing exercise to determine whether the effects on intra-Community trade were out of proportion to the purpose of measures such as the Shops Act 1950. It was submitted by the local authority that the aim pursued by section 47 was a non-economic, intangible one, rendering the application of the balancing test impossible since that would involve a comparison between two incomparable matters. This is in line with Hoffmann J's argument that non-justiciable issues were involved in the Sunday trading litigation. The real reason for denying the application of the balancing test is that there might be less restrictive means of achieving the aim at issue, for example by permitting the choice of any one closing day rather than imposing Sunday as the closing day.

It was further submitted that, if the ECJ held that the proportionality test was for the national courts to apply, the national courts were equally confined to the application of the necessity test in accordance with their own rules of procedure and evidence. Yet, the primary submission of the local authority was that, following the ECJ's rulings

[137] Case C-155/80, *Oebel* [1981] ECR 1993; [1983] 1 CMLR 340.

[138] Case 145/88, *Torfaen Borough Council* v. *B&Q plc* [1989] ECR 3851; [1990] CMLR 337.

in *Conforama* and *Marchandise*, the prohibition contained in Article 28 (ex Article 30) did not apply to national rules such as the Shops Act 1950.

Clarification of the local authorities' position in the *Stoke-on-Trent* case

The ruling of the ECJ in *Stoke-on-Trent* finally put an end to the uncertainty of the local authorities in relation to their duty under section 71(1) of the Shops Act 1950. After a discussion of the decisions in *Conforama* and *Marchandise*, the ECJ held that:

> [Article 28 (ex Article 30)] of the Treaty is to be interpreted as meaning that the prohibition which it lays down does not apply to national legislation prohibiting retailers from opening their premises on Sunday.[139]

As a consequence, local authorities were free to secure the observance of the Shops Act 1950 and to fulfil their duty under section 71(1). Any past or present attempts to enforce the Act, that is, by criminal or civil proceedings against Sunday traders, were lawful. Any fines and any injunctions which had been imposed or granted were lawful. Where interim injunctions had been granted, the ruling relieved the local authorities from their liability to pay damages if a cross-undertaking in damages had been given. Even if the ECJ did not follow counsel's argument exactly, it was a victory for the local authorities in the sense that it clarified for the time being their position.

However, this is not to say that the local authorities did not see which way the wind was blowing. Throughout the litigation, they were well aware of the fact that sooner or later the Shops Act would be reformed.

The 'Keep Sunday Special Campaign'

The formation of the campaign and the failure of its first strategy

Having been formed to oppose the Shops Bill in 1986, the first target of the 'Keep Sunday Special Campaign' (KSSC) was, naturally, Parliament.[140] However, the defeat of the Shops Bill and the ensuing Sunday

[139] Case C-169/91, *Stoke-on-Trent City Council* v. *B&Q plc* [1992] ECR I-6635; [1993] 1 CMLR 426, para. 17.

[140] For a more in-depth analysis of the defeat of the Shops Bill, see F. Brown, 'The Defeat of the Shops Bill, 1986' in M. Rush (ed.), *Parliament and Pressure Politics* (Oxford, 1990), 213 at 219 (on the professional character of the lobbying).

trading litigation required the campaign to change its strategy if it did not want to lose the struggle for reform on another battlefield. First, unsuccessful attempts were made to pressurise local authorities as well as central government into enforcing the law, the KSSC being in constant contact with the Attorney-General. Secondly, and equally unsuccessfully, campaigners were sent to Brussels in order to strengthen the position of the KSSC by having Sunday specified as the normal day of rest in the Working Time Directive.[141] Such a provision was eventually included in the Directive, though it was later annulled by the ECJ.[142] Thirdly, after the commencement of the Sunday trading litigation, the KSSC resorted to indirect means to influence the Euro-litigation.

Shadow-boxing

Paul Diamond, legal adviser to the KSSC, was the leading figure trying to influence the Euro-litigation. Targeting practitioners as well as academics, he argued in a series of articles that, even though the Shops Act was *prima facie* caught by Article 28 (ex Article 30), it could be justified under the 'rule of reason' established in *Oebel*.[143] In addition, the 'public morality' provision of Article 30 (ex Article 36) was wide enough to 'encompass the desire of a significant proportion of the population to maintain a distinct Sunday'.[144] More importantly, he relied on the 'public policy' provision, arguing that, by rejecting the Shops Bill 1986, Parliament had unequivocally shown a wish not to deregulate Sunday trading.

In the light of this reasoning, the judgment of the ECJ in *Torfaen* was interpreted as meaning that any restrictive effects on intra-Community trade as a result of section 47 of the Shops Act 1950 could not constitute a breach of Community law. The fact that the ECJ had decided that the restrictions in the Shops Act were justified with regard to Community law was taken to mean that such restrictions could not go beyond what was necessary to be effective. It was argued that, by holding legislation such as the Shops Act 1950 to be justified, the ECJ was implying that it

141 Council Directive 93/104/EC of 23 November 1993 concerning certain aspects of the organisation of working time, OJ 1993 No. L307, 13 December 1993, 18.

142 Case C-84/94, *United Kingdom* v. *Council* [1996] ECR I-5755.

143 Case C-155/80, *Oebel* [1981] ECR 1993; [1983] 1 CMLR 340.

144 P. Diamond, 'Dishonourable Defences: The Use of Injunctions and the EEC Treaty – Case Study of the Shops Act 1950' (1991) 54 *Modern Law Review* 72 at 80. The KSSC argued that Sunday was a day of rest the character of which should be maintained for social and cultural reasons. B&Q characterised the KSSC as 'religious fanatics'. Paul Diamond, legal adviser to the KSSC, in an interview on 7 January 2000.

was proportionate. The application of the proportionality doctrine in national courts was denied on the ground that this would – at least potentially – be to declare an Act of Parliament void and thus infringe the supremacy of Parliament. The KSSC's reasoning was thus in line with Hoffmann J's decision in *Stoke-on-Trent City Council* v. *B&Q plc*,[145] which was welcomed as settling the law: the issue of Sunday trading had to be resolved by a sovereign legislature rather than by the judiciary.

The interpretation of Article 28 (ex Article 30) in *Conforama*, *Marchandise* and *Stoke-on-Trent* as such was well in tune with Paul Diamond's line of reasoning. Similarly, the outcome in *Stoke-on-Trent*, that is, the compatibility of the Shops Act 1950 with Article 28 (ex Article 30), was in accordance with the short-term interests of the KSSC to prevent Sunday trading. However, the overall consequences of the Sunday trading litigation sat rather uneasily with the long-term interests of the KSSC. The litigation had created a favourable climate among the population in relation to reform of the Shops Act. But, due to widespread Sunday opening during the period when the litigation was ongoing, people had become so accustomed to Sunday opening that a prohibition of Sunday trading had become a very unpopular option for reform. The origins of the KSSC's defeat ultimately lie here.

Nevertheless, after the judgment in *Stoke-on-Trent* had been rendered by the ECJ, Parliament was once again to become the target of the KSSC's campaign. After the House of Lords judgment in *Stoke-on-Trent*[146] in March 1993, it was widely felt that reform was due. It was at this stage that the KSSC launched its last campaign against total and partial deregulation of Sunday trading by introducing into Parliament a Private Member's Bill in the name of Ray Powell MP. The Bill was sabotaged in May 1993, so paving the way for reform by the government. The following analysis will show that the KSSC might have done better by concentrating on the Euro-litigation rather than by lobbying Parliament or half-heartedly targeting lawyers.

The KSSC's missed opportunities

Even though it decisively influenced the social, economic and political dimensions of what Rawlings calls the 'Euro-law Game',[147] the KSSC did not join the Euro-litigation itself. In theory, there were two opportunities for the KSSC to enter the litigation: first, on a national

[145] [1990] 3 CMLR 897. [146] [1993] 2 All ER 297.

[147] R. Rawlings, 'The Euro-Law Game: Some Deductions from a Saga' (1993) 20 *Journal of Law and Society* 309.

level, and, secondly, on the European level. The KSSC missed both opportunities.

Rawlings offers an explanation of why the KSSC did not intervene as a third party in the proceedings before the ECJ. He argues that it has never been conclusively decided whether third party interventions are permissible in relation to Article 234 (ex Article 177) references. The third party intervention procedure under Article 37 of the Protocol to the Statute of the ECJ[148] does not apply to Article 234 (ex Article 177) references in cases in which the individual is not represented or is not permitted to appear in the national court.[149] The correctness of this line of argument is doubtful. It is suggested that a representative of the KSSC could certainly have established 'an interest in the result of [the] case',[150] in view of the fact that the KSSC had support from the Labour Party, from some of the larger retailers,[151] from the unions and from churches. Thus, a third party intervention procedure under Article 37 of the Protocol could have been an effective means for the KSSC to ensure its voice was heard. In the event, the KSSC did not intervene as a third party in the proceedings before the ECJ.

Equally, it is suggested that the KSSC did not take advantage of the law on a national level to make its voice heard. Considering the sporadic enforcement of the Shops Act – if there was enforcement at all – the KSSC could have applied for judicial review of local authority decisions not to enforce the Shops Act.

If the KSSC had applied for judicial review, it would have had to establish that it had *locus standi* to make such an application. According to Order 53, rule 3, of the Rules of the Supreme Court, an applicant must obtain leave to apply for judicial review. Order 53, rule 3(7), states that the court shall not grant leave unless it considers that the applicant has a 'sufficient interest' in the matter. It may be speculated as to whether the KSSC had 'sufficient interest' to meet the leave requirement. Potential applicants might have been shopowners whose business and – eventually – turnover were seriously affected by illegal Sunday opening, special interest groups such as the KSSC, and individuals like Paul Diamond who could have pursued a public interest action.

148 As amended by Council Decision of 24 October 1988 establishing a Court of First Instance.

149 C. Harlow and R. Rawlings (eds.), *Pressure Through Law* (London, 1992), 281.

150 Protocol to the Statute of the Court of Justice of the European Economic Community, Art. 37(II).

151 E.g. Co-operative Union Ltd and Iceland Foods.

In the *National Federation* case,[152] which was decided in 1982, that is, before the Sunday trading litigation had ever begun, it was held that standing should not be viewed as a preliminary or threshold issue. Rather, the question of standing should be treated as a mixed question of law and fact for the courts to decide at the oral hearing. *National Federation* was therefore hailed as indicative of a liberalisation of the rules of standing which would have been helpful to shopowners.

As the *National Federation* case shows, the interpretation of the phrase 'sufficient interest' is of particular importance to campaign groups such as the KSSC which, by its very nature, may not be directly affected by the decision being challenged, but will represent those who have concerns about the issues involved. It is suggested that, *at the time of writing*, pressure groups such as those involved in the issue of Sunday trading would almost certainly be able to establish sufficient interest. This is due to the fact that recent case law – namely, the decisions of the High Court in *ex parte Greenpeace*[153] and in *ex parte World Development Movement Ltd*[154] and the House of Lords' decision in *ex parte Equal Opportunities Commission*[155] – indicates a more lenient approach. However, the position seems to have been less clear in the late 1980s and early 1990s. One could argue that, in the wake of the decision in *ex parte Child Poverty Action Group*,[156] there might have been a possibility for campaign groups to succeed in establishing sufficient interest. On the other hand, the decision in *R. v. Secretary of State for the Environment, ex parte Rose Theatre Trust Company Ltd*,[157] in

[152] *Inland Revenue Commissioners* v. *National Federation of Self-Employed and Small Businesses* [1982] AC 617.

[153] *R.* v. *Inspectorate of Pollution, ex parte Greenpeace* [1994] 4 All ER 329. In this case, Otton J held that Greenpeace had *locus standi* to challenge a decision of the Inspectorate of Pollution and the Ministry of Agriculture acting pursuant to the Radioactive Substance Act 1990.

[154] *R.* v. *Secretary of State for Foreign and Commonwealth Affairs, ex parte World Development Movement Ltd* [1995] 1 WLR 386. The applicant, a pressure group, was held to have sufficient interest to challenge the provision of grants to the Malaysian government for the building of the Pergau Dam.

[155] *R.* v. *Secretary of State for Employment, ex parte Equal Opportunities Commission* [1994] 2 WLR 409. The EOC was held to have standing.

[156] *R.* v. *Secretary of State for Social Security, ex parte Child Poverty Action Group*; *R.* v. *Secretary of State for Social Security, ex parte Greater London Council* [1990] 2 QB 540 The Child Poverty Action Group, a pressure group which purports to represent the interest of social security claimants, was held to have standing for judicial review of decisions in the area of social security.

[157] *R.* v. *Secretary of State of the Environment, ex parte Rose Theatre Trust Co. Ltd* [1990] 1 All ER 754.

which a campaign group was denied standing to challenge a minister's decision, indicates that it could equally well have been possible that the time would not (yet) have been ripe for campaign groups such as the KSSC to establish sufficient interest in Sunday opening. It seems as if a campaign group indeed would have been denied standing on the basis of the law as it then stood.

Finally, an application for judicial review by an individual or organisation who or which comes to court not to protect its or their own interests but to protect the interests of other parties not before the court – such as would have been the case with Paul Diamond, for instance – amounts to 'representative' standing. 'Representative standing' could include 'associational' standing and (possibly) 'citizen' standing. 'Associational standing' arises in a situation in which the applicant purports to represent a *group of individuals* who have a personal interest in the claim. By contrast, 'citizen standing' (also referred to as 'public interest standing') refers to a situation in which the applicant purports to represent the *public interest* as opposed to the interests of any particular individual. Considering the differing opinions on the issue of Sunday trading, it can safely be assumed that a court would have classified such a case as one of 'associational standing'. The decision in the *Fleet Street Casual* case[158] in 1982 is indicative of the fact that the English courts are willing to recognise associational standing. Thus, an individual might very well have established *locus standi* when seeking judicial review on behalf of a group interested in the prohibition of Sunday trading. The courts, however, have not drawn a clear distinction between associational standing and citizen standing. However, considering the outcome in *R.* v. *Felixstowe Justices, ex parte Leigh*[159] in 1987, the English courts would very likely have been prepared to entertain 'citizen' or 'public interest' actions. Thus, an individual could have challenged a local authority's failure to comply with section 71(1) of the Shops Act 1950 by way of judicial

[158] *Inland Revenue Commissioners, ex parte Federation of Self-Employed and Small Businesses Ltd* [1982] AC 617. Even though the applicant, a trade association, challenging a tax amnesty granted by the Inland Revenue to casual workers in the newspaper industry, was *not* granted standing, the case is seen as the starting-point of representative standing since the court did not consider the representative nature of the applicant a reason not to accord the applicant standing.

[159] [1987] QB 582 a journalist was entitled to represent the public interest as a 'private Attorney-General'.

review.[160] This would have been a further opportunity for the KSSC to take an active part in the litigation.

Backing the wrong horse

Even if a challenge by the KSSC to the local authorities' failure to enforce the law, or equally a third party intervention by the KSSC before the ECJ, had ultimately been unsuccessful, it would nevertheless surely have been an opportunity for the KSSC to make its voice heard. Strict enforcement of the Shops Act by the local authorities would have lent support to the rule of law. Continuous litigation against the local authorities would have drawn the attention of the public away from the opportunity of going shopping on Sundays to the harm caused to the rule of law by the systematic breach of the Shops Act by the Sunday traders. Thus, a more aggressive strategy on a national level by the KSSC could have prevented the decriminalisation of the breach of the Shops Act and could have given public interests a voice in the Sunday trading saga. However, the KSSC did not notice the shift away from the legislature to the judiciary.[161] It backed the political horse at a time when strong and highly professional skills were needed to join the Euro-litigation game.

The UK government: caught between loyalty and politics

The Shops Bill 1986 was the government's attempt to reform the Sunday trading law. The Bill followed the recommendations of the Auld Committee.[162] Yet, the Bill had been Mrs Thatcher's only Parliamentary defeat of a major piece of legislative reform during her term of office, probably because she tried to balance the conflicting interests involved. This defeat led to the government's retreat from the Parliamentary stage for the time being as regards Sunday trading. The conflict was left to be resolved by the judiciary. The extent to which

[160] Note that R. Rawlings suggests that an individual would not have been allowed to appear in the national court. Rawlings, 'The Euro-Law Game', 309.

[161] Paul Diamond, legal adviser to the KSSC, in an interview on 7 January 2000, defended the KSSC's strategy, claiming that the strategy would have succeeded had there not been 'a tacit agreement between the Sunday traders to break the law' and had the large majority of local authorities not been supportive of the Sunday traders.

[162] Cmnd 9376, Report of the Committee of Inquiry, *The Shops Act: Late-Night and Sunday Opening* (London, 1984).

the government allowed the rule of law to be negated by refusing to act can best be illustrated by the situation in autumn 1991.[163] It will be recalled for present purposes that the judgments in *Conforama*[164] and *Marchandise*[165] had already been delivered. The Court of Appeal decision in *Kirklees*[166] was binding until the House of Lords reversed it on appeal in June 1992. Furthermore, in *Rochdale*[167] and *Stoke-on-Trent*, references for preliminary rulings had already been made. The law as it then stood was that, as a matter of Community law cross-undertakings in damages had to be given by local authorities who sought interlocutory injunctions against Sunday traders. As has already been seen, the requirement to give cross-undertakings in damages was one of the main reasons for the negation of the rule of law in the Sunday trading litigation. The question of what role the Attorney-General and the government could have played, and indeed did play, in upholding the rule of law in the Sunday trading saga will now be considered.[168]

The Attorney-General's role

The Attorney-General's powers

The Attorney-General is the chief Law Officer of the Crown. In substance, he represents the Crown in the courts in all matters in which rights of a public character come into question. This is a power which he could have used in the Sunday trading saga. If the Crown had brought civil action against the Sunday traders, the Attorney-General would have been the person to reach that decision and would have been the plaintiff in those proceedings. At some stage in the Sunday trading litigation, it seemed as if the Attorney-General could have stepped in – or maybe even *should* have stepped in – in order to emphasise the duty to obey the law and to reaffirm the rule of law. However, he chose not

[163] See Figure 2.2, p. 97 above.

[164] Case C-312/89, *Union Departmentale des Syndicats CGT de l'Aisne* v. *Sidef Conforama* [1991] ECR I-997.

[165] Case C-332/89, *Ministère Public* v. *Marchandise* [1991] ECR I-1027.

[166] [1991] 3 WLR 985.

[167] *Rochdale Borough Council* v. *Anders* [1988] 3 All ER 490 at 491.

[168] Weatherill has raised the question of whether all these references to the 'rule of law' assume the Art. 28 (ex Art. 30) argument would inevitably fail. Upholding the rule of law depends on an authoritative ruling on what the law requires, which did not exist until the ECJ's decision in *Stoke-on-Trent*. I disagree with this argument. The 'rule of law' existed long before the ECJ's decision in *Stoke-on-Trent*. The UK government was supportive of the strategy of the Sunday traders in using EC law to change national law.

Table 2.2 *Chronology of references in the Sunday trading litigation*

Case	1988	1989	1990	1991	1992	1993
Torfaen	25/04 Reference	29/06 Opinion 23/11 Judgment				
Rochdale Reading Stoke-on-Trent			05/10 Reference (Rochdale)	20/05 Reference (Stoke-on-Trent)	08/07 Opinion 16/12 Judgment	31/03 House of Lords' Judgment in Stoke-on-Trent
Kirklees			14/05 High Court	30/04 Court of Appeal	25/06 House of Lords	
Marchandise Conforama Francovich		05/10 Reference	22/11 Opinion	28/02 Judgment 28/05 Opinion 19/11 Judgment		
Factortame			19/06 Judgment 11/10 House of Lords			

to do so. The question of why and when he could have so stepped in will now be considered.

Pressuring the Attorney-General into taking action

As already indicated above, it was the Court of Appeal decision in *Kirklees* which put the local authorities into a quandary. The situation of total deregulation following the Court of Appeal decision in *Kirklees* triggered a rebellion by advocates of the rule of law who turned to the Attorney-General. Faced with the inability of the local authorities to enforce the provisions of the Shops Act 1950, the Attorney-General as the chief Law Officer of the Crown was the proper person to take action. On 27 November 1991, he was asked by a private notice[169] in the House of Commons what steps he intended to take to prevent the breach of the Sunday trading laws by seeking a nationwide injunction.

The Attorney-General's missed opportunity to uphold the rule of law

The Attorney-General made it explicitly clear that he had decided not to intervene for four reasons. First, the laws were not suspended, and Sunday traders remained liable to criminal proceedings. Secondly, Parliament had placed 'primary responsibility'[170] for laws passed by Parliament such as the Shops Act 1950 on the local authorities. Thirdly, if he were now to intervene, he would have to bring a very large number of actions. Finally, he would be required to give a cross-undertaking in damages in any of those proceedings, which might prove to be contrary to the public interest if he lost the actions.

Even though the Attorney-General himself denied any connection with matters of political policy which should be left to government in general and ministerial responsibility in particular, it can safely be stated that his decision not to take action was well in tune with the overall strategy of the government. The Attorney-General's refusal to intervene – though politically wise, as the majority of the population wanted to see the law changed[171] – raises significant issues concerning the underlying policy of the government in relation to the use or

[169] By Ivor Stanbrook, Conservative MP for Orpington.

[170] Official Reports 6th series, Parliamentary Debates, House of Commons, vol. 199, col. 914, 27 November 1991.

[171] Tony Askham, solicitor for the retailers, in an interview on 26 July 1999.

misuse of Article 28 (ex Article 30) in order to attain long-term political objectives.

Co-ordination with government policy

Overall policy goal

The long-term policy goal of the government was clearly deregulation. The large-scale campaign of the Sunday traders against the prohibition of Sunday trading, the numerous proceedings in the national courts as well as the Euro-litigation itself and, finally, the reluctance of the local authorities to enforce the law following the Court of Appeal decision in *Kirklees*, indirectly promoted this long-term policy goal. It explains the reluctance of the government and the Attorney-General to intervene. The rule of law was ruled out by political calculation.[172] However, the government was thwarted in its calculation by another ruling of the ECJ, as well as by political reality. The policy goal of deregulation must be seen in the context of the defeat in Parliament of the Shops Bill in 1986, the ratification of the Maastricht Treaty and, most importantly, the issue of state liability following the decision in *Francovich* in November 1991.

Political reality

The significance of the pending ratification of the Maastricht Treaty can be described as follows. One essential amendment made by the Maastricht Treaty was the introduction of the principle of subsidiarity in Article 5 (ex Article 3b). It is arguable that, from a British point of view, the principle of subsidiarity promised to prevent further movement towards a federalist Community while ensuring that the Community would act within the limits of its powers. This was one of the incentives intended to induce the UK Parliament to adopt a favourable attitude towards the ratification of the Maastricht Treaty. Leaving matters of domestic law – as the issue of Sunday trading (mostly) was – to

[172] Again, Weatherill raised the point as to whether that is really true. He admits that the government would not have been sorry to see the Shops Act 1950 defeated by litigation. But for him, this does not amount to a defeat for the rule of law. At this stage, before the ECJ's *Stoke-on-Trent* ruling, he understands the law not to be settled. Again, I disagree. The argument is based on the premise that *Stoke-on-Trent* was needed to clarify the rule of law.

Community institutions to decide would have undermined the credibility of the government's argument about the significance of the principle of subsidiarity. Thus, since sensitive issues of a socio-cultural and political nature were involved, the official position of the government can be seen as support for the national law.

Support for the national law

In *Torfaen*, the UK government made it expressly clear that, regardless of the Community element in the proceedings, the defendants had committed an offence in relation to domestic goods. The fear of the government of the national law being declared incompatible with Community law can also be seen by the fact that the necessity for a reference was denied.

Further, the UK government denied any causal link between a restriction on the period during which shops may sell goods and a reduction of imports. It was argued that it had not been established that section 47 affected imports. This was for the following reasons. First, there was insufficient evidence to support such an allegation. Secondly, if there was evidence, it merely pointed to a wide divergence between the effect of Sunday closing in particular cases. Thus, the evidence underpinned the allegation that a reduction in the defendant's turnover had no effect on the pattern of imports into the UK generally. Thirdly, it was argued that, following the case law on Article 28 (ex Article 30), the rules at issue could not be regarded as measures affecting particular imported products. Therefore, they did not qualify as indistinctly applicable measures subject to the requirement of justification laid down by the ECJ in *Cassis de Dijon*. In essence, what the UK was arguing was therefore that the rules at issue were *equal-burden* rules, not being discriminatory against or disadvantageous to imported goods and as such outside Article 28 (ex Article 30).

Alternatively, it was submitted that, if the relevant provision were held to be within Article 28 (ex Article 30), it would be justifiable and proportionate either under Article 30 (ex Article 36) or under *Cassis de Dijon* as a mandatory requirement, notwithstanding the absence of corresponding legislation in Scotland. In any event, both lines of reasoning – whether the provision was held to be *prima facie* within Article 28 (ex Article 30) or not – show the government's concern to establish the compatibility of the relevant provisions of the Shops Act 1950 with Community law.

Francovich as a potential threat to the government's policy

The government's position was decisively influenced by the development of the principle of state liability in *Francovich*. In 1991, the ECJ had held that Community law laid down a principle according to which a Member State is obliged to pay compensation for harm caused to individuals by breaches of Community law for which the Member States can be held responsible.[173] Even though the decision left many questions to be clarified by subsequent case law, it was quite conceivable that, on the basis of *Francovich* and the Court of Appeal decision in *Kirklees*, an adverse decision of the ECJ could open the floodgates for claims in damages for infringement of Article 28 (ex Article 30) against the UK government. Therefore, in order to influence the proceedings in the ECJ in *Stoke-on-Trent*, the Attorney-General himself was sent to Luxembourg. Considering the outcome of the case, this mission must have been interpreted as a success by the government.

The government's position in the *Stoke-on-Trent* case

In the *Stoke-on-Trent* case before the ECJ, the UK government relied heavily on the gist of the Opinion of the Advocate-General in *Conforama*[174] and *Marchandise*[175] and on the judgments in those cases. In essence, the Sunday trading legislation in the UK was said to be indistinguishable from the employment legislation in France and Belgium (which was in issue in *Conforama* and *Marchandise*) for the purposes of Article 28 (ex Article 30). The reason for this submission was to ensure that the ECJ would hold the legislation at issue justified with regard to Community law so as to satisfy the first limb of the *Torfaen* test.

The UK government further maintained that the measures at issue did not exceed what was necessary in order to ensure the attainment of the objective in view, *inter alia*, the protection of national or regional socio-cultural characteristics. It was of the utmost importance for the UK to obtain a final ruling as to section 47. Thus, it was argued that the question of proportionality was a matter for the ECJ to decide rather than for the national courts. The motive behind this submission was certainly the expectation that, in the wake of the judgments in *Conforama* and *Marchandise*, the ECJ would come to a conclusion to the

[173] Cases C-6 and 9/90, *Francovich and Bonifaci* v. *Italy* [1991] ECR I-5357, para. 37.

[174] Case C-312/89, *Union Departmentale des Syndicats CGT de l'Aisne* v. *Sidef Conforama* [1991] ECR I-997.

[175] Case C-332/89, *Ministère Public* v. *Marchandise* [1991] ECR I-1027.

same effect. The UK government urged the ECJ to dismiss the argument that the legislation was disproportionate because of the Member States' exceeding their powers to regulate trading and working on Sunday. First, it was argued, the measure was necessary in the pursuit of an aim held by the ECJ to be justified under Community law. Secondly, the balancing test could not and should not be based on the estimated additional sales of imported goods, on the one hand, or the objectives of the legislation, on the other. As a result, the legislation could not be held to be disproportionate on the basis on which the Sunday traders alleged that it could. In any event, having regard to the discretion left to the Member States to regulate arrangements of working hours, the legislation at issue was merely the expression of a power of evaluation of national and regional socio-cultural characteristics.

In summary, it was argued that Article 28 (ex Article 30) did not apply to national legislation prohibiting Sunday trading since it was both justified with regard to Community law and proportionate with regard to the powers of the Member States to regulate working hours. Considering that the ECJ held that Article 28 (ex Article 30) was to be interpreted as meaning that the prohibition which it laid down did *not* apply to national legislation prohibiting retailers from opening their premises on Sundays, the submissions of the UK government must be regarded as having been successful in the sense of lending support to the national law. However, for the attainment of deregulation, a solution in Parliament had become inevitable, following the outcome of the Sunday trading litigation.

Resolving the matter in Parliament

Once it was out of danger of excessive damages claims, the UK government once again focused on the issue of deregulation. This can be seen in the fact that the Attorney-General refused to act even after the decision of the ECJ on 16 December 1992 in *Stoke-on-Trent*.[176] However, the lesson which the government had learnt from the instrumentalisation of Article 28 (ex Article 30) was that re-regulation of the market could not be achieved without taking into account the underlying socio-moral issues. This can be seen in the Sunday Trading Act 1994, which put an end to the Sunday trading saga, and took into account changes in consumer expectations. In essence, the new Act combines

[176] Official Reports 6th series, Parliamentary Debates, House of Commons, vol. 216, cols. 219–20, 16 December 1992.

deregulation with employment protection. It thus illustrates the shift in government policy from total deregulation to re-regulation coupled with the recognition of the underlying socio-moral and socio-cultural issues.

The European Commission's position in the Sunday trading litigation

The European Commission's overall strategy

Even though the European Commission used various lines of reasoning, it always tried to ensure the validity of the national measure. The question which therefore arises is how this position fits into the wider policy of the Commission to act as a 'motor of integration', on the one hand, and as the Community 'watchdog', on the other.

The Commission as a 'motor of integration'

As a 'motor of integration', it is the Commission's responsibility according to Article 211 (ex Article 155) to 'ensure the proper functioning and development of the common market'. To this end, the Commission has powers of a legislative, administrative, executive and judicial nature. For present purposes, it is worth considering how the Commission's judicial activity complements its legislative role in relation to Article 28 (ex Article 30). According to its powers and duties under Article 211 (ex Article 155), it is the Commission's duty to ensure and further the process of achieving single market integration. This it did, for instance, by giving guidance as to the interpretation of Community law in Directive 70/50/EEC.[177] In general, however, as will be seen when discussing the role of the ECJ, in the absence of harmonisation measures it was by and largely left to the ECJ to ensure the free movement of goods. This is not to say that the Commission stopped acting as a 'motor of integration' in light of the ECJ's jurisprudence. Rather, it reoriented its own legislative programme so as to complement the jurisprudence of the ECJ.[178]

It should, however, be noted that integration is only one of the Commission's many objectives. It is the task of the Commission to reconcile conflicting objectives such as integration, on the one hand and a desire

[177] Directive 70/50/EEC of 22 December 1969, OJ 1969 No. L13, 29.

[178] Commission Communication, 3 October 1980, OJ 1980 No. C256, 2.

for national regulation on the other. In the Sunday trading cases, the Commission's objective was not to make inroads into national affairs such as the regulation of Sunday as a non-working day, which is as such not necessary to achieving the objectives of the Treaty. In light of the 'Maastricht debate' in general and the debate about the 'principle of subsidiarity'[179] in particular, it must have been a central concern of the Commission not to urge a rigorous application of Article 28 (ex Article 30) to national rules which are clearly outside the scope of Article 28 (ex Article 30) and thus arguably outside the exclusive competence of the Community. Yet, this is not to say that the Commission lost sight of its integration policy. Its concern about integration can be discerned throughout its submissions, as, for example, in *Stoke-on-Trent* where on the facts of the case a unified interpretation by a single court at Community level was considered to be preferable to differing interpretations by national courts.

To summarise, the Commission clearly indicated that it was not willing to exercise its powers for the furtherance of unmeritorious claims beyond Community objectives. It was not willing to act as a watchdog where matters of purely domestic law were involved.

The Commission as a watchdog

This latter proposition is further corroborated by the fact that the Commission did not take enforcement action under Article 226 (ex Article 169). A direct action before the ECJ under Article 226 (ex Article 169) is the principal remedy provided by the Treaty for an infringement of EC law by Member States. The Commission has a discretion to bring such an action if it 'considers that a Member State has failed to fulfil an obligation under [the] Treaty'.[180] In the majority of cases the failure is non-compliance with the requirements of the Treaty.[181] It should be noted that, before the Maastricht Treaty, which revised Article 228 (ex Article 171),[182] the only sanction against a state which had failed to comply with a ruling from the ECJ under Article 226 (ex

[179] Art. 5 (ex Art. 3b). [180] Art. 226 (ex Art. 169).

[181] E.g. Case C-178/84, *Commission* v. *Germany* [1987] ECR 1227; [1988] 1 CMLR 780 (the 'German Beer Case'). These were infringement proceedings against Germany for its failure to fulfil certain obligations under Art. 28 (ex Art. 30) of the Treaty.

[182] Art. 228 (ex Art. 171) provides: 'If the Court of Justice finds that the Member State concerned has not complied with its judgment it may impose a lump sum or penalty payment on it.' It is the task of the Commission to bring such cases before the ECJ.

Article 169) was a second action under Article 226 (ex Article 169) for failure to comply with its obligations under Article 228 (ex Article 171). Even though the ECJ had over the years provided for remedies for individuals via the principles of direct and indirect effect and state liability under *Francovich*,[183] the law as it then stood was far from being a satisfactory weapon, especially when a preliminary reference had already been made on the same issue. The merit of the *Francovich* judgment lies primarily in co-operation and dispute resolution between the Member State concerned and the Community. However, political dialogue between the Commission and the Member State is pointless if the Member State has not breached Community law. It is for this reason that it is very unlikely that, even after the Maastricht Treaty, the Commission would have brought an action under Article 226 (ex Article 169) since the UK was not considered to be in breach of Community law.

Reshaping the scope of Article 28 in *Torfaen*

The position of the Commission in *Torfaen* was influenced to a considerable extent – if not determined entirely – by E. L. White, a member of its legal department, who acted as Agent for the Commission. His position and wider academic interests were set out in an article in 1989.[184] The overall object of White's approach was to prevent the overstretching of Article 28 (ex Article 30) which had begun in *Cinéthèque* by distinguishing between restrictions on the *characteristics* of products, on the one hand, and restrictions on the *circumstances* in which goods may be sold, on the other.[185]

In *Torfaen*, the Commission argued that, following *Dassonville* and *Cassis de Dijon*, all state measures which had a restrictive effect on imports were contrary to Article 28 (ex Article 30) unless they were justifiable as mandatory requirements or under one of the categories listed in Article 30 (ex Article 36). The measures in issue did not constitute restrictions having an effect on trade between the Member States. Rather, they should be classified as measures restricting the place, the time and the manner in which goods may be sold or used and the persons by whom they may be sold or used.

[183] Cases C-6 and 9/90, *Francovich and Bonifaci* v. *Italy* [1991] ECR I-5357.

[184] E. L. White, 'In Search of the Limits of Art. 30 of the EEC Treaty' (1989) 26 *Common Market Law Review* 235.

[185] For a discussion of his academic view, see p. 154 below.

This argument was supported by reference to the *Oebel*,[186] *Blesgen*[187] and *Forest*[188] cases. The Commission was thus drawing on a line of cases in which the ECJ had held that equal-burden rules, which did not relate to the *characteristics* of goods but merely to the *conditions* under which all goods were sold, were outside Article 28 (ex Article 30). In *Oebel*, the ECJ held that Article 28 (ex Article 30) did not apply to national rules which prohibited the production and distribution of bakery products during certain hours of the night. Equally, in *Blesgen*, the ECJ decided that an indistinctly applicable measure restricting the sale of drinks of a certain alcoholic strength for consumption on the premises in all places open to the public was outside Article 28 (ex Article 30). And, in *Forest*, the ECJ decided that a national system of wheat-milling quotas did not affect intra-Community trade and was thus outside Article 28 (ex Article 30).

By analogy, the Commission argued that restrictions on shop-opening hours would not restrict the importation or marketing of goods from Member States. Thus, it was argued that the link with the importation of goods was too remote. The Commission, however, conceded that, by limiting the *times* at which certain goods may be sold, such measures might reduce the *demand* for the goods. Yet, this effect would not be equivalent to an adverse effect on trade between Member States. On the contrary, it was argued that disparities in shop-opening hours within the Community were capable of increasing trade.

In summary, it was submitted by the Commission that the measure in issue fell outside the scope of Article 28 (ex Article 30), thus rendering unnecessary a consideration of a justification under Article 30 (ex Article 36) or of a mandatory requirement. However, if the ECJ held that those measures were within Article 28 (ex Article 30), it was submitted that justifying the measure either under Article 30 (ex Article 36) or as a mandatory requirement would be difficult. Justifications based on, for example, employee protection, respect for the traditional English Sunday or control of competition would probably fail the proportionality test or would constitute arbitrary discrimination within the meaning of the second sentence of Article 30 (ex Article 36).

[186] Case C-155/80, *Oebel* [1981] ECR 1993; [1983] 1 CMLR 340.

[187] Case C-75/81, *Belgium* v. *Blesgen* [1982] ECR 1211; [1983] 1 CMLR 431.

[188] Case 148/85, *Direction Générale des Impôts and Procureur de la République* v. *Forest* [1986] ECR 3449.

Adjustment of the Commission's arguments after *Torfaen*

In the *Conforama*[189] and *Marchandise*[190] proceedings, the Commission adjusted its line of argument to take into account the judgment in *Torfaen*. Here, as well as in the subsequent case of *Stoke-on-Trent*, the criterion for keeping the concept of measures of equivalent effect within its proper bounds, as advocated by White in *Torfaen*, did not feature, as White was no longer involved in the matter. To a large extent, in *Conforama* and *Marchandise*, the Commission drew on White's arguments.

The Commission now argued that a two-stage approach was necessary when analysing whether a measure was caught by Article 28 (ex Article 30). First, did the legislation pursue an objective which was justified under Community law? Secondly, did the legislation satisfy the requirements of proportionality? It was argued that *Torfaen* had laid down a general 'principle' for employee protection on Sunday, as well as for the preservation of the special character of Sundays. This general principle would be applicable to social welfare legislation such as that in issue in *Conforama* and *Marchandise*. It is submitted that this reasoning amounts essentially to the introduction of a new head of mandatory requirement which is subject to the proportionality test. In relation to the proportionality requirement, the Commission's argument seems to embody the experience gained in national court proceedings following the judgment in *Torfaen*. For the sake of consistency, it was submitted by the Commission that the application of the proportionality test should not be left to national courts. On the facts of the case, the Commission did not consider the prohibition on the employment of staff on Sunday disproportionate to the result sought.

To sum up, it was argued by the Commission that the national measure in question fell within Article 28 (ex Article 30). However, it was said to be justified as well as proportionate, and therefore was not caught by the prohibition in Article 28 (ex Article 30). While *Conforama* and *Marchandise* were evidence of the Commission's intention not to leave too much leeway to the national courts, this intention became even more apparent in *Stoke-on-Trent*.

[189] Case C-312/89, *Union Departmentale des Syndicats CGT de l'Aisne* v. *Sidef Conforama* [1991] ECR I-997.

[190] Case C-332/89, *Ministère Public* v. *Marchandise* [1991] ECR I-1027.

The Commission's position in *Stoke-on-Trent*

In *Stoke-on-Trent*, the Commission proceeded on the assumption that the measure in question fell within Article 28 (ex Article 30). On that basis, it was argued that the two-stage test (justification with regard to Community law, and the proportionality test) laid down by the ECJ in *Torfaen*, as subsequently modified in *Conforama* and *Marchandise*, should be followed. First, as regards the question of whether the measure at issue was justified, it was submitted that, on the basis of the ECJ's judgments in *Oebel*, *Conforama* and *Marchandise*, it must be concluded that section 47 of the Shops Act 1950 pursued an objective which was justified by reference to Community law. By analogy with those cases, section 47 should be considered to be a rule ensuring the accordance of the opening hours of retail premises with national or regional socio-cultural characteristics. Secondly, it was submitted that the question of proportionality in the present case could not be left to be determined by the national courts. Thus, the approach in *Oebel*, *Conforama* and *Marchandise*, rather than that in *Torfaen*, should be followed. Considering that a complete deregulation of Sunday opening would result in only a 1–2 per cent increase in the sales of imported goods, it was argued that the restrictive effects of section 47 were not excessive with regard to the purpose in view.

To conclude, the Sunday trading cases and the alleged non-compliance of the UK with Community law were not considered to be an area where it was appropriate for the Commission to act as guardian of Community law as such. By refusing to act as 'watchdog' for Community law, the Commission gave a helping hand to the Member States to act as 'watchdogs' for their own national laws.

The Advocates-General and the ECJ: principal characters or merely supporting roles?

The role of the ECJ and that of the Advocates-General can only be properly understood if they are set in their wider political and institutional contexts.

The Advocates-General

The role of the Advocates-General

In general, when a case arrives at the ECJ, it is assigned to one of the Advocates-General by the First Advocate-General. When designating an Advocate-General to review the case, it is the aim of the First Advocate-General to achieve a balanced workload but not to produce any particular specialisation by way of subject-matter. However, considering that, in *Torfaen*, *Conforama*, *Marchandise* and *Stoke-on-Trent*, it was always Advocate-General van Gerven who delivered the Opinion, it seems to have been the case that, at least in those cases, specialisation was indeed intended. In view of this, one might even speculate whether the timing of the references was planned by counsel for the Sunday traders. The aim of the Sunday traders might well have been to avoid having Advocate-General Slynn assigned to the case. To appreciate this argument, we need briefly to look at the role of Advocate-General Slynn in the *Cinéthèque* case.

The significance of the choice of advocate-general in *Torfaen*

Lord Slynn was designated Advocate-General in *Cinéthèque*. In contrast to the ECJ itself, Advocate-General Slynn advocated a new approach. In his Opinion, the rule in issue was not caught by Article 28 (ex Article 30). Rather, he contended that the type of rule in issue constituted a separate category, even if it did in fact lead to a restriction of imports. This approach was markedly different to that subsequently adopted by the ECJ. In view of his reasoning in *Cinéthèque*, the Sunday traders would not have wanted Lord Slynn to be designated Advocate-General in *Torfaen*.

Bearing in mind that Lord Slynn's term of office as an Advocate-General came to an end in 1988,[191] when the first references from the English courts were being made, it is (just about) possible that the Sunday traders took account of this fact when deciding *when* to ask for a reference. It is more likely, however, that they simply took advantage of the unwritten rule that the judge-rapporteur should not be a judge from a Member State concerned in the case. Even though in theory this rule does not apply to the appointment of the Advocate-General, it is likely that, in cases in which 'impartiality and independence' are in doubt, the case is assigned to another Advocate-General. Considering the significance of the Sunday trading litigation, and its wider constitutional and political implications in the UK, it was to be expected that a non-British Advocate-General would be selected in order to ensure that he or she would act 'with complete impartiality and

[191] He was appointed to the Court in 1988.

independence' as required by Article 222 (ex Article 166). In any event, it was van Gerven who was chosen to act as Advocate-General in *Torfaen, Marchandise, Conforama* and *Stoke-on-Trent*.

Advocate-General van Gerven's threshold definition in *Torfaen*

The first issue in *Torfaen* to be dealt with by van Gerven was the question of whether the reference should be reworded. He rejected the contention that the national court's factual assumption was irrelevant, and thus refused to reword the reference. He subsequently focused on the question of whether, and if so which, national rules found to have a certain restrictive effect on imports may fall outside the scope of Article 28 (ex Article 30). In doing so, he advocated what Mortelmans called 'van Gerven's threshold definition'.[192]

His starting-point was the situation in which national rules lead to a national market being 'screened off' or rendering market access unacceptably difficult for operators from other Member States. Relying on the decisions in *Cinéthèque*,[193] *Warner Brothers*,[194] *Buet*[195] and *Pharmaceutical Society*,[196] he considered the case law in relation to what he called this 'new' situation. From these cases, he drew the conclusion that the interpretation of Article 28 (ex Article 30) was not based on the restriction on imported goods but rather on the partitioning of the common market into separate national markets. In order to arrive at that conclusion, he drew an analogy to Article 81 (ex Article 85). The basis for this analogy was found essentially in the underlying purpose of Article 28 (ex Article 30) and Article 81 (ex Article 85), that is, the establishment of the Community market as laid down in Articles 2 and 3. Despite the differences between Article 81 (ex Article 85) and Article 28 (ex Article 30), including, *inter alia*, in the presence or absence of the *de minimis* rule and the parties to whom they are addressed, van Gerven advocated the application of the ECJ's approach in Article 81 (ex Article 85) cases to Article 28 (ex Article 30).

192 K. Mortelmans, 'Article 30 of the EEC Treaty and Legislation Relating to Market Circumstances: Time to Consider a New Definition?' (1991) 28 *Common Market Law Review* 115.

193 Cases 60 and 61/84, *Cinéthèque SA* v. *Fédération Nationale des Cinémas Francais* [1985] ECR 2605; [1986] 1 CMLR 365.

194 Case 158/86, *Warner Brothers Inc.* v. *Christiansen* [1988] ECR 2605.

195 Case 382/87, *Buet* v. *Ministere Public* [1989] ECR 1235.

196 Cases 266 and 267/87, *The Queen* v. *Pharmaceutical Society of Great Britain* [1989] ECR 1295.

For present purposes, we need to consider the expression 'affect trade between Member States' in Article 81 (ex Article 85). In the competition law context, there are two situations concerning the partitioning of the market that may be distinguished. First, there is the situation in which an agreement renders *access* to a national market more difficult, that is, it creates a threshold to the national market. In this situation, the prohibition laid down in Article 81(1) (ex Article 85(1)) applies only if it can be shown that the agreement at issue reinforces the compartmentalisation of markets on a national basis. As was held in *Cementandelaren* v. *Commission*,[197] the essential condition was that the economic interpenetration of the national market which the Treaty is designed to bring about is hindered, thus rendering it more difficult for producers or sellers from other Member States to operate in that market. Secondly, there is the situation in which a horizontal or vertical agreement in itself 'screens off' a national market. In this case, the prohibition in Article 81(1) (ex Article 85(1)) applies automatically. Therefore, the essential distinction drawn in the field of competition law is that between the screening off of national markets and the erection of thresholds to the national markets.

Based on this analysis, van Gerven advocated a similar distinction being made in relation to the application of Article 28 (ex Article 30). First, there were cases such as *Warner Brothers*, *Buet* and *Pharmaceutical Society* in which the contested rule constituted merely a barrier to the national market, thus increasing the difficulty in penetrating it. In those cases, Article 28 (ex Article 30) should only be applicable if on the basis of the whole legal and economic context the economic interpenetration was thereby threatened. According to van Gerven, it had to be sufficiently probable that the national rule rendered the market so inaccessible that the majority of imported goods would disappear from the market. Secondly, there were cases like *Cinéthèque* in which the national rule itself screened off the national market. It was suggested by the Advocate-General that, in those cases, Article 28 (ex Article 30) was automatically applicable. By classifying previous cases according to his suggested categories, van Gerven intended to restate the approach already taken by the courts.

On the facts of the case, van Gerven came to the conclusion that the national measure at issue neither screened off nor unacceptably increased the difficulty of penetrating the market. Even though a

[197] Case 8/72, *Vereeniging van Cementhandelaren* v. *Commission* [1972] ECR 977.

reduction in turnover was undeniable, according to van Gerven this would not have the effect of partitioning the Community market. His proposed reply to the preliminary question started off accordingly:

> A national rule which prohibits retail premises from being open on Sunday for the sale of goods to customers, save in respect of certain specified items, is not covered by the prohibition laid down in Article 28 (ex Article 30) if the rule does not cause imported goods to be discriminated against or placed at an actual disadvantage compared with domestic goods and if it does not screen off the domestic market of the Member State in question or make access to that market substantially more difficult or unattractive for imported goods to which the rule applies.[198]

In the alternative, if the ECJ should decide that the measure *was* covered by Article 28 (ex Article 30), the Advocate-General submitted that it could not be justified under one of the exceptions in Article 30 (ex Article 36). Further, he analysed whether 'protecting Sunday as a non-trading day' could be introduced as a novel category of mandatory requirement. In theory, he accepted the validity of such an attempt; however, he stressed the difficulty of proving that, in practice, such a new mandatory requirement was necessary and proportionate to the aim pursued. Equally, whether the measure could qualify as an exception under one of the established categories of mandatory requirements depended on its being necessary for the fulfilment of, and proportionate to, the mandatory requirement relied on. He contended that, in either case, such an investigation would involve policy considerations for the assessment of which Community law did not provide sufficient and adequate tools. Therefore, he suggested that such an inquiry be avoided at Community level. The second part of his proposed reply to the preliminary question was phrased accordingly:

> [Articles 28 and 30 (ex Articles 30 and 36)] of the Treaty do not preclude a national rule which prohibits retail premises from being open on Sunday for the sale of goods to customers, save in respect of certain specified articles, if the rule does not cause imported goods to be discriminated against or placed at an actual disadvantage compared with domestic goods and if any obstacles to intra-Community trade which may be caused by the application of that prohibition are not greater than is necessary for encouraging non-working activities and social contracts on a specified day which is already devoted to those purposes by a large part of the population.[199]

[198] Case 145/88, *Torfaen Borough Council* v. *B&Q plc* [1989] ECR 3851 at 3884.
[199] *Ibid.*

Van Gerven's primary submission can therefore be summarised as follows. He concluded that – in general – a restriction on Sunday trading did not constitute a measure of equivalent effect within the meaning of Article 28 (ex Article 30). A restriction on Sunday trading would, however, constitute such a measure if it discriminated against imports in some way or 'screened off' the domestic market or rendered it unacceptably difficult to penetrate that market.

Was van Gerven's new approach a success or a failure?

As will be seen, van Gerven's approach was forcefully rejected by the ECJ. Yet, the outcome in *Torfaen* may be seen as demonstrating van Gerven's success in advocating a fundamental change of direction in the development of the ECJ's approach to the free movement of goods. What van Gerven clearly intended was to limit the application of Article 28 (ex Article 30) so as to exclude Sunday trading-type cases from being held to be in violation of Article 28 (ex Article 30). This he did by proposing a new methodology in relation to Article 28 (ex Article 30) by analogy to Article 81 (ex Article 85). This self-imposed task made him the 'intellectual hero of a new phase in writing and rewriting of the economic constitution of Europe'.[200]

Van Gerven's about-turn after *Torfaen*

In *Conforama* and *Marchandise*, van Gerven proceeded on the basis of the decision in *Torfaen*, that is, on the assumption that, with regard to commercial legislation applicable to imported and domestic products alike, the ECJ had held in favour of the *Dassonville* rule. Acknowledging the similarity between national legislation concerning a general prohibition on Sunday trading and national legislation concerning a prohibition on employing workers on Sunday, he submitted that the prohibition in Article 28 (ex Article 30) was applicable *in principle* to a rule prohibiting the employment of staff on Sundays. Whether or not a national rule was *in fact* caught by Article 28 (ex Article 30) was, however, dependent on the need for and proportionality of the legislation in question. Van Gerven further argued – for the sake of a uniform application of Community law – that in relation to the latter issues a solution in a general context was necessary and desirable; it

[200] J. H. H. Weiler, 'The Constitution of the Common Market Place: The Evolution of the Free Movement of Goods' in P. Craig and G. de Búrca (eds.), *The Evolution of EU Law* (Oxford, 1999), 369.

was for the ECJ to assess the need for and the proportionality of the specific legislation at issue.

According to van Gerven, any attempt to justify the contested national legislation in *Conforama* and *Marchandise* under the heading of mandatory requirement would require the creation of a new justification to be added to the list of existing mandatory requirements based on the decision in *Cassis de Dijon*. Pointing to the judgments in *Oebel* and *Torfaen*, van Gerven perceived a readiness on the part of the ECJ to recognise further mandatory requirements in addition to the classic grounds of justification. This led him to turn his attention to the proper division of tasks between the national courts and the ECJ.

Taking into account the difficulty of classifying possible justifications under the existing categories, and – above all – the difficulty of establishing general guidelines with regard to justifications, van Gerven argued that there were three steps involved in considering whether a measure *prima facie* within Article 28 (ex Article 30) could be justified. First, it was a matter for the ECJ to determine whether a new justification which had been relied on in a national court was acceptable. It was then for the national court to decide whether the national legislation could in fact be justified, that is, whether it pursued the objective recognised by the ECJ to be in keeping with the Treaty. Secondly, it had to be determined whether the legislation did not exceed what was necessary in order to ensure the attainment of the objective in view in light of the extent and nature of the obstacles created by the legislation. The requirement of necessity demanded, according to van Gerven, the consideration of two issues: whether the national legislation was in fact relevant for the attainment of the objective pursued; and whether there was a suitable alternative measure. Thirdly, it was necessary to analyse whether the potential obstacle to intra-Community trade was out of proportion to the objective pursued. Both of the latter tasks were, according to van Gerven, for the ECJ itself. This position was not altered by the fact that, in *Torfaen*, the ECJ did not explicitly rule on the proportionality of the measure in question since it was 'immediately apparent' that it was proportionate to the legitimate objective pursued by the measure.

It is clear from this exposition that van Gerven urged the ECJ to decide conclusively on the admissibility of the objective pursued by the legislation at issue, on its necessity, and on its proportionality. Applying this approach to the proceedings before him, van Gerven stated that designation of a single day of rest for employees could be regarded as a legitimate objective under Community law, that the measures at issue did not jeopardise the integration of the market, and that it automatically followed as a matter of fact that the obstacles created by the legislation were not out of proportion to the attainment of the objective pursued. In summary, it was therefore submitted that the national legislation was not in breach of Article 28 (ex Article 30).

Van Gerven in *Stoke-on-Trent*

The last of the three Opinions delivered by Advocate-General van Gerven in this series of cases was that in *Stoke-on-Trent*. For the fourth time in two years, it was van Gerven who had to take into account the differing interests of all parties involved (the referring courts, the two parties to the conflict and those who had prepared submissions for the hearing) and to combine them all into one proposal in order to put an end to a long-standing conflict not only on the substance of the matter but also on the interrelationship between national and European law. His task was not easy. The mere fact that the lowest and the highest courts of the land were involved necessarily had implications for the domestic judicial system, irrespective of the outcome of the cases. Van Gerven felt called upon to follow the course he had already chosen in *Conforama* and *Marchandise*, that is, defining the proper division of tasks between the national courts and the ECJ. As will be seen, van Gerven again tried to shape rules for future co-operation between the national courts and the ECJ.[201]

For the purpose of our analysis, it is important to analyse how and why the Advocate-General regrouped the set of questions; what he regarded as being the ground rules of co-operation between the courts; and how he applied these criteria to *Stoke-on-Trent* in the light of *Torfaen*, *Conforama* and *Marchandise*.

Rearranging the questions: from a vertical to a horizontal perspective

After reviewing the questions referred by the three national courts, van Gerven went on to rearrange the questions so that they could be

[201] See Opinion of Advocate-General van Gerven, Case C-169/91, *Stoke-on-Trent City Council* v. *B&Q plc* [1992] ECR I-6635; [1993] 1 CMLR 426, para. 3: '[G]reat uncertainty continues to prevail at least in Great Britain with regard to the compatibility of the Shops Act with Community law.' This statement demonstrates an unwillingness on the part of the Advocate-General to deal repeatedly with the same issue, but it also demonstrates a certain lack of understanding of the issue on the part of the Advocate-General.

considered, not from a vertical perspective, but from a horizontal perspective. National courts, to a greater or lesser extent, formulate their referred questions with a view to obtaining an answer from the ECJ in order to decide a national issue (here, the compatibility of the Shops Act with European law). This approach recognises the supremacy of European law. European law, the ECJ and the Advocate-General are thus forced into a position they do not wish to be in the ECJ becomes the court of final instance to decide on the issue of the opening hours of shops in the UK on Sundays. By rearranging the referred questions, van Gerven broadened the perspective from a national, vertical perspective to a horizontal, European perspective.

The approach he chose is one that followed the logic of European law by linking the referred questions to the relevant European law issues: (1) the significance of *Conforama* and *Marchandise* for the UK Sunday trading legislation; (2) placing the three judgments into the context of the ECJ's recent case law on the applicability of Article 28 (ex Article 30); (3) the question of who is to carry out the assessment of justification and proportionality; (4) the requirement of an objective which is justifiable under Community law; (5) the Community proportionality requirement; and (6) other questions. The Opinion is structured along the lines of van Gerven's horizontal perspective. The Advocate-General thereby maintained the sovereignty of European law and avoided falling into the temptation too closely and too directly to intervene (vertically!) by means of Article 28 (ex Article 30) into the Member States' Sunday trading law. Each referring court would find its particular questions under the relevant heading, and thus van Gerven recognised the role and importance of the national courts. The national courts, in turn, before they were able to discern answers to their questions in the Opinion of the Advocate-General, had to make the intellectual effort to reorientate their perspective from a vertical perspective to the horizontal perspective of European law.

Placing *Stoke-on-Trent* into the context of *Conforama*, *Marchandise* and *Torfaen*

First, van Gerven elaborated on the effect of the *Conforama* and *Marchandise* judgments for the UK Sunday trading laws. The first effect of these cases was that the provisions in question were to be regarded as trading rules within the *Dassonville* formula. From a further comparison between the judgment in *Torfaen* and those in *Conforama* and

Marchandise, it may be deduced that the relevant provisions could not properly be distinguished. By concentrating on the effect of the provisions at issue and their impact on the sales of national as well as imported products, van Gerven suggested that the legal bases in *Torfaen*, *Conforama* and *Marchandise* were comparable. Equally, he did not consider it possible to distinguish *Torfaen* from *Conforama* and *Marchandise* on account of factual differences. The essential difference found by van Gerven between the two judgments as such was that, in *Conforama* and *Marchandise*, the ECJ itself had decided the question of proportionality, whereas, in *Torfaen*, the question had been dealt with by the national court. However, instead of stressing the differences between the cases, van Gerven noted their common background – in particular the effect of the decisions in *Oebel*, *Cinéthèque* and *Quietlynn*[202] in relation to the objective justification of national laws as well as their proportionality. On the facts of the case and in light of the developed ground rules, van Gerven was convinced that the legislation in question was neither discriminatory nor intended to regulate trade. Resorting back to his 'threshold definition', he argued that the measures at issue did not lead to partitioning of the market. Further, the Sunday trading rules themselves as well as the barriers to trade caused by Sunday trading did not exceed what was necessary in order to ensure the attainment of the objective justified under Community law. Implicit in this statement is therefore the argument that the relevant provisions could not be said to be disproportionate.

Yet, it is apparent from van Gerven's Opinion that he did not want proportionality to be the decisive criterion for deciding on the compatibility of national provisions with Community law. Even though in *Stoke-on-Trent* he did not expressly advocate the view and approach he put forward in *Torfaen*, it is apparent that he reasoned along those lines. It was his intention to keep the application of Article 28 (ex Article 30) within its proper boundaries. This was stressed in his conclusion, in which he claimed that:

> the prohibition contained in [Article 28 (ex Article 30)] of the EEC Treaty was not applicable to a purely *domestic* situation in a Member State.[203]

[202] Case C-23/89, *Quietlynn Ltd and Brian James Richards* v. *Southend-on-Sea Borough Council* [1990] ECR I-3059; [1990] 3 CMLR 55.

[203] Case C-169/91, *Stoke-on-Trent City Council* v. *B&Q plc* [1992] ECR I-6635 at 6685 (emphasis added).

The Advocate-General's concept of *who* is to apply the justification and the proportionality test

The Advocate-General could not avoid tackling the issue on which the ECJ had not yet given a clear ruling, that is, the question of who is to apply the proportionality test.[204] He thereby legitimises the referring courts' questions as far as they purport not to have understood how the tasks should be shared between the national courts and the ECJ. According to van Gerven, this question of principle was not as such submitted by the national courts. [205] The question is, however, inherent in the national courts' difficulties in applying *Torfaen*. Therefore, the next issue addressed by van Gerven was the issue of who is responsible for what. He distinguishes three lines of argument, the first dealing from a more general perspective with what co-operation in the application of the proportionality principle should look like.

Co-operation in principle[206] For van Gerven, it is the joint task of the ECJ and the national courts to determine whether a national measure is compatible with Community law, just as the ECJ had reiterated in *Conforama* and *Marchandise*:

> It must be observed *in limine* that, although the Court has no jurisdiction in preliminary reference proceedings to rule on the compatibility of a national provision with the Treaty, it is nevertheless empowered to provide a national court with all the criteria for the interpretation of Community law which will enable the latter to assess that compatibility for the purpose of giving judgment in the case before it.

The ECJ's statement, taken as a starting-point, allowed van Gerven to have a closer look at the collaboration between the ECJ and the national courts. The national court must, first, it is suggested, in the formulation of the question, provide the ECJ with all the necessary factual information and the national legal framework so that the ECJ is afforded the possibility of laying down a rule with full knowledge of the facts. The ECJ cannot, however, rule on the correctness of that information or legal framework. Secondly, the ECJ must provide the national court with all relevant information with regard to Community law, including the criteria to be used in assessing the issues of

[204] Opinion of the Advocate-General van Gerven, *ibid.*, para. 17, last sentence.
[205] *Ibid.*, para. 18. [206] *Ibid.*, para. 19.

justification and proportionality. Finally, it is for the national court, on the basis of the reply given to it by the ECJ, to assess the compatibility or incompatibility of national legislation with Community law and to determine the necessary consequences under national law. This three-step approach does not provide much guidance for deciding clear-cut cases. That is why the question of how van Gerven applied these general observations to the assessment of justification is much more important.

Co-operation in the assessment of justification[207] For van Gerven, it is for the national court, with the assistance of the parties, to identify as clearly as possible the policy objectives pursued by national legislation and to bring them to the ECJ's attention. The Advocate-General therefore referred in his Opinion to an article by Koopmans,[208] in which the latter proposed that the ECJ contact the national court if relevant information is missing, although Koopmans admits that the national rules of procedure make it impossible for most of the national courts to reopen the case after having suspended it when they first referred their questions to the ECJ. Van Gerven then went on to conclude that it is for the ECJ ultimately to decide whether the objectives thus identified are consistent with an objective pursued by Community law or – where they fall within areas which in the current state of Community law are within the competence of the Member States – whether Community law is in any way opposed to the objectives pursued by the national measure.

Co-operation in the assessment of proportionality Here, van Gerven considered the abstract question of how EC law may be further developed. Although the principle may be clear, difficulties will arise when co-operation is put into practice. According to van Gerven, 'it is . . . for the Court and for the Court alone, clearly and imperatively to indicate in its case law the criteria to be used in that assessment'. These are quite strong words, and they may be read as contradicting Hoffmann J's reasoning[209] when he claimed the supremacy of Parliament.

[207] *Ibid.*, para. 20.

[208] T. Koopmans, 'The Technique of the Preliminary Question – A View from the Court of Justice' in H. Schermers *et al.* (eds.), *Article 177: Experiences and Problems* (The Hague, 1987), 327.

[209] *Stoke-on-Trent City Council* v. *B&Q* [1990] 3 CMLR 31.

The Advocate-General is on safe European law ground here, and therefore could be explicit in his language. Much more difficult were the further steps he suggested. He saw it as:

> [a] joint task of the Court and the national court to apply those criteria drawn from existing case law to the concrete legal and factual context. In that connection the national court in its order for reference, must give the fullest possible description of the legislation in issue (legal basis, scope, detailed rules and practice governing its application) and its restrictive effects on intra-Community trade.

What exactly is 'the fullest possible description'? And who decides when 'full' is 'fullest'. The ECJ may have doubts as to the quality of the information or the correctness of the facts presented. That is why there may be a certain preparedness on the part of the ECJ, where basic Community law issues are at stake, to decide the case itself, and this is what van Gerven seemed to have in mind when he said in *Stoke-on-Trent*:

> If it appears from the findings of the national court and the arguments submitted to the Court that there is no room for any doubt, the Court itself . . . will state the results of the assessment under Community law.

If, however, the ECJ sticks to the general concept of task-sharing, in which the ECJ does not make an assessment on the basis of the information provided to it, then the national court, where necessary after further examination of the legislative and factual context, and in light of the ECJ's reply to the preliminary question, must arrive at its own decision regarding the application of the proportionality requirement.

Van Gerven's impact on the scope of Article 28

An Advocate-General's Opinion is not binding in any respect on the ECJ. The ECJ is free to disregard it entirely. As will be seen, this is what actually happened in *Torfaen*, despite the fact that – from the late 1980s onwards – there has been a general tendency on the part of the ECJ to refer to the Opinion of the Advocate-General or even to approve of it and to incorporate it into the judgment. Yet, even though van Gerven's approach was not followed in the instant case, it did, nevertheless, influence the ECJ in subsequent proceedings. It is suggested that the influence of the Advocate-General's Opinion on the general development of the law reflects the most important aspect of his office. This is all the more true in light of van Gerven's ground-breaking views on the proportionality principle as a means to lay down ground rules for the division of tasks between the national courts and the ECJ. It is the latter aspect of his Opinion in *Stoke-on-Trent* that has been neglected in the whole Sunday trading saga and its legal aftermath, maybe because the ECJ itself did not decide on the issue of proportionality.

The ECJ

Precedent and judicial activism

The ECJ's decisions in *Torfaen, Conforama*, *Marchandise* and *Stoke-on-Trent* have to be considered in the context of the ECJ's role within the framework of the Community institutions. In particular, two aspects are of special interest: first, the question of precedent; and, secondly, the interrelationship between legislative and judicial initiatives.

In theory, the ECJ is not bound by its previous decisions, that is, it is not under an obligation to apply the doctrine of precedent.[210] However, like any other court – especially in common law jurisdictions – the ECJ prefers to follow its own previous decisions, that is, it *does* in practice apply the doctrine of precedent. In its more recent case law, a tendency for the ECJ to refer to its own previous decisions by name has become evident. It is therefore suggested that the ECJ has now arrived at what is called a *jurisprudence constante* in cases in which it has already considered a similar problem. Yet, the ECJ will not hesitate to depart from its previous decisions if it thinks it necessary, although it has seldom done so. Where it does so, it is worth analysing the underlying reasons for its departure from its previous decisions.

The ECJ's approach to the doctrine of precedent can be explained by the role which was assigned to it in the Treaty. For present purposes, we must ignore developments such as the creation of the Court of First Instance and the increasing tendency for chambers (rather than the full court) to hear cases, which may lead to delicate problems of precedent. It should be noted at the outset that *Conforama*, *Marchandise* and *Stoke-on-Trent* were heard in full court, while *Torfaen* was argued in the Sixth Chamber. More importantly, however, it is not the court's structure itself which determines the ECJ's approach to precedent. Rather, it is the difficulty of amending and changing the Treaty or creating new legislative instruments which led to the creation of a court which is not bound by the doctrine of *stare decisis*. The Treaty

[210] A. Arnull, 'Owning Up to Fallibility: Precedent and the Court of Justice' (1993) 30 *Common Market Law Review* 247.

of Rome – as the law stood at that time – was a framework treaty with many lacunae which needed to be filled. And generally, where a cumbersome process such as the legislative process in the European Union is required to change existing legislation or even the Treaty itself, it is often necessary for a court of first and last resort to depart from its previous decisions. In the absence of an effective single Community legislative organ, the ECJ necessarily had to use judicial activism in order to do justice.

The ECJ's reasoning in *Torfaen*

In *Torfaen*, the ECJ was faced with the following situation. Despite the fact that it had long been accepted that Article 28 (ex Article 30) was wide enough to cover non-discriminatory legislation, the UK and the local authority argued that the Sunday trading legislation was of such a character that it fell wholly outside the scope of Article 28 (ex Article 30). Van Gerven and the Commission each submitted an argument to the same effect, although based on different reasoning. As will become clear when discussing the impact of the judgment, the ECJ intended to render judgment to the same effect as proposed by White, van Gerven, the local authority and the UK government. It was open to the ECJ to reach this result in different ways.

It could simply have followed the Advocate-General's Opinion, thus adapting the ECJ's approach to Article 28 (ex Article 30) to the model offered by Article 81 (ex Article 85). It could equally have followed White's approach, distinguishing between restrictions on the *characteristics* of products, on the one hand, and restrictions on the *circumstances* in which goods may be sold, on the other. Further, the ECJ could simply have rendered judgment along traditional lines, that is, it could have applied the *Cassis de Dijon* test. It is arguable that the ECJ in *Cassis de Dijon* had accepted that the protection of national or regional socio-cultural characteristics constituted a newly identified mandatory requirement, and simply left the national court to determine whether the provision at issue satisfied the requirement of proportionality.[211] Yet, as will be seen, neither in *Torfaen* nor in *Stoke-on-Trent* did the ECJ mention mandatory requirements as such, and its reference to Directive 70/50/EEC[212] indicates that it argued along pre-*Cassis de Dijon* lines relying heavily on *Cinéthèque*.

[211] Interpretation by C. Greenwood, 'European Community Law' (1991) *All England Annual Review* 141 at 148.

[212] Directive 70/50/EEC of 22 December 1969, OJ 1969 No. L13, 29.

In fact, the ECJ followed its previous decision in *Cinéthèque*. It pointed out that, even though the case related to a measure which applied without distinction to both national and imported goods, in light of the ruling in *Cinéthèque* this did not prevent it constituting a measure of equivalent effect. The ECJ acknowledged that the measure concerned was covered by the expression used in the *Dassonville* formula, that is, a trading rule capable of hindering, directly or indirectly, actually or potentially, intra-Community trade. Taking this proposition as a starting-point, the ECJ propounded a twofold approach to the legislation at issue.

First, the compatibility with Community law of such legislation depended on whether the legislation pursued an objective which is justified with regard to Community law. On that question, the ECJ observed that it had already been stated in *Oebel*[213] that national rules governing the hours of work, delivery and sale in the bread and confectionery industry constituted a legitimate part of economic and social policy, consistent with the objectives of public interest pursued by the Treaty. Considering that national rules governing the opening hours of retail premises equally reflected 'certain political and economic choices in so far as their purpose is to ensure that working and non-working hours are so arranged as to accord with national or regional socio-economic cultural characteristics',[214] it was felt that the same justification had to apply to the Sunday trading legislation.

Secondly, the compatibility with Community law of such national rules depended on whether the obstacle to Community trade created by such legislation exceeded what was necessary for the attainment of the objective in view.[215] This latter aspect of the two-stage test was a matter for the national court to determine.[216] It will be recalled that the ECJ held accordingly in answer to the first question, declining to answer the second and third question:

> [Article 28 (ex Article 30)] of the Treaty must be interpreted as meaning that the prohibition which it lays down does not apply to national rules prohibiting retailers from opening their premises on Sunday where the restrictive effects on Community trade which may result therefrom do not exceed the effects intrinsic to rules of that kind.[217]

213 Case C-155/80, *Oebel* [1981] ECR 1993; [1983] 1 CMLR 340.

214 *Ibid.*, para. 14.

215 The ECJ expressly referred to Art. 3 of Directive 70/50/EEC, OJ English Special Edition 1970 (I) 17.

216 Case C-155/80, *Oebel* [1981] ECR 1993, para. 16.

217 Case C-145/88, *Torfaen Borough Council* v. *B&Q plc* [1989] ECR 3851 at 3890.

The ECJ's position in *Conforama* and *Marchandise*

The judgment in *Torfaen* was relied on in *Conforama* and *Marchandise.* It was held that, following *Torfaen*, the legislation pursued an aim which was justified with regard to Community law. In relation to the question of proportionality, the ECJ stated that the restrictive effects on trade which stem from such rules did not 'seem' disproportionate to the aim pursued. In answer to the questions referred, the ECJ therefore held that:

> The prohibition contained in [Article 28 (ex Article 30)] of the Treaty, properly construed, does not apply to national legislation prohibiting the employment of staff on Sundays.[218]

This decision was explained in *Stoke-on-Trent* as resting on the principle established in *Torfaen*. However, while in *Torfaen* the issue of proportionality was considered to be a question of fact for the national court, in *Conforama* and *Marchandise* the ECJ – having all the necessary factual information at its disposal – found it necessary to rule on the question of proportionality itself.

The ECJ's ruling in *Stoke-on-Trent*

In contrast to the Advocate-General, the ECJ did not make any effort to sort the referred questions into any order. The reason for this might be that, in view of the position the ECJ took, most of the questions did not need to be answered. Therefore, there was no need to reorder the questions. All the ECJ did was to extend *Conforama* and *Marchandise* to the UK Sunday trading legislation, and to decide the issue of proportionality itself. In the words of the ECJ with regard to *Conforama* and *Marchandise*:[219]

> The Court considered that it had all the information necessary for it to rule on the question of the proportionality of such rules and that it had to do so in order to enable national courts to assess their compatibility with Community law in a uniform manner since such an assessment cannot be allowed to vary according to the findings of fact by individual courts in individual cases.

[218] Case C-312/89, *Union Departmentale des Syndicats CGT de l'Aisne* v. *Sidef Conforama* [1991] ECR I-997 at 1026.

[219] Case C-169/91, *Stoke-on-Trent City Council* v. *B&Q plc* [1992] ECR I-6635; [1993] 1 CMLR 426, paras. 14–16.

> Appraising the proportionality of national rules which pursue a legitimate aim under Community law involves weighing the national interest in attaining that aim against the Community interest in ensuring the free movement of goods. In that regard, in order to verify that the restrictive effects on intra-Community trade of the rules at issue do not exceed what is necessary to achieve the aim in view, it must be considered whether those effects are direct, indirect or purely speculative and whether those effects do not impede the marketing of imported products more than the marketing of the national products.
>
> It was on the basis of those considerations that, in its judgments in the *Conforama* and *Marchandise* cases the Court ruled that the restrictive effects on trade of national rules prohibiting the employment of workers on Sundays in certain retailing activities were not excessive in relation to the aim pursued. For the same reasons, the ECJ must make the same finding with regard to national rules prohibiting shops from opening on Sundays.

The three consecutive judgments raise fundamental questions as to the interpretation of the ECJ's approach. Moreover, they raise interesting issues in relation to the proposition that the ECJ is not bound by its previous decisions, but that it nevertheless follows previous case law where appropriate. While the interpretation of the ECJ's decisions will be considered further below, it is worth elaborating on how the Sunday trading cases fit into the ECJ's practice as regards the doctrine of *stare decisis.*

The trilogy of cases: a prime example of the ECJ's struggle to cope with the doctrine of *stare decisis*

It is beyond dispute that, in *Conforama* and *Marchandise*, the ECJ took on a task which in *Torfaen* it had assigned to the national courts, that is, the application of the proportionality test. It thus departed from its previous case law, thereby causing confusion – especially in England and Wales, where the doctrine of *stare decisis* is well recognised. The problems arising from this departure from its previous case law arose from the fact that the ECJ did not explicitly overrule *Torfaen*, as would have happened in a national common law jurisdiction. Rather, it obscured the status of its previous decision to such an extent that the House of Lords in *Stoke-on-Trent* felt obliged to make a further reference in order to clarify the state of the law. The difficulty apparent in this line of cases may be ascribed to the fact that it is still not universally recognised that the ECJ's judgments constitute a source of law in its own right. It is still widely felt that the effect of judicial decisions is to render justice in the particular proceedings before the ECJ. However, the Sunday trading litigation is a perfect example of how a single judgment of the ECJ affects a considerable number of cases in national courts. Therefore, the conclusion to be drawn is that – particularly in light of the ECJ having jurisdiction over common law countries – a departure from previous case law has to be clearly indicated by the ECJ.

The attitude of the judges in the referring proceedings

Before embarking on a discussion of how academics interpreted and reacted to the judgments in *Torfaen*, *Conforama*, *Marchandise* and *Stoke-on-Trent*, it is essential to analyse how the national courts interpreted the judgment in *Torfaen*.[220] In essence, apart from the interpretation of Article 28 (ex Article 30) itself, the application of the judgment in national courts involved two delicate issues: first, the question of the supremacy of Parliament; and, secondly, the application of the proportionality principle in the English courts. It will be seen how the English courts interpreted the ECJ's judgment in relation to Article 28 (ex Article 30) as such.

The interpretation of Article 28

Difficulties arising out of the judgment in *Torfaen*

Considering the nature of the judgment rendered in *Torfaen*, it is hardly surprising that it gave rise to a number of conflicting judgments in the national courts. In relation to Article 28 (ex Article 30), there was the difficulty of whether the question of potentially restrictive effects was a question of law or fact, and whether or not Sunday trading legislation fell wholly outside the scope of Article 28 (ex Article 30) or whether it was *prima facie* a breach of Article 28 (ex Article 30) which could be justified by application of the ECJ's jurisprudence. First, the English courts' approach to Article 28 (ex Article 30), as demonstrated in *Wellingborough*,[221] *Peterborough*,[222] *Stoke-on-Trent*[223]

[220] See Figure 2.3, p. 127 below.
[221] *Wellingborough Borough Council* v. *Payless DIY Ltd*; *Kettering Borough Council* v. *W. H. Smith Do-It-All Ltd* [1990] 1 CMLR 773.
[222] *W. H. Smith Do-It-All* v. *Peterborough City Council (No. 2)* [1990] 2 CMLR 577.
[223] *Stoke-on-Trent City Council* v. *B&Q plc* [1990] 3 CMLR 31 (High Court).

Table 2.3 *The relationship between the UK courts and the ECJ*

	1988	1989		1990				1991	1992
References by the UK courts in the Sunday trading litigation	Torfaen 25.4.88						Stoke House of Lords 20.5.91	Rochdale House of Lords 13.6.91	
Torfaen in the UK courts			Wellingborough 16.2.90	Peterborough 4.6.90	Stoke 8.7.90	Shrewsbury 20.7.90			
Judgments of the ECJ		Torfaen 23.11.89		Factortame 19.6.90			Marchandise and Conforama 28.2.91	Francovich 19.11.91	Stoke 16.12.92
The issue of cross-undertakings in damages in the UK courts				High Court 14.5.90			Court of Appeal 30.4.91	House of Lords 25.6.92	

and *Shrewsbury*,[224] will be considered. The most important of these decisions is the High Court decision of Hoffmann J in *Peterborough*.

Potentially restrictive effects: a question of law or fact?

In *Wellingborough*, Judge Francis Allen treated the issue of whether section 47 had restrictive effects on imports as a 'factual issue'[225] dependent on whether sufficient evidence had been adduced by the appellants. He held that the appellants had not proved that section 47 had a potentially restrictive effect on imports.

In *Peterborough*, in contrast, Schiemann J treated the question of whether section 47 was a measure having equivalent effect to quantitative restrictions as a question of mixed law and fact.[226] Mustill LJ, on the other hand, considered the question to be purely a question of law. He referred to *Torfaen*, claiming that that case had decided conclusively that section 47 did not contravene Article 28 (ex Article 30). Similar results were reached in *Stoke-on-Trent* as well as in *Shrewsbury*. Thus, the majority of judges relied to a great extent, if not conclusively, on the authority of the ECJ in *Torfaen*, treating the issue under consideration as a question of law. Closely linked with the question of law or fact is the question of whether the measure was caught by Article 28 (ex Article 30) or whether it was *prima facie* outside Article 28 (ex Article 30).

Section 47: outside or within Article 28?

The Wellingborough Justices and the Kettering Justices[227] had ruled that section 47 of the Shops Act did not in fact have a potentially restrictive effect on imports from other Member States. Thus, they had held that section 47 was *prima facie* outside Article 28 (ex Article 30). Following their convictions in those cases, the defendant companies appealed, arguing before Judge Francis Allen in the Northampton Crown Court that section 47 in fact *was* a measure having equivalent effect to a quantitative restriction on imports within Article 28 (ex Article 30) because it did, at least potentially, hinder intra-Community trade. Judge Francis Allen, treating the issue as a factual issue, held that the appellants had not proved that section 47 had a potentially

[224] *B&Q Ltd* v. *Shrewsbury and Atcham Borough Council* [1990] 3 CMLR 535.

[225] [1990] 1 CMLR 773 at 777, para. 14.

[226] [1990] 2 CMLR 577 at 608, para. 89.

[227] Three appeals, two from the Wellingborough Justices, one from the Kettering Justices, were heard together in the Northampton Crown Court because the same point was argued by the appellants in relation to each case.

restrictive effect on imports. Thus, section 47 was regarded as wholly outside Article 28 (ex Article 30).

In *Peterborough*, however, the opposite result was reached. The appellant companies were convicted of trading in prohibited goods on Sunday contrary to section 47. On appeal, the Crown Court found that section 47 was not caught by Article 28. Therefore, the High Court had to examine whether or not the relevant provision fell within Article 28 (ex Article 30). Judgment was rendered by Mustill LJ and Schiemann J. It was held that section 47 was *prima facie* caught by Article 28 (ex Article 30). Both judges reached the same conclusion even though they treated the question of whether it was law or fact differently.

Next comes the judgment in *Stoke-on-Trent*. Both the Crown Court and Hoffmann J in the High Court held section 47 to be *prima facie* within Article 28 (ex Article 30) even though capable of justification. Equally, in *Shrewsbury*, Northcote J in the Crown Court proceeded on the assumption that section 47 was *prima facie* caught by Article 28 (ex Article 30).

It may, therefore be concluded that *Wellingborough* is the only decision in which – based on a factual interpretation of the issue – section 47 was considered to be completely outside Article 28 (ex Article 30). The uncertainty of the national courts as to the meaning of the judgment in *Torfaen* can clearly be seen.

The place of *Torfaen* in the ECJ's jurisprudence

In essence, there were three possible interpretations open to the national courts. They could decide that *Torfaen* was merely an application of the *Cassis de Dijon* line of authority; they could interpret the judgment as constituting an individual, wholly novel line of authority; or they could avoid commenting on this question at all, focusing rather on the task left to them by the ECJ, that is, the application of the proportionality principle.

In *Wellingborough*, Judge Francis Allen relied entirely on the approach of the ECJ in *Torfaen* and *Cinéthèque*, the only exception being that the question of whether or not section 47 was within Article 28 (ex Article 30) was treated as a factual issue. Once it had decided that section 47 did not have a potential restrictive effect on imports, the court went through the two-stage approach laid down in *Torfaen*. It held that – following *Torfaen* – section 47 had an objective which was justified in Community law and that it did not exceed that which was intrinsic in rules preserving the traditional English and Welsh Sunday as a non-trading day. Judge Francis Allen thus contended that *Torfaen* was a reformulation of the law in relation to the exceptions to Article 28 (ex Article 30), that is, that it created a new general category of measures which constituted an exception to the prohibition in Article 28 (ex Article 30).

However, in *Peterborough*, Mustill LJ rejected the idea that the decision in *Torfaen* radically altered the law on equivalent measures or even departed from well-established principles by creating a wholly new doctrine. He held that *Torfaen* was in a direct line of descent, *inter alia*, from *Cassis de Dijon* to *Cinéthèque. Torfaen* was regarded as an illustration of the kind of national measure which the ECJ might be willing to regard as potentially consistent with Community law subject to fulfilling the requirement of proportionality. Judgment to the same effect was rendered by Schiemann J. He held that the ECJ in *Torfaen* had expressly reaffirmed the criteria established in *Cassis de Dijon* in order for a measure to be exempt from the prohibition in Article 28 (ex Article 30): the non-discrimination criterion, the justification criterion and the proportionality criterion.

Equally, Hoffmann J in *Stoke-on-Trent* held that *Torfaen* should be regarded as being governed by *Cinéthèque*, and thus in a direct line of authority from *Cassis de Dijon*. He explicitly relied on the discussion of this question in the *Peterborough* case.[228] The weight of authority which has to be attributed to the High Court decision in *Peterborough* suggests the correctness of this interpretation. It can therefore be assumed that the last decision, *Shrewsbury*,[229] implicitly approved this interpretation even though Northcote J did not express an opinion on this matter.

In conclusion, it seems therefore that the weight of authority in the English courts tended to regard *Torfaen* as being in a direct line of authority from *Cassis de Dijon*. Although the English courts attempt to fully apply the decisions of the ECJ, the divergent interpretations of this issue expose the uncertainty surrounding the correct meaning of the decision in *Torfaen*.

The proportionality requirement

The proportionality principle in Community law

In Community law, proportionality is a general principle of law. General principles of law are derived from various sources, but the most

[228] [1990] 3 CMLR 31 at 43, para. 33.
[229] *B&Q Ltd* v. *Shrewsbury and Atcham Borough Council* [1990] 3 CMLR 535.

important sources are the Community Treaties and the legal systems of the Member States. This issue was discussed by Advocate-General Duteillet de Lamothe in *Internationale Handelsgesellschaft.*[230] He considered that proportionality could have three possible sources in Community law: the German Basic Law;[231] general principles of Community law; and an express and clear provision of the Treaty. According to the Advocate-General, proportionality could be traced back both to the general principles of Community law and to express Treaty provisions. The ECJ in *Internationale Handelsgesellschaft* clearly accepted the first view, leaving in doubt the issue of the incorporation of the concept of proportionality into the Treaty. The incorporation was subsequently effected beyond doubt by virtue of the Community competence and legislative capacity in conjunction with the concept of subsidiarity. According to the guidelines of the Edinburgh European Council of December 1992, Article 5 (ex Article 3b) of the EC Treaty incorporates the principle of proportionality, defined as requiring 'that the means to be employed by the Community should be proportional to the objective pursued'.[232] But the European Council cannot amend the Treaty or even issue an authoritative interpretation on it. It was only at Amsterdam – with the Protocol on the Application of the Principles of Subsidiarity and Proportionality – that proportionality was formally written into the text of the Treaty. However, at the time of the decisions in *Torfaen*, *Marchandise*, *Conforama* and *Stoke-on-Trent*, the Maastricht Treaty was still under discussion so that it can safely be stated that the principle of proportionality at that time was to a large extent a *judicial* doctrine for the ECJ to apply in reviewing the legality of Community action and Member State action.

The proportionality requirement and the free movement of goods

It is now well established that national measures which a Member State seeks to justify under Article 30 (ex Article 36) not only must be justified[233] in light of their objective but also must be proportionate to

[230] Case C-11/70, *Internationale Handelsgesellschaft GmbH* v. *Einfuhr- und Vorratsstelle für Getreide und Futtermittel* [1970] ECR 1125 at 1147.
[231] In German, *Grundgesetz*.
[232] 'Overall Approach to the Application by the Council of the Subsidiarity Principle and Art. 3b of the Treaty on European Union', Annex 1 to Part A of the 'Conclusions of the Presidency', European Council in Edinburgh, 11–12 December 1992, 2.
[233] Art. 30 (ex Art. 36), first sentence.

their purpose.[234] In this area, the proportionality test takes the form of a 'least restrictive alternative' test: in *Duphar*,[235] it was held that, if the interest involved could be as adequately protected by measures which were significantly less restrictive of intra-Community trade, the contested measures would not be upheld unless it could be shown that, in the absence of these measures, the administrative burden on the Member State would exceed the limits of what should reasonably be required.

It follows from the wording of the 'least restrictive alternative' test that the ECJ approaches the proportionality inquiry in stages. The interest or objective must be classified as, and thus justified on, one of the grounds listed in Article 30 (ex Article 36); in essence, this involves an evaluation of whether the challenged measure was a suitable or effective means of achieving the objective at issue. One must ask whether there is a measure which would be less restrictive of intra-Community trade. If there is no such less restrictive means of achieving the justified aims, it will be necessary to inquire into whether the measure has an excessive or disproportionate effect on intra-Community trade. The first two stages are often considered to constitute a necessity test, while the third stage is usually described as a 'balancing test' or 'proportionality *stricto sensu*'.

Yet, even though it is possible to describe the proportionality inquiry in general terms, it is important to emphasise that the test will differ considerably from case to case: the nature of the objectives pursued will differ from case to case; the intensity of scrutiny will vary depending on the particular interest at issue; and matters such as the financial or political implications in Member States will be taken into account. What is also of relevance is what might be called the 'federalist dimension',[236] to which van Gerven devoted so much attention in his Opinion in *Stoke-on-Trent*. Where a measure is considered to be within the competence of a nation-state, the ECJ will be reluctant or may even refuse to apply the proportionality test. This may account for the fact that the ECJ refused to apply the proportionality test in *Torfaen*, leaving it instead to the national courts to decide. It equally indicates that the proportionality test applied to measures falling

[234] Case C-7/68, *Commission* v. *Italy* [1968] ECR 423 at 431 *per curiam*.

[235] Case C-238/82, *Duphar* v. *Netherlands* [1984] ECR 523 at 542 *per curiam*.

[236] G. de Búrca, 'The Principle of Proportionality and Its Application in EC Law' (1993) 13 *Yearbook of European Law* 105 at 112, for a more detailed analysis, see p. 146 below.

within the mandatory requirements laid down in *Cassis de Dijon* is similar to that taken as regards Article 30 (ex Article 36). A measure falling within the 'rule of reason' has to pass the proportionality test.

The proportionality test as defined in *Torfaen*

In *Torfaen*, the test was formulated in the following terms:

> It is necessary to ascertain whether the effects of such national rules exceed what is *necessary* to achieve the *aim* in view . . . [T]he prohibition laid down in [Article 28 (ex Article 30)] covers national measures governing the marketing of products where the restrictive effect of such measures on the free movement of goods *exceeds the effects intrinsic to trade rules*. The question of whether the effects of specific national rules do in fact remain within that limit is a *question of fact* to be determined by the *national court*.[237]

The test involves the determination of the objective pursued, an evaluation of whether it is necessary to achieve the aim and a balancing exercise of whether the restrictive effects at issue exceed the effects intrinsic to trade rules. In its judgment, the ECJ laid down the following guidelines for the application of this test. The ECJ stressed that the rules at issue 'reflect certain political and economic choices in so far as their purpose [was] to ensure that working and non-working hours [were] so arranged as to accord with national or regional socio-cultural characteristics'.[238] This amounts to explicitly recognising that the purpose of the Shops Act was, *inter alia*, of a socio-cultural and socio-economic nature. Yet, the ECJ did not make precisely clear what in its view was the objective of the Shops Act. It may have been employment protection as well as preserving the special character of Sunday. The ECJ left this decision to the national courts. The courts in England and Wales, however, took differing views on this matter, as we shall now see.

The determination of the objective of the Shops Act in the national courts

In *Shrewsbury*,[239] Northcote J considered the aim of the Shops Act to be employment protection, that is, the protection of employees who might not wish to work on Sundays. He rejected the submission of the respondents that the objective was the preservation of the traditional

[237] Para. 15 (emphasis added). [238] Para. 14 (emphasis added).
[239] *B&Q Ltd* v. *Shrewsbury and Atcham Borough Council* [1990] 3 CMLR 535.

character of Sunday as a day of worship. This conclusion was based on the ground that, at the time of the enactment of the Shops Act, the existing Sunday Observance Act 1780[240] was intended to fulfil that function. Clearly, he treated the issue as a matter of fact rather than as a matter of law. Concentrating therefore on employment protection, Northcote J felt that this objective could be achieved in other ways which would be less of a hindrance to trade. Accordingly, the prohibition contained in the Act was held to be disproportionate.

The first judgment rendered to the opposite effect was *Wellingborough*. In that case, Judge Francis Allen took the view that the Shops Act had as its main objective the preservation of the special character of Sunday. This conclusion was based on paragraphs 13 and 14 of the *Torfaen* decision, and he therefore treated the issue as a question of law. Judge Francis Allen conceded that the objective could be stated in a variety of ways. Yet, supporting his legal argument with factual evidence, he rejected any submission claiming that the objective of the Act could not be ascertained. It is clear from the wording of his judgment that he himself felt very strongly about the preservation of the special character of Sunday:

> The objective is the preservation of the special and traditional character of Sunday in England and Wales as a day for rest, relaxation, socialising and, for a significant part of the population, worship. It is a day when the pace of life is different from that on other days, a day on which most people appreciate being spared the business of other days.[241]

Judgment to the same effect, though in less emphatic terms, was rendered in *Peterborough*. Schiemann J identified the aim of the legislation at issue as being 'to keep Sunday a non-working day'.[242] Similarly, Mustill LJ voiced his opinion that the aim to which the ECJ referred was the 'ordering of working and non-working hours'[243] so as to accord with national socio-cultural characteristics. Both Schiemann J and Mustill LJ therefore treated the question of the objective of the legislation as a matter of law.

This aspect of the decision in *Peterborough* was explicitly approved by Hoffmann J in *Stoke-on-Trent*. For him, it was apparent from the wording in *Torfaen* that the ECJ was satisfied that the purpose of section 47 was to arrange working and non-working hours in England and Wales so as to accord with national or regional socio-cultural

[240] Now repealed. [241] [1990] 1 CMLR 773 at 779, para. 24.
[242] [1990] 2 CMLR 577 at 609, para. 98. [243] *Ibid.*, para. 64.

characteristics. This was 'plain and obvious'.[244] He therefore treated the question of the objective of section 47 primarily as a question of law supported by factual evidence.

In the majority of the reported decisions, judges in national courts held that the objective of the legislation was the protection or preservation of the special character of Sunday. The only odd one out seems to be the decision in *Shrewsbury*. In that case, Northcote J held that the objective was determinative of the outcome of the case, while in all the other decisions the judges went on to apply the balancing limb of the proportionality test. It seems to follow that Northcote J deliberately put an emphasis on this aspect so as to reach the outcome that the measure was disproportionate.

The objectives of the Shops Act in light of the ECJ's approach to Article 28

Both objectives (that is, employment protection, and preservation of the special character of Sunday) are in line with the ECJ's approach to exceptions to Article 28 (ex Article 30) at the time of the Sunday trading litigation. The ECJ has always stressed that Article 30 (ex Article 36) only covers justifications of a non-economic nature.[245] The preservation and protection of the special character of Sunday is clearly a non-economic purpose. Similarly, the ECJ at the time of the Sunday trading litigation had recognised or was about to recognise the following non-economic mandatory requirements: the protection of consumers,[246] the prevention of unfair commercial practices,[247] the effectiveness of fiscal supervision,[248] the need to protect the environment[249] and the improvement of working conditions.[250] The ECJ has also referred to the protection of public health[251] as being a mandatory

[244] [1990] 3 CMLR 31 at 43, para. 31.

[245] Case C-7/61, *Commission* v. *Italy* [1982] ECR 2187 at 2204: 'It must be recalled that ... [Art. 30 (ex Art. 36)] refers to matters of a non-economic nature.'

[246] Case C-382/87, *R. Buet and Educational Business Services (EBS) SARL* v. *Ministère Public* [1989] ECR 1235.

[247] Case C-6/81, *BV Industrie Diensten Groep* v. *J. A. Beele Handelmaatschappij BV* [1982] ECR 707.

[248] Case C-823/79, *Criminal Proceedings Against Giovanni Carciati* [1980] ECR 2773.

[249] Case C-302/86, *Commission* v. *Denmark* [1988] ECR 4607 (the 'Danish Beer Bottles' case).

[250] Case C-155/80, *Oebel* [1981] ECR 1993 *per curiam*.

[251] Case C-120/78, *Rewe-Zentrale AG* v. *Bundesmonopolverwaltung für Branntwein* [1979] ECR 649; [1979] 3 CMLR 494; Case C-193/80, *Commission* v. *Italy* (*Re Wine Vinegar*) [1981] ECR 3019.

requirement, although this is expressly covered by Article 30 (ex Article 36) in any event.

It is arguable whether the objective of the Act established in *Torfaen* falls within one of these heads. This question ties in with the question of whether *Torfaen* was decided on the basis that the objective of the Shops Act fell within one of the existing mandatory requirements or constituted a new mandatory requirement. Whatever view is taken of this, it is clear that the objective of the Act had been established as a matter of law by the ECJ to be applied mechanically by the national courts. By contrast, the ECJ made it explicitly clear that the question of whether the effects of the Shops Act on imports exceeded the effects intrinsic to rules of that kind was a question of fact to be determined by the national court. Consequently, the final decision on whether section 47 was proportionate and thus in accordance with Community law was left to the judges in the national courts.

The role of the supremacy of Parliament in the Sunday trading litigation

The principle of the supremacy of Parliament has always been regarded as *the* basic principle of the constitution of the UK – at least prior to the European Communities Act 1972. The legislative supremacy of Parliament is a legal doctrine which refers to the relationship between the courts and Acts of Parliament. The classical exposition of this doctrine was given by Dicey,[252] who labelled it 'Parliamentary sovereignty'. By 'Parliamentary sovereignty' is meant that there are no legal limitations on the legislative competence of Parliament. Parliament here refers to the constitutional phenomenon known as the 'Queen in Parliament', namely, the legislative process by which a Bill approved by the House of Lords and the House of Commons may receive the royal assent and thus become an Act of Parliament. Thus defined, Parliament, according to Dicey, has

> under the English constitution, the right to make or unmake any law whatever; and further that no person or body is recognised by the law of England as having a right to override or set aside the legislation of Parliament.[253]

[252] A. Dicey, *Introduction to the Study of the Law of the Constitution* (10th edn, London, 1959). However, for a critical analysis of the omnipotence of Parliament, see S. Sedley, 'The Sound of Silence: Constitutional Law Without a Constitution' (1994) 110 *Law Quarterly Review* 270.

[253] Dicey, *Law of the Constitution*, 39–40.

In Dicey's formulation, the legislative supremacy of Parliament therefore has two aspects: the positive and the negative. The positive aspect of legislative supremacy is taken to mean that power to legislate on any matter whatsoever is vested in Parliament. In relation to the Shops Act 1950, this doctrine validates the enactment of the Act. Furthermore, it confirms the power of Parliament to change the law as to Sunday trading. This, however, entails the question of whether courts may ascribe a legal force to other instruments which fall short of being an Act of Parliament. It is well established that the courts do not attribute legislative supremacy to international treaties (such as the Treaty of Rome) entered into by the government under prerogative powers unless the treaty is specifically incorporated into national law. However, as stated above, by the European Communities Act 1972 legal effect was given within the UK to those provisions of Community law which were, according to the European Treaties, intended to have direct effect within Member States. It follows that legal effect has to be given to Article 28 (ex Article 30) despite the fact that it was not made by Parliament itself, that is, by an Act of Parliament as such.

According to the negative aspect of the legislative supremacy of Parliament, there exists no competing authority with the power either to legislate for the UK or to impose limits upon the legislative competence of Parliament. Thus, on an orthodox reading of the doctrine, neither national courts nor the ECJ would have the power to override or set aside an Act of Parliament. The courts would be under a duty to apply the legislation made by Parliament and would not be in a position to hold an Act of Parliament to be invalid or unconstitutional. If this was the end of the matter, then certainly – in the wake of *Torfaen* – a national court would not be in a position to hold the Shops Act 1950 to be disproportionate. Yet again, the European Communities Act 1972, in conjunction with the jurisprudence of the ECJ, comes into play. Thus, if a national court following the decision in *Torfaen* decided that the restrictive effects on Community trade which may result from the 1950 Act exceeded the effects intrinsic to rules of that kind, it would defer to the primacy of Community law.

English courts *do* have the power to override and set aside Parliamentary legislation.[254] This is a limitation on the principle of

[254] Even this position can be reconciled with the orthodox Diceyan view of Parliamentary sovereignty. This states that the English courts apply EC law as a 'higher law' than

Parliamentary sovereignty, which is and was at that time well recognised in English law. Lord Bridge noted in *R.* v. *Secretary of State for Transport, ex parte Factortame Ltd* that:

> [i]f the supremacy within the European Community of Community law over the national law of Member States was not always inherent in the EEC Treaty . . . it was certainly well established in the jurisprudence of the ECJ long before the UK joined the Community. Thus whatever limitation of its sovereignty Parliament accepted when it enacted the European Communities Act 1972 was entirely voluntary.[255]

Whether or not the courts made use of this power is another matter.

Sunday trading: a matter for the courts or for Parliament?

The only reported decision in which an English court was indeed prepared to use the powers granted to it by the European Communities Act 1972 was the Crown Court decision in *Shrewsbury*. Also, in *Stoke-on-Trent*,[256] Hoffmann J referred to an unreported decision in which the same conclusion was reached. In that case, the stipendiary magistrate at Pendle identified the protection of Sunday leisure activities as the objective of the Shops Act. The magistrate concluded that many people regarded Sunday shopping in DIY and garden centres as a leisure activity so that a ban on such shopping had to be regarded as disproportionate. In both cases – *Shrewsbury* and the unreported decision – the judges seemed to sympathise with the traders and were reluctant to apply the incriminated provision. In both cases, the issue of Parliamentary sovereignty did not seem to be uppermost in the judges' minds.

By contrast, in *Stoke-on-Trent*, the supremacy of Parliament came to the fore. Hoffmann J was seriously concerned about the proper boundary between Community law and national law, while acknowledging Parliamentary sovereignty. While recognising the priority of Community law, Hoffmann J undermined the supremacy of Community law by stressing a different aspect of the matter, namely, the division of

English law – but only because Parliament, which is supreme, has told them to do so in the European Communities Act 1972. The question of whether EC membership *per se* of the European Community has limited Parliamentary sovereignty would only be tested if Parliament passes a statute explicitly stated to apply in the UK even if it is contrary to EC law.

[255] [1991] 1 AC 603 at 659. [256] [1990] 3 CMLR 31 at 237.

powers between legislature and judiciary.[257] He answered this question by stating that:

> The fact that the European Court had said that a particular question is one for decision by the national court does not endow that court with quasi-legislative powers. It must confine itself within the area of judicial intervention required by the Treaty and not trespass on questions which are for democratic decision in Parliament.[258]

Hoffmann J therefore narrowed down the duty of the court. In detail, he defined it as no more than deciding whether it was a reasonably tenable view that preventing shop-workers from having to work on Sundays was a sufficiently important objective to justify the consequent reduction in Community trade and that no other means would achieve the same objective with less hindrance to trade. In essence, this amounts to a denial of the application of the balancing test in the national courts and thus a denial of the task imposed on national courts by the ECJ in *Torfaen* for the sake of Parliamentary sovereignty.[259] Hoffmann J's view was supported by Diamond, who equally claimed that it was 'the very sovereignty of Parliament'[260] which was at stake. It is, however, submitted that it was not Parliamentary sovereignty which was at stake in the Sunday trading litigation. Rather, the Sunday trading saga exemplifies the limitation of Parliamentary sovereignty

[257] [1990] 3 CMLR 31 at 34, para. 1.

[258] [1990] 3 CMLR 31 at 34–5, para. 3.

[259] It has to be underlined that such a reading does not fully catch Lord Hoffmann's argument. He is not denying EC law's supremacy; rather, it is for him a question of the separation of powers between the courts and Parliament as to how to give effect to supremacy. If we look at decisions of the ECJ applying the proportionality principle in cases of challenges to the validity of acts of the Community institutions, we see how cautious the ECJ is. The ECJ allows the Community institutions a wide discretion, particularly as regards matters of economic policy. The ECJ is wary of second-guessing the legislature; it is respectful of the separation between its powers and those of the legislature. One may wonder whether this is so different from Lord Hoffmann's view. However, proportionality performs a different function in cases of review of EEC acts by the ECJ as compared with cases before national courts involving national restrictions on free movement. It is not a precise analogy. But the general issue is similar: how far should the courts go in reviewing legislative choices. So Lord Hoffmann's approach is probably wrong as a matter of EC law. But he is raising a major issue. Perhaps if we look at national courts and then at the ECJ, proportionality operates as a 'double standard'.

[260] P. Diamond, 'Sunday Trading and the Sovereignty of Parliament' (1990) 7 *Trading Law* 216.

which Parliament accepted when it voluntarily enacted the European Communities Act 1972. His decision must be seen in the context of the decisions in the English courts rendered immediately after the judgment in *Torfaen*.

Confusion in the national courts on proportionality

In *Wellingborough*, Judge Francis Allen took on the task of applying the balancing test to the measure at issue. He stated that the courts could not simply follow the choice made by Parliament as to specific national rules. Rather, they had to enquire 'as to whether or not the effects are limited to those intrinsic to rules of that kind'. Judge Francis Allen found that there was no basis for saying that section 47 had any restrictive effects which went beyond those which might be intrinsic to rules of its type. The following reasoning was meant to support his conclusion. Section 47 constituted an 'unembellished ban'.[261] The intrinsic effects on Community trade of a prohibition on Sunday trading could not be exceeded by an unembellished ban. Hence, section 47 did not have any restrictive effects which went beyond those which might be intrinsic to rules of its type. Section 47 thus satisfied the *Torfaen* test; it did not fail the proportionality test.

In *Peterborough*, Mustill LJ pointed to the difficulties involved in the application of the balancing test. In the case before him, the application of the balancing test would involve the measuring of the desire to keep Sunday holy against the free-trade economic objectives of the common market. Hence, the balancing exercise called for by the *Cassis de Dijon* exception required the attribution of weight to socio-cultural objectives, on the one hand, and economic objectives, on the other. It further required a balance to be struck between a national, moral, social or cultural norm, on the one hand, and the Community free trade interest, on the other. This, according to Mustill LJ, amounted to an impossibility and was thus not what the jurisprudence of the ECJ required. The solution to this problem would be to set aside the notion of the balancing exercise and to replace it with a more qualitative test at the necessity test stage.

A further problem addressed by Mustill LJ was that the factual approach to the issue of proportionality – and the balancing test in particular – opened up the possibility that different courts faced with

[261] [1990] 1 CMLR 773 at 778, para. 19.

different evidence or no evidence at all could reach differing conclusions on the potential effect of section 47 on the free movement of goods. Equally, section 47 had to be regarded as a general measure whose application in particular circumstances would have more or less perceptible effects on intra-Community trade. Hence, if the question were approached on a case-by-case basis, this would inevitably open up the possibility of different outcomes in different proceedings. Again, according to Mustill LJ, the solution lay in a less exact and more qualitative assessment of the effect on the free movement of goods rather than in a reliance on factual evidence in individual cases. However, Mustill LJ did not consider it necessary to apply the proportionality test in the proceedings before him since the respondents had focused on whether Article 28 (ex Article 30) applied to section 47, thus considering that it was not a trading rule. Therefore, Mustill LJ did not go further than holding that Article 28 (ex Article 30) *did* apply to section 47 and that it could only be saved if it satisfied the *Cassis de Dijon* criteria.

Schiemann J, however, went further than that. He considered the application of the proportionality test in cases such as the one before him to be 'obvious'[262] and therefore as not requiring evidence. Clearly, this finding does not take account of the problems pointed out by Mustill LJ. Rather, it ignores the possibility of different outcomes depending on the particular facts and circumstances of individual cases. This evaluation of the application of the proportionality test therefore avoids the complexity of and the problems arising out of the application of the proportionality criteria.

The above judgment in *Peterborough* having been rendered on 4 June 1990, a rather different approach was taken when the *Torfaen* case returned to the referring court on 11 June 1990. Unlike the High Court in *Peterborough*, the Cwmbran Magistrates' Court in *Torfaen* was prepared to balance the aim of the national legislation against the impact on intra-Community trade. First, the magistrates made it explicitly clear that whether or not section 47 was incompatible with Article 28 (ex Article 30) hinged only on the question of whether or not it was proportionate. They then held that, as a question of fact, the effects on intra-Community trade were not excessive in the context of the balance between the need to preserve the special character

[262] [1990] 2 CMLR 577 at 610, para. 102.

of Sunday and such impact as there was upon that trade. It followed, according to the magistrates, that section 47 was not out of proportion and thus not incompatible with Article 28 (ex Article 30).

Like the Cwmbran Magistrates' Court, most national courts treated the question of proportionality as a question of fact. This position resulted in a problem correctly pointed out by Mustill LJ in *Peterborough*: the problem of consistency in adjudication. Jarvis termed it 'fragmentation of justice'.[263] Indeed, throughout the country, whenever the judgment in *Torfaen* was interpreted in national courts, B&Q – or the companies concerned – presented a mass of factual and expert evidence so as to discharge the burden of proof that the restrictive effects of the measure on Community trade exceeded the effects intrinsic to rules of that kind. A 'troupe of experts'[264] toured the country on behalf of the Sunday traders, spending several days in any one place giving evidence. Traders had requested up to twenty-five-day hearings in order to have sufficient time available to adduce factual evidence supporting their appeals. Thus, in light of the foregoing discussion, Hoffmann J's judgment in *Stoke-on-Trent* is properly regarded as a reaction to the situation in the English and Welsh national courts.

Hoffmann J's attempt to settle the law

In theory, Hoffmann J paid tribute to the ECJ's view that proportionality was a question of fact. In practice, however, he stressed the following aspect:

> If the court is satisfied on the basis of judicial notice that the requirements of proportionality have been met, there is no need for the prosecution to adduce oral or documentary evidence.[265]

The doctrine of judicial notice in relation to the Sunday trading litigation, according to Hoffmann J – relying on Professor Cross – is important because it tends to produce uniformity of decisions on matters of fact. Reliance on the doctrine of judicial notice would prevent different outcomes in the various cases and would allow the question of Sunday opening to be settled authoritatively 'by the normal rules of precedent'.[266] He therefore held that the burden of justifying the

[263] M. Jarvis, 'The Sunday Trading Episode: In Defence of the Euro-Defence' (1995) 44 *International and Comparative Law Quarterly* 451 at 458.
[264] [1990] 3 CMLR 31 at 44; Barnard, 'Sunday Trading', 449 at 454.
[265] [1990] 3 CMLR 31 at 44. [266] *Ibid.*, 45.

proportionality of the measure was fully discharged 'on the basis of facts of which the court is entitled to take judicial notice'.[267] In applying the proportionality test, Hoffmann J stated that:

> the duty of the court is only to enquire whether the compromise adopted by the UK Parliament, so far as it affects Community trade, is one which a reasonable legislature could have reached ... [I]n this case the duty of the court goes no further than to decide whether it is a reasonably tenable view that preventing shop-workers from having to work on Sundays is a sufficiently important objective to justify the consequent reduction in Community trade and that no means other than requiring shops to shut would achieve the same objective with less hindrance to trade.[268]

Hoffmann J concluded that section 47 could not be considered to be unreasonable; he considered that it would be 'presumptuous'[269] to hold otherwise. In conclusion, he was firmly convinced that section 47 was proportionate and therefore compatible with Article 28 (ex Article 30).

This judgment was regarded with the greatest respect by lawyers, the local authorities and the Sunday traders. It was the first case in which a higher court had looked at the merits of the arguments of the Sunday traders. According to Tony Askham, solicitor for B&Q, it was the first time that the 'European defence' was tested against a judge with a thorough knowledge of the issues involved. In addition, most lawyers at that time were very well aware of Hoffmann J's considerable reputation.[270] Therefore, his judgment in *Stoke-on-Trent* should be regarded as an important authority. It was considered to be capable of bringing an end to the Sunday trading war. According to Lord Goff, there was a huge sigh of relief among first-instance judges when Hoffmann J had given his 'very best'[271] in *Stoke-on-Trent*.

The effect of Hoffmann J's judgment in *Stoke-on-Trent*

Hoffmann J's judgment effectively prevented any court which is bound by High Court precedent from coming to a different conclusion in subsequent proceedings. The only way to avoid the binding force of the this decision was by way of an appeal to a higher court or by a reference to the ECJ. The latter approach was taken by a stipendiary magistrate in *Reading Borough Council* v. *Payless DIY Ltd*.[272] The magistrate referred

[267] *Ibid.*, 52. [268] *Ibid.*, 49. [269] *Ibid.*, 51.
[270] He eventually became a member of the House of Lords.
[271] Lord Goff of Chieveley in an interview, 22 July 1999.
[272] 23 July 1990 (unreported).

several issues to the ECJ, including the question of whether Hoffmann J was correct. The precise wording of this aspect of the reference was as follows:

> Is it the function of the national court to examine the facts (as proved by evidence) and come to its own conclusion regarding the applicability of those criteria, or is the function of the national court limited to deciding whether or not a national legislature acting reasonably could have adopted the legislative measure in question having regard to those criteria?[273]

This reference to the ECJ effectively questioned the correctness of Hoffmann J's decision in *Stoke-on-Trent*. For this reason, the House of Lords accepted the leapfrog appeal, and passed the case straight to the ECJ. The House of Lords referred three questions:

1. Is the effect of the Court of Justice's rulings in Case C-312/89 *Conforama* and C-332/89 *Marchandise* to determine that the prohibition contained in [Article 28 (ex Article 30)] of the EEC Treaty does not apply to national rules, such as those in issue in Case 145/88 *Torfaen Borough Council* v. *B&Q plc*, which prohibit retailers from opening their premises on Sunday for the serving of customers with certain goods?
2. If not, is it nevertheless immediately apparent, whether or not evidence is adduced, that the restrictive effects on intra-Community trade which may result from national rules such as those in question 1 above do not exceed 'the effects intrinsic to rules of that kind', as that phrase is used in the ruling of the Court of Justice in [*Torfaen*]?
3. If not, on what criteria and by reference to what, if any, factual or other evidence must the national court determine the question of whether or not the restrictive effects on intra-Community trade which may result from national rules such as those in question 1 above exceed 'the effects intrinsic to rules of that kind' within the meaning of that phrase as used in the ruling of the Court of Justice [in *Torfaen*]?

The three questions referred by the House of Lords are in themselves highly questionable. The ECJ had in *Conforama* and *Marchandise* given an answer to at least the first two questions, and the third question provoked the Advocate-General's forceful complaint about the role and function of the proportionality principle. One may wonder why the

[273] Case C-304/90 [1992] ECR I-6493 at 6496.

House of Lords did not answer the questions itself, particularly as the House of Lords had already discussed the effects of *Conforama* and *Marchandise* in the Appellate Committee before the final referral.[274] It is suggested that the explanation is to be found in the House of Lords' intention 'to kill the case'[275] once and for all. And the House of Lords relied heavily here on its future member, Hoffmann J. The idea, therefore, was to get Hoffmann J's judgment in *Stoke-on-Trent* confirmed by the ECJ. The degree of consistency of adjudication already introduced into national courts should be maintained. It is worth pausing here in order to consider the possible reasons for the difficulties of the national courts in applying the proportionality test.

The proportionality requirement: a scapegoat for the chaos in the national courts?

It is arguable whether the reason for the chaos in the national court should be attributed to the problems relating to the availability of injunctive relief to enforce the Shops Act. This issue has already been elaborated on.[276] It is suggested that the availability of injunctions, in conjunction with the issue of cross-undertakings in damages, accounts to a large extent for the problems with the application of the *Torfaen* judgment in the national courts.

It is equally arguable whether the underlying reason for the difficulties in the national courts stem from the fact that judges in English courts – most notably Hoffmann J – resorted to the principle of sovereignty of Parliament when in fact no such principle was at issue. Even if the vital constitutional principle for Hoffmann J was the separation of powers between judges and the legislature, and not the sovereignty of Parliament,[277] the *effect* of such a reference to the proportionality principle in its two limbs is to obscure its application while challenging the full supremacy of Community law. Yet, considering that in most judgments the issue of Parliamentary sovereignty did not feature as highly as in Hoffmann J's judgment, it would be overstating the significance of the doctrine if the reason for the chaos in the national courts were to be sought in the doctrine of Parliamentary sovereignty. Rather, it should be sought in the application of the proportionality criterion in the English courts and the role of the doctrine of proportionality in English law as such.

[274] See p. 116 above. [275] Lord Goff of Chieveley in an interview, 22 July 1999.
[276] See p. 130 above.
[277] On the two ways to read Lord Hoffmann, see note 209 above.

It is undeniable that the judgment in *Torfaen* gave little guidance to national courts as to how the proportionality test should be applied in practice. This would certainly not have been decisive for the application of the principle in civil law courts, yet it was decisive for the application in English courts for the following reason. While the proportionality principle is well established in the ECJ's case law, English courts were at that time – and indeed still are – less experienced in its practical application than are courts in civil law jurisdictions. It has been pointed out that the Sunday trading cases were the first occasion on which the English courts were confronted head-on with the proportionality principle.[278] This indicates that responsibility for the difficulties of applying the principle is not to be sought merely in the judgment of the ECJ as such. Instead, the reason should be sought in the English legal system itself and the admission of a new principle into English administrative law.

Proportionality in English law

Proportionality in English law is a contentious doctrine. It is beyond doubt that proportionality already plays a part in English law, in which the English courts have regard to the principles of the European Convention on Human Rights. It is equally beyond doubt that English courts are bound to give effect to the principle of proportionality in cases involving directly effective Community law.[279] To what extent the principle of proportionality will find its way into English law by way of what Lord Irvine of Lairg calls the 'spillover effect'[280] remains to be seen and was uncertain at the time of the Sunday trading litigation.

However, the fact that courts are obliged to give effect to the principle of proportionality in cases involving directly effective Community law does not mean that they are well experienced in doing so. This is due to the fact that the doctrine of proportionality is not firmly established in English administrative law. On the one hand, there are some cases in which the courts have applied a concept of proportionality. In those cases, it is arguable that it was not of relevance merely in

[278] Jarvis, 'The Sunday Trading Episode', 451 at 457.

[279] Case 222/84, *Johnston* v. *Chief Constable of the Royal Ulster Constabulary* [1986] ECR 1651; [1986] 3 CMLR 240; *Rainey* v. *Greater Glasgow Health Board* [1987] AC 224; [1986] 3 WLR 1017; [1987] 1 All ER 65 (House of Lords).

[280] Q. Lairg, 'Judges and Decision-Makers: The Theory and Practice of Wednesbury Review' (1996) *Public Law* 59 at 75.

establishing '*Wednesbury* unreasonableness'.[281] Examples include cases in which proportionality is unequivocally referred to,[282] cases which indirectly reflect the concept[283] and cases in which the idea is merely implicitly present.[284] On the other hand, it is now well established that it is not open to a court below the House of Lords to depart from the traditional grounds of *Wednesbury* unreasonableness while the status of proportionality remains uncertain.

There are in essence three different positions which have been advocated. First, it has been argued that proportionality simply does not exist in English law. This is the view of Millett J in *Allied Dunbar (Frank Weisinger) Ltd* v. *Frank Weisinger*.[285] Indeed, Millett J even argued that the doctrine of proportionality is 'a novel and dangerous doctrine',[286] and consequently declined to apply it as a test of the validity of a covenant in restraint of trade.[287] Secondly, it has been argued that proportionality is not a separate ground of review but is part of the reasoning process that might lead a court to conclude that a decision was *Wednesbury* unreasonable or irrational.[288] Thirdly, it has been suggested that proportionality is a separate ground of review in English law. Lord Diplock indicated this in the *GCHQ* case.[289]

In the *GCHQ* case, he classified the three grounds of judicial review of administrative action as illegality, procedural impropriety, and irrationality. Yet, he left open the possibility of further development on a case-by-case basis. In particular, what he had in mind was the

281 *Associated Provincial Picture Houses Ltd* v. *Wednesbury Corporation* [1948] 1 KB 223. 'Wednesbury unreasonableness' in the narrow sense, or irrationality, is one of the three grounds of review recognised in English administrative law. In essence, a decision or rule is liable to be quashed if an authority's decision is 'so unreasonable that no reasonable authority could ever have come to it'. *Associated Provincial Picture Houses Ltd* v. *Wednesbury Corporation* [1948] 1 KB 223 *per* Lord Greene MR. Very rarely is such unreasonableness found to have occurred.

282 *R.* v. *Barnsley Metropolitan Borough Council, ex parte Hook* [1976] 1 WLR 1052 at 1057.

283 *Wheeler* v. *Leicester City Council* [1985] AC 1054.

284 *Bromley London Borough Council* v. *Greater London Council* [1983] 1 AC 768 (the so-called 'Fares Fair' case).

285 [1988] IRLR 60.

286 *Ibid.*, para. 44.

287 However, that is a private law matter, not public law, and therefore arguably is not the same issue as is under examination here.

288 *R.* v. *Secretary of State for the Home Department, ex parte Brind* [1991] 1 AC 696.

289 *Council of the Civil Service Unions* v. *Minister of State for the Civil Service* [1985] AC 374.

'possible adoption in the future of the principle of proportionality'.[290] In the wake of *GCHQ*, several academics took the lead and argued for the introduction or recognition of the doctrine in English law.[291] It is at this stage that the Sunday trading cases fell to be decided in the English courts. One might even be tempted to argue that the future of the proportionality principle in English administrative law depended to a large extent on the success or failure of the application of the principle in the Sunday trading litigation. This view is supported by the fact that immediately following the bulk of the decisions in the national courts the House of Lords rendered judgment in *R.* v. *Secretary of State for the Home Department, ex parte Brind.*

Ex parte Brind is the leading authority on the status of proportionality in English law. Their Lordships, in particular Lord Ackner and Lord Lowry, rejected the notion that proportionality was a separate ground of review, but accepted that it could well be part of the reasoning process that might lead a court to establish *Wednesbury* unreasonableness. The decision is usually regarded as the high-water-mark of the courts' adherence to the *Wednesbury* principle. In view of the chaos in the national courts following the application of the *Torfaen* criteria, it is arguable that the decision in *ex parte Brind* constitutes a reaction by the House of Lords to what was going on in the lower courts in order to prevent the same happening in the context of English administrative law.

The proper reading of the proportionality principle seems to be that it plays different roles in different cases, and that it might be dangerous to try to distil a general rule out of the existing case law.[292]

Proportionality: a novel and dangerous doctrine?

The potential remedies available to the judge oblige him to act as an administrator, and on occasion give him the power to command the administrative authorities to act in a particular way. The introduction of the doctrine of proportionality into English law would undoubtedly increase these controlling powers of the judge. Moreover, it would

[290] *Ibid.*, 410.

[291] J. Jowell and A. Lester, 'Proportionality: Neither Novel nor Dangerous' in J. Jowell and D. Oliver (eds.), *New Directions in Judicial Review* (London, 1988), 51–73. With regard to the constitutional context in a historical perspective, see Sedley, 'The Sound of Silence', 270 at 277 and 278.

[292] See especially the contributions in E. Ellis (ed.), *The Principle of Proportionality in Europe* (Oxford, 1999).

bring him to the verge of dealing with the merits of the case, thus blurring the fundamental distinction in English law between appeal and review. Judicial review is concerned merely with the *legality* of a decision as opposed to its *merits*. Thus, the fundamental objection to proportionality is that it leads to review of the merits of public decisions while the standard of review is considerably lower than that of *Wednesbury* reasonableness. The danger lies in the court getting involved in a process of policy evaluation which lies far outside its allotted constitutional role. It is here that Hoffmann J's warning that the application of the proportionality test 'involves compromises between competing interests which in a democratic society must be resolved by the legislature' is most relevant.[293]

It has, however, been argued that this is overstating the effect of the introduction of proportionality into English law, and that some of these objections are even ill-conceived.[294] The increasing influence and significance of EC law as well as developments within the European Convention on Human Rights have already 'acclimatised' UK lawyers to the concept and required them to apply it in any event. Further, it has been argued that the restatement and interpretation of the decision in *Wednesbury* has gradually led to the development of a test which inevitably leads to the same outcome as the application of the principle of proportionality. It should be noted, for example, that, when an English judge states that byelaws made by local authorities would probably be held void on the ground of unreasonableness if they involved 'such oppressive or gratuitous interference with the rights of those subject to them as could find no justification in the minds of reasonable men',[295] he reaches the same result a German lawyer would reach by applying the principle of proportionality.[296] In *ITF*,[297] Lord

[293] *Stoke-on-Trent City Council* v. *B&Q* [1990] 3 CMLR 31 at 49; even clearer expositions (because they were written for an academic audience) are A. Hoffmann, 'A Sense of Proportion' in M. Andenas and F. Jacobs (eds.), *European Community Law in English Courts* (Oxford, 1998), 149; and A. Hoffmann, 'The Influence of the European Principle of Proportionality upon UK Law' in E. Ellis (ed.), *The Principle of Proportionality* (Oxford, 1999), 106 at 113.

[294] P. Craig, *Administrative Law* (5th edn, London, 2003).

[295] *Kruse* v. *Johnson* [1898] 2 QB 91 at 99–100.

[296] Cases of byelaws have always been treated as special. They attract unusually intensive judicial review. Therefore, their importance for the development of a general rule should not be overestimated.

[297] *R.* v. *Chief Constable of Sussex, ex parte International Trader's Ferry Ltd* [1999] 1 All ER 129.

Cooke suggested that the test was 'whether the decision in question was one which a reasonable authority could reach'.[298] According to Craig, this requires the local authority to embark on the same exercise as is required when applying the proportionality test. This analysis leads to the conclusion that it is doubtful whether it was indeed the uncertain status of the principle of proportionality in English law which led to the chaos in national courts. Yet, even though there were undeniably problems with the application of the *Torfaen* judgment in national courts, the tendency towards more stability and consistency of adjudication following the decision in *Stoke-on-Trent* should not be overlooked.

Coping with proportionality

There were several signs that stability and consistency of adjudication had made their way into the English courts after Hoffmann J's judgment in *Stoke-on-Trent*. The conclusion reached by Hoffmann J was supported by judges in subsequent proceedings. For instance, in the unreported decision in *Stoke-on-Trent* v. *Toys 'R' Us Ltd*,[299] Sir Nicholas Browne-Wilkinson supported Hoffmann J's conclusion that the Shops Act did meet the proportionality requirement. In *Coventry City Council* v. *Woolworths plc*,[300] Hoffmann J emphasised the significance of his earlier decision in *Stoke-on-Trent*. The decision in *Coventry* was given after an appeal to the House of Lords in *Stoke-on-Trent*[301] had been granted leave, though before the merits of the case were actually heard by the House of Lords.[302] In *Coventry*, Hoffmann J stated that it had been the consistent practice of High Court judges, pending a decision in such an appeal, to proceed on the 'assumption that the earlier decision [was] correct'.[303] Similarly, in *Kirklees*, Lord Goff stated that Hoffmann J's decision in *Stoke-on-Trent* was regarded as 'definitive'[304] by first-instance judges as to the application of the *Torfaen* principle. In conclusion, the weight of authority points to a relatively stable position in the national courts following Hoffmann J's decision in *Stoke-on-Trent*.

Yet, it was not until the ECJ's subsequent decision in *Stoke-on-Trent* that the English courts considered the issue of proportionality to be finally and authoritatively settled. This was then confirmed by the House

298 [1999] 1 All ER 129 at 157. 299 Judgment of 18 October 1990.
300 [1991] 2 CMLR 3 at 4. 301 [1990] 3 CMLR 31.
302 Judgment in the House of Lords was rendered on 31 March 1991.
303 [1991] 2 CMLR 3 at 4. 304 [1992] 3 WLR 170 at 183.

of Lords in *Stoke-on-Trent*[305] when the case was returned to them. The appellants invited the House of Lords to comment on the judgment of Hoffmann J, in particular on his invocation of the principle of judicial notice. Lord Goff declined to do so on the following grounds:

> In view of the answer of the Court of Justice of the European Communities, these matters are no longer relevant. Any comments upon them which your Lordships might make would be *obiter*; and in these circumstances, it would, in my opinion, be undesirable for your Lordships to respond to this invitation of the appellants.[306]

However, the main issues of the EC proportionality rule in the English courts have not been clarified. *Stoke-on-Trent* released the ECJ from the sensitive task of deciding on the question of where the power lies, in Parliament or in the courts. The answer to this question might be evident under EC law; it is, however, not yet accepted by the House of Lords.[307] This is even more true with regard to the fourth dimension of the proportionality rule, the federalist dimension. Advocate-General van Gerven's considerations in *Stoke-on-Trent* are still hanging in the air. Clarification is needed more than ever on the correct division of power between the national and the European courts.[308] The English courts did not touch the issue, as they did not overcome the threshold erected by Hoffmann J. So far, his decision has provided consistency far beyond the case at issue.

To conclude, it can safely be stated that the chaos in the English courts contributed to the willingness and determination of the ECJ to step in and to decide on the reach of Article 28 (ex Article 30) itself. This decision left no more to the national courts than what Barnard calls the 'rubber-stamping'[309] of the ECJ's decision in *Stoke-on-Trent*.

305 In which the House of Lords had to implement the ECJ's decision; see [1993] 2 All ER 297.

306 [1993] 2 All ER 297 at 299.

307 Hoffmann, 'A Sense of Proportion' in Andenas and Jacobs (eds.), *European Community Law*, 149; Hoffmann, 'The Influence of the European Principle of Proportionality' in Ellis (ed.), *The Principle of Proportionality*, 106 at 113.

308 W. van Gerven, 'The Effect of Proportionality on the Actions of Member States of the European Community: National Viewpoints from Continental Europe' in Ellis (ed.), *The Principle of Proportionality*, 37 at 46, referring to *Stoke-on-Trent*, said: 'Proportionality was used therefore as a factor to determine the allocation of powers between the Community and the national law.'

309 Barnard, 'Sunday Trading', 449 at 457.

Reactions to the Euro-litigation

In the previous section, it was demonstrated that the discussion of the judgment in *Torfaen* in the national courts focused very much on the principle of proportionality. However, the academic discussion of the judgment was primarily concerned with the interpretation of Article 28 (ex Article 30) and its wider practical and theoretical implications. The ECJ's approach to measures of equivalent effect to quantitative restrictions which apply to domestically produced and imported products alike, that is, indistinctly applicable measures, in the Sunday trading cases was taken as a starting-point in order to enter into a more general discussion of the breadth of Article 28 (ex Article 30). The approach taken by academics to the correct interpretation of Article 28 (ex Article 30) is most accurately characterised as 'diverse'. It is nevertheless possible to identify general lines of argument, although it should be noted that most commentators did not merely comment on the decisions as such but put forward proposals as to the proper scope of Article 28 (ex Article 30).

Support for the orthodox approach to Article 28

There were some writers who continued to advocate the orthodox approach to Article 28 (ex Article 30) in relation to indistinctly applicable measures, by which I mean a mechanical application of the *Dassonville* formula. Such writers include Gormley and Arnull.

Gormley commented, immediately after the judgment in *Torfaen*, that the ECJ's reasoning was unclear while the outcome as such should be welcomed. According to Gormley, the case should have been dealt with by a 'straightforward application of the basic principle in *Dassonville* accompanied by the rule of reason'.[310] He stated that, on a mechanical application of the *Dassonville* formula, one would inevitably arrive at the conclusion that section 47 of the Shops Act was capable of hindering, actually or potentially, directly or indirectly, trade between Member States. The next test would then be whether the measure could be justified either under the rule of reason or under Article 30 (ex Article 36). Even though this approach might not be designed to reduce the number of references to the ECJ, Gormley contended that it would

[310] L. Gormley, 'Case Study of Torfaen Borough Council v. B&Q plc' (1990) 27 *Common Market Law Review* 149.

not result in the ECJ being flooded with cases. On the contrary, a wide application of the basic principle in *Dassonville*, coupled with the use of the rule of reason and Article 30 (ex Article 36), should be welcomed by the Member States. Nevertheless, he pointed out that:

> it is important ... that litigants should not simply see [Article 28 (ex Article 30)] as a panacea to attack every local regulation of economic life willy-nilly. Disputes alleging interference with inter-state trade should always have a genuine inter-state element.[311]

On this basis, Gormley – in reliance on *Oebel* – argued that a strong case could have been made out on the basis of employment protection as a mandatory requirement. This would have avoided the situation in which national courts had to engage in 'difficult and painful policy evaluations',[312] namely, whether Sunday closing could be justified on the grounds of socio-economic policy.

Like Gormley, Arnull supported the traditional approach to Article 28 (ex Article 30).[313] Even though the ECJ did not mention the *Dassonville* formula in its judgment as such, he argued that *Torfaen* should be viewed as an example of the mechanical application of that rule. According to Arnull, it was beyond doubt that, whatever the exact nature of the test, it would be satisfied in *Torfaen*. He supported this contention by reference to Advocate-General van Gerven's submission in *Stoke-on-Trent* in which van Gerven maintained that recent case law demonstrated that 'the [ECJ's] broad *Dassonville* and *Cassis de Dijon* formula continues to apply with undiminished scope'. However, the fact that the exact nature of the test had been clarified neither in *Torfaen* nor in the subsequent decisions in *Conforama*, *Marchandise* and *Stoke-on-Trent*, was deeply regretted by Arnull. Referring to *Torfaen*, he stated:

> The disappointing feature of the judgment is that the terms in which it is couched create considerable confusion as to the scope of a fundamental provision of the EEC Treaty.[314]

The lesson to be learnt from the Sunday trading litigation, according to Arnull, was that the mandatory requirements invented in *Cassis de*

[311] *Ibid.*, 150. [312] *Ibid.*, 148.

[313] Arnull, 'What Shall We Do on Sunday?', 112; A. Arnull, 'Current Survey: Anyone for Tripe?' (1993) 18 *European Law Review* 314.

[314] Arnull, 'What Shall We Do on Sunday?', 112 at 124.

Dijon merely constituted further derogations from Article 28 (ex Article 30) rather than a test for determining whether a national rule fell within the scope of Article 28 (ex Article 30). Following the Sunday trading litigation, it was therefore not correct to insist on a strict construction of Article 30 (ex Article 36) or to argue that the mandatory requirements were not true derogations. Consequently, the only way to restore some measure of order would, according to Arnull, be the recognition of the concept of precedent by the ECJ.

In *Keck*,[315] Advocate-General van Gerven proceeded on the assumption that, following the Sunday trading cases, the broad *Dassonville* formula still remained the cornerstone of the ECJ's case law concerning the scope of application of Article 28 (ex Article 30). He noted, however, that this was not made sufficiently clear by the ECJ. He appreciated the ECJ's efforts to clarify the law on the issue of proportionality, particularly in *Stoke-on-Trent*. Nevertheless, he denied that the ECJ had wished to restrict the fundamental scope of the prohibition laid down in Article 28 (ex Article 30). According to van Gerven, it was now high time to give, in *Keck*, a ruling on the significance of the *Dassonville* formula concerning the sphere of application of Article 28 (ex Article 30), and accordingly he invited the ECJ to spell out its approach:

> In order to avoid any confusion, I think, that the Court owes a duty to the national courts to make this quite clear.[316]

Criticism of the mechanical application of the Dassonville *formula*

On the other hand, there were some writers who were firmly opposed to a mechanical application of the *Dassonville* rule, notably Advocate-General van Gerven, and Advocate-General Lenz in *Quietlynn*.[317] Similarly, White[318] was critical of the mechanical application of the *Dassonville* formula.

In essence, White argued for a different approach in relation to measures relating to the *characteristics* of the products, in contrast to

[315] Judgment of 24 November 1993, Cases C-267 and 268/91, *Keck and Mithouard* [1993] ECR I-6097.

[316] *Ibid.*, 6121.

[317] Case C-23/89, *Quietlynn Ltd and Brian James Richards* v. *Southend-on-Sea Borough Council* [1990] ECR 3059; [1990] 3 CMLR 55.

[318] E. White, 'In Search of the Limits to Article 30 of the EEC Treaty' (1989) 26 *Common Market Law Review* 235.

measures which merely regulate the *circumstances* in which the goods with the same characteristics are sold or used. While the former – according to White – should fall within Article 28 (ex Article 30), the latter should not. White's starting-point was the warning that Article 28 (ex Article 30) should not be allowed to 'become a quasi-constitutional instrument which complainants and courts can use to question the justification and "proportionality" of virtually all State measures regulating society'.[319] Rather, the effectiveness of Article 28 (ex Article 30) 'as a weapon against measures which really stand in the way of the creation of the Common Market'[320] should be preserved. He then proceeded to define measures of equivalent effect as 'all those measures which hinder the establishment of the Common Market but . . . not . . . those measures in respect of which Member States can safely be allowed to take divergent paths without endangering this objective'.[321] This modification of the *Dassonville* formula was necessary since the *Dassonville* formula was far too wide. He suggested an approach which drew a distinction between rules relating to the *circumstances* in which certain goods may be sold or used and rules relating to the *characteristics* of the products. The decisive criterion – according to White – should be whether imported products enjoy 'equal access'[322] to the market of the importing Member State compared with national goods. Considering that White concentrates on the nature of the rules themselves, that is, on the legislation relating to the market, it is obvious that his argument is based on a legal criterion, whereas van Gerven, in his Opinion in *Torfaen*, concentrated on whether the national market had been 'screened off' by the erection of thresholds to national markets. Thus, in contrast to White, his argument is based on an economic criterion.

It should be recalled that White's approach was not followed in *Torfaen*. It should equally be noted that it was also White who acted as Agent for the Commission in *Quietlynn*. In that case, the question was whether section 2 of the Local Government (Miscellaneous Provisions) Act 1982, which prohibited the sale of lawful sex articles from unlicensed sex establishments, constituted a measure having an effect equivalent to a quantitative restriction on imports. White argued that the national provision merely regulated 'in a general and neutral manner the circumstances in which sex shops may be used and

[319] *Ibid.*, 239. [320] *Ibid.*, 239. [321] *Ibid.*, 242. [322] *Ibid.*, 246.

thus indirectly the circumstances in which sex articles may be sold'.[323] As in *Torfaen*, this approach was not relied on by the ECJ. The ECJ held instead that the rule in question was a rule concerning the 'distribution'[324] of the products in question. As such, it did not have any connection with intra-Community trade. Thus, the national provision was not held to be in breach of Article 28 (ex Article 30). Yet, even if his theory was accepted by the ECJ neither in *Torfaen* nor in *Quietlynn*, it will be seen further below that his approach was eventually accepted to a large extent by the ECJ in *Keck*.

Mortelmans, in reviewing both White's and van Gerven's approaches as well as the decision in *Torfaen* and subsequent developments, sought to strike a balance. As with White, Mortelmans drew a distinction between rules concerning the 'composition, characteristics and presentation of products' and rules concerning the 'market circumstances surrounding the sale of products'.[325] But, even though approving of White's categorisation, he stated that his market circumstances theory had 'too many loopholes'[326] since it went too far. It would exclude far too many rules from the scope of Article 28 (ex Article 30). In particular, Mortelmans pointed to door-to-door selling rules and consumer credit rules. He contended that there would be no justification for their harmonisation on the basis of Article 95 (ex Article 100a) if they were excluded from Article 28 (ex Article 30). After all, this Article required the measures to realise the objectives of the internal market. An exclusion of those rules from Article 28 (ex Article 30) would be an unacceptable position since it would mean the high level of consumer protection in Article 95(3) (ex Article 100a(3)) would not apply.

As a consequence, he proposed a slightly altered definition for Article 28 (ex Article 30). He further subdivided the market circumstances category into rules 'with a territorial element' and rules of a general nature 'without a territorial element'.[327] While rules without a territorial element are very likely to pose a real threat to the completion of the internal market, rules with a territorial element are not so likely to do so. Therefore, the latter rules fell outside Article 28 (ex Article 30) altogether. According to Mortelmans, the trading hours law in *Torfaen* and other cases should be regarded as a rule on market circumstances

[323] Case C-23/89, *Quietlynn Ltd and Brian James Richards* v. *Southend-on-Sea Borough Council* [1990] ECR 3059 at 3067.

[324] *Ibid.*, para. 9.

[325] Mortelmans, 'Article 30 of the EEC Treaty', 115.

[326] *Ibid.*, 129.

[327] *Ibid.*, 130.

relating to a fixed location where the goods are only a secondary consideration. Thus they should be regarded as outside Article 28 (ex Article 30). Mortelmans also mentioned rules which do not have any links with Community law, so-called 'internal situation rules'.[328] The Shops Act 1950 was not considered to be such a rule. Rather, rules such as those in *Oosthoek*[329] and *Gauchard*[330] may be regarded as internal situation rules. Yet, Mortelmans recognised the difficulty of drawing a line between cases with and cases without a territorial element. Where there is doubt, the measure should be held to fall within Article 28 (ex Article 30) so as to be able to promote the internal market: *in dubio pro communitate.*[331]

Qualifying the Dassonville *formula*

Steiner equally rejected the mechanical application of the *Dassonville* formula as 'too wide'.[332] She did not call into question the application of the *Dassonville* formula as such. According to Steiner, it was the appropriate test, and should remain so, in assessing whether an indistinctly applicable measure was *prima facie* incompatible with Article 28 (ex Article 30). However, it was in need of modification so as to restrict the 'scope for a difference of view'.[333] This modification should be aimed at reducing the abuse of Article 28 (ex Article 30) and thus the workload of the ECJ. There were, said Steiner, two ways of achieving this aim: first, by a more rigorous application of the *Dassonville* formula as opposed to a mechanical application; and, secondly, by taking the test as a mere starting-point while qualifying it. The latter approach was the one eventually advocated by Steiner. Essentially, this was the approach taken by White, Advocate-General van Gerven and

328 *Ibid.*, 130.

329 Case C-286/81, *Oosthoek's Uitgeversmaatshcappij BV* [1982] ECR 4575; [1983] 3 CMLR 428. The case concerned the prohibition of the offer of free gifts to buyers of encyclopaedias. Contrary to White's approach, the ECJ held the prohibition to be within Art. 28 (ex Art. 30).

330 Case C-20/87, *Ministère Public* v. *André Gauchard* [1987] ECR 4879. The case involved legislation requiring prior authorisation for the opening and extension of commercial premises exceeding a certain floor area. Note, however, that this case did not concern Art. 28 (ex Art. 30) but former Art. 52.

331 Mortelmans, 'Article 30 of the EEC Treaty', 115 at 131.

332 J. Steiner, 'Drawing the Line: Uses and Abuses of Article 30 EEC' (1992) 29 *Common Market Law Review* 749 at 767.

333 *Ibid.*, 767.

Mortelmans, the difference being the shaping of the qualifications to the test.

The qualifications proposed by Steiner run as follows. Rather than putting the emphasis on the *effects*[334] of the measure at issue, she advocated an approach which essentially constitutes an assessment of whether the measure constitutes, actually or potentially, a *hindrance*[335] to inter-state trade. The question to be asked was whether the measure was capable of operating as a deterrent to imports. The test would be satisfied if the channels of trade *between Member States* were closed or trading opportunities *within the importing Member State* were markedly or substantially restricted. It should be noted that Steiner's proposed test was not intended to be subject to the *de minimis* rule. This approach, it was suggested, had the advantage of avoiding the mechanical application of the *Dassonville* formula.

The essential distinction between a focus on effects and a focus on hindrance is the following. On the one hand, a focus on effects equates to a focus on the anticipated loss of profits or turnover suffered *by individual undertakings* in the importing state. On the other hand, a focus on hindrance equates to a focus on the loss of marketing opportunities or advantages *for the product* at issue. While it is beyond doubt that section 47 of the Shops Act 1950 had substantially reduced the imports *by the defendants concerned*, it is equally clear that it did not hinder the importation of *gardening and DIY products into the UK*. In addition, there was no restriction on the marketing opportunities for the goods concerned, since the goods could be sold during the week. Thus, applied to the Sunday Trading cases, Steiner's proposal would lead to the conclusion that section 47 of the Shops Act 1950 could not be said to be in breach of Article 28 (ex Article 30), the advantage being that an application of the proportionality criteria in national courts would have been avoided.

The need to lay down the law

Commentaries on and evaluations of the decisions in the Sunday trading litigation were critical of the outcome. The essence of those commentaries was that the application of Article 28 (ex Article 30) had not been facilitated by *Torfaen* and subsequent decisions. Certainly, the

[334] *Ibid.*, 768. [335] *Ibid.*, 773.

ECJ's judgment in *Stoke-on-Trent* did make the application of Article 28 (ex Article 30) easier than did the decision in *Torfaen*. But still, the stage had not been reached where the law had been clarified and simplified. What was needed in relation to indistinctly applicable equal-burden rules was a general approach to all market circumstances cases no matter which particular prohibition was concerned. It was rightly pointed out by Mortelmans that the chance to do so had already arisen in *Conforama* and *Marchandise*. He suggested that the ECJ should delay judgments in those cases until van Gerven had delivered his Opinion in the trio of cases which would subsequently be decided together in *Stoke-on-Trent*. Yet, the judgments in *Conforama* and *Marchandise* were given on 28 February 1991, that is, five months before the Advocate-General gave his Opinion in *Stoke-on-Trent* on 8 July 1992.[336]

Similarly, Advocate-General Tesauro, in his Opinion in *Hünermund* v. *Landesapothekerkammer Baden-Württemberg*,[337] addressed frankly the difficulties in the ECJ's case law on Article 28 (ex Article 30) and pointed to the uncertainties on the scope of Article 28 (ex Article 30). He finally invited the ECJ to define precisely the scope of Article 28 (ex Article 30):

> It is as well, then, to clear the field of all exercises in dialectics and to remove from the ambit of [Article 28 (ex Article 30)] those national laws which have nothing to do with trade, still less with the integration of the markets.[338]

It therefore comes as no surprise that, soon after the Sunday trading litigation ended, the ECJ was again called upon to clarify the case law and to determine the exact scope of Article 28 (ex Article 30). It can even be argued that the Sunday trading litigation made a change of direction in the ECJ's jurisprudence inevitable. It set the stage, in *Keck*, for a rethinking of the law.

Keck: *more than just another episode in the Sunday trading saga?*

The opportunity to clarify the law in *Keck* was eagerly seized by the ECJ. Yet, it was not until the initial hearing that the ECJ realised the

336 See Figure 2.2, p. 97 above.

337 Case 292/92, *Hünermund* v. *Landesapothekerkammer Baden-Württemberg* [1993] ECR I-6787.

338 *Ibid.*, 6812.

opportunity presented by the facts of *Keck* to reverse part of its earlier case law. As a result, the case was transferred to the full court consisting of all thirteen judges, pursuant to Article 95(3) of the ECJ's Rules of Procedure dated 19 June 1991.[339] This supports the view that *Keck* was meant to clarify previous case law and to redraw the boundaries of Article 28 (ex Article 30).

The case concerned the compatibility with European law of a French provision[340] prohibiting the resale of goods at a loss. The defendants were prosecuted for reselling products in an unaltered state at prices lower than their actual purchase price contrary to that law. They defended themselves by, *inter alia*, contending that a general prohibition on resale at a loss was incompatible with Article 28 (ex Article 30). Even though other defences had been raised, the ECJ rightly focused on Article 28 (ex Article 30). The ECJ stated that, with a view to giving 'a useful reply'[341] to the French court, the appropriate course was to 'look at the prohibition of resale at a loss from the perspective of the free movement of goods'.[342]

Legislation prohibiting resale at a loss is often regarded as a means to prevent unfair competition. It is therefore common practice in the Member States to enact legislation prohibiting resale at a loss. Oliver[343] even points out that the prevention of unfair competition is one of the recognised requirements justifying restrictions on imports. Similarly, van Gerven, in his first Opinion in *Keck*, pointed out that it would appear that the national rules under considerations relied on two of the mandatory requirements recognised by the ECJ, namely, 'fair trading and protection of consumers'.[344] In his second Opinion in *Keck*, van Gerven explicitly stated that the penalisation of resale at a loss

> may be judged to be necessary by a Member State in order to achieve the aim – recognised by the Court as a mandatory requirement under [Article 28 (ex Article 30)] – of ensuring fair trading or of preventing competition from being distorted.[345]

[339] OJ 1991 No. L176, 7.

[340] Art. 1 of French Law No. 63-628 of 2 July 1936, as amended by Art. 32 of Order No. 86-1243 of 1 December 1986.

[341] Case C-267 and 268/91, *Keck and Mithouard* [1993] ECR I-6097 at 6130.

[342] *Ibid.*, 6130.

[343] P. Oliver, *Free Movement of Goods in the EC* (3rd edn, London, 1996), 100.

[344] Case C-267 and 268/91, *Keck and Mithouard* [1993] ECR I-6097 at 6114.

[345] *Ibid.*, 6119.

On the basis of common practice and the significance of the prevention of unfair competition within Community law, it is arguable that it would have been open to the ECJ to uphold the prohibition at issue. Indeed, the ECJ *did* uphold the legislation. However, it did not seem to attribute any importance to the above-mentioned considerations, but instead decided *Keck* on novel grounds while trying to clarify its case law.

The judgment in Keck

In essence, the ECJ held that:

> [Article 28 (ex Article 30)] of the Treaty is to be interpreted as not applying to legislation of a Member State imposing a general prohibition on resale at a loss.[346]

The ECJ held that national legislation prohibiting the reselling of goods at a loss was not designed to regulate trade in goods between Member States.[347] Such legislation might restrict the volume of sales of products from other Member States. However, this did not necessarily lead to its being a measure having equivalent effect to a quantitative restriction on imports. In addition, the ECJ took into account that there was an

> increasing tendency of traders to invoke [Article 28 (ex Article 30)] of the Treaty as a means of challenging any rules whose effect is to limit their commercial freedom even where such rules are not aimed at products from other Member States.[348]

This is undoubtedly a reference to the Sunday trading litigation even though none of the cases was explicitly mentioned in the judgment itself.

The ECJ drew a distinction between rules which lay down 'requirements to be met'[349] and rules 'restricting or prohibiting certain selling arrangements'.[350] While rules governing requirements to be met falling within the *Dassonville* formula constituted measures of equivalent effect prohibited by Article 28 (ex Article 30) unless justifiable, the ECJ proposed a different approach to rules governing selling arrangements. It was held that, 'contrary to what [had] previously been decided',[351] the latter rules did not fall within the *Dassonville* formula. National

346 *Ibid.*, 6132, para. 17. 347 *Ibid.*, para. 12. 348 *Ibid.*, para. 14.
349 *Ibid.*, para. 15. 350 *Ibid.*, para. 16. 351 *Ibid.*, para. 16.

rules restricting or prohibiting certain selling arrangements were not such as to hinder, directly or indirectly, actually or potentially, intra-Community trade. The ECJ went on to state the further requirement that those provisions had to apply to all relevant traders operating within the national territory and had to affect in the same manner, in law and in fact, the marketing of domestic products and the marketing of products from other Member States. Provided those conditions were fulfilled, the effect of the application of such rules was not such as to prevent or impede the market access of products from other Member States.[352] Consequently, such rules were held to fall outside the scope of Article 28 (ex Article 30).

This approach was subsequently affirmed by the ECJ in *Hünermund* v. *Landesapothekerkammer Baden-Württemberg*[353] in relation to rules concerning selling arrangements. The ECJ held, on the basis of *Keck*, that Article 28 (ex Article 30) did not apply to a rule of professional conduct which prohibited all pharmacists from advertising outside the pharmacy quasi-pharmaceutical products which they are authorised to sell. This finding underlines the increasing feeling that the magic formula seems to be the distinction between selling arrangements and rules that lay down requirements to be met by goods.

The relationship between Keck *and the Sunday trading cases*

Even though subsequent case law has shed some light on the judgment in *Keck*, it is still the focus of ongoing academic discussion, the analysis of which is beyond the scope of this book. Attention has already been drawn to the fact that the ECJ did not mention any of the Sunday trading cases in its judgment in *Keck*, even though it clearly indicated that the decision was 'contrary to what [had] previously been decided'.[354] Therefore, it seems to be impossible to reconcile subsequent decisions with the Sunday trading cases. Any attempt to analyse how the ECJ dealt with the Sunday trading litigation in *Keck* remains to a large extent pure speculation.

It is now generally accepted that the ECJ has strictly adhered to its distinction between selling arrangements, on the one hand, and

[352] *Ibid.*, para. 17.
[353] Case C-292/92, *Hünermund* v. *Landesapothekerkammer Baden-Württemberg* [1993] ECR I-6787.
[354] *Ibid.*, para. 16.

measures of the kind envisaged in paragraph 15 of the judgment in *Keck*, on the other. However, it is also widely acknowledged that the ECJ did not sufficiently define the concept of 'selling arrangements' in *Keck*. Oliver rightly points out that the judgment was badly drafted, particularly because the concept of selling arrangements in paragraph 16 was not defined.[355] This is crucial for an assessment of the Sunday trading cases, since it seems as if section 47 of the Shops Act 1950 should properly be classified as a rule affecting selling arrangement of the kind most likely contemplated by the ECJ in *Keck*. Section 47 does not relate to matters intrinsic to the product such as inherent characteristics, but rather matters extrinsic to the products, that is, the time when the goods may be sold. Following Craig and de Búrca's distinction between 'static . . . and non-static or dynamic selling arrangements',[356] section 47 could further be classified as a static selling arrangement. It is a measure relating to the hours at which shops may be open rather than a measure relating to the ways in which a specific product is marketed. Thus, had the Sunday trading litigation been decided in the wake of *Keck*, the ECJ would certainly have reached the same result as it did, with one notable difference. In *Stoke-on-Trent*, the ECJ had to decide on the issue of proportionality in order to deny the applicability of Article 28 (ex Article 30), whereas under *Keck* Sunday trading would have fallen outside the scope of application of Article 28 (ex Article 30). Thus, *Keck* allows the ECJ to circumvent the fourth dimension of the proportionality rule, or, to put it another way, to avoid getting involved in the federalist dimension.

However, it is not always the legal decision as such which is significant for the outcome of litigation. Timing can be equally important – and this seems to have been part of the Sunday traders' recipe for success. Even before the Sunday trading litigation, there were what Weiler calls 'subterranean cracks'[357] appearing in the *Dassonville* formula. The Sunday traders can take the credit for having exposed the cracks. It was the task of the ECJ subsequently to decide whether to patch up the cracks or to tear the whole *Dassonville* structure down altogether. *Keck* should be seen as the ECJ's attempt to try to save what

[355] Oliver, *Free Movement of Goods in the EC*, 106.

[356] P. Craig, and G. de Búrca (eds.), *EU Law: Text, Cases and Materials* (3rd edn, Oxford, 1998).

[357] Weiler, 'The Constitution of the Common Market Place' in Craig and de Búrca (eds.), *The Evolution of EU Law*, 369.

could be saved by rethinking the merits of the *Dassonville* structure. Or, in Maduro's (slightly altered) words,[358] Article 28 (ex Article 30) was never meant as an economic due-process clause controlling the degree of public intervention in the market. Thus, the ECJ used *Keck* to reinforce the original importance of Article 28 (ex Article 30).

[358] M. Maduro, 'Never on a Sunday – What Has (EU) Law Got To Do With It' in S. Sciarra (ed.), *Labour Law in the Courts: National Judges and the European Court of Justice* (Oxford, 2001), 281, writes: 'The aim was not to construct Article 28 judicially as an economic due process clause controlling the degree of public intervention in the market.'

3

The reconstruction of the equal treatment litigation

The approach chosen in the area of equal treatment differs considerably from that used to study the area of Sunday trading. The equal treatment litigation was not one single case, nor indeed a series of related cases, but rather a whole series of unrelated cases in which the English courts referred issues of equal treatment to the ECJ.[1] However, all these cases have one common factor: they were referred to the ECJ under Article 234 (ex Article 177) of the EC Treaty. This has made it possible for official equality-promotion agencies, trade unions and non-governmental organisations to become involved in the litigation.[2] The choice of case law, however, is not an arbitrary one, but one which has been guided by the following assumptions:

(1) The cases should focus principally on labour law (social security cases are included only if they are of a paradigmatic nature) so as to facilitate a better understanding of the EC law on equal treatment.
(2) The cases should involve the Equal Opportunities Commission,[3] which plays a major role in Great Britain[4] in implementing equal treatment.[5]

[1] Equal treatment here is used to refer to cases covered by Art. 141 (ex Art. 119) and all those cases coming under Directives 75/117/EEC and 76/207/EEC. For the purpose of this study, there is no need to embark on a discussion of the various theoretical concepts of equal treatment, the principle of equality and/or the principle of non-discrimination; see, however, C. Barnard, 'The Principle of Equality in the Community Context: P, Grant, Kalanke and Marschall: Four Uneasy Bedfellows?' (1998) 57 *Cambridge Law Journal* 352.

[2] See C. Docksey, 'The Principles of Equality between Women and Men as a Fundamental Right under Community Law' (1991) 20 *Industrial Law Journal* 258, who underlines that the ECJ has developed the law in this area mainly by way of preliminary rulings under Art. 234 (ex Art. 177).

[3] See www.eoc.org.uk. [4] Northern Ireland has its own, separate agency.

[5] C. Barnard, 'A European Litigation Strategy: The Case of the Equal Opportunities Commission' in J. Shaw and G. More (eds.), *New Legal Dynamics of the European Union* (Oxford, 1995), 253.

(3) The cases should document the development of EC law on sex discrimination and its growing impact on national law. This is why the case law of interest here covers more than two decades, largely from 1979 to 1999.

Ultimately, the set of reconstructed cases allows for a greater insight into the input of UK law into European law. The findings presented are not aimed at providing a comprehensive picture of the law on equal treatment at either a UK or a European level. Instead, the reconstruction of the Euro-litigation on equal treatment serves to elucidate the rules and procedures which guide the achievement of equality in the European legal order.

The legal structure for achieving equality between men and women

The first pillar in the European legal structure governing equality between men and women, and the basic rule which serves as a driving force in the Euro-litigation, has been and still is Article 141 (ex Article 119), as amended by the Treaty of Amsterdam. Article 141 (ex Article 119) has been complemented by Council Directive 75/117/EEC [6] of 10 February 1975 on the approximation of the laws of the Member States relating to the application of equal pay for women. The second legal pillar takes the form of Council Directive 76/207/EEC of 9 February 1976[7] on the implementation of the principle of equal treatment of men and women as regards access to employment, vocational training and promotion, and working conditions, as amended by Council Directive 2002/73/EC.[8] One Treaty Article and two Directives cover all the legal means, rights and remedies at the heart of the Euro-litigation on equal treatment. They determine the scope of application of the European law on sex discrimination – *sedes materiae* and *sedes personae* – with regard to the form of discrimination covered, be it direct or indirect, justifiable or not, and, last but not least, with regard to

[6] OJ 1975 No. L45, 19. [7] OJ 1976 No. L39, 40.

[8] OJ 2002 No. L269, 23 September 2002, 15. In addition, there is Council Directive 2000/78/EC of 27 November 2000 establishing a general framework for equal treatment in employment and occupation, OJ 2000 No. L303, 27 November 2000, 16. The European legislator has mostly codified the rulings of the ECJ as described here.

the set of legal remedies available to implement the principle of equal treatment.[9]

The European legal background and the national law on equal treatment in 1979

Macarthys Ltd v. *Smith*[10] was decided by the ECJ on 27 March 1979, and *R.* v. *Secretary of State for Employment, ex parte Seymour-Smith and Perez*[11] was decided by the ECJ on 9 February 1999. The time span between these two cases covers two decades of intensive development of EC law, and its effect on domestic law. For a better understanding of the conflicts which arose between EC law and national law, it might be helpful to recall the jurisprudence of both legal systems in 1979, when the English courts first began to refer such cases to the ECJ.

The Equal Pay Act 1970[12] and the Sex Discrimination Act 1975 constitute the national legislation adopted in the field governed by Article 141 (ex Article 119), the Equal Pay Directive 75/117/EEC and the Equal Treatment Directive 76/207/EEC. The two Acts were enacted in order to implement the UK's obligations under the European provisions.[13] Both the 1975 Act and certain amendments to the 1970 Act came into force on 29 December 1975, during the one year period provided for by Article 8 of the Equal Pay Directive. The 1970 Act has been amended on a number of occasions when it has been found to fall short of the requirements of Article 141 (ex Article 119) and the Equal Pay Directive.[14] Thus, in 1979, at the time when *Macarthys Ltd* v. *Smith* was decided, the UK law on equal treatment was fully settled.

[9] This classification is drawn mainly from N. Reich, *Bürgerrechte in der Europäischen Union, Subjektive Rechte von Unionsangehörigen und Drittstaatsangehörigen unter besonderer Berücksichtigung der Rechtslage nach der Rechtsprechung des EuGH und dem Vertrag von Amsterdam* (Baden-Baden, 1999), 212.

[10] Case 129/79, *Macarthys Ltd* v. *Smith* [1980] ECR 1275.

[11] Case C-167/97, *R.* v. *Secretary of State for Employment, ex parte Seymour-Smith and Perez* [1999] ECR I-623.

[12] As amended by the Sex Discrimination Act 1975.

[13] That the 1970 Act and the 1975 Act form the national legislation passed by the UK in order to implement its obligations under Art. 119, the Equal Pay Directive 75/117/EEC and the Equal Treatment Directive 76/207/EEC was confirmed by the ECJ in Case 61/81, *Commission* v. *United Kingdom* [1982] ECR 578 at 587, and by the House of Lords in *R.* v. *Secretary of State for Employment, ex parte Equal Opportunities Commission* [1995] 1 AC at 23C–D.

[14] For example, following decision of the ECJ in Case 61/81, *Commission* v. *United Kingdom* [1982] ECR 578 at 587, the 1970 Act was amended in order to permit claims

The EC case law on Article 141 (ex Article 119) and the respective Directives was quite limited. The ECJ had only a few opportunities to shape the meaning of Article 141 (ex Article 119). The most important decision taken at that time was certainly *Defrenne II*,[15] on 8 April 1976, in which the ECJ ruled that Article 141 (ex Article 119) had direct effect. Appellants and their advisers were now given a legal platform which could be used and tested in terms of its reach. In the same decision, the ECJ set out its understanding of Article 141 (ex Article 119). It is worth quoting this in full:[16]

> [Article 141 (ex Article 119)] pursues a double aim. First in light of the different stages of the development of social legislation in the various Member States, the aim of [Article 141 (ex Article 119)] is to avoid a situation in which undertakings established in the States which have actually implemented the principle of equal pay suffer a competitive disadvantage in intra-Community competition as compared with undertakings established in States which have not yet eliminated discrimination against women workers as regards pay. Secondly, this provision forms part of the social objectives of the Community, which is not merely an economic union, but is at the same time intended, by common action, to ensure social progress and seek the constant improvement of the living and working conditions of their people, as is emphasised by the Preamble to the Treaty.

The ECJ went beyond the economic imperatives of Article 141 (ex Article 119). France, with its more advanced anti-discrimination laws, was concerned at the competitive disadvantage which would result if similar laws were not introduced in the other Member States.[17] Two years later, in *Defrenne III*,[18] the ECJ expanded the principle of equal treatment into a general fundamental right.

At the heart of the question of the meaning of 'pay' were the three *Defrenne* decisions, *Defrenne I*[19] in 1971, *Defrenne II*[20] in 1976 and

for equal pay for work of equal value to be brought in circumstances in which no job evaluation scheme had been carried out. Further amendments which were prompted by judgments of the ECJ presented here will be discussed separately where appropriate.

15 Case 43/75, *Defrenne II* [1976] ECR 455 at 472.

16 *Ibid.*, paras. 8–10.

17 S. Fredman, 'European Community Discrimination Law: A Critique' (1992) 21 *Industrial Law Journal* 119.

18 Case 149/77, *Defrenne III* [1978] ECR 1365, para. 12; Docksey, 'The Principles of Equality', 258 at 259.

19 Case 80/70, *Defrenne I* [1971] ECR 445.

20 Case 43/75, *Defrenne II* [1976] ECR 455.

Defrenne III[21] in 1978. The conflict turned around the question of whether and to what extent retirement pensions may come within the meaning of pay. The ECJ originally had a relatively narrow view of this, but this view was overruled in *Garland*[22] in 1982 and then confirmed in *Barber*[23] in 1990. The wide reach of Article 141 (ex Article 119) became even more important after the ECJ denied the horizontal direct effect of Directive 76/207/EEC in *Marshall I*.[24] Proactive claimants then tested Article 141 (ex Article 119) in *Birds Eye*,[25] *Smith* v. *Advel Systems*,[26] *Grant*[27] and *Lawrence*[28] as an instrument to equalise the 'pay' of men and women – though in vain.

The potential addressees of EC law on equal treatment – *sedes personae* – were likewise undefined. There was considerable litigation over the question of whether Article 141 (ex Article 119) applied to the public sector. In *Johnston*,[29] in 1986, the ECJ held that a police officer may rely on Directive 76/207/EEC. This second series of cases concerned not so much 'equal pay' as 'equal treatment'. In *P* v. *S*,[30] in 1996, the ECJ extended the scope of Directive 76/207/EEC to transsexuals. *Grant*,[31] decided in 1998, dealt with the equal treatment of homosexuals under Article 141 (ex Article 119).

No relevant case law existed at that time concerning the question of the distinction between direct and indirect discrimination. It was not at all clear whether indirect discrimination was covered by Article 141 (ex Article 119). The breakthrough came in *Jenkins*,[32] which was decided following a referral by the Employment Appeal Tribunal on 31 March 1981. One major battlefield of equal treatment concerned – and still concerns – discrimination related to pregnancy and motherhood. This was due to the UK government's efforts to neutralise

[21] Case 149/77, *Defrenne III* [1978] ECR 1365.
[22] Case 12/81, *Garland* v. *British Rail Engineering Ltd* [1982] ECR 359.
[23] Case C-262/88, *Barber* v. *Guardian Royal Exchange* [1990] ECR I-1889.
[24] Case 152/84, *Marshall* v. *Southampton and South West Hampshire Area Health Authority* [1986] ECR 723 (*Marshall I*).
[25] Case C-132/92, *Birds Eye Walls Ltd* v. *Roberts* [1993] ECR I-5599.
[26] Case C-408/92, *Smith* v. *Advel Systems Ltd* [1994] ECR I-4435.
[27] Case C-249/96, *Grant* v. *South West Trains Ltd* [1998] ECR I-623.
[28] Case C-320/00, *Lawrence* v. *Regent Office Care Ltd* [2002] ECR I-7325.
[29] Case 222/84, *Johnston* v. *Chief Constable of the Royal Ulster Constabulary* [1986] ECR 1651.
[30] Case C-13/94, *P* v. *S and Cornwall County Council* [1996] ECR I-2145.
[31] Case C-249/96, *Grant* v. *South West Trains Ltd* [1998] ECR I-623.
[32] Case 96/80, *Jenkins* v. *Kingsgate (Clothing Productions) Ltd* [1981] ECR 911.

Directive 92/85/EC governing the protection of pregnant women at work.[33] *Webb*[34] was decided in 1994, though it dealt only with contracts concluded for an *indefinite* term. It took another seven years before the ECJ, in *Melgar*[35] and *Tele Danmark*,[36] held that pregnant workers are equally protected under fixed-term contracts.[37]

Rights and remedies were not a major issue in the late 1970s. The relevant law needed to be settled before it became possible to take a closer look at the opportunities for women to take advantage of the rights granted under EC law. The UK courts started the series of referrals in 1983 with *Marshall I*. The ECJ granted vertical direct effect to Article 5 of Directive 76/207/EEC on equal treatment, but refused to grant horizontal direct effect to it. There is certainly a link between the denial of horizontal direct effect and the wide interpretation of public sector employment in *Foster* in 1990, so that function and not form is the determinant of a body's status.[38] *Marshall II* in 1993, and *Coote*[39] and *Levez*,[40] both decided in 1998, focused on the correct interpretation of Article 6 of Directive 76/207/EEC and (the equivalent) Article 2 of Directive 75/117/EEC. In *Comet*,[41] the ECJ introduced the principle of *efficiency* and *comparability* as a yardstick for assessing national legal remedies to implement EC law. In *Levez*,[42] the ECJ gave shape to the two principles as constituents of effective legal protection. *Preston*[43] was another milestone in the ECJ's involvement in rights and remedies.

It is evident therefore that the EC law on equal treatment, as it stood in 1979, pales in comparison with today's elaborate and sophisticated

[33] B. Bagilhole and P. Byrne, 'From Hard to Soft Law and From Equality to Reconciliation in the United Kingdom' in L. Hantrais (ed.), *Gendered Policies in Europe: Reconciling Employment and Family Life* (Basingstoke, 2000), 130.

[34] Case C-32/93, *Webb* v. *EMO Air Cargo (UK) Ltd* [1994] ECR I-3569.

[35] Case C-438/99, *Melgar* v. *Ayuntamiento de Los Barrios* [2001] ECR I-6915.

[36] Case C-109/00, *Tele Danmark A/S* v. *Handels- og Kontorfunktionaerernes Forbund i Danmark* [2001] ECR I-6993.

[37] Case C-438/99, *Melgar* v. *Ayuntamiento de Los Barrios* [2001] ECR I-6915; and Case C-109/00, *Tele Danmark A/S* v. *Handels- og Kontorfunktionaerernes Forbund i Danmark* [2001] ECR I-6993; see D. Stott, 'What Price Certainty?' (2002) 3 *European Law Review* 351. The same issue was discussed by P. Matthews, Principal Legal Officer to the Equal Opportunities Commission, in a speech given on 31 March 1999 at the Academy of European Law, Trier, on 'New Developments in Labour Law of the EC, Sex Equality Law and Positive Action' (unpublished).

[38] Docksey, 'The Principles of Equality', 258 at 276.

[39] Case C-185/97, *Coote* v. *Granada Hospitality Ltd* [1998] ECR I-5199.

[40] Case C-326/96, *Levez* v. *T. H. Jennings (Harlow Pools) Ltd* [1998] ECR I-7835.

[41] Case 45/76, *Comet BV* v. *Produktschap voor Siergewassen* [1976] ECR 2043.

[42] Case C-326/96, *Levez* v. *T. H. Jennings (Harlow Pools) Ltd* [1998] ECR I-7835.

[43] Case C-78/98, *Preston* v. *Wolverhampton Healthcare NHS Trust* [2000] ECR I-3201.

body of rules. The analysis below will consider how and why the appellants referred issues to the ECJ in order to overcome barriers set by national rules, at the same time stretching EC law on equal treatment beyond its original boundaries.

Directive 2000/43/EC implementing the principle of equal treatment between persons irrespective of racial or ethnic origin,[44] Directive 2002/78/EC establishing a general framework for equal treatment in employment and occupation[45] and Directive 2002/73/EC amending Directive 76/207/EEC on the implementation of the principle of equal treatment for men and women as regards access to employment, vocational training and promotion, and working conditions,[46] although relevant, will not be considered in detail here, except to the extent that they are incidentally relevant to the overall analysis.

The structure of the analysis and the fourteen referrals

The core of the analysis is based on the fourteen referrals from the English courts to the ECJ between 1979 and 1999 – four from industrial tribunals, three from the Employment Appeal Tribunal and the remaining seven from the Court of Appeal and the House of Lords. The fourteen referrals analysed here predetermine the scope and the structure of the analysis. The referrals are grouped around three main issues: (1) the scope, *sedes materiae* and *sedes personae*; (2) the form of discrimination, whether direct or indirect; and (3) the remedies.

The fourteen referrals are analysed in Figures 3.1 and 3.2. Figure 3.1 shows the degree to which the individual national courts were involved in the three main issues, that is, the scope of application, the form of discrimination, and the remedies. Table 3.1 builds on the hierarchy of references in equal treatment cases, and links the case in question to the referring court.

The two figures serve as a guide throughout the reconstruction of the equal treatment litigation. The structure of the analysis is largely comparable to that used in Chapter 2 above for the Sunday trading litigation. The analysis starts with a presentation of the national and EC background in equal treatment; it then considers the arguments of the appellants, the respondents and the UK government; it then considers the views of the Commission, the Advocates-General and the ECJ; it then concludes with a consideration of the views of the national courts.

[44] OJ 2000 No. L180, 19 July 2000, 22.
[45] OJ 2000 No. L303, 2 December 2000, 16.
[46] OJ 2002 No. L269, 5 October 2002, 15.

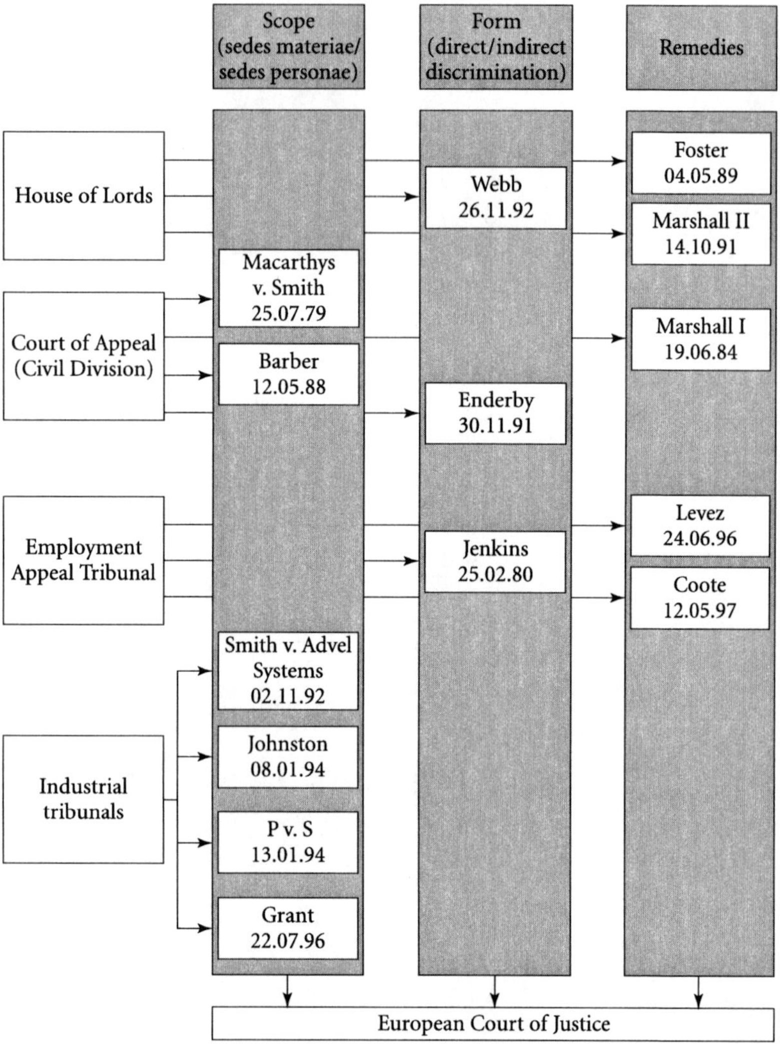

Figure 3.1 Scope, form and remedies in equal treatment litigation.

The appellants

The appellants' role in the equal treatment cases

The appellants in the equal treatment cases are individuals who claim to have suffered discrimination. Each case involves either a single individual or a group of individuals. The appellants are named individuals,

Table 3.1 *The hierarchy of references in equal treatment litigation*

Court	Case
House of Lords	Foster
	Marshall II
	Webb
Court of Appeal	Barber
	Enderby
	Macarthys v. Smith
	Marshall I
Employment Appeal Tribunal	Coote
	Jenkins
	Levez
Industrial tribunals	Grant
	Johnston
	P v. S
	Smith v. Advel Systems

that is, they are not presented simply as 'appellants' or 'respondents', as is the German practice. The 'report of the hearing' will remind us that there is a human being behind the litigation. There is one notable exception here, which is *P* v. *S and Cornwall Country Council.* The need for anonymity here may result from the specific facts of the case, which concerned the dismissal of transsexuals. The ECJ showed less concern for the anonymity of the appellants in *Grant* v. *South West Trains Ltd*, in which the ECJ had to consider an employer's refusal to provide travel concessions to same-sex cohabitees.

Individuals who have suffered discrimination often feel strongly about the issue. The Euro-litigation on equal treatment therefore has a specific emotional aspect. This can be seen in the language of all parties concerned, not only that of the appellants and the respondents, but sometimes also that of the national judges and the Advocates-General. For example, in *P* v. *S*, Advocate-General Tesauro criticised the dismissal of the appellant in strong words:

> To maintain that the unfavourable treatment suffered by [the appellant] was not based upon grounds of sex because in such a case it is not possible to speak of discrimination between the two sexes, would be a

> quibbling formalistic interpretation and a betrayal of the true essence of that fundamental and inalienable value which is equality.[47]

Emotions, however, may work the other round. In *Webb*,[48] Glidewell LJ was not prepared to accept counsel's submission on behalf of Ms Webb. Counsel suggested that, if a pregnant woman applies for a job, and, but for her pregnancy (which must for this purpose be disregarded), she would be the best qualified applicant for the job, the potential employer would be required by the Sex Discrimination Act 1975 to engage her. This might be so even though she may be so advanced in her pregnancy that she would have to leave a month later or, indeed, if from the start she is unable because of her physical condition, resulting from her pregnancy, to perform the job for which she was engaged. Glidewell LJ rejected this submission in the following terms:

> In my view such a result would be lacking in fairness and in what I regard as the proper balance to be struck in relations between the employer and employees.

The strategy is to win the case

Appellants intend to win *their* case in order to get *their* particular problem resolved. All appellants pin their hopes on European law to overturn national rules. The industrial tribunal in *Coote* v. *Granada Hospitality Ltd*[49] had to decide on a woman's claim of victimisation on the basis that the respondent (her former employer) had failed to provide references for her when requested, and that this was preventing her from obtaining employment. The point at issue was whether the right under section 4(1)(a) of the Sex Discrimination Act 1975 was linked to the existence of a valid employment contract. The appellant had left the respondent's employment before bringing an action for victimisation. The chairman of the industrial tribunal expressed his sympathy with the appellant's claim, but rejected jurisdiction and dismissed the claim:[50]

> This is a decision which I reach with some regret as it seems to me that there may here be a gap in the legislation. If the applicant cannot

[47] Case C-13/94, *P* v. *S and Cornwall County Council* [1996] ECR I-2145 at 2155.

[48] *Webb* v. *EMO Air Cargo (UK) Ltd* [1992] 2 All ER 43 at 52, Court of Appeal.

[49] Decision of 7 September 1995, not reported. Made available by the Equal Opportunities Commission.

[50] *Ibid*.

> bring herself within section 29 [of the Sex Discrimination Act 1975] by showing that the provision of a reference is the provision of goods, facilities or services, then it seems to me that, in a situation which may be extremely unjust to the employee, she has no remedy.

Neither the chairman nor the applicant referred to EC law, in particular to Article 6 of Directive 76/207/EEC. It was left to the Equal Opportunities Commission in the Employment Appeal Tribunal to raise the issue and to ask that the case be referred to the ECJ.[51]

Coote v. *Granada Hospitality* is of paradigmatic importance. Industrial tribunals and even the Employment Appeal Tribunal often rely entirely on national law and do not consider the implications of European law. This phenomenon is due mainly to the majority of the applicants not being legally represented in industrial tribunals (since these tribunals are supposed to have relatively informal rules of procedure and evidence, and therefore in theory there is no need for lawyers and no legal aid is available). However, the situation changes if and when the Equal Opportunities Commission becomes involved in the case. But the EOC will and is allowed to step in only on request. The EOC has the resources and the necessary skills to use European law.

The appellant's financial resources

The appellant, even if she knows from the outset that she may need to go to the ECJ, has no legal means at hand to compel a national court to make a referral. Instead, she must persuade the judges sitting in the national court that the case cannot be properly decided without seeking advice from the ECJ on the correct interpretation of the EC law on sex discrimination. Even though one of the lowest courts in the land, an industrial tribunal may refer a case directly to the ECJ, but there is no guarantee that these tribunals will do so. It may take an appeal to the Employment Appeal Tribunal at the very least, or even an appeal to the Court of Appeal or the House of Lords, with all the concomitant expense and delay involved, to obtain a reference to the ECJ. Bringing a case to the ECJ takes time and costs money, and, even if the appellants succeed in having their case referred to the ECJ, the outcome may not be satisfactory, and may leave the national judges

[51] Equal Opportunities Commission, outline submissions for the appellant in the Employment Appeal Tribunal, *Coote* v. *Granada Hospitality Ltd*, 10 July 1996.

and the parties in further uncertainty as to how to interpret or apply the ECJ's judgment – as is often the case.[52]

It is usually not clear from the records where the appellants' financial resources come from. One may wonder whether and to what extent trade unions are behind the applicant, supporting her morally and financially, with the aim ultimately of benefiting their memberships as a whole.[53] Usually, the only actor willing to disclose its role in the proceedings is the Equal Opportunities Commission, which has provided financial assistance in a number of the cases being examined here. Such financial assistance, however, usually does not suffice to cover the entire costs of the litigation, and quite often its support may even be limited to the provision of free legal expertise by the legal officers of the Commission.

The appellants' arguments in the courts

The *sedes materiae* of European law on equal treatment: stretching the boundaries of equal pay

The scope of application of EC law on equal treatment has been steadily enlarged over the last two decades. The case law focused on the notion of 'equal pay'. In *Macarthys Ltd* v. *Smith*,[54] the ECJ had to decide whether discrimination in pay necessarily results from an actual or theoretical comparison of women's and men's salaries. In *Barber* v. *Guardian Royal Exchange*,[55] the ECJ had to define the borderline between 'equal pay' in employment and 'equal treatment' in social security payments. The Equal Opportunities Commission was involved in both cases, and helped to highlight the paradigmatic character of the litigation.

EC legislation contains no express definition of the relevant comparator. In *Macarthys Ltd* v. *Smith*, the ECJ was confronted directly

[52] Barnard, 'A European Litigation Strategy', in Shaw and More (eds.), *New Legal Dynamics of the European Union*, 253 at 271, with regard to Case C-262/88, *Barber* v. *Guardian Royal Exchange* [1990] ECR I-1889 and the need for subsequent referrals to clarify the scope of the decision.

[53] See C. Kilpatrick, 'Community or Communities of Courts in European Integration? Sex Equality Dialogues between UK Courts and the ECJ' (1998) 4 *European Law Journal* 121 at 134.

[54] Case 129/79, *Macarthys Ltd* v. *Smith* [1980] ECR 1275.

[55] Case C-262/88, *Barber* v. *Guardian Royal Exchange* [1990] ECR I-1889.

with the problem of the substitution of cheaper female labour.[56] Mrs Smith took over the management of the Wembley warehouse from Mr Cullough. The salary paid to Mrs Smith was £50 per week whereas Mr Cullough had received a salary of £60 per week. Mrs Smith brought proceedings first in the industrial tribunal, then in the Employment Appeal Tribunal, claiming that her contract should be treated as entitling her to the same salary as Mr Cullough used to have. The Employment Appeal Tribunal dismissed her appeal, the principal reason being that the Equal Pay Act 1970 restricted the equality of treatment to the case of contemporaneous employment of men and women whose actual duties (and not the abstract title of the post) are to be compared.[57] On appeal, the Court of Appeal referred the following question to the ECJ:

> Is the principle of equal pay for equal work, contained in [Article 141 (ex Article 119)] of the EEC Treaty and Article 1 of [Directive 75/117/EEC], confined to situations in which men and women are contemporaneously doing equal work for their employer?

A restrictive interpretation was said to result in manifest anomalies and absurdities and to permit the arbitrary segregation of workers of one sex in particular sectors of employment.[58] In the language of Article 141 (ex Article 119), the appellant submitted, there is nothing to suggest a restriction of the equal pay principle to men and women who are contemporaneously doing equal work for their employer. She felt that her argument was supported by Article 1 of Directive 75/117/EEC which extended the criterion of equal pay in Article 141 (ex Article 119) in accordance with the International Labour Organization's Convention No. 100 concluded in 1951 to 'rates of remuneration established without discrimination based on sex' and by the European Court of Human Rights' judgment of 23 July 1968.[59] As is well known, the ECJ[60] decided in favour of the appellant, and held that Article 141

[56] Fredman, 'European Community Discrimination Law', 119 at 123.

[57] For the historical background, see Bagilhole and Byrne, 'From Hard to Soft Law', in Hantrais (ed.), *Gendered Policies in Europe*, 125.

[58] Case 129/79, *Macarthys Ltd* v. *Smith* [1980] ECR 1275, as presented and documented in the report of the hearing, *ibid.*, 1278.

[59] *Ibid.*, 1279 and 1280. The ECHR case referred to is the *Belgian Linguistic Case (No. 2)*, ECHR Series A No. 6, judgment of 23 July 1968, (1979–80) 1 EHRR 252, para. 10.

[60] Case 129/79, *Macarthys Ltd* v. *Smith* [1980] ECR 1275 at 1296.

(ex Article 119) was not confined solely to cases in which men and women were contemporaneously employed. Thus, the way was open for a further enlargement of the notion of pay. The most striking example, however, involved occupational social security schemes.

Barber was decided ten years later, in 1990. It has a peculiarly British background.[61] Historically, a distinctive feature of UK employment-related equality measures was that pension matters were initially excluded from the scope of the non-discrimination principle. Employers were permitted to apply unequal treatment in death and retirement provision.[62] These exclusions were partly removed in 1978, but only to the extent of prohibiting direct discrimination on the grounds of sex, in relation to age and length-of-service conditions governing membership of a scheme. *Marshall I* pushed the UK into action to explicitly prohibit different compulsory retirement ages for men and women, but the 1975 Act continued to maintain unequal pension ages, contributions and pension benefits and to apply scheme-eligibility rules even when they were indirectly discriminatory. So the question remained whether pension schemes and redundancy payments were to be regarded as 'pay' within the meaning of Article 141 (ex Article 119) or 'conditions' within the meaning of Directive 76/207/EEC.

Mr Barber was dismissed by reason of redundancy at the age of 52. In the case of redundancy, members of the pension scheme were entitled to an immediate pension subject to having attained the age of 55 (for men) or 50 (for women). Other staff were entitled to a number of cash benefits calculated on the basis of their years of service and a deferred pension payable at the normal retirement date. All staff also received an amount equal to the statutory redundancy payment, increased, where appropriate, so as to take account of the years of service notionally credited in the event of early retirement. The pension scheme granted Mr Barber a sum consisting of the cash benefits provided for in the severance terms and an amount equal to the statutory redundancy payment. As he had not attained the age of 55 at the time of his dismissal, Mr Barber did not receive an immediate pension but was granted a deferred pension only. It is not disputed that a woman of the same age and in the same position as Mr Barber would have been entitled to an immediate pension plus the statutory redundancy payment. It

[61] G. Moffat and L. Luckhaus, 'Occupational Pension Schemes, Equality and Europe: A Decade of Change' (1998) 20 *Journal of Social Welfare and Family Law* 1.

[62] Equal Pay Act 1970, section 6(1); and Sex Discrimination Act 1975, section 6(4).

was also agreed that the value of such compensation would have been greater than the total amount received by Mr Barber. The industrial tribunal dismissed Mr Barber's claim. On appeal, the Employment Appeal Tribunal held that, although there was discrimination, it was legal under national law since it was covered by the exception relating to 'provision in relation to death or retirement' referred to in section 6(4) of the Sex Discrimination Act 1975. On the basis of *Burton*,[63] the Employment Appeal Tribunal held that the question was one of access to pension benefits, and therefore fell to be decided not by principles relating to equal pay but by principles relating to equal treatment. Accordingly, Article 141 (ex Article 119) was not applicable, and Directive 76/207/EEC useless, due to its lacking horizontal direct effect. The Court of Appeal took the view that the dispute raised questions concerning the interpretation of EC law, and asked the ECJ for a preliminary ruling, *inter alia*, on the following questions:[64]

1. When a group of employees are made compulsorily redundant by their employer in circumstances similar to those in this case and receive benefits in connection with that redundancy, are all those benefits 'pay' within the meaning of [Article 141 (ex Article 119)] and Directive 75/117/EEC or do they fall within the Equal Treatment Directive 76/207/EEC?
2. Is it material to the answer to 1 that one of the benefits in question is a pension paid in connection with a private occupational pension scheme operated by the employer ('a private pension')?
3. Is the principle of equal pay referred to in [Article 141 (ex Article 119)] and the Equal Pay Directive infringed in the circumstances of the present case if: (a) a man and a woman of the same age are made compulsorily redundant in the same circumstances and, in connection with that redundancy, the woman receives an immediate private pension but the man receives only a deferred pension, or (b) the total value of the benefits received by the woman is greater than the total value of the benefits received by a man?

In *Burton*, the ECJ had used the following criteria to distinguish between equal treatment and equal pay: the first principle applies to the *conditions of eligibility* for a benefit, while the second applies to the

[63] Case 19/81, *Burton* v. *British Railways Board* [1982] ECR 555.

[64] The Court of Appeal referred five questions. The final two dealt with social security issues, which are not of interest in the context of this analysis.

actual benefit given to those who satisfy the qualifying conditions. On behalf of the appellant, it was contended with regard to the first question that the logical basis falls short of being a complete account of the distinction since it is frequently used to describe the same systems of employee benefits in different ways, so that a particular component of the system may in turn appear as a qualifying condition or as an aspect of the benefit itself. Therefore, the appellant relied on *Bilka-Kaufhaus*,[65] in which the ECJ is said to have held that the qualifying conditions for entitlement to a supplementary retirement pension financed by an employer raised an issue of equal pay rather than equal treatment. The ECJ's reason is said to be that pay cannot be 'itemised' into its component parts: there is only one integral concept of pay and the principle of equal pay requires that a comparison be made between all the components.

With regard to the second question, the appellant had to demonstrate that private pensions were covered by Article 141 (ex Article 119). It is submitted that private pensions provided by employers constitute pay, because the relevant legislation in the UK has as its sole purpose to ensure that private pension schemes are properly managed and organised, but it does not have the effect of making them a part of the statutory social security system. This is all the more so as today's private pension schemes result largely from collective bargaining between employers and trade unions. Pension schemes are taken into account in the overall settlement resulting from those negotiations, alongside pay increases or holiday arrangements. They constitute a significant *competitive* factor.[66]

[65] Case 170/84, *Bilka-Kaufhaus GmbH* v. *Weber von Hartz* [1986] ECR 1607; [1986] 2 CMLR 701; the submissions of the appellant are taken from the report of the hearing in Case C-262/88, *Barber* v. *Guardian Royal Exchange* [1990] ECR I-1889 at 1898, written by Mancini.

[66] The only feature which may raise doubts as to whether private pension benefits can be considered as 'pay' is the fact that certain elements of the private pension can act as a 'substitute' for certain state pension benefits (i.e. certain elements of the state pension are 'contracted-out'). Under certain conditions, an employee covered by a private pension scheme may be exempted from having to pay certain social security contributions which he would otherwise have to pay (and consequently forego entitlement to certain state pension benefits which he would otherwise have received). The state permits such substitutions to be made only when it is sure that the employee is a member of a pension scheme which provides sufficient benefits on retirement in lieu of the state pension benefits which the employee has chosen to forego. However,

As to the third question, counsel for Mr Barber submitted that, even if it were correct to say that a claim to pension entitlement was a claim to access to a particular form of benefit and therefore raised an issue of equal treatment, the fact is that he was entitled to a pension, albeit a deferred pension. Accordingly, his claim was that the pension benefit conferred upon him was not equal to that conferred upon comparable female employees. It therefore raised an issue of equal pay rather than equal treatment. The appellant claimed that it would be necessary to impose some sort of valuation upon benefits which take very different forms, and thus to compare, for example, the value of a period of extra holiday with the value of a particular bonus or the use of a car. Each component part of employee benefits would have to be equal for comparable male and female employees.

The ECJ[67] took a courageous decision, and confirmed that benefits paid by an employer to a worker in connection with the latter's compulsory redundancy fall within the scope of Article 141 (ex Article 119), that pensions paid under a contracted-out private pension scheme fall within the scope of Article 141 (ex Article 119), that pension schemes which apply an age condition that varies according to sex are contrary to Article 141 (ex Article 119), and that the principle of equal pay must be ensured in respect of each element of remuneration and not only on the basis of an assessment of the total consideration paid to workers.

The *Barber* judgment led to five further references to the ECJ to clarify the scope of the so-called *Barber* principle.[68] However, more important for the development of the EC law on equal treatment has been *Smith* v. *Advel Systems*.

the fact that such substitutions may be made does not make those private pension benefits a part of the state benefits system. There are private pension schemes in relation to which no contracting-out has occurred either because the employer has not sought exemption from the obligation to pay contributions to the state scheme for his employees or because such exemption has been refused. It would be artificial to maintain that contracted-out private pensions are not 'pay' but that non-contracted-out private pensions are 'pay'.

67 Case C-262/88, *Barber* v. *Guardian Royal Exchange* [1990] ECR I-1889 at 1957.

68 Case C-109/91, *Ten Oever* [1993] ECR I-4879; Case C-152/91, *Neath* [1993] ECR I-6935; Case C-200/91, *Coloroll* [1994] ECR I-4389; Case C-110/91, *Moroni* [1993] ECR I-6591; and Case C-167/97, *Seymour-Smith* [1999] ECR I-623. For the EOC's policy, see Barnard, 'A European Litigation Strategy' in Shaw and More (eds.), *New Legal Dynamics of the European Union*, 271.

The *sedes materiae* of European law on equal treatment: levelling up equal pay

The central question in the sequel to *Barber* concerns the *manner* in which discrimination is being removed from pension schemes. Those administering pension schemes have opted to *raise* the normal pensionable age for women to that applying to men. Mrs Smith and the other applicants in *Smith* v. *Advel Systems*[69] were members of a contracted-out occupational pension scheme, the Advel Pension and Life Assurance Plan, run by their employer, Advel Systems Ltd. Until 1 July 1991, the pension scheme provided that the normal pensionable age was 65 for men and 60 for women. The pension scheme was amended with effect from 1 July 1991 to provide for a normal pensionable age of 65 for both men and women. Seventy-eight female employees challenged the new rules of the pension scheme before the Bedford Industrial Tribunal. Their complaint was based in particular on Article 141 (ex Article 119). By a decision of 2 November 1992, the industrial tribunal referred a whole set of questions to the ECJ for a preliminary ruling:[70]

1. Where an occupational pension scheme has different normal pensions ages for men and women (65 and 60 respectively) and where an employer seeks in light of *Barber* to eliminate that discrimination, is it inconsistent with [Article 141 (ex Article 119)] for the employer to adopt a common pension age for men and women?
2. If the answer to question 1 is in the negative whether [Article 141 (ex Article 119)] imposes an obligation on the employer to minimise the adverse consequences to women whose benefits are affected by the employer's decision to eliminate the differences in pension ages?

Raising the pensionable age for female employees instead of lowering the pensionable age for male employees is certainly disadvantageous for female workers. The outcome of the proceedings depended solely on whether Article 141 (ex Article 119) requires positive action to raise the standards of equal treatment to the highest level available.

Counsel for the appellants drew a line between benefits based on periods of service completed in the past to which discriminatory rules

[69] Case C-408/92, *Smith* v. *Advel Systems Ltd* [1994] ECR I-4435.

[70] As quoted in Advocate-General van Gerven's conclusion in Case C-408/92, *Smith* v. *Advel Systems Ltd* [1994] ECR I-4439 at 4440.

applied, and benefits based on periods of service to be completed in the future to which equal standards as laid down in the new rules apply. For past benefits, the appellants relied heavily on cases involving sex discrimination in which the ECJ has consistently held that the more favourable rules must be applied to the less favoured sex, those rules forming 'the only valid frame of reference' for immediate implementation of the principle of equal treatment.[71] The appellants, however, had to take account of the time limits set down in the *Barber* judgment.

For future benefits, counsel for the appellants relied on *Defrenne II*, in which the ECJ held that:

> the objection that the terms of this Article may be observed in other ways than by raising the lowest salaries may be set aside.[72]

The method selected for abolishing the prohibited discrimination should not lead to lower pension benefits for women than are strictly necessary to eliminate the discrimination. One must take into account, *inter alia*, any surpluses in the pension fund or alternative methods of financing, such as increasing premiums, to the extent to which the employer has profited in the past from the maintenance of a discriminatory pension scheme.

The ECJ answered the essence of the question referred to it in the negative.[73] Article 141 (ex Article 119) does not prevent the employer from raising the retirement age of women to that of men in the future. However, Article 141 (ex Article 119) precludes an employer from taking such a step in respect of the past, that is, in relation to periods of service completed between the date of the *Barber* judgment (17 May 1990) and the date on which those measures came into force (1 July 1991). Appellants who fall into this category benefit unconditionally from the principle of equal treatment. All in all, the proponents of

[71] The ECJ first developed this criterion in its judgment on Joined Cases 75/82 and 117/82, *Razzouk and Brydoun* v. *Commission* [1984] ECR 1509, para. 19, in the context of the right to equal treatment of male and female European Community officials. In its judgments in *Kowalska* and *Nimz*, the ECJ extended the criterion to Art. 141 (ex Art. 119) of the EC Treaty. See Case C-33/89, *Kowalska* v. *Freie und Hansestadt Hamburg* [1990] ECR I-2591, para. 20; and Case C-184/89, *Nimz* v. *Freie und Hansestadt Hamburg* [1991] ECR I-297, para. 18.

[72] Case 43/75, *Defrenne II* [1976] ECR 455, para. 15.

[73] Case C-408/92, *Smith* v. *Advel Systems Ltd* [1994] ECR I-4469.

using EC law to promote equal treatment suffered a severe setback from this judgment.[74]

The *sedes personae* of the EC law on equal treatment: extending the principle to discrimination in matters of public policy

The definition of the *sedes personae* reaches beyond the equal pay principle into broader issues of equal treatment. *Johnston*[75] was decided in 1986. At that time, there was considerable uncertainty surrounding what was and what was not part of the 'public sector'.[76] Reading *Marshall I*, in which the ECJ held that Directives bind only 'organs of the state' as distinct forms of 'public authorities', and equating the state with the legal definition of the Crown in UK law, the industrial tribunal ruled that the ECJ did not intend that bodies of an 'intermediate category' between state organs on the one hand and private employers on the other, should have Directives enforced against them by private individuals.

Mrs Johnston was a member of the Royal Ulster Constabulary (RUC) in Northern Ireland. The RUC was placed under the authority of its Chief Constable. Under the Police Act (Northern Ireland) 1970, the Chief Constable had the power to appoint reserve constables to the Royal Ulster Constabulary Reserve ('RUC Reserve'). Whereas in England and Wales, police officers are not generally armed and there is no general policy against the training of women officers in the use of firearms or against their deployment on duties requiring the carrying of firearms, a different policy had been adopted in Northern Ireland by the Chief Constable of the RUC. Male officers carry firearms in the regular course of their duties. However, female members of the RUC did not carry firearms, save in exceptional cases, and female members of the RUC Reserve were never issued with firearms and did not

[74] Another recent setback for the equal treatment movement concerning the scope of Art. 141 (ex Art. 119) is Case C-320/00, *Lawrence* v. *Regent Office Care Ltd* [2002] ECR I-7325. Here, the ECJ decided that a case 'in which the differences identified in the pay conditions of workers of different sex performing equal work or work of equal value cannot be attributed to a single source [i.e. the same employer] does not come within the scope of Art. 141(1)'.

[75] Case 222/84, *Johnston* v. *Chief Constable of the Royal Ulster Constabulary* [1986] ECR 1651.

[76] P. Morris, 'Sex Discrimination, Public Order and the European Court' (1987) *Public Law* 334.

receive training in the use of firearms. The reason for this policy was that the Chief Constable considered that, if female officers were armed, it would increase the risk of their becoming targets for assassination.

In 1980, the Chief Constable decided that contracts for women members of the RUC's full-time reserve could be entered into or renewed only in cases in which the duties to be performed were capable of being performed by women pursuant to this policy (that is, the duties did not require the use of firearms). The reasons for this decision were as follows. At the material time, the RUC had a sufficient number of women officers for the duties normally assigned to women members. The only duties for the performance of which recruits for the full-time reserve were required were general police duties, that is, security duties such as guard and escort duties, which frequently involved the use of firearms, and therefore were only open to male officers. Mrs Johnston became a member of the full-time reserve in 1974. Her second contract for full-time employment expired in 1980. Due to the new policy, Mrs Johnston's contract was not further renewed. She was subsequently employed on a part-time basis in the RUC Reserve as a communications assistant. It was accepted by all the parties that Mrs Johnston was an efficient and valuable member of the RUC full-time reserve and that the reason why her full-time contract was not renewed was the policy decision taken by the Chief Constable. If she had been a man, the Chief Constable would have offered her a new full-time contract.

Mrs Johnston complained to the industrial tribunal, basing her application on the Sex Discrimination Order (Northern Ireland) 1976. Before the first hearing of the case, the Secretary of State issued a certificate as provided for in Article 53 of the Order, stating that the refusal to offer full-time employment to Mrs Johnston in the RUC Reserve was for the purpose of safeguarding national security and protecting public safety and public order. By virtue of Article 53, when read in isolation, the issue of that certificate deprived Mrs Johnston of any remedy. However, she relied on Article 6 of Directive 76/207/EEC. Therefore, she had to meet the conditions set out in Article 6:

> This Directive shall apply without prejudice to the right of Member States to exclude from its field of application those occupational activities and, where appropriate, the training leading thereto, for which, by reason of their nature or the context in which they are carried out, the sex of the workers constitutes a determining factor.

The industrial tribunal submitted a set of seven questions to the ECJ for a preliminary ruling of which four are of interest for the determination of the *sedes personae* of Directive 76/207/EEC:[77]

1. ... Can a Member State exclude from the Directive's field of application acts of sex discrimination as regards access to employment done for the purpose of safeguarding national security or of protecting public safety or public order?
2. Is full-time employment of a police reserve force, or training in the handling and use of firearms for such employment capable of constituting one of those occupational activities and, where appropriate, the training leading thereto, for which, by reason of their nature or the context in which they are carried out, the sex of the worker constitutes a determining factor, within the meaning of Article 2(2)?
3. What are the principles and criteria by which Member States should determine whether 'the sex of a worker constitutes a determining factor' within the meaning of Article 2(2) in relation to (a) the occupational activities of an armed member of such a force and (b) 'the training leading thereto' whether by reason of their nature or by reason of the context in which they are carried out?

...

6. Is the applicant entitled to rely on the principle of equal treatment contained in the relevant provisions of the Directive before the national courts and tribunals of Member States in the circumstances of the present case?

The *sedes personae* of Directive 76/207/EEC is not directly addressed, although all the questions referred to the ECJ are guided by a common philosophy. The referring court had difficulties in accepting that Directive 76/207/EEC could intervene to such an extent in a nation's sovereignty. Mrs Johnston's claim was supported by the Equal Opportunities Commission. For such an organisation, this was the perfect test case. Possibly, Mrs Johnston had no real interest in full-time employment as an armed officer but was willing to support the equal treatment movement. The involvement of the EOC explains the high quality of the legal arguments presented to the industrial tribunal.

Concerning the first question, Mrs Johnston considered that such a far-reaching derogation was not covered by Article 2(2) of the

[77] Case 222/84, *Johnston* v. *Chief Constable of the Royal Ulster Constabulary* [1986] ECR 1651 at 1668.

Directive. Otherwise, a Member State could determine the scope of the Directive unilaterally without being subject to control by the Community institutions.[78] The second question is criticised as being ill-conceived. Whether full-time employment as an armed member of a police reserve force is capable of coming within Article 2(2) of the Directive is said to depend upon the particular occupational activity within the general category of the employment in question. The mere fact that the Chief Constable required members of the RUC Reserve to be armed did not alter the nature of her occupational activities nor did it change the context in which they were carried out. Employment such as that in question might be capable of coming within the scope of Article 2(2) only insofar as particular occupational activities within the category of employment in question are activities for which the sex of the police officer constitutes a determining factor. This, however, has not been demonstrated. Derogations might be possible but only if they are founded on objective reasons. That is why, in the circumstances of the present case, it is suggested with regard to the third question that the sex of a police officer will only be a 'determining factor' if the nature of the particular activity would be different if carried out by a woman or if the context in which it is carried out makes it essential for it to be done by a man in order to ensure respect for the fundamental right of privacy, for example in carrying out body searches. The purposes asserted in the Secretary of State's certificate and the reasons given by the Chief Constable are seen as not being sufficient for this purpose. As regards the sixth question, Mrs Johnston argued that Article 53 of the Sex Discrimination Order (Northern Ireland) 1976 was contrary to the clear, complete and precise provision of Article 6 of Directive 76/207/EEC and cannot therefore preclude her from relying on the provisions of the Directive before the national court. The Chief Constable and the Secretary of State did not act as private persons but as persons exercising statutory powers or entrusted with public duties. The Directive is therefore directly binding on them. At the time of the reference, *Marshall I*[79] had not yet been decided, which is why the appellants were not able to rely on the direct effect of Article 6.

The ECJ decided in favour of Mrs Johnston, although it may be necessary for the national courts to take into consideration requirements of public safety in order to restrict general policing duties. The scope

[78] Case 41/74, *Van Duyn* v. *Home Office* [1974] ECR 1337.

[79] *Marshall I* was decided on 26 February 1986, *Johnston* on 15 May 1986.

of potential addressees of Directive 76/207/EEC was thus considerably enlarged. From 1986 onwards, there were no more 'sheltered areas' in national law where the principle did not apply. Following *Johnston*, *Sirdar*[80] in 1999 and *Kreil*[81] in 2000 came as no surprise. It was only a matter of time before the restrictions on the employment of women in the armed services of Member States were challenged.

The *sedes personae* of the EC law on equal treatment: from formal equality to substantive justice?

The next attempt to extend the scope of EC law on equal treatment was made in *P* v. *S*[82] and *Grant* v. *South West Trains Ltd.*[83] Any attempt to apply existing UK legislation to transsexuals and homosexuals had failed in the national courts.[84] Therefore, EC law was the last resort as a means of achieving 'equal treatment' under the existing legal rules.[85] There is a particular interrelationship between the two referrals: by the time *P* v. *S* was decided by the ECJ, the *Grant* case had already begun.[86]

P v. *S* concerned the equal treatment of transsexuals under Directive 76/207/EEC. *Grant* concerned equal pay for homosexuals under Article 141 (ex Article 119). Both cases ventured into new areas of Community law. Sexual orientation has always been regarded as a matter of privacy. It was only in relatively recent times that transsexuals and homosexuals discovered the fertile ground of EC law and in particular the ability of EC law to transform their political concerns into legal arguments. The Treaty of Amsterdam, however, changed the legal environment considerably. Article 141 (ex Article 119) as amended by the Treaty of Amsterdam allows the Council under certain conditions (that is, after a unanimous vote on a proposal from the Commission after

[80] Judgment of 26 October 1999, Case C-273/97, *Sirdar* v. *(1) Army Board and (2) Secretary of State for Defence* [1999] ECR I-7403, para. 27.

[81] Judgment of 11 January 2000, Case C-285/98, *Kreil* v. *Germany* [2000] ECR I-69, para. 17.

[82] Case C-13/94, *P* v. *S and Cornwall County Council* [1996] ECR I-2145.

[83] Case C-249/96, *Grant* v. *South West Trains Ltd* [1998] ECR I-623.

[84] For a brief discussion of the UK law prior to *P* v. *S*, see P. Skidmore, 'Sex, Gender and Comparators in Employment Discrimination' (1997) 26 *Industrial Law Journal* 51, who distinguishes between (1) true sex issues, (2) sex and gender and (3) sex and sexual orientation.

[85] *Ibid.*, 56.

[86] L. Flynn, 'Case Note on C-13/94, P v. S and Cornwall County Council' (1997) 34 *Common Market Law Review* 367 at 383; *Grant* v. *South West Trains Ltd* [1996] IRLR 342, Employment Appeal Tribunal.

consulting the European Parliament), to take appropriate action to eliminate various forms of discrimination, including discrimination based on sexual orientation. The scene was therefore set for the development of EC law in this area. The appellants had to overcome the argument that the issues in question did not yet come under Community law, at least not until further legislative changes were introduced.

P v. *S* involved the dismissal of a transsexual, on account of gender reassignment. The person concerned stated her intention of undergoing surgery in order to change her biological sex (male) to suit her sexual identity (female). In April 1991, P was taken on as a manager at an educational establishment operated by Cornwall County Council. A year later, P told S, the principal and chief executive of the establishment, that she intended to undergo a 'sex-change operation'. At first, S appeared supportive and tolerant, but later changed his attitude, essentially due to the opposition of the board of governors. P was finally dismissed. She therefore brought an action before an industrial tribunal claiming that she had suffered discrimination on the grounds of sex. The tribunal considered that English law provided no helpful answer in the circumstances, and in particular that no discrimination against P could be identified on the basis of sex discrimination. However, the tribunal was of the opinion that Article 3 of Directive 76/207/EEC may allow for a broader interpretation that would cover discrimination against transsexuals.

It seems that the applicant first tried to show why gender reassignment might be the only way to harmonise biological sex and sexual identity. The applicant thereby produced a large number of scholarly articles claiming that the causes of the condition at issue were to be found in biological dysfunctions which were thus already present at birth, or else in psychological disorders linked to the environment. The second line of reasoning went even further, by asking for a redefinition of sex.[87] Medical and scientific circles proposed that it was necessary to go beyond the traditional classification and recognise that, in addition to the man/woman dichotomy, there is a range of characteristics, behaviour and roles shared by men and women, so that sex itself ought rather to be thought of as a continuum.

The legal reasoning of the applicant was quite different from the usual submissions in equal treatment cases. As there was as yet no

[87] Case C-13/94, *P* v. *S and Cornwall County Council* [1996] ECR I-2153, para. 17.

precedent set by the ECJ, the applicant referred to relevant legislation and case law in the Member States as well as to judgments of the European Court of Human Rights. The debate on the proper application of Directive 76/207/EEC shifted somewhat away from Article 3 (as introduced by the industrial tribunal) to Article 5(1). Article 5(1) provides:

> Application of the principle of equal treatment with regard to working conditions, including the conditions governing dismissal, means that men and women shall be guaranteed the same conditions without discrimination on grounds of sex.

The applicant frequently referred to the fact that she would not have been dismissed if she had remained a man. The ECJ accepted the argument that, in view of the objective pursued by Directive 76/207/EEC, Article 5(1) precludes dismissal of a transsexual for a reason related to gender reassignment.[88]

P v. *S* was only a starting-point for more far-reaching litigation on the equal treatment of homosexuals. In *Grant*, the appellant was engaged as a clerical officer by the British Railways Board. In 1995, the employment was transferred to South West Trains Ltd, a wholly owned subsidiary of the British Railways Board, which was privatised in 1996. Clause 18 of her contract of employment entitled her to travel concessions. Those travel concessions were further regulated in the Staff Travel Facilities Privilege Ticket Regulations. Clause 8 of the Ticket Regulation provided, *inter alia*, that 'privilege tickets are granted for one common law opposite sex spouse of a member of staff, subject to a statutory declaration being made that a meaningful relationship has existed for a period of two years or more'. It is clear from the facts that South West Trains granted concessions to non-married couples. Lisa Grant applied for travel concessions for her female partner. When her application was rejected by reference to clause 8 of the Ticket Regulation, she brought a case against her employer before an industrial tribunal. She claimed that this denied her a part of her pay (consisting in obtaining travel concessions for her female cohabitee), in circumstances in which a male employee would obtain travel concessions for his female cohabitee, and was a breach of Article 141 (ex Article 119). The industrial tribunal referred the case to the ECJ. The test case character of *Grant* is obvious. The appellant's strategy was clearly to bring the case to the ECJ as soon as possible.

[88] *Ibid.*

Counsel for the appellant submitted four principal arguments in support of the appellant:[89]

(1) The refusal constitutes discrimination directly based on sex. Her employer's decision would have been different if the benefits in issue had been claimed by a man living with a woman, and not by a woman living with a woman.
(2) The mere fact that the male worker who previously occupied her post had obtained travel concessions for his female partner, without being married to her, is enough to identify direct discrimination based on sex. If a female worker does not receive the same benefits as a male worker, all other things being equal, she is the victim of discrimination based on sex.
(3) A refusal constitutes discrimination based on sexual orientation, which is included in the concept of discrimination based on sex in Article 141 (ex Article 119), as laid down in *P* v. *S*, in the resolutions of Community institutions and in international human rights standards.
(4) The refusal to allow her the benefits is not objectively justified.

The ECJ denied there was any discrimination prohibited by Article 141 (ex Article 119), and referred the issue of the equal treatment of homosexuals back to national and European legislators.[90] The expensive and burdensome attempt by the appellant to push the ECJ beyond equal treatment to substantive justice failed. There is a strong linkage between *Grant* and *Smith* v. *Advel Systems*. Article 141 (ex Article 119) allows for the establishment of equal opportunities for men and women but does not set standards for substantive justice.

The form of discrimination: from the prohibition of direct discrimination to the prohibition of indirect discrimination in equal pay

We have arrived in the late 1970s. *Dassonville* had been decided. The notion of 'measures having equivalent effect' had been shaped. *Cassis de Dijon* was about to be decided. There is obviously a link between the ECJ's broad understanding of barriers to trade and efforts to bring

[89] The submissions are taken here from the decision of the ECJ in Case C-249/96, *Grant* v. *South West Trains Ltd* [1998] ECR I-643, paras. 16–19.
[90] *Ibid*.

indirect discrimination under the notion of pay.[91] In *Jenkins*, Kingsgate Clothing Productions paid full-time workers 10 per cent more per hour than part-time employees in order to discourage absenteeism in their factory and to achieve a more efficient use of their machinery. All but one of the part-time workers were women. The applicant, Mrs Jenkins, a female part-time worker, complained that the difference in pay between herself and a full-time male employee contravened the equality clause in her contract of employment. The industrial tribunal dismissed her complaint on the ground that, although she was employed on like work as the man, the fact that the man was full-time was a material difference other than the difference of sex within the meaning of section 1(3) of the Equal Pay Act 1970, which justified a different rate of pay. On appeal, the Employment Appeal Tribunal referred the following questions to the ECJ:[92]

1. Does the principle of equal pay, contained in [Article 141 (ex Article 119)] of the EEC Treaty and Article 1 of the Council Directive 75/117/EEC require that the pay for work at time rates shall be the same, irrespective: (a) of the number of hours worked each week; or (b) of whether it is of commercial benefit to the employer to encourage the doing of the maximum possible hours of work and consequently to pay a higher rate to workers doing forty hours per week than to workers doing fewer than forty hours per week?
2. If the answer to Question 1(a) or (b) is in the negative, what criteria should be used in determining whether or not the principle of equal pay applies where there is a difference in the time rates of pay related to the total number of hours worked each week?
3. Would the answer to Question 1(a) or (b) or 2 be different (and, if so, in what respects) if it were shown that a considerably smaller amount of male workers is able to perform the minimum number of hours each week required to qualify for the full hourly rate of pay?

Mrs Jenkins pointed out that Article 141 (ex Article 119) and Article 1 of Directive 75/117/EEC applied to *part-time workers* as well.[93]

[91] G. More, 'The Principle of Equal Treatment: From Market Unifier to Fundamental Right?' in P. Craig and G. de Búrca (eds.), *The Evolution of EU Law* (Oxford, 1999), 517.

[92] Case 96/80, *Jenkins* v. *Kingsgate (Clothing Productions) Ltd* [1981] ECR 911.

[93] The arguments are taken from the written observations submitted to the ECJ in Case 96/80, *Jenkins* v. *Kingsgate (Clothing Productions) Ltd* [1981] ECR 911 at 915.

She presented her issue within its wider context, recalling that by far the majority of part-time workers in the Community at that time were women, and that, in the UK, the proportion of women in part-time work was even greater than in the other Member States. Section 1(3) of the Equal Pay Act 1970 provided that a variation between a woman's contract and that of a man is justifiable if the employer proves that it is due to a material difference (other than sex) between her case and his. Then she drew attention to the principle enunciated by the United States Supreme Court in *Griggs* v. *Duke Power Co.*,[94] according to which what must be prohibited are not only practices which are *intended* to discriminate but equally those which are discriminatory *in their effect*, irrespective of the intentions of their authors, thereby refuting the counter-argument of the respondents who were strongly relying on 'intention' as a necessary requirement for the assumption of indirect discrimination. The only reference point in EC law on equal treatment at that time was *Defrenne*.[95] Therefore, Mrs Jenkins recalled the double aim, economic and social, of Article 141 (ex Article 119) and asserted that that aim would be frustrated if the principle of equal pay was effectively confined to full-time workers. If an employer wished to encourage his employees to work longer hours, he should pay a suitable overtime rate and not reduce the pay of those working part-time. Basically, she relied on the wording of Article 141 (ex Article 119), paragraph (2)(b) of which states that 'pay for work at time rates shall be the same for the same job'. The deciding factor as to whether the job is the same is the nature of the work performed by the workers concerned and not the hours worked each week.

The appellant conceded, however, that there might be reasons such as superior skills or qualifications and a longer period of service which would justify a pay difference. Such exceptions to the principle of equal pay, however, need to be strictly confined to real and relevant differences. Mrs Jenkins put emphasis on 'job-related' justifications in order to refute the argument that the extra costs incurred as a result of part-time workers were sufficient justification for the pay difference.

The ECJ had no difficulty in applying Article 141 (ex Article 119) directly to part-time work. The ECJ said that discrimination occurred

[94] Case 96/80, *Jenkins* v. *Kingsgate (Clothing Productions) Ltd* [1981] ECR 911 at 916, as quoted in the report of the hearing.

[95] Case 43/75, *Defrenne II* [1976] ECR 455.

if the difference in pay was an indirect way of reducing the pay of part-time workers who were exclusively or predominantly women.[96] Where the national courts are able to establish that the payment of lower hourly rates of remuneration for part-time work than for full-time work represents discrimination based on a difference of sex, the provisions of Article 141 (ex Article 119) will apply directly to such a situation.[97] The ECJ thereby brought Article 141 (ex Article 119) into line with its case law on freedom of trade under Article 28 (ex Article 30).

The determination of discrimination: direct discrimination and pregnancy

Since the early 1990s, a series of cases before the ECJ has arisen on the applicability and reach of Article 2(1) of Directive 76/207/EEC in cases in which women contended that they had been discriminated against on the grounds of pregnancy and motherhood.[98] *Webb* v. *EMO Air Cargo (UK) Ltd*[99] was referred to the ECJ by the House of Lords in 1992 to clarify possible contradictions between the Dutch *Dekker*[100] and the Danish *Hertz*[101] cases, which were both decided in 1990. Mrs Dekker had applied for a job with Vormingscentrum voor Jong Volwassenen (VJV), and informed the selection committee that she was three months pregnant. The committee recommended her to the board as being the most suitable candidate for the job, but the board decided not to employ her. The reason was that, under the applicable Dutch law, VJV would have been required to pay Mrs Dekker 100 per cent of her salary while she was absent owing to her confinement, but would not have been in a position to recover the amount so paid from its insurers because her pregnancy was a condition which was known about at the time her employment would have commenced. Mrs Hertz gave birth to her child after a complicated pregnancy during which she was

[96] Case 96/80, *Jenkins* v. *Kingsgate (Clothing Productions) Ltd* [1981] ECR 911 at 928.

[97] The true significance of *Jenkins* then is that it binds the national courts to the directly applicable Art. 141 (ex Art. 119); see D. Krimphove, *Europäisches Arbeitsrecht* (2nd edn, Munich, 2001), 182.

[98] With regard to the particular UK background, see Bagilhole and Byrne, 'From Hard to Soft Law', in Hantrais (ed.), *Gendered Policies in Europe*, 130.

[99] Case C-32/93, *Webb* v. *EMO Air Cargo (UK) Ltd* [1994] ECR I-3569.

[100] Case 177/88, *Dekker* v. *Stichting Vormingscentrum voor Jonge Volwassenen Plus* [1990] ECR I-3941.

[101] Case C-179/88, *Handels- og Kontorfunktionaerernes Forbund i Danmark (Union of Clerical and Commercial Employees) (for Hertz)* v. *Dansk Arbejdsgiverforening (Danish Employers Association) (for Aldi Marked K/S)* [1990] ECR I-3979.

on sick leave with the consent of her employer. She was given maternity leave, but later took frequent periods of sick leave due to complications arising from her confinement. After these had amounted to 100 days in one year, her employer gave her notice of dismissal. The ECJ had decided *Dekker*, but not *Hertz*, in favour of the appellant.

Webb lasted for more than six years. The decision of the Court of Appeal,[102] the reference by the House of Lords[103] and the final decision of the House of Lords[104] after the ECJ had given its answer, raised much concern in the UK. In 1987, EMO Air Cargo engaged Mrs Webb to replace another employee who had become pregnant and who had been given three months' maternity leave. The employer required the appellant to start working immediately in order to undertake six months' training. Two weeks after starting work, the appellant discovered that she was pregnant and when she informed her employer of the fact she was dismissed. The industrial tribunal dismissed her claim, holding that the real reason for her dismissal had been the fact that it was impossible for her to carry out the primary task for which she had been recruited, namely, to replace Mrs Stewart during the latter's absence on maternity leave.[105] A male employee in the same situation would have been dismissed too, if he had requested leave of absence during the period in question. Mrs Webb's subsequent appeals, first to the Employment Appeal Tribunal and then to the Court of Appeal, were both unsuccessful. She finally appealed to the House of Lords, which sought answers from the ECJ on the following questions:

> Is it discrimination on grounds of sex contrary to Council Directive 76/207/EEC for an employer to dismiss a female employee:
>
> (a) whom he engaged for the specific purpose of replacing (after training) another female employee during the latter's forthcoming maternity leave;
> (b) when, very shortly after appointment, the employer discovers that the appellant herself will be absent on maternity leave during the maternity leave of the other employee, and the employer dismisses her because he needs the job holder to be at work during that period;

102 *Webb* v. *EMO Air Cargo (UK) Ltd* [1992] 2 All ER 43, Court of Appeal.
103 *Webb* v. *EMO Air Cargo (UK) Ltd* [1992] 4 All ER 929, House of Lords.
104 *Webb* v. *EMO Air Cargo (UK) Ltd* [1995] 4 All ER 577, House of Lords.
105 As quoted in *Webb* v. *EMO Air Cargo (UK) Ltd* [1992] 2 All ER 43 at 48, Court of Appeal.

(c) had the employer known of the pregnancy of the appellant at the date of appointment, she would not have been appointed; and

(d) the employer would similarly have dismissed a male employee engaged for this purpose who required leave of absence at the relevant time for medical and other reasons?

For a better understanding of the issues to be decided at the EC level, it might be useful briefly to present the national background to the case. The Sex Discrimination Act 1975 distinguishes between *direct* discrimination under section 1(1)(a) (discrimination on the grounds of sex, that is, situations in which a woman is accorded, on account of her sex, less favourable treatment than that accorded to men) and *indirect* discrimination under section 1(1)(b) (which consists in applying to a woman a requirement or condition which, although applying equally to a man, is to the woman's detriment or is in any event more difficult for her to comply with). Section 5(3) of the Act is of particular interest here as it provides that a comparison of persons of different sex or marital status with regard to direct *and* indirect discrimination 'must be such that the relevant circumstances in the one case are the same, or not materially different, in the other'. Two main controversies on the reach of the national law dominated the course of litigation in the national courts: whether there was direct or indirect discrimination, and whether Mrs Webb was treated less favourably than a hypothetical man.

Counsel for the appellant argued as follows:[106]

(1) The correct test for determining whether a woman has been discriminated against on the ground of her sex is to ask whether the woman would have received the same treatment as a man but for her sex.[107]

(2) It follows therefore that a woman who is dismissed for any reason related to her pregnancy would not have been dismissed but for her sex, and is thus discriminated against on the ground of her sex.

[106] *Webb* v. *EMO Air Cargo (UK) Ltd* [1992] 2 All ER 43 at 51, Court of Appeal.

[107] This test derives from the speech of Lord Goff in *Equal Opportunities Commission* v. *Birmingham City Council* [1989] 1 All ER 769 at 774; [1989] AC 1155 at 1194, a speech with which all the other members of the House agreed. The *dictum* was quoted and applied by Lord Bridge in *James* v. *Eastleigh Borough Council* [1990] 2 All ER 607 at 611; [1990] 2 AC 751 at 764.

(3) It is incorrect to make a comparison with a man who is suffering from medical condition. Pregnancy is not an illness.
(4) If this were to be wrong and not every dismissal of a pregnant woman related to her condition of pregnancy amounts to discrimination, then nevertheless in Mrs Webb's case the only proper conclusion to draw is that the employer has discriminated against her.

It was left to the Court of Appeal to fully consider the implications of national and EC law. The Court of Appeal took ample time to consider carefully the implications of *Dekker* and *Hertz* for the present case. It perceived an equivocation in the ECJ's case law. Whereas *Dekker* clearly excluded any comparison of a pregnant woman with a man in a similar position, *Hertz* was read so as to reintroduce the need for a male comparator where pregnancy-related illness extended beyond the period of maternity leave, arguing that illness at this time was no different from that of men.[108] Mrs Webb relied on *Dekker* as the appropriate reference case to conclude that there was *direct* discrimination in her case and that there was no means under EC law to justify her dismissal.[109] Such a reading, however, would have created difficulties in English law. The relevant sections of the Sex Discrimination Act 1975 do not allow for such a conclusion. The House of Lords noted in particular the fact that the pregnant woman who was dismissed had been recruited precisely in order to replace, at least initially, an employee who was herself due to take maternity leave.[110]

The ECJ held that Article 2(1) of Directive 76/207/EEC precludes dismissal of an employee who was recruited for an unlimited term with a view initially to replacing another employee during the latter's maternity leave and who cannot do so because, shortly after her recruitment, she is herself found to be pregnant.[111] There seems to be no means to justify direct discrimination against a pregnant woman by reference to a hypothetical man in a comparable position. Since *Webb*, further

[108] There is ample evidence that the difference between *Dekker* and *Hertz* must be seen as the justification for why the Court of Appeal did not refer the case to the ECJ, Fredman, 'European Community Discrimination Law', 119 at 122 and 123; N. Burrows, 'Maternity Rights in Europe – An Embryonic Legal Regime' (1991) 11 *Yearbook of European Law* 273 at 282; Docksey, 'The Principles of Equality', 259 at 267 and 275.

[109] *Webb* v. *EMO Air Cargo (UK) Ltd* [1992] 2 All ER 43 at 55, Court of Appeal, where it is clear from the facts that counsel relied on para. 12 of the *Dekker* judgment.

[110] Case C-32/93, *Webb* v. *EMO Air Cargo (UK) Ltd* [1994] ECR I-3583, para. 14; see also Advocate-General Tesauro's Opinion, *ibid.*, 3569, para. 1 and *ibid.*, 3773, para. 9.

[111] Case C-32/93, *Webb* v. *EMO Air Cargo (UK) Ltd* [1994] ECR I-3589.

cases, such as *Brown*,[112] have been brought before the ECJ in order to test the reach and forms of direct discrimination resulting from pregnancy. These cases may be read as an attempt to break the taboo[113] of whether or not direct sex discrimination may be justifiable. Although the story is not yet over, Article 2(7) of Directive 2002/73/EC[114] is quite clear about the unlawfulness of pregnancy-related discrimination.

The threshold of indirect discrimination: the justification requirement

Prior to Directive 2002/73/EC, EC law on equal treatment laid down different standards for the justification of *direct* and *indirect* discrimination.[115] Direct discrimination on grounds of sex had a high threshold of justification.[116] Justification was not excluded, but was bound to a strict regime. The baseline of the ECJ's understanding was made clear in *Johnston*,[117] and was confirmed in *Sirdar*[118] and *Kreil*.[119] Directive 76/207/EEC formulates a number of derogations which may justify discrimination. These have been subject to Euro-litigation, not by way of references from the UK but by references from Germany, where 'positive discrimination' is a governmental policy. Two of the German *Länder* had adopted specific legislation on 'women's quotas' in order to remove imbalances in the employment rates between men and women. In *Kalanke*,[120] the ECJ read into Articles 2 and 4 of Directive 76/207/EEC a prohibition on so-called 'hard quotas'. However, the ECJ

[112] Case C-394/96, *Brown* v. *Rentokil* [1998] ECR I-4185; [1998] 2 CMLR 1049; on this case, see M. Wynn, 'Pregnancy Discrimination: Equality, Protection or Reconciliation' (1999) 62 *Modern Law Review* 435.

[113] J. Bowers and E. Moran, 'Justification in Direct Sex Discrimination Law: Breaking the Taboo' (2002) 31 *Industrial Law Journal* 307.

[114] OJ 2002 No. L269, 5 October 2002, 17. Art. 2(7) provides as follows: 'Less favourable treatment of a woman related to pregnancy or maternity leave within the meaning of Directive 92/85/EC shall constitute discrimination within the meaning of this Directive.'

[115] The new Directive is meant to establish a coherent concept, thereby providing for a legal definition of what might constitute direct and indirect discrimination.

[116] E. Szyszczak, '"The Status to Be Accorded to Motherhood": Case C-32/93, *Webb* v. *EMO Air Cargo (UK) Ltd*' (1995) 58 *Modern Law Review* 860 at 864, therefore concludes that the term 'justification' is confusing in the context of direct discrimination, and that it would be better to talk of 'derogations'.

[117] Case 222/84, *Johnston* v. *Chief Constable of the Royal Ulster Constabulary* [1986] ECR 1651.

[118] Judgment of 26 October 1999, Case C-273/97, *Sirdar* v. *(1) Army Board and (2) Secretary of State for Defence* [1999] ECR I-7403.

[119] Judgment of 11 January 2000, Case C-285/98, *Kreil* v. *Germany* [2000] ECR I-69.

[120] Case C-450/93, *Kalanke* v. *Freie Hansestadt Bremen* [1995] ECR I-3053.

modified its position in *Marschall* v. *Land Nordrhein-Westfalen*[121] by clarifying that the phrase 'same qualifications' does not mean 'same chances'. Therefore, soft quotas are compatible with EC law. It is a subject of great debate in Germany as to what a state may do in order actively to promote substantive justice. There is no comparable development of 'positive discrimination' in the UK.[122]

The UK's contribution to equal treatment focused on *indirect* discrimination and the possible objective justifications of indirect discrimination. Again, a parallel can be drawn with the *Dassonville* and *Cassis de Dijon* case law on Article 28 (ex Article 30). Once the ECJ admitted that indirect discrimination is covered by Article 141 (ex Article 119), it became necessary to define the scope and reach of the possible derogations therefrom. The point first appeared in *Jenkins*, although in retrospect one may wonder whether the ECJ realised at the time that it was dealing with indirect discrimination, and that there was a need to clarify whether the 'extra costs' incurred as a result of employing part-time workers may be regarded as sufficient justification.[123] However, since *Jenkins*, the UK courts have permitted *economic* arguments to justify indirect discrimination.[124] *Bilka-Kaufhaus*,[125] a German case, provided the ECJ with an opportunity to give shape to the scope and reach of measures which might legitimise indirect discrimination. The so-called *Bilka* test that any reasons which justify indirect discrimination on economic grounds must (a) meet a genuine need of the enterprise, (b) be suitable for attaining the objective pursued by the enterprise and (c) be necessary for that purpose.[126] *Bilka-Kaufhaus* served to raise UK standards of equal treatment beyond *Jenkins*. *Enderby*[127] allowed the ECJ to consider the scope of objective justifications afresh, and

[121] Case C-409/95, *Marschall* v. *Land Nordrhein Westfalen* [1997] ECR I-6363; for a UK perspective, see Barnard, 'The Principle of Equality', 352 at 366; for a German perspective, see Reich, *Bürgerrechte in der Europäischen Union*, para. 18 Diskriminierungsschutz, 225.

[122] E. Szyszczak, 'Positive Action after Kalanke' (1996) 59 *Modern Law Review* 876.

[123] T. Hervey, 'Justification for Indirect Sex Discrimination in Employment: European Community and United Kingdom Law Compared' (1991) 40 *International and Comparative Law Quarterly* 807.

[124] Fredman, 'European Community Discrimination Law', 119 at 131.

[125] Case 170/84, *Bilka-Kaufhaus GmbH* v. *Weber von Hartz* [1986] ECR 1607; [1986] 2 CMLR 701; see Hervey, 'Justification for Indirect Sex Discrimination', 807 at 810.

[126] Case 170/84, *Bilka-Kaufhaus GmbH* v. *Weber von Hartz* [1986] ECR 1607; [1986] 2 CMLR 701, paras. 31 and 37.

[127] Case C-127/92, *Enderby* v. *Frenchay Health Authority and Secretary of State for Health* [1993] ECR I-5535.

to address the suggested discriminatory effect of collective bargaining agreements directly – which is not possible under UK law.[128]

Dr Enderby was employed as a speech therapist by the Frenchay Health Authority, part of the UK's National Health Service. She considered herself to be a victim of *indirect* sex discrimination due to the fact that, at her level of seniority within the National Health Service, members of her profession – overwhelmingly a female profession – were appreciably less well paid than members of comparable professions in which, at an equivalent professional level, there were more men than women. In 1989, an industrial tribunal dismissed her application on the ground that the differences in pay were the result of structures specific to each profession, in particular to separate collective bargaining arrangements, which were not discriminatory. The industrial tribunal rejected the health authority's argument that the difference in pay between speech therapists and pharmacists was merely a consequence of the market forces in employment.[129] The Employment Appeal Tribunal, by contrast, considered that market forces played some part in the difference in pay between speech therapists and pharmacists, and that that was enough to justify the difference in pay. The Court of Appeal finally referred a set of questions to the ECJ:[130]

1. Does the principle of equal pay enshrined in [Article 141 (ex Article 119)] require the employer to justify objectively the difference in pay between job A (speech therapy) and job B (pharmacy)?
2. If the answer to question 1 is in the affirmative, can the employer rely as sufficient [justification for the] difference in pay upon the

[128] UK law at that time dealt with grievances arising out of collective bargaining agreements as individual complaints: see Sex Discrimination Act 1975, section 77; and Fredman, 'European Community Discrimination Law', 119 at 133.

[129] The underlying issue was whether the Equal Pay Act 1970 was designed to equalise pay or merely to prevent discrimination. If the latter was the case, the court might legitimately take the narrow view of discrimination adopted by the Sex Discrimination Act 1975, section 1(1)(b), which required the claimant to identify a requirement or condition which fewer women than men could comply with. Wood J took the view that the UK legislation was never intended to eliminate all wage differences; rather, it was meant to prohibit discrimination on the ground of sex. Unless discrimination was found in the process of wage-fixing itself, the statute was not contravened. The policy behind the decision was to limit the intervention of law in wage structuring. M. Wynn, 'Equal Pay and Gender Segregation' (1994) 110 *Law Quarterly Review* 556 at 558.

[130] Case C-127/92, *Enderby* v. *Frenchay Health Authority and Secretary of State for Health* [1993] ECR I-5535 at 5541.

fact that the pay of jobs A and B respectively have been determined by different collective bargaining processes which (considered separately) do not discriminate on grounds of sex and do not operate so as to disadvantage women because of their sex?

3. If the employer is able to establish that at times there are serious shortages of suitable candidates for job B and that he pays the higher remuneration to holders of job B but it can be established that only part of the difference in pay between job B and job A is due to the need to attract suitable candidates to job B, (a) is the whole difference of pay objectively justified; (b) is the part (but only that part) of the difference which is due to the need to attract suitable candidates to job B objectively justified; or (c) must the employer equalise the pay of jobs A and B on the grounds that he has failed to show that the whole of the difference is objectively justified?

Dr Enderby submitted in respect of the first question that there was indirect discrimination under the circumstances set out by the Court of Appeal unless the employer could objectively justify the difference in pay. That followed from the mere fact that a group of workers consisting almost exclusively of women was paid less than a group of workers consisting mainly of men and the two groups did work of equal value. In support of her argument, she cited *Bilka-Kaufhaus*,[131] *Teuling*,[132] *Rinner-Kühn*,[133] *Ruzius-Wilbrink*,[134] *Kowalska*,[135] *Nimz*[136] and *Commission* v. *Belgium*[137] in order to demonstrate that only objective justifications which meet the three-pronged approach of the *Bilka* test were acceptable.

As to the second question, Dr Enderby argued that the employer cannot rely on the fact that the pay rates derive from two different, non-discriminatory, collective bargaining processes as a sufficient justification for the difference in pay. She referred to the identical position taken on this point by the UK in *Danfoss*,[138] that is, that the existence

[131] Case 170/84, *Bilka-Kaufhaus GmbH* v. *Weber von Hartz* [1986] ECR 1607; [1986] 2 CMLR 701.

[132] Case 30/85, *Teuling* [1987] ECR 2497.

[133] Case 171/88, *Rinner-Kühn* v. *FWW Spezial-Gebäudereinigung GmbH & Co. KG* [1989] ECR 2743.

[134] Case 102/88, *Ruzius-Wilbrink* [1989] ECR 4311.

[135] Case C-33/89, *Kowalska* v. *Freie und Hansestadt Hamburg* [1990] ECR I-2591.

[136] Case C-184/89, *Nimz* v. *Freie und Hansestadt Hamburg* [1991] ECR I-297.

[137] Case C-229/89, *Commission* v. *Belgium* [1991] ECR I-2205.

[138] Case 109/88, *Danfoss* [1989] ECR 3199.

of different collective bargaining agreements cannot in itself provide an objective justification for a serious adverse impact on women.

On the third question, Dr Enderby submitted that, since only a very small part of the pay difference was due to the state of the employment market, the employer could not rely on that factor to justify the difference in whole or in part (solution (c) in question 3). Just as a woman claiming equal pay had to show that her work is of equal value, the employer had to show that the whole of the difference is due to a gender-neutral factor. If the employer succeeded in providing evidence, only that part would be justified (solution (b) in question 3).

The ECJ was quite outspoken in its views.[139] Statistics sufficed to demonstrate that there was indirect discrimination (question 1), and the use of separate collective bargaining processes was not a sufficient objective justification for the difference in pay (question 2). However, it was for the national courts to determine, if necessary by applying the principle of proportionality, whether and to what extent the shortage of candidates for a job and the need to attract them by higher pay constituted an objectively justified economic ground for the difference in pay (questions 3).

It is questionable whether *Enderby* provides sufficient guidance for the English courts to handle indirect discrimination.[140] However, the codification of the case law in Directive 2002/73/EC may be the turning point in the battle to eliminate indirect discrimination through the ECJ – although Article 2(2), second indent, and Article 2(6) of the Directive provide enough leeway for further litigation.[141]

Rights and remedies: the development of effective legal protection

Previously, two Articles of Directive 76/207/EEC constituted the basis of EC law on rights and remedies in equal treatment litigation. Article 5 provided as follows:[142]

[139] Case C-127/92, *Enderby* v. *Frenchay Health Authority and Secretary of State for Health* [1993] ECR I-5535 at 5576.

[140] M. Connolly, 'How an ECJ Decision on Equal Pay May Affect British Indirect Discrimination Law' (1996) 1 *Web Journal of Current Legal Issues* 1, with reference to UK case law.

[141] For a first analysis, see pp. 265–8 below.

[142] They have now been merged into one single Article, Art. 6, by Directive 2002/73/EC, OJ 2002 No. L269, 5 October 2002, 15.

> 1. Application of the principle of equal treatment with regard to working conditions, including the conditions governing dismissal, means that men and women shall be guaranteed the same conditions without discrimination on grounds of sex.
> 2. To this end, Member States shall take the measures necessary to ensure that:
>   (a) any laws, regulations and administrative provisions contrary to the principle of equal treatment shall be abolished;
>   (b) any provisions contrary to the principle of equal treatment which are included in collective bargaining agreements, individual contracts of employment, internal rules of undertakings or in rules governing the independent occupations and professions shall be, or may be declared, null and void or may be amended;
>   (c) those laws, regulations and administrative provisions contrary to the principle of equal treatment when the concern for protection which originally inspired them is no longer well founded shall be revised; and that where similar provisions are included in collective bargaining agreements labour and management shall be requested to undertake the desired revision.

Article 6 provided as follows:

> Member States shall introduce into their national legal systems such measures as are necessary to enable all persons who consider themselves wronged by failure to apply to them the principle of equal treatment within the meaning of Articles 3, 4 and 5 to pursue their claims by judicial process after possible recourse to other competent authorities.

In *Marshall I*, the ECJ ruled that Article 5 has direct effect. Article 6, however, had a longer and more inconsistent history. Although in *von Colson*[143] the ECJ at first denied any direct effect to Article 6, it later accepted, in *Johnston*, that the first limb of Article 6, that is, in respect of the availability of appropriate judicial remedies, had direct effect. The question of the direct effect of the second limb of Article 6, that is, the obligation to impose sanctions, was also raised in *Johnston*, and even more pressingly in *Foster*. In *Marshall II*, the ECJ reversed the

[143] Case 14/83, *Von Colson and Kamann* v. *Land Nordrhein-Westfalen* [1984] ECR 1891 at 1908; on this case, see J. Shaw, 'European Community Judicial Method: Its Application to Sex Discrimination Law' (1990) 19 *Industrial Law Journal* 228, n. 33.

position it took in *von Colson* and *Johnston* and granted direct effect to both limbs of Article 6.

The German and English courts have for a long time been engaged in efforts to give shape to the notion of adequate sanctions as set out in *von Colson*.[144] The uncertainties and inconsistencies of the law, especially in the German and English courts, may have been the reason why the ECJ reversed its earlier case law and gave Article 6 a much clearer 'European interpretation'. *Coote*,[145] *Levez*[146] and *Preston*[147] document the ongoing efforts of the ECJ to define more clearly the reach of 'effective legal protection' in equal treatment litigation. However, the ECJ's interpretation has now been codified in the revised Article 6(1) of Directive 76/207/EEC as amended by Directive 2002/73/EC.[148] The revised Article 6(1) of Directive 76/207/EEC now provides as follows:

> Member States shall ensure that judicial and/or administrative procedures, including where they deem it appropriate conciliation procedures, for the enforcement of obligations under this Directive are available to all persons who consider themselves wronged by failure to apply the principle of equal treatment to them, even after the relationship in which the discrimination is alleged to have occurred has ended.

The vertical direct effect of Article 5 of Directive 76/207/EEC

The facts of the *Marshall* litigation are as follows. Mrs Marshall worked from July 1966 to March 1980 as a senior dietician for the Southampton and South West Hampshire Area Health Authority, a part of the UK's National Health Service. At the age of 62, she was dismissed on the ground that she had passed the age of 60, the normal retirement age for women and the age at which women in the UK were entitled to collect a state pension. In the course of the proceedings which Mrs Marshall brought against her employer on grounds of discrimination,

[144] See *ibid.*, 228, on the – indirect – interplay between the German and the UK courts in legitimising the ECJ in its efforts to 'grasp the nettle' and reverse its earlier case law.

[145] Case C-185/97, *Coote* v. *Granada Hospitality Ltd* [1998] ECR I-5199.

[146] Case C-326/96, *Levez* v. *T. H. Jennings (Harlow Pools) Ltd* [1998] ECR I-7835; [1999] All ER (EC) 1.

[147] Case C-78/98, *Preston* v. *Wolverhampton Healthcare NHS Trust* [2000] ECR I-3201.

[148] See also recital 17 to Directive 2002/73/EC.

the Court of Appeal made a reference to the ECJ under Article 234 (ex Article 177).

The ECJ held[149] that a general policy concerning the dismissal of a woman solely because she had attained or passed the qualifying age for a state pension, which age is different under national legislation for men and for women, constitutes discrimination on the ground of sex and is contrary to Article 5(1) of Directive 76/207/EEC. The ECJ, however, did not confine itself to determining the case at hand, but in addition went on to develop the far-reaching principle that Directives may have direct effect, more specifically that an individual may rely on Article 5(1) against a state authority acting in its capacity as employer, in order to avoid the application of any national provision which does not conform to that Article.

The facts of *Foster* highlight the overwhelming importance of rights granted under Article 5(1). Mrs Foster and five other appellants were former employees of the British Gas Corporation (BGC). Upon its privatisation, the rights and liabilities of the BGC were transferred to British Gas plc. At the material time, the BGC was governed by the Gas Act 1972. As a matter of English law, the BGC was a 'public body' and a 'public authority' for the purposes of various domestic statutes and in English common law. The BGC was not regarded as a state agent of the Secretary of State, and its employees were not in Crown employment for the purposes of UK employment law. The appellants were required by the BGC to retire on attaining the age of 60. This was in accordance with the BGC's general retirement policy, which stated that employees had to retire when they were entitled to a state pension. In the UK, that age was 60 for women and 65 for men. Since the appellants wished to continue working beyond the age of 60 and were not allowed to do so, they presented complaints to the industrial tribunal, claiming that they had been subject to unlawful discrimination on the ground of sex, which, although not prohibited by national rules, was contrary to Article 5(1) of Directive 76/207/EEC. The industrial tribunal dismissed their applications on the ground that the BGC was not a 'state authority' within the meaning of the operative part of the judgment in *Marshall* and therefore Directive 76/207/EEC could not be relied on in this instance. That decision was confirmed by

149 Case 152/84, *Marshall* v. *Southampton and South West Hampshire Area Health Authority* [1986] ECR 723 (*Marshall I*).

the Employment Appeal Tribunal and by the Court of Appeal. It was left to the House of Lords to refer the case to the ECJ with a remarkable reference:

> Whether the British Gas Corporation (at the material time) was a body of such a type that the appellants are entitled in English courts and tribunals to rely directly upon the equal treatment Directive 76/207/EEC of 9 February 1976 so as to be entitled to a claim for damages on the ground that the retirement policy of the British Gas Corporation was contrary to the Directive.

In the order referring the case to the ECJ, the House of Lords stated that it was not in dispute between the parties that, if Directive 76/207/EEC was applicable, the BGC's practice of making men and women retire at different ages was illegal. It was further common ground that, if the Directive did not have direct effect, there was nothing unlawful in the BGC's retirement policy.

For the applicants, the challenge was to show that the BGC had to be regarded as a 'State authority' within the meaning of EC law. They considered that, in deciding whether a body is a 'State authority', the term 'State' had to be taken broadly as including all organs of the state that are engaged in commercial and similar activities. The applicants referred to the Opinion of Advocate-General Slynn in *Marshall I*[150] and to *Fratelli Costanzo SpA*.[151] The applicants pointed out that, in *Marshall* and *Johnston*, the ECJ used the words 'State', or 'organ of the State' 'emanation of the State', 'State authority' and 'public authority' interchangeably. In the applicants' opinion, the ECJ had ruled out completely the existence of any intermediate form between state organs and private bodies.[152] The English courts had raised a number of arguments to narrow down the notion of 'State', which were all rejected by the applicants. First, the Court of Appeal intended to limit the direct effect of Directives to public authorities 'charged by the State with the performance of any of the classic duties of the State'. However, such a limitation is said to be incompatible with *Marshall*, in which

[150] Advocate-General Slynn, *ibid.*, 725.

[151] Case 103/88, *Fratelli Costanzo SpA* v. *Comune di Milano* [1989] ECR 1839.

[152] In so far they refer to Case 222/84, *Johnston* v. *Chief Constable of the Royal Ulster Constabulary* [1986] ECR 1651, Case 152/84, *Marshall* v. *Southampton and South West Hampshire Area Health Authority* [1986] ECR 723 (*Marshall I*) and Case C-80/86, *Criminal proceedings against Kolpinghuis Nijmegen BV* [1987] ECR 3969.

the ECJ stated that direct effect was necessary to prevent the state from taking advantage of its own failure to comply with Community law. Secondly, the idea that the direct effect of the Directive should be limited to bodies exercising powers of the Crown is rejected by reference to *Johnston*, in which the ECJ held that the Chief Constable of the Royal Ulster Constabulary was a state authority even though he was constitutionally independent of the state. Thirdly, the applicants did not see any grounds for limiting the application of the direct effect of Directives to public authorities of a non-commercial character. Again, such a limitation was said to be incompatible with *Marshall*. Last but not least, the applicants rejected any effort to equate a state authority solely to the legislator. They cited *Becker*,[153] *Marshall* and *Johnston*, in which the respondents were able to rely on direct effect although none of the bodies in those cases had any legislative power.

The ECJ held for the first time that Article 5(1) may be relied on against a body, whatever its legal form, which has been made responsible, pursuant to a measure adopted by the state, for providing a public service under the control of the state and has for that purpose special powers beyond those which result from the normal rules applicable in relations between private individuals.

Judicial protection and adequate sanctions to compensate for discrimination: the direct effect of Article 6 of Directive 76/207/EEC

In *von Colson*,[154] the ECJ held that Article 6 was insufficiently clear and too conditional to have direct effect, and cannot therefore be relied on directly by the victim of discrimination in a national court. However, it also held that a sanction must be 'such as to guarantee real and effective judicial protection' and 'must also have a real deterrent effect on the employer'.[155] The ruling provided sufficient grounds for the German labour courts to set aside Article 611 of the German Civil Code, which allowed the victim to be compensated only for his expenses in applying for the job (postage, photocopying etc.).[156]

The next occasion on which the ECJ was able to reconsider the question of the direct effect of Article 6 of Directive 76/207/EEC was

[153] Case 8/81, *Becker* v. *Finanzamt Münster-Innenstadt* [1982] ECR 53.
[154] Case 14/83, *Von Colson and Kamann* v. *Land Nordrhein-Westfalen* [1984] ECR 1891.
[155] *Ibid.*, 1908. [156] Krimphove, *Europäisches Arbeitsrecht*, 252.

in *Johnston*.[157] Contrary to its position in *von Colson*, the ECJ was now ready to grant direct effect to the first limb, that is, effective judicial protection. As far as the obligation to impose *sanctions* for unjustified discrimination in the sense of Directive 76/207/EEC is concerned, the ECJ held in the same judgment that the second limb of Article 6 did not contain an unconditional and sufficiently precise obligation on which individuals could rely when national law did not provide for compensation. This ruling was in line with the earlier *von Colson* and *Harz* cases.[158]

This was the EC law as it stood when *Marshall II* made its way to the ECJ. *Marshall II* allowed the ECJ to address the question of whether and under what conditions the second limb of Article 6 of Directive 76/207/EEC could be granted direct effect. The reason for this may be found in the facts of the *Marshall* litigation. Subsequent to *Marshall I*, the Court of Appeal sent the case back to the industrial tribunal in order to determine the compensation to be awarded to Mrs Marshall. The health authority had already paid Mrs Marshall £6,250 under section 65(2) of the Sex Discrimination Act 1975, that being the maximum compensation payable by an industrial tribunal under the provisions of that Act. However, the industrial tribunal assessed Mrs Marshall's financial loss at £19,405, which included £1,000 in respect of injury to her feelings. The House of Lords could not, under the present law, award compensation beyond the statutory limit and therefore referred the following questions to the ECJ:

1. Where the national legislation of a Member State provides for the payment of compensation as one remedy available by judicial process to a person who has been subject to unlawful discrimination of the kind prohibited by Council Directive 76/207/EEC, is the Member State guilty of a failure to implement Article 6 of the Directive by reason of the imposition by the national legislation of an upper limit of £6,250 on the amount of compensation recoverable by such a person?
2. Where the national legislation provides for the payment of compensation as aforesaid, is it essential to the due implementation of

157 Case 222/84, *Johnston* v. *Chief Constable of the Royal Ulster Constabulary* [1986] ECR 1651, paras. 18, 19 and 58.

158 Case 14/83, *Von Colson and Kamann* v. *Land Nordrhein-Westfalen* [1984] ECR 1891, para. 27; Case 79/83, *Harz* v. *Deutsche Tradax* [1984] ECR 1921, para. 27.

Article 6 of the Directive that the compensation to be awarded (a) should not be less than the amount of the loss found to have been sustained by reason of unlawful discrimination, and (b) should include an award of interest on the principal amount of the loss so found from the date of the unlawful discrimination to the date when the compensation is paid?

3. If the national legislation of a Member State failed to implement Article 6 of the Directive in any of the respects referred to in questions 1 and 2, is a person who has been subjected to unlawful discrimination as aforesaid entitled as against an authority which is an emanation of the Member State to rely on the provision of Article 6 as overriding the limits imposed by the national legislation on the amount of compensation recoverable?

As regards the *adequacy of compensation*, Mrs Marshall considered that sanctions for breaches of Community law must be effective, proportionate and dissuasive. In particular, they must punish breaches under conditions both procedural and substantive, which are analogous to those applicable to breaches of national law of a similar nature and importance.[159] Any amount less than the full amount of compensation calculated and awarded by the industrial tribunal would fail to place Mrs Marshall in the position in which she would have been had she not been the victim of unlawful discrimination. As regards the *principle of comparability*, Mrs Marshall contended that, by virtue of the statutory limit, compensation for unlawful sex discrimination in employment was not as favourable as compensation in other, comparable fields. Claims in domestic law for unlawful discrimination other than within the realm of employment, for which the county courts in England and Wales have jurisdiction, are not subject to the statutory limits; the same applies to claims for dismissal other than by reason of discrimination alone for which the industrial tribunals have jurisdiction. Mrs Marshall pointed out that, according to the established EC case law, a national court is obliged to set aside a national rule which would prevent it from taking the necessary measures to ensure the full effectiveness of Community law rights.[160] In her opinion, the

[159] Case 199/82, *Ammistrazione delle Finanze dello Stato* v. *San Giorgio SpA* [1983] ECR 3595.

[160] Case C-106/89, *Marleasing* v. *La Comercial Internacional de Alimentacion* [1990] ECR I-4156.

industrial tribunal therefore was obliged to award her compensation which it assessed as adequate to remedy the breach of her Community law rights, setting aside where necessary the provisions of domestic law which would otherwise prevent it from doing so.

In its interpretation of Article 6, the ECJ went beyond *von Colson* and *Johnston*. A remedy may not be limited either by establishing a fixed upper limit or by excluding an award of interest. The ECJ then held that a person who had been injured as a result of a discriminatory dismissal may rely on Article 6 in order to set aside a national provision which imposed limits on the amount of compensation recoverable. Thus, Article 6 has direct effect, even with regard to the type of sanctions to be imposed. The new Article 6(2), as substituted by Directive 2002/73/EC, codified the case law, but introduced an exception.[161] The new Article 6(2) provides:

> Member States shall introduce into their national legal systems such measures as are necessary to ensure real and effective compensation or reparation as the Member States so determine for the loss and damage sustained by a person injured as a result of discrimination contrary to Article 3, in a way which is dissuasive and proportionate to the damage suffered; such compensation or reparation may not be restricted by the fixing of a prior upper limit, except in cases in which the employer can prove that the only damage suffered by an applicant as a result of discrimination within the meaning of this Directive is the refusal to take his or her job application into consideration.

Post-contractual direct effect of Article 6 of Directive 76/207/EEC: judicial protection in *Coote*

Once the ECJ had ruled that both elements of Article 6 (that is, the availability of effective judicial remedy, and the obligation to impose sanctions) had direct effect, further issues inevitably arose. Appellants read Article 6 as providing for effective judicial protection even after termination of the contract.

In *Coote*, Ms Coote was employed by Granada Hospitality between December 1992 and September 1993. During her employment, she brought proceedings alleging that she had been dismissed because of pregnancy. Those proceedings ended with a settlement between Ms

[161] One may wonder whether this ruling is compatible with EC law; see the analysis of the case law at pp. 265–8 below.

Coote and her former employer. In July 1994, Ms Coote tried to find a new job through employment agencies. Her attempts to return to employment ran into difficulties, which she attributed to a refusal by her former employer to provide a reference to one of the employment agencies. Ms Coote then brought proceedings in the industrial tribunal arguing that she had been wronged by Granada's refusal to provide references. The proceedings were dismissed when the industrial tribunal held that it had no jurisdiction. The alleged discrimination, even assuming it to be proved, had taken place *after* the end of the employment relationship.

The key notion in English law is the concept of 'victimisation', more or less identically defined in the Sex Discrimination Act 1975 and the Race Relations Act 1976. National courts had held that the Race Relations Act 1976 did not apply to acts of discrimination (including victimisation) committed by an employer against a former employee *after* the termination of the contract of employment.[162] Section 4(2) of the Race Relations Act 1976 (the equivalent provision to section 6(2) of the Sex Discrimination Act 1975) was said to be limited to events occurring during the subsistence of the relevant employment. In *Post Office* v. *Adekye*,[163] the Court of Appeal approved the Employment Appeal Tribunal's reasoning:

> It does seem unsatisfactory to us that discrimination at an appeal hearing following summary dismissal should not be covered by the [Sex Discrimination Act 1975] unless the contract of employment expressly saves the employment, pending appeal. We suspect that, if Parliament had thought about the issue, it would have wished to outlaw discrimination both at dismissal and at an appeal hearing. But, in our view, Parliament failed to do so.[164]

When hearing *Coote*, the Employment Appeal Tribunal was prepared to follow that line of argument. Nevertheless, the Employment Appeal Tribunal was uncertain whether, in light of Directive 76/207/EEC, the Sex Discrimination Act 1975, unlike the Race Relation Act 1976, had to be interpreted as prohibiting retaliatory measures whose harmful

[162] *Nagarajan* v. *Agnew*, *Nagarajan* v. *Swiggs and London Regional Transport* and *Swiggs & London Regional Transport* v. *Nagarajan* [1994] IRLR 61, Employment Appeal Tribunal; *Post Office* v. *Adekeye* [1995] IRLR 297, Employment Appeal Tribunal.

[163] *Ibid.* [164] *Ibid.*

effects were produced after the employment had ended.[165] By asking the ECJ for a preliminary ruling, the Employment Appeal Tribunal sought to ascertain whether, on the basis of Directive 76/207/EEC, Member States are obliged to introduce the measures necessary to allow a worker to bring proceedings against a former employer, if the worker considers that the motive for the employer's refusal to provide references was that the employer resented having been made a defendant in sex discrimination proceedings brought by the worker.[166]

Counsel for the appellant relied heavily on *von Colson*[167] and *Marshall II.*[168] According to counsel, the purpose of the Directive was to ensure that real equality of opportunity for women and men in the labour market was understood as a fundamental right which could not be upheld unless effective remedies were available for employees who had suffered discrimination whether during employment or after the employment had been terminated. There is, it was submitted, nothing in Directive 76/207/EEC to suggest that its scope is limited to acts of discrimination or victimisation by an employer against a current employee. If an employer is free to victimise a former employee who has brought proceedings against him for sex discrimination by, for example, refusing to provide that employee with a reference, the objective of the Directive is severely undermined. Employees will be deterred from pursuing claims of sex discrimination for fear that their future employment prospects may be permanently blighted if their employer chooses to victimise them in this way.

The ECJ held,[169] contrary to the view advocated by Advocate-General Mischo,[170] that Article 6 of Directive 76/207/EEC requires Member States to introduce into their legal systems such measures as are necessary to ensure judicial protection for workers whose employer, after the employment relationship has ended, refuses to provide references as a reaction to legal proceedings brought to enforce compliance with the principle of equal treatment within the meaning of

[165] Case C-185/97, *Coote* v. *Granada Hospitality Ltd* [1998] ECR I-5199.

[166] Advocate-General Mischo, *ibid.*, para. 2.

[167] Case 14/83, *Von Colson and Kamann* v. *Land Nordrhein-Westfalen* [1984] ECR 1891, paras. 15–18 and 22–3.

[168] Case C-271/91, *Marshall* v. *Southampton and South West Hampshire Area Health Authority* (*Marshall II*) [1993] ECR I-4367.

[169] Case C-185/97, *Coote* v. *Granada Hospitality Ltd* [1998] ECR I-5199 at 5223.

[170] *Ibid.*, 5210.

that Directive. The ruling in *Coote* has not, however, been codified in the revised Article 6(2) of Directive 76/207/EEC.

The principle of equivalence and the principle of effectiveness in Article 6 of Directive 76/207/EEC: *Levez*

Levez v. *Jennings*[171] was the first decision in which the principles of equivalence and effectiveness were fully discussed. There were early attempts by the ECJ to get to grips with possible differences of national and EC law remedies, particularly in *Comet.*[172] None of these cases, however, had required the ECJ to decide on the issue of the equivalence and effectiveness of national and EC judicial remedies. In *Levez*, the point at issue was in relation to differences in *time limits* between, on the one hand, claims under the Equal Pay Act 1970 (two years) and, on the other, claims under the Limitation Act 1980 and the Race Relations Act 1976 (six years). The Equal Opportunities Commission had tried to convince the UK government that UK law was in breach of Community law. However, in line with the UK government's policy at the time, the Equal Opportunities Commission was first required to take the case to the ECJ.[173]

In February 1991, the appellant, Mrs Levez, was employed by the respondent, Jennings (Harlow Pools) Ltd, as the manager of a betting shop in Cheltenham, at a salary of £10,000 per annum. In October 1991, the appellant was appointed manager of another of the respondent's shops, situated in Billericay, Essex. She replaced a male manager, Mr Albert Fuller, in that job. Mrs Levez became aware that Mr Fuller had received a higher salary than herself, and consequently asked for a pay increase. She was informed by the respondent's operations manager that Mr Fuller had been paid £10,800 and her salary was raised to that level from 30 December 1991. In fact, Mr Fuller had been paid £11,400 since September 1990. In April 1992, Mrs Levez's salary was increased to £11,400, as a part of a salary review conducted by the respondent. Mr Fuller had left the respondent's employment by that date. Mrs Levez left the respondent's employment in 1993. Having

[171] Case C-326/96, *Levez* v. *T. H. Jennings (Harlow Pools) Ltd* [1998] ECR I-7835; [1999] All ER (EC) 1.

[172] Case 45/76, *Comet BV* v. *Produktschap voor Siergewassen* [1976] ECR 2043, paras. 12–19.

[173] B. Napier, 'Proving Equal Value – The European Court Lends a Hand' (1993) 19 *New Law Journal* 1648.

subsequently discovered the true level of Mr Fuller's salary, Mrs Levez brought a claim of equal pay on 16 September 1993, under the Equal Pay Act 1970. The industrial tribunal first confirmed her claim but at the request of the respondent ruled in accordance with section 2(5) of the 1970 Act that Mrs Levez was not entitled to arrears of pay for any period prior to 17 September 1991, that being the date two years prior to the date on which her claim was lodged. The case thus concerned the comparability and effectiveness of national and EC judicial remedies. The appellant had to demonstrate the non-compliance of section 2(5) of the 1970 Act (two years) with Article 2 of the Equal Pay Directive 75/117/EEC, which is materially equivalent with Article 6 of Directive 76/207/EEC (that is, there is no explicit time limit laid down).

The Employment Appeal Tribunal felt unable to agree on the meaning and effect of Article 2 of the Equal Pay Directive 75/117/EEC, or on whether or not it could strike out the two-year time limit in section 2(5) of the 1970 Act, and therefore sought advice from the ECJ. Counsel for the appellant submitted that section 2(5) of the 1970 Act complied neither with the principle of comparability nor with the principle of effectiveness. The ECJ is said to have consistently held, since *Comet*, that, in the absence of Community rules on the matter, national procedural conditions, including rules relating to time limits for bringing actions, are also applicable to actions based on Community law, provided that, first, they are no less favourable for such actions than for similar actions of a domestic nature (the principle of comparability or equivalence) and, secondly, they do not render the exercise of rights conferred by Community law impossible in practice (the principle of effectiveness).[174]

The ECJ had not at that point yet considered the scope of the principle of comparability. However, the manner in which that principle should be applied was considered by Advocate-General van Gerven in *Marshall II*, though in the event his view on this was not followed by the ECJ.[175] He stated that, if greater compensation is provided for comparable infringements of national law than the adequate compensation

[174] Case C-28/93, *Fissher* v. *Voorhuis Hengelo BV* [1994] ECR I-4583, para. 39; Case 33/76, *Rewe Zentralfinanz eG* v. *Landwirtschaftskammer für das Saarland* [1976] ECR 1989, para. 5, 6; Case 45/76, *Comet BV* v. *Produktschap voor Siergewassen* [1976] ECR 2043, paras. 12–19.

[175] Case C-271/91, *Marshall* v. *Southampton and South West Hampshire Area Health Authority* (*Marshall II*) [1993] ECR I-4367, paras. 9–10 and 20–1.

required by Community law, the same greater compensation should also apply to infringements of Community law.

Counsel for the appellant used van Gerven's interpretation of the principle of comparability to claim that UK law proceeded less diligently against infringements of Community law than it did against comparable infringements of domestic law. Therefore, the ECJ should compare the national procedural conditions, including time limits, applicable to claims for equal pay under the 1970 Act with the procedural conditions for similar claims in the employment field, including other claims for breach of the contract of employment, claims for racial discrimination in pay, claims for sex discrimination outside the contract of employment, and claims arising out of unlawful deductions from an employee's pay, all of which may be brought before industrial tribunals.

Secondly, counsel argued that Member States violate their obligation to provide full and effective remedies if they define different time limits for comparable domestic actions. The principle of effectiveness can clearly be discerned in *von Colson* and in *Marshall II*.[176] In the present case, section 2(5) of the 1970 Act would prevent the payment of full compensation or the provision of an effective remedy for failure to apply the principle of equal pay, as required by Articles 2 and 6 of Directive 76/207/EEC. It could not be argued that Mrs Levez was free to pursue a separate action against her employer for misrepresentation in the county court. Such a course would require a complainant to incur costs, and the delay and uncertainty of two separate sets of legal proceedings, whereas claimants seeking to rely on any similar domestic right in the employment field would be required to bring only one set of proceedings.

The ECJ[177] decided in favour of Mrs Levez, though for a somewhat different reason to that submitted by counsel for the appellant. It held that the two-year limitation period was contrary to Community law where the delay in bringing a claim was attributable to the fact that the employer deliberately misrepresented to the employee the level of remuneration received by persons of the opposite sex performing equal work. The action in the county court does not suffice to provide an effective legal remedy, if the latter is likely to entail procedural conditions which are less favourable than those applicable to similar domestic

[176] *Ibid.*, para. 30.

[177] Case C-326/96, *Levez* v. *T. H. Jennings (Harlow Pools) Ltd* [1998] ECR I-7835; [1999] All ER (EC) 1.

actions (in the industrial tribunal). Whether this is the case or not has to be decided by the national courts. Two conclusions may be drawn from the judgment. First, the ECJ avoided deciding on the scope of the two principles. Instead, it emphasised the concrete circumstances of the case. Secondly, the ECJ seemed inclined to accept that, in the case at hand, the principle of comparability was not met in UK law.

The Equal Opportunities Commission

The Equal Opportunities Commission[178] is one of the foremost expert bodies on equality for women and men in the UK. It was created in 1976 pursuant to the Sex Discrimination Act 1975 and is modelled on the United States' Equal Employment Opportunity Commission[179] as a quasi-autonomous non-governmental organisation (or 'quango'). While it is constitutionally separate from central government, it is funded by a grant-in-aid, originally paid by the Home Office and now by the Department for Education and Employment. Although the EOC has official status, it acts and behaves more as a pressure group, and in this respect might be considered more a non-governmental organisation. However, contrary to the position of most NGOs, the EOC has a stable financial basis and an official mandate. The EOC sees its own tasks as follows: working to end sex discrimination; promoting equal opportunities for women and men; and reviewing and suggesting improvements to the Sex Discrimination Act 1975 and the Equal Pay Act 1970.

The powers of the EOC which are relevant to our discussion are provided for under section 75 of the Sex Discrimination Act 1975. The EOC may grant 'assistance' to complainants under both the Sex Discrimination Act 1975 and the Equal Pay Act 1970, either because it is unreasonable to expect the applicant to deal with the case unaided due to the complexity of the issues involved, or because of the applicant's position in respect of the respondent, or by reason of any other special consideration, for example, clarification of the law. The EOC has *locus standi* under English law,[180] and is therefore entitled to use judicial

[178] Barnard, 'A European Litigation Strategy' in Shaw and More (eds.), *New Legal Dynamics of the European Union*, 253. See www.eoc.org.uk.

[179] See www.eeoc.gov.

[180] There has been disagreement in the English courts. However, in *R.* v. *Secretary for State of Employment, ex parte EOC* [1994] 1 All ER 910, the House of Lords confirmed that the EOC does have sufficient standing.

review to achieve its aims. The EOC acts mainly in the national legal environment, although it does use EC law to seek to have national law overruled. However, the EOC has not yet brought its own cases before the ECJ via Article 234 (ex Article 177). In all the cases discussed here, the EOC at most provided 'assistance' to the litigants.

The EOC as a 'repeat player'

Due to its stable basis, the EOC must be understood as a 'repeat player' in Galanter's terminology.[181] Once *Defrenne* had demonstrated the potential of EC law for dealing with equal treatment, the EOC entered the arena of Euro-litigation. Advocate-General Warner, giving his Opinion in *Jenkins*,[182] referred explicitly to the support Mrs Jenkins had received from her trade union and from the EOC. For nearly twenty years, the EOC was able to develop and sharpen its skills in handling EC law. Whenever the EOC was approached by applicants seeking advice, the European dimension was always in the background. If the applicants failed in the national courts, the EOC tested the scope of European law. European law could therefore overcome a deadlock situation in national law, if necessary. The EOC's legal officers not only broadened their own understanding of equal treatment as a supranational issue but also established a network of expert solicitors and barristers, such as Dinah Rose, Michael Beloff and David Pannick,[183] to act for applicants. The EOC has a unique position in Europe: there is no comparable organisation with the same stable basis in any other Member State, and there is probably no other organisation in any other Member State which has been able to steadily increase its skills in using EC law as an instrument for improving equal treatment as effectively as the EOC has done.

The strategy of the EOC: there is no strategy

The EOC claims it has no strategy to develop a systematic approach to instrumentalise EC law on equal treatment to overcome shortcomings

[181] Barnard, 'A European Litigation Strategy' in Shaw and More (eds.), *New Legal Dynamics of the European Union*, 260; see pp. 44–5 above; and, for a more in-depth analysis of repeat players, see pp. 15–16 above.

[182] Case 96/80, *Jenkins* v. *Kingsgate (Clothing Productions) Ltd* [1981] ECR 911 at 932.

[183] Interview with Pauline Matthews, Principal Legal Officer at the EOC, on 5 January 2000.

in the national law.[184] However, an analysis of the cases brought before the ECJ over a period of twenty years with the assistance of the EOC seems to contradict such a claim. The EOC has indeed contributed to extending the scope of EC law on equal treatment – *sedes materiae* and *sedes personae*. It has helped to implement indirect discrimination as a principle of EC law, and it has heavily influenced the development of judicial remedies. The impression is left that there *is* a strategy lying behind the EOC's use of EC law.

The EOC's own understanding has been formulated by Pauline Matthews. She calls the EOC's tactics 'opportunistic', rather than planned.[185] The EOC does not act as a litigant in its own right. Instead, it assists individuals who seek their advice. Thus, all the applications which reach the EOC may be understood as reflecting the basic problems women meet in daily life. The EOC officer in charge, and at a later stage the Commission itself, have to decide which cases to take up. The EOC has obviously made good choices in the past about which cases to support. From a sociological point of view, the EOC's opportunistic approach may produce better results than would result from following a set strategy, because the cases they take up have not been 'invented' by the EOC but are instead the result of real conflicts between employer and employee.

However, even such a finding does not provide a full picture of the EOC's involvement in Euro-litigation. It is possible to categorise the cases discussed here. Each category contains different elements of what might broadly be termed as the EOC's strategy.

(1) There are cases with an overt *strategic* character. This is mainly true with regard to the unequal treatment of men and women in national pension schemes. Even prior to *Barber* the EOC had implemented a test-case strategy, supporting litigants in carefully selected cases before UK courts and persuading the courts to refer questions to the ECJ under the preliminary reference procedure.[186] *Barber* was the breakthrough in removing differences in

[184] For a different view, see C. Kilpatrick, 'Community or Communities of Courts in European Integration?', 134.

[185] Interview with Pauline Matthews, Principal Legal Officer at the EOC, on 5 January 2000.

[186] D. Curtin, 'Scalping the Community Legislator: Occupational Pensions and "Barber"' (1990) 27 *Common Market Law Review* 479, n. 22, where she mentions Case 69/80, *Worringham*, Case 19/81, *Burton*, Case 12/81, *Garland* and Case 192/85, *Newstead*, and

pensionable ages. *Smith* v. *Advel Systems* provided a sequel to *Barber* by implementing the ECJ's ruling into the national legal system.[187] A comparable strategic element may be detected in *P* v. *S* and *Grant* in order to broaden the meaning of sex discrimination either by the European judiciary or if necessary by the national legislator. However, *P* v. *S* and *Grant* raise complicated issues even on the role and function of the EOC itself. Is it an organisation for realising the equal treatment of men and women or is it also competent to recognise equal treatment for transsexuals and homosexuals?

(2) Euro-litigation may simply be the *product of chance*. This is true of *Coote*, in which the idea of basing the action on Article 6 arose haphazardly. The strategy is one of 'let us try the European way and see what happens'. *Levez* comes near to being one such case.

(3) There are cases in which there is considerable pressure from the individuals involved in the case, who may have suffered in a literal sense from sex discrimination. Such pressure may also come from women not only in the UK but also in the other Member States. This is particularly true for discrimination on the grounds of pregnancy and maternity. *Webb* was decided in 1994 on the basis of the Dutch *Dekker* case. In its aftermath, a whole series of cases have been referred to the ECJ from all the Member States.[188]

(4) Indirect sex discrimination as an issue of equal treatment was introduced into the European legal environment by the EOC in *Jenkins* on the basis of relevant US case law. The EOC deliberately used Euro-litigation as a platform to extend the scope of Article 141

refers to Lord A. Lester, 'The Uncertain Trumpet, References to the Court of Justice from the United Kingdom: Equal Pay and Equal Treatment Without Sex Discrimination' in H. G. Schermers *et al.* (eds.), *Article 177 EEC: Experiences and Problems* (The Hague, 1987), 164.

187 Barnard, 'A European Litigation Strategy' in Shaw and More (eds.), *New Legal Dynamics of the European Union*, 261.

188 P. Matthews, Principal Legal Officer at the EOC, in a speech given on 31 March 1999 at the Academy of European Law, Trier, on 'New Developments in Labour Law of the EC, Sex Equality Law and Positive Action' (unpublished), who, in discussing equal treatment, refers to Case C-394/96, *Brown* v. *Rentokil* [1998] ECR I-4185, Case C-66/96, *Pederson* v. *Kvickly Skive* [1998] ECR I-7327; [1999] 2 CMLR 326, Case C-207/98, *Mahlberg* v. *Land Mecklenburg* [2000] ECR I-549; [2001] 3 CMLR 40, and who, in discussing pay and benefits, refers to C-411/96, *Boyle* v. *Equal Opportunities Commission* [1998] ECR I-6401; [1998] 3 CMLR 1133, Case C-218/98, *Abdoulaye* v. *Regie Nationale des Usines Renault SA* [1999] ECR I-5723; [2001] 2 CMLR 18 and Case C-333/97, *Lewen* v. *Denda* [1999] ECR I-7243; [2000] 2 CMLR 38.

(ex Article 119) from direct to indirect discrimination.[189] The case and the arguments may have much to do with the establishment of the EOC modelled after its US counterpart. At the time, however, the EOC did not fully realise that two factors were crucial to the development of disparate impact cases in the US context – class actions and statistics.[190] While it seems fair to conclude that the EOC might have believed it could overcome the lack of class actions through its particular legal status and its political role in the UK legal system, the EOC was not able to fully utilise statistics as a tool in uncovering indirect discrimination. Unintentionally, the EOC had opened the floodgates and indirectly invited appellants to rely on statistics in order to prove indirect discrimination, a strategy which finally ended in deadlock.[191]

The EOC before the ECJ: keeping a low profile

In the cases discussed here, the EOC is mentioned only three times, in *Jenkins*,[192] *Coote*[193] and *Smith* v. *Advel Systems*.[194] In *Jenkins*, Advocate-General Warner compared the degree of support enjoyed by the employer and the employee in the case at hand. Whereas the Advocate-General expressed some sympathy with the respondent, 'a relatively small company, which is not in a strong financial position', he seemed to be quite convinced that Mrs Jenkins was in a relatively strong position as she was supported by her trade union, the National Union of Tailors and Garment Makers, and by the EOC. Advocate-General Warner concluded, with a slightly pejorative undertone, that 'her case has, consequently, been very fully presented to us'.[195] In *Coote*, Pauline Matthews of the EOC is only referred to with regard to her role in

[189] Case 96/80, *Jenkins* v. *Kingsgate (Clothing Productions) Ltd* [1981] ECR 911 at 916 with references.

[190] C. Barnard and B. Hepple, 'Indirect Discrimination: Interpreting Seymour-Smith' (1999) 58 *Cambridge Law Journal* 399.

[191] Connolly, 'British Indirect Discrimination Law', 1; and see more specifically two decisions of the Court of Appeal, *British Coal Corporation* v. *Smith* [1994] ICR 810; [1994] IRLR 342, and *North Yorkshire County Council* v. *Ratcliffe* [1994] IRLR 342 as quoted in Wynn, 'Equal Pay and Gender Segregation', 556 at 560.

[192] Case 96/80, *Jenkins* v. *Kingsgate (Clothing Productions) Ltd* [1981] ECR 911 at 932.

[193] Case C-185/97, *Coote* v. *Granada Hospitality Ltd* [1998] ECR I-5199 at 5212.

[194] Case C-408/92, *Smith* v. *Advel Systems Ltd* [1994] ECR I-4435.

[195] Case 96/80, *Jenkins* v. *Kingsgate (Clothing Productions) Ltd* [1981] ECR 911 at 932.

instructing the barrister, Dinah Rose;[196] in *Smith* v. *Advel Systems*, the same is true of Verena Jones of the EOC, as regards instructing Michael Beloff QC.[197]

In all other cases, the EOC is not mentioned at all, either by the judge-rapporteur, or by the Advocate-General, or by the ECJ itself, even as regards the EOC's role in instructing the barrister in the proceedings. This may be because the EOC wished to maintain a low profile following criticisms of its role in the *Jenkins* case. The EOC selects which case to support, and – if it is paying – chooses the barrister. The EOC also uses its own expertise to contribute to the legal submissions presented on behalf of the applicant in the proceedings, and even lends moral support during lengthy litigation.[198] Nevertheless, it remains very much in the background. In academic writing, the EOC is commonly understood as a 'public interest group'. While it may superficially appear to act as a public interest group, its funding from central government and its statutory basis make it very different from the usual public interest group.

Hidden or open international co-operation?

When reconstructing the equal-treatment cases, one is tempted to conclude that there must have been some sort of co-operation between the EOC and non-governmental organisations, trade unions and similar groups outside the UK. This is particularly true of the possible co-operation between the UK, German and Danish appellants before the ECJ. The interplay seems obvious with regard to direct discrimination and the development of judicial remedies on the basis of Articles 5 and 6 of Directive 76/207/EEC. However, the EOC denies that any such international co-operation has ever occurred. The least that can be said is that there is a forum run by the European Commission where 'repeat players' may exchange ideas. However, such information exchange and mutual consultation has not yet resulted in a joint

[196] Case C-185/97, *Coote* v. *Granada Hospitality Ltd* [1998] ECR I-5199 at 5212.

[197] Case C-408/92, *Smith* v. *Advel Systems Ltd* [1994] ECR I-4435.

[198] This must have been the case in *Enderby*, where the case encountered almost unprecedented judicial hostility, lasted for more than seven years and where substantial financial and moral support was needed to keep the litigant going: E. Ellis, 'Case Note on Case C-127/92, Enderby v. Frenchay Health Authority and the Secretary of State for Health, Judgment of 27 October 1993, not yet reported' (1994) 31 *Common Market Law Review* 387.

strategy being developed by the litigants or other actors. The EOC, as well as their counterparts in the other Member States, seem to start from the idea that, although equal treatment is international in its nature, the appropriate solutions to overcome discrimination must be found in the national legal system. Such an understanding does not exclude co-operation: these non-governmental organisations each refer their own cases to the ECJ, thus mutually building on the overall 'progress' achieved. International co-operation is certainly a field which the repeat players have not yet fully explored.

The respondents and the governments

The degree to which respondents and governments are involved in Euro-litigation differs considerably from case to case. This might be due partly to differences in the publicity policy of the ECJ and that of national courts. Not all of the decisions reported here contain a report of the hearing; sometimes the submissions of the parties have to be deduced from the Opinion of the Advocate-General, from the judgment of the ECJ itself or from the files of the EOC. However, even if the report of the hearing is published, there is no general scheme of presenting the case and the submissions of the parties. The report might provide a full picture of the case, or it might be a mere summary of the case. The Opinion of the Advocates-General will often give more detail than the report, or may simply repeat the report. However, again, there is no common policy.

Decisions of the lower courts in England and Wales are not regularly reported. A full picture of the cases, all of which will have started off in one or another lower court, may therefore be available only where the reference has been made by the Court of Appeal or the House of Lords. The submissions of the appellants are usually presented more fully than those of the respondents or the UK government as *amicus curiae* in the UK courts or in the ECJ. Therefore, it is much more difficult to reconstruct the arguments of the respondents and those of the UK government. The analysis below will therefore concentrate on the common factors of the submissions in the cases.

The government as the true respondent

It is often the case that, in practice, the true opponent of the appellants before the ECJ is not the employer but the UK government. In

Macarthys Ltd v. *Smith*, *P* v. *S*, *Webb*, *Jenkins*, *Coote* and *Levez*, the respondents did not submit any written submissions to the ECJ.[199] Generally, no explanation was given for this omission by the respondents.

This gap was partly filled by the UK government, which provided submissions as if it were the respondent. The UK government was often either directly or indirectly involved, for example in *Johnston* (the Chief Constable of the Royal Ulster Constabulary), *P* v. *S* (Cornwall County Council), *Enderby* (Frenchay Health Authority and the Secretary of State for Health), *Marshall I* and *Marshall II* (Southampton and South West Hampshire Area Health Authority), or through its privatised emanations, for example in *Grant* (South West Trains Ltd) and *Foster* (British Gas plc).

The reasons for such involvement by the UK government are complex. Moral pressure can be more easily put on the state which has adopted the respective legislation. Whenever a reference is made to the ECJ, the UK – as is any other Member State – is 'accused' of non-compliance with EC law obligations. A number of cases have long-term implications for government policy.[200] For example, in a privatisation, the UK government, even though no longer directly concerned in the privatised undertaking, is often confronted with the social impact of its policy before the courts and cannot escape its political responsibility. Last but not least, EC law itself sets boundaries for Euro-litigation. Directives benefit from vertical direct effect alone, and therefore private appellants may enforce their rights under EC law only in cases in which the respondent may be regarded as part of the 'State' within the meaning the ECJ has given to that term.

Private respondents played a major role in two cases only, that is, in *Barber* and *Smith* v. *Advel Systems*. Both cases concerned the concept of 'equal pay' under Article 141 (ex Article 119) with regard to private pension schemes. Here, the respondents took a strong position in the Euro-litigation, although it did appear that the pension industry, and indeed the UK government, had been caught 'on the hop' by *Barber*.

[199] Although, in *Levez*, oral observations were made by the former employer. See Case C-326/96, *Levez* v. *T. H. Jennings (Harlow Pools) Ltd* [1998] ECR I-7835; [1999] All ER (EC) 1 at 3.

[200] For the socio-political background of the privatisation policy, see N. Johnson, 'The Judicial Dimension in British Politics' (1998) 21 *West European Politics* 148.

The *Barber* ruling initially created 'something close to panic in the pension industry'.[201]

However, other than in *Barber* and *Smith* v. *Advel Systems*, the respondents tended to keep a low profile and seemed to rely on the representations of the government. There are even cases in which the respondents are not represented at all. However, there is no evidence of any direct co-operation between the UK government and the respondents, perhaps with the exception of *Barber*, where Arthur Hugh Vaughan QC submitted a comprehensive submission to the ECJ on behalf of the respondent which fitted together very well with the rather short submission of the UK government.[202] Indirectly, there might well have been some sort of co-ordination between the barristers, at least in their oral submissions.

Member States seem to treat the cases which come before the ECJ merely as national cases. In principle, they avoid getting involved in cases referred from other Member States. Occasionally, however, Member States may give support to the respondents and the UK government. In the cases of interest to us here, the German government intervened in *Enderby*,[203] and the French government intervened in *Levez*.[204] Here, the two Member States' positions differed from that of the UK government, though both of the former avoided openly contradicting the latter. There seems to be a tacit agreement to consider equal treatment as a national issue.

The respondents' and the governments' construction of the EC law on equal treatment

Despite the long timespan of two decades between the first and the last of the cases under analysis here,[205] the respondents' and the governments' construction of EC law on equal treatment demonstrates a

[201] Moffat and Luckhaus, 'Occupational Pension Schemes', 1 at 16.

[202] Case C-262/88, *Barber* v. *Guardian Royal Exchange* [1990] ECR I-1889 at 1903 and 1906.

[203] Case C-127/92, *Enderby* v. *Frenchay Health Authority and Secretary of State for Health* [1993] ECR I-5535 at 5547.

[204] Case C-326/96, *Levez* v. *T. H. Jennings (Harlow Pools) Ltd* [1998] ECR I-7835; [1999] All ER (EC) 3 at 10.

[205] The cases concern the scope of the EC law on equal treatment, direct and indirect discrimination and the rights and remedies to enforce equal treatment.

remarkable consistency in the way EC law is instrumentalised and in the way the arguments are built.

The losers' strategy

The respondents lost the vast majority of the cases. So did the UK government. The respondents and the government succeeded only in *Smith* v. *Advel Systems* and in *Grant*. *Smith* was initiated by the EOC to raise the standards of equal treatment; *Grant* was finally resolved by the Treaty of Amsterdam. Here, the respondents and the government had a winning strategy. They were in an exceptionally strong position. However, all the other cases under consideration here may be divided into two categories: first, the self-evidently 'unwinnable' cases such as *Macarthys Ltd* v. *Smith*, *Webb* and *Jenkins*; and, secondly, the borderline cases in which the outcome was not foreseeable such as *Johnston*, *Barber*, *P* v. *S*, *Enderby*, *Foster*, *Marshall*, *Coote* and *Levez*. Here, litigation tactics may lead to a 'relentless exploitation of the national appeals procedure'.[206]

Setting aside *Barber* (the notion of equal pay) and *Enderby* (the boundaries and requirements of indirect discrimination), the respondents' and the government's submissions create the impression that they were not interested at all, or only to a limited degree, in the final outcome of the litigation.[207] The respondents might have felt at a certain point that they would lose the case in any event. The attitude of the UK government is even more striking. Losing the case in the ECJ was considered as a pretext for amending the national law, as far as necessary, but only after the ECJ found UK law to violate EC law. The overall political climate in the 1980s certainly played a role. There was a strong anti-EC attitude.[208] Cases lost in the ECJ in such a sensitive field as equal treatment could provide fertile ground to nourish antipathy towards 'Europe', at least in business circles. Business and

[206] With regard to *Johnston*, see A. Arnull, 'Social Policy: The Beat Goes On' (1987) 12 *European Law Review* 56.

[207] Case C-262/88, *Barber* v. *Guardian Royal Exchange* [1990] ECR I-1889 at 1906: 'If the Court came to a different conclusion [i.e. equal to pay to cover pension schemes], it would offend the principle of legal certainty and cause enormous disruption and expense to many occupational schemes which have been funded on the basis of legislation providing for different pensionable ages for men and women.' This is the only time the UK government raises the scenario of a catastrophe.

[208] See the conclusions, p. 475 below.

the UK government were bound together in their anti-EC feelings. These findings can be further explored by analysing the way in which the respondents and the UK government built their arguments. This highlights the fact that their strategy is not a purely legal one, but is linked to non-legal, non-judicial factors.

Denial of the EC's competence

The most powerful argument the respondents and the government could raise was a denial of the EC's competence to intervene in the particular field. However, there is a certain danger in this argument. The more often it is used, the less can it be taken seriously. The respondents and the government are well aware of this risk. That is why competence is often denied in an indirect way, that is, it is linked to a different set of legal arguments.

One of the most important cases in this respect is *Johnston*.[209] The UK considered that Directive 76/207/EEC was inapplicable to action taken by the Member States for the purpose of safeguarding national security or for protecting public safety or public order. Member States are said to be free to exclude such matters from the scope of their legislation on equal treatment. That conclusion was drawn first from the principle of interpreting the Directive in conformity with the rules of the Treaty and with general principles of law. The Treaty itself leaves intact the power of the Member States to take such measures as they consider necessary or expedient for the above-mentioned purposes, as is shown by the safeguard clauses contained in Articles 30, 39, 46, 55, 296 and 297 (respectively, ex Articles 36, 48, 56, 66, 223 and 224). It is inconceivable that a Directive may be interpreted as restricting a power which the Treaty itself leaves intact. With regard to Article 297 (ex Article 224), the UK government was supported by the Danish government.[210] The Danish government's representative stated that Article 297 (ex Article 224) makes it possible to neutralise any rule of Community law, and leaves the Member States a wide margin of appreciation in this respect. A Member State's exercise of its discretion in this respect is not subject to judicial review, save in the case of abuse. These are strong arguments, but they were all rejected by the ECJ.

[209] Case 222/84, *Johnston* v. *Chief Constable of the Royal Ulster Constabulary* [1986] ECR 1651 at 1671.
[210] *Ibid.*, 1676.

In *Barber*, both the respondent and the UK government openly disputed the EC's competence to intervene in the regulation of pension schemes pursuant to the principle of equal pay under Article 141 (ex Article 119). The respondent, Guardian Royal Exchange, submitted that the discrimination alleged by Mr Barber related to the terms governing his dismissal and did not give rise to any question of equal pay. Accordingly, Mr Barber's case fell within the scope of 'working conditions' or 'social security' within the meaning of Article 140 (ex Article 118) and not within the scope of Article 141 (ex Article 119).[211] The applicability of Article 141 (ex Article 119) is to be excluded by virtue of the interpretation given by the ECJ in *Defrenne*[212] and *Newstead*.[213] The financial aspects of an occupational pension scheme are said to fall within Article 140 (ex Article 118) of the Treaty.[214] The submissions of the UK government were to the same general effect, although the UK government attempted to justify the non-applicability of Article 141 (ex Article 119) by reference to the specific nature of the pension schemes at issue as contracted-out pension schemes.[215]

Levez raises complex questions on the principle of equivalence, a principle which requires that domestic law remedies should safeguard Community law 'without discrimination'.[216] The UK government tried to defend the idea of two separate systems to guarantee effective judicial protection. It therefore submitted that, for the purposes of the non-discrimination requirement, a claim under the Equal Pay Act 1970 is a form of action under domestic law which is similar to a claim brought in reliance upon Article 141 (ex Article 119). Accordingly, the UK government maintained that a comparison should be made between, on the one hand, the procedural rules governing actions relying on the principle of equal pay for men and women without discrimination on the ground of sex – as provided for and safeguarded by Community

[211] Case C-262/88, *Barber* v. *Guardian Royal Exchange* [1990] ECR I-1889 at 1903.
[212] Case 149/77, *Defrenne II* [1978] ECR 1365, paras. 19 and 23.
[213] Case 192/85, *Newstead* v. *Department of Transport and Her Majesty's Treasury* [1987] ECR 4753.
[214] Case C-262/88, *Barber* v. *Guardian Royal Exchange* [1990] ECR I-1889 at 1904.
[215] *Ibid.*, 1906. A similar reference to that of a lack of competence of the EC can be found in *Coote* in which the UK government stressed the importance of Art. 7 of Directive 76/207/EEC against the applicant's reference to Art. 6 of the same Directive.
[216] Case C-326/96, *Levez* v. *T. H. Jennings (Harlow Pools) Ltd* [1998] ECR I-7835; [1999] All ER (EC) 1, para. 28 *per* Advocate-General Léger.

law – and, on the other hand, those governing an action relying on the same principle, as provided for and safeguarded by domestic law. This reasoning presupposed that two separate principles of equal pay for men and women without discrimination on the ground of sex can exist concurrently at two different levels, national and Community.[217]

The failure to recognise the *acquis communautaire*

There are a few cases in which the respondents and the government were not able or did not want to recognise the links between the EC law on equal treatment and the EC law on freedom of trade. In *Jenkins*, the ECJ held for the first time that indirect discrimination comes under Article 141 (ex Article 119). The UK government was prepared to accept the applicability of Article 141 (ex Article 119) and Article 1 of Directive 75/117/EEC only 'where the difference in pay between a male and a female employee was the *result* of discrimination based on sex; where the discrimination was the consequence of other factors, *ex hypothesi* it is not "based on sex" and therefore not within the ambit of either of those Articles'.[218] *Jenkins* was decided in 1981 and *Cassis de Dijon* in 1979. No cross-reference can be found in the submissions of the respondent or the UK government to the ECJ's case law on the freedom of trade. If they had been able to test their result-oriented argument against the *Cassis de Dijon* doctrine, they would have been able to foresee the ECJ's judgment.[219]

A less emphatic version of the same argument may be found in *Enderby*. Both the respondent and the UK government concluded that indirect discrimination required more than just the existence of discriminatory *effects* on women, that is, that the applicant has to prove the existence of a 'requirement' or a 'condition' with which substantially fewer women than men could comply.[220] The respondent argued that an adverse impact on a group consisting mainly of women is not sufficient in itself to trigger the requirement to provide objective justification. According to the respondent, the applicants could not rely on

[217] *Ibid.*, paras. 41–2.
[218] Case 96/80, *Jenkins* v. *Kingsgate (Clothing Productions) Ltd* [1981] ECR 911 at 918 (emphasis added).
[219] It is fair to say, however, that the ECJ itself did not make such a cross-reference: see Case 96/80, *Jenkins* v. *Kingsgate (Clothing Productions) Ltd* [1981] ECR 911 at 932.
[220] S. Fredman, 'Equal Pay and Justification' (1994) 23 *Industrial Law Journal* 37.

Jenkins and *Danfoss* because these were cases in which the adverse impact was not the only issue.[221] In the respondent's view, it is only where there is *prima facie* indirect discrimination that the employer must objectively justify the hurdle imposed.[222] The UK law required that the applicant had to show that the difference in pay was attributable to a factor that was causally related to sex in order to establish a *prima facie* case of indirect discrimination.[223]

Defence of the *status quo ante* of EC law

One common denominator of submissions to the ECJ in these cases was the attempt to prevent EC law being stretched beyond the *status quo* of the established case law. In *Foster*, the success or failure of the appellants' claim depended on whether or not the respondent, British Gas plc, was to be regarded as an 'emanation of the State'. Both British Gas and the UK government rejected the broad meaning given to the notion of the state by the appellant. British Gas considered[224] that, in order to determine the definition of the state, it was necessary to examine the principle which enables individuals to rely on a Directive in a municipal forum. It is said to be clear from the judgments that the basis for this principle is that a state may not take advantage of its own failure to perform the obligations imposed on it by the Directive. In *von Colson*,[225] the ECJ held that a Member State's obligations arising from a Directive are also binding on the national courts, for matters within their jurisdiction. As far as other organs or emanations of the state are concerned, the respondent contended that individuals may rely on a Directive in claims against them only because they are agents of the state and the state has delegated certain functions to them. Michael Beloff QC, acting for the respondent, referred to *Snupat*[226] and *Worms*,[227] in which the ECJ defined the concept of an 'organ' of

[221] Case C-127/92, *Enderby* v. *Frenchay Health Authority and Secretary of State for Health* [1993] ECR I-5535 at 5543.
[222] *Ibid.*, 5543. [223] *Ibid.*, 5544.
[224] Case C-188/89, *Foster* v. *British Gas plc* [1990] ECR I-3313 at 3319.
[225] Case 14/83, *Von Colson and Kamann* v. *Land Nordrhein-Westfalen* [1984] ECR 1891.
[226] Joined Cases 32 and 33/58, *Snupat* v. *High Authority of the European Coal and Steel Community* [1959] ECR 127.
[227] Case 18/60, *Worms* v. *High Authority of the European Coal and Steel Community* [1962] ECR 195.

the High Authority by reference to the existence of a delegation of powers.

The UK government argued in the same vein, although it undermined its narrow understanding mainly with reference to secondary Community law, trying to find consistency in the EC law.[228] First, reference was made to Article 2 of Directive 80/723/EEC on the transparency of financial relations between Member States and public undertakings,[229] in which a distinction is made between 'public authorities or local authorities' and 'public undertakings' (defined as 'any undertaking over which the public authority may exercise directly or indirectly a dominant influence by virtue of their ownership of it, their financial participation therein or the rules which govern it'). The UK government then pointed to Directive 71/305/EEC concerning the coordination of procedures for the award of public works contracts.[230] Here, the term 'a body governed by public law' is defined as any body 'established for the specific purpose of meeting needs in the general interest, not having an industrial or commercial character'. British Gas plc was not included in Annex 1 to the Directive as a body governed by public law. The UK government neglected the ECJ's case law on public undertakings within the meaning of Article 86 (ex Article 90).[231] Thus, the effort to look for consistency lacked consistency within itself.

Defence of the power of the national courts to decide the case

The respondents and the governments did not contend that EC law was not applicable. However, for them, the national courts were the only bodies competent to apply EC law and the rulings of the ECJ. The real point at issue was how the responsibilities between the national courts and the ECJ should be divided. This issue was raised by the UK government in *Enderby*, *Foster* and *Levez*.

In *Enderby*, both the respondent and the UK government argued that it is for the *national* court to decide whether and to what extent a pay difference is justified where a higher salary is paid in order to

[228] Case C-188/89, *Foster* v. *British Gas plc* [1990] ECR I-3313 at 3321.

[229] OJ 1980 No. L195, 29 July 1980, 35.

[230] OJ English Special Edition, 1971 (II), 682, as amended by Council Directive 89/440/EEC of 18 July 1980, OJ 1989 No. L210, 1.

[231] However, Case C-41/90, *Höfner and Elsner* v. *Macrotron* [1991] ECR I-1979 was decided on 23 April 1991, nearly one year after *Foster* on 12 July 1990.

attract suitable candidates.[232] The respondent, however, made a strong argument challenging even the national courts' jurisdiction:

> It is unrealistic, illogical and artificial to ask an employer to establish what part of the wage is attributable to market forces. Since such forces constrain an employer to agree to a particular level of pay in order to attract candidates it is that total amount which is entirely explained by the state of the employment market.[233]

Foster is interesting because it was one of the few cases in which the UK government explicitly challenges the jurisdiction of the ECJ. The UK government stated that it was not a matter for the ECJ but for the national courts to determine whether British Gas plc was a part of the state in the context of the UK legal system. The UK government referred to the judgment in *Marshall I*, in which the ECJ stated that it was for the national court to apply the considerations referred to by the ECJ to the circumstances of each case.[234] The UK government then went on to prepare alternative arguments should the ECJ decide that this was a matter of Community law. This submission is somewhat misleading, however, as the UK government did not appear to challenge the ECJ's competence to decide the notion of 'the State' under EC law. What the UK government really wanted was to insist that the final decision on whether British Gas plc complied with the requirements of EC law lay in the hands of the national courts.

In *Levez*,[235] the UK government claimed that it was for the national courts to decide whether the domestic actions available to guarantee effective judicial protection were similar to those which were required under Articles 2 and 6 of Directive 75/117/EEC. Again, the UK government relied on the standards laid down by the ECJ in *von Colson*. If the ECJ intervenes and defines the standards for determining the existence of 'similar domestic actions', this would in effect take away powers from the national courts and reduce their discretion regarding the comparability of actions. In its intervention in *Levez*, the French

[232] Case C-127/92, *Enderby* v. *Frenchay Health Authority and Secretary of State for Health* [1993] ECR I-5535 at 5548.

[233] *Ibid.*, 5548.

[234] Case C-188/89, *Foster* v. *British Gas plc* [1990] ECR I-3313 at 3321.

[235] Case C-326/96, *Levez* v. *T. H. Jennings (Harlow Pools) Ltd* [1998] ECR I-7835; [1999] All ER (EC) 1.

government argued that the national courts should make these decisions; however, it also argued for a comparison to be made between equal pay and race relations (as did the appellant).[236]

Defence of the national methodology to set aside European law

Steiner and Woods[237] explain the disproportionate number of UK cases on equal treatment as follows:

> EC sex discrimination law has been invoked more frequently before domestic courts and tribunals in the UK than in any other Member State. The reason for [the UK's] apparent deficiencies in this field does not necessarily lie in any greater reluctance, or a greater failure on [its] part, to observe Community law, but rather in the different styles of drafting and interpretation prevailing under the two legal systems. The broad general principles of EC law are enacted in [the UK's] Equal Pay Act 1970 and Sex Discrimination Act 1975 as precise and detailed rules. Such rules lend themselves to, and often receive, a literal interpretation by [UK] courts. As a result, action which is plainly discriminatory may fail to fall within the specific wording of the Act.

Respondents and the UK government remain closely bound to the so-called 'British'[238] style of drafting and interpretation. *Macarthys Ltd* v. *Smith* was decided in 1979, *Webb* in 1994 and *Levez* in 1998. In *Macarthys Ltd* v. *Smith*, the UK government noted that Article 141 (ex Article 119) did not define precisely the meaning of the terms 'the same work' and 'the same job'. Do they mean a job performed at the same time as that with which it is being compared, or at a different time? If a comparison may be made between jobs performed at different times, is there any limit to the timespan between the two jobs? In the absence of detailed Community rules in this respect, and if the principle of Article 141 (ex Article 119) were to be held to extend to cover the comparison of non-contemporaneous employment, the criteria would have to be worked out and regulated at national level.[239]

236 *Ibid.*, paras. 52 and 64.

237 J. Steiner and L. Woods, *Textbook on EC Law* (5th edn, London, 1996).

238 J. Levitski, 'The Europeanization of British Style' (1994) 42 *American Journal of Comparative Law* 347.

239 Case 129/79, *Macarthys Ltd* v. *Smith* [1980] ECR 1275 at 1282. A similar problem arose in *Coote*. The case concerned whether an employee could claim a reference from her employer after the employment had terminated. The UK government argued that legal proceedings brought to enforce the principle of equal treatment do not fall within

A similar issue arose in *Webb*. The UK government argued as *amicus curiae* in the Court of Appeal that the Sex Discrimination Act 1975 explicitly required a comparison to be made between the dismissal of the complainant (a pregnant woman) and what would have happened to a male employee in the nearest comparable situation.[240] Counsel for the government saw no difficulty in comparing a pregnant woman with a man who has a medical condition which would require him to be absent for the same period of time and at the same time as the pregnant woman.[241] The 'inconsistencies' between *Dekker*[242] and *Hertz*[243] served as a fertile ground to insist on the comparison requirement under English law.

Defence of the autonomy of the respondents

The autonomy of the parties is primarily a legal concept. However, the concept has economic and moral implications. All three dimensions (legal, economic and moral) play an important role in the way in which the respondents construct their arguments.

First and foremost, equal treatment cases challenge the 'private autonomy' (*Privatautonomie*) of the respondents in deciding whom they want to engage, a man or a woman, on what terms and conditions and at what salary. EC law overrides this private autonomy, and obliges respondents to submit to the dictates of EC law. This might even be true with regard to 'collective autonomy' by way of collective bargaining agreements made between employers and trade unions.[244] Secondly, equal treatment cases challenge the degree to which employers may rely on economic reasons ('economic autonomy') to justify discrimination in whatever form, whether direct or indirect. Private autonomy and economic autonomy are interrelated. Employers as respondents use

the scope of Directive 76/207/EEC if they are taken *after* the employment relationship has ended. This was, in effect, a covert attempt to impose the interpretation given to an English statute by an English court onto European law.

240 *Webb* v. *EMO Air Cargo (UK) Ltd* [1992] 2 All ER 43 at 51–2.

241 An argument described by Szyszczak, 'The Status to Be Accorded to Motherhood', 860 at 862, as 'drawing inherently wrong comparisons'.

242 Case 177/88, *Dekker* v. *Stichting Vormingscentrum voor Jonge Volwassenen Plus* [1990] ECR I-3941.

243 Case C-179/88, *Handels- og Kontorfunktionaerernes Forbund i Danmark (Union of Clerical and Commercial Employees) (for Hertz)* v. *Dansk Arbejdsgiverforening (Danish Employers Association) (for Aldi Marked K/S)* [1990] ECR I-3979.

244 Case C-309/99, *Wouters* v. *Algemene Raad van de Nederlandse Ordre vor Advocaten* [2002] ECR I-1577.

legal arguments to defend their economic autonomy. Nevertheless, the meaning is different. The third dimension of autonomy turns on questions of *morality*. Here, the respondents tend to impose mainstream morality on the appellants.

It is often difficult for a respondent to accept that the EC law on equal treatment intervenes directly or indirectly in its private autonomy.[245] Even more difficult for UK lawyers to accept is the overarching interference of EC law in collective bargaining agreements[246] and its linkage to 'participative social democracy'.[247] In *Enderby*, the point at issue was whether the employer could rely, as sufficient justification for the difference in pay, on the fact that the level of pay for similar jobs had been determined by different collective bargaining processes which, considered separately, did not discriminate on the ground of sex. In the respondent's view, since the collective bargaining processes were reasonable and uninfluenced, directly or indirectly, by gender considerations, the employer should be able to rely on those collective-bargaining processes to defend himself against a claim that it had discriminated in pay rates. For each of the relevant professions in *Enderby*, many years of negotiations, supported by exhaustive studies, enabled the parties to take into account various factors, in particular the qualifications required and the state of the employment market.[248] *Enderby* is one of the rare cases in which a Member State intervened in order to support, at least partly, the appellant against the respondent. The German government considered that, where an employer has concluded a number of collective bargaining agreements with the same union, the fact that those agreements are otherwise legally valid does not in itself automatically justify the difference in pay set under each agreement. Otherwise, the employer could easily, by separate bargaining processes, circumvent the principle of equal pay. The German government went on to conclude that, nevertheless, it would be possible for different collective bargaining agreements to be concluded on the basis of an objective criterion of differentiation, and accordingly for any comparison between the jobs to be precluded.[249]

245 Wynn, 'Pregnancy Discrimination', 435 at 438: 'equality must take precedence over freedom of contract.'

246 Fredman, 'European Community Discrimination Law', 119 at 133.

247 J. Kentridge, 'Direct and Indirect Discrimination after Enderby' (1994) *Public Law* 198.

248 Case C-127/92, *Enderby* v. *Frenchay Health Authority and Secretary of State for Health* [1993] ECR I-5535 at 5546.

249 *Ibid.*, 5547.

The major *economic* concern of the respondents was the possibility of increased costs as a knock-on effect of equal treatment, in particular as a result of equal pay for men and women. The extension of the EC law to all forms of indirect discrimination has increased the financial burden on employers. Therefore, respondents tend to devote their full attention to the issue of whether and under what conditions the different treatment of men and women is allowed. The issue first arose in *Jenkins*. The employer in that case argued that the extra costs incurred as a result of employing part-time workers were sufficient justification for the pay difference.[250] The rather 'confusing'[251] judgment was interpreted by the English courts largely to allow economic justifications. *Bilka-Kaufhaus* also gave rise to the issue of economic justification. The full-time employees of Bilka were given a non-contributory pension on retirement. Part-time employees did not qualify for the pension unless they had been employed full-time for at least fifteen years. The employer contended that the exclusion of part-time workers from the pension scheme was to discourage part-time employment. This was necessary, as the employer had to employ several full-time workers to cover the evening and Saturday opening times which were unpopular among part-timers, and so had to make full-time work more attractive than part-time work. The policy therefore was thought to be justified by economic reasons as referred to in *Jenkins*.

There is, however, no direct evidence that German and UK employers were co-operating in their arguments before the ECJ defending economic reasons as legitimate and objective justifications. However, clearly employers have a common interest in keeping costs down. The employers therefore succeeded in defending their economic freedom. It remains to be seen whether and to what extent the English courts handle the *Bilka* test in the future.

There were far-reaching economic implications in *Smith* v. *Advel Systems*, in which, in the aftermath of *Barber*, the respondents found themselves challenged for directly discriminating against women by raising the pensionable age for female employees (rather than lowering it for men). Other potential respondents had no difficulty in recognising the far-reaching implications of the case.

[250] Case 96/80, *Jenkins* v. *Kingsgate (Clothing Productions) Ltd* [1981] ECR 911: 'The fewer hours worked entail additional charges (principally financial) for the employer which may be taken into consideration to give the female part-time employee a lower time rate.'

[251] Hervey, 'Justification for Indirect Sex Discrimination', 807 at 809.

P v. *S* and *Grant* concerned the applicability of EC law to the equal treatment of transsexuals and homosexuals. Here, different concepts of morality clashed. The facts of the cases and the submissions of the parties have been only partly made public. However, it is clear from the respective Opinions of the Advocates-General that in both cases the respondents argued against the applicability of the principle of equal treatment based on their own private conceptions of morality.[252]

The European Commission's position in equal treatment cases

The European Commission does not have a 'position' as such in equal treatment litigation, and therefore it is not one of the major players in this area of law. However, there has been a remarkable consistency in the Commission's attitude over the last two decades. In general, the Commission favours a broad understanding of the ECJ's jurisdiction; however, it does not want the ECJ to intervene too deeply in the Member States' legal orders. Member States should, in the Commission's view, benefit from discretion.

The Commission strongly supports the idea of using Article 141 (ex Article 119) as the principal weapon to fight sex discrimination. It relies on a *Cassis de Dijon*-type approach. The notion of 'pay' is to be given a broad meaning, encompassing both direct and indirect forms of discrimination. Article 141 (ex Article 119) is seen as a means to improve access by women to the labour market. The Commission advocates an interpretation of EC law which extends its scope of application *sedes materiae*. The Commission, however, rejects efforts to transform the principle of equal treatment into a principle of 'substantive justice', that is, to establish material standards on equal treatment once access to the labour market is guaranteed. The starting-point is similar with regard to the scope of application *sedes personae*. Whenever the 'State' is the addressee of the appellants' attempts to achieve equal treatment, appellants will find that the Commission is a strong supporter of their case. Last but not least, the Commission strongly advocates the availability of judicial protection. There should be no 'sheltered areas' of national law beyond the reach of EC law.

252 Advocate-General Elmer in Case C-249/96, *Grant* v. *South West Trains Ltd* [1998] ECR I-623 at 633 and Advocate-General Tesauro in Case C-13/94, *P* v. *S and Cornwall County Council* [1996] ECR I-2145 did not explicitly blame the respondents for their behaviour. However, the Advocates-General's intentions are nevertheless clear.

However, the Commission is much more supportive of respondents and the Member States when it comes to justifying exemptions, in particular with regard to all forms of indirect discrimination. The broader the jurisdiction of the ECJ in the scope of application *sedes materiae*, the wider should be the scope of the Member States to justify exemptions from the principle of equal treatment. The same is true with regard to judicial protection. While the Commission supports appellants in their attempts to shape judicial protection as a substantive part of the European legal order, it nevertheless maintains the freedom of the Member States to give shape to the principle of equal treatment.

The Commission's strong support for a broad understanding of 'equal pay'

As early as 1980, in *Macarthys Ltd* v. *Smith*,[253] the Commission had an opportunity to set out its position. The point at issue in that case was whether the applicability of Article 141 (ex Article 119) depended on whether men and women are *contemporaneously* doing equal work for their employer. The Commission took a strong position: the requirement of contemporaneity was neither justified either by the purpose or by the language of the text, nor supported by the case law of the ECJ, and furthermore had no foundation in common sense or in policy.[254] Whether the jobs are done simultaneously or successively, both employees are to be paid on the same basis. Discrimination would be encouraged if the principle of equal pay required the work to be done contemporaneously. Following *Defrenne*,[255] the Commission argued that the economic and social aims of Article 141 (ex Article 119) would be hindered by any requirement for contemporaneity. For example, one employer could undercut a competitor by employing only female employees at cheaper rates of pay.[256] The Commission highlighted some of the possible consequences of permitting such discrimination: an employer could dismiss all his male employees and replace them by female employees at lower rates of pay. A female employee in such a situation would be unable to make any claim for equal pay because there were no contemporaneously employed male workers to act as comparators.

Following *Macarthys Ltd* v. *Smith*, it was clear that the Commission supported the use of Article 141 (ex Article 119) as a means to make

253 Case 129/79, *Macarthys Ltd* v. *Smith* [1980] ECR 1275.
254 *Ibid.*, 1283.
255 Case 43/75, *Defrenne II* [1976] ECR 455, paras. 8–10.
256 Case 129/79, *Macarthys Ltd* v. *Smith* [1980] ECR 1275 at 1284.

equal treatment between men and women a reality. The next occasion on which equal treatment was in issue was in *Barber*, in which the notion of pension benefits as 'pay' within the meaning of Article 141 (ex Article 119) and Directive 75/117/EEC was discussed. The Commission was well aware of the legal and political implications of a decision in favour of the appellants in *Barber*, and made such implications clear in its submission. It considered that, in order to resolve the issues submitted to the ECJ, it was necessary to ascertain whether the fact that men and women of the same age had differing entitlements to statutory redundancy pay, in effect solely because of their sex, was compatible with Community law. If it was not compatible with Community law, the further issue had to be considered of whether the incompatibility derived from Article 141 (ex Article 119) or from the application of Article 5(1) of Directive 76/207/EEC. The Commission recognised that the Guardian Royal Exchange, the respondent in the case, as a private employer, could only be subject directly to EC law if Article 141 (ex Article 119) applied.

However, the practical consequences for the dispute vary greatly, depending on whether the matter is covered by Article 141 (ex Article 119), which has direct effect, or by Directive 76/207/EEC, which cannot be relied on in disputes between individuals. In order to resolve that issue, the Commission pointed out that *Roberts*[257] merely interpreted the Directive and left open the question of Article 141 (ex Article 119). *Worringham*[258] implied that compensation paid in the event of redundancy, other than the immediate pension, is covered by Article 141 (ex Article 119). And, in *Bilka-Kaufhaus*,[259] the ECJ applied Article 141 (ex Article 119) to an occupational pension scheme. Accordingly, the Commission identified two possible approaches:[260]

(1) A broad approach, based on the view that the judgment in *Bilka-Kaufhaus* has eliminated the distinction between the amount of the benefits and access thereto, with the result that Article 141 (ex Article 119) applies on the same condition both to access to occupational retirement schemes and to the benefits which they provide.

[257] Case C-132/92, *Birds Eye Walls Ltd* v. *Roberts* [1993] ECR I-5599.

[258] Case 69/80, *Worringham* v. *Lloyds Bank Ltd* [1981] ECR 767.

[259] Case 170/84, *Bilka-Kaufhaus GmbH* v. *Weber von Hartz* [1986] ECR 1607; [1986] 2 CMLR 701.

[260] Case C-262/88, *Barber* v. *Guardian Royal Exchange* [1990] ECR I-1889 at 1908.

(2) A narrow approach which leads to the result that compensation for redundancy is covered by Article 141 (ex Article 119), so that the same compensation must be paid to men and women in the same situation, even if it includes immediate payments under an occupational pension scheme in which normal retirement is fixed at different ages for men and women.

The Commission advocated the broad approach. To do otherwise would look like a retreat from *Bilka-Kaufhaus*, in which the ECJ specifically held that occupational pensions and other benefits are covered by Article 141 (ex Article 119).

The Commission's half-hearted support for transforming equal treatment into a general principle of substantive justice

The Commission demonstrated its unwillingness to argue before the ECJ in favour of a general principle of 'substantive justice' on three occasions. *Smith* v. *Advel Systems*, *P* v. *S* and *Grant* have in common that the appellants wanted to stretch the notion of equal pay and equal treatment beyond the mere abolition of discrimination in its formal sense. As a consequence of *Barber*, the effect of *Smith* v. *Advel Systems* was to raise the normal pensionable age for women to that applicable to men. In line with the arguments of the UK and German governments, the Commission had argued that Community law does not preclude the reduction of such benefits as long as the benefits are set at an equal level for both men and women.[261] *P* v. *S* concerned the equal treatment of transsexuals under Directive 76/207/EEC, and *Grant* concerned the equal pay of homosexuals under Article 141 (ex Article 119). Both the UK government and the Commission submitted that, to dismiss a person because he or she is a transsexual or because he or she has undergone a gender-reassignment operation, does not constitute sex discrimination for the purposes of Directive 76/207/EEC.[262] The Commission's arguments were more fully developed in *Grant*, which concerned the definition of a 'common law spouse' and was thus a family law issue, and therefore did not fall under the EC Treaty.

[261] Case C-408/92, *Smith* v. *Advel Systems Ltd* [1994] ECR I-4435.
[262] Case C-13/94, *P* v. *S and Cornwall County Council* [1996] ECR I-2145 at 2164.

The Commission argues for the integration of indirect discrimination

The Commission argued forcefully in favour of the appellants in their claims to have been subject to various forms of indirect discrimination. There is a strong similarity between the Commission's position in *Macarthys* and *Barber* (direct discrimination) on the one hand, and *Jenkins* (indirect discrimination) on the other. For the Commission, the question in *Jenkins* was whether the expression 'the same job' required a male employee and a female employee to work the same number of hours per week. Language versions other than English seem to suggest that it is in fact the 'post' and not the number of hours worked which determines whether or not the two jobs are 'the same'. The Commission referred to *Macarthys*, in which the ECJ decided that the nature of the services is the decisive factor. Moreover, according to the Commission, it is somewhat artificial to classify two jobs that were previously considered to be different from one another as similar just because there had been a reduction in the standard working week.

As to the extra costs imposed on employers, the position of the Commission has always been that 'factors affecting the cost or yield of female labour shall not be taken into consideration in the case of work paid by time'.[263] Any other approach, unless it were based on an objective, expert and detailed analysis, would leave the door open for discrimination based on sex. For the Commission, practical experience proves that the employment of part-time workers is in fact neither more nor less costly for the employer than the employment of full-time workers.[264]

In *Enderby*, the Commission had a further occasion to set out its position. It referred to the ECJ's case law, which made it clear that, where a disadvantage is imposed on a group composed predominantly of women, that disadvantage constitutes discrimination contrary to Article 141 (ex Article 119) unless the rule from which it derives can be objectively justified on the basis of factors unrelated to sex. No distinction should be made between situations in which the disadvantage

263 The role of the Commission with regard to the 'cost argument' is not fully considered by Hervey, 'Justification for Indirect Sex Discrimination', 807 at 809, n. 13.

264 Quoting a resolution of the conference of the Member States of 30 December 1961 on the equalisation of rates of pay for men and women, and an Opinion of 1 June 1978 of the Economic and Social Committee, both to the effect that pay for part-time work must be proportional to that for full-time work.

derives directly from a 'rule' and those in which the disadvantage derives from historical discriminatory assumptions. The fact that nothing indicates that on average women are less well paid than men in the professions in issue, or even the fact that those professions are in general predominantly female, should not be regarded as significant. The comparison must be made solely between persons doing an equivalent job who are at the same grades of their respective professions. The Commission points out that such an approach is needed to fight indirect discrimination, even if this means that it becomes necessary to compare the objective worth of various jobs and to justify pay differences only on the basis of statistics, which may or may not be reliable.

However, the Commission has made no attempt to transform the principle of equality into a principle of 'substantive justice'. The Commission considers that, in order to avoid the danger of raising the rule against sex discrimination into a general obligation of equal pay independent of such discrimination, the ECJ may limit the requirements of its case law to cases in which the rule in issue has a substantially more harmful impact on women than on men.[265]

The price for the integration of indirect discrimination: broadening the scope of objective justifications

There have only been a few cases in which the Commission has had an opportunity to set out its position on what objective justifications there may be for sex discrimination. In *Enderby*, the employer sought to argue for the non-applicability of Article 141 (ex Article 119) by referring to the fact that separate collective bargaining agreements had been concluded with each of the professions in issue. A point at issue therefore was whether the mere existence of such collective bargaining processes sufficed to justify any discrimination in the pay agreed by those collective bargaining processes. The Commission submitted that it is the *result* which has to be justified not the *process* by which that result was reached. In *Kowalska*[266] and *Nimz*,[267] the ECJ, it is said, recognised that the fact that a rule unfavourable to women has been agreed upon by employers and workers is not a sufficient reason to

[265] Case C-127/92, *Enderby* v. *Frenchay Health Authority and Secretary of State for Health* [1993] ECR I-5535 at 5545.

[266] Case C-33/89, *Kowalska* v. *Freie und Hansestadt Hamburg* [1990] ECR I-2591.

[267] Case C-184/89, *Nimz* v. *Freie und Hansestadt Hamburg* [1991] ECR I-297.

allow the *result* to stand if, in itself, the result is not justifiable. The Commission admitted that, occasionally, higher rates of pay for different professions are justified, in particular where there is a serious shortage of suitable candidates. The Commission submitted that only that part of the difference in the pay levels which is due to the particular need to attract suitable candidates can be justified.[268] To allow an employer to justify the *whole* difference in pay by claiming that a part of it may be explained by recruitment difficulties would evidently lead to an undervaluing of the female job.[269]

Effective and adequate judicial protection as basic elements of EC law

In *Johnston*, *Marshall II* and *Coote*, the Commission had the opportunity to develop its position on the role and importance of effective and adequate judicial protection in the European legal order. *Johnston* can be read as a case in which the ECJ enlarged the scope of application, *sedes personae*, of Article 141 (ex Article 119). One may also read *Johnston* as an outspoken *dictum* of the ECJ on the role and importance of effective judicial protection. This is how the Commission constructed its arguments. In *Johnston*, the appellant had been excluded from working as an armed officer in the Royal Ulster Constabulary and was permitted to work only in an unarmed role. The Commission was willing to assume that Directive 76/207/EEC had to be interpreted in light of Article 297 (ex Article 224),[270] that is, the unequal treatment may be justifiable. An exception created by an unchallengeable administrative decision, such as that provided for in Article 53 of the Sex Discrimination Order (Northern Ireland) 1976, is, however, said not to be permissible. A Member State which alleges that its action

[268] See Case C-127/92, *Enderby* v. *Frenchay Health Authority and Secretary of State for Health* [1993] ECR I-5535 at 5548.

[269] *Macarthys Ltd* v. *Smith* rules out hypothetical comparisons in favour of concrete situations. It therefore follows that the choice between totally equal pay and no equality at all is an approach which should clearly be applied both to a woman claiming equal pay and to an employer trying to justify the inequality. However, according to the Commission, the development of the ECJ's case law on the different effects of Art. 141 (ex Art. 119) in cases of disguised discrimination should, according to the Commission, culminate in allowing an employer to justify that part of the difference corresponding to the extra amount he has to pay in order to attract suitable candidates.

[270] Case 222/84, *Johnston* v. *Chief Constable of the Royal Ulster Constabulary* [1986] ECR 1651 at 1674.

was taken on the basis of an exception referred to in the Treaty or in secondary legislation must show that the necessary conditions are met, subject to review by the ECJ.[271]

It is worth noting that the Commission supports the concept of judicial review even in sensitive areas such as national security and public order. After *Johnston*, it was clear that judicial review would become and would remain an issue which the Commission would have to defend against any attempt by the Member States to restrict its reach. In *Marshall II*, the question arose of whether it was possible for a Member State to define an upper limit for compensation paid to women who had suffered discrimination. The upper limit also excluded the payment of interest on compensation. The Commission first reiterated the ECJ's case law, set out mainly in *von Colson* and *Harz*, from which it deduced that the Member States remained free to determine the redress to be provided. If a Member State opts for a sanction in the form of compensation, the compensation must nevertheless be adequate in relation to the damage sustained and have a real deterrent effect. Based on the ECJ's case law, the Commission then developed its own position on the restrictions on compensation imposed by UK law:[272]

(1) Even though it is not entirely unforeseen by Community legislation,[273] introducing limitations on liability in the implementation of Community law is said to be extremely rare, and such instances as exist relate to situations which are not comparable to those covered by the Directive in question.
(2) With regard to the exclusion of payment of interest, the Commission observed that, in the case at hand, as a result of the delay caused by the legal proceedings, over a decade had elapsed since the appellant's cause of action first arose. The Commission considered that, in such circumstances, the payment of interest was an

[271] *Ibid.*, 1674.

[272] Case C-271/91, *Marshall* v. *Southampton and South West Hampshire Area Health Authority* (*Marshall II*) [1993] ECR I-4367 at 4378.

[273] See Council Directive 85/374/EEC on the approximation of the laws, regulations and administrative provisions of the Member States concerning liability for defective products, OJ 1985 No. L210, 7 August 1985, 29, Art. 16; in the field of employment, see Council Directive 80/987/EEC on the approximation of the laws of the Member States relating to the protection of the employees in the event of insolvency of their employer, OJ 1980 No. L283, 28 October 1980, 23 and Council Directive 2000/43/EC implementing the principle of equal treatment between persons irrespective of racial or ethnic origin, OJ 2000 No. L180, 19 July 2000, 22, Art. 15.

essential element in ensuring that the damages awarded fulfilled their purpose of restoring the original position of the appellant. In the absence of express national provisions allowing an award of interest, the national courts should be guided by comparable situations for which such provisions exist.

The Commission's reluctance to allow the direct effect of Article 6 of Directive 76/207/EEC

The Commission did not support the direct effect of either Directive 76/207/EEC or Directive 75/117/EEC. The Commission gave way to the Advocates-General and the ECJ, choosing instead to keep a low profile. Such an interpretation becomes evident from the position the Commission took in *Marshall II*[274] on the question of whether the second limb of Article 6 of Directive 76/207/EEC benefited from direct effect.

(1) For the Commission, *von Colson* seems to be the bottom line of a feasible interpretation. Since Article 6 does not specify the nature of the sanction sought, it does not provide a directly effective right to override the limits of national law.
(2) An interpretation of national law based on Article 6 allowing EC law to override the limits of national legislation would offend the principles of legal certainty and non-retroactivity. In light of the ECJ's recognition in *Francovich*[275] of a cause of action against the state for the non-transposition of the provisions of a Directive not having direct effect, such an interpretative approach is said to be rendered unnecessary.

The Advocates-General and the ECJ: who is pushing whom in the development of equal treatment?

The position of the Advocates-General

Each Advocate-General is independent of the other Advocates-General, and therefore it is misleading to analyse whether they have a particular policy in equal treatment cases brought before the ECJ. The least that can be said is that the Advocates-General are usually some years ahead of the ECJ's position. However, the Opinions to be

[274] Case C-271/91, *Marshall* v. *Southampton and South West Hampshire Area Health Authority* (*Marshall II*) [1993] ECR I-4367 at 4377–80.

[275] Cases C-6 and 9/90, *Francovich and Bonifaci* v. *Italy* [1991] ECR I-5357.

analysed here demonstrate that there are substantial differences in the way in which the Advocates-General define their role and in which they present their views on equal treatment. Contrary to the submissions of the appellants, the respondents and the governments, the Advocates-General are expected to place the legal issues raised in their formal European legal contexts. The manner in which they do this, and the style and presentation of their Opinions, differ considerably from one Advocate-General to another, and sometimes from one case to another.

There are two striking features in the Opinions: the way Advocates-General handle the issue of the equal treatment of transsexuals and homosexuals; and the attention they devote to judicial remedies. The Advocates-General seem to feel particularly strongly about the issue of the equal treatment of transsexuals and homosexuals, so much so that one wonders if they are able to remain objective on the issue: they express sympathy for the appellants beyond the limits of what might be thought to be compatible with their impartial role in European litigation. The Advocates-General are here arguing much more like lawyers acting for appellants. The second issue is much less emotive than the first, though nevertheless of utmost importance in practice. After the ECJ had confirmed the direct effect of the second limb of Article 6 of Directive 76/207/EEC, the Advocates-General struggled hard to give shape to judicial remedies under EC law. The effectiveness of judicial protection and the comparability of judicial remedies are at the heart of the matter.

The notion of pay: *Macarthys* and *Barber*

The Opinions analysed below demonstrate how far the development of the European legal order has gone in a single decade. In *Macarthys Ltd* v. *Smith*,[276] Advocate-General Capotorti provided a rather technical view of the notion of equal pay. His main point was that a restriction on the application of the principle of Article 141 (ex Article 119), in the sense indicated by the question referred by the Court of Appeal, is not warranted by the wording of that provision, which requires only a similarity in the work done, and thus there is no mention of any criterion of *contemporaneity*. The Advocate-General backed up his position by reference to the objectives of Article 141 (ex Article 119) as set out in *Defrenne*.

[276] Case 129/79, *Macarthys Ltd* v. *Smith* [1980] ECR 1275 at 1291.

Advocate-General van Gerven faced more difficulties in *Barber*,[277] when it came to defining the notion of pay with regard to pension benefits. It was clear from the outset that the decision of the ECJ would depend ultimately on whether the ECJ would follow *Burton*[278] or *Bilka-Kaufhaus*.[279] The Advocate-General defined three possible solutions for resolving this issue:[280]

(1) Either the scope of Article 141 (ex Article 119) is limited, in accordance with *Burton*, to conditions governing pay *stricto sensu* which relate to the amount of remuneration and thus to the benefit itself, in which case the judgment in *Bilka* cannot be regarded as a precedent in this respect.
(2) Or, the scope of Article 141 (ex Article 119) is to be viewed as encompassing all working conditions which directly or indirectly affect the amount of remuneration and which, in other words, have financial consequences for the employee, in which case *Bilka* may be regarded as foreshadowing an interpretation which breaks with the – on that point restrictive – view taken by the ECJ in *Defrenne III*.
(3) Or, the principles in *Bilka* and *Defrenne III* are to be reduced to their common denominator, from which an interpretation may be deduced that gives full effect to that provision while taking account of the matters covered by Article 139 (ex Article 117) and Article 140 (ex Article 118).

Advocate-General van Gerven favoured the third solution as an attractive compromise. His distinction amounts to bringing within Article 141 (ex Article 119) working conditions (including conditions governing dismissal or other forms of redundancy) which directly govern *access* to remuneration (including a payment or pension benefit in connection with redundancy), but not the *conditions* precedent thereto which govern the inception, continuation or termination of the employment relationship, even though those conditions are attended by financial consequences or are accompanied by financial provision (such as terminal payments or pension benefits). Such an understanding goes hand in hand with van Gerven's Opinion in *Stoke-on-Trent*, and brings *Barber* within Article 141 (ex Article 119) as long as the

[277] Case C-262/88, *Barber* v. *Guardian Royal Exchange* [1990] ECR I-1889 at 1912.
[278] Case 19/81, *Burton* v. *British Railways Board* [1982] ECR 555.
[279] Case 170/84, *Bilka-Kaufhaus GmbH* v. *Weber von Hartz* [1986] ECR 1607; [1986] 2 CMLR 701.
[280] Case C-262/88, *Barber* v. *Guardian Royal Exchange* [1990] ECR I-1889 at 1925.

age condition does not have as its purpose the selection of staff whose employment relationship is to be terminated (in which case it would fall within the Directive on equal treatment as a condition governing dismissal) but rather constitutes a condition for the grant of a payment or pension benefit in connection with redundancy which takes effect once the employment relationship has been terminated.

In addition to the definition of what constitutes 'pay', the Advocate-General had to give his opinion on whether and to what extent the total value of the benefits is the same, even though the benefits were made up of components which differ according to sex but which are equally valuable. The Advocate-General followed the appellant's arguments in understanding 'pay' as a normative category. According to the Advocate-General, the principle of equal pay implies equality at the level of each component of remuneration. If it were otherwise, the enforceability of that principle by national courts would be seriously jeopardised, as national courts would be required to evaluate and compare a large number of diverse forms of remuneration which employers confer on their employees. That would call for a complex factual analysis, which would not guarantee the equality of total pay as effectively as it would guarantee the equality of each component of pay separately. Therefore, the principle of equal pay implies equality at the level of each component of remuneration.

Formal equality and substantive justice: are there inconsistencies?

The Advocates-General had three occasions on which to give their views on the possible transformation of the principle of equal treatment into a general principle of substantive justice. The first occasion arose in *Smith* v. *Advel Systems*. Advocate-General van Gerven raised the question without leaving any doubt as to his negative answer:

> Although the matter in issue is delicate, my view is that the *fundamental* answer is quite clear under Community law.[281]

Advocate-General van Gerven referred to his Opinions in *Ten Oever*,[282] *Moroni*,[283] *Neath*[284] and *Coloroll*,[285] in which he made a distinction

[281] Case C-408/92, *Smith* v. *Advel Systems Ltd* [1994] ECR I-4435 at 4443 (emphasis added).

[282] Case C-109/91, *Ten Oever* [1993] ECR I-4879.

[283] Case C-110/91, *Moroni* [1993] ECR I-6591.

[284] Case C-152/91, *Neath* [1993] ECR I-6935.

[285] Case C-200/91, *Coloroll Pension Trustees Ltd* v. *Russell* [1994] ECR I-4389.

between pension benefits according to whether the services for which the benefit was or is to be paid were performed before or after the *Barber* judgment. The Advocate-General shared the view taken by Advel Systems (the respondent), the UK and German governments and the Commission that Community law does not preclude the reduction of such benefits as long as the benefits are set at the same level for both men and women. Any different conclusion would amount to undesirable Community interference in a policy area which at present is the province of the Member States. What remains, according to the Advocate-General, is equal treatment in terms of 'equal access' and definitely not 'substantive' in terms of equal conditions.

Gender reassignment (*P* v. *S*) and homosexuality (*Grant* v. *South West Trains*) are issues which reach beyond the proper scope of EC law and imply the existence of human rights. That is why in both cases Advocate-General Tesauro, in *P* v. *S*, and Advocate-General Elmer, in *Grant*, had to deal with the interrelationship of EC law and the European Convention on Human Rights. Advocate-General Tesauro delivered his Opinion in December 1995.[286] He did not limit his presentation to EC law, maybe because EC law does not provide much guidance on the issue. He started by stating that the phenomenon of transsexuality constitutes a reality today which has been discussed by various bodies, not only scientific but also legal, in particular from the point of view of fundamental human rights. Moreover, a quick look at the situation in the various Member States reveals a clear tendency, particularly since the early 1980s, towards an ever wider recognition of transsexuality, both by legislation and by judicial decision. Advocate-General Tesauro then turned to transsexuality as a subject-matter for the European Convention on Human Rights. He referred to *B* v. *France*,[287] in which the European Court of Human Rights stated that the prohibition in French law on adopting a feminine name or changing one's civil status after surgery constituted a violation of Article 8(1)[288] of the European Convention on Human Rights.[289]

Advocate-General Tesauro then took a closer look at Directive 76/207/EEC. For him, the point was whether gender reassignment was

[286] Case C-13/94, *P* v. *S and Cornwall County Council* [1996] ECR I-2145.

[287] *B* v. *France* (A/232-C) [1992] 2 FLR 249; (1993) 16 EHRR 1; [1992] Fam Law 491.

[288] Art. 8(1) provides: 'Everyone has the right to respect for his private and family life, his home and his correspondence.'

[289] Case C-13/94, *P* v. *S and Cornwall County Council* [1996] ECR I-2145, para. 11.

covered by Article 2(1) of the Directive.[290] First, he reiterated that the Directive prohibits any discrimination whatsoever on the ground of sex. The wording of the principle of equal treatment laid down in the Directive refers to the traditional male/female dichotomy. In order to ascertain whether the Directive also covers discrimination against transsexuals, as the industrial tribunal suggested, one must determine whether the unfavourable treatment of transsexuals constitutes discrimination on the ground of sex. The Advocate-General answered this question in the affirmative,[291] and invited the ECJ to make a 'courageous' decision. He left the final word to Advocate-General Trabucchi in an Opinion he delivered nearly thirty years ago:

> [I]f we want Community law to be more than a mere mechanical system of economics and to constitute instead a system commensurate with the society which it has to govern, if we wish it to be a legal system responding to the concept of social justice and European integration, not only of the economy but of the people, we cannot disappoint the [national] courts' expectations, which are more than those of legal form.[292]

Advocate-General Elmer's Opinion in *Grant* v. *South West Trains* followed the reasoning of Advocate-General Tesauro in *P* v. *S* quite closely, though with less enthusiasm, maybe with less impact on human rights and certainly without reference to the appellant's arguments. He began with general remarks concerning gender discrimination in society. He reiterated the ECJ's decision in *P* v. *S*, in which the ECJ held that the right not to be discriminated against on the ground of sex is a fundamental human right whose observance the ECJ had a duty to ensure. In Advocate-General Elmer's view, the ECJ interpreted the Community principle of equal treatment in such a way as to allow him to find gender discrimination in *Grant*. A provision in the rules of an employer's pay scheme, under which travel concessions are granted to a cohabitee

[290] Art. 2(1) of Directive 76/207/EEC provides as follows: 'For the purposes of the following provisions, the principle of equal treatment shall mean that there shall be no discrimination whatsoever on grounds of sex either directly or indirectly by reference in particular to marital or family status.'

[291] Case C-13/94, *P* v. *S and Cornwall County Council* [1996] ECR I-2145: 'To my mind where unfavourable treatment of a transsexual is related to (or rather is caused by) a change of sex, there is discrimination by reason of sex or on grounds of sex, if that is preferred.'

[292] Opinion of Advocate-General Trabucchi in Case 7/75, *F* v. *Belgium* [1975] ECR 679 at 697, as quoted in the Opinion of Advocate-General Tesauro in Case C-13/94, *P* v. *S and Cornwall County Council* [1996] ECR I-2145 at 2157.

of the opposite sex but not to a cohabitee of the same sex, constitutes discrimination on the basis of gender and falls within the scope of Article 141 (ex Article 119).[293]

The Advocate-Generals' unwavering views on pregnancy and motherhood

For Advocate-General Tesauro, *Webb*[294] was a clear-cut case. He stated that termination of an employment contract because of pregnancy applied only to women and therefore constituted direct discrimination on the grounds of sex. He based his understanding on the ECJ's judgment in *Dekker*[295] with respect to the refusal to appoint a pregnant woman, and in *Hertz*[296] with respect to the dismissal of a pregnant woman. The Advocate-General suggested that, following *Dekker* and *Hertz*, the Directive must be construed so as to achieve substantive equality and not mere formal equality, which would constitute the denial of the very concept of equality. The Advocate-General rejected the view of the national courts that a pregnant woman is comparable to a male employee who is unable, for medical or other reasons, to work during a given period.[297]

Early uncertainties on indirect discrimination

Jenkins[298] provided the first occasion for an Advocate-General to give an Opinion on whether *indirect* discrimination is covered by Article 141 (ex Article 119). The Employment Appeal Tribunal had referred the question of whether the wording of Article 141 (ex Article 119) required that the rate of pay for work must be the same irrespective of the number of hours an employee works each week. Advocate-General Warner denied that a part-time worker and a full-time worker had the 'same' job even though they may do equal work. He found support for his argument in *Macarthys Ltd* v. *Smith*, in which the ECJ said:

> It must be acknowledged, however, that . . . it cannot be ruled out that a difference in pay between two workers occupying the same post but

[293] Case C-249/96, *Grant* v. *South West Trains Ltd* [1998] ECR I-623 at 628–30.

[294] Case C-32/93, *Webb* v. *EMO Air Cargo (UK) Ltd* [1994] ECR I-3569.

[295] Case 177/88, *Dekker* v. *Stichting Vormingscentrum voor Jonge Volwassenen Plus* [1990] ECR I-3941.

[296] Case C-179/88, *Handels- og Kontorfunktionaerernes Forbund i Danmark (Union of Clerical and Commercial Employees) (for Hertz)* v. *Dansk Arbejdsgiverforening (Danish Employers Association) (for Aldi Marked K/S)* [1990] ECR I-3979.

[297] Case C-32/93, *Webb* v. *EMO Air Cargo (UK) Ltd* [1994] ECR I-3569 at 3576.

[298] Case 96/80, *Jenkins* v. *Kingsgate (Clothing Productions) Ltd* [1981] ECR 911.

> at different periods in time may be explained by the operational factors which are unconnected with any discrimination on the grounds of sex. That is a question of fact which is not for the Court or tribunal to decide.[299]

The Advocate-General underlined that this was the correct approach even though it was difficult to monitor in practice. This was a quite narrow understanding, which the ECJ did not accept. However, the Advocate-General was correct in underlining the importance of 'facts' in deciding on questions of indirect discrimination.

The burden of proof in direct and indirect discrimination

In *Enderby*, Advocate-General Lenz attempted to draw a clear line between direct and indirect discrimination, in particular on the different requirements on the burden of proof.[300] He distinguished cases of direct and indirect discrimination, and referred to his Opinion in *Danfoss*.[301]

In cases of *direct* discrimination, it is said to be necessary and sufficient to carry out an actual comparison of the pay received by a female employee and a male employee performing work, which is the same or of equal value, for the same employer. During the course of the proceedings, the plaintiff must introduce evidence of a male comparator employed by the same employer who is doing work which is the same as or of equal value to that done by the plaintiff and who is being paid more than the plaintiff. It is then for the employer to furnish counter-evidence, for example by adducing objective grounds for the unequal pay which are not based on the sex of the recipients. It may be concluded therefore that, in cases of direct discrimination, the employer must objectively justify differences in pay.

The concept of 'indirect discrimination' is a legal one, which enables cases of unequal treatment, for which there is an objective justification but which in fact results in the woman being disadvantaged, to be characterised as unlawful sex discrimination. In the context of indirect discrimination, the plaintiff can, by proving objective facts, raise a rebuttable presumption of sex discrimination. The structure of the reasoning for both direct and indirect discrimination is comparable with regard to the evidentiary aspect of the proceedings in as much as

[299] Case 129/79, *Macarthys Ltd* v. *Smith* [1980] ECR 1275, para. 12.

[300] Case C-127/92, *Enderby* v. *Frenchay Health Authority and Secretary of State for Health* [1993] ECR I-5535 at 5556.

[301] Case C-109/88, *Danfoss* [1989] ECR 3209, para. 25.

the rebuttable presumption of discrimination can be raised, in one case by means of a specific comparison and, in the other, by a comparison of groups, which places the onus on the employer to adduce evidence to rebut that presumption or to produce a justification.

For the Advocate-General, the principle of equal pay enshrined in Article 141 (ex Article 119) requires the employer to justify objectively the differences in pay between pharmacists and speech therapists employed by the UK's National Health Service.[302] The Advocate-General did not challenge the notion that the existence of indirect discrimination is a matter of fact. This is why appellants and respondents will continue to dispute over the facts, more specifically over statistics. The law divides the burden of proof. The appellant seems to be in a more favourable situation if she succeeds in proving the facts; the respondent, however, has the opportunity to refute the presumption by bringing forward objective reasons to justify unequal treatment. However, since then, Directive 97/80/EC has settled the issue in favour of employees.[303]

The direct effect of Article 6 of Directive 76/207/EEC: providing a ground for EC law-based sanctions

The question raised by the appellant in *Marshall II* was whether the existing case law of the ECJ on Article 6 of Directive 76/207/EEC could be further extended in order to give direct effect also to the second limb of Article 6, that is, in relation to the requirement imposed on Member States to provide for *appropriate sanctions*. Ms Marshall wanted the ECJ to set standards for the notion of judicial protection. Advocate-General van Gerven divided his Opinion into three principal parts, each of which was headed by a specific question:

(1) May individuals rely on Article 6 of the Directive before national courts?

[302] Advocate-General Lenz in Case C-127/92, *Enderby* v. *Frenchay Health Authority and Secretary of State for Health* [1993] ECR I-5535 at 5558, paras. 19, 25, 26, 27, 38, 39 and 40.

[303] OJ 1998 No. L14, 15 December 1997, 6. Art. 4(1) provides: 'Member States shall take such measures as are necessary, in accordance with their national judicial systems, to ensure that, when persons who consider themselves wronged because the principle of equal treatment has not been applied to them establish, before a court or other competent authority, facts from which it may be presumed that there has been direct or indirect discrimination, it shall be for the respondent to prove that there has been no breach of the principle of equal treatment.'

(2) Is a statutory upper limit on compensation compatible with Article 6 of the Directive?
(3) Is the inability to award interest compatible with Article 6 of the Directive?

He admitted that *von Colson*[304] and *Harz*[305] had taken for granted that the answer to the first question could only be that a victim of discrimination *cannot* rely on Article 6 of the Directive *inter alia* against a public body of a Member State in order to have the limits imposed by national legislation on the amount of compensation recoverable set aside.[306] He added that *he* would have come to a different conclusion. The starting-point of his analysis was the general obligation imposed on Member States by Article 10 (ex Article 5) of the EC Treaty to guarantee the application and effectiveness of Community law. He then went on to reiterate the key paragraphs of the judgments in *von Colson* and *Harz*.[307] However, he drew a different conclusion from the baseline of the latter two judgments, instead relying on *Zuckerfabrik*.[308]

He then turned to the question of whether a *statutory upper limit* on compensation was compatible with Article 6 of the Directive. He sought the answer on the basis of the two basic requirements against which national remedies have to be measured: the criterion of *sufficient enforceability*; and the criterion of *comparability* in *von Colson* and *Hertz*. National upper limits on compensation are not regarded as unlawful provided that the limit is set high enough not to deprive the sanction of its deterrent nature and did not prevent its being adequate in relation to the damage normally sustained as a result of an infringement.[309] The more important aspect was the criterion of comparability. The appellant relied on it, the respondent and the UK government rejected it. For van Gerven *Marshall II* was not a hard case: he recognised good reasons for the distinction made by UK law in its redress scheme. Industrial tribunals in the UK deal with all complaints relating to race and sex discrimination in employment,

[304] Case 14/83, *Von Colson and Kamann* v. *Land Nordrhein-Westfalen* [1984] ECR 1891.
[305] Case 79/83, *Harz* v. *Deutsche Tradax* [1984] ECR 1921.
[306] Case C-271/91, *Marshall* v. *Southampton and South West Hampshire Area Health Authority* (*Marshall II*) [1993] ECR I-4367 at 4384.
[307] *Ibid.*, paras. 7 and 8.
[308] With regard to national rules concerning the suspension of the enforcement of national administrative measures, see Case C-143/88 and C-92/89, *Zuckerfabrik Süderdithmarschen* [1991] ECR I-415, para. 25.
[309] Case C-271/91, *Marshall* v. *Southampton and South West Hampshire Area Health Authority* (*Marshall II*) [1993] ECR I-4367 at 4391.

and the compensation which may be awarded in race discrimination cases was subject to the same upper limits as those laid down in section 65(2) of the Sex Discrimination Act 1975.

Instead of opting for a legal system in which all complaints relating to sex discrimination (irrespective of whether they relate to employment or some other field) are dealt with by one court, the UK legislator opted for a system in which all claims based on unfair dismissal *in the field of employment* are dealt with by one court (the industrial tribunals, with appeal to the Employment Appeal Tribunal) irrespective of whether the dismissal was based on discrimination on the grounds of sex, race or some other unlawful criterion, or was unlawful for other reasons, and irrespective as to whether the complaint was based on national or Community law. Both options appear to van Gerven to be of equal validity, and it cannot be inferred from the option chosen by the UK that less effective sanctions are imposed in that country in respect of Community law than are imposed in respect of corresponding national law. He therefore considered that, as far as the criterion of comparability is concerned, the limit on compensation imposed by section 65(2) of the Sex Discrimination Act 1975 does not conflict with Article 6 of the Directive.

Advocate-General van Gerven then pointed out that there is an obligation to pay interest under Article 6 of the Directive. His argument focused on the *principle of efficiency*. In *Johnston*, the ECJ had held that 'the requirement of judicial control stipulated by Article 6 of the Directive reflects a general principle of law [to the effect that] all persons have the right to obtain an effective remedy in a competent court against discrimination prohibited by the Directive'. According to van Gerven, the principle of efficiency requires that, insofar as the national legal order gives people a right of appeal or other legal remedies against the decision of the first court, they must be able to avail themselves of those avenues without being disadvantaged financially.[310]

The power and the limits of the principle of efficiency and the principle of comparability to shape judicial protection

EC law provides two principles, based on *Comet*,[311] for giving shape to judicial protection: the principle of efficiency; and the principle of

[310] *Ibid.*, para. 26.

[311] Case 45/76, *Comet BV* v. *Produktschap voor Siergewassen* [1976] ECR 2043, paras. 12–19.

comparability. In theory, *Coote*[312] and *Levez*[313] provided fertile ground for the Advocates-General to discuss and shape these principles. The Opinions of the Advocates-General differ considerably in their outlook. In *Coote*, Advocate-General Mischo said that the concept of 'efficiency' is a concept which should be left in the hands either of the legislator or of the parties themselves. However, in *Levez*, Advocate-General Léger concentrated on the principle of comparability, a principle van Gerven applied in *Marshall II*, though without being too explicit about doing so.

In *Coote*, Advocate-General Mischo had no difficulties in accepting that the provision of references fell within the scope of the Directive. In contrast to the Commission, he started from the idea that the appropriate legal basis is Article 3 of Directive 76/207/EEC. Based on *Kowalska*,[314] he concluded that the protection provided for under the Directive did not cease with the termination of the employment relationship. However, he added three qualifications to dispel misunderstandings:[315]

1. It is only where the employer is required by law or by an express or implied term of the contract to provide references, or in practice habitually accedes to requests for references, that the principle of equal treatment must be observed.
2. The provision of references for former employees falls within the scope of the Directive and in no way interferes with any rules of national law concerning the extent of the employer's obligation to provide such references.
3. The employer remains entirely unfettered as regards the assessment to be made of the quality of the services rendered, provided that it remains within the limits imposed by the duty of objectivity.

Advocate-General Mischo's Opinion then considered whether the requirements to provide judicial remedies imposed by Article 6 apply in cases in which the employee claims to have suffered not from discrimination on the ground of sex but rather from victimisation for having exercised the right to bring proceedings challenging alleged discrimination on the ground of sex. Based on a literal reading of the Directive,

[312] Case C-185/97, *Coote* v. *Granada Hospitality Ltd* [1998] ECR I-5199.
[313] Case C-326/96, *Levez* v. *T. H. Jennings (Harlow Pools) Ltd* [1998] ECR I-7835.
[314] Case C-33/89, *Kowalska* v. *Freie und Hansestadt Hamburg* [1990] ECR I-2591.
[315] Case C-185/97, *Coote* v. *Granada Hospitality Ltd* [1998] ECR I-5199 at 5206.

he concluded that this was not the case. As would an English judge, the Advocate-General stuck to the wording of the Directive, and rejected the opportunity of reaching a different conclusion on the basis of the 'richly promising seam of case law, which has recourse to the concept of *effet utile*'.[316]

In *Levez*, Advocate-General Léger's Opinion is much more in line with van Gerven's presentation in *Marshall II*. Advocate-General Léger attempted to get to grips with the principle of equivalence and the principle of effectiveness under the existing case law of the ECJ. First, he referred explicitly to Advocate-General Mancini in *San Giorgio*[317] and Advocate-General Jacobs in *BP Supergas*[318] to demonstrate that generally it is for the national court to ensure that the principle of equivalence is observed. However, the question is whether European law may provide guidelines on the expression 'similar domestic action' which national courts must respect.[319] Advocate-General Léger confirmed that it remained incumbent upon EC law to define *standards of comparability*. He promoted the idea of a *vertical* comparison. Therefore, Mrs Levez's claim had to be compared with similar claims for salary arrears in the field of employment. Advocate-General Léger rejected the approach of the UK government that a claim under the Equal Pay Act 1970 is a form of action under domestic law which is similar to a claim brought under Article 141 (ex Article 119) – a circular argument.[320] He was willing to accept neither the proposal of the French government, the European Commission and the appellant, nor that, if a comparison is to be made, then the field of domestic law in which the protection is most akin to that of the Equal Pay Act 1970 – that is, the Race Relations Act 1976 – should be the correct point of comparison. Such an approach may be criticised for focusing on the broadest possible interpretation of the general principle of non-discrimination. In the end, the Advocate-General confirmed the responsibility of the national courts to determine whether similar actions are being treated differently, depending on whether the cause of action is discrimination on ground of sex, and therefore safeguarded

[316] *Ibid.*, 5208.

[317] Case 199/82, *Ammistrazione delle Finanze dello Stato* v. *San Giorgio SpA* [1982] ECR 3595, para. 11.

[318] Case C-62/93, *BP Supergas* v. *Greece* [1995] ECR I-1883, para. 58.

[319] Case C-326/96, *Levez* v. *T. H. Jennings (Harlow Pools) Ltd* [1998] ECR I-7835; [1999] All ER (EC) 1, para. 49.

[320] *Ibid.*, para. 43.

by Community law, or whether the action is one which is not linked to Article 141 (ex Article 119).

Secondly, the Advocate-General then turned to the *principle of effectiveness*. Essentially, the ECJ was asked whether the fixing of a time limit such as that laid down by section 2(5) of the Equal Pay Act 1970 made it impossible to exercise the rights conferred by Community law. The Advocate-General recalled that there is a certain tension between the principle of effectiveness and the Member States' independence in procedural matters, insofar as the former requires that the rules governing domestic actions should not make it virtually impossible or excessively difficult to exercise rights conferred by Community law. In a long line of cases, the ECJ had made clear its position. Under EC law, time limits are justified if they serve 'to ensure that the legality of administrative decisions cannot be challenged indefinitely'.[321] The Advocate-General then turned to Mrs Levez, who had been prevented from taking action because her employer had concealed from her the discrimination of which she was a victim. It was the unusual circumstances of the particular case, rather than the existence of the time bar in the Equal Pay Act 1970, that led the Advocate-General to conclude that the fact that the national court was prevented by the terms of section 2(5) of the Equal Pay Act 1970 from extending the time limit in exceptional cases was contrary to the principle of effectiveness as well as to the principle of equivalence.

The position of the ECJ

While it might be an overstatement to conclude that the case law of the ECJ fully sets out the Court's views on any particular matter, it is nevertheless possible to perceive certain consistent tendencies in the ECJ's views. The ECJ has shown a preparedness to permit a broad understanding of the scope of application *sedes materiae*. This is particularly true for the notion of equal pay within Article 141 (ex Article 119). *Barber* must certainly be analysed in light of the ECJ's denial of horizontal direct effect to the two Directives on equal treatment. Thus, the only way to enhance its policy of eliminating sex discrimination was to broaden the scope of Article 141 (ex Article 119). A clear statement to this effect cannot, however, be found in the case law on the scope of application *sedes personae*. The least that can be said is that the ECJ

[321] Case C-338/91, *Steenhorst-Neerings* [1993] ECR I-5475, para. 22.

has made great efforts to extend the applicability of EC law into areas Member States tend to shelter from interference by European law. The contrary is true for the potential addressees of sex discrimination. The ECJ seems bound to the classical male–female conflict areas. Sex discrimination is understood as gender discrimination and not discrimination based on sexual orientation. Here, the ECJ leaves the matter to the policy-makers.

The ECJ had no difficulties in attacking all direct forms of sex discrimination. *Webb* may serve as a classic example in which a woman was dismissed when she informed her employer that she was pregnant. Since *Melgar*[322] and *Tele Danmark*,[323] it has been clear that the question of whether the contract of employment was for a fixed term or for an indefinite term has no bearing on the discriminatory character of a dismissal or refusal to employ on account of pregnancy. By contrast, the ECJ met more difficulties in dealing with forms of indirect discrimination. Although it was prepared to accept indirect forms of discrimination coming under primary and secondary EC law, it maintained that, in principle, it was for the national courts to decide, on the basis of the facts in the case, whether there is indirect discrimination or not. It did not, however, provide much in the way of guidance as to the criteria the national courts should apply. The same is true of the matters that employers may put forward to objectively justify the indirect discrimination. Again, the ECJ relied on the national courts to apply EC law. However, quite the contrary is true for matters involving judicial protection: on this issue, the ECJ was keen to strengthen effective judicial protection and to minimise the role of the national courts.

The ECJ has developed a particular technique to deal with questions referred to it. National courts tend to frame their questions in a form which they believe will best induce the ECJ to set out clear guidance on the issues. This approach is common to all national courts, whatever their position in the legal hierarchy.[324] The ECJ, on the other hand, is

[322] Case C-438/99, *Melgar* v. *Ayuntamiento de Los Barrios* [2001] ECR I-6915.

[323] Case C-109/00, *Tele Danmark A/S* v. *Handels- og Kontorfunktionaerernes Forbund i Danmark* [2001] ECR I-6993.

[324] Barnard and Hepple, ‘Indirect Discrimination’, 399 at 403, where the authors note how carefully the House of Lords drafted ‘five detailed and carefully constructed questions’ in *Seymour-Smith* and how poor the answer of the ECJ was.

inclined to resist any effort to force it to be too precise or too specific in its answers. It does this by broadening the questions and/or by combining them so as to give them a wider scope. This has the effect of divorcing the national legal issues from the facts of the individual cases, and of making European law unclear and therefore in need of further clarification. EC law is thus reduced to an absolute minimum and the arguments of the appellants and the respondents vanish into the fog.

Broadening the scope of application *sedes materiae*

In *Macarthys Ltd* v. *Smith*, the ECJ followed the conclusions of Advocate-General Warner, although the ECJ's judgment is clearer and less beset by exceptions than is the Advocate-General's Opinion. For the ECJ, the decisive test lies in establishing whether there is a difference in treatment between a man and a woman performing 'equal work' within the meaning of Article 141 (ex Article 119). The scope of that concept – which is entirely qualitative in character, in that it is exclusively concerned with the nature of the services in question – may not be restricted by the introduction of a requirement of contemporaneity. The ECJ accepts, however, that there might be circumstances in which a difference in pay between two workers occupying the same post but at different periods in time may be explained by factors which are unconnected with any sex discrimination. Here, it would remain for the national court to decide the case. The second question referred to the ECJ concerned the yardstick against which the potential salary of the discriminated woman could and should be measured. The ECJ relies on the concept of 'a hypothetical male worker'.[325] Statistical comparisons between professions are seen as an appropriate means to determine whether women receive lower pay than men in a comparable job. This is a task best done by the national courts.

Barber was a good opportunity to define the notion of equal pay. Although competence issues did not really come to the fore in the *Barber* case, these issues were nevertheless present in the background. Although the *Barber* decision was a landmark decision, the ECJ did not follow Advocate-General van Gerven in his attempt to distinguish

[325] Case 129/79, *Macarthys Ltd* v. *Smith* [1980] ECR 1275 at 1289, para. 14.

between, on the one hand, conditions concerning *access* to remuneration and, on the other hand, *conditions* precedent thereto on the inception, continuation or termination of the employment relationship. Contrary to the Advocate-General's approach, the ECJ did not answer the referred questions in a cumulative form but answered them as separate, unconnected questions. In reply to the first question,[326] the ECJ relied on *Garland*,[327] in which it held that the concept of pay within the meaning of Article 141 (ex Article 119) comprised all forms of remuneration. Certain benefits paid after the termination of the employment relationship therefore constituted 'pay'. By relying on *Defrenne II*,[328] the ECJ rejected the UK government's argument that a statutory redundancy payment fell outside the scope of Article 141 (ex Article 119) because it constituted a social security benefit and not a form of pay.

The ECJ then turned to the second question.[329] It is notable that the ECJ did not discuss *Burton*,[330] which raised the same issue. *Defrenne I*[331] reminded the ECJ that Article 141 (ex Article 119) did not cover social security schemes or benefits directly governed by legislation without any element of agreement within the undertaking or the occupational branch concerned. The ECJ then referred to *Bilka-Kaufhaus* in order to justify the conclusion that a pension paid under a contracted-out occupational pension scheme did fall within the scope of Article 141 (ex Article 119). Transposed to the terminology of Advocate-General van Gerven, the ECJ chose the most comprehensive option on the notion of pay.[332]

[326] '1. When a group of employees are made compulsorily redundant by their employer in circumstances similar to those in this case and receive benefits in connection with that redundancy, are all those benefits "pay" within the meaning of [Art. 141 (ex Art. 119)] and Directive 75/117/EEC or do they fall within the Equal Treatment Directive 76/207/EEC?'

[327] Case 12/81, *Garland* v. *British Rail Engineering Ltd* [1982] ECR 359, para. 5.

[328] Case 43/75, *Defrenne II* [1976] ECR 455, para. 40.

[329] '2. Is it material to the answer to 1 that one of the benefits in question is a pension paid in connection with a private occupational pension scheme operated by the employer ("a private pension")?'

[330] Case C-19/81, *Burton* v. *British Railway Board* [1982] ECR 555, thereby avoiding the difficulty of reconciling *Barber* with *Burton*; see S. Honeyball and J. Shaw, 'Social Policy: Sex, Law and the Retiring Man' (1991) 16 *European Law Review* 47.

[331] Case 80/70, *Defrenne I* [1971] ECR 445, paras. 7 and 8.

[332] Curtin, 'Scalping the Community Legislator', 475 at 482, n. 32.

The third[333] and fifth[334] questions were dealt with together by the ECJ.[335] If national courts were under an obligation to make an assessment and a comparison of all the various types of remuneration received by employees, judicial review would become difficult in practice, and the effectiveness of Article 141 (ex Article 119) would be diminished as a result. It follows that effective judicial review is ensured only if the principle of equal pay applies to each and every element of remuneration. The ECJ followed the arguments of the Advocate-General closely here.

The ECJ rejects an extension of the scope of application *sedes personae*

Johnston[336] constituted yet a further occasion for the ECJ to underline its position that there are no realms of national law that may remain 'sheltered' from the scope of application of EC law. For the ECJ, the most important question was whether the UK could legitimately deny judicial review of the appellant's claim on the ground of public safety. Therefore, the ECJ started with the sixth question[337] referred by the national court. The ECJ held that the requirement of judicial review stipulated by Article 6 of Directive 76/207/EEC reflects a general principle of law which underlies the constitutional traditions of the Member States and which is laid down in Articles 6 and 13 of the European Convention on Human Rights. For the ECJ, it is therefore clear that,

[333] '3. Is the principle of equal pay referred to in [Art. 141 (ex Art. 119)] and the Equal Pay Directive infringed in the circumstances of the present case if: (a) a man and a woman of the same age are made compulsorily redundant in the same circumstances and, in connection with that redundancy, the woman receives an immediate private pension but the man receives only a deferred pension, or (b) the total value of the benefits received by the woman is greater than the total value of the benefits received by a man?'

[334] 'Is it material to the answer to Question 3 that the woman's right to access to an immediate pension provided for by the Severance Term could only be satisfied if she qualified for an immediate pension under the provisions of the private occupational scheme in that she was being treated as retired by the Guardian because she was made redundant within seven years of her normal pension date under the pension scheme?'

[335] Case C-109/88, *Danfoss* [1989] ECR 3199, para. 12.

[336] Case 222/84, *Johnston* v. *Chief Constable of the Royal Ulster Constabulary* [1986] ECR 1651.

[337] '6. Is the applicant entitled to rely on the principle of equal treatment contained in the relevant provisions of [Directive 76/207/EEC] before the national courts and tribunals of Member States in the circumstances of the present case?'

by virtue of Article 6, all persons have the right to obtain an effective remedy in a competent court against measures which they consider to be contrary to the principle of equal treatment laid down in Directive 76/207/EEC. The ECJ was very explicit:

> It follows that the application of the principle of equal treatment for men and women is not subject to any general reservation as regards measures taken on grounds of the protection of public safety apart from the possible application of [Article 297 (ex Article 224)] of the Treaty which concerns a wholly exceptional situation and is the subject-matter of the seventh question. The facts which induced the competent authority to invoke the need to protect public safety must therefore if necessary be taken into consideration in the first place in the context of the application of the specific provisions of the Directive.

Such specific provisions may be found in Article 2(2) of the Directive, provided the circumstances of the case may be understood as constituting a 'determining factor'. Although all derogations have to be interpreted strictly, the ECJ was willing to recognise that, in the serious civil disturbances in Northern Ireland at the time, the carrying of firearms by female police officers might increase the risk of their being assassinated, and might therefore be contrary to the requirement of public safety.[338] In such circumstances, the sex of the police officer may constitute a determining factor. Due regard, however, has to be given to the principle of proportionality.[339]

In its fourth[340] and fifth[341] questions, the Industrial Tribunal asked the ECJ for an interpretation of the expressions 'protection of women' in Article 2(3) of the Directive and 'concern for protection' in Article 3(2)(c).[342] The ECJ rejected a broad interpretation of these exemptions. For the ECJ it was clear from the express reference to pregnancy and maternity that the Directive was intended to protect a woman's biological condition and the special relationship which exists between a woman and her child.[343]

338 Case 222/84, *Johnston* v. *Chief Constable of the Royal Ulster Constabulary* [1986] ECR 1651 at 1686, para. 36.

339 *Ibid.*, 38.

340 'Are Art. 119 and the Equal Pay Directive of direct effect in the circumstances of this case?'

341 See note 334 above. 342 See p. 186 above.

343 Case 222/84, *Johnston* v. *Chief Constable of the Royal Ulster Constabulary* [1986] ECR 1651 at 1688, para. 44.

In comparison to the forceful (and even emotional) Opinions of the Advocates-General in *P* v. *S*[344] and *Grant*,[345] the ECJ's reasoning appears rather sober. *P* v. *S* is a very short judgment in which the ECJ set aside all references to human rights and Member States' legislation with regard to gender reassignment. According to the ECJ, the Directive covers not only discrimination based on the fact that a person is of one or the other sex but also discrimination arising from gender reassignment:

> Such discrimination is based, essentially if not exclusively, on the sex of the person concerned. Where a person is dismissed on the ground that he or she intends to undergo, or has undergone, gender reassignment, he or she is treated unfavourably by comparison with a person of the sex to which he or she was deemed to belong before undergoing gender reassignment.[346]

This reading also guided the ECJ in *Grant*, although *P* v. *S* concerned Directive 76/207/EEC and *Grant* Article 141. Maybe the different treatment of transsexuals and homosexuals results from the simple fact that transsexuals form a fairly easily identifiable group.[347] The ECJ, sitting in full Court, devoted much more attention to the human rights dimension and the policy considerations highlighted by the appellant and by the Advocate-General. Instead of responding to the questions one by one, the ECJ again considered all six referred questions together, although it did divide them into three issues.

The first essential point raised by the national court was whether an employer's refusal to grant travel concessions to a person of the same sex with whom an employee has a stable relationship constitutes discrimination prohibited by Article 141 (ex Article 119) and Directive 75/117/EEC, where such concessions are granted to an employee's spouse or the person of the opposite sex with whom an employee has a stable relationship outside marriage. The ECJ rejected any effort to extend the scope of application of Article 141 (ex Article 119) to differences in treatment based on sexual orientation, thus taking an extremely formal perspective. In referring to the above-quoted paragraph in *P* v. *S*, the ECJ held at, since the condition imposed by the

[344] Case C-13/94, *P* v. *S and Cornwall County Council* [1996] ECR I-2145.
[345] Case C-249/96, *Grant* v. *South West Trains Ltd* [1998] ECR I-623.
[346] Case C-13/94, *P* v. *S and Cornwall County Council* [1996] ECR I-2145 at 2165.
[347] *Ibid.*, para. 16.

respondent's regulations applied in the same way to female and male workers, it cannot be regarded as constituting discrimination directly based on sex.[348]

Secondly, the ECJ considered whether, with respect to the application of a condition such as that at issue, persons who have a stable relationship with a partner of the same sex are in the same situation as those who are married or have a stable relationship outside marriage with a partner of the opposite sex. The ECJ referred to Member States' legislation, to the European Commission of Human Rights and to the European Court of Human Rights, and concluded that, in the present state of the law within the Community, stable relationships between two persons of the same sex are not regarded as equivalent to marriages or stable relationships outside marriage between persons of opposite sex. The ECJ concluded that, in these circumstances, it is for the legislature alone to adopt measures which may affect that position.

Last but not least, the ECJ considered the appellant's submission that it follows from *P* v. *S* that differences of treatment based on sexual orientation are included in the prohibition of sex discrimination in Article 141 (ex Article 119). The ECJ tried to distinguish this case from the position it had taken in *P* v. *S* by saying that, in *Grant*, 'discrimination was in fact based, especially if not exclusively, on the sex of the person concerned'.[349] Again, the ECJ considered national and international regulations, conventions and policy statements and concluded that the solution must be found in the Treaty of Amsterdam, which allows the Council under certain conditions (a unanimous vote on a proposal from the Commission after consulting the European Parliament) to take appropriate action to eliminate various forms of discrimination, including discrimination based on sexual orientation.[350] The first measure to be adopted under the new Article 13 of the EC Treaty was Directive 2000/78/EC which, *inter alia*, realises politically what the ECJ felt unable to determine on the basis of Directive 76/207/EEC alone.[351]

348 Case C-249/96, *Grant* v. *South West Trains Ltd* [1998] ECR I-623 at 646, para. 28.

349 *Ibid.*, para. 42. 350 *Ibid.*, para. 48.

351 As laid down in Art. 2(2)(b); on the content and the policy behind this, see M. Bell and L. Waddington, 'Reflecting on Inequalities in European Equality Law' (2003) 28 *European Law Review* 349; on the possible implications of the new legal basis, see R. Whittle and M. Bell, 'Between Social Policy and Union Citizenship: The Framework Directive on Equal Treatment in Employment' (2002) 27 *European Law Review* 677.

Direct and indirect discrimination

The ECJ's position in challenging all forms of *direct* discrimination has been quite consistent since 1990, at least in the eyes of the ECJ itself. This may explain the unwillingness on the part of the ECJ in *Webb* to consider the questions referred by the House of Lords, as they considered that the same issues had already been dealt with in *Hertz*[352] and *Habermann-Beltermann*.[353] Just as in the Sunday trading cases, the ECJ started from the position that it had already said what had to be said, and that any fine-tuning should remain in the hands of the national courts. However, *Webb*, and later *Brown*,[354] demonstrated that the ECJ was wrong.

The decision in *Webb* concerned a contract of employment concluded for an *indefinite* term. According to the ECJ, there can be no question of comparing the situation of a woman who finds herself incapable, by reason of pregnancy of performing the task for which she was recruited, with that of a man similarly incapable for medical or other reasons. The ECJ referred explicitly to Mrs Webb's submission that pregnancy is not in any way comparable with a pathological condition and even less so with an unavailability for work on non-medical grounds, both of which are situations that may justify the dismissal of a woman without discriminating on the ground of sex. Furthermore, and contrary to the submission of the UK government, dismissal of a pregnant woman recruited for an indefinite period is said not to be justifiable on grounds relating to her inability to fulfil a fundamental condition of her employment contract. The availability of an employee is necessarily, for the employer, a pre-condition for the proper performance of the employment contract.

The ECJ had many more difficulties in dealing with *indirect* discrimination. *Jenkins*[355] shows that the ECJ was fully aware of the far-reaching implications of putting both direct and indirect discrimination under the jurisdiction of Article 141 (ex Article 119). The ECJ could have taken *Jenkins* as a 'testing ground' in which it could take

[352] Case C-179/88, *Handels- og Kontorfunktionaerernes Forbund i Danmark (Union of Clerical and Commercial Employees) (for Hertz)* v. *Dansk Arbejdsgiverforening (Danish Employers Association) (for Aldi Marked K/S)* [1990] ECR I-3979.

[353] Case C-421/92, *Habermann-Beltermann* [1994] ECR I-1657.

[354] Case C-394/96, *Brown* v. *Rentokil* [1998] ECR I-4185; [1998] 2 CMLR 1049; on this case, see Wynn, 'Pregnancy Discrimination', 435.

[355] Case 96/80, *Jenkins* v. *Kingsgate (Clothing Productions) Ltd* [1981] ECR 911.

a first step into the difficult field of indirect discrimination. Although the judgment is extremely short, it contains the basic elements which the ECJ then developed in subsequent judgments. The ECJ recognised that indirect discrimination is covered by Article 141 (ex Article 119), although the discrimination may be justified if the difference in pay between part-time work and full-time work is attributable to factors which are objectively justifiable. The ECJ therefore necessarily had to decide the issue of *how* any such discrimination could be objectively justified and *who* was to make that determination. To this end, the ECJ, in a statement which has raised concerns not only in the UK, stated:

> Where the hourly rate of pay differs according to whether the work is part-time or full-time it is for the national courts to decide in each individual case whether, regard being had to the facts of the case, its history and the employer's *intention*, a pay policy such as that which is at issue in the main proceedings although represented as a difference based on weekly working hours is or is not in reality discrimination based on the sex of the worker.[356]

The key word here is 'intention'. Read literally, this excludes all sorts of discrimination that the employer has no intention of committing.[357] With hindsight, it seems relatively clear, however, that the ECJ did not intend to put so much emphasis on the employer's intention to discriminate. In *Enderby*,[358] the ECJ had a further opportunity to set out what should be understood by 'objective justification' and on whom the burden of proof should rest.[359] The latter question had already been decided in *Bilka-Kaufhaus*,[360] *Kowalska*,[361] *Nimz*[362] and *Danfoss*[363] to the benefit of the potential victims. The ECJ followed the Advocate-General in his reasoning that it is not the *procedure* but the *result* that

356 *Ibid.*, para. 14 (emphasis added).

357 Barnard, 'A European Litigation Strategy' in Shaw and More (eds.), *New Legal Dynamics of the European Union*, 270.

358 Case C-127/92, *Enderby* v. *Frenchay Health Authority and Secretary of State for Health* [1993] ECR I-5535.

359 A. Abanulo, 'Equal Pay for Work of Equal Value: The "Result-Oriented" Approach that Never Was' (1999) 28 *Industrial Law Journal* 365.

360 Case 170/84, *Bilka-Kaufhaus GmbH* v. *Weber von Hartz* [1986] ECR 1607; [1986] 2 CMLR 701.

361 Case C-33/89, *Kowalska* v. *Freie und Hansestadt Hamburg* [1990] ECR I-2591.

362 Case C-184/89, *Nimz* v. *Freie und Hansestadt Hamburg* [1991] ECR I-297.

363 Case 109/88, *Danfoss* [1989] ECR 3199.

should decide whether discrimination was present or not.[364] Therefore, the mere existence of collective bargaining agreements is not *per se* a justification. The key point in *Enderby*, however, is encapsulated in the third referred question which required a decision as to whether Community law should provide guidelines and criteria which the national courts would have to respect when assessing whether discrimination was objectively justified. The ECJ first reiterated its consistent case law under which it held that it is for the national courts to determine whether and to what extent the reasons put forward by an employer as justification for adopting a practice which was discriminatory on the ground of sex may be regarded as being objectively justified on economic grounds.[365] The ECJ continued:

> Those grounds may include, if they can be attributed to the needs and objectives of the undertaking, different criteria such as the worker's flexibility or adaptability to hours and places of work, his training or his length of service.[366]

While the ECJ accepted in principle the validity of the argument that the shortage of candidates might present such an objective justification, it delegated the final decision to the national courts. Directive 76/207/EEC, as amended by Article 1(2) of Directive 2002/73/EC, now defines, in Article 2(2), second indent,[367] and Article 2(6),[368] the reasons which might justify *indirect* discrimination. While the EC legislator has undertaken a major effort to implement the ECJ's case law,

[364] See Fredman, 'Equal Pay and Justification', 39.

[365] Case 170/84, *Bilka-Kaufhaus GmbH* v. *Weber von Hartz* [1986] ECR 1607; [1986] 2 CMLR 701, para. 36; and Case C-184/89, *Nimz* [1991] ECR I-297 at 319, para. 14.

[366] Case C-127/92, *Enderby* v. *Frenchay Health Authority and Secretary of State for Health* [1993] ECR I-5535 at 5575, para. 25.

[367] Art. 2(2), second indent, defines indirect discrimination as 'where an apparently neutral provision, criterion or practice would put persons of one sex at a particular disadvantage compared with persons of the other sex, unless that provision, criterion or practice is objectively justified by a legitimate aim, and the means of achieving that aim are appropriate and necessary'.

[368] Art. 2(6) now provides: 'Member States may provide, as regards access to employment including the training leading thereto, that a difference of treatment which is based on a characteristic related to sex shall not constitute discrimination where, by reason of the nature of the particular occupational activities concerned or of the context in which they are carried out, such a characteristic constitutes a genuine and determining occupational requirement, provided that the objective is legitimate and the requirement is proportionate.'

in particular *Sirdar*[369] and *Kreil*,[370] the new wording may give rise to further litigation.[371]

A firm commitment to judicial protection

The ECJ had two occasions, in *Marshall I* and *Marshall II*, to state and reiterate the importance of judicial protection under Articles 5 and 6 of Directive 76/207/EEC. Following Advocate-General van Gerven, the ECJ fully considered the three questions raised by the House of Lords in *Marshall II* – although in a different order and only after having highlighted the meaning and scope of Article 6 of Directive 76/207/EEC.[372] In its answer to the first question,[373] the ECJ deduced from Article 6 that the fixing of an upper limit for compensation cannot by definition constitute a proper implementation of Article 6 of the Directive, since it limits the amount of compensation *a priori* to a level which is not necessarily consistent with the requirement of ensuring real equality of opportunity through adequate reparation for the loss and damage sustained as a result of a discriminatory dismissal. On the second question,[374] the ECJ is likewise quite clear on the need to award interest as an essential component of compensation for the purposes of restoring real equality of treatment.

The most important part of the ECJ's judgment concerns the third question[375] as to whether the second limb of Article 6 of the Directive

[369] Case C-273/97, *Sirdar* v. *(1) Army Board and (2) Secretary of State for Defence* [1999] ECR I-7403.

[370] Case C-285/98, *Kreil* v. *Germany* [2000] ECR I-69.

[371] Recital 12 to the Directive explicitly refers to *Johnston*, *Sirdar* and *Kreil*.

[372] Case C-271/91, *Marshall* v. *Southampton and South West Hampshire Area Health Authority* (*Marshall II*) [1993] ECR I-4367 at 4406, para. 17.

[373] '1. Where the national legislation of a Member State provides for the payment of compensation as one remedy available by judicial process to a person who has been subject to unlawful discrimination of the kind prohibited by Council Directive 76/207/EEC, is the Member State guilty of a failure to implement Art. 6 of the Directive by reason of the imposition by the national legislation of an upper limit of £6,250 on the amount of compensation recoverable by such a person?'

[374] '2. Where the national legislation provides for the payment of compensation as aforesaid, is it essential to the due implementation of Art. 6 of the Directive that the compensation to be awarded (a) should not be less than the amount of the loss found to have been sustained by reason of unlawful discrimination, and (b) should include an award of interest on the principal amount of the loss so found from the date of the unlawful discrimination to the date when the compensation is paid?'

[375] '3. If the national legislation of a Member State failed to implement Art. 6 of the Directive in any of the respects referred to in questions 1 and 2, is a person who

benefits from direct effect. The three decisive paragraphs of the judgment deserve close attention:

> Accordingly, the combined provisions of Article 6 and Article 5 of the Directive give rights, on the part of a person who has been injured as a result of discriminatory dismissal, which that person must be able to rely on before the national courts as against the State and authorities which are an emanation of the State.
>
> The fact that Member States may choose among different solutions in order to achieve the objective pursued by the Directive depending on the situations which may arise, cannot result in individuals being prevented from relying on Article 6 in a situation such as that in the main proceedings where the national authorities have no degree of discretion in applying the chosen solution.
>
> It should be pointed out in that connection that, as appears in particular from the judgment in Joint Cases C-6/90 and C-9/90 *Francovich* v. *Italian Republic* [1991] ECR I-5357, at 17, the right of the State to choose among several possible means of achieving the objectives of a Directive does not exclude the possibility for individuals of enforcing before national courts rights whose content can be determined sufficiently precisely on the basis of the provisions of the Directive alone.

This judgment of the ECJ is quite outspoken, and invites appellants to push the development of judicial protection further along. This they did. In *Coote*, the ECJ began its judgment by referring to *von Colson*[376] and *Marshall I*,[377] in which it reiterated the key role of Article 6 for victims of discrimination in pursuing their claims through a judicial process, here understood as a principle which underlies the constitutional traditions common to the Member States and enshrined in Article 6 of the European Convention on Human Rights.[378] It continued with a clear-cut statement of the principle of effective judicial protection, which would be deprived of an essential part of its effectiveness if the protection which it provided did not cover measures which

has been subjected to unlawful discrimination as aforesaid entitled as against an authority which is an emanation of the Member State to rely on the provision of Art. 6 as overriding the limits imposed by the national legislation on the amount of compensation recoverable?'

[376] Case 14/83, *Von Colson and Kamann* v. *Land Nordrhein-Westfalen* [1984] ECR 1891.

[377] Case 152/84, *Marshall* v. *Southampton and South West Hampshire Area Health Authority* [1986] ECR 723 (*Marshall I*).

[378] Case C-185/97, *Coote* v. *Granada Hospitality Ltd* [1998] ECR I-5199 at 5220, paras. 20 and 21.

an employer might take as a reaction to legal proceedings brought by an employee with the aim of enforcing compliance with the principle of equal treatment. Fear of such measures,

> where no legal remedy is available against them, might deter workers who considered themselves the victims of discrimination from pursuing their claims by judicial process, and would consequently be liable to seriously jeopardise the implementation of the aim pursued by the Directive.[379]

In *Levez*,[380] the ECJ recognised that, in general, it is compatible with Community law for national rules to prescribe reasonable limitation periods for bringing proceedings, as this is in the interests of legal certainty. Nevertheless, in the present case the ECJ held the principle of *efficiency* had been violated due to the particular circumstances of the case. Mrs Levez had been deliberately misinformed about the salary of her male predecessor. Mrs Levez discovered the true situation only after the time period for bringing a claim under English law had passed. This law thus made it virtually impossible or excessively difficult to obtain arrears of remuneration in respect of sex discrimination. For the ECJ, it was therefore plain that the ultimate effect of this rule would be to facilitate the breach of Community law by an employer whose deception caused the employee's delay in bringing proceedings for enforcement of the principle of equal pay.

In theory, there would have been no reason in *Levez* for the ECJ to discuss the principle of *equivalence*. However, the UK government had argued that Mrs Levez could have successfully claimed full compensation for the damage suffered by bringing a claim under the Equal Pay Act 1970 in proceedings before the county court. For the ECJ, these arguments served as a pretext for a closer look at the principle of equivalence. While the ECJ confirmed that, in principle, it is for the national courts to ascertain whether the procedural rules intended to ensure that the rights granted to individuals by Community law were safeguarded under national law comply with the principle of equivalence,[381] nevertheless the ECJ may provide the national court with *guidance* as to the interpretation of Community law. The ECJ thus introduced three elements into the assessment of whether the principle

[379] *Ibid.*, para. 24.
[380] Case C-326/96, *Levez* v. *T. H. Jennings (Harlow Pools) Ltd* [1998] ECR I-7835.
[381] Case C-261/95, *Palmisani* [1997] ECR I-4025, para. 33.

of equivalence was violated or not: (1) the similarity of the purpose and the cause of action; (2) the purpose and the essential characteristics of allegedly similar domestic actions; and (3) the operation and any special features of that procedure before the various national courts.[382]

Based on these criteria, and by an explicit reference to the Advocate-General's Opinion, the ECJ rejected the UK government's submission that the same procedural rules, namely, the limitation period laid down by section 2(5) of the Equal Pay Act 1970, applied to two comparable claims, one relying on a right conferred by Community law, the other on a right conferred by domestic law, is sufficient to ensure compliance with the principle of equivalence. The ECJ was not, however, willing to indicate the types of claim that should be compared. One may read into the final conclusions of the ECJ a certain scepticism over whether the claim before the county court may be regarded as equivalent, due to the fact that an action before the industrial tribunal is simpler and generally cheaper.[383] The important issue that the case highlights is whether the national courts are really willing to accept the responsibility offered to them by the ECJ or whether the ECJ must continue to monitor national proceedings in order to determine whether the national courts are applying EC law correctly.

Preston[384] was the next occasion on which the ECJ was able to test English remedies against the requirements of EC law. More than 60,000 part-time workers claimed to have been victims of discrimination on the ground of sex as a result of being excluded from occupational pension schemes, membership of which, in the UK, was often available only to full-time workers. English law, however, limited to two years prior to the date of initiating proceedings the period for which a person may secure the right to retroactive membership of the pension scheme from which they were excluded. Such workers have to initiate proceedings within a period of six months after each employment ceased, even where a series of fixed-term contracts had been concluded. The full Court ruled in favour of the claimants. Legally, *Preston* largely confirms *Levez*. The effects of the two limitation periods in *Preston* were found to undermine the principle of efficiency. While the ECJ did not

[382] Case C-326/96, *Levez* v. *T. H. Jennings (Harlow Pools) Ltd* [1998] ECR I-7845, paras. 41, 43 and 44.
[383] *Ibid.*, para. 51.
[384] Case C-78/98, *Preston* v. *Wolverhampton Healthcare NHS Trust* [2000] ECR I-3201.

rule out national limitation periods as such, it took a hard look at their impact on part-time workers. Just as in *Levez*, the application of the principle of comparability raised many difficulties. While the ECJ reiterated the above-mentioned three elements to assess the comparability of remedies meant to implement EC law with those meant to implement similar national rules, it put much more emphasis on the national courts' obligation to verify objectively, in the abstract, whether the rules at issue were similar, taking into account the role played by those rules in the legal procedure as a whole, as well as the operation of that procedure and any special features of those rules.[385]

The attitude of judges in national courts and of legal doctrine

The basis of analysis here is relatively limited, as most decisions of the referring courts are not publicly available. If the Equal Opportunities Commission was involved in a case, then information about that case is usually more readily available from the EOC's files. Not surprisingly, the decisions of the Court of Appeal and the House of Lords are much more likely to be reported in full than those of the lower courts, particularly those of industrial tribunals and the Employment Appeal Tribunal. However, despite the difficulty of obtaining information on some decisions, it is still possible to derive from the cases a set of hypotheses on the role and function of the referring courts. The referring courts are set out in Table 3.2.

The willingness of the national courts to refer questions to the ECJ

The degree to which the English courts are willing to refer cases to the ECJ differs widely. The lower courts seem more willing to refer sex discrimination cases than the higher courts. This difference in attitude may be partly due to the dominant role of the EOC in litigation before the industrial tribunals and the Employment Appeal Tribunal. Beyond the issue of the willingness of courts to refer cases, however, there are differences in the role the courts play in the development of equal treatment litigation. Each level of the courts system seems to fulfil a

[385] *Ibid.*, para. 63.

Table 3.2 *Enforcement of the ECJ's equal treatment decisions in the national courts*

	Case	ECJ	National courts
Scope *sedes materiae*	Macarthys v. Smith	(+)[a]	(+) Court of Appeal[b]
	Barber	(+)	large follow-up[c]
	Smith v. Advel Systems	(−)	
Scope *sedes personae*	Johnston	(+)	(+)[d]
	P v. S	(+)	(+)[e] follow-up
	Grant	(−)	
Direct and indirect discrimination	Webb	(+)	(+) House of Lords[f]
	Jenkins	(+)	(−) Employment Appeal Tribunal[g]
	Enderby	(+)	(−) follow-up[h]
Judicial protection	Marshall I	(+)	(+) House of Lords
	Foster	(+)	(+) House of Lords
	Marshall II	(+)	(+) House of Lords
	Coote	(+)	
	Levez	(+)	

[a]A '(+)' symbol indicates a positive outcome/follow-up for the appellant(s); a '(−)' symbol indicates a negative outcome/follow-up for the appellant(s).

[b][1981] QB 180; [1980] 3 WLR 929; [1981] 1 All ER 111, Court of Appeal, *per* Lord Denning.

[c]On the English law background, see in particular G. Moffat and L. Luckhaus, 'Occupational Pension Schemes, Equality and Europe: A Decade of Change' (1998) 20 *Journal of Social Welfare and Family Law* 1.

[d]See P. Morris, 'Sex Discrimination, Public Order and the European Court' (1987) *Public Law* 334 at 343. The industrial tribunal subsequently awarded Mrs Johnston (and other women police officers) substantial damages.

[e]On the immediate, yet positive, effect of *P v. S*, see P. Skidmore, 'Can Transsexuals Suffer Sex Discrimination?' (1997) 19 *Journal of Social Welfare and Family Law* 105 at 109.

[f]The House of Lords decided in favour of Mrs Webb, [1995] 4 All ER 577, and remitted the case to the industrial tribunal for an assessment of compensation; see C. Boch, 'Case Note on Case C-32/93, Webb v. EMO Air Cargo (UK) Ltd [1994] ECR I-3567 in the House of Lords [1995] 1 WLR 1454' (1996) 33 *Common Market Law Review* 547.

[g]See C. Barnard and B. Hepple, 'Indirect Discrimination: Interpreting Seymour-Smith' (1999) 58 *Cambridge Law Journal* 399 at 401 and 402. When *Jenkins* returned to the Employment Appeal Tribunal, the President, Sir Nicholas Browne-Wilkinson, stated that the ECJ's judgment was so unclear that he would apply his own reinterpretation of national law, and held that unintentional discrimination against part-time female workers was contrary to the Equal Pay Act 1970, even if not unlawful under Article 141 (ex Article 119): see [1981] IRLR 388.

[h]On the effects of *Enderby* in the English courts, see M. Connolly, 'How a European Court of Justice Decision on Equal Pay May Affect British Indirect Discrimination Law' (1996) 1 *Web Journal of Current Legal Issues* 1.

quite specific function within the overall picture of equal treatment litigation.

Policy-making in industrial tribunals

Some of the principal cases in the area of equal treatment have been referred to the ECJ by industrial tribunals. In *Smith* v. *Advel Systems*,[386] the EOC set out to transform the principle of equal treatment into a principle of substantive justice. *Smith* must be seen in the context of a line of cases in which the EOC attempted to shape the implementation of the *Barber* doctrine in English law. *P* v. *S*[387] and *Grant* v. *South West Trains*[388] fit very well into such a picture. Industrial tribunals were prepared to extend Directive 76/207/EEC and Article 141 (ex Article 119) to transsexuals and homosexuals respectively. Unfortunately, these two cases are not very well documented, even in the reports of the hearings and the Opinions of the Advocates-General. Thus, little information can be found on the background to the cases, that is, on the 'why' and 'how' the cases made their way to the ECJ. It seems as if the EOC did not directly assist the appellants before the industrial tribunals, and therefore it does not have full information on these cases.

An analysis of *Smith* v. *Advel Systems*, *P* v. *S* and *Grant* v. *South West Trains* reveals that industrial tribunals are prepared to consider new issues in which the case law is not yet settled and in which the law is not clear. The Article 234 (ex Article 177) procedure is clearly used by appellants as a means to push the ECJ into action in order to improve the legal position of those in society suffering discrimination.

The Employment Appeal Tribunal: developing existing EC law

The Employment Appeal Tribunal devotes more attention to the strict legal aspects of litigation than to the 'sensational' facts of cases like *P* v. *S* and *Grant*. Nevertheless, the Employment Appeal Tribunal may be more open to an appellant's arguments (because it is much closer to everyday employment practices) than the higher courts. This was the case in *Levez*,[389] in which the two lay members of the Employment

[386] Case C-408/92, *Smith* v. *Advel Systems Ltd* [1994] ECR I-4435.
[387] Case C-13/94, *P* v. *S and Cornwall County Council* [1996] ECR I-2145.
[388] Case C-249/96, *Grant* v. *South West Trains Ltd* [1998] ECR I-623.
[389] Case C-326/96, *Levez* v. *T. H. Jennings (Harlow Pools) Ltd* [1998] ECR I-7835.

Appeal Tribunal outvoted the judicial president.[390] On the other hand, the Employment Appeal Tribunal seems unprepared to allow itself to be used to stretch equal treatment law beyond its boundaries. Instead, the Employment Appeal Tribunal considers that it refers cases only when there are good legal reasons for doing so.

These findings result from an analysis of the three cases of interest to use here which industrial tribunals have referred to the ECJ: *Jenkins*, *Levez* and *Coote*. *Jenkins* raised for the first time the question of whether indirect discrimination comes under the notion of equal treatment in Article 141 (ex Article 119). *Levez* and *Coote* must be understood as sequels to *Marshall II*. Once the ECJ had accepted the direct effect of both limbs of Article 6 of Directive 76/207/EEC, there was ample room to test the actual scope of Article 6. The three referrals, however, would probably not have been made if the EOC had not been involved in the litigation. In all three cases, the EOC stepped in after the industrial tribunal had made its decision. In all three cases, the EOC provided considerable input on the role and importance of Community law in overcoming deficiencies in national equal treatment rules.

The Court of Appeal: clarifying the legal issues

The Court of Appeal's function seems to lie in bringing those cases to the ECJ where clarification of the correct interpretation of Treaty rules and of the relevant Directives is needed and where questions concerning the proper implementation of Directives in the national legal system arise. The Court of Appeal has referred four cases of interest to us here, that is, *Macarthys Ltd* v. *Smith*,[391] *Barber*,[392] *Enderby*[393] and *Marshall I*.[394] In all four cases, the Court of Appeal sought clarification of the EC law on equal treatment. In *Macarthys*, the Court of Appeal sought a decision on whether men and women had to be *contemporaneously* employed in order for a valid comparison to be made of rates

[390] C. Kilpatrick, 'Gender Equality: A Fundamental Dialogue' in S. Sciarra (ed.), *Labour Law in the Courts: National Judges and the European Court of Justice* (Oxford, 2001), 31 at 50.

[391] Case 129/79, *Macarthys Ltd* v. *Smith* [1980] ECR 1275.

[392] Case C-262/88, *Barber* v. *Guardian Royal Exchange* [1990] ECR I-1889.

[393] Case C-127/92, *Enderby* v. *Frenchay Health Authority and Secretary of State for Health* [1993] ECR I-5535.

[394] Case 152/84, *Marshall* v. *Southampton and South West Hampshire Area Health Authority* [1986] ECR 723 (*Marshall I*).

of pay. *Barber* concerned whether social security payments fell outside the scope of application of Article 141 (ex Article 119) and therefore beyond the jurisdiction of the ECJ. In *Enderby*, the Court of Appeal sought guidance on what reasons employers may put forward to objectively justify differences in pay between men and women. *Marshall I* evidences a shift in the emphasis of equal treatment litigation from the scope of application of Article 141 (ex Article 119) to matters of enforcement.

The House of Lords: seeking a final decision from the ECJ

Appellants must travel a long way from the industrial tribunal to the House of Lords. However, once they get there, they are usually successful in persuading the House of Lords to refer equal treatment issues to the ECJ. The House of Lords has done so in *Webb*, *Foster* and *Marshall II*. All three cases have one aspect in common, that is, that the House of Lords appears to have referred the three cases to the ECJ not to seek advice on a specific legal issue, but rather to seek guidance on how to decide a particular case under established EC law. By doing so, the House of Lords is pushing the ECJ to act as a court of final instance, that is, as the highest court of the country, rather than to observe its normal role as a horizontal supranational body that has to take into consideration twenty-five different legal orders in its interpretation of European legal concepts.

In *Foster*, the outcome of the litigation depended entirely on whether the appellants were entitled to rely directly on Directive 76/207/EEC before the English courts and tribunals in order to claim damages on the ground that the policy of the British Gas Corporation on the age of retirement of its employees was contrary to the Directive. There was agreement between all parties concerned, including the courts, that the appellants had suffered from discrimination. However, the question which arose and which was referred to the ECJ, was whether the British Gas Corporation must be understood as an 'emanation of the State'; if so, the appellants would succeed; if not, the appellants would fail. This was a clear-cut 'yes' or 'no' situation, in which the House of Lords relied on the ECJ to determine the appropriate solution.

In *Webb*, it was held unanimously by the industrial tribunal, the Employment Appeal Tribunal, the Court of Appeal and the House of Lords that, on a proper construction of the relevant provision of the Sex Discrimination Act 1975, the dismissal of the appellant did not constitute unlawful discrimination against her on the ground of sex.[395] The ECJ was asked to decide on the question of whether the dismissal of a pregnant woman must be regarded in each and every case as a prohibited form of direct sex discrimination. All the English courts concerned had difficulties in accepting a concept of fairness, which does not fit in well with the legal and cultural traditions in the UK.

Marshall II was somewhat different, in that the ECJ had not yet had the opportunity definitively to decide on the possible direct effect of the second limb of Article 6 of Directive 76/207/EEC. Thus, there was clearly a legal issue in the background which needed to be investigated by the ECJ. However, the length of the *Marshall* litigation, lasting more than a decade, with two referrals to the ECJ, should have provoked the House of Lords into putting an end to the debate and to take a decision on its own.

European legal requirements and national facts

There seems to be a tension between broad European legal requirements and the need for the national courts to decide on the facts by reference to these requirements. English courts devote much effort to determining whether the case is covered by codified equal treatment law. Most of the references result from deficiencies, or *lacunae*, in English law, which invite appellants to seek their rights in the broader and more purposive language of the EC law on equal treatment.[396] If pushed to the European legal level, or if prepared to embark on determining the EC law on equal treatment, English courts look at comparable cases decided by the ECJ in order to provide guidance in the case at hand. If there is no relevant case law at hand, or if the EC law is too broad to provide clear-cut guidance, the English courts tend to refer the issue to the ECJ.

There are two cases in which the difficulties of the English courts in dealing with the peculiarities of EC law arose. In *Webb*, the English courts all agreed that, under the English rules on equal treatment, there was no sex discrimination. Whether the reasoning under English law was correct may be left to those who are familiar with English law. What

[395] *Webb* v. *EMO Air Cargo (UK) Ltd* [1995] 4 All ER 579.
[396] Steiner and Woods, *Textbook on EC Law*, 360 and 361.

is more important here is that none of the English courts felt capable of seeking the answer in the case law of the ECJ at the time. Neither *Dekker*[397] nor *Hertz*[398] were perceived as giving an answer to the question of whether the dismissal of a pregnant woman must be regarded *per se* as sex discrimination. The reasoning of the English courts was that *Webb* on the one hand and *Dekker* and *Hertz* on the other were not comparable. In *Dekker*, a woman was not offered employment because she was pregnant and because her employer would not receive state funding to pay for a replacement during her maternity leave, due to the rather confused Dutch social security rules on the matter. In *Hertz*, a woman suffered from post-confinement complications, and was dismissed after being ill for more than a hundred days within a period of one year, well outside the maternity protection period. Both cases held that pregnancy-related discrimination constitutes direct sex discrimination, but in *Hertz* the ECJ left the length of the maternity protection period to be determined by national law.[399] This difference led the English courts to conclude that *Dekker* could not help to decide *Webb*.

As the ECJ had identified only two permissible reasons for dismissal,[400] there was ample room for claimants to continue to bring cases before the courts. *Brown*[401] was one such case, decided while *Webb* was still pending. Mrs Brown was employed as a driver by Rentokil, servicing 'Sanitact' units in retail outlets. When she became pregnant in August 1990, she informed her employer. She was absent from work from the middle of August onwards, and submitted certificates for symptoms described as 'bleeding in pregnancy'. She never worked again. Under Rentokil's rules, employees may be dismissed if

397 Case 177/88, *Dekker* v. *Stichting Vormingscentrum voor Jonge Volwassenen Plus* [1990] ECR I-3941.

398 Case C-179/88, *Handels- og Kontorfunktionaerernes Forbund i Danmark (Union of Clerical and Commercial Employees) (for Hertz)* v. *Dansk Arbejdsgiverforening (Danish Employers Association) (for Aldi Marked K/S)* [1990] ECR I-3979.

399 Docksey, 'The Principles of Equality', 258 at 267; Fredman, 'European Community Discrimination Law', 119 at 122; Burrows, 'Maternity Rights in Europe', 273 at 282.

400 C. Boch, 'Case Note on Case C-32/93, Webb v. EMO Air Cargo (UK) Ltd [1994] ECR I-3567 in the House of Lords [1995] 1 WLR 1454' (1996) 33 *Common Market Law Review* 547, who distinguishes two situations in which pregnancy is not going to be treated as the reason for dismissal: (1) pregnancy-related illness arising after the end of the maternity leave period; and (2) treatment of pregnancy in relation to the duration of the contract of employment.

401 Case C-394/96, *Brown* v. *Rentokil* [1998] ECR I-4185; [1998] 2 CMLR 1049.

they are absent for reasons of sickness for more than twenty-six weeks continuously. The employer so informed her, and, as Mrs Brown decided not to come back to work, she was dismissed in February 1991 while still pregnant. The litigation arose as a result of the fact that Mrs Brown was not entitled to any statutory maternity rights as she did not have the requisite two-year period of continuous employment, and therefore she had no right to return to work within the twenty-nine weeks following birth. For the national courts, *Webb* had not sufficiently clarified the possible differences between dismissal for pregnancy itself and dismissal for illness. Therefore, *Brown* was eventually referred by the House of Lords to the ECJ.[402] The ECJ agreed with Advocate-General Colomer that the condition of pregnancy encompassed those disorders arising from pregnancy itself. The entire period of pregnancy was subject to the same risks, and a dismissal for any such condition was held to be directly discriminatory as it was based on the fact of pregnancy. As a result, 'the principle of non-discrimination' required similar protection throughout the period of pregnancy. One may wonder whether *Brown* has indeed clarified the difference between *Dekker* and *Hertz* or whether additional references will be needed to further clarify the exact meaning of direct discrimination. The real problem was not whether the facts are different – each case is different – but what shape the co-operation between the national courts and the European courts should take. Article 2(7) of Directive 76/207/EEC as amended by Directive 2002/73/EC is meant to clarify the boundaries. It seems as if the legislator has chosen to set aside the considerations raised by the Advocate-General and in legal doctrine to allow exceptionally for unequal treatment related to pregnancy.

Coote differed insofar as the lacunae resulted from deficiencies in the English law itself, which were highlighted by the Employment Appeal Tribunal thus:

> It does seem unsatisfactory to us that discrimination at an appeal hearing following summary dismissal should not be covered by the [Sex Discrimination Act 1975] unless the contract of employment expressly saves the employment, pending appeal. We suspect that, if Parliament had thought about the issue, it would have wished to outlaw discrimination both at dismissal and at an appeal hearing. But, in our view, Parliament failed to do so.[403]

[402] Wynn, 'Pregnancy Discrimination', 435 at 436.
[403] *Post Office* v. *Adekeye* [1995] ICR 548E–F, Employment Appeal Tribunal.

For a German lawyer, such a lacuna could easily be removed either by reference to the national law itself and the purpose behind it or by reference to the spirit of the EC law on equal treatment.

The loyal application of EC law by the national courts

Once the ECJ has answered the referred questions, national courts demonstrate a remarkable loyalty in striving for a correct application of the EC law to the case at hand, at least insofar as the UK legislation was intended to implement EC law.[404] This is true even in cases where the national courts have difficulty in accepting the findings of the ECJ. Lord Templeman said in *Foster*:

> I decline to apply the ruling of the European Court, couched in terms of broad principle and purposive language characteristic of Community law in a manner which is for better or worse, sometimes applied to enactments of the United Kingdom Parliament.[405]

Loyalty even persuades judges to admit that, after having sought advice from the ECJ, they were wrong in the way they construed the relationship between national law and EC law. In *Macarthys*,[406] Cumming-Bruce LJ had been criticised for stating that

> if the terms of the Treaty are judged in [the ECJ] to be inconsistent with the provisions of the Equal Pay Act 1970, European law will prevail over that municipal legislation. But such a judgment in [the ECJ] cannot affect the meaning of the English statute.[407]

He later accepted that he had gone too far with this statement. Generally speaking, the English courts make sincere efforts to apply the judgments of the ECJ to the case at hand.

This was particularly true in those referrals where the English courts were seeking a clear-cut answer from the ECJ such as *Macarthys*, *Webb*, *Foster* and *Marshall II*. In *Macarthys*, Lord Denning confirmed that the ECJ had decided that men and women need not be employed contemporaneously in order to compare rates of pay. That interpretation, Lord Denning went on to say, must now be applied by all the courts

[404] G. de Búrca, 'Giving Effect to European Community Directives' (1992) 55 *Modern Law Review* 215; Boch, 'Case Note on Case C-32/93', 547 at 564.

[405] *Foster* v. *British Gas plc* [1991] 2 All ER 705 at 711, House of Lords.

[406] [1981] 1 All ER 121.

[407] See [1979] 3 All ER 325 at 335–6.

in England.[408] Lord Keith of Kinkel[409] faced many more difficulties in altering the position which had been so firmly held by all national courts over the years. He stated:

> It seems to me that the only way of doing so is to hold that, in a case in which a woman is engaged for an indefinite period, the fact that the reason why she will be temporarily unavailable for work at a time when to her knowledge her services will be particularly required is pregnancy is a circumstance relevant to her case, being a circumstance which could not be present in the case of the hypothetical man.

This is simply a roundabout way of confessing that the position of the English courts can no longer be maintained in light of the ECJ's decision. The only way for their Lordships to save face was to emphasise the difference between employment for an indefinite period and employment for a fixed term. *Melgar*[410] and *Tele Danmark*[411] put an end to the debate.[412] What is more important in *Webb* is that the House of Lords declared Directive 76/207/EEC to be horizontally directly effective – otherwise Mrs Webb would never have received compensation.[413]

Disharmonies

If the ECJ does not provide the guidance sought by the referring court, then that court will find itself in a much more difficult position. A striking example of this is *Jenkins*. The Employment Appeal Tribunal had referred the question to the ECJ of whether indirect discrimination comes under the scope of Article 141 (ex Article 119). The question was very carefully prepared, due, *inter alia*, to the input of the Equal Opportunities Commission. The Employment Appeal Tribunal broke down the ECJ's decision into four questions, one of which was whether 'it is sufficient for the purposes of section 1(3) of the [Equal

408 *Macarthys Ltd* v. *Smith* [1981] 1 All ER 111 at 120, Court of Appeal.

409 *Webb* v. *EMO Cargo Air Cargo (UK) Ltd* [1995] 4 All ER 582.

410 Case C-438/99, *Melgar* v. *Ayuntamiento de Los Barrios* [2001] ECR I-6915.

411 Case C-109/00, *Tele Danmark A/S* v. *Handels- og Kontorfunktionaerernes Forbund i Danmark* [2001] ECR I-6993.

412 On the problem of drawing a line between a definite and an indefinite employment contract, see S. Moore, 'Sex, Pregnancy and Dismissal' (1994) 19 *European Law Review* 653; and Szyszczak, 'The Status to Be Accorded to Motherhood', 860 at 861.

413 Boch, 'Case Note on Case C-32/93', 547 at 565.

Pay Act 1970] and [Article 141 (ex Article 119)] for the employer to show only that he had no *intention* of discriminating or [whether he] must . . . also show that the difference in pay is objectively justified for some other reason'.[414] The Employment Appeal Tribunal was in considerable doubt as to the effect of Article 141 (ex Article 119) in relation to *unintentional* indirect discrimination. There are said to be passages in the ECJ's judgment which support the view that it was not enough for the employer simply to show that he had no intention of discriminating. The Employment Appeal Tribunal assumes, without deciding the issue, that Article 141 (ex Article 119), as construed by the ECJ, does not apply to cases of unintentional indirect discrimination. The result was that the correct solution could only be found in English law. It is striking that the Employment Appeal Tribunal confined itself to a consideration of the decision of the ECJ in the case at hand without considering any of the other case law of the ECJ. Had it done so, it would have made it easier for the Tribunal to assume that the ECJ was mistaken in referring to *intentional* discrimination.

Jenkins indirectly triggered off two further cases with far-reaching implications for UK law – 'indirectly' because it needed *Bilka-Kaufhaus* and *Rinner-Kühn* to pave the way for the two cases in question.[415] In *R.* v. *Secretary of State for Employment, ex parte EOC*,[416] the House of Lords, without making a reference to the ECJ, ruled that the provisions of the Employment Protection (Consolidation) Act 1978, pursuant to which employees who worked for less than sixteen hours a week were subject to less favourable conditions for claiming compensation for unfair dismissal and redundancy pay than those working more than sixteen hours a week, were indirectly discriminatory and incompatible with Directive 75/117/EEC and Article 141 (ex Article 119). Statistics show that 87 per cent of part-time workers were women. The second challenge was the requirement of two years' continuous service in order to qualify for the right not to be unfairly dismissed.

The second case was *R.* v. *Secretary of State for Employment, ex parte Seymour-Smith and Perez*.[417] The House of Lords referred a set of carefully worded questions to the ECJ to try to extract from the ECJ a full

[414] *Jenkins* v. *Kingsgate (Clothing Productions) Ltd* [1981] 1 WLR 1485 at 1493.

[415] Barnard and Hepple, 'Indirect Discrimination', 399 at 402.

[416] [1995] 1 AC 1; [1994] 2 WLR 409; [1994] 1 All ER 910.

[417] Case C-167/97, *R.* v. *Secretary of State for Employment, ex parte Seymour-Smith and Perez* [1999] ECR I-623.

answer as to what is the legal test for establishing whether a measure has such a degree of disparate impact between men and women as to amount to indirect discrimination, and at what point in time this test is to be applied, that is, either when the measure is adopted or when the employee is dismissed. The ECJ[418] accepted the UK government's argument that the correct comparison is between, on the one hand, the proportion of men in the workforce able to satisfy the two-year continuous employment requirement and, on the other hand, the proportion of women in the workforce able to satisfy the two-year continuous employment requirement. It is not sufficient simply to consider the number of those affected. The ECJ then went on to say that the test is whether a considerably smaller proportion of women than men are able to satisfy the two-year continuous employment requirement. The crunch came when the ECJ stated that the statistics in this case (77.4 per cent of men and 68.9 per cent of women could comply with the two-year continuous employment requirement) do not on the face of it demonstrate that a considerably smaller proportion of women are able to fulfil the requirement imposed by the disputed rule. The final decision was left for the national courts, and it was also for the national courts to determine the time at which to apply the test. The outcome was a disappointment for those fighting for equal treatment. However, in the event, the ruling is now of limited importance for the UK, as the two-year rule in national law has since been revoked.

Co-operation and co-responsibility?

The greatest challenge for national courts arises when the ECJ relies on the co-operation and co-responsibility of the national courts to give shape to the EC law on equal treatment. This burden on the national courts is less onerous in cases of direct discrimination. More difficulties arise in cases of indirect discrimination, in which the national courts have to decide whether the reasons put forward by the employer are objectively justified.[419] *Enderby* was one such case because of the reluctance to accept the idea of *prima facie* evidence resulting from wage differences rather than from the cause of the discrimination.[420]

418 *Ibid.*, paras. 59, 60, 62 and 64.

419 Hervey, 'Justification for Indirect Sex Discrimination', 807; Fredman, 'European Community Discrimination Law', 119 at 127; and C. McCrudden, 'The Effectiveness of European Equality Law: National Mechanisms for Enforcing Gender Equality Law in the Light of European Requirements' (1993) 13 *Oxford Journal of Legal Studies* 320.

420 Wynn, 'Equal Pay and Gender Segregation', 556 at 558.

According to Wood J, the chairman of the Employment Appeal Tribunal, it was a fundamental misreading of the Equal Pay Act 1970 to maintain that its purpose was to provide equal pay for men and women:

> It is only if a women is paid less because she is a woman that she has suffered from discrimination. The purpose of the Act was to prevent discrimination – not to provide equal pay.[421]

Subsequent cases which attempted to apply the *Enderby* doctrine in English law demonstrate that the national courts face great difficulties in applying the *Enderby* doctrine.[422] One might be tempted to conclude that the ECJ's desire for co-operation and co-responsibility is misunderstood by the national courts. The leeway given to the national courts is taken as a pretext for maintaining the national rules while pretending that the decision is in line with EC law.

Legal doctrine

The interplay between national and EC law on equal treatment is a matter of much concern in UK legal doctrine. Every key decision of the national or European courts is the subject of much academic and other comment. Thus, there is a large body of legal doctrine which may help the reader to better understand the reasons why equal treatment issues reach the ECJ and why women in the UK and their support organisations have put so much trust in the ECJ to remedy the deficiencies in the national law on equal treatment.

However, the 'strategic' use of EC law, as initiated by the EOC and supported by legal doctrine, has over-stretched the inherent boundaries of the European legal order. After a relatively long 'honeymoon' period for the prospects of European law on equal treatment, a certain disappointment set in in the aftermath of *Barber*, and even more so

421 *Enderby* v. *Frenchay Health Authority and Secretary of State for Health* [1991] IRLR 53, Employment Appeal Tribunal; Fredman, 'Equal Pay and Justification', 37 at 39.

422 For a more general analysis, see Connolly, 'British Indirect Discrimination Law', 1; and more specifically two decisions of the Court of Appeal, *British Coal Corporation* v. *Smith* [1994] ICR 810; [1994] IRLR 342, and *North Yorkshire County Council* v. *Ratcliffe* [1994] IRLR 342 as quoted in Wynn, 'Equal Pay and Gender Segregation', 556 at 560.

after *Grant*, *Brown* and *Seymour-Smith*. For example, in discussing the judgment in the *Seymour-Smith* case, Barnard and Hepple conclude by saying:[423]

> The one virtue of the ECJ's judgment is that it leaves the House of Lords and other courts and tribunals in the UK virtually free to step boldly back into the domain of indirect discrimination, and to make their own assessments rather than hang on the many nuances of nebulous words from [the ECJ].

It seems as if the trust in EC law is declining and that there will be more political pressure on the UK government to take legislative steps. The national judiciary, as has been shown, is sticking very much to its 'British style' of interpretation, thus effectively preserving the relatively low-cost labour market in the UK.[424]

The male comparator

The principle of equal treatment, the principle of equality and/or the principle of non-discrimination[425] all have a common factor, which is that they all require a comparator to be identified, and a comparison then to be made. Equal treatment has to be distinguished from 'unequal' treatment, equality from 'inequality' and non-discrimination from 'discrimination'. The question then arises of whether the comparator must necessarily be a *male* comparator, or whether it could equally be a *female* comparator, or whether a comparator should be used at all, that is, whether it may be better to uncouple the principle of equal treatment from *any* comparator. The ECJ has been heavily criticised, especially by female academic writers, for using the male comparator as the appropriate yardstick to decide discrimination issues, regardless of the form the discrimination may take.[426]

The prime example is *Barber*, in which the ECJ's arguments were implicitly determined by the educational and professional backgrounds

[423] Barnard and Hepple, 'Indirect Discrimination', 399 at 412.

[424] Bagilhole and Byrne, 'From Hard to Soft Law' in Hantrais (ed.), *Gendered Policies in Europe*, 141.

[425] Much could be said on the differing philosophical backgrounds. See Barnard, 'The Principle of Equality', 352 at 363; and Bell and Waddington, 'Reflecting on Inequalities', 349.

[426] See Fredman's harsh critique 'The Poverty of Equality: Pensions and the ECJ' (1996) 25 *Industrial Law Journal* 91 at 102.

of the male judges.[427] The situation is more complex with regard to the *sedes personae* of equal treatment provisions. Academics unanimously criticised the ECJ for its assumption that female armed police officers were more vulnerable to assassination than their male colleagues.[428] In *P* v. *S*, the comparison was made between the treatment given to the transsexual claimant (a woman) and the treatment which men generally could expect to receive in similar circumstances. Therefore, it may be suggested that there is no need to identify an individual comparator,[429] and that a comparison may be made between persons of the same sex.[430] Such an understanding would have the potential for introducing a new dimension into the ECJ's equality jurisprudence,[431] moving away from the Aristotelian approach to equality and the requirement for a comparator of the opposite sex to be used, and towards an analysis based on disadvantage and detriment.[432] However, a different reading of *P* v. *S* is possible. The Advocate-General was happy to treat the transsexual appellant in *P* v. *S* as a woman, thus denying that transsexuals were in law 'a third sex'. The ECJ was said to go even further in treating sex as relevant by adopting a comparative approach. According to the ECJ's reasoning, the appellant had to show that, as a woman, she had been treated less favourably than a man (perhaps her former self).[433] After *P* v. *S*, some commentators were

[427] Fredman, 'European Community Discrimination Law', 119 at 123.

[428] V. Shrubsall, 'Protective Practices and the Equal Treatment Directive' (1987) 16 *Industrial Law Journal* 118; Arnull, 'Social Policy', 56 at 61 ('the idea that armed policewomen would more frequently be subject to assassination attempts than male officers and that their guns might fall into the hands of their attackers seems somewhat fanciful'); E. Ellis, 'Can Public Safety Provide an Excuse for Sex Discrimination?' (1986) 102 *Law Quarterly Review* 496 ('[n]o explanation whatsoever is provided as to why policewomen might be more likely to be assassinated than policemen'); Morris, 'Sex Discrimination', 334 at 338 ('[n]o evidence was placed before the Court to justify its implicit assumption that, in a situation characterised by serious civil disorder, women officers are more vulnerable to assassination than their male colleagues').

[429] A. Campbell and H. Lardy, 'Discrimination against Transsexuals in Employment' (1996) 21 *European Law Review* 412.

[430] L. Flynn, 'Case Note on C-13/94', 367 at 377; for a similar reading see K. A. Armstrong, 'Legal Integration: Theorizing the Legal Dimension of European Integration' (1998) 36 *Journal of Common Market Studies* 155 at 164–6.

[431] C. Barnard, 'P v. S: Kite Flying or a New Constitutional Approach?' in S. O'Leary and A. Dashwood (eds.), *The Principle of Equal Treatment in EC Law* (London, 1997), 59.

[432] L. Flynn, 'Case Note on C-13/94', 367 at 377 and 378.

[433] P. Skidmore, 'Can Transsexuals Suffer Sex Discrimination?' (1997) 19 *Journal of Social Welfare and Family Law* 105; Skidmore, 'Sex, Gender and Comparators', 59 at 60.

hopeful that the ECJ would now be able to set aside discrimination resulting from sexual orientation. When a suitable case, *Grant*, came before the ECJ, however, this hope was revealed to be wishful thinking. In *Grant*, the ECJ signalled decisively that the traditional comparison between persons of the opposite sex was the appropriate comparator to adopt.[434] Although the ECJ was again strongly criticised for its decision,[435] there was nevertheless some preparedness on the part of legal writers to accept that including sexual orientation under the EC law of equal treatment was 'a bridge too far'.[436] The amendment of the Treaty of Amsterdam has deprived the ECJ of its ability to step in and to adopt a 'gung-ho' approach to the development of equal treatment.[437]

The question of the appropriate comparator is still open for debate. *Dekker* is seen as the only case in which there was no need to use a comparator.[438] Therefore, it has been argued that 'the essentially feminist principle that discrimination on the grounds of pregnancy is *per se* unlawful sex discrimination' has helped to 'transcend the male norm'.[439] However, there is some disagreement as to this interpretation of *Dekker*. It has been argued that the ECJ implicitly held in *Dekker* that 'sex' includes pregnancy. A comparator is therefore said still to be required, which in *Dekker* was a non-pregnant (male) person. If *Dekker* is understood in this way, then *P* v. *S* lacked any potential for reaching beyond the traditional approach, because in *P* v. *S* the ECJ held that references to sex include changing sex or changing physical sexual characteristics.[440] Thus one may well wonder whether the ECJ ever intended to go beyond formal equality.[441]

[434] T. Connor, 'Community Discrimination Law: No Right to Equal Treatment in Employment in Respect of Same Sex Partner' (1998) 23 *European Law Review* 378.

[435] S. Terrett, 'A Bridge Too Far? Non-Discrimination and Homosexuality in European Community Law' (1998) 4 *European Public Law* 487 at 505; Connor, 'Community Discrimination Law', 378 at 382; Barnard, 'The Principle of Equality', 352 at 364 and 366.

[436] Terrett, 'A Bridge Too Far?' 487 at 505.

[437] *Ibid.*

[438] Skidmore, 'Can Transsexuals Suffer Sex Discrimination?' 105 at 109.

[439] Boch, 'Case Note on Case C-32/93', 547 at 557, referring to E. Ellis, 'Discrimination on the Ground of Pregnancy in EEC Law' (1991) *Public Law* 159.

[440] R. Wintemute, 'When Is Pregnancy Discrimination Indirect Sex Discrimination?' (1998) 27 *Industrial Law Journal* 23.

[441] Barnard and Hepple, 'Indirect Discrimination', 399 at 412, who conclude that the ECJ is only capable of pronouncing on questions of formal equality.

'Frailty thy name is woman'[442]

There is a connection between the ECJ's emphasis on the male comparator and the underlying philosophy that discrimination has to be eliminated because 'women need to be protected'. The idea of protection implies a limitation of self-determination and self-responsibility. This became abundantly clear in *Johnston*, in which the ECJ, after having emphasised Mrs Johnston's basic right to equal treatment, nevertheless went on to accept all too easily her employer's justification for the unequal treatment she received. The ECJ was guided by its basic belief that women are weaker than men and that their weakness justifies special treatment. The ECJ was perhaps reluctant to see armed women police officers on the streets. Ten years later, views have changed, and so has the ECJ, as evidenced in *Sirdar*[443] and *Kreil*,[444] although the principle of equal treatment within the police and the armed forces is still not yet fully recognised by the ECJ. This exclusion from the principle of equal treatment of certain jobs deprives women of their full self-determination and self-responsibility. Whether one does or does not approve of armed female police officers, one should question whether it is for the courts to maintain deeply rooted societal beliefs and traditions. Similar issues arise in relation to pregnancy discrimination. The ECJ has repeatedly used instrumental reasons as the basis for the protection of pregnancy and maternity, with the consequence that paternalistic ideology has emphasised women's vulnerabilities rather than their rights to be treated equally as workers.[445]

The costs of equal treatment

It is generally agreed that the realisation of equal treatment is expensive, and that somebody has to pay for it, whether the employer directly or the state indirectly (for example, by reimbursing statutory maternity pay). It is likewise generally agreed that the ECJ may take into

[442] *Hamlet*, Act I, Scene ii, line 146. I have borrowed the reference from Advocate-General Darmon in Case 222/84, *Johnston* v. *Chief Constable of the Royal Ulster Constabulary* [1986] ECR 1651 at 1659.

[443] Case C-273/97, *Sirdar* v. *(1) Army Board and (2) Secretary of State for Defence* [1999] ECR I-7403.

[444] Case C-285/98, *Kreil* v. *Germany* [2000] ECR I-69.

[445] Wynn, 'Pregnancy Discrimination', 435.

consideration only the specific costs of the individual employer and that it cannot weigh up the possible savings in unemployment benefit and social security payments against the costs of anti-discrimination policies.[446] There is a clear contradiction between the ECJ's settled case law, under which economic factors are disregarded, and the practical effects of the ECJ's judgments, which seem to indicate quite the contrary.[447] The economic consequences of *Barber* led the ECJ to limit its retrospective application.[448] However, there was a lot of confusion on the economic burden of the judgment for pension funds and for the UK government.[449] The common thread in the post-*Barber* cases was the question of the temporal limitation of the judgment,[450] and these cases served to challenge the ECJ on the economic impact of its own jurisprudence.[451] *Smith* v. *Advel Systems* cannot be fully understood without considering the costs of equalising the ages for pension entitlement between men and women. The economic implications are less obvious in the cases of the equal treatment of transsexuals and homosexuals. The ECJ implicitly indicated in *P* v. *S* that transsexuals form a small group in society, which might help to explain its decision.[452] In *Barber*, the ECJ limited the retrospective implications of the judgment. *Smith* v. *Advel Systems* raised the issue of equalising the ages of pension entitlement between men and women. Even in the field of maternity protection, the economic factor cannot be ignored. The

[446] Boch, 'Case Note on Case C-32/93', 547 at 554.

[447] Fredman, 'The Poverty of Equality', 91 at 94.

[448] S. Moore, '"Justice Doesn't Mean a Free Lunch": The Application of the Principles of Equal Pay to Occupational Pension Schemes' (1995) 20 *European Law Review* 159.

[449] 'EC Rules on Pensions Equality' (1990) *European Industrial Relations Review*, No. 198, 20 at 21, estimates that the elimination of sexual discrimination from all benefits deriving from occupational pension schemes could cost employers an additional £3 billion a year. Other estimates ranged from £45 billion (the UK government) to £6–12 billion spread over a period of 10–15 years: see Moore, 'Justice Doesn't Mean a Free Lunch', 159 at 165.

[450] *Ibid.*, 177; Comment, 'Equality in Occupational Pension Schemes: Still Waiting for Coloroll' (1994) 23 *Industrial Law Journal* 155 at 158.

[451] Moore, 'Justice Doesn't Mean a Free Lunch', 159 at 177.

[452] According to Advocate-General Tesauro in Case C-13/94, *P* v. *S and Cornwall County Council* [1996] ECR I-2143 at 2145, in Europe 1 in 30,000 males and 1 in 100,000 females seek to have a sex change operation. Advocate-General Elmer in Case C-249/96, *Grant* v. *South West Trains Ltd* [1998] ECR I-621 at 623, estimates that there are 33 million homosexuals in the European Union.

reading of *Hertz*[453] and *Dekker*[454] by the national courts prior to *Webb* has a clear economic basis. *Brown*, which was decided in the aftermath of *Webb*, made the costs of pregnancy protection calculable, in that the entire period of pregnancy was subject to the same risks and a dismissal for any such condition was directly discriminatory.[455] However, there is no protection granted outside the period of pregnancy, even if the illness is related to pregnancy.

Whereas economic implications underlie the decisions in the above cases, they are a central issue in equal value claims. The success of an equal value claim depends crucially upon being able to establish a rate of pay at odds with external market forces but justified by fairness between grades within an organisation. Although it is possible to establish an equal value claim even in the absence of comparable employees, by engaging experts to conduct a job-evaluation exercise, the whole legal approach may be nullified if the employer is permitted to rely on rates of pay in the external labour market in order to justify departures from pay levels set by the job evaluation. In the development of the law of equal pay, a critical step in the process occurred when, as early as 1981, in *Jenkins*, the ECJ accepted that a defence of 'objective justification' could be permitted under Article 141 (ex Article 119). However, such an objective justification could in the long term only undermine the effectiveness of the principle of equal pay for equal value.[456] That explains why, in *Enderby*, the ECJ's preparedness to largely accept the 'market forces defence' was so heavily criticised.[457] The restriction of the *Bilka* test in recent court rulings seems to confirm such a reading of the objective justification requirement.[458] The question has already been raised as to whether and to what extent

[453] Case C-179/88, *Handels- og Kontorfunktionaerernes Forbund i Danmark (Union of Clerical and Commercial Employees) (for Hertz)* v. *Dansk Arbejdsgiverforening (Danish Employers Association) (for Aldi Marked K/S)* [1990] ECR I-3979.

[454] Case 177/88, *Dekker* v. *Stichting Vormingscentrum voor Jonge Volwassenen Plus* [1990] ECR I-3941.

[455] Wynn, 'Pregnancy Discrimination', 437 at 438.

[456] H. Collins, 'CCT, Equal Pay and Market Forces' (1994) 23 *Industrial Law Journal* 341.

[457] Fredman, 'Equal Pay and Justification', 37 at 40 and 41; Wynn, 'Equal Pay and Gender Segregation', 556 at 562; Kentridge, 'Direct and Indirect Discrimination', 198 at 205; H. Fenwick, 'Indirect Discrimination in Equal Pay Claims: Backward Steps in the European Court of Justice?' (1995) 1 *European Public Law* 331.

[458] Barnard and Hepple, 'Indirect Discrimination', 399 at 409.

direct discrimination even on grounds of pregnancy might be justifiable in particular situations.[459]

The ECJ's ability to evaluate statistics

When the ECJ demonstrated its preparedness, in *Jenkins*, to include indirect discrimination under the EC law of equal treatment, the question naturally arose as to how women could demonstrate that their pay was less than that of men. Academic writers are becoming increasingly sceptical about the usefulness of statistics as evidence of such inequality in pay.[460] Furthermore, the ECJ is said to lack the requisite statistical and social science expertise which is needed to assess arguments about disparate impact and objective justifications. Therefore, the ECJ may not be the most appropriate forum for evaluating the facts of a case. Indeed, *Seymour-Smith* documents the inherent limits of statistical evidence; in that case, there was no substantial difference in the percentage of women affected by the allegedly discriminatory acts as compared to the percentage of men affected. Thus, the appellant's reliance on statistics failed.

An alternative to statistical evidence may be to increase transparency.[461] In *Barber*, the ECJ used the transparency principle to determine whether each element of the overall pay package must be equal as between men and women or whether it is sufficient that the overall pay packages are of equal value. It has been argued that, in *Danfoss*, the ECJ had already developed a novel use of the concept of transparency, which had earlier been used to reduce the burden of proof on the employee, and to increase the burden of proof on the employer, whereas transparency was used in the same case to ascertain what needs to be examined in order to determine discrimination.[462] Unfortunately, Directive 2000/43/EC perpetuates the problematic reliance on statistics to demonstrate racial or ethnic discrimination.[463]

[459] Advocate-General van Gerven in Case C-132/92, *Birds Eye Walls Ltd* v. *Roberts* [1993] ECR I-5579 at 5592, paras. 12–17, as quoted in Bowers and Moran, 'Justification in Direct Sex Discrimination Law', 309, n. 7.

[460] Barnard and Hepple, 'Indirect Discrimination', 399 at 400.

[461] Abanulo, 'Equal Pay for Work of Equal Value', 365 at 369 and 370.

[462] Honeyball and Shaw, 'Social Policy', 51 at 52.

[463] D. Schiek, 'Diskriminierung wegen "Rasse" oder "ethnischer Herkunft": Probleme bei der Umsetzung der Richtlinie 2000/43/EG im Arbeitsrecht' (2003) 2 AuR 50.

4

The reconstruction of good faith in the control of unfair terms in consumer contracts

Introduction: the reach and nature of the conflict between civil law, common law and European law

> If good faith has been taken away, all intercourse among men ceases to exist.[1]

In 1993, the European Community adopted Directive 93/13/EEC on unfair terms in consumer contracts.[2] The reactions in the legal community to the Directive were similar to the reaction to the *Cassis de Dijon* decision. After *Cassis de Dijon*, lawyers were obliged to accept that national laws and regulations would henceforth be measured against the basic freedom to trade. In 1993, fourteen years after *Cassis de Dijon*, the even more sensitive area of private law came under scrutiny from EC law. Private law is tied up with national traditions and cultures. Any attempt to subject private law to EC law would therefore be fraught with difficulties and would therefore meet opposition. The common law countries were particularly keen to oppose such a development, because the concept of good faith, as used in the Directive to exercise control over unfair terms in consumer contracts, was so alien to common law traditions. The understanding of good faith, and its role and function in common law and civil law, varies greatly among the legal communities of the Member States.[3] Legal doctrine can, however, shed light on the extent to which a common law understanding of good faith fits into a 'true' European understanding of the concept. However, there is as yet no such European understanding, and there

[1] Grotius, *De Jure Belli ac Pacis* (Lugduni Batavorum, 1919).

[2] OJ 1993 No. L095, 21 April 1993, 29.

[3] The extensive comparative study by Zimmermann and Whittaker on the handling of good faith issues in the legal orders of the Member States of the European Union and beyond explicitly excludes the use of notions of good faith in the control of standard contract conditions; see S. Whittaker and R. Zimmermann (eds.), *Good Faith in European Contract Law* (Cambridge, 2000), 59.

are no references to the ECJ by the English courts and subsequent rulings of the English courts on good faith issues which may be analysed here. This does not mean, however, that the ECJ has not yet considered the scope and reach of Directive 93/13/EEC. There is a growing body of case law from the ECJ which sheds light on how good faith issues will be handled in the ECJ.[4] Our reconstruction of good faith will of necessity be of a somewhat speculative nature.

The conflict: the differing concepts used in the Directive, the UCTA and the UTCCR

There is statutory law in England and Wales on the control of unfair terms in consumer contract which can be analysed here. Such statutory law includes the Unfair Contract Terms Act 1977 (UCTA), the Unfair Terms in Consumer Contracts Regulations 1994[5] (UTCCR 1994) and the Unfair Terms in Consumer Contracts Regulations 1999[6] (UTCCR 1999). The latter two instruments implement Directive 93/13/EEC.[7] An analysis of these three pieces of legislation will highlight the changing pattern of the regulation of unfair terms in consumer contracts. It will be shown that the common law and the statutes, prior to the adoption of Directive 93/13/EEC, focused very much on controlling *limitation and exclusion clauses*. The Directive widened the scope of this control in two ways: first, it introduced a general clause on good faith; and, secondly, it shifted the emphasis from the control of unfair terms generally to the control of unfair *standard* business terms and conditions.

This 'Europeanisation' of English law will obviously have long-term effects in English law, as the English courts will clearly need to respect the supremacy of European law. Possible areas of conflict will have to

[4] J. Stuyck, 'Judgment of 27 June 2000 Joined Cases C-240/98 to C-244/96 Océano Grupo Editorial SA v. Rocio Murciano Quintero, and Salvat Editore SA v. José M. Sánchez Alcón Prades, nyr' (2001) 38 *Common Market Law Review* 719; Judgment of 10 May 2001, Case C-144/99, *Commission* v. *Netherlands* [2001] ECR I-3541; Judgment of 7 May 2002, Case C-478/99, *Commission* v. *Sweden* [1999] ECR I-4147; Judgment of 21 November 2002, Case C-473/00, *Cofidis SA* v. *Fredout* [2002] ECR I-875; Judgment of 1 April 2004, Case C-237/02, *Freiburger Kommunalbauten GmbH Baugesellschaft & Co. KG* v. *Ludger Hofstetter et Ulrike Hofstetter* [2004] 2 CMLR 13.

[5] SI 1994 No. 3159.

[6] SI 1999 No. 2083. The UTCCR 1999 replaced the UTCCR 1994.

[7] The Law Commissions of England and Wales and Scotland have made a proposal to merge the UTCCR and the UCTA. See the Law Commission, Consultation Paper No 166, and the Scottish Law Commission, Discussion Paper No 119, 'Unfair Terms in Contracts: A Joint Consultation Paper' (London, 2002).

be defined. To this end, a first insight into possible areas of conflict may be provided by an analysis of the enforcement activities of the Office of Fair Trading (OFT).[8] Furthermore, the first case to reach the House of Lords under the new law, *Director-General of Fair Trading* v. *First National Bank plc*,[9] may also be analysed.[10] Although *First National* was not referred to the ECJ, the House of Lords set out its understanding of the notion and concept of good faith as a means of exercising control over unfair terms in consumer contracts.

The deeper conflict: the struggle over 'good faith' in contract law

There is nothing in the common law comparable to the extent of control exercised over contracts in civil law countries, usually on the basis of the concept of good faith.[11] Contract law in common law does not recognise those concepts which permit the courts in civil law countries to exercise control over agreements made between private parties. Lord Goff summed up the basic understanding of the role of judges in common law countries with regard to commercial contracts as follows:

> Our [i.e. the judges'] only desire is to give sensible commercial effect to the transaction. We are there to help businessmen, not to hinder them, we are there to give effect to their transactions, not to frustrate them, we are there to oil the wheels of commerce, not to put a spanner in the works, or even grit in the oil.[12]

Commercial contract law and consumer contract law cannot be equated. However, as consumer law cases have been middle order cases so far, Lord Goff's definition of the role of judges seems to mirror the approach taken by judges in common law countries in controlling contracts of whatever nature. The reluctance of the common law to interfere, and the limited role of judges in litigation, do not mean that there is no control over contracts at all. English lawyers have long experience in using the interpretation of the parties as a means of

[8] See www.oft.gov.uk. [9] [2002] 1 AC 481; [2001] 3 WLR 1297; [2002] 1 All ER 97.

[10] *Ibid*; for more detail, see pp. 413–23 below.

[11] S. Whittaker and R. Zimmermann, 'Good Faith in European Contract Law: Surveying the Legal Landscape' in Whittaker and Zimmermann (eds.), *Good Faith in European Contract Law*, 39.

[12] Robert Goff, 'Commercial Contracts and the Commercial Court' (1984) 100 *Law Quarterly Review* 382 at 391.

achieving a variety of results. However, the approach of English law to the interpretation of contracts is said to be largely *objective* in its approach, whereas civil law regimes are said to be largely *subjective* in their approach. The objective approach strictly excludes evidence of prior negotiations and subsequent conduct as an aid to interpretation.[13] The legal certainty and predictability that the objective approach produces is seen by the English courts as an advantage over the uncertainty inherent in the subjective approach of the civil law regime.[14] Thus, there is a certain apprehension among English lawyers that the introduction of the concept of good faith might introduce uncertainty and an element of arbitrariness into English contract law, thus negating the competitive advantage of the objective approach.

For a German lawyer, it is impressive to see how carefully English courts reconstruct the wording, and the meaning behind the wording, in the interpretation of exclusion and limitation clauses in contracts. The criticism may be made that the English courts have become so adept at 'twisting' the meaning of words, that they can arrive at whatever interpretation they choose in order to reach the desired result. Thus, interpretation could be regarded as the 'functional equivalent' of content control.[15] Seen this way, the question arises as to whether there is any substantial difference between contract control in English law and that in civil law. However, while the differences should not be over-emphasised, the underlying philosophy behind the objective and subjective approaches remains real and should not be overlooked by focusing too closely on the *outcome* of cases.[16] The debate over the correct interpretation of a European concept of good faith in contract law is dominated by the question of objective versus subjective

[13] J. Steyn, 'The Role of Good Faith and Fair Dealing in Contract Law: A Hair-Shirt Philosophy?' (1991) *Denning Law Journal* 131 at 132; J. Steyn, 'Contract Law: Fulfilling the Reasonable Expectations of Honest Men' (1997) 113 *Law Quarterly Review* 433.

[14] Steyn, 'The Role of Good Faith', 433.

[15] At a more technical level, comparative lawyers do not so much analyse whether different national legal orders provide identical rules in respect of a particular legal issue but rather devote more attention to determining whether the legal rules which have been established are 'functionally equivalent'.

[16] For the legal background in Germany, see U. Reifner, 'Good Faith: Interpretation or Limitation of Contracts? The Power of German Judges in Financial Services Law' in R. Brownsword, N. Hird and G. Howells (eds.), *Good Faith in Contract: Concept and Context* (Aldershot, 1999), 269 at 271, who refer to R. Samek, 'The Objective Theory of Contract and the Rule in L'Estrange v. Graucob' (1974) 52 *Canadian Bar Review* 351.

Table 4.1 *The interplay between cooperativism and individualism, and objective and subjective interpretation*

	Cooperativism = collective justice	Individualism = freedom of contract
Objective interpretation		Procedural good faith
Subjective interpretation	Substantive good faith	

interpretation, or, more broadly, the weight the legal order should give to the parties' intentions and their particular circumstances. In the final analysis, the question may be reduced to the essential ethic of contracting, that is, either 'individualism' or 'co-operativism'.[17]

Hence there is a need to demonstrate the way in which English law uses objective interpretation as a means to exercise control over exclusion and limitation clauses in contracts. It is simply impossible to understand the difficulties English law faces in its application of good faith as a means to control unfair terms, without understanding the scrutiny that English law devotes to the traditional task of interpreting exclusion and limitation clauses. The particular English approach to the control of unfair terms is reflected in the handling of the good faith notion in the UTCCR. It will be demonstrated that English lawyers tend to read *procedural* elements into the principle of good faith as established by Directive 93/13/EEC that reflect the traditional means of control by way of 'incorporation' and 'construction' of a contract term. *Substantive* elements in the principle of good faith – the civil law perspective – require subjective interpretation. The interplay between the two elements of good faith (objective and subjective interpretation) and the two different ethics of contract law (co-operativism and individualism) can be seen in Table 4.1. The traditional English concept of contract law may be found at the right-hand side of the figure, and the European concept of contract law at the left-hand side. In essence, this is what the reconstruction of good faith in unfair terms in consumer contracts is all about.

[17] Using the terminology of R. Brownsword, 'Individualism, Co-operativism and an Ethic for European Contract Law' (2002) 64 *Modern Law Review* 628 at 630.

No solution, but a better understanding of the role and function of good faith in European contract law

The reconstruction of good faith must start with an analysis of the position at common law. Since the adoption of the UCTA and the implementation of Directive 93/13/EEC in the UTCCR 1994, the scope of application of the common law in the control of unfair terms has been considerably reduced. In essence, the common law is now restricted to determining how terms are incorporated into contracts, and how terms are to be interpreted. The key role of freedom of contract is best felt in the strong rejection of any legal means to control the content of unfair terms. This is the first part of our analysis.

A major change in English contract law resulted from the enactment of the UCTA in 1977. The UCTA must be seen as legislative interventionism into the freedom of contract, though here limited to the control of exclusion and limitation clauses. While the UCTA clearly constitutes a means to import elements of justice into contract law, the UCTA was not meant and has not been used as a comprehensive concept to remedy unfairness, be it procedural or substantive in nature, in contract law. While it was possible under common law to remedy unfairness by using the 'reasonableness test', the higher courts in England were unwilling to infringe on the freedom of contract outside the boundaries of exclusion and limitation clauses. This is the second part of our analysis.

Thus, it remained for the European Community to bring the issue to the fore. After the enactment of the UTCCR 1994, the deeper conflict over the ethics of contract law resurfaced. Since then, legal doctrine, the Office of Fair Trading (as the key enforcement authority) and the English courts have been struggling hard over the correct understanding of the concept of good faith in contract law. Legal doctrine clearly recognises the deeper issues hidden within the conflict over the correct understanding of good faith (although it is divided over the practical implications). The enforcement authorities and the courts clearly show a tendency to 'reduce' good faith, following the common law tradition, to procedural good faith only. This finding will be developed step-by-step below, beginning with a doctrinal analysis of the UTCCR 1994, then turning to a stocktaking of the OFT's activities and finally culminating in an analysis of the *First National Bank* case. The particular way in which the OFT and the courts read procedural good faith might well pave the way for the development of a true European ethic on contract law.

The wider picture: standards of good faith and effective legal protection

Usually, the two limbs of civil law substantive law and procedural law – are kept separate. It is for each individual, whether a consumer or a businessperson, to negotiate the terms of his or her contract and to decide whether he or she will enforce his or her rights. Private autonomy in substantive law, and the autonomy in deciding whether to enforce one's rights in court, are mutually dependent. In Germany, for example, standard contract terms have become the focus of judicial activism. In 1976, the *Gesetz zur Regelung des Rechts der Allgemeinen Geschäftsbedingungen* (Act on Standard Business Conditions) was adopted only after agreement had been reached between the various interested parties (consumers, business and the government) over effective redress mechanisms. A political consensus emerged that the traditional means of enforcement would not suffice and that additional means were needed to eliminate unfair terms. However, the debate in Germany was entirely focused on the control of *standard* contract terms. In the end, the German legislator relied on the established regulatory model which governed unfair competition issues. Consumer and trade organisations were therefore given a collective right to seek an injunction against traders using unfair standard business terms. At that time, most countries (Germany and Austria excepted) relied on administrative enforcement. The UK, in theory, ought to have done the same. The UCTA, however, did not grant public authorities any enforcement power. The traditional concept of individual law-enforcement prevailed over any form of collective redress.

It was at this point that Directive 93/13/EEC was enacted. The Directive stimulated the development of new and Europe-wide individual and collective enforcement mechanisms. There is no area of EC law, certainly not in the field of consumer protection, in which any rights granted are not accompanied by effective legal protection. The UTCCR 1994, enacted to implement the Directive, granted powers to the Office of Fair Trading to enforce the new law. For the first time in the UK, there was therefore an enforcement authority which focused its activities on the issue of unfair terms in consumer contracts. An analysis of the OFT's reports will demonstrate that the agency is using its powers to enforce the regulatory concepts of the UCTA.

Therefore, the Directive, as implemented in the UTCCR 1994, may be seen as filling the gap in the UCTA's enforcement regime. However, this is only half the story. Directive 93/13/EEC is read by consumer advocates as also obliging Member States to introduce *collective* redress mechanisms which could be used by consumer organisations. This issue was at the heart of a reference made by the High Court to the ECJ.[18] Before the case was heard by the ECJ, however, the UK government remedied the deficient enforcement structure by replacing the UTCCR 1994 with the UTCCR 1999. The latter instrument essentially re-enacted the former instrument, but with amendments which allowed public bodies and the Consumers' Association (the leading non-governmental organisation in the field of consumer protection in the UK) to take collective enforcement measures in the courts.[19] Because the UK government indicated its intention to do this, the reference to the ECJ was suspended and later withdrawn by the appellant, the Consumers' Association.

There were good reasons, based on EC law, why the UK government was well advised to prevent the case being heard by the ECJ. Superficially, UK law was in line with EC law requirements. The true conflict, however, went much deeper. The UK has a strong tradition of relying on public law-enforcement agencies to eliminate unfair trading practices (not just unfairness in contract terms, but unfairness in any type of trading practice). Trade and consumer organisations were traditionally not involved in law-enforcement. Because of this deeply ingrained tradition in the UK legal order, simply amending the statutory regulations is not in itself sufficient to establish an ethos of collective law-enforcement by consumer and trade organisations. In short, it will be demonstrated below that the European concept of collective redress has not yet become established in the UK legal order. In the end, it may be necessary for consumer organisations to take the initiative to implement substantive good faith in UK contract law.

The common law position: *caveat emptor* and the freedom of contract

In order for a contracting party to include an exclusion clause in a contract, three requirements must be satisfied. First, it must be shown that the exclusion clause is properly incorporated into the contract

[18] Judgment of 28 February 1996, *R. v. Secretary of State for Trade and Industry, ex parte Consumers' Association and Which?*, High Court, unreported (available on Lexis).

[19] The 'Explanatory Notes' to the UTCCR 1999 state: 'The Regulations provide for the first time that a qualifying body named in Schedule 1 (statutory regulators, trading standards departments and [the] Consumers' Association) may also apply for an injunction to prevent the continued use of an unfair contract term . . .'

Table 4.2 *Individual, administrative and collective redress under the common law, the UCTA, the UTCCR and Directive 93/13/EEC*

	Common law	UCTA	UTCCR	Directive 93/13/EEC
Individual redress	Traditional concept	Traditional concept	Traditional concept	Subjective rights under the Directive
Administrative control			Office of Fair Trading	
Collective redress				Action for injunction

(incorporation); secondly, it must be shown that, properly interpreted, the exclusion clause covers the breach which has occurred and the resulting loss or damage (construction); and, thirdly, it must be shown that there is no other rule of law which would invalidate or render inoperative the exclusion clause. The first two requirements might be termed 'indirect control' mechanisms: 'indirect', because there is no control of the *content* of the contract; 'control', because there *is* an impact on the content despite the overt rejection of content control.

Formally speaking, Directive 93/13/EEC does not, *prima facie*, appear to regulate the incorporation of contract terms.[20] This is consistent with the approach of the European Community not to intervene into the national legal rules governing the conclusion of contracts. However, the Directive *does* contain rules on construction the application of which is limited to *standard* business terms and conditions. The emphasis of the Directive is on *content control*. Thus, it may be asked why our analysis should consider indirect forms of control. For a German lawyer, it is precisely here that the differences in the two approaches become clear. German courts tend not to consider the question of whether a particular term is incorporated in the contract but rather to consider the question of control over the contract. Thus, to a lawyer in the civil law tradition, English law and English legal doctrine seem to be somewhat old-fashioned in this respect. At the

[20] However, it will need to be demonstrated that the particular way in which English law reads the Directive is evidence that the Directive contains elements dealing with the incorporation procedure.

risk of simplifying the argument, it may be that a rule invalidating the so-called 'surprise clause' (that is, clauses which one would not necessarily expect to find in a contract of the type in question) similar to that of Article 305(c) of the BGB[21] could help the English courts to avoid having to use artificial reasoning to ensure the parties are not bound by 'unusual' contract terms.

Control of the incorporation of a clause

The three requirements which must be met in order to include an exclusion clause in a contract (incorporation, construction, and no contrary rule of law) were noted above. As regards the first requirement (incorporation of a clause), there are three ways of incorporating a clause: by signature, by notice, and by course of dealing. All three ways are governed under English law by an objective approach.[22] It seems fair to say that English doctrine does not overtly differentiate between the integration of 'contract terms' and 'standard business terms and conditions'. The way in which the rules on incorporation are applied makes such a distinction superfluous. In this respect, the particular facts of a case are much more important in determining the question of incorporation than any all-embracing legal principle. Civil law regimes have followed a different development route. In civil law countries, the third method of incorporation, that is, by a course of dealing, is of much greater importance in relation to standard commercial contracts.

Incorporation by signature

The first method of incorporating a clause is by signature. If a document is to be regarded as an integral part of a contract, it must be determined whether or not it has been signed by the party against whom the exclusion or limitation clause is being pleaded. A person who signs a contractual document is bound by its terms, even if he has not read them. In *L'Estrange* v. *F. Graucob Ltd*,[23] it was held by the

[21] 'Bestimmungen in Allgemeinen Geschäftsbedingungen, die nach den Umständen, insbesondere nach dem äußeren Erscheinungsbild des Vertrags, so ungewöhnlich sind, dass der Vertragspartner des Verwenders mit ihnen nicht zu rechnen braucht, werden nicht Vertragsbestandsteil.'

[22] R. Bradgate, 'Unreasonable Standard Terms' (1997) 60 *Modern Law Review* 582 at 584, referring to Guideline C in Schedule 2 to the UCTA.

[23] [1934] 2 KB 394. This decision was criticised in *McCutcheon* v. *David MacBrayne Ltd* [1964] 1 WLR 125 at 133; G. Treitel, *The Law of Contract* (11th edn, London, 2003),

High Court that the owner of a cafe was bound by an exclusion clause which was written in a 'regrettably small print', and that it would have made no difference had she had not been able to read English.[24]

Incorporation by notice

The second method of incorporating a clause into a contract is by notice. If the documents in question is consigned by the person against whom the term is sought to be enforced, the question will arise as to whether reasonable notice of the term had been given to that person. Under German law, a number of potential problems may be resolved by the application of Article 305(c) of the BGB. Consumers are protected from the application of terms which go beyond what the parties might reasonably expect to find in the type of contract in question. Terms which go beyond what the parties might reasonably expect will therefore not form part of the contract.[25] Under common law, if an exclusion clause is included, or referred to,[26] in a document which is simply handed over by one party to the other party, or is displayed where the contract is made (for example, behind the counter of a shop), that exclusion clause will be incorporated in the contract only if reasonable notice of its existence was given to the party adversely affected by it. The document in which the exclusion clause is set out (or referred to) must be intended to have contractual effect. This will happen only if the party to whom it was handed (or to whose attention it was brought) knows it was intended to have this effect, or if it was delivered to him or brought to his attention in such circumstances as to give him reasonable notice of the fact that it contained binding contractual terms.[27] Generally, in order to decide if a document contains contractual terms, reference should be made to current commercial

216, suggests that, on the facts of *L'Estrange* v. *F Graucob Ltd*, the Regulations would not apply as the buyer was not a 'consumer'.

24 *The Luna* [1920] P 22.

25 J. Basedow, 'Gestaltung rechtsgeschäftlicher Schuldverhältnisse' in *Münchener Kommentar Bürgerliches Gesetzbuch* (4th edn, Munich, 2003), para. 305(c) at 3. There is considerable uncertainty in German law over the degree to which so-called surprise clauses may be submitted to the good faith test, i.e. may become the subject of content control.

26 The principle of incorporation by reference to another document is usually combined with incorporation by notice, but it may equally be applied to incorporation by signature: *Thompson* v. *London, Midland and Scottish Railway Co.* [1930] 1 KB 41; *Smith* v. *South Wales Switchgear Ltd* [1978] 1 WLR 165; *Circle Freight International Ltd* v. *Medeast Gulf Exports Ltd* [1988] 1 Lloyd's Rep 427.

27 *Harling* v. *Eddy* [1951] 2 KB 739; *The Polyduke* [1978] 1 Lloyd's Rep 211.

practice.[28] Therefore, a document will be considered as contractual if it is obvious to a reasonable person that it was intended to have this effect. This will be the case if the document is of a kind that generally contains contractual terms.[29]

A good illustration is provided by *Chapelton* v. *Barry Urban District Council*,[30] in which the plaintiff wished to hire two deckchairs from the defendant council on a beach. The deckchairs were stacked near a notice which read, *inter alia*, 'Hire of chairs 2d *per* session of 3 hours', and which requested the public to obtain tickets from the deckchair attendant. The plaintiff took two deckchairs and obtained two tickets from the attendant, which he put in his pocket without reading. When he sat on one of the deckchairs, it collapsed and he was injured. He sued the council, who relied on a clause printed on the tickets excluding liability for any injury arising from the hire of the deckchair. The Court of Appeal held that, since no reasonable man would assume that the ticket was anything but a receipt for the money, the defendant had failed to satisfy the preliminary requirement of identifying the ticket as a contractual document.

In *Burnett* v. *Westminster Bank Ltd*,[31] the plaintiff had for some years maintained accounts at two of the defendant's branches, branch A and branch B. A new chequebook was issued to him by branch A, on the front cover of which was a notice that 'the cheques in this book will be applied to the account for which they have been prepared'. These cheques were in fact designed for use in a computer system operated by branch A, and 'magnetised ink' was used which the computer could 'read'. The plaintiff knew that there were words on the cover of the chequebook, but had not read them. He drew a cheque for £2,300, but crossed out branch A and substituted branch B. The computer could not 'read' the amendment to the plaintiff's cheque. He later wished to stop the cheque and told branch B to do so. Meanwhile, the computer had debited his account at branch A. He sued the bank for breach of contract. The bank pleaded the limitation term on the cover of the chequebook. Mocatta J gave judgment for the plaintiff. The chequebook was not a document which could reasonably be assumed

[28] Treitel, *The Law of Contract*, 217.

[29] *Hood* v. *Anchor Line* [1918] AC 837 (ship ticket); *Thompson* v. *London, Midland and Scottish Railway Co.* [1930] 1 KB 41 (railway ticket); *Taylor* v. *Glasgow Corp.* [1952] SC 440 (ticket at baths); *Thornton* v. *Shoe Lane Parking Ltd* [1971] 2 QB 163 (car park ticket issued by automatic machine).

[30] [1940] 1 KB 532; [1940] 1 All ER 356.

[31] [1966] 1 QB 742; [1965] 3 All ER 81.

to contain any terms of the contract, and the defendant had not in fact given notice of the limitation to the plaintiff. The defendant was, in effect, seeking, without the plaintiff's consent, to alter the terms of the contract.

Incorporation presupposes that the limiting term has been adequately brought to the attention of the other party *before* the contract is made (a belated notice is ineffective).[32] The effectiveness of pre-contractual notice depends principally on two factors: first, the steps taken to give notice; and, secondly, the nature of the exempting conditions. As regards the first factor, where the notice is contained in a contractual document, it is normally sufficient for the exempting condition to be prominently set out or referred to on the face of the document.[33] A person wishing to rely on the clause does not have to prove that he actually succeeded in bringing the clause to the notice of the other party, but that reasonable steps were taken to bring the terms to the attention of the other party.[34] On the other hand, a clause is unlikely to be incorporated if there are no words on the face of the document drawing attention to it,[35] or if, for example, there are such words but they are made illegible by a date stamp,[36] or the exclusion clause is buried in a mass of advertisements.[37] It is not necessary, as a matter of law, to print words such as 'see back' or 'see inside' on the face of the document.[38]

As regards the second factor (the nature of the exempting conditions), the leading case is *Parker* v. *South Eastern Railway Co.*[39] In this

[32] *Olley* v. *Marlborough Court Ltd* [1949] 1 KB 532; [1949] 1 All ER 127.

[33] *Thompson* v. *London, Midland and Scottish Railway Co.* [1930] 1 KB 41. In this case, the plaintiff asked her niece to buy a railway excursion ticket for her. The ticket (cost 2s 7d) had on its face the words 'see back' and on the back a statement that it was issued subject to the conditions set out in the company's timetables, which could be bought for 6d. The plaintiff could not read the words on the ticket as she was illiterate. The plaintiff was injured by the alleged negligence of the defendant railway company. The jury found that the defendant had not taken reasonable steps to bring the conditions to the plaintiff's notice. However, the Court of Appeal reversed the decision and held that the clause was incorporated in the contract as the notice was clear and the ticket was a common form of contractual document. The fact that the traveller was illiterate was of no importance since the ticket had been bought on the plaintiff's behalf by her niece and it was found that the niece's father had ascertained, before the ticket was taken, that there were conditions for excursion tickets.

[34] *Birch* v. *Thomas* [1972] 1 WLR 294.

[35] *Richardson, Spence & Co.* v. *Rowntree* [1894] AC 217.

[36] *Sugar* v. *London, Midland & Scottish Railway Co.* [1941] 1 All ER 172.

[37] *Stephen* v. *International Sleeping Car Co. Ltd* (1903) 19 TLR 620.

[38] *Burke* v. *South Eastern Railway Co.* (1879) 5 CPD 1.

[39] (1877) 2 CPD 416.

case, the plaintiff deposited a bag in the defendant's station cloakroom. He received a paper ticket which said on its face 'See back', and on the back were a number of printed conditions, including a condition limiting the defendant's liability for any package to £10. The plaintiff admitted that he knew there was writing on the ticket, but stated that he had not read it, and did not know or believe that the writing contained conditions. The bag was lost, and the plaintiff claimed £24 10s for its value. In the Court of Appeal, three questions were posed: (1) Did the plaintiff know that there was printing on the ticket? In the instant case, he did. (2) Did he know that the ticket contained or referred to conditions? In the instant case, he did not know. (3) Had the defendant taken sufficient steps to draw the plaintiff's attention to the relevant conditions? In the instant case, the condition was designed to exempt the defendant from liability for loss caused to the customer. The exclusion was so wide and unusual that it required an unusually explicit warning. Since the defendant had not given such a warning, they could not rely on the exclusion. If the notice complied with these two requirements, the fact that a particular plaintiff suffers from some non-legal disability, for example he is unable to speak English or is blind or illiterate,[40] is irrelevant.

In conclusion, therefore, it can be said that the more unusual a particular term is, the greater will be the degree of notice required to incorporate it. In *Thornton* v. *Shoe Lane Parking Ltd*,[41] the plaintiff wished to park his car in the defendant's automated car park. He had not been there before. Outside the car park was a notice stating the charges and adding the words 'All cars parked at owners' risk'. As the plaintiff drove into the car park, a traffic control light turned from red to green, and a ticket was issued by a machine. No supervisor was in attendance. The plaintiff took the ticket and saw the time on it. He also saw that it contained other wording, but put it into his pocket without reading it. The words in fact stated that the ticket was issued subject to conditions displayed on the premises. To read these conditions, the plaintiff would have had to walk round the car park until he reached a panel on which they were displayed. The plaintiff never thought to look for them. One condition purported to exempt the defendant from liability not only for damage to parked cars, but also for injury

[40] *Thompson* v. *London, Midland and Scottish Railway Co.* [1930] 1 KB 41, in which the defendant was illiterate.

[41] [1971] 2 QB 163.

to customers, however caused. When the plaintiff returned to collect his car, there was an accident in which he was injured. The defendant pleaded the exempting terms. The Court of Appeal gave judgment for the plaintiff. Lord Denning summarised the law as follows:

> The customer pays his money and gets a ticket. He cannot refuse it. He cannot get his money back. He may protest to the machine, even swear at it. But it will remain unmoved. He is committed beyond recall. He was committed at the very moment when he put his money into the machine. The contract was concluded at that time. It can be translated into offer and acceptance in this way: the offer is made when the proprietor of the machine holds it out as being ready to receive the money. The acceptance takes place when the customer puts his money into the slot. The terms of the offer are contained in the notice placed on or near the machine stating what is offered for the money. The customer is bound by these terms as long as they are sufficiently brought to his notice beforehand, but not otherwise. He is not bound by the terms printed on the ticket if they differ from the notice, because the ticket comes too late. The contract has already been made.

Although a term must be construed in its context, it is not enough to look at a set of printed conditions as a whole. If the particular condition relied on is one which is unusual in that class of contract, special measures may be required to bring it to the notice of the other party. As Lord Denning put it in *J. Spurling Ltd* v. *Bradshaw*:[42]

> Some clauses I have seen would need to be printed in red ink on the face of the document with a red hand pointing to it before the notice could be held to be sufficient.

In *Interfoto Picture Library Ltd* v. *Stiletto Visual Programmes Ltd*,[43] the test was slightly reformulated. The plaintiffs ran a photographic transparency lending library. Following a telephone inquiry by the defendant, the plaintiff delivered to the defendant forty-seven transparencies, together with a delivery note containing nine printed conditions. Condition 2 stipulated that all the transparencies had to be returned within fourteen days of delivery; otherwise, a storage fee of £5 per day plus VAT would be charged for each transparency retained thereafter. The defendant, who had not used the plaintiff's services before, did not read the conditions, and returned the transparencies four weeks later,

[42] [1956] 1 WLR 461. [43] [1989] QB 433.

whereupon the plaintiff invoiced the defendant for £3,783.50. The defendant refused to pay and the plaintiff brought an action to recover the sum. At first instance, the court gave judgment for the plaintiff for the amount claimed. On appeal, the Court of Appeal reversed this decision. The Court of Appeal had evidence of the terms of supply used by other businesses in the same business as the plaintiff. Although many businesses in the industry imposed a charge for the late return of material, the charges were all significantly lower than that charged by the plaintiff, and therefore, in the absence of special notice, the clause was not incorporated. Dillon and Bingham LJJ emphasised the 'unusual' nature of the plaintiff's term, but it was clear to them that it was the amount of the charge, not the nature of the term, which was unusual. Dillon LJ stated that special notice would be required where a clause was 'particularly onerous or unusual'. The clause failed because the amount charged was 'extortionate', although of a common type.[44] This case involved business parties, and therefore, in the consumer context, it is likely that even greater efforts would need to be made in order to bring such a clause sufficiently to the attention of a consumer.[45]

For a German lawyer, 'incorporation by notice' reflects the twofold nature of so-called 'surprise clause' (that is, clauses which one would not necessarily expect to find in a contract of the type in question). First, there must be a means of invalidating such 'surprise clauses'. Secondly, the borderline between control by way of incorporation and control by way of content control is sometimes difficult to draw. A 'surprise clause' may easily contain an element of 'unfairness', simply by overstepping the contracting parties' reasonable expectations of the possible content of the contract terms. German courts circumvent the systematic difficulties in deciding whether the 'surprise clause' deals only with incorporation or also with content control, by viewing the 'surprise clause' as a part of 'procedural' good faith. Thus, the good faith test includes elements of the incorporation test. This is procedural good faith as it is understood in the UK.

Incorporation by a course of dealing

The third method of incorporating a clause into a contract is by a course of dealing. The courts have never defined what constitutes a

44 Bradgate, 'Unreasonable Standard Terms', 586 at 587.

45 This is the conclusion drawn by G. Howells and S. Weatherill, *Consumer Protection Law* (Aldershot, 1995), 308.

course of dealing with any degree of precision, since what constitutes a 'regular' course of dealing depends on the facts of the particular case.[46] Some general guidance, however, was given by the House of Lords in *McCutcheon* v. *David MacBrayne Ltd*.[47] In that case, a ferry belonging to the defendant sank, and the plaintiff's car was lost. The defendants sought to rely on an exclusion clause contained in a note which, contrary to their usual practice, they had not asked the plaintiff to sign. In the House of Lords, it was held that the course of dealing must be both regular and consistent. As regards the expression 'consistent', Lord Devlin said that 'previous dealings were relevant only if they prove knowledge of the terms, actual and not constructive, and consent to them'. Lord Pearce added that there was no consistent course of dealing in this case because the previous transactions had always been in writing (the note was always signed) whereas in the present case the transaction was entirely oral.

Therefore, the law is in a state of some uncertainty. It is suggested[48] that, if there is a lengthy and consistent course of dealing on terms incorporating an exclusion clause, then those terms may apply to a particular transaction even though, in relation to the particular transaction, the usual steps needed to incorporate the clause were not taken.[49] Thus, the primary rule should be that a term will not apply if:

(1) the transaction in question was not part of a consistent course of dealing;[50]

[46] For example, in *Henry Kendall Ltd* v. *William Lillico Ltd* [1969] 2 AC 31, the House of Lords held that 100 similar contracts over a period of three years constituted a course of dealing. In *Hollier* v. *Rambler Motors (AMC) Ltd* [1972] 2 QB, however, it was held that three or four contracts over a period of five years was not a course of dealing between a consumer and a garage. An important factor is whether the contracting parties have equal bargaining power. In *British Crane Hire Corporation Ltd* v. *Ipswich Plant Hire Ltd* [1975] QB 303, it was held that a clause had been incorporated into the contract on the basis of two previous transactions and the custom of the trade. The facts that the parties were of equal bargaining power, they were both in trade and such conditions were habitually incorporated into these contracts influenced this decision.

[47] [1964] 1 WLR 125. [48] Treitel, *The Law of Contract*, 220.

[49] *Hardwick Game Farm* v. *Suffolk Agricultural etc. Association* [1969] 2 AC 31 at 90, 104, 105, 113 and 130; *SIAT di dal Ferro* v. *Tradax Overseas SA* [1980] 1 Lloyd's Rep 53; *George Mitchell (Chesterhall) Ltd* v. *Finney Lock Seeds Ltd* [1983] QB 284 at 295, affirmed [1983] QB 284; *Circle Freight International Ltd* v. *Medeast Gulf Exports Ltd* [1988] 2 Lloyd's Rep 427.

[50] *McCutcheon* v. *David MacBrayne Ltd* [1964] 1 WLR 125.

(2) past transactions were spread over a long period of time and their number was so small that they could not be said to give rise to a course of dealing;[51]
(3) the steps which are necessary to incorporate the clause had never been taken at any stage of the dealings between the parties;[52] or
(4) the terms of each transaction in the series had been separately negotiated and expressly agreed between the parties.[53]

Control of the construction of a clause

The three requirements which must be met in order to include an exclusion clause in a contract (incorporation, construction, and no contrary rule of law) were noted above. For the second requirement, construction, it must be shown that the exclusion clause, properly interpreted, covers the damage which was caused. The general principle is that contract terms are construed strictly against the party seeking to rely on them (the *contra proferentem* rule).[54] This principle applies in cases in which a party relies on an exclusion clause to protect him or her from liability for negligence or for certain other breaches. The application of these rules of construction does not, however, render exclusion clauses generally ineffective. If the clause is appropriately drafted so as to exclude or limit the liability in question, then the courts must (subject to the powers conferred on them by the UCTA and the UTCCR) give effect to it.

The wide reach of the *contra proferentem* rule

The *contra proferentem* rule is well known in all legal systems. Therefore, the European Community had no difficulty in obtaining agreements to having the rule inserted into Directive 93/13/EEC, at least

[51] *Hollier* v. *Rambler Motors (AMC) Ltd* [1972] 2 QB 71 (three or four transactions in five years not sufficient). *The Havprins* [1983] 2 Lloyd's Rep 356 at 362 (three transactions in five years sufficient, though incorporation was 'not by course of dealing alone'). See, however, *Hardwick Game Farm* v. *Suffolk Agricultural etc. Association* [1969] 2 AC 31, in which three or four contracts a month for three years were held to be sufficient.

[52] *Smith* v. *Taylor* [1966] 2 Lloyd's Rep 231.

[53] *Johnson Matthey Bankers Ltd* v. State *Trading Corp. of India* [1984] 1 Lloyd's Rep 427 at 433.

[54] *Verba chartarum fortius accipiuntur contra proferentem* (the words of written documents are construed more forcibly against the party putting forward the document). In the case of exclusion clauses, this is the party seeking to impose the exclusion.

with regard to enforcement action taken by individuals. The rule does not apply to preventive action.[55] The Directive covers only standard business terms, whereas the common law also deals with exclusion and limitation clauses in all contracts regardless of their nature. Contract control by or through 'construction' is certainly the most uniquely 'English' element in the field of contract law. Construction is the true battleground between the lawyers drafting the contract terms and the judges submitting those terms to judicial scrutiny. The art of drafting often consists in devising a form of wording which will defy any attempt by the courts to construe it in a manner contrary to that intended by its drafter. From a civil law lawyer's perspective, 'construction' must be understood as a means of avoiding a fully fledged content control. The requirement to use 'plain and intelligible language' is in effect already a legal requirement by virtue of its being inherent in the common law doctrine of construction.

The *contra proferentem* rule in action

The effect of the *contra proferentem* rule is that any ambiguity in the exclusion clause is resolved against the party seeking to rely on it.[56] 'If a person is under a legal liability and wishes to get rid of it, he can only do so by using clear words.'[57] As a result, the words of the exclusion clause must exactly cover the liability which it is sought to exclude; otherwise, any doubt or ambiguity will be resolved against the party seeking to rely on it. Therefore, a clause stating that a seller gives 'no warranty, expressed or implied' does not protect the seller from liability for a breach of contract;[58] nor does a provision protecting him

[55] Art. 5(2) of the Directive.

[56] In *Wallis, Son and Wells* v. *Pratt and Haynes* [1911] AC 394 and in *Andrews Bros. (Bournemouth) Ltd* v. *Singer and Co. Ltd* [1934] 1 KB 17, the court adopted a restrictive interpretation of the exclusion clauses and held that they did not exclude the sellers' liability.

[57] *Alison (J. Gordon) Ltd* v. *Wallsend Shipway and Engineering Co. Ltd* (1927) 43 TLR 323 at 324 *per* Scrutton LJ.

[58] *Harling* v. *Eddy* [1951] 2 KB 739. The distinction between *conditions* and *warranties* in English law is of vital importance. In brief, a condition may be defined as a statement of fact, or a promise, which forms an essential term of the contract. If the statement of fact proves to be untrue, or the promise is not fulfilled, the innocent party may treat the breach as a repudiation which discharges him from further performance of the contract. A good example is the case of *Behn* v. *Burness* (1841) 2 M&G 257, in which a ship was stated in the contract of charterparty to be 'now in the port of Amsterdam'. The fact that the ship was not in the port at the date of the contract discharged

from liability for a breach of implied conditions and warranties cover the breach of an express term of the contract;[59] nor does a provision in a hire-purchase agreement stating that 'no warranty, condition or description or representation is given' exclude liability for breach of a collateral undertaking previously given.[60]

In the leading case of *Wallis, Son & Wells* v. *Pratt & Haynes*,[61] the respondents sold seed to the appellants as 'common English sainfoin' on the condition that the 'sellers give no warranty expressed or implied as to growth, description or any other matters'. The seed delivered to the appellants was not in fact 'common English sainfoin', but the appellants, believing it to be 'common English sainfoin', resold it as such to third parties, to whom the appellants were obliged to pay damages once the error came to light. The respondents pleaded the exclusion clause. It was held by the House of Lords that, even though the appellants had accepted the goods and could therefore only sue for breach of warranty *ex post facto*, there was nevertheless originally a breach of the condition implied by section 13 of the Sale of Goods Act 1893,[62] and this had not been successfully excluded. As Lord Loreburn LC succinctly put it:

> If a man agrees to sell something of a particular description he cannot require the buyer to take something which is of a different description, and a sale of goods by description implies a condition that the goods shall correspond to it. But if a thing of different description is accepted in the belief that it is according to the contract, then the buyer cannot

the carter from performance. On the other hand, a warranty, being a less important term, does not entitle the innocent party to treat the contract as repudiated in the event of its breach, but only to claim damages. In *Chanter* v. *Hopkins* (1838) 4 M&W 399, a warranty was defined as 'an express or implied statement of something which the party undertakes shall be part of a contract; and though part of the contract, yet collateral to the express object of it'. Because of this rigid distinction between conditions and warranties, case law in the more recent times has developed a third category, namely, 'intermediate' (or 'innominate') terms, the breach of which does not necessarily entitle the innocent party to terminate the contract; see *Hongkong Fir Shipping Co. Ltd* v. *Kawasake Kisen Kaisha Ltd* [1962] 2 QB 26, at 70 *per* Lord Diplock. For a more detailed analysis, see J. Beatson, *Anson's Law of Contract* (28th edn, Oxford, 2002), 132–41.

59 *Andrew Bros. (Bournemouth) Ltd* v. *Singer & Co. Ltd* [1934] 1 KB 17.

60 *McCullagh* v. *Lane Fox & Partners Ltd* (1994) 1 EGLR 48.

61 [1911] AC 394.

62 Section 13 of the Sale of Goods Act 1893 provides: 'Where there is a contract for the sale of goods by description, there is an implied condition that the goods shall correspond with the description; and if the sale be by sample, as well as by description, it is not sufficient that the bulk of the goods corresponds with the sample if the goods do not also correspond with the description.'

> return it after having accepted it; but he may treat the breach of the condition as if it was a breach of warranty, that is to say, he may have the remedies applicable to a breach of warranty . . . There is no doubt that, when you are dealing in a commodity the inspection of which does not enable you to distinguish its exact nature, there are risks both on the buyer and on the seller if they think fit to sell by description. But *if it is desired by a seller to throw the risk of any honest mistake on the buyer, then he must use apt language, and I should have thought the clearer he tries to make the language the better.* I do not think he has done so in the clause to which I have referred.[63]

In *Lee (John) & Son (Grantham) Ltd* v. *Railway Executive*,[64] goods stored in a railway warehouse let to a tenant were damaged by fire. The tenant brought an action against the Railway Executive alleging that the accident was due to their negligence because a spark or other combustible material ejected from their railway engine had caused the fire. The Railway Executive relied on a clause in the tenancy agreement, which provided that:

> The tenant shall be responsible for and shall release and indemnify the company and their servants from and against all liability for personal injury (whether fatal or otherwise) loss of or damage to property and any other loss damage costs and expenses however caused or incurred (whether by the act or neglect of the company or their servants or agents or not) which but for the tenancy hereby created or anything done pursuant to the provisions hereof would not have arisen.

In the Court of Appeal, the application of the clause was confined by the words 'but for the tenancy hereby created' to liabilities which arose only by reason of the relationship of landlord and tenant created by the lease. The clause was capable of a wider meaning, but it had to be construed against the grantor, *contra proferentem*, and thus the defendants were not protected. It is worth quoting from the judgment of Lord Evershed MR:

> The difficulty is the exact extent of the former words, 'the tenancy hereby created'. The allegation in the statement of claim is that the defendants were negligent either in that their engine was unsafe or because for other reasons sparks were emitted from it . . . Because of the extravagant result, which the former view involves, I think that the latter construction is the one which the court ought to adopt. We are presented with two

[63] [1911] AC 394 at 395–6 (emphasis added). [64] [1949] 2 All ER 581.

> alternative readings of this document and the reading, which one should adopt is to be determined, among other things, by a consideration of the fact that the defendants put forward the document. They have put forward a clause which is by no means free from obscurity and have contended that, on the view for which they argued, it has a remarkably, if not an extravagantly, wide scope, and I think that the rule *contra proferentem* should be applied and that the result is that the present claim is not one which obliges the first plaintiffs to give to the defendants a release and an indemnity.[65]

Courts have sometimes gone so far as to find ambiguity where none existed in using the *contra proferentem* rule as *de facto* content control.[66] An example is *Hollier* v. *Rambler Motors (AMC) Ltd.*[67] The plaintiff agreed with the manager of the defendant's garage that his car would be towed to the garage for repair. While at the garage, the car was substantially damaged by fire as a result of the defendant's negligence. The defendant argued that the transaction was subject to their usual terms which included a clause stating: 'The Company is not responsible for damage caused by fire to customers' cars on the premises.' The Court of Appeal held that, even if this clause was incorporated into the contract, it would not operate to provide a defence. The defendant argued that, in the circumstances, the only way in which it could be liable for damage by fire was if it were negligent, and that the wording of the clause was therefore appropriate to exclude liability for negligence. The court held that the clause could be read by a reasonable customer as a warning that the defendant would not be responsible for a fire caused without negligence. It was not therefore sufficiently unambiguous to exclude liability for negligence.

The extensive scope of application of the *contra proferentem* rule has been somewhat narrowed in more recent judgments. In *Ailsa Craig Fishing Co. Ltd* v. *Malvern Fishing Co. Ltd*,[68] the House of Lords held that the *contra proferentem* rule did not apply with the same rigour to limitation clauses as it did to exclusion clauses. Lord Wilberforce summarised the law as follows:

> Whether a clause limiting liability is effective or not is a question of construction of that clause in the context of the contract as a whole. If it is to exclude liability for negligence, it must be most clearly and

[65] *Ibid.*, 582H–583B and 583F–H.
[66] Howells and Weatherill, *Consumer Protection Law*, 309.
[67] [1972] 2 QB 71; [1972] 1 All ER 399. [68] [1983] 1 WLR 964.

> unambiguously expressed, and in a contract such as this, must be construed *contra proferentem*. I do not think that there is any doubt so far. But I venture to add one further qualification, or at least clarification: one must not strive to create ambiguities by strained construction, as I think that the appellants have striven to do. The relevant words must be given, if possible, their natural, plain meaning. *Clauses of limitation are not regarded by the courts with the same hostility as clauses of exclusion: this is because they must be related to other contractual terms, in particular to the risks to which the defending party may be exposed, the remuneration which he receives, and possibly also the opportunity of the other party to insure.*[69]

Finally, in *George Mitchell (Chesterhall) Ltd* v. *Finney Lock Seeds Ltd*,[70] Lord Diplock agreed with Lord Denning in the Court of Appeal that recent legislation had

> removed from judges the temptation to resort to the device of ascribing to the words appearing in exclusion clauses a tortured meaning so as to avoid giving effect to an exclusion or limitation of liability when a judge thought that in the circumstance to do so would be unfair.[71]

Courts seem to accept a limitation clause more easily than exclusion clauses. A contracting party will indeed be much more reluctant to accept an exclusion clause than a limitation clause. This differentiation fits very well into the overall approach of the English law in which the parties' autonomy and the parties' intentions are objectively defined. There is indeed a difference between an exclusion of liability and a limitation of liability. Civil law legal systems tend to devote less attention to the differences and treat both forms alike.[72]

Special cases in which particular rules of construction apply

There remain at least two special cases in which particular rules of construction are employed by the courts. The first is where a party seeks to exclude liability for his own negligence. The second is where

[69] *Ibid.*, 966G–H (emphasis added). [70] [1983] 2 AC 803. [71] *Ibid.*, 809.

[72] In the Australian case of *Darlington Futures Ltd* v. *Delco Australia Pty Ltd* [1987] 1 ALJR 76, the High Court of Australia refused to differentiate between exclusion clauses and limitation clauses in this manner. Instead, the court held that 'the interpretation of an exclusion clause is to be determined by construing the clause according to its natural and ordinary meaning, read in light of the contract as a whole, thereby giving due weight to the context in which the clause appears including the nature and the object of the contract and, where appropriate, construing the clause *contra proferentem* in case of ambiguity'.

a party seeks to exclude liability for a 'fundamental breach'. The readiness of the courts to strictly control exclusion and limitation clauses which seek to exclude liability for the contracting parties' own negligence comes close to being a type of 'fairness' or 'reasonableness' test. The 'fundamental breach' doctrine goes one step further in that it generalises the fairness or reasonableness test and turns it into a general principle that comes close to content control in civil law regimes. However, while the so-called Lord Morton doctrine survives to maintain liability for one's own negligence, the fundamental breach doctrine, after a promising start on exclusion and limitation clauses in contracts for the purchase of used cars, was struck down by the House of Lords in *Photo Production Ltd* v. *Securicor Transport Ltd*.[73]

Cases in which a party relies on an exclusion clause to protect him from liability for negligence

The ability of the contracting parties to exclude liability for negligence causing personal injury or death has been substantially restricted by legislation.[74] Nevertheless, cases will still occur in which a party will seek to exclude or limit its liability for negligence in situations other than those of personal injury or death (for example, liability arising under the tort of conversion). Although it is possible to exclude liability in negligence, the courts have traditionally approached clauses which are said to exclude such liability on the assumption that it is 'inherently improbable that one party to a contract should intend to absolve the other party from the consequences of the latter's own negligence'.[75] The courts will therefore conclude that a term does not exclude liability for negligence because, quite often, the drafters of the contract will avoid alerting the other contracting party by using milder expressions.[76] Only where clear and unambiguous words are used will the court be ready to conclude that a clause excludes liability for negligence.

[73] [1980] 1 Lloyd's Rep 545 at 549–51 *per* Lord Wilberforce; the reasoning has been analysed by N. Palmer and D. Yates, 'The Future of the Unfair Contract Terms Act 1977' (1981) 40 *Cambridge Law Journal* 108.

[74] UCTA, section 2; UTCCR 1994, Schedule 3, para. 1(a).

[75] *Gillespie* v. *Bowles (Roy) Transport Ltd* [1973] QB 400 at 419 *per* Buckley LJ.

[76] 'Why was an express reference to negligence not inserted? Similar questions have been posed on a number of occasions. Why do draftsmen not take note of the impact of a clear and consistent line of judicial decisions? For my part, I have no doubt that the off-the-record reason would be "one does not want to frighten off one or other of the parties". Omissions of express references to negligence tend to be deliberate.' *E. E. Caledonia Ltd* v. *Orbit Valve Co. Europe plc* [1994] 2 Lloyd's Rep. 239 at 246 *per* Lord Steyn.

What the courts are really doing is submitting such exclusion clauses to a strict 'comprehensibility' test which encompasses elements of fairness.

The harsh approach may be found in an old authority which was later overruled. In *Rutter* v. *Palmer*,[77] the plaintiff left his car at the defendant's garage to be sold. The contract provided that 'customers' cars are driven by your [the defendant's] servants at customers' sole risk'. The car was taken for a trial run by one of the defendant's drivers. There was a collision, and the car was damaged. It was held that the clause effectively placed the risk of negligence on the plaintiff, and so his claim failed. The clear and unambiguous wording of an exclusion or limitation clause is all the more necessary where the liability sought to be excluded or limited arises from tort. Thus, it has been held that a term in a contract for the hire of a bicycle, purporting to exempt the owner from liability for personal injury, only extended to liability in contract and not to liability in negligence. It is necessary therefore for a term to specifically refer to negligence, or at least to be widely expressed, in order to cover liability in tort. Phrases such as 'will not be liable for any damage, however caused',[78] 'will not in any circumstance be responsible',[79] 'arising from any cause whatsoever',[80] and so on, will ordinarily be construed to cover liability for negligence.[81]

Taking into consideration the fact that it is inherently unlikely that one contracting party will agree to allow the other contracting party to exclude liability for his own negligence, the courts have evolved specific rules of construction in relation to clauses concerning the exclusion or limitation of liability for negligence. The origin of these rules may be found in *Canada Steamship Lines Ltd* v. *King*.[82] In that case, by clause 7 of a lease by which the Crown leased a freight shed to the appellant company, it was provided that 'the lessee shall not have any claim ... against the lessor for ... damage ... to ... goods ... being ... in the said shed', and by clause 8 the Crown undertook to keep the shed in repair. Clause 17 provided that 'the lessee shall at all times indemnify ... the lessor from and against all claims ... by whomsoever made ... in any manner based upon, occasioned by or attributable to the execution of these presents, or any action taken or things done ... by virtue hereof, or the exercise in any manner of rights arising

[77] [1922] 2 KB 87. [78] *White* v. *Blackmore* [1972] 2 QB 651.
[79] *Harris Ltd* v. *Continental Express Ltd* [1961] 1 Lloyd's Rep 251.
[80] *A. E. Farr Ltd* v. *Admiralty* [1953] 1 WLR 1285.
[81] Beatson, *Anson's Law of Contract*, 171. [82] [1952] AC 192.

hereunder'. Owing to the negligence of the Crown's servants while using an oxyacetylene torch to effect certain repairs to the shed, a fire broke out which destroyed the shed and its contents. The appellant company and others, whose goods were destroyed in the fire, presented petitions of right against the Crown for damages. The Crown pleaded that the appellant company's claim was barred by clause 7 of the lease, and in third party proceedings relied on clause 17 as giving rise to a right of indemnity from the appellants against the claims of the other appellants.

It was held, first, that the Crown had failed in clause 7 to limit its liability in respect of negligence in clear terms, and that accordingly the clause was to be construed as relating only to liability not based on negligence, examples of such liability being found in certain of the obligations imposed on lessors by the Civil Code of Lower Canada. Secondly, it was held that clause 17 did not cover negligent acts of the Crown's servants, because (1) it was at least doubtful whether the words 'any action taken or things done ... by virtue hereof' could be applied to a negligent act done in the course of carrying out an obligation; (2) even if these words were wide enough to include such a negligent act, the principle must be applied on the ground that the head of damage might be based on some other ground than that of negligence; and (3) the meaning and effect of clause 17 were far from clear, and such a liability may be excluded only by clear words. The Crown's claim to an exclusion of liability under clause 17 was therefore not established. The lessor was accordingly liable for the destruction of the goods. Lord Morton summarised the law as follows:

> (1) If the clause contains language which expressly exempts the person in whose favour it is made (hereinafter called 'the proferens') from the consequences of the negligence of his own servants, effect must be given to that provision ... (2) If there is no express reference to negligence, the court must consider whether the words used are wide enough, in their ordinary meaning, to cover negligence on the part of the servants of the proferens. If a doubt arises at this point, it must be resolved ... (3) If the words used are wide enough for the above purpose, the court must then consider whether 'the head of damage may be based on some ground other than that of negligence'. The 'other ground' must not be so fanciful or remote that the proferens cannot be supposed to have desired protection against it; but subject to this qualification ... the existence of a possible head of damage other than that of negligence is fatal to the proferens even if the words used are *prima facie* wide enough to cover negligence on the part of his servants.

This test has subsequently been followed by the courts. In order to satisfy the first limb of the test, there must be a clear reference to the word 'negligence' or to a synonym of it.[83] The safest course is to use the word 'negligence'.[84] In the absence of any such express reference, the court will proceed to apply the second and third limbs of the test. Under the second limb of the test, the court must consider whether the words used are wide enough, in their ordinary meaning, to cover negligence on the part of the party relying on the exclusion clause. If doubt arises as to whether the words are wide enough, the doubt must be resolved against the party relying on the clause. Under the third limb of the test, the courts will have to consider whether the exclusion clause may cover some kind of liability other than negligence. If there is such a liability, the clause will generally be confined in its application to that alternative source of liability and will be held not to extend to negligence. If this alternative ground is not so fanciful or remote that the person seeking exclusion cannot be supposed to have desired exclusion against it, the exclusion clause will be construed as extending to that ground alone, even if the words used are *prima facie* wide enough to cover negligence.[85]

Lord Morton's test, although criticised by a relatively recent Australian case,[86] is currently applied by English authorities. In *E. E. Caledonia Ltd* v. *Orbit Valve Co. Europe plc*,[87] by a contract made between the plaintiff (the operators and occupiers of an oil-drilling platform in the North Sea) and the defendant for the carrying out of work to the plaintiff's order on the platform, each party agreed to indemnify the other against 'any claim . . . or liability . . . arising by reason of . . . [the] death of any employee . . . of the indemnifying party, resulting from or . . . connected with the performance of this order'. One of the defendant's employees died in a fire on the platform. The plaintiff made a payment in settlement of the claims of the deceased's estate and of the defendant on the basis that the death was caused by the

[83] *Lamport & Holt Lines Ltd* v. *Coubro & Scrutton (M&I) Ltd* [1982] 2 Lloyd's Rep 42; *Spriggs* v. *Sotheby Parke Bernet & Co.* [1986] 1 Lloyd's Rep 487.

[84] *E. E. Caledonia Ltd* v. *Orbit Valve Co. Europe plc* [1994] 1 WLR 1515.

[85] *Shell Chemicals UK Ltd* v. *P&O Roadtanks Ltd* [1995] 1 Lloyd's Rep 297 at 301; *Alderslade* v. *Hendon Laundry Ltd* [1945] KB 189 at 192; *Canada Steamship Lines Ltd* v. *King* [1952] AC 292; *The Raphael* [1982] 2 Lloyd's Rep 42.

[86] *Schenker & Co. (Aust) Pty Ltd* v. *Malpas Equipment and Services Pty Ltd* [1990] VR 834 at 836 *per* McGarvie J.

[87] [1978] 1 WLR 221 at 228 and 232 *per* Hobhouse J, approved by the Court of Appeal in *E. E. Caledonia Ltd* v. *Orbit Valve Co. Europe plc* [1994] 1 WLR 1515 at 1521.

negligence of the plaintiff's servants and by breaches of the plaintiff's statutory duty. In the Court of Appeal, Steyn LJ started his analysis by mentioning that the court should construe the contractual terms objectively and should attempt to determine whether they contain any reference to negligence or synonymous words, which in the present case was not the case (and thus the first two limbs of Lord Morton's test had not been satisfied). He proceeded to apply the third limb of the test, thereby slightly modifying its message:

> [I]n my judgment even in the case of a bilateral clause, such as the one before us, it is *prima facie* implausible that the parties would wish to release one another from the consequences of the other's negligence and agree to indemnify the other in respect of such consequences. The point is a matter of first impression and capable of elaboration. But I would hold that Lord Morton's third proposition equally applies to a bilateral clause such as [the one in question].[88]

There is one further matter to be considered. The third limb of Lord Morton's test is horn-book construction law. The printed conditions in the agreement in this case were evidently drafted by a lawyer. Why therefore was an express reference to negligence not inserted? Similar questions have been posed on a number of occasions. Why do draftsmen ignored the clear and consistent case law on this subject? Perhaps it is the case that draftsmen do not wish to provoke the second party to the contract to withdraw before the contract is concluded by making the terms of the contract too favourable to the first party. Omissions of express reference to negligence may therefore be deliberate.[89]

Here, Steyn LJ reveals the true purpose of the third limb of Lord Morton's test: if a contracting party is unwilling openly to declare in clear and unequivocal language that he is seeking to limit all his liability, even that caused by his own negligence, then he must pay the price for his unwillingness by having the contract construed in favour of the other party to the contract.

The same approach was employed in *Shell Chemicals UK Ltd* v. *P&O Roadtanks Ltd.*[90] A gap needed to be bridged between Lord Morton's test and the transparency principle enshrined in Directive 93/13/EEC. Transparency, too, relies on autonomy and responsibility. If the contracting parties openly state in plain and intelligible language what

[88] *Ibid.*, 1523A–D. [89] *Ibid.*, 1523G–H.
[90] [1995] 1 Lloyd's Rep 297. See also *The Fiona* [1994] 2 Lloyd's Rep 506.

terms they wish to see included in the contract, they will be in a position to make a fully informed decision as to whether or not to enter into the contract. The essential principle is party autonomy. However, the courts might take a stand to make autonomy a realistic feature. This exactly is the tiny bit of 'fairness' that makes party autonomy work – with the support of transparency.

The 'fundamental breach' doctrine does not provide sufficient content control in common law

From about 1950 onwards, the courts evolved rules of interpretation to cover the situation in which a party to a contract commits a fundamental breach of that contract but then seeks to rely on an exclusion clause to exclude his liability for that breach. These rules of interpretation became known as the 'fundamental breach' doctrine. This doctrine has been applied by the courts in all areas of the law of contract. The practical effect of the doctrine was that a party who had committed a fundamental breach of contract was sometimes unable to rely on an exclusion clause in the contract. Thus, in a number of well-known cases, a person who had committed a serious breach of contract was not permitted to rely on an exclusion clause drafted in very wide terms.[91] In summary, the effect of this doctrine was that 'when one party has been guilty of a fundamental breach of contract and the other side accepts it, so that the contract comes to an end . . . then the guilty party cannot rely on an exception or limitation clause to escape from his liability for the breach'.[92]

Two different approaches have been adopted as to the nature of this doctrine. The first approach suggests that there was actually a *rule of law* preventing the operation of exclusion clauses in situations of fundamental breach.[93] The second approach may be called the *rule of construction* approach, according to which the question of whether an exclusion clause covers a fundamental breach is one of construction. The clause is interpreted against the party seeking to rely on it. The

[91] *Alexander* v. *Railway Executive* [1951] 2 KB 882; *Karsales (Harrow) Ltd* v. *Wallis* [1956] 1 WLR 936; *Sze Hai Tong Bank Ltd* v. *Rabler Cycle Co. Ltd* [1959] AC 576 at 587 and 588; *Yeoman Credit Ltd* v. *Apps* [1962] 2 QB 508 at 520; *Charterhouse Credit Ltd* v. *Tolly* [1963] 2 QB 683.

[92] *Harbutt's 'Plasticine' Ltd* v. *Wayne Tank & Pump Co. Ltd* [1970] 1 Lloyd's Rep 15 at 25; followed in *Suisse Atlantique Société d'Armement Maritime SA* v. *NV Rottersdamsche Kolen Centrale* [1966] 1 Lloyd's Rep 529; [1967] AC 361.

[93] *Karsales (Harrow) Ltd* v. *Wallis* [1956] 1 WLR 936; *Yeoman Credit Ltd* v. *Apps* [1962] 2 QB 508 at 520; *Charterhouse Credit Ltd* v. *Tolly* [1963] 2 QB 683.

House of Lords set the tone of the fundamental breach doctrine as early as 1967 in *Suisse Atlantique Société d'Armement Maritime SA* v. *NV Rotterdamsche Kolen Centrale.*[94] Thirteen years later, and after conflicting decisions in the lower courts, the House of Lords determined once and for all the question of the availability of the fundamental breach doctrine in *Photo Production Ltd* v. *Securicor Transport Ltd.*[95]

In *Suisse Atlantique*,[96] the respondent agreed to charter a vessel from the appellant for the carriage of coal from the United States to Europe, the vessel returning in ballast after each voyage. The charter was to remain in force for two years. Fixed periods of lay time were provided during which the respondents were obliged to load or discharge the vessel, and demurrage was payable, subject to certain exceptions, at the rate of US$1,000 per day. Between 16 October 1957 and the end of the charter, the vessel made eight round trips between the United States and Europe. The appellant alleged that a further six round trips could have been completed within the lay time or a further nine round trips if the respondent had loaded and discharged the vessel with reasonable despatch. Before the House of Lords, the appellant contended, *inter alia*, that its claim for the loss of freight on the lost trips was not limited to the demurrage payments, and that the breaches of contract which caused the delays amounted to a fundamental breach of contract entitling the appellant to repudiate the contract, and that, accordingly, such a breach prevented the respondent from relying on the demurrage clause to limit its liability. After holding that the demurrage clause was not an exclusion clause but an 'agreed damages' provision, the House of Lords went on to state that, even if the clause were an exclusion clause, it plainly covered the alleged breach, whether or not this was 'fundamental' in the sense that it would have entitled the shipowner to be discharged from his contractual obligations.[97] The House of Lords was clearly of the opinion that the fundamental breach doctrine was not in principle a *rule of law*, particularly in light of previous authority.[98] Viscount Dilhorne analysed the law as follows:

> In a number of cases . . . there are judicial observations to the effect that exempting clauses, no matter how widely they are drawn, only avail a party when he is carrying out the contract in its essential respects. In my view it is not right to say that the law prohibits and nullifies a clause

[94] [1967] 1 AC 361. This opinion was also shared by Lord Pearson in *UGS Finance Ltd* v. *National Mortgage Bank of Greece* [1964] 1 Lloyd's Rep 446 at 450.
[95] [1980] 1 Lloyd's Rep 545 at 549–51 *per* Lord Wilberforce.
[96] [1967] 1 AC 361.
[97] *Ibid.*, 395, 407, 413, 426 and 437.
[98] *Ibid.*, 392, 399, 405, 410, 425 and 431–2.

> exempting or limiting liability for a fundamental breach or breach of a fundamental term. Such a rule of law would involve a restriction on freedom of contract and in the older cases I can find no trace of it . . .
>
> In my view no such rule of law ought to be adopted . . . Exclusion clauses differ greatly in many respects. Probably the most objectionable are found in the complex standard conditions, which are now so common. In the ordinary way the customer has no time to read them, and if he did read them he would probably not understand them . . . Freedom of contract must surely imply some choice or room for bargaining . . . I have no doubt that exemption clauses should be construed strictly and I think that this case must be decided by considering whether there is any ground for adopting any but the natural meaning of the demurrage clause . . . It is impossible to hold that these words are not wide enough to apply to the circumstances of the present case, whether or not there was a fundamental breach. So the only question is whether there is any reason for limiting their scope. The authorities are against the appellants, but, even putting them aside, I can find no such reason.[99]

In *Photo Production Ltd* v. *Securicor Transport Ltd*,[100] the House of Lords disappointed all those who were hoping for a major change in the way the courts dealt with exclusion clauses under the fundamental breach doctrine. Securicor had agreed to provide a visiting patrol service to the respondent's factory at a charge of £8 15s per week. The contract contained an exclusion clause which read: 'Under no circumstances shall the company [Securicor] be responsible for any injurious act or default by any employee . . . unless such act or default could have been foreseen and avoided by the exercise of due diligence on the part of the company.' An employee of Securicor, while on patrol, deliberately started a fire in the factory. The fire spread, and a large part of the premises was burned down. The House of Lords held that, on the true nature of the contractual task, the modest amount of the charge, and the ability of the factory owner to insure against fire more economically, the risk assumed by Securicor was a modest one.[101] Accordingly, Securicor had effectively modified their obligation under the contract in the exercise of due diligence in their capacity as employers, and there was no evidence of any attempt to escape liability. The House of Lords once again affirmed their view that the question of whether or not an exclusion clause protected a party to a contract in the event of

[99] *Ibid.*, 392B–G, 405G–406A and 406B–407E. [100] [1980] 1 Lloyd's Rep 545.
[101] [1980] AC 827 at 846, 851 and 852.

a breach, or in the event of what would have been a breach, depended upon the construction of the contract. As Lord Diplock put it:

> I agree with Lord Wilberforce's analysis of the speeches in *Suisse Atlantique*, and with his conclusion that this House rejected the argument that there was any such rule of law. I also agree that *Harbutt's Plasticine*[102] and the subsequent cases in which the so-called 'rule of law' was applied to defeat exclusion clauses, should be overruled, though the actual decisions in some of the later cases might have been justified on the proper construction of the particular exclusion clause on which the defendant relied. Even if the breach was so serious as to entitle the injured party to treat the contract as repudiated, or to render further performance impossible, the other party was not prevented from relying on the clauses. Since the exclusion clause covered the damage, which had arisen, the defendants were not liable.[103]

In the Court of Appeal in *George Mitchell (Chesterhall) Ltd* v. *Finney Lock Seeds Ltd*, Oliver LJ came dangerously near to reintroducing by the backdoor the doctrine of fundamental breach.[104] However, Lord Bridge of Harwich in the House of Lords once again reached the conclusion that this doctrine should not apply.[105] The applicable principles are those of interpretation, perhaps with the modification that actual exclusions from liability are more strictly interpreted than clauses (as in the instant case) which merely limit the amount of damages recoverable. Common law contract law seems to start from the premise that exclusion clauses represent, if correctly drafted and if the parties are mutually so informed, the parties' chosen risk-allocation.

The adoption of the UCTA in 1977 has, however, changed the way in which exclusion and limitation clauses are handled. Statutory intervention has made it unlikely that the judges will ever again resort to their former extremes of interpretation.[106]

The control of unfair terms under the common law and the potential influence of European law

The UCTA and the UTCCR make no reference to the incorporation of exclusion and limitation clauses in contracts. This might have left the

[102] *Harbutt's 'Plasticine' Ltd* v. *Wayne Tank & Pump Co. Ltd* [1970] 1 Lloyd's Rep 15.
[103] [1980] 1 Lloyd's Rep 545 at 551.
[104] [1983] 1 QB 284 at 302. [105] [1983] 2 AC 803 at 813–14.
[106] Howells and Weatherill, *Consumer Protection Law*, 310; C. Willett, 'Good Faith and Consumer Contract Terms' in R. Brownsword, N. Hird and G. Howells (eds.), *Good Faith in Contract*, 67 at 69.

way open for the common law to continue to govern this issue. However, as will be demonstrated below, Directive 93/13/EEC has been read by the UK courts to include both incorporation control and content control in a concept of procedural good faith, and such a reading permits the intrusion of European law into the issue of the incorporation of exclusion and limitation clauses. Such a reading goes hand in hand with the 'Europeanisation' of interpretation control. Directive 93/13/EEC formulates the *contra proferentem* rule. However, it will be for the ECJ to establish a Europe-wide understanding of the *contra proferentem* rule. One such conflict might arise over the meaning and importance of the *contra proferentem* rule with regard to preventive actions such as injunctions.[107]

The Unfair Contract Terms Act 1977: legislative intervention in the freedom of contract

If an exclusion clause successfully meets the requirements of the first two tests (incorporation and construction), then content control will have been established regardless of whether or not the clause was rendered inoperative due to the existence of a particular statutory rule. Until recently, the control of exclusion and limitation clauses by statute in the field of the sale of goods was rare (although it has existed for some time in the field of hire-purchase agreements).[108] A small number of statutes have included provisions governing the sale of particular types of goods.[109] Major changes were brought about by section 3 of the Misrepresentation Act 1967 and the Supply of Goods and Services Act 1973. The subsequent case law elucidated the relationship between the regulation of unfair terms and misrepresentation. In *Curtis* v. *Chemical Cleaning & Dyeing Co. Ltd*,[110] the plaintiff took a dress to the defendant to be cleaned. She signed a receipt after being informed, incorrectly, that it exempted the defendant from liability for certain specified kinds of damage. In fact, the receipt exempted liability 'for any damage, however arising'. It was held that the defendant could not rely on the clause, as it had induced the plaintiff to sign the receipt by misrepresenting its contents. Lord Denning[111] said that a mere failure

[107] Case C-144/99, *Commission* v. *Netherlands* [2001] ECR I-3541, para. 19.

[108] Hire-Purchase Act 1938, section 8(3).

[109] Agriculture Act 1970, sections 68(6), 71(4) and 72(3); Plant Varieties and Seeds Act 1964, section 17(1).

[110] [1951] 1 KB 805. [111] *Ibid.*, 809.

to draw attention to the existence or extent of the exclusion clause might in some circumstances amount to misrepresentation.

There has been ample discussion in civil law regimes of whether and to what extent the rules on misrepresentation suffice to deal with certain forms of exclusion and limitation clauses. However, in the UK, the Misrepresentation Act 1967 did not have the effect of controlling limitation and exclusion clauses. The development of the law in the UK in this area took a different direction. Based on a Law Commission report on exclusion clauses, a Bill entitled the Avoidance of Liability (England and Wales) Bill was introduced into Parliament. The original title of the Bill is much more descriptive than its final short title, the Unfair Contract Terms Act 1977. The intention of the Act is to restrict the exclusion and limitation of liability in contracts. Generally speaking, the Act appears to be very much in line with the common law approach, and therefore may be understood as a continuation of the traditional approach of seeking a balance between maintaining freedom of contract and misusing the very same freedom to incorporate unfair exclusion and limitation clauses.[112] Thus the common law never took the approach adopted in civil law regimes, in which judges were able to correct the content of 'unfair' contract terms. The focus under the common law has always been on using interpretation and construction as a means of eliminating unfair exclusion and limitation clauses. To put it another way, it is not the unfairness of contract terms which has been at issue, but the correct construction of the contract. Seen thus, the UCTA is certainly a major step forward in English contract law, yet at the same time is thoroughly in line with the common law approach of concentrating on exclusion and limitation clauses. The adoption of the UCTA constitutes the third step after interpretation and construction, a step, however, which the English courts were reluctant to take without guidance from statutory law.

Lord Denning described the UCTA as 'one of the most important reforms in our times in the civil law'.[113] He felt his life-long efforts to have been vindicated by the development of appropriate statutory

[112] According to H. Beale, 'Legislative Control of Fairness: The Directive on Unfair Terms in Consumer Contracts' in J. Beatson and D. Friedman (eds.), *Good Faith and Fault in Contract Law* (Oxford, 1997), 231 at 237, the absolute bans on certain types of exclusion clauses seem to have been justified by the Law Commissions primarily on the basis of bargaining power or the misleading nature of the term.

[113] Parliamentary Debates, House of Lords, 1976–7 Session, vol. 936, col. 1119.

rules to outlaw the misuse of freedom of contract. In 1977, the English legal environment seemed harmonious. The newly adopted Act paved the way for getting to grips with exclusion and limitation clauses and maybe even for putting an end to the long-standing battle between the lawyers who draft exclusion and limitation clauses and the judges who seek to restrict their ambit. Twenty-seven years later, this relatively optimistic view of the Act's potential needs to be reconsidered. It seems as if the legislative approach, although it fitted well into common law thinking, neglected the reality of how exclusion and limitation clauses were used in practice. In theory, and again looking at the UCTA through the eyes of a German lawyer, the regulatory framework should and could have sufficed to develop a coherent concept on the control of unfair terms, simply by giving exclusion and limitation clauses a broad understanding.[114] To some extent, each and every term which seeks to restrict the freedom of contract might be understood as excluding or limiting liability. Such considerations, however, have remained wishful thinking. It will be demonstrated below that the English courts tend to pursue strictly the common law approach, that is, they confine themselves to controlling exclusion and limitation clauses in the traditional common law sense without attempting to move towards a more general concept of content control. It was therefore left to the European Community to take that step in Directive 93/13/EEC and to push the UK into action. The true deficiency in the UCTA turned out to be the lack of any mechanism for collective redress for challenging exclusion and limitation clauses. The UTCCR 1994 and 1999 remedied this latter deficiency by providing that collective action may be taken either by specified public bodies or by the Consumers' Association.

The scope of the UCTA

The UCTA re-enacted section 3 of the Misrepresentation Act 1967 and the Supply of Goods and Services Act 1973, albeit in a slightly amended form. The Act also established a new set of general controls on exclusion and limitation clauses. The Consumer Protection Act 1987, which deals with consumer safety,[115] and the Fair Trading

[114] See Howells and Weatherill, *Consumer Protection Law*, 321.

[115] Part I of this Act was introduced with a view to implementing the Product Liability Directive 85/374/EEC, OJ 1988 No. L307, 54.

Act 1973[116] also contain provisions which may affect the validity of exclusion and limitation clauses.[117]

The UCTA came into force on 1 February 1978,[118] and cut across the dichotomy between fact and law established by the previous tests of incorporation and construction.[119] It reduced the freedom of the parties to settle their own terms in contract, mainly by prohibiting or confirming earlier statutory prohibitions under the Supply of Goods (Implied Terms) Act 1973 of certain types of exclusion clause, and by making a large number of other such clauses subject to a requirement of reasonableness. The Act applies to the exclusion of liability in tort as well as in contract. It does not apply to the regulation of *all* contract term but generally only to those that attempt to exclude or restrict liability.[120] The Act is confined almost entirely to what is termed 'business liability',[121] and therefore little of it applies to purely private transactions. It is, however, very much concerned with consumer contracts and contracts in which one party deals on the other's written standard terms.[122] Certain types of contract are wholly outside the scope of the Act, for example contracts of employment, contracts of insurance and contracts for the carriage of goods by sea.

[116] Under the Fair Trading Act 1973, a Director-General of Fair Trading has been appointed and a Consumer Protection Advisory Committee has been set up. The Director-General, or the Secretary of Sate for Trade and Industry or any other minister, may refer to the Advisory Committee the question of whether a consumer trade practice specified in the reference adversely affects the economic interests of consumers in the UK. The Advisory Committee will consider this reference and formulate a report, which may then be followed by legislative action (i.e. a statutory instrument) by the Secretary of State.

[117] F. Reynolds, 'Classification of Statements' in A. Guest (ed.), *Benjamin's Sale of Goods* (5th edn, London, 1997), 13.

[118] A large number of articles were published after the enactment of the Act, which present a detailed analysis of the UCTA; see, for example, L. Sealy, 'Unfair Contract Terms Act 1977' (1978) 37 *Cambridge Law Journal* 15; and F. Reynolds, 'The Unfair Contract Terms Act 1977' (1978) *Lloyd's Maritime and Commercial Law Quarterly* 201.

[119] M. Bridge, *The Sale of Goods* (Oxford, 1998), 383.

[120] For a clear analysis of the areas outside the UCTA, see the Law Commissions' Joint Consultation Paper, 'Unfair Terms in Contracts', 2, 12 and 17; and on the issue of clauses against which businesses (unlike consumers) are not protected under the UTCCR, see *ibid.*, 122.

[121] Section 1(3) defines 'business liability' as 'liability for breach of obligations or duties arising (a) from things done or to be done by a person in the course of a business (whether his own business or another's), or (b) from the occupation of premises used for business purposes of the occupier'.

[122] Reynolds, 'The Unfair Contract Terms Act', 201.

If we set aside the issue of the application of the Act to exclusion and limitation clauses, the regulatory approach of the UCTA seems to be very much in line with civil law legislation enacted in the other Member States in the 1970s.[123] This is most evident when one considers the differences in the approaches to, first, the control of business-to-business contracts, secondly, the control of business-to-consumer contracts and, thirdly, the control of consumer-to-consumer contracts. The legislator appeared to start from the premise that consumers are most in need of protection. Thus, section 3 of the Act is said to be the provision with potentially the most profound impact. Section 3 is confined to business liability and to situations in which one party deals as a consumer or on the other's written standard terms of business.[124] Here, however, the civil law lawyer becomes puzzled. While it is obvious that the consumer might need protection in his or her dealings with businesspersons, it seems strange to equate the scope of application *sedes personae* and the scope of application *sedes materiae*. The intention of the legislator seemed to have been to protect small businesses in their dealings with more sophisticated, larger businesses.[125] Contrary to the usual legislative practice in the UK, no definition is given of what might constitute 'written standard terms of business'.[126] So what remains is that written standard terms of business trigger the need for the protection of businesspersons, but *only* businesspersons. Civil law regimes start from a different premise: the nature of the contract term as a standard business condition legitimises the need for content control regardless of the personal status of the contracting party, or whether he or she is dealing as a consumer or as a businessperson. The UK approach is different: the justification for statutory intervention is based on the existence of 'unreasonable' exclusion and limitation clauses. Emphasis has to be put on 'clauses' instead of 'written standard terms of business'. That is why the reference to 'written standard

[123] See the overview of the Member States' laws on unfair contract terms in Basedow, 'Schuldverhältnisse' in *Münchener Kommentar*, para. 305, at 22–38.

[124] Reynolds, 'The Unfair Contract Terms Act', 201 at 204; J. Adams and R. Brownsword, 'The Unfair Contract Terms Act: A Decade of Discretion' (1988) 104 *Law Quarterly Review* 94, state: 'judges by and large will see the UCTA as a statutory endorsement of the post-war policy of consumer protection'; see also the further references, *ibid.*, n. 2.

[125] Reynolds, 'The Unfair Contract Terms Act', 201 at 204.

[126] Parliament preferred to give no guidance: Reynolds, 'The Unfair Contract Terms Act', 201 at 204, n. 14; Law Commissions' Joint Consultation Paper, 'Unfair Terms in Contracts', 137.

terms of business' in section 3[127] constitutes a somewhat 'alien element' in the UCTA, which explains, at least to some extent, why legal doctrine has not devoted much attention to the importance of written standard terms of business in the overall legal approach.[128] There is only one Court of Appeal case. In *St Albans City and District Council* v. *International Computers Ltd*,[129] Nourse LJ, with whom the other members of the court agreed, said that to deal on the other's standard terms means simply to make the final contract on those terms. Standard terms seem to be those which remained 'effectively untouched'.[130] The lower courts take a flexible approach to this issue,[131] feeling no need to define the notion of 'written standard terms of business' clearly.

The concepts of 'deals as consumer' and 'course of business'

The Act provides special rules for consumers which apply only if one party deals as a consumer, while the other makes the contract in the course of business. Therefore, a statutory definition of who 'deals as consumer' is necessary. Section 12(1) provides as follows:

> A party to a contract 'deals as consumer' in relation to another party if (a) he neither makes the contract in the course of a business nor holds himself out as doing so; and (b) the other party does make the contract in the course of a business; and (c) ... the goods passing under or in pursuance of the contract are of a type ordinarily supplied for private use or consumption.[132]

In accordance with subsections (a) and (b) of this definition, it is obvious that the Act will not apply if both parties are dealing as consumers, for example where a car is sold privately. To this extent, the UCTA fully complies with EC law. However, there is a grey area as to where the borderline lies between those who deal as consumers and those who

[127] Section 3(1) provides: 'This section applies as between contracting parties where one of them deals as consumer or on the other's written standard terms of business.'

[128] One of the authors who devotes attention to written standard terms of business is Reynolds, 'The Unfair Contract Terms Act', 201 at 204.

[129] [1996] 4 All ER 481. [130] *Ibid.*, 491 g.

[131] Law Commissions' Joint Consultation Paper, 'Unfair Terms in Contracts', 137 and 138.

[132] Requirement (c) applies only to sections 6 and 7; see Law Commissions' Joint Consultation Paper, 'Unfair Terms in Contracts', 52, 53, 56.

deal in the course of business. This issue has been the subject of some concern in the Member States. One potential problem area is where a party makes a sale only occasionally,[133] what the French term *non-professionnel.*[134] Are such sales to be considered as having been done in the course of a business? While the ECJ took a narrow view in *di Pinto* and considered that such sales were done in the course of a business,[135] the Member States' legal orders, including that of the UK, tend to treat such 'non-professionals' as consumers.

The Act applies only if one party deals as a consumer while the other party makes the contract in the course of a business. In *R&B Customs Brokers Co. Ltd* v. *United Dominions Trust Ltd*,[136] the fact that a company purchased a car partly for business use and partly for private use was not enough to persuade the Court of Appeal that the company operated in the course of a business. Although Dillon LJ initially accepted that where a company which carries on a business makes a contract it makes that contract in the course of business, he subsequently distinguished the facts and held that, since the purchase of the car was an activity merely incidental to the carrying on of a business ('a one-off adventure in the nature of trade'), a degree of regularity had to be established before it could be said that the activity was an integral part of the business and so carried on in the course of business; since the necessary regularity had not been shown in this particular case, the company was dealing as a consumer and not in the course of business.[137] As a result, the implied term of fitness for purpose, implied by section 14(3) of the Sale of Goods Act 1979, could not be excluded.[138]

The importance of the characterisation of this sale as a consumer sale is evident from the subsequent statement of Dillon LJ. He stated that, if the company had been dealing in the course of a business, and had the defendant never taken possession of or inspected the car, then in his view the 'reasonableness test' under section 6(3) of the UCTA would have been satisfied, and therefore the finance company would have been able to exclude its liability.[139] This surprisingly narrow view

[133] *Ibid.*, 56.

[134] H.-W. Micklitz, in *Münchener Kommentar Bürgerliches Gesetzbuch*, para. 13 at 17–20.

[135] Judgment of 14 March 1991, Case C-361/89, *Ministere Public* v. *Patrice Di Pinto* [1991] ECR I-1206.

[136] [1988] 1 WLR 321.

[137] [1988] 1 WLR 321 at 328–9 and 331 *per* Dillon LJ.

[138] Sections 12(1) and 6(2) of the UCTA.

[139] [1988] 1 WLR 321 at 332A–B.

of when something occurs in the course of a business[140] set the tone for subsequent judgments. In *Oval (717) Ltd* v. *Aegon Insurance Co. (UK) Ltd*,[141] the plaintiff, a private company owned by the University of Bristol, entered into a contract with an insurance company which issued performance bonds in connection with a contract to construct new halls of residence for the university. The judge, Colin Reese QC, found that:

> the *R&B Customs Brokers* case is properly distinguishable from the present case and that this plaintiff obviously contracted with the defendant in the ordinary mainstream course of the business which it had been established to undertake.[142]

Although this seems a correct interpretation of the *R&B Customs Brokers* case, the judge did not comment extensively on the case, because he proceeded instead on the alternative submission that the contract was made on the defendant's written standard terms of business. Section 3 of UCTA is confined to business liability where one party deals as a consumer 'or on the other's written standard terms of business'.[143] In *Lease Management Services Ltd* v. *Purnell Secretarial Ltd*,[144] it was held that the appellant, a printer and office supply business, was not dealing in the course of a business when it hired a photocopier in order to produce 'photo plates' and 'paper plates'. In *Stevenson* v. *Rogers*,[145] the defendant, who carried on the business of a fisherman, sold a fishing boat to the plaintiff. The plaintiff brought an action against the defendant in relation to the sale of the boat. At first instance, the judge held, on a preliminary issue, that the sale of the boat by the defendant to the plaintiff was not a sale 'in the course of a business' for the purposes of section 14(2) of the Sale of Goods Act 1979, since it did not have any element of regularity.

Thus, the meaning given to the notion of 'dealing as a consumer' seems to be well settled in English law. Hence, it is all the more important to note that in *Stevenson* v. *Rogers*[146] in the Court of Appeal, Porter LJ found that the words of section 14(2) of the Sale of Goods Act 1979 should be construed to give them their widest possible meaning. He then went on to say that the change in the statutory wording

140 Howells and Weatherill, *Consumer Protection Law*, 326.
141 (1997) 85 BLR 97; (1997) 54 Con LR 74.
142 (1997) 54 Con LR 74 at 106.
143 Reynolds, 'The Unfair Contract Terms Act', 201 at 204.
144 [1994] *Consumer Credit Law Reports* 127.
145 [1999] 1 All ER 613.
146 *Ibid.*

between, on the one hand, section 3 of the Sale of Goods (Implied Terms) Act 1973, which was re-enacted as section 14(2) of the Sale of Goods Act 1979, and, on the other hand, the statutory predecessor to those two sections in the Sale of Goods Act 1893, was intended to widen the protection afforded to a purchaser by section 14(2) from a situation in which the seller was a dealer in the type of goods sold, to one in which the seller simply made a sale 'in the course of a business', thus removing the requirement for regularity of dealing, or indeed any dealing in the goods.

Terms rendered ineffective, and terms subjected to a reasonableness test

The UCTA clearly distinguishes between terms rendered totally ineffective and terms subjected to a reasonableness test. Again, the distinction is not unfamiliar in civil law regimes. Much of the debate in the 1970s on this matter centred on the question of whether there should be a 'blacklist' of unfair terms, or a 'grey list' which would list terms which were presumed to be unfair. The idea of drawing up such lists was to give guidance to the public and to the enforcement authorities and the courts on what types of term would be considered unfair. Much of the debate in several more countries turned around the question of whether, in addition to the drawing up of black and grey lists, a general test should be set out in order to determine whether terms not specifically included in those lists were also unfair. At first sight, the distinction in the UCTA between totally ineffective terms and terms subject to a reasonableness test seems in line with the approach of civil law regimes, at least if the reasonableness test is understood and interpreted as some sort of general clause. The UCTA, however, cannot be and has not been used as a general means of content control.[147]

It is common ground that the UCTA is difficult to read and fully comprehend. For this reason, among others, the Law Commissions were given a mandate to consider whether the legislation needs to be re-enacted in clear and accessible terms.[148] The UCTA deals with two types of clause: those which need not be subject to a reasonableness test

[147] Adams and Brownsword, 'The Unfair Contract Terms Act', 94.
[148] Law Commissions' Joint Consultation Paper, 'Unfair Terms in Contracts', 156.

because they are always invalid, and those which require a reasonableness test. The difficulty is that the scope of application *sedes materiae* and *sedes personae* has to be linked to the type of term. Setting aside special rules on sales and hire-purchase, in essence the distinction is this:

(1) A contractual term will come under the first category (those terms which are always invalid) if:
  (a) it purports to exclude or limit liability for death or personal injury (section 2(1) of the UCTA)[149] where this is done as part of a business transaction (section 1(3) of the UCTA);[150] or
  (b) it purports to exclude or limit liability for breach of the implied conditions in sections 12–15 of the Sale of Goods Act 1979 (description, satisfactory quality, fitness for purpose, correspondence with sample)[151] where the buyer deals as a consumer; or
  (c) it purports to exclude or limit liability for loss or damage in the case of goods of a type ordinarily supplied for private use or consumption where the loss or damage (i) arises from the goods proving defective while in consumer use and (ii) results from the negligence of a person concerned in the manufacture or distribution of the goods, or (in contracts other than contracts of sale or hire purchase under which possession or ownership passes[152]) in respect of the goods' correspondence with description or sample, or their quality or fitness for any particular purpose where the buyer deals as a consumer.

[149] This section primarily attacks terms that attempt to exclude or limit tort-based liability for injury caused by negligence. Nevertheless, it does not apply: (1) if a provision excludes strict liability for death or personal injury, and (2) where death or personal injury results from breach of contract or duty which can be committed without negligence (for example, where a producer incurs 'product liability' in respect of defective products). Clauses purporting to exclude liability for such breaches may be ineffective under other provisions of the Act (sections 6 and 7) or under other Acts (for example, the Consumer Protection Act 1987).

[150] Section 1(3) defines 'business liability' as 'liability for breach of obligations or duties arising (a) from things done or to be done by a person in the course of a business (whether his own business or another's) or (b) from the occupation of premises used for business purposes of the occupier'.

[151] As, for example, in *Rasbora Ltd* v. *JCL Marine Ltd* [1977] 1 Lloyd's Rep 645, which concerned 'consumer sale' litigated under section 55 of the Sale of Goods Act 1893.

[152] For example, contracts of hire or exchange, or for work and materials.

(2) Other contractual terms will be subjected to the reasonableness test. The reasonableness test will be applied if:
   (a) a contract term purports to exclude or restrict liability for negligence (section 2(2) of the UCTA) (other than death or personal injury) regardless of the parties' qualifications; or
   (b) a contract term purports to permit a party to render a contractual performance substantially different from that which was reasonably expected of him (where one party deals as a consumer or deals on the other's written standard business terms) (section 3(2)(b)(i) of the UCTA); or
   (c) a contract term purports to permit a party, in respect of the whole or any part of his contractual obligations, to render no performance at all (where one party deals as a consumer or deals on the other's written standard business terms) (section 3(2)(b)(ii) of the UCTA).[153]

The reasonableness test

When is the test applied?

Section 11(1) of the UCTA provides that, in order for a term to be fair and reasonable, regard must be had 'to the circumstances which were, or ought reasonably to have been, known to or in the contemplation of the parties[154] *when the contract was made*'.[155] It is therefore clear that the reasonableness of contract terms is to be judged at the time of making the contract, not at the time of reliance on the clause, and its effectiveness will not therefore be impaired by subsequent events.[156] This rule has been criticised. Although a clause may seem reasonable at the time of the conclusion of the contract, the same clause may seem

[153] In this situation it is for the party seeking to impugn the term to allege the existence and nature of the different performance reasonably expected of the other party: *Circuit Systems Ltd (in liquidation) and Basten* v. *Zuken-Redac (UK) Ltd (formerly Racal-Redac (UK) Ltd)* (1994) 42 ConLR 120 at 142.

[154] I.e. the parties to the particular contract and the circumstances known to or in contemplation of both: *Edmund Murray Ltd* v. *BSP International Foundations Ltd* (1992) 33 ConLR 1.

[155] Emphasis added. In relation to a notice not having contractual effects, section 11(3) provides that the test is to be applied 'having regard to all the circumstances obtaining when the liability arose or (but for the notice) would have arisen'.

[156] Treitel, *The Law of Contract*, 258. The position was different under the Misrepresentation Act 1967 and the Supply of Goods (Implied Terms) Act 1973.

unfair and unreasonable at the time of reliance due to changed circumstances.[157] Nevertheless, Directive 93/13/EEC adopted the same rule.

Burden of proof

The general rule, laid down in section 11(5) of the Act, is that 'it is for those claiming that a contract term or notice satisfies the requirement of reasonableness to show that it does'.[158] It has been held that the question of reasonableness must be raised in the pleadings by the person who wishes to prevent the term being held to be reasonable.[159] In some situations, the burden of proof may be shared. For example, in section 3(2)(b)(i) of the UCTA, it is for the party alleging a 'substantially different' performance to prove that the performance was substantially different.[160]

Guidelines for the application of the test

The guidelines for determining the reasonableness of contract terms are to be found in section 11 of and Schedule 2 to the Act. The guidelines set out in Schedule 2 apply only to the cases prescribed in section 6 (sale and hire purchase) and section 7 (miscellaneous contracts under which goods pass). It is doubtful whether the guidelines in Schedule 2 should be taken into consideration in deciding the question of reasonableness for the purposes of section 3.[161] The guidelines, however, are not exhaustive.[162]

[157] The UCTA solution was favoured by the Scottish Law Commission, but not by the English Law Commission. Benjamin, *Benjamin's Sale of Goods*, para. 13-75.

[158] *Smith* v. *Bush* [1990] 1 AC 831 at 858; *Sheffield* v. *Pickfords Ltd* [1997] CLC 648; (1997) 16 Tr LR 337 *The Times*, 17 March 1997.

[159] *Ibid.*

[160] *Circuit Systems Ltd (in liquidation) and Basten* v. *Zuken-Redac (UK) Ltd (formerly Racal-Redac (UK) Ltd)* (1994) 42 ConLR 120 at 142; for a fuller view, see Law Commissions' Joint Consultation Paper, 'Unfair Terms in Contracts', 50.

[161] In *Rees Hough Ltd* v. *Redland Reinforced Plastics Ltd* (1984) 27 BLR 136; (1984) Const LJ 67, Judge Newey QC thought that it would be sensible for the purposes of section 3 to take into account the Schedule 2 matters. Furthermore, his opinion was supported by Clarke J in *Monarch Airlines Ltd* v. *London Luton Airport Ltd* [1998] 1 Lloyd's Rep 403 at 412, and by Judge Colin Reese QC in *Oval (717) Ltd* v. *Aegon Insurance Co. (UK) Ltd* (1997) 54 Con LR 74 at 104. Nevertheless, Staughton J, in the *The Zinnia* [1984] 2 Lloyd's Rep 211 at 222, found that, for the purposes of sections 2 and 3, it is not required to have regard to the matters specified in Schedule 2 to the Act.

[162] *Oval (717) Ltd* v. *Aegon Insurance Co. (UK) Ltd* (1997) 54 Con LR 74 at 104; Howells and Weatherill, *Consumer Protection Law*, 321 and 322.

Section 11 provides further guidance. Section 11(1) provides:

> In relation to a contract term, the requirement of reasonableness ... is that the term shall have been a fair and reasonable one to be included having regard to the circumstances which were, or ought reasonably to have been, known to or in the contemplation of the parties when the contract was made.

Section 11(4) provides:

> Where by reference to a contract term or notice a person seeks to restrict liability to a specified sum of money and the question arises whether the term or notice satisfies the requirement of reasonableness, regard shall be had in particular ... to (a) the resources which he could expect to be available to him for the purpose of meeting the liability should it arise; and (b) how far it was open to him to cover himself by insurance.[163]

Thus, section 11(4) applies to terms purporting to limit a person's liability to a specified sum of money. It does not apply to terms that exclude liability generally.[164] Both elements of section 11(4) underpin a modern understanding of contract law, at least from the perspective of an economic analysis of law. One can read into section 11(4) the principle of the 'cheapest cost-avoider',[165] an 'economics and law' principle which does not yet appear to have been fully accepted in Europe as a means of balancing the conflicting interests arising out of risk-allocation. German courts do not openly address economic considerations in their reasoning, although such considerations may nevertheless guide the courts in their behind-the-scenes decision-making process.

English law differs here. The English courts have a long history of taking into consideration the availability of insurance as a means of risk-allocation, and thus indirectly as a means of interpretation of limitation and exclusion clauses. For example, in *George Mitchell (Chesterhall) Ltd* v. *Finney Lock Seeds Ltd*, the fact that the sellers could

[163] *Monarch Airlines Ltd* v. *London Luton Airport Ltd* [1998] 1 Lloyd's Rep 403 at 412.

[164] *Flamar Interocean Ltd* v. *Denmac Ltd (The Flamar Pride)* [1990] 1 Lloyd's Rep 434 at 438 *per* Porter J.

[165] A principle originating in 'law and economics' analysis. The principal states that liability arising out of an event should be imposed on the person who can most cheaply avoid the occurrence of the event.

insure against the risk of crop failure caused by supplying the wrong variety of seeds without materially increasing the price of seeds, was one of the relevant factors that weighed the scales in favour of the buyers.[166] In *The Flamar Pride*,[167] the question of the *availability* of insurance, rather than whether any insurance was actually taken out, seems to have been taken into account by the court in its judgment. In *Singer Co. (UK) Ltd* v. *Tees and Hartlepool Port Authority*, the defendant port authority limited its liability for any loss or damage caused to goods consigned to it to a specified sum of money per ton. Although the port authority had the financial means to take out insurance to cover the *full* cost of any loss or damage, and although such insurance was available, and therefore, under section 11(4), the limitation clause ought to have been considered unreasonable, nevertheless the clause was held to be reasonable. The fact that the clause was unreasonable under section 11(4) was outweighed by the fact that the port authority had limited knowledge of the nature and value of the goods consigned, and therefore a limitation on its liability was not unreasonable in those circumstances.[168]

Schedule 2 to the UCTA contains a non-exhaustive list of guidelines. Although the guidelines in Schedule 2 apply, strictly speaking, only to decisions under sections 6(3) and 7(3) of the UCTA, nevertheless the courts seem to take them into account in deciding other cases.[169]

[166] [1983] 2 AC 803 at 817D–F *per* Lord Bridge (although this case was decided under section 55(3) and (4) of, and Schedule 1, para. 11, to the Sale of Goods Act 1979, it is still good law for the interpretation of the UCTA). Similarly, in *Phillips Products Ltd* v. *Hyland and Hampstead Plant Hire Co. Ltd* [1987] 1 WLR 659; [1987] 2 All ER 620, the fact that the defendant was in the best position to take out insurance and bear the loss (along with the fact that, because the plaintiff – who hired an excavator from the defendant – hired the excavator for a very short period of time, they had little opportunity to arrange for insurance and had no control in the choice of the driver) resulted in the term failing to satisfy the requirement of reasonableness.

[167] *Flamar Interocean Ltd* v. *Denmac Ltd (The Flamar Pride)* [1990] 1 Lloyd's Rep 434 at 439; see also *Monarch Airlines Ltd* v. *London Luton Airport Ltd* [1998] 1 Lloyd's Rep 403 at 413.

[168] *Singer Co. (UK) Ltd* v. *Tees and Hartlepool Port Authority* [1988] 2 Lloyd's Rep 164 at 170 *per* Stein J. Similarly, in *R&B Customs Brokers Co. Ltd* v. *United Dominions Trust Ltd* [1988] 1 WLR 321 at 332A–B, Dillon LJ stated that the fact that the defendant finance company had never had possession of or inspected the car sold would had been an essential point in determining that the reasonableness test had been satisfied.

[169] Beale, 'Legislative Control of Fairness' in Beatson and Friedman (eds.), *Good Faith and Fault*, 231 at 235, referring to *Phillips Products Ltd* v. *Hyland and Hampstead Plant Hire Co. Ltd* [1987] 1 WLR 659; [1987] 2 All ER 620.

Schedule 2 specifies the following matters to be taken into account in deciding the question of reasonableness:

(a) the strength of the bargaining positions of the parties relative to each other, taking into account (among other things) alternative means by which the customer's requirements could have been met;
(b) whether the customer received an inducement to agree to the term, or in accepting it had an opportunity of entering into a similar contract with other persons, but without having to accept a similar term;
(c) whether the customer knew or ought reasonably to have known of the existence and extent of the term (having regard, among other things, to any custom of the trade and any previous course of dealing between the parties);
(d) where the term excludes or restricts any relevant liability if some condition is not complied with, whether it was reasonable at the time of the contract to expect that compliance with that condition would be practicable;
(e) whether the goods were manufactured, processed or adapted to the special order of the customer.

From a more analytical point of view, the main intention of the five guidelines seems to be to maintain or to restore freedom of contract (understood here as freedom to choose one's own contract terms).[170] The fact that one party to the contract had a much stronger bargaining position than the other does not in itself lead to the conclusion that the terms of the contract are unreasonable. Rather, the question is whether the other party to the contract had any alternative but to accept those contract terms, for example a customer purchasing from a supplier who had a monopoly. The legislator seems to have had in mind that contract terms are negotiated between the parties. Individually negotiated terms are still the overall objective of contract-formation, at least from the perspective of the apparent aim of the UCTA. Standard terms imposed by one contracting party upon the other are largely outside the focus of the law. In combination with standard terms, the reference to the strength of the bargaining power of the parties gains much more impetus. It is then possible to understand why the strength

[170] See Beale, 'Legislative Control of Fairness' in Beatson and Friedman (eds.), *Good Faith and Fault*, 231 at 237; Howells and Weatherill, *Consumer Protection Law*, 321.

of a party's bargaining position may lead to the presumption that the terms of the contracts are unreasonable, a presumption which may of course be rebutted. It was left to the European Community, in Directive 93/13/EEC, to introduce reform. The liberal tradition of the English law, which is evident from the UCTA, could only be strengthened by the introduction of a subjective element obliging the English courts to look at the *reality* of the consent to contractual terms.[171]

Cases in which the guidelines under Schedule 2 have played a role are scarce. It is not clear, however, whether the reason for this is that so many clauses in consumer contracts are automatically invalid,[172] or whether the lack of a collective redress mechanism was preventing cases from being brought before the courts. The new enforcement role of the Office of Fair Trading, established by the UTCCR 1994, seems to confirm that the latter reason is the cause of the dearth of cases. It is also the case that such cases often get no further than the lower courts, and are therefore not reported.[173] The first set of cases in which the courts laid down their understanding of the reasonableness test dealt with *commercial contracts*. The second set of cases concerns *consumer contracts*. Both sets of cases are highly indicative of the way in which the UK courts apply the reasonableness test. The first set seems to challenge Lord Goff's understanding of the role and function of judges in commercial law, as the House of Lords seems to have altered its policy substantially. It has even been said that the House of Lords has generated a state of uncertainty in commercial contracts under the UCTA.[174] Such a conclusion, taking for granted commercial contract law, would have suffered from continental legal intrusion since 1983, when *George Mitchell (Chesterhall) Ltd* v. *Finney Lock Seeds Ltd*,[175] the first case under the UCTA, was decided. The second set of decisions highlights the overall importance of the concrete facts of the case to

[171] Bradgate, 'Unreasonable Standard Terms', 582 at 584 (referring to *AEG (UK) Ltd* v. *Logic Resource Ltd* [1995] CLC 265 at 278 *per* Hobhouse LJ) is of the opinion that such a duty already exists. I wonder, however, whether it is already well established.

[172] Beale, 'Legislative Control of Fairness' in Beatson and Friedman, *Good Faith*, 231 at 235.

[173] N. Palmer, 'Exclusions of Liability under Non-Contractual Bailments and Unfair Contract Terms Act – II' (1978) 128 *New Law Journal* 915; N. Palmer, 'Clarifying the Unfair Contract Terms Act' (1986) 7 *Business Law Review* 57; and R. Lawson, 'The Unfair Contract Terms Act: A Progress Report' (1981) 131 *New Law Journal* 933 (with references to unpublished case law).

[174] Adams and Brownsword, 'The Unfair Contract Terms Act', 94 at 95.

[175] [1983] 2 AC 803.

which English judges devote so much attention. A subjective, reality-related approach would require the courts to use the guidelines in Schedule 2 to determine whether there was a 'weaker party' in need of protection. *Smith* v. *Bush* and *Harris* v. *Wyre Forest District Council*[176] support such a reading, and have been understood as representing a policy of creating a social market.[177] Each set of cases, that is, the commercial contract cases and the consumer contract cases, will now be considered in turn.

Commercial contract cases

R. W. Green Ltd v. *Cade Bros. Farms*[178] was decided in 1978 under section 55(4) and (5) of the Sale of Goods Act 1893. The cause of action arose prior to the coming into force of the UCTA.[179] Nevertheless, it is still good law, as the criteria used to decide the case reflect those prescribed in the UCTA. In this case, Green sold twenty tons of uncertified seed potatoes to Cade for £634. When the potatoes began to grow, Cade discovered that the potatoes were affected with a virus. Cade therefore claimed that the seed potatoes had not been of 'merchantable quality' or 'fit for their purpose' within the meaning of section 14 of the Sale of Goods Act 1893, and claimed damages for loss of profit of £6,000. Green replied that, by clause 5 of the contract of sale, its liability was limited to the price of the seed potatoes, that is, £634.

Griffiths J, after commenting that each commercial contract must be considered and construed against the background of the trade in which the parties operate, concluded that the clause in the contract which limited the compensation to the contract price was reasonable because it was not imposed by a strong party upon a weak party. This sort of clause had been in use for over twenty years in the industry,[180] and had evolved over a much longer period as a result both of trade

[176] [1990] 1 AC 831; [1989] 2 All ER 514.

[177] H. Collins, 'Good Faith in European Contract Law' (1994) 14 *Oxford Journal of Legal Studies* 246 at 247.

[178] [1978] 1 Lloyd's Rep 602.

[179] The UCTA came into force on 1 February 1978.

[180] The use of trade terms over a long period of time was among the factors considered by Judge Hallgarten QC in *Sonicare International Ltd* v. *East Anglia Freight Terminal Ltd and Neptune Orient Lines Ltd* [1997] 2 Lloyd's Rep 48 at 55, who mentioned that the problematic terms were accepted not only by Neptune Orient Lines but by all other port users who sought to use East Anglia Freight Terminal's services. Furthermore, in *Monarch Airlines Ltd* v. *London Luton Airport Ltd* [1998] 1 Lloyd's Rep 403, the fact that the problematic term, under which the operator of Luton Airport excluded its

practice and of discussions between the National Association of Seed Potato Merchants and the National Farmers' Union.[181] In addition to the parties' equal bargaining power, other factors that favoured the reasonableness of the terms included the fact that (a) the buyer received no inducement to accept the term, (b) the buyer could avoid the risk by buying certified seed, but he chose not to do so and (3) the language of the exclusion clause was clear and readily comprehensible.[182] The condition, which obliged the buyer to give notice of any defect within three days of purchase, however, was found to be unreasonable, as it would have been impossible for the farmer to discover the presence of the virus within such a short time.[183]

George Mitchell (Chesterhall) Ltd v. *Finney Lock Seeds Ltd*[184] was the first case to be decided by the House of Lords under the UCTA. Given the scarcity of decisions concerning the UCTA and the importance of

liability for loss or damage to aircraft occurring in the course of taking off had been in use in almost identical terms by the carriers' international organisation, IATA, was a very important factor. As Clarke J pointed out: 'In my judgment, viewed overall, the similarity between the provisions of clause 10 and other provisions which are apparently acceptable in international aviation (and indeed elsewhere) is a pointer to the conclusion that the clause is and was reasonable.'

181 [1978] 1 Lloyd's Rep 602 at 607 and 608; see also *The Zinnia* [1984] 2 Lloyd's Rep 211.

182 The importance of 'clear language' is obvious also in the Scottish case of *Knight Machinery (Holdings) Ltd* v. *Rennie*, 1995 SLT 166 at 171, where the court said that a clause obliging the buyer to give notice within seven days was not clear (and thus unreasonable) business sense as 'the businessman buying the machine sold could not tell from the clause what the notice is to contain, on what it is to be based, and whether or not he should send such a notice when he encounters what appear to be fairly typical, apparently minor, possibly temporary, probably remediable problems, particularly when he has no means of determining whether they are symptomatic of some defect in the machine or simply of maladroitness in those attempting to operate it or are perhaps related to the emulsions, inks, papers or other materials being used in the operation of the machine or to some combination of such factors'. Then the Court went to hold that '*prima facie* it would not be reasonable at the time of the contract to expect that it would be practicable for the buyer to send a written notice to the sellers within seven days of delivery of the machine in circumstances such as could reasonably be expected to obtain in this type of contract in relation to this type of machine'. The same factor was considered by Staughton J in *The Zinnia* [1984] 2 Lloyd's Rep 211, who mentioned that the term would be unreasonable because (1) the conditions were in such small print that one could barely read them and (2) the draftsmanship was so convoluted and prolix that one almost needed a degree in law to understand them. This argument, however, was not raised in the court, and as a result it was not taken into account. As regards the 'clear language' factor and its importance in construction of contracts, see pp. 310–14 above.

183 [1978] 1 Lloyd's Rep 602 at 608.

184 [1983] 2 AC 803.

the House of Lords in the UK legal order, the decision was guaranteed to be a landmark decision, one which would determine the correct application of the reasonableness test for many years to come. One might have expected that, given the similarity in the facts and in the applicable law between *George Mitchell (Chesterhall) Ltd* v. *Finney Lock Seeds Ltd* and *R. W. Green Ltd* v. *Cade Bros. Farms*,[185] inasmuch as both involved commercial contracts for the supply of seeds, and both used similar legal criteria, the former under the UCTA and the latter under the Sale of Goods Act 1893, the House of Lords would have based its decision in the later case on the precedent set by the earlier case. Instead, the House of Lords rewrote the handling of exclusion and limitation clauses in commercial contracts.

The facts of *George Mitchell (Chesterhall) Ltd* v. *Finney Lock Seeds Ltd* were as follows. The plaintiff, a firm of seed merchants, contracted to sell to the defendant 30 lbs of 'Late Dutch Special' cabbage seed for £201.60. Owing to errors by the defendant's suppliers and employees, the seed supplied was not late cabbage seed, and after planting by the plaintiff it germinated and grew but was commercially useless. The loss of profit was over £61,000. The plaintiff claimed damages and the defendant relied on its terms and conditions, which provided, *inter alia*:

> In the event of any seeds or plants sold or agreed to be sold by us not complying with the express terms of the contract of sale . . . or any seeds or plants proving defective in variety purity we will, at our option, replace the defective seeds or plants, free of charge to the buyer or will refund all payments made to us by the buyer in respect of the defective seeds or plants and this shall be the limit of our obligation.[186]

The House of Lords found that this clause, if 'read as a whole, unambiguously limits the appellants' liability to replacement of the seeds or a refund of the price'. The condition was clear, and even a layman would have had no difficulty in understanding it. Furthermore, a similar limitation of liability was for many years universally embodied in the terms of trade between seed suppliers and farmers. Although these terms had never been negotiated between representative bodies, they had not been the subject of any protest by the National Farmers' Union. So far, the House of Lords' reasoning seems to be very much in line with *R. W. Green Ltd* v. *Cade Bros. Farms*. The critical argument against the limitation clause hinged upon the fact that the seed supplier, in

[185] [1978] 1 Lloyd's Rep 602. [186] [1983] 2 AC 803 at 811D–F.

line with the usual practice, had attempted an informal compromise of the farmer's claim, by offering a sum of money in excess of that set as the ceiling of liability by their limitation clause. As Lord Bridge put it:

> The decisive factor appeared to be the practice of the appellants . . . to negotiate settlements of farmers' claims for damages in excess of the price of the seeds, if they thought that the claims were 'genuine' and 'justified'. This evidence indicated a clear recognition by seedsmen in general, and the appellants in particular, that reliance on the limitation of liability imposed by the relevant condition would not be fair or reasonable.[187]

One might argue that this reasoning is not convincing, because the seed supplier knew the rules and could make their own risk-allocation. However, another reading might also be possible. It seems that the House of Lords recognises a link between the non-negotiated limitation clause and the preparedness of the defendants to enter into negotiations on improved compensation. However that might be, the result of the judgment is strikingly clear. Parties to a commercial contract can no longer be certain that they have effectively limited their liability simply by meeting the incorporation and construction requirements. The UCTA, and more specifically the 'reasonableness test', introduces an element of uncertainty into commercial contract law. Parties now have to make allowance for judicial discretion – a situation which may be relatively alien to English lawyers, but which is well accepted by lawyers in civil law regimes.

Consumer contract cases

The same uncertainty might have prevailed in consumer contracts. However, the effects of the UCTA and the interpretation given to it by the courts seem to raise less concerns. The two principal cases in this area may be read as confirming the well-established practice of

[187] *Ibid.*, 816–817G–D *per* Lord Bridge. The previous practice that had developed between the parties was also considered as a decisive factor in *Rees Hough Ltd* v. *Redland Reinforced Plastics Ltd* (1984) Const LJ 67 at 69–70, where Judge Newey QC found that '[o]bviously, some considerations carry much more weight than others; for example that [the plaintiff] did not lack the ability to look after themselves is probably the weightiest in favour of upholding the Terms; and, for example, that [the defendant] ha[d] never in the past sought to rely on the Terms in its dealing with [the plaintiff] may well be the weightiest against'. He finally found that the defendant could rely on the standard 'Terms of Sale' to invalidate the express and implied terms between itself and the plaintiff, as the plaintiff had failed to prove that the 'Terms of Sale' were reasonable.

emphasising the context in which the conflict arose.[188] In a consumer contract, it is the concrete circumstances of the case which will decide whether a limitation clause is valid or not, rather than any more nebulous notion of 'injustice'. Thus, the same term may be held to be reasonable in one set of circumstances, but unreasonable in another. This is because, in English law, the control of contracts is determined by contract terms and not by *standard* contract terms. Thus, two cases in which consumers bought a house are of paradigmatic importance. The two cases, *Smith* v. *Bush* and *Harris* v. *Wyre Forest District Council*,[189] were heard together, because the legal issues involved were materially identical. In *Smith* v. *Bush*, the first and more important of the two, the plaintiffs had applied to a building society for a mortgage to assist them in purchasing a house. The building society instructed the defendants, a firm of surveyors and valuers, to carry out a visual inspection of the house and to report on its value and any matter likely to affect its value. The plaintiffs, consequently, after receiving this professional valuation of the house, agreed to purchase it. The valuer, however, was careless and failed to notice major defects in the house, which in effect made the house valueless. When the plaintiffs discovered the defects, they sued the valuer for damages in tort. The defendants relied, *inter alia*, on the disclaimer in the report and the application form to exempt them from liability. The plaintiffs claimed that the disclaimer did not exclude the defendants' liability and that the defendants were in any event precluded by section 2 the UCTA from so excluding their liability since the disclaimer did not satisfy the requirement of reasonableness set out in section 11(3) of the Act. The judge at first instance gave judgment for the plaintiffs.

In the Court of Appeal, after having made clear that a list of factors cannot be exhaustive, Griffiths LJ considered a number of factors in favour of the plaintiffs. First, the parties were not of equal bargaining power. Secondly, the purchasers were young, first-time buyers at the bottom end of the market, and it would not have been reasonably practicable for them to obtain advice as to valuation from an alternative source, as they would be required to pay twice the price. Thirdly, the undertaking by the valuers to value the house was not such an

[188] See T. Kaye, 'Surveying the Scene: A Valuer's Duty of Care' (1989) 52 *Modern Law Review* 841; and Collins, 'Good Faith', 246 at 247. There might even be a link to 'fiduciary' duties. See Whittaker and Zimmermann, 'Good Faith' in Whittaker and Zimmermann (eds.), *Good Faith in European Contract Law*, 46.

[189] [1990] 1 AC 831; [1989] 2 All ER 514.

inherently commercially dangerous proposition as to render the exclusion of liability reasonable. Fourthly, the consequences for each party of losing the case were markedly imbalanced. If the defendants were to lose the case, then they would be expected to compensate the plaintiffs for the value of the house, a value which was in the larger picture quite a modest amount, and for which the defendants would be insured. If the plaintiffs were to lose the case, it would be a financial catastrophe for them, since they would be left with a valueless house, a mortgage to repay and no money with which to buy another house. Fifthly, throwing the risk onto one buyer would mean that all the risk would be borne by one person,[190] whereas throwing the risk onto the valuer would result in distributing the risk among all house purchasers through an increase in his fees to cover insurance.[191] Finally, if the plaintiff had employed and paid the valuer himself, it would have been reasonable for the surveyor to exclude liability for negligence.[192]

This case, however, should be clearly distinguished from situations such as industrial property, large blocks of flats or very expensive houses. In these latter situations, since the risk undertaken by the valuer is much higher, the purchaser is more likely to obtain his own valuer to guide him in his purchase, and, since a much larger sum of money is involved, it will be more reasonable for the valuer, valuing the property on behalf of those who are providing the finance, either to exclude or to limit his liability to the purchaser.[193] In general, it seems that, if large sums of money are dependent on *any* kind of professional advice (not just with regard to mortgage valuations) against which it would be impossible for the adviser to obtain adequate insurance cover and which would ruin him if he were to be held personally liable, it would be more reasonable for the surveyor to limit his liability to the extent of his insurance cover.[194]

Such a reading also follows from *McCullagh* v. *Lane Fox & Partners Ltd*,[195] in which the plaintiff and his wife were persuaded by the

[190] Similar 'justice' considerations were taken into account in *Rasbora Ltd* v. *JCL Marine Ltd* [1977] 1 Lloyd's Rep 645 at 651, in which Lawson J found that, since the sellers were responsible for electrical engineering defects which caused the total loss of a boat within twenty-seven hours of her being handed over, a situation in which, if the exclusion applied, the buyer would be left without any remedy at all; the term was therefore held to be unreasonable (however, this case concerned a consumer sale, and therefore the term was void *ab initio*).

[191] *Smith* v. *Bush* [1990] 1 AC 831 at 858B–H and 859A–D.

[192] *Ibid.*, 859E–G.

[193] *Ibid.*, 859H and 860A–B.

[194] *Ibid.*, 859.

[195] (1994) 1 EGLR 48; (1994) 49 Con LR 124.

associate of an estate agents firm to buy a house whose gardens were described as being 0.92 acres in extent. However, the size of the garden proved to be only 0.48 acres in extent. Hobhouse LJ, in the Court of Appeal, held that it was fair and reasonable for the defendants to be allowed to rely on a disclaimer since, *inter alia*:

> Mr McCullagh did not even trouble to read the document, he had more than an ample opportunity to do so and to inform himself fully of what it contained . . . He had ample opportunity to regulate his conduct having regard to the disclaimer. He could have obtained, had he so chosen, an independent check of the acreage . . . Mr McCullagh had, and would have been assumed by all concerned to have, the benefit of legal advice and representation.[196]

In the 'estate agent' cases, the court's judgment is not only based on the actual contractual clause but to a large extent also relates to the actual position of the buyer and the relevant land market. It seems to be fair and just to distinguish between the young, first-time buyer and the experienced businessperson who purchases an expensive property. Where the parties are of equal bargaining power, the requirement of reasonableness can be more easily discharged than in a case in which the disclaimer is imposed upon a purchaser who has no effective power to object.[197]

Section 3(2) of the UCTA: the key provision on consumer protection

Section 3(2) of the UCTA provides:

> As against that party, the other cannot by reference to any contract term—
>
> (a) when himself in breach of contract, exclude or restrict any liability of his in respect of the breach; or

[196] *Ibid.*, 157.

[197] *Smith* v. *Bush* [1990] 1 AC 831 at 858C–D. See also *Sonicare International Ltd* v. *East Anglia Freight Terminal Ltd and Neptune Orient Lines Ltd* [1997] 2 Lloyd's Rep 48 at 54, in which Judge Hallgarten QC said: 'The relevant relationship to be examined was that between EAFT and NOL, and so far as those parties were concerned, they had without any problem traded upon the NAWK conditions for several years subject only to negotiation of tariffs from time to time. The bargaining position of EAFT and NOL was broadly equal, and there was no suggestion that the NAWK conditions were in any way imposed on NOL.'

(b) claim to be entitled—
   (i) to render a contractual performance substantially different from that which was reasonably expected of him, or
   (ii) in respect of the whole or any part of his contractual obligation, to render no performance at all,

except in so far as (in any of the cases mentioned above in this subsection) the contract term satisfies the requirement of reasonableness.

First, section 3(2) requires in essence the distinguishing of contract terms from written standard terms. Therefore, in theory, in the absence of any guidance from Parliament on how to make this distinction, there is ample room for the courts to fill this gap in the UCTA. More interesting and more important is the extension of the scope of control to contract terms beyond exclusion and limitation clauses in section 3(2)(b).[198] The law clearly distinguishes between (i) the claim to render a contractual performance substantially different from that promised and (ii) to render no performance at all. With regard to the former, the UCTA introduces a 'reasonable expectations test'. The law does not explain what 'reasonable expectations' are. However, for the first time, the courts seem to be expressly directed to consider the point of view of the person against whom the clause is pleaded.[199] It will need to be demonstrated whether the 'reasonable expectations test' comes close to the good faith test under Directive 93/13/EEC.[200] If the reasonable expectations test leads to the conclusion that the contractual performance promised in the contract has been met, a further test needs to be met, which may be considered as a second reasonableness test, which is that the clause must meet the requirements of reasonableness under Schedule 2 to the UCTA. While this regulatory technique may seem logical – as the term would otherwise have to be regarded as invalid – its application might create confusion. How can the reasonable expectation be weighed against reasonableness under Schedule 2? One may well agree with the findings of the Law Commissions that there should be only one test.[201]

[198] B. Coote, 'Statutes, Unfair Contract Terms Act 1977' (1978) 41 *Modern Law Review* 312 at 318; Reynolds, 'The Unfair Contract Terms Act', 204.

[199] Coote, 'Statutes', 312 at 318; Reynolds, 'The Unfair Contract Terms Act', 204.

[200] The Directive, however, calls for the application of the 'legitimate expectations test', see pp. 420–1 below.

[201] Law Commissions' Joint Consultation Paper, 'Unfair Terms in Contracts', 40.

A dispute between *Zockoll Group Ltd and Mercury Communications Ltd* led to two decisions of the Court of Appeal. The first of these two cases is of particular interest, as Phillips LJ attempted to build a bridge between section 3 of the UCTA and the notion of good faith. In the second of the two cases, Bingham MR commented more clearly on reasonable expectations.

In *Zockoll Group Ltd* v. *Mercury Communications Ltd (No. 1)*,[202] the plaintiff anticipated the introduction of alphanumeric telephone numbers in the UK and acquired from the defendant about 3,000 choice generic 'phonenames'. One of those numbers was 0500 354448, which could be converted into the phonename 0500 FLIGHT and was of obvious value to travel agents. Under the contract for the supply of the telephone numbers, the defendant was entitled to withdraw any number on giving reasonable notice. The plaintiff had owned the 0500 FLIGHT number for about four years but had made little use of it. In March 1997, the defendant wrote to the plaintiff withdrawing the number, as it had been requested by one of its other customers. The plaintiff sought an interlocutory injunction to restrain the defendant from transferring the number. The judge at first instance held that the plaintiff had no arguable case for breach of contract and refused to grant an injunction. The plaintiff appealed and sought a mandatory injunction ordering the defendant to withdraw the number from the other customer and to restore it to the defendant. The plaintiff argued that Mercury were precluded from acting as they did by section 3(2) of the UCTA. Phillips LJ said that section 3(2) would only avail the plaintiff if

> [(i)] clause 8(1) [of the contract] is unreasonable and (ii) Mercury's action in reliance upon that clause will have the effect of rendering their contractual performance substantially different from what was reasonably expected of them when the contract was concluded or, indeed, of rendering no performance at all of all or part of their contractual obligation.

In the last paragraph, Phillips LJ made an indirect reference to good faith,[203] by referring to Bingham MR's well-known summary of the

[202] [1998] FSR 354.

[203] For another reference to good faith in insurance contracts, see *Orakpo* v. *Barclays Insurance Services* [1995] *Lloyd's Reinsurance Law Reports* 443 *per* Lord Hoffmann. See also *Laceys Footwear (Wholesale) Ltd* v. *Bowler International Freight Ltd* [1997] 2 Lloyd's Rep 369 *per* Lord Brooke at 384.

law in *Timeload Ltd* v. *British Telecommunications plc.*[204] In *Timeload*, Bingham MR had said:[205]

> As I ventured to observe in *Interfoto Picture Library Ltd* v. *Stiletto Visual Programmes Ltd*,[206] the law of England, while so far eschewing any broad principle of good faith in the field of contract, has responded to demonstrated problems of unfairness by developing a number of piecemeal solutions directed to the particular problem before it. It seems to me at least arguable that the common law could, if the letter of the statute does not apply, treat the clear intention of the legislature expressed in the statute as a platform for invalidating or restricting the operation of an oppressive clause in a situation of the present, very special kind. I say no more that that there is, I think, a question here which has attracted much attention in Commonwealth jurisdictions and on the continent and may well deserve to be further explored here.

Phillips LJ then went on to say that he could not ignore these observations on the potential operation of the law when he decided that the defendant's conduct either had rendered performance of the contract substantially different from what had been reasonably expected, or had resulted in non-performance of part of the contractual obligation.[207] Thus, despite his effort to build a bridge to good faith, Phillips LJ in the end based his decision on a reasonable expectations test.

In *Zockoll Group Ltd* v. *Mercury Communications Ltd (No. 2)*,[208] the Court of Appeal clarified the meaning of section 3. Bingham MR stated that what was 'reasonably expected' cannot be determined simply by relying on a proper construction of the contract, but rather must be derived from all the circumstances of the case, including the way in which the contract was presented by the party seeking to rely on the clause to the other party. According to the Law Commissions, this appears to mean that, if it was made reasonably clear to a consumer that the business had the right to and might in fact perform its obligations in the way it is now seeking to do, then section 3 will have no application.[209] Such an understanding does not reach beyond procedural good faith, because whether a party will be able successfully to rely on

[204] [1995] EMLR 459.

[205] See *Timeload Ltd* v. *British Telecommunications plc* [1995] EMLR 459 at 468; and Phillips LJ in *Zockoll Group Ltd* v. *Mercury Communications Ltd (No. 1)* [1998] FSR 354 at 362.

[206] [1989] QB 433 at 439.

[207] [1998] FSR 354 at 362–3.

[208] [1999] EMLR 385.

[209] Law Commissions' Joint Consultation Paper, 'Unfair Terms in Contracts', 27, n. 53, referring to three cases.

an exclusion or limitation clause will still depend very much on the concrete circumstances of the case.

Terms partly reasonable and partly unreasonable

A question of great practical importance is whether or not it is possible for the court to sever parts of a clause, when examining its reasonableness, thus allowing part of the clause to be reasonable but deciding that the other part of the clause is unreasonable. This will depend on an interpretation of section 11(1) of the UCTA.[210] In *Stewart Gill Ltd* v. *Horatio Myer & Co. Ltd*, Donaldson MR summarised the law as follows:

> In the face of this wording [of section 11(1)] it seems to me to be impossible to contend that we should look only at that part of the clause which is relied on. The issue is whether 'the term [the whole term and nothing but the term] shall have been a fair and reasonable one to be included'.[211]

Similarly, in the same case, Stuart-Smith LJ added:

> Nor does it appear to me to be consistent with the policy and purpose of the Act to permit a contractor to impose a contractual term which taken as a whole is completely unreasonable, to put a blue pencil through the most offensive parts and say that what is left is reasonable and sufficient to exclude or restrict his liability in the manner relied on.[212]

Therefore, we may conclude that a term is either reasonable as a whole, or not at all. The legal doctrine on this point in England is similar to the position in Germany, where the courts have consistently rejected any attempt to allow clauses to be severed.[213]

The appellate courts' respect for decisions of the lower courts: the real reason for the small number of cases

In *George Mitchell (Chesterhall) Ltd* v. *Finney Lock Seeds Ltd*,[214] the first case to be decided under the UCTA, the House of Lords made it

[210] Section 11(1) of the UCTA provides: 'In relation to a contract term, the requirement of reasonableness for the purposes of this Part of this Act ... is that the term shall have been a fair and reasonable one to be included having regard to the circumstances which were, or ought reasonably to have been, known to or in the contemplation of the parties when the contract was made.'

[211] [1992] 1 QB 600 at 607A–C. [212] *Ibid.*, 609C–E.

[213] This is the so-called *geltungserhaltende Reduktion*; for more detail, see Basedow, in *Münchener Kommentar*, para. 306, at 12–20.

[214] [1983] 2 AC 803.

abundantly clear that the higher courts in the country must in general respect the judgment of the first-instance court and be reluctant to reverse the judgment, unless it is plainly and obviously wrong. As Lord Bridge of Harwich put it in his judgment in that case:

> There will be sometimes room for a legitimate difference of judicial opinion as to what the answer should be, where it will be impossible to say that one view is demonstrably wrong and the other demonstrably right. It must follow, in my view, that . . . the appellate court should treat the original decision with the utmost respect and refrain from interference with it unless satisfied that it proceeded upon some erroneous principle or was plainly and obviously wrong.[215]

A decision as to the reasonableness of a clause, while not being an 'exercise of discretion', at least not in the eyes of Lord Bridge,[216] requires the court to take into account a whole range of considerations, to weigh them in the balance, and to reach a decision based thereon.[217] This is the direct consequence of a context-related control of contract terms, whether those terms are negotiated or are in a standard form. The fact that the list of factors in Schedule 2 is non-exhaustive increases the relevance of the individual circumstances of the case in determining reasonableness.[218] It has already been mentioned that criticism has been made of the House of Lords' interpretation of the reasonableness test, in particular that their interpretation has introduced an element of uncertainty into the interpretation of commercial contracts, and this uncertainty necessarily leads to an exercise of discretion.[219] However, the House of Lords' true intention was to discourage appeals. Any decision regarding the invalidity of contract terms will take into account, first and foremost, the context of the case, that is to say the individual circumstances. Seen thus, the role of the Court of Appeal and

[215] *Ibid.*, 816A–C, followed by Nourse LJ in *St Albans City and District Council* v. *International Computers Ltd* [1996] 4 All ER 481 at 491J–492C.

[216] [1983] 2 AC 803 at 805.

[217] *Ibid.*, 816A–C. It seems that, as a general rule, whenever a court has to come to a judgment after taking into account a number of factors, the vaguer the standard and the greater the number of factors which the court has to weigh up, the more reluctant the appellate court will be to interfere with the trial judge's decision: *Re Grayan Building Services Ltd* [1995] Ch 241 at 254; *Pro Sieben Media AG* v. *Carlton UK Television Ltd* [1999] 1 WLR 605 at 612.

[218] *Smith* v. *Bush* [1990] 1 AC 831 at 858B.

[219] J. Adams and R. Brownsword, 'The Unfair Contract Terms Act: A Decade of Discretion', 94 at 103.

the House of Lords will remain a minor one. Such an interpretation accords with the way in which the English courts have assessed exclusion and limitation terms for decades. The consequence, however, is that the lower courts are granted a 'broad discretion',[220] though to the detriment of legal certainty and to the efficiency of the legal regime of the UCTA.

The relationship between statutory and common law unreasonableness, objective and subjective interpretation, and procedural and substantive good faith

'Incorporation' and 'construction' control under the common law is applied prior to statutory 'content control'. As noted above, one method of incorporation is by notice. To incorporate a clause by notice, the person seeking to rely on the clause has to show that he took reasonable steps to bring the clause to the attention of the other party, although not that the other party *actually* took notice of the clause.[221] 'Special notice' is required if a contracting party wishes to rely on a 'particularly onerous or unusual' term. The special notice requirement means that the contracting party may have to take special steps to bring that term 'fairly and reasonably' to the attention of the other contracting party. The special notice test was applied in *Thornton* v. *Shoe Lane Parking*[222] by Megaw LJ and in *Interfoto Picture Library Ltd* v. *Stiletto Visual Programmes Ltd*[223] by Dillon and Bingham LJJ. It seems as if the test applied by Megaw LJ is more restricted, as it refers to the nature of the clause, whereas Dillon and Bingham LJJ do not refer to the nature of the term but rather (on the facts of the case) to the extent of the charge for the late return of the material. More recently, in *AEG (UK) Ltd* v. *Logic Resource Ltd*,[224] Hobhouse LJ prefers the more restricted test propounded by Megaw LJ in *Thornton*.

The problem here is not so much which particular variety of the special notice test is to be preferred, but rather the quality and the nature of the test itself. Whichever version of the special notice test one adopts, there is inevitably some overlap between the statutory

[220] These are the words used by Collins, 'Good Faith', 245.
[221] *Birch* v. *Thomas* [1972] 1 WLR 294.
[222] [1971] 2 QB 163; [1971] 2 WLR 585; [1971] 1 All ER 686.
[223] [1989] QB 433.
[224] [1996] CLC 265. See also Bradgate, 'Unreasonable Standard Terms', 582 at 587.

reasonableness test and the common law special notice test.[225] It is difficult to see how a court, having first considered factors similar to those used to determine the statutory reasonableness test in order to decide that a clause needs special notice, and then, having decided that sufficient notice of the clause was given to meet the special notice test, could, in effect, reverse its first assessment and hold the clause to be unreasonable under the UCTA.[226] Civil law regimes resolve this issue by understanding the incorporation of the contract term as a more technical process, in which knowledge or the opportunity to acquire knowledge is required, and in which value-judgments on the content of the term are largely excluded. Treitel's finding that common law *dicta*[227] allow the submission of a properly incorporated clause to the reasonableness test and thus allow for it then to be declared invalid,[228] comes quite close to the distinction drawn in civil law regimes. However, Treitel's views are not supported by any particular decision.[229] The great majority of English courts and legal doctrine is far removed from such an understanding.

Therefore, there seems an obvious need to define the relationship between the common law and the statutory test. It has been suggested that, whereas the common law takes a purely *objective* approach to consent, paragraph (c) of Schedule 2 to the UCTA, by contrast,[230] is concerned with the *subjective* reality of the consent to the term. The difficulty is that paragraph (c) is not purely subjective. It asks not only whether the customer knew (the subjective element), but also whether he 'ought reasonably to have known' (the objective element), of the existence and extent of the term. Therefore, the distinction between paragraph (c) and the common law is more subtle than simply that between a subjective and an objective test of consent. The main difference seems to be that, whereas the common law looks to the

[225] Howells and Weatherill, *Consumer Protection Law*, 308.

[226] Bradgate, 'Unreasonable Standard Terms', 582 at 591.

[227] Treitel, *The Law of Contract*, 243–4.

[228] *Thornton* v. *Shoe Lane Parking Ltd* [1971] 2 QB 163 at 170 *per* Denning MR; *Standard Chartered Bank Ltd* v. *Walker* [1982] 1 WLR 1410 at 1416.

[229] *Luddit* v. *Ginger Coote Airways Ltd* [1947] AC 233 at 242.

[230] 'The matters to which regard is to be had in particular for the purposes of sections 6(3), 7(3) and (4), 20 and 21 are any of the following which appear to be relevant – (c) whether the customer knew or ought reasonably to have known of the existence and extent of the term (having regard, among other things, to any custom of the trade and any previous course of dealing between the parties).'

profferor, the statute looks to the profferee and asks whether he ought reasonably to have known of the terms.[231] Even where the profferor has taken reasonable steps to draw the profferee's attention to the terms (thus satisfying the common law requirements), the profferee may reasonably say that he was not aware of them (thus rendering the term unreasonable under the UCTA).[232] Such a distinction might be helpful to highlight the differences between common law and statutory law. However, it cannot overcome the remaining uncertainties in the application of the law. The uncertainty in how to handle the two tests is also manifest in the interpretation of the UTCCR 1994 and 1999.[233]

What remains to be considered is the question of the interrelationship between subjective interpretation and substantive good faith. The link between objective interpretation and procedural good faith has already been considered above. Much more difficult is the question of the interrelationship between subjective interpretation and substantive good faith. English doctrine and English courts seem to equate subjective interpretation with substantive good faith. Seen from a European perspective, such a reading is problematic. English law understands subjective interpretation as a means to take the parties' expectations into account. In contrast to the common law, subjective interpretation is much more concerned with the specific circumstances of the case, and therefore the specific circumstances of the case dominate the value-judgments of the courts. However, the way in which the courts apply the reasonableness test, and the way in which the parties' reasonable expectations are balanced, are evidence of a strong focus on procedural fairness. The expectations of the parties are bound to their knowledge of the terms and to their bargaining power. This is certainly not substantive good faith. More is needed here than simply assessing and weighing the parties' abilities and interests. Substantive good faith reaches beyond procedural good faith. In the latter, elements of justice are brought to bear independently of the actual capacity of consumers to understand and negotiate the terms of the contract and their implications. It is an irony that the reasonableness test laid down

[231] See Willett, 'Good Faith' in Brownsword, Hird an Howells (eds.), *Good Faith in Contract*, 85; for a discussion of the changes resulting from the enactment of the UTCCR, see pp. 379–82 below.

[232] Bradgate, 'Unreasonable Standard Terms', 582 at 592.

[233] See the analysis of the OFT at pp. 383–99 below.

in the UCTA (which can be equated to procedural good faith) brings with it legal uncertainty, whereas substantive good faith enhances legal certainty.

The Unfair Terms in Consumer Contracts Regulations

The UCTA was not the last step to be taken in relation to unfair contract terms, but it was the last step to be initiated on a purely national level. On 5 April 1993, Directive 93/13/EEC on unfair terms in consumer contracts was adopted,[234] with the twofold objective of setting standards on the control of unfair contract terms and providing for adequate and effective means to control such terms. The UK government fulfilled its Community obligation to implement the Directive into national law by adopting the Unfair Terms in Consumer Contracts Regulations 1994[235] (UTCCR 1994). Five years later, the Unfair Terms in Consumer Contracts Regulations 1999[236] (UTCCR 1999) replaced the UTCCR 1994. With the enactment of the UTCCR 1994, UK law on unfair terms shifted from the control of *exclusion and limitation clauses* to the control of *standard business terms and conditions*.[237] The yardstick of analysis is no longer the reasonableness test but rather good faith, at least in standard business terms and conditions. The first part of the analysis will therefore consider whether and to what extent EC law has succeeded in implementing into the English legal order the concept of 'substantive good faith'. The second part of the analysis will focus on the power of the Office of Fair Trading and the Consumers' Association to take enforcement action under the UTCCR.

Historical background

In 1993, the European Council adopted Directive 93/13/EEC on unfair terms in consumer contracts. The Directive required Member States to adapt their legislation accordingly by the end of 1994. As Directives in general allow Member States a great deal of discretion as to how they implement European law into their national legislation, the various Member States adopted different approaches when implementing

[234] Directive 93/13/EEC, OJ 1993 No. L95, 21 April 1993, 29.

[235] SI 1994 No. 3159. [236] SI 1999 No. 2083.

[237] See Beale, 'Legislative Control of Fairness' in Beatson and Friedman (eds.), *Good Faith*, 231, who writes: 'I hope it is now accepted that the problems caused by standard form contracts are rather different to those confronted in traditional cases of victimisation.'

the Directive. Generally speaking, the method of implementation depended on the pre-existing legislation in the particular field. Usually, two different approaches are possible: either to transpose the Directive as it is, or to integrate it into existing legislation. As the UK had already enacted the UCTA in 1977, it opted for the first method. The Directive was transposed into UK law by enacting the UTCCR 1994. The UCTA and the UTCCR 1994 differ with regard to the scope of their application, as well as on various other points, the UTCCR being at the same time both broader and narrower than the UCTA. The technique chosen allowed the UK to formally meet its obligation to implement the Directive.[238]

On 1 October 1999, the UTCCR 1999 came into force, replacing the UTCCR 1994. The main reason for the enactment of the UTCCR 1999 was to meet the Directive's requirement to implement adequate and effective procedures to prevent the use of unfair terms. Under the UTCCR 1994, this function was originally assigned only to the Director-General of Fair Trading, the only institution empowered to seek injunctions in appropriate cases. Consumer organisations therefore argued that the Directive had not been fully implemented into UK law, and initiated proceedings against the UK government before the High Court. Hidden J referred the case to the ECJ, raising the question as to whether Article 7 of Directive 93/13/EEC imposes an obligation on the Member States to grant consumer organisations the right to take action.[239] The new UK government, political control of which had passed from the Conservative Party to the Labour Party, promised to amend the UTCCR 1994 accordingly. The reference to the ECJ was therefore withdrawn. Thus, it can be seen that the reference to the ECJ directly led to the introduction of the UTCCR 1999.

In January 2001, the Law Commission of England and Wales and the Scottish Law Commission were mandated to consider the desirability and feasibility of, first, merging the UCTA and UTCCR into a unified regime, secondly, extending the legislation to protect business, in particular small business, and, thirdly, making any replacement legislation clearer and more accessible to the reader. In August 2002, the two Law Commissions presented their joint consultation paper on 'Unfair

[238] E. Hondius, 'Unfair Contract Terms: Towards a European Law' (1997) 5 *European Review of Private Law* 121.

[239] Judgment of 28 February 1996, *R.* v. *Secretary of State for Trade and Industry, ex parte Consumers' Association and Which?*, High Court, unreported (available on Lexis).

Terms in Contracts'.[240] In essence, the Law Commissions respond to all three questions raised in the affirmative. However, the future of the initiative is far from clear.

The content of the UTCCR: technical inconsistencies

The UTCCR 1994 implemented the provisions of the Directive almost verbatim.[241] However, in implementing the Directive into the UTCCR 1994, it was rewritten in a format and wording supposedly more suited to the UK.[242] The problem is that even slight changes of wording create subtle changes of meaning. The UTCCR had an immediate influence on the substantive private law that governs the relationship between the supplier and the consumer. The UTCCR 1994 contained substantive provisions that guaranteed the consumer's protection and declared unfair contract terms to be non-binding and void (regulation 5). At the same time, the UTCCR 1994 established a new enforcement mechanism in order to promote the enforcement of the UTCCR 1994. Regulation 8 offered for the first time a specific provision to control standard terms.[243]

The UTCCR do not amend or replace the UCTA, and therefore the latter is still applicable in full. Even if the UCTA and the UTCCR have at least partly the same goal, namely, to ensure consumer protection, they are not fully complementary. The UTCCR and the UCTA do not have the same scope of application, and they provide for different control mechanisms. Thus, the relationship between the UCTA and the UTCCR is complex. It may be thought regrettable that these two sources of control were not combined into one coherent piece of legislation. As one learned scholar stated: 'This seems likely to produce a situation of nightmarish complexity in the area of consumer law, where simple and user-friendly rules should be the order of the day.'[244] The

[240] Law Commissions' Joint Consultation Paper, 'Unfair Terms in Contracts'.

[241] C. Willett, 'The Directive on Unfair Terms in Consumer Contracts and Its Implementation in the United Kingdom' (1997) 5 *European Review of Private Law* 223 at 229.

[242] R. Bragg, 'Implementation of the EC Directive on Unfair Contract Terms in Consumer Contracts. The Department of Trade and Industry Consultation Document' (1994) 53 *Cambridge Law Journal* 30.

[243] P. Sobich, 'Verfahrensrechtliche Kontrolle "unfairer" AGB in Großbritannien: The Unfair Terms in Consumer Contracts Regulations 1994' (1998) RIW 684.

[244] F. Reynolds, 'Unfair Contract Terms' (1994) 110 *Law Quarterly Review* 1.

possible areas of conflict are indeed of considerable importance.[245] Such areas of potential conflict include:

(1) *Objective*: the UCTA is intended to address exclusion and limitation clauses notwithstanding their context, whether contractual or non-contractual, or whether in business-to-business relations, business-to-consumer relations or consumer-to-consumer relations. The UTCCR covers only standard business terms and conditions between businesses and consumers.
(2) *Reach of control*: the UCTA only covers exclusion and limitation clauses, while the UTCCR covers all types of clauses including agreed remedies[246] and price-related matters.[247] The Department of Trade and Industry considered the matter but concluded that a combination of the two regimes was not possible for the time being.[248] This view might change if the Law Commissions' proposal finds political support.
(3) *Core terms*: the UCTA reasonableness test applies to an exclusion clause even if it is one that defines the main subject-matter of the contract. Under the UTCCR, a 'main subject-matter term' must be written in plain and intelligible language, and only under special circumstances will it be subject to the unfairness test under regulation 4 of the UTCCR 1994 (regulation 5 of the UTCCR 1999).
(4) *Intensity of control*, or *which test applies*: the UCTA standard of reasonableness and the UTCCR standard of unfairness can be considered to be similar, but not identical. Application of the two standards might lead to the same result, but this is not necessarily the case.[249]
(5) *Standard terms or individually negotiated terms*: the UTCCR apply only to terms that have not been individually negotiated, that is, to *standard form contracts* or *standard business terms and*

[245] See the useful comparison of the major fields of conflict in Howells and Weatherill, *Consumer Protection Law*, 312; and the conclusions of the Law Commissions' Joint Consultation Paper, 'Unfair Terms in Contracts', 66.
[246] Collins, 'Good Faith', 241.
[247] Beale, 'Legislative Control of Fairness' in Beatson and Friedman (eds.), *Good Faith and Fault*, 240.
[248] Department of Trade and Industry, 'Implementation of the EC Directive on Unfair Terms in Consumer Contracts (93/13/EEC): A Consultation Document' (London, October 1993).
[249] The Department of Trade and Industry argues, however, that the tests of fairness are sufficiently similar to reduce any problems arising from a potential overlap. See Collins, 'Good Faith', 241.

conditions.[250] The UCTA is broader than the UTCCR, in that it covers individually negotiated contract terms, at least in the form of exclusion and limitation clauses.

(6) *Types of contract covered*: certain types of contract are excluded from the scope of the UCTA (see sections 26, 28 and Schedule 1) as well as from that of the UTCCR, but the two lists of exclusions are not identical.[251]

(7) *The notion of a 'consumer'*: the UTCCR defines 'consumer' (regulation 2(1) of the UTCCR 1994; regulation 3(1) of the UTCCR 1999) along the lines of EC law, whereas the UCTA states the circumstances in which a person 'deals as consumer' (section 12). Again, the tests are not the identical.[252]

(8) *Burden of proof*: the burden of proof in the UTCCR differs from that in the UCTA. While it is not clear whether the consumer bears the burden of proof that a term is unfair under the UTCCR, it is the supplier that has to show that a term is reasonable under the UCTA (section 11(5)).[253]

The scope of application: terms and contracts

The scope of application of the UTCCR comprises 'any term in a contract concluded between a seller or supplier and a consumer where the [term in question] has not been individually negotiated'. Regulation 3(3) of the UTCCR 1994 and regulation 5(2) of the UTCCR 1999 presume that a term has not been individually negotiated where the term has been drafted in advance and the consumer has not been able to influence the substance of the contract. The fact that there is an individually negotiated term does not bar the application of the fairness test to the contract, as regulation 3(4) of the UTCCR 1994 and regulation 5(3) of the UTCCR 1999 will apply if an overall assessment

[250] C. Miller, B. Harvey and D. Parry, *Consumer and Trading Law: Text, Cases and Materials* (Oxford, 1998), 337.

[251] For example, the UCTA does not apply to insurance contracts, while the UTCCR 1994 do not apply to contracts of employment. This limitation in the scope of application of the UTCCR 1994 stems from the powers under Art. 95 (ex Art. 100a) and is not replicated in the UCTA; see *Johnstone* v. *Bloomsbury Health Authority* [1992] QB 333, Court of Appeal.

[252] Cf. Collins, 'Good Faith', 240.

[253] C. Wagner and R. Althen, 'Umsetzung der Richtlinie des Rates über missbräuchliche Klauseln in Verbraucherverträgen im Vereinigten Königreich' (1995) RIW 548; T. Kaye, 'Implementing an EC Directive on Unfair Terms' (1995) 3 *Web Journal of Current Legal Issues* 3.

of the contract indicates that the contract was a pre-formulated standard contract.[254] However, the UTCCR then applies only to that part of the contract which has not been individually negotiated. The UCTA does not differentiate between whether or not such a term has been individually negotiated, provided that it is an exclusion or limitation clause. Due to pressure from the German government,[255] the Directive, and therefore the UTCCR, exempt so-called 'core terms' from the scope of control.[256] This category is unknown to the UCTA, as section 3(2)(b) covers terms which purport to permit a contractual performance substantially different from that which might have been reasonably expected by the other party, or no performance at all. In areas of potential overlap, consumers will seek to rely on the provision which provides the greatest protection wherever it might be found.[257] It is not always an easy task to determine which provision offers the greater protection, and more research would have to be done in order to elucidate the differences in the degree of protection. Of course, if a term is void and ineffective under the UCTA, there is no point in arguing whether it is unfair under the UTCCR. However, the term may be of a type which is not within the scope of the UCTA and yet is within the scope of the UTCCR, for example a penalty clause.[258]

Schedule 1 to the UTCCR 1994 excluded contracts relating to employment, succession rights, rights under family law and the incorporation or organisation of companies and partnerships. Thus, in contrast to the UCTA, contracts of insurance, contracts relating to intellectual property and contracts relating to land were not expressly

[254] Regulation 3(4). Often, clauses concerning the price, and similar terms, are individually negotiated and would therefore be exempt from control under the UTCCR 1994. But these core terms are excluded from control in any event by regulation 3(2). According to that regulation, 'core terms' can only be subject to the fairness test if they are not drafted in plain and intelligible language. Therefore, the formal requirement of plain and intelligible language determines whether the substantial fairness test is applied.

[255] The corresponding German provision is Art. 8 of the AGBG, which creates a lot of difficulties in its application. There are no clear borderlines between terms that are subject to control and those that are outside control because they regulate price and performance. German courts struggle hard to apply the provision correctly. However, these decisions are inconsistent and therefore cause legal uncertainty. It remains to be seen whether the revised formula in Art. 307 of the BGB will lead to greater certainty.

[256] The difficulties came to the fore in the House of Lords in *Director-General of Fair Trading* v. *First National Bank plc* [2001] 3 WLR 1297; [2002] All ER 97; for more detail, see pp. 413–23 below.

[257] Miller, Harvey and Parry, *Consumer and Trading Law*, 337.

[258] Willett, 'The Directive on Unfair Terms', 223 at 230.

excluded from the UTCCR 1994. Insurance contracts were certainly covered by the UTCCR 1994, as, probably, were contracts in which an interest in land was transferred from a business to a consumer (that is, a sale by a developer to a consumer, or a lease by a business landlord to a consumer). The applicability of the UTCCR 1994 to contracts relating to land was not considered very clear.[259] This resulted from the Directive's language: The English text says that the Directive applies to sales and supplies of 'goods' and 'services', neither of which would be considered by an English lawyer to include land.[260] Land is clearly not 'goods', but might conceivably come within the notion of 'services'.[261] The issue was, however, resolved in the UTCCR 1999.

The non-application of the UTCCR 1994 to contracts of employment was grounded in Article 95 (ex Article 100a) of the EC Treaty. However, it is interesting to note that, in 2002, Germany amended its unfair contract terms legislation specifically in order to include contracts of employment.[262] The UCTA applies to such contracts, as long as the criteria of section 12(1)(a) and (b) are met. In *Brigden* v. *American Express Bank Ltd*, the claimant was dismissed without the usual disciplinary procedures having been followed. The employee claimed that this was a breach of his employment contract. The employer relied on a clause in the employee handbook (which formed part of the contract of employment) which provided that 'an employee may be dismissed by notice and/or payment in lieu of notice during the first two years of employment without any implementation of the disciplinary procedure'.[263] The UCTA was considered in principle as applicable, but the claimant nevertheless lost his claim for breach of contract, as he did not come within section 3(2) of the UCTA. The disputed clause was not a term excluding or restricting the liability of the employer in respect of breach of contract or entitling the employer to render a

259 C. Maggs, 'Consumer Concerns – There Is Room for Improvement to the Unfair Terms in Consumer Contracts Regulations, Coming into Force in July' (1995) 92(21) *Law Society's Gazette* 23 at 24.

260 In comparison, the French understanding is broader. The French version talks about 'biens', which includes, according to the Civil Code, both movable and immovable property.

261 Other scholars have no problems including contracts relating to land in the scope of application of the UTCCR 1994: see, for example, M. Dean, 'Unfair Contract Terms: The European Approach' (1993) 56 *Modern Law Review* 581.

262 However, collective bargaining agreements between trade unions and employers are excluded: Art. 310 of the BGB.

263 [2000] IRLR 94.

contractual performance substantially different from that which was reasonably expected of it or to render no performance in respect of any part of its contractual obligation as required by the UCTA.[264] *Brigden* has, however, remained the only judgment so far advocating a broad reading of consumer contracts.[265]

The applicability of the UTCCR to standard business terms and conditions used in the financial services industry is less clear. Some practitioners feared that the UTCCR might have unexpected consequences for the financial services industry. For example, one commentator noted: 'Where a bank lends one person money on the basis of a guarantee from a third party consumer, arguably the guarantee must be fair even though the guarantor does not himself receive anything from the bank.'[266] In general, the UTCCR is considered not to apply to the creation and issue of financial securities.[267] But, almost all other financial transactions could be considered to be within the definition of 'service' and thus within the scope of application of the UTCCR. This is particularly true for ancillary or subsidiary terms meant to amend or supplement interest rates. In *Director-General of Fair Trading* v. *First National Bank plc*,[268] the House of Lords gave the notion of 'core terms' a narrow meaning to prevent the financial sector from being exempted from the scope of the legislation. Otherwise, there would have been no need for the special guidance, contained in the Annex to the Directive, on the application of the fairness test to transactions in which the price is linked to fluctuations in a stock exchange quotation.[269]

The concept of consumer

By regulation 2 of the UTCCR 1994, 'consumer' is defined as 'a natural person who, in making a contract to which these Regulations apply, is acting for purposes which are outside his business'. The definition in

264 In any event, it was likely that the clause would have passed the reasonableness test; see S. Gold, 'District Judge Stephen Gold Explains This and That in the Civil Way: Part 2' (1999) 149 *New Law Journal* No. 6910, 1589 at 1590.

265 Law Commissions' Joint Consultation Paper, 'Unfair Terms in Contracts', 37, with references in n. 107.

266 P. Watts, 'Consumer Concern – The New Regulations on Unfair Terms in Consumer Contracts Are Disappointingly Unclear in Their Drafting and Scope' (1995) 92(02) *Law Society's Gazette* 13 at 14.

267 Bragg, 'Implementation of the EC Directive', 31.

268 [2002] 1 AC 481; [2001] 3 WLR 1297; [2002] 1 All ER 97; for more detail, see pp. 413–23 below.

269 Collins, 'Good Faith', 242.

the UTCCR 1999 is slightly amended. By regulation 2 of the UTCCR 1999, 'consumer' is defined as any natural person who, in contracts covered by these Regulations, is acting for purposes which are outside his trade, business or profession'. The aim of the Directive is to protect only consumers. Businesses, no matter how small, are not protected at all by the Directive.[270] In accordance with well-established EC standards, the UTCCR defines 'consumer' more narrowly than the UCTA does.[271] A company can be a consumer under the UCTA,[272] but under the UTCCR a consumer must be a 'natural person'. Under section 12 of the UCTA, a party who is not acting 'in the course of a business' may have consumer status.[273] The UTCCR 1994 took a different approach. The person must be 'acting for purposes which are outside his business' in order to qualify as a consumer. Acting 'in the course of a business' is understood as an action integral to the business, that is, part of the normal trading activities of that business. A business entity (sole trader, partnership or company) which is not acting 'in the course of a business', even though the purchase in question is wholly or partly for business purposes, may be regarded as a 'consumer'. If a solicitor buys a vehicle for use in his business, the car will probably not have been bought 'in the course of a business'. The solicitor will be defined as a consumer under the UCTA. Under the UTCCR 1994 and 1999, however, it is the *purpose* of the purchase of the car which is critical. Because the car would have been bought for the purposes of the business, the solicitor would not qualify as a 'consumer' under the UTCCR. Such buyers will nevertheless continue to benefit from the protection of the UCTA.[274]

The content of the UTCCR: procedural and substantive good faith

The Directive and the UTCCR 1994 introduced into English contract law a general legislative framework for exercising control over standard contract terms. Central to this is the notion of 'good faith'. The notion

[270] Bragg, 'Implementation of the EC Directive', 30.

[271] Beale, 'Legislative Control of Fairness' in Beatson and Friedman, *Good Faith and Fault*, 239.

[272] Businesses engaged in a transaction outside their normal business purposes can claim to be 'dealing as consumer' since the decision in *R&B Customs Brokers Ltd* v. *United Dominions Trust Ltd* [1988] 1 WLR 321; see Kaye, 'Implementing an EC Directive', 2.

[273] Willett, 'The Directive on Unfair Terms', 223 at 229.

[274] Law Commissions' Joint Consultation Paper, 'Unfair Terms in Contracts', 54, para. 3.85.

of 'good faith' in legal doctrine is commonly understood to have two aspects, a procedural aspect and a substantive aspect, which are usually referred to respectively as 'procedural good faith' and 'substantive good faith'. There is, however, considerable disagreement as to where the borderline lies between these two aspects. Either the procedural aspect might be used to exclude certain types of unacceptable conduct, or it might be a mechanism for determining the issue of the incorporation of contract terms.[275] The substantive aspect might be used to determine that any significant imbalance in the contract terms either was caused by the absence of good faith or was contrary to good faith, and therefore the term would be deemed to be unfair.[276]

In order to understand the implications of the distinction between procedural good faith and substantive good faith, we must consider more fully the relationship between the common law approach (the incorporation rule, the construction rule, and fairness or reasonableness) and the approach of Directive 93/13/EEC. The latter does not, at least not explicitly, deal with incorporation, although it does establish the construction rule (the *contra proferentem* rule), but instead it puts emphasis on content control through the notion of 'good faith'.

In theory, the borderline between procedural and substantive good faith is clearly drawn. However, it may be incorrect to draw too sharp a distinction between procedural and substantive good faith, in that procedural good faith might, depending on the meaning given to it, cover construction as well as incorporation. Problems arise, however, if one tries to include incorporation control in procedural good faith. It seems as if the EC legislator has caused confusion by introducing a requirement of *transparency* into the Directive. Transparency tends to be understood in English doctrine as a principal element of procedural good faith. Such an understanding seems to be confirmed by the inclusion of paragraph (i) of the indicative list in the Annex to the Directive as well as by limiting the application of the good faith test to the time at which the contract was concluded.[277] If reduced to its procedural implications, the transparency requirement is doing nothing more than setting out rules of incorporation. It seems as if English law puts considerable emphasis, maybe too much emphasis,

275 Beale, 'Legislative Control of Fairness' in Beatson and Friedman, *Good Faith and Fault*, 245, n. 90.

276 Beale, 'Legislative Control of Fairness' in Beatson and Friedman, *Good Faith and Fault*, 245, n. 91; Collins, 'Good Faith', 229 at 250.

277 Law Commissions' Joint Consultation Paper, 'Unfair Terms in Contracts', 42, para. 3.54, 47, para. 3.67.

on the procedural aspect of good faith. The question then arises of what exactly remains within the scope of substantive good faith.

A correct understanding can only be found by reading 'substantive good faith' together with the requirement for there to be 'a significant imbalance in the parties' rights and obligations arising under the contract'.[278] There is a tendency in UK law to conflate the substantive aspect of the Directive and the UTCCR with the reasonableness test under the UCTA. The consequences of reducing good faith to procedural good faith might lead – for good or for bad – to a conflict with EC law. The Directive distinguishes between contract terms which may be controlled by individual litigants and standard contract terms which may be controlled by collective (and preventive) action. The control of standard contract terms must necessarily disregard the question of incorporation. While it is true that the House of Lords in *Director-General of Fair Trading* v. *First National Bank plc*[279] clearly recognised the different requirements to be applied to contract terms as between individual litigation and standard contract terms in collective, preventive action, and while the House of Lords also left the door open for a substantive good faith test,[280] there is no reported case in which substantive good faith may be said to have been the decisive factor.

The substance of contract control: substantive good faith and the 'significant imbalance' test

Regulation 4 of the UTCCR 1994 defines what is to be considered as unfair:

> '[U]nfair term' means any term which contrary to the requirement of good faith causes a significant imbalance in the parties' right and obligations under the contract to the detriment of the consumer.

Regulations 4(2), (3) and (4) provide further guidance on how to use the unfairness test. In addition to referring to the indicative list in Schedule 3, an assessment of the unfairness of a term shall be made by taking into account, first, the nature of the goods or services for which the contract was concluded, secondly, all the circumstances attending the conclusion of the contract, and, thirdly, all the other terms of the

278 UTCCR 1994, regulation 4; UTCCR 1999, regulation 5.

279 [2002] 1 AC 481; [2001] 3 WLR 1297; [2002] 1 All ER 97.

280 *Ibid.*; see Law Commissions' Joint Consultation Paper, 'Unfair Terms in Contracts', 46. para. 3.65.

contract or of another contract on which it is dependent. The unfairness test combines 'objective' control standards (significant imbalance, contrary to good faith) with 'subjective' control standards (the taking into consideration of the individual circumstances of the case). The latter aspect has caused no problem in English law, as English law has long emphasised the importance of the particular circumstances of each case. A closer analysis, however, reveals that this subjective control largely reduces objective control to a mere procedural fairness test.

English law, and those who comment thereon, focus on the language of regulation 4, which is said to establish a two-limb test.[281] Thus, not only must the term cause a significant imbalance (the first limb), but also the imbalance must be contrary to the requirement of good faith (the second limb). Those who argue that the 'significant imbalance' must be caused by the absence of good faith should in theory assume a term to be void only if the requirements of both limbs are met separately.[282] The point, however, seems to be whether the existence of the two sets of criteria in the two limbs means that there is a two-stage test to apply under different conditions, possibly with differing results.

Of particular importance is the question of whether a term which represents a significant imbalance is *automatically* contrary to good faith.[283] This is certainly the view of Mário Tenreiro, former head of the legal department of Directorate-General XXIV of the European Commission and one of the progenitors of Directive 93/13/EEC: his statement[284] to this effect is often quoted in the literature.[285] The

[281] G. Howells, 'Good Faith in Consumer Contracting' in Brownsword, Hird and Howells (eds.), *Good Faith in Contract*, 91 at 95; Law Commissions' Joint Consultation Paper, 'Unfair Terms in Contracts', 54. para. 3.58.

[282] Willett, 'The Directive on Unfair Terms', 223 at 232; Miller, Harvey and Parry, *Consumer and Trading Law*, 338; Collins, 'Good Faith', 245 *et seq.*; Dean, 'Unfair Contract Terms', 581 at 583.

[283] The views on this matter do not seem to be fully consistent: Howells, who defends the two hurdle model, starts from the presumption that imbalance implies good faith; see Howells, 'Good Faith in Consumer Contracting' in Brownsword, Hird and Howells (eds.), *Good Faith in Contract*, 91 at 95; the same is true for Willett, 'The Directive on Unfair Terms', 223 at 232.

[284] 'Let us be clear: there is no way that a contractual term which causes "a significant imbalance in parties' rights and duties arising under the contract to the detriment of the consumer" can conform with the requirement of "good faith". Indeed, the opposite is true: a term is always regarded as contrary to the requirement of "good faith" when it causes such an imbalance.' Mário Tenreiro, 'The Community Directive on Unfair Terms and National Legal Systems' (1995) 3 *European Review of Private Law* 273 at 279.

[285] For example, by the Law Commissions' Joint Consultation Paper, 'Unfair Terms in Contracts', 44, n. 131.

intellectual effort devoted to distinguishing 'imbalance' from 'good faith' stands in stark contrast to the legislative history and even possibly to its practical importance.[286] Anecdotal evidence suggests that the wording of Article 3 of the Directive (which establishes the 'significant imbalance' criteria) resulted from an agreement reached between officials of the Commission and the Member States late at night in a cocktail bar. The German representative insisted on good faith as a condition for his approval; the UK representative similarly insisted on an imbalance test. The outcome was a general clause merging both concepts into a unique 'European' concept. It is unlikely that this anecdote is true, however, as the concept of a 'significant imbalance' was unknown to English contract law prior to the Directive. The UK point of view at that time seems to be more fully reflected in the recitals than in the wording of Article 3.

The imbalance test Of the two tests under the UTCCR used to determine whether a contract is unfair (that is, the imbalance test and the good faith test), the imbalance test is said to be the more important for making that determination.[287] The strength of the bargaining positions of the parties is a familiar tool of English law, at least in the context of determining reasonableness under the UCTA,[288] and the concept is referred to in Recital 16 of Directive 93/13/EEC.[289] The concept is aimed at maintaining the freedom of contract.[290] Therefore, it is no surprise that the imbalance test should be the starting-point in a determination of whether a contract is unfair. One may even speculate whether there are any substantial differences between the approach of the UTCCR and that of the UCTA, or whether the UTCCR should be regarded merely as a more developed and more finely tuned version of the UCTA. The reasonableness test in the UCTA is guided by the criteria in Schedule 2, which refers, *inter alia*, to the relative strengths of the bargaining power of the parties. The guidance in Schedule 2 is aimed at the courts, and therefore grants considerable discretion to the courts.[291] An assessment of reasonableness under the UCTA can

[286] *Ibid.*, 47. [287] Willett, 'The Directive on Unfair Terms', 223 at 232.

[288] Dean, 'Unfair Contract Terms', 584.

[289] '[I]n making an assessment of good faith, particular regard shall be had to the strength of the bargaining positions of the parties . . . '

[290] This is exactly what most of the German case law on unfair contract terms is all about. The courts are doing no more than re-establishing the freedom of contract to the benefit of the weaker party.

[291] Collins, 'Good Faith', 245.

therefore easily be viewed as a *balancing* of the rights and obligations of the parties, and thus perhaps differs little in practice from the imbalance test under the UTCCR. Regulation 4 of the UTCCR 1994 defines the imbalance test, and refers to the indicative list in Schedule 3 to the Regulations (which implements the Annex to the Directive) which provides guidance on the issue of when the rights and obligations of the parties to the contract may be considered as significantly imbalanced. For lawyers in the UK, it is all too tempting to try to integrate the imbalance test into the well-established reasonableness test in the UCTA. Therefore, we need to consider how the two tests differ in their practical application.

Imbalance under the UTCCR is founded on the fact that, either the consumer does not have the same rights as the seller or supplier, or the consumer cannot make an effective response to a right exercised by the seller or supplier.[292] This is clear from the indicative list in the Annex to the Directive, which seeks to guide the application of the balancing test. For example, item (c) in the indicative list provides that a contract term may be unfair if it 'mak[es] an agreement binding on the consumer whereas provision of services by the seller or supplier is subject to a condition whose realisation depends on his own will alone'. Thus, the liability of the consumer in one set of circumstances is compared to the liability of the seller or supplier in a different set of circumstances. One commentator has described this test as a 'mirror image scenario'.[293] The UCTA's reasonableness test does not look at the positions of both parties to the contract, but rather seeks to determine whether the term, regardless of the viewpoints of the buyer or the seller, can be considered as reasonable. For the UTCCR, it is the interaction of all the contract terms that is important in determining unfairness. The UCTA does not deal with the whole contract but rather considers the terms in isolation.[294]

One provision in the UCTA is, however, more in the nature of a balancing test. Section 3(2)(b)(i) of the UCTA requires a court to consider the point of view of the party against whom the clause is pleaded.[295] Although this is not a fully fledged balancing test as such, there are elements in it which come close to the 'mirror image scenario'.

[292] Willett, 'Good Faith' in Brownsword, Hird and Howells (eds.), *Good Faith in Contract*, 86.

[293] *Ibid.* [294] Dean, 'Unfair Contract Terms', 583.

[295] Reynolds, 'The Unfair Contract Terms Act', 201 at 204; and Bradgate, 'Unreasonable Standard Terms', 584 at 585.

However, there are formal limits to such a comparison. The UTCCR set some limits to the balancing exercise. For example, a supplier cannot use the defence that use of the clause resulted in a cheaper deal for the consumer, and that this fact negates any perceived imbalance.[296] The UCTA, however, expressly accepts that the giving of an inducement (for example, in the form of cheaper goods to be supplied under the contract) to a consumer which the consumer would not have been able to obtain elsewhere under less onerous contractual terms is a factor tending to make the exclusion or limitation clause more fair.[297]

The balancing test combines subjective and objective standards. Because the balancing test under the UTCCR is used to determine whether standard business terms are fair, rather than to determine whether individually negotiated terms are fair, this necessarily implies that the test is inherently an objective test. German law emphasises objective standards in contract law, and this gives contract terms the status of 'quasi-legal rules'.[298] English law, by contrast, is more flexible, and seeks to combine objective and subjective standards in contract law. Schedule 2 to the UCTA lists a number of guidelines to be considered in the reasonableness test. The courts do not consider only what is reasonable in the eyes of the public at large (an objective test) but also what would be reasonable in the particular circumstances of this contract for these parties (a subjective test).[299] This is in line with the traditional common law position of a case-by-case analysis. Over the years, a number of criteria have been developed in case law which influence the determination of reasonableness.[300] The UTCCR's indicative list of unfair terms is more than a mere guideline like those in the UCTA. The indicative list in the UTCCR allows each term to be

[296] Beale, 'Legislative Control of Fairness' in Beatson and Friedman, *Good Faith*, 242.

[297] Schedule 2, para. (b), to the UCTA.

[298] H.-J. Pflug, *Kontrakt und Status im Recht der Allgemeinen Geschäftsbedingungen* (Munich, 1986).

[299] *Woodman* v. *Photo Trade Processing Ltd*, Judgment of 7 May 1981, Exeter County Court, unreported.

[300] The key criteria being a resistance to the exclusion of liability for negligence to consumers, an insistence upon a reasonable opportunity to familiarise oneself with the terms being offered, uncovering cartels by demonstrating the similarity of terms used in a particular trade, the fairness of the bargain if the exclusion clause substantially devalues the worth of the promise, the fairness of a limitation of damages in light of the likely losses arising from breach, the efficiency of the allocation of the burden of insurance, and a reluctance to permit a contracting party to grant itself a discretion with respect to the remedies it will give for its own breach of contract; see Collins, 'Good Faith', 245.

considered in light of the particular circumstances of the case, even where such terms are *prima facie* unfair.[301] In theory, regulation 6(1) of the UTCCR requires the setting aside of individual circumstances in the control of standard terms, which lies in the hands of the Office of Fair Trading. However, the enforcement strategy seems to be different.

The good faith test The second element involved in the test of fairness under the Directive and under the UTCCR introduces the notion of good faith into English law, and is therefore the most novel aspect of the legislation. At first glance, the second test (that is, the good faith test) is as necessary as the first test (that is, the balancing test) in order to declare a term unfair because, even if a term causes a significant imbalance in the rights and obligations to the consumer's detriment, it will nevertheless only be unfair if this is contrary to the requirement of good faith.[302] The key question is whether the good faith test is a test which can stand on its own or whether it is inextricably interlinked with the imbalance test.

There is considerable debate (and confusion[303]) on the notion of good faith under the UTCCR. A narrow reading of the concept of good faith views the concept simply as meaning the absence of bad

[301] Dean, 'Unfair Contract Terms', 587. As the Directive's list is expressly stated to be non-exhaustive, the possibility remained for the Member States to extend that list if they so wished. The legislation in the various Member States has not always followed the grey list approach. Some of this legislation has established lists of terms that are regarded as unfair (black lists; for example, Luxembourg, Spain and Belgium) while other legislation has opted for black and grey lists (for example, Italy and Germany); in fact, it is only a minority of states that has provided a non-binding list like the one in the Directive. See Report from the Commission on the Implementation of the Council Directive 93/13/EEC of 5 April 1993 on Unfair Terms in Consumer Contracts, COM (2001) 398 final, 11 July 2001.

[302] There was some discussion on how to interpret the role of the 'good faith' requirement – it certainly could not survive as a stand-alone test. Nevertheless, it must be emphasised that it is an important element of the fairness test, and that the fairness test is a single test consisting of both elements mentioned cf. S. Bright, 'Legal Studies – Winning the Battle Against Unfair Contract Terms' (2000) 20 *Journal of Society of Public Teachers of Law* 331 at 347.

[303] For example, the suggestion was made to assimilate the test as much as possible with the UCTA reasonableness test (see Dean, 'Unfair Contract Terms', 585, referring also to the House of Lords Select Committee on the European Communities (Session 1991–2), Sixth Report, House of Lords Paper 28, 74 and 91); another suggestion was to refer to the idea of 'acting in good conscience' or 'not unconscionably' (see Collins, 'Good Faith', 250).

faith.[304] Good faith is taken to connote a particular (innocent) state of mind, namely, one free from suspicion or notice – good faith in the sense of 'the pure heart and the empty head' as Lord Kenyon once described it.[305] This narrow interpretation of the requirement of good faith could easily be met simply by providing the consumer with the appropriate information. But, permitting such an interpretation would not give any real substance to the good faith test, but would instead turn it into a mere procedural rule relying on subjective standards. By contrast, at the other end of the interpretation spectrum, there have been attempts to read into the notion of good faith an element of *contractual justice*. Such a reading reaches beyond the imbalance test, and views the overall purpose of the good faith test as not to reinstitute the freedom of contract but rather to guarantee an objective set of 'just' rights and duties.[306] One's understanding of good faith therefore will have implications which reach far beyond the realm of consumer contract law into commercial contract law.

The difficulty in analysing good faith begins at an early stage of the analysis. Whereas a civil law lawyer applies the test of good faith to the substance of a contract, an English lawyer, by contrast, would give the notion of good faith a much wider understanding. Good faith is understood by a common law lawyer as a concept that may be applied, first, to the bargaining process leading to the contract, secondly, to the substance of the contract, thirdly, to the performance of the contract, and, fourthly, to the enforcement of the contract.[307] There is a common factor in these two approaches, which is that both

[304] See the references in Brownsword, Howells and Wilhelmsson, 'Between Market and Welfare' in Willett (ed.), *Aspects of Fairness*, 25 at 39, and to some extent Howells, 'Good Faith in Consumer Contracting' in Brownsword, Hird and Howells (eds.), *Good Faith in Contract*, 91.

[305] *Lawson* v. *Weston* (1801) 4 Esp 56; 170 ER 806.

[306] H. MacQueen, 'Good Faith in the Scots Law of contract: An Undisclosed Principle' in A. Forte (ed.), *Good Faith in Contract and Property* (Oxford, 1999), writes: 'Nevertheless, it is probably fair to say that the proponents of a good faith principle have seen it as an instrument of social welfare in contract law as against the market and commercial transactions', referring to Brownsword, Howells and Wilhelmsson, 'Between Market and Welfare' in Willett (ed.), *Aspects of Fairness*, 25. Even stronger is M. Bridge, 'Good Faith in Commercial Contracts, in Contract, Concept and Context' in Brownsword, Hird and Howells (eds.), *Good Faith in Contract*, 145: 'He [Brownsword] favours something of a Kantian categorical imperative in the pursuit of contractual interest – I am free to pursue my interest to the extent that this is compatible with the legitimate interests of others.'

[307] Willett, 'The Directive on Unfair Terms', 223 at 232.

approaches focus on the application of good faith to the substance of the contract. Directive 93/13/EEC therefore focuses on the substance of what has been agreed.[308] All other elements of good faith, if any, are left to the national legislator or more broadly to national law. It is not unreasonable to expect the legislator to provide guidance on the scope and reach of good faith. However, just like the Directive, the UTCCR does not define what exactly constitutes good faith. The UTCCR, in Schedule 2, merely requires the court to *have regard* in particular to the parties' relative bargaining power, any inducement given to the consumer, whether goods were made to special order, and whether the consumer has been treated fairly and equitably. These criteria are similar to the reasonableness guidelines in the UCTA, although not identical.[309] To assimilate the good faith test to the reasonableness test of the UCTA is incorrect.[310] The concept of good faith includes notions of reasonableness.[311] However, it should not be forgotten that the good faith requirement was introduced into English law prior to the adoption of Directive 93/13/EEC. The notion of good faith can no longer be determined purely by reference to English law alone, but must also take into account Community law.[312] Therefore, it is likely that, in time, the ECJ will have its say on how the notion of good faith should be understood and whether it has a meaning distinct from the imbalance test. The House of Lords is well aware of the Community influence on UK contract law and has explicitly confirmed that – at least in theory – a contract term may be unfair purely as a matter of substance.[313]

The civil law concept of good faith requires a consideration of the variety of ways in which one party may abuse a society's notion of how promises are to be made and kept.[314] Such abuse may involve *taking advantage* of another's trust either by encouraging misplaced

[308] Steyn, 'The Role of Good Faith', 131 at 136, who underlines that the then proposed Directive did not create a duty of good faith in the performance of contracts.

[309] G. Howells and S. Weatherill, *European Consumer Law* (Dartmouth, 1995), 324; E. Burroughs, 'The Seller Is Not Liable for' (1995) 145 *New Law Journal* 1368.

[310] Bragg, 'Implementation of the EC Directive', 33; M. Dean, 'Consolidation or Confusion? – The EC Directive on Unfair Contract Terms' (1995) 145 *New Law Journal* 31.

[311] In the same sense, see Dean, 'Unfair Contract Terms', 584.

[312] Howells and Weatherill, *European Consumer Law*, 325; Bragg, 'Implementation of the EC Directive', 33; as the Directive is very similar to the German Standard Contracts Law (AGBG), the German approach might serve as an interpretation aid.

[313] *Director-General of Fair Trading* v. *First National Bank plc* [2001] 3 WLR 1297; [2002] All ER 97, para. 17 *per* Lord Bingham and, even more clearly, para. 36 *per* Lord Steyn.

[314] Collins, 'Good Faith', 250.

reliance or by securing an unduly advantageous transaction[315] (this is the language of Lord Bingham in *Director-General of Fair Trading* v. *First National Bank plc*). It differs from a good faith test, in which a supplier is encouraged to take into account and respect the *legitimate interests of the consumer*[316] (this is the language of the Directive in Recital 16).[317] The civil law understanding of good faith should enrich the debate in the UK, although concern has been expressed that the civil law concept of good faith does not fit in well with the UK's legal and cultural traditions.[318]

In addition to Schedule 2, further factors may be taken into consideration to give a clearer definition of the notion of good faith in order to comply with the notion of good faith in Community law. The Directive provides, in its Annex, for an indicative list of clauses which are presumed to be unfair. The legal value of the list has recently been boosted by the ECJ in *Océano*.[319] In that case, the ECJ had little difficulty in taking the indicative list as a yardstick to determine the validity of jurisdiction clauses, and this decision has effectively ended the debate over the legal quality of the indicative list.[320] The UTCCR's indicative list may therefore be presumed to have full legal validity.[321] The nature of certain types of contract term might be such that it is obvious that the term is contrary to the requirement of good faith, for example terms excluding or limiting liability for personal injury or death.[322] Last but not least, the transparency requirement should also enrich the concept of good faith, as it covers not only procedural fairness but also substantive fairness. A non-transparent contract term may be unfair simply because no meaning can be given to a term which

[315] *Ibid.*, 250. [316] Willett, 'The Directive on Unfair Terms', 223 at 232.

[317] For a possible conflict between the two, see E. Macdonald, 'Scope and Fairness of the Unfair Terms in Consumer Contracts Regulations: Director-General of Fair Trading v. First National Bank' (2002) 65 *Modern Law Review* 763 at 769.

[318] G. Teubner, 'Legal Irritants: Good Faith in British Law or How Unifying Law Ends Up in New Divergences' (1998) 61 *Modern Law Review* 11.

[319] Stuyck, 'Judgment of 27 June 2000 Joined Cases C-240/98 to C-244/96', 719; and S. Whittaker, 'Judicial Interventionism and Consumer Contracts' (2001) 117 *Law Quarterly Review* 215.

[320] N. Reich and H.-W. Micklitz, *Europäisches Verbraucherrecht* (4th edn, Baden-Baden, 2003), 519–22.

[321] Terms giving the seller or supplier rights or remedies against the consumer, which the consumer does not have against the seller or supplier (paras. (c), (d) and (f)); terms imposing penalties (para. (e)); and terms binding consumers to other terms which they have not seen (para. (i)): Willett, 'The Directive on Unfair Terms', 223 at 233.

[322] *Ibid.*, 233.

is not expressly written down in the contract. In this, the transparency principle reaches beyond procedural rules and has an impact on the substance of the contract.[323] The standard to be applied is that of the average consumer.[324] However, the question of whether a certain term satisfies the good faith requirement can only be answered if an overall assessment is made of, for instance, whether the lack of equal bargaining power can be outweighed by the fact that the consumer had a real choice of terms.[325]

The formal aspects of contract control: procedural aspects of good faith and transparency

There is a view that the bargaining process leading up to the contract is at the heart of the procedural aspect of good faith. Such an understanding comes close to the principle of open and fair dealing under the common law.[326] Such an understanding would, however, come as a surprise to a civil law lawyer, because the latter would clearly distinguish the process of incorporation from content control. Good faith is seen as an essential part of content control. Incorporation and the rules which govern the inclusion of contract terms are not considered as part of a test of good faith. The background to such an understanding may be found in the limited role that the incorporation test plays in the overall concept of controlling unfair terms. Civil law puts an emphasis on the control of the substance of the contract, and devotes much less attention to the question of whether the terms in question have been incorporated into the contract. Common law had to rely on the incorporation test as a primary means of eliminating unfair terms. That is why the so-called procedural aspects of good faith are very much in line with common law thinking. In a way, the understanding of good faith typically reflects common law traditions and cultures.

Further uncertainty arises out of the role of the transparency principle and its interrelationship with the procedural aspects of good faith.

323 For a more in-depth analysis, see F. Brunetta d'Usseaux, 'Formal and Substantive Aspects of the Transparency Principle in European Private Law' (1997) 5 *Consumer Law Journal* 231.

324 In *Director-General of Fair Trading* v. *First National Bank plc* [2001] 3 WLR 1297; [2002] All ER 97, Lord Bingham does not really discuss the issue; however, he does state that 'in judging the fairness of the term it is necessary to consider the position of typical parties when the contract is made' (*ibid.*, para. 20).

325 Regulation 4(2) of the UTCCR 1994.

326 *Director-General of Fair Trading* v. *First National Bank plc* [2001] 3 WLR 1297; [2002] All ER 97, para. 20 *per* Lord Bingham.

The transparency principle is enshrined in Articles 4(2) and 5 of Directive 93/13/EEC.[327] However, there is no judicial remedy provided to enforce transparency.[328] That is why the transparency principle may gain legal efficacy only in combination with the principle of good faith. In other words, obscure and opaque contract terms may be determined to be contrary to good faith, and thus be regarded as unfair. In Germany, the transparency principle has become a fallback position which the courts may use to declare terms void. In the recently revised German Civil Code, the transparency principle has been given a formal legal status in Article 307(1)(2).[329] However, if the supplier clearly and fully informs the consumer, and if no express provision in the law provides otherwise, the term may very well be legal and effective. The UK had to face the challenge of how to incorporate the transparency principle into the control of unfair terms and how to link it legally to the notion of good faith. In the view of the present author, the UTCCR do not provide a sufficient means of incorporating the transparency principle into English law. This has been done, if at all, by the enforcement activities of the Office of Fair Trading.[330]

The UTCCR are very much in line with Articles 4(2) and 5 of the Directive. Therefore, in essence, the UTCCR do not contain any direct link between the transparency principle and the notion of fairness – here understood as covering imbalance and good faith. However, transparency appears indirectly at two different levels, and under two different circumstances. Regulation 3 of the UTCCR 1994 defines the terms to which the Regulations apply. Regulation 3(2) exempts what may be termed 'core terms' from the scope of application 'in so far as it [the core term] is in plain, intelligible language'. The provision reflects Article 4(2) of the Directive. Neither the Directive nor regulation 3(2) provides specific guidance on what to do with terms which do

[327] For a discussion of the transparency principle in a European context, see H.-W. Micklitz, 'Obligation of Clarity and Favourable Interpretation to the Consumer (Art. 5)' in European Commission (ed.), *The 'Unfair Terms Directive', Five Years On – Evaluation and Analysis* (Brussels, 2000), 147–59.

[328] There has been little discussion of whether the transparency principle must be understood as a right given to consumers in the sense of the *Francovich* doctrine; see, however, Beale, 'Legislative Control of Fairness' in Beatson and Friedman, *Good Faith*, 242 at 247, who discusses the lack of remedies.

[329] The UK may well follow suit if the Law Commissions' ideas find support.

[330] See the enlightening comment by P. Gurowich, 'Comment' in Micklitz, 'Obligation of Clarity and Favourable Interpretation' in European Commission (ed.), *The 'Unfair Terms Directive'*, 147 at 156.

not meet the 'plain, intelligible language' requirement. The 'plain, intelligible language' requirement in regulation 3(2) must be read with regulation 6, although the latter regulation operates in a quite different context. The heading of regulation 6, 'Construction of written contracts', is critical here. Taken literally, regulation 6 does not deal with the control of the content of the contract. Instead, it has to be understood as a more developed version of the well-known 'construction rule' which is used by the courts to eliminate exclusion and limitation clauses.[331] Any written term of a contract has to be expressed in plain, intelligible language, and, if there is doubt about the meaning of a term, the interpretation which is the most favourable to the consumer shall prevail. The problem with the 'plain, intelligible language' requirement, however, is that no yardstick exists by which to judge the plainness and the intelligibility of the language used. The same is true for the construction rule. What, therefore, is the 'most favourable' interpretation? Unlike the traditional *contra proferentem* rule, the most favourable interpretation might not always be the one that makes the term more favourable to the consumer. A term may be made more favourable to the consumer and yet still be prejudicial to him.[332]

Splitting good faith into procedural and substantive aspects necessarily results in conflating procedural aspects of good faith with the transparency principle. This need not be a problem as long as objective standards are applied. One may wonder whether the procedural aspects of the good faith principle when combined with the transparency rule represent the true strength of Directive 93/13/EEC by leading to a diffusion of consumer contract law principles into commercial law.[333]

The preventive control of unfair terms

The UTCCR increased the amount of substantive law governing the relationship between the consumer and the supplier. The UTCCR contain substantive provisions protecting the consumer against unfair standard terms and declaring unfair terms void and therefore non-binding on the consumer. But there is more in the UTCCR than these basic protective terms.[334] The UTCCR also provide for an injunction as

[331] See pp. 309–14 above. [332] Willett, 'The Directive on Unfair Terms', 223 at 231.

[333] Brownsword, Howells and Wilhelmsson, 'Between Market and Welfare' in Willett (ed.), *Aspects of Fairness*, 25 at 58.

[334] Sobich, 'Verfahrensrechtliche Kontrolle', 684.

a means of controlling unfair terms in order to ensure the effectiveness of the substantive provisions of the UTCCR. This element of control is a considerable improvement on the previous situation, but there is controversy over whether these control provisions in the UTCCR fully meet the requirements of the Directive.

This means of control was first provided for in regulation 8 of the UTCCR 1994. Regulation 8 was based on Article 7 of Directive 93/13/EEC. Article 7 requires Member States to adopt 'adequate and effective means . . . to prevent the continued use of unfair terms'.[335] Article 7 goes on to say that the means chosen by the Member States 'shall include provisions whereby persons or organisations, having a legitimate interest under national law in protecting consumers, may take action according to the national law concerned before the courts or before competent administrative bodies for a decision as to whether contractual terms drawn up for general use are unfair, so that they can apply appropriate and effective means to prevent the continued use of such terms'. Originally, the Department of Trade and Industry had argued that no new legislation was necessary in order to implement Article 7 of the Directive as domestic law already guaranteed that unfair terms were not enforceable against the consumer.[336] After protests on the part of several consumer organisations, regulation 8 was included in the UTCCR 1994 as a means of implementing Article 7.

The UTCCR empower the Director-General of Fair Trading (the head of the Office of Fair Trading) with the general duty of controlling unfair terms. The post of Director-General has been in existence since the Fair Trading Act 1973 came into force. The Director-General's main duty consists in establishing a fair balance between the interests of commerce and those of consumers. Regulation 8 of the UTCCR 1994 obliged the Director-General to consider any complaint made to him that a contract term drawn up for general use was unfair, unless the complaint appeared to be frivolous or vexatious. The UTCCR do not provide any definition of what is to be considered as 'frivolous or vexatious'. What seems to be clear, however, is that there is no distinction

[335] Although the Directive allowed the Member States to choose between a legal procedure and an administrative one, all the Member States, including the UK, opted for a legal procedure.

[336] Department of Trade and Industry, 'Implementation of the EC Directive on Unfair Terms in Consumer Contracts (93/13/EEC): A Consultation Document' (October 1993).

to be drawn between different complainants so that even a non-party to the contract could complain.[337] Therefore, a complaint could be made by individual consumers, private consumer organisations, public consumer organisations, and even competitors of the supplier.[338] This kind of action was entirely novel to English law, and ran counter to the doctrine of privity of contract.[339] However, as is clearly evident from the language of the UTCCR 1994, the Director-General *cannot act on his own initiative*. He must wait for a complaint.[340] The Director-General therefore is nothing more than a long arm of the complainant.[341]

If the Director-General considers a term to be unfair, he may, according to regulation 8(2) of the UTCCR 1994, bring proceedings for an injunction against any person appearing to him to be using or recommending the use of this term in contracts concluded with consumers. An injunction can be brought against anyone, such as a trade association, who is recommending the use of the unfair terms.[342] Regulation 8(2) also permits the Director-General to apply for an interlocutory injunction. As is evident from the language of regulation 8, the initiation of proceedings for injunctive relief is within the *discretion* of the Director-General, and is therefore not an *obligation*. The only obligation on the Director-General is to *consider* any complaint brought to him. For years, the Director-General refrained from seeking injunctions. According to regulation 8(3) of the UTCCR 1994, the Director-General may, if he considers it appropriate, have regard to any undertakings given to him as to the continued use of such a term in consumer contracts. This provision can therefore be understood as not *requiring* formal legal action.[343] However, there are no direct legal consequences where such an undertaking is violated. The only available redress for the Director-General seems to be for the Director-General to begin formal legal proceedings. Regulation 8(3) of the UTCCR 1994 thus permitted an element of flexibility and

337 Sobich, 'Verfahrensrechtliche Kontrolle', 684 at 685.

338 To date, apart from consumers themselves, local authority trading standards departments have been the main source of the complaints that have been received; see Miller, Harvey and Parry, *Consumer and Trading Law*, 379.

339 Dean, 'Unfair Contract Terms', 590. However, the law has been changed in the meanwhile and the privity doctrine no longer applies.

340 H. Wilkinson, 'Unfair Contract Terms – Hydra-Headed Monsters' (1999) 149 *New Law Journal* 773.

341 Sobich, 'Verfahrensrechtliche Kontrolle', 684 at 685.

342 Miller, Harvey and Parry, *Consumer and Trading Law*, 380.

343 Sobich, 'Verfahrensrechtliche Kontrolle', 684 at 685.

compromise in the approach of the Director-General to the enforcement of the provisions of the UTCCR.[344]

If the Director-General decided to bring formal legal proceedings, he had to give reasons for doing so, under regulation 8(4) of the UTCCR 1994. The purpose of this provision was to ensure transparency of the control mechanism. Regulation 8(4) thus enabled a complainant to seek judicial review of a negative decision by the Director-General concerning his enforcement of the legislation. The UTCCR 1994 did not explicitly provide for such a judicial review, but the Office of Fair Trading recognises such a possibility. However, as judicial review is granted in respect of every decision of an administrative body, it cannot be considered as an effective means of control within the meaning of Directive 93/13/EEC.[345] The court is not bound to follow the Director-General's opinion ('*may* grant an injunction on such terms as it thinks fit'), and may also, according to regulation 8(6), apply the injunction to similar terms. Last but not least, regulation 8(7) permitted the Director-General to 'arrange for the dissemination in such form and manner as he considers appropriate of such information and advice concerning the operation of these Regulations as may appear to him to be expedient to give to the public and to all persons likely to be affected by these Regulations'. Due to the high profile in consumer affairs of the Office of Fair Trading, such publication may have a greater impact on a company than a court's decision. The UTCCR 1994 did not confer on consumer organisations any right to take action in their own name. Consumer organisations only had the right to collect consumer complaints and send them to the Office of Fair Trading. There is no representative action in the UK.[346]

The Unfair Terms in Consumer Contracts Regulations 1999

Consumer organisations were not given a right under the UTCCR 1994 to take action directly in the courts. The consumer organisations argued that the Directive specifically gave such organisations a right to take action, and that consequently the UK government had failed to fully implement the terms of the Directive. Article 7 of the Directive states that 'adequate and effective means' should 'include provisions whereby persons or organisations, having a legitimate interest under national law in protecting consumers, may take action ... for a

[344] Beale, 'Legislative Control of Fairness' in Beatson and Friedman, *Good Faith*, 252.
[345] Sobich, 'Verfahrensrechtliche Kontrolle' 684 at 685.
[346] Dean, 'Unfair Contract Terms', 589.

decision as to whether contractual terms drawn up for general use are unfair'. It was this provision which consumer organisations alleged the government had failed to implement fully.[347] They initiated proceedings in the national courts, and convinced the High Court to refer the question to the ECJ. However, before the ECJ heard the case, the newly elected Labour government announced an amendment to the UTCCR 1994 in order to deal with the concerns raised. On 1 October 1999, the UTCCR 1999 came into force, replacing the original UTCCR 1994. The UTCCR 1999 are largely identical to the UTCCR 1994, but follow the language of the Directive more closely and grant various statutory bodies and the Consumers' Association (the leading non-governmental organisation in the field of consumer protection in the UK) the right to bring formal legal proceedings.

The bodies empowered to enforce the UTCCR 1999

The most important change arising from the UTCCR 1999 is the introduction of the notion of 'qualifying bodies' listed in Schedule 1 to the UTCCR 1999. The UTCCR 1999 considerably enlarges the number of persons able to control standard terms. These include the Data Protection Registrar, the Rail Regulator and the various Directors-General responsible for regulating the supply of gas, electricity, water and telecommunications. The UTCCR 1999 empower these qualifying bodies, when considering complaints, to apply for injunctions in appropriate cases and to demand copies of standard form contracts and other information relating to their use. The Consumers' Association is also included as a qualifying body. According to regulation 12, the qualifying bodies have the same powers as the Director-General of Fair Trading in seeking an injunction. However, the powers of the qualifying bodies are to some extent dependent on the Director-General. The qualifying bodies must notify the Director-General of any intention to apply for an injunction.[348] Even if they do not *need*

[347] The Consumers' Association sought to have the exclusion of bodies such as itself declared unlawful in *R.* v. *Secretary of State for Trade and Industry, ex parte Consumers' Association and Which?*, Judgment of 28 February 1996, High Court, unreported (available on Lexis); other bodies addressed the question to the European Commission of whether local authorities and local courts should have enforcement powers (E-2827/95 WQ, 96/C 40/98).

[348] The same idea is behind the UK's proposal to implement Directive 98/27/EC on injunctions into EC law: see P. Rott, 'Injunctions for the Protection of Consumers' Interests after the Implementation of Directive 98/27/EC into German and English Law' (2001) 24 *Journal of Consumer Policy* 401.

the Director-General's permission to act, this requirement nevertheless effectively restricts their power. The number of qualifying bodies empowered to act for the benefit of consumers has certainly been increased. However, the reform should be nothing more than a first step to a wider reform. Because UK law does not recognise a representative action, the restrictions on the power of the qualifying bodies to seek an injunction were probably a political necessity.

There are two further substantive changes in the UTCCR 1999. Regulation 13 confers upon the Director-General and the qualifying bodies the right to request disclosure of documents in order to assist them in determining the validity of a complaint. This right, however, cannot be used to compel a person to supply any document or information which the person would be entitled to refuse to disclose in civil proceedings before a court. Last but not least, the UTCCR 1999 enlarged the Director-General's power of publication. Regulation 8(7) of the UTCCR 1994 gave the Director-General a *discretion* to publish certain information; regulation 15(1) of the UTCCR 1999 now *obliges* the Director-General to publish certain information. Regulation 15(2) now requires the Director-General on request, to supply certain information to members of the public. This power of publication is given only to the Director-General, not to the qualifying bodies.

Changes on the substantive level

The scope of application *sedes materiae* of the UTCCR 1999 remains the same as in the UTCCR 1994, in that they both apply to unfair terms in contracts concluded between a seller or a supplier and a consumer. However, the scope of application *sedes personae* has been changed. The UTCCR 1999 broaden the definition of consumers and suppliers. The UTCCR 1994 only applied to a consumer acting outside his or her business. The UTCCR 1999 defines a 'consumer' as 'any natural person who, in contracts covered by these Regulations, is acting for purposes which are outside his trade, business or profession'. The UTCCR 1999 defines a 'seller or supplier' as 'any natural or legal person who, in contracts covered by these Regulations, is acting for purposes relating to his trade, business or profession, whether publicly owned or privately owned'. The definition is thus much more precise in comparison to the UTCCR 1994, which did not, in relation to a seller or supplier, specify the category of person but simply referred to 'person' and did not make any distinction between trade, business and profession nor between the type of business.

The UTCCR 1994 were not subject to extensive litigation. It is commonly assumed that the qualifying bodies will, following the practice of the Office of Fair Trading, seek to negotiate informal resolutions to disputes and will co-operate with the Director-General to ensure that businesses do not face multiple or repeated approaches on the same or related issues.

The conformity of the UTCCR 1994 and 1999 with the Directive

The UK restricted the UTCCR 1994 to contracts concerning 'goods and services'. Other Member States, however, adopted a broader approach by including *all* consumer contracts.[349] The UTCCR 1994 led to unnecessary complications in its applicability to contracts concerning land. The term 'goods' does not necessarily include the sale of immovable property. The UTCCR 1999 resolved this issue by providing that the Regulations cover *all* consumer contracts, including those relating to land.[350] Certain types of contracts, for example, contracts of employment, were expressly excluded from the UTCCR 1994, and from the Directive.[351] There was, however, felt to be no need to re-enact these exclusions, as these contracts are of a type that cannot inherently be concluded between a seller/supplier and a consumer.

There is a slight difference between the Directive and the UTCCR regarding the definition of a consumer. The UTCCR 1994 defined a 'consumer' as a 'natural person . . . who is acting for purposes which are outside his business'. This could be considered to be a broader notion than that in the Directive, which defines a 'consumer' as a person who is acting not only for purposes outside his business, but also for purposes outside his trade or profession. Therefore, a wider range of buyers were covered by the UTCCR 1994 than by the Directive. The notion of consumer differs from that in the UCTA. The UTCCR 1994 reflected the Community law viewpoint that businesspersons are well

[349] Bright, 'Winning the Battle', 331 at 339.

[350] The Regulatory Impact Assessment states: 'This is intended to remove any uncertainty that, to the extent that the Directive applies to contracts to land, including leasehold and tenancy agreements and licenses, the Regulations also apply to such contracts' (22 July 1999). See also Bright, 'Winning the Battle', 331 at 341.

[351] Contracts relating to employment, succession rights, rights under family law, incorporation and organisation of companies or partnership agreements. However, these contracts might be covered by the UCTA, as was recently the case with an employment contract that qualified as a consumer contract: cf. *Brigden* v. *American Express Bank Ltd* [2000] IRLR 94.

able to look after their own interests, whatever the type of transaction.[352] The reason why the UTCCR 1994 did not implement the Directive's definition of a consumer verbatim probably derives from the fact that English law traditionally did not make a distinction between the protection of consumers and businesspersons.[353] In certain circumstances, a company is capable of being a consumer.[354] By contrast, the UTCCR 1999 more closely reflects the wording of the Directive. These and other amendments were intended to bring the definitions much more into line with those in the Directive.

Last but not least, the question has been raised as to whether the non-implementation of Article 5[355] conforms with the Directive.[356] In *Commission* v. *Netherlands*,[357] the ECJ answered this question in the affirmative. Therefore, the Law Commissions' proposals to enshrine the transparency principle in new legislation is in reality nothing more than an implementation of existing EC law.[358]

The concept of good faith as understood by the Office of Fair Trading

The Office of Fair Trading

The Director-General of Fair Trading has the power to publish information relating to the UTCCR and the work of the OFT. He does so regularly by publishing 'Bulletins'. This task of information-dissemination is considered by the OFT[359] to be one of its most

352 Judgment of 14 March 1991, Case C-361/89, *Ministere Public* v. *Patrice Di Pinto* [1991] ECR I-1206.

353 See, for example, *R&B Customs Brokers Co. Ltd* v. *United Dominion Trust Ltd* [1988] 1 All ER 847, in which the Court of Appeal interpreted the UCTA as giving protection to companies where the transaction in question was not entered into in the course of their regular business.

354 Dean, 'Consolidation or Confusion?', 29.

355 Art. 5 provides: 'In the case of contracts where all or certain terms offered to the consumer are in writing, these terms must always be drafted in plain, intelligible language. Where there is doubt about the meaning of a term, the interpretation most favourable to the consumer shall prevail.'

356 Beale, 'Legislative Control of Fairness' in Beatson and Friedman, *Good Faith*, 247.

357 Judgment of 10 May 2001, Case C-144/99, *Commission* v. *Netherlands* [2001] ECR I-3541.

358 Law Commissions' Joint Consultation Paper, 'Unfair Terms in Contracts', 48–50 and 95.

359 Office of Fair Trading, Unfair Contract Terms, Bulletin No. 1, May 1996, 1.

important functions. These publications provide considerable scope for an analysis of how and when the OFT exercises its powers of control. The extent to which the OFT became involved in the control of unfair terms came as a surprise to commentators. The threat of consumer organisations insisting on being granted *locus standi* might have helped to push the OFT into greater efforts than it otherwise would have done, although in practice consumer organisations are not making much use of their new rights.

It must be recalled that the Director-General cannot determine categorically whether a term is unfair. Only the High Court has such authority. While the OFT mainly seeks voluntary change,[360] it has frequently made clear to suppliers its willingness to take court action. Thus, voluntary agreements dominate the OFT's administrative practice. However, when undertakings are given, formal or otherwise, the OFT makes clear to the supplier that revised contracts and terms are not immune from further action.[361]

The risks and challenges in the interpretation of the notion of good faith

When in 1995 the OFT first became empowered to control *standard* contract terms under the UTCCR, it had only little, general guidance on how to apply the UTCCR.[362] It therefore had to develop its own policy, which it then set out in its publications. The basic approach of the policy quickly became clear: the decision as to whether a standard term in a contract will be regarded as unfair within the meaning of regulation 4 depends on the answers to two questions. First, does the term create a significant imbalance in the parties' rights and obligations under the contract, to the detriment of the consumer, that is, do the terms of the contract unduly weigh the contract against the consumer and in favour of the business?[363] Secondly, if there is such an imbalance, does that imbalance amount to a breach of the requirement of good faith?[364] The UTCCR refer to the nature of the goods and services which are the

360 *Ibid.*, point 1.8, 6.

361 Office of Fair Trading, Unfair Contract Terms, Bulletin No. 6, April 1999.

362 Office of Fair Trading, Briefing, July 1995.

363 *Ibid.*, 2. Regulation 4 provides: '[An] "unfair term" means any term which contrary to the requirement of good faith causes a significant imbalance in the parties' rights and obligations under the contract to the detriment of the consumer.'

364 Office of Fair Trading, Briefing, July 1995, 2.

subject of the contract, to all the other terms of the contract (including core terms) and to all the circumstances attending the making of the contract.[365] From the outset, the relationship between 'the good faith test' in regulation 4 of the UTCCR 1994 and the requirement that standard terms must be written in plain and intelligible language in regulation 3(2) of the UTCCR 1994[366] raised concerns in the OFT. Although the plain and intelligible language requirement is not directly linked to the fairness test, the OFT considered that the fairness test was much more likely to be met if the contract was written in plain and intelligible language.[367] A contract which is printed in a typeface which is too small to read, or is worded in a manner which is convoluted or unnecessarily legalistic, is more likely to fail to meet the requirement of good faith.[368]

There is an obvious tendency in the OFT briefing papers to link the UTCCR 1994 to the already existing legislation on the control of unfair terms. This is particularly true with regard to Schedule 2 to the UTCCR 1994, which provided guidance on what was meant by the requirement of good faith. Similar criteria are set out in the UCTA,[369] and the similarity between the two sets of criteria may be a result of the UK government's input into the negotiations of the Directive. Thus, the OFT has, by a circuitous route, been given powers under the UCTA. Difficulties may arise, however, if the OFT were to attempt to introduce the good faith requirement into the control of contracts under common law. Under Schedule 2 to the UTCCR 1994, a supplier would be able to avoid an assessment of unfairness by showing that he had acted in good faith by disclosing all the contract terms in full and explaining their effect clearly.[370] This provision in Schedule 2 might be read so as to bar the introduction of 'bad faith' as an element of the fairness test. However, six months after the UTCCR 1994 came into force, the OFT said in an interview that it would take into account the good faith of the supplier. 'Good faith' here is regarded as the fair-mindedness and reasonableness of the supplier.[371] Such an understanding seems to be subjective (that is, relating to the conscience of the supplier) rather than objective (that is, relating only to the wording of the contract). According to the OFT, fair-mindedness and reasonableness should be

[365] *Ibid.*, 2. [366] *Ibid.*, 2. [367] The rule in question is regulation 6. [368] *Ibid.*

[369] Sections 11(2) and 24(2) of the UCTA. [370] Schedule 2 to the UTCCR 1994.

[371] Schedule 2, para. (d), refers to the 'extent to which the supplier has dealt fairly and equitably with the consumer'.

evident in standard contract terms.[372] These rather broad statements might imply a lot of things, in between a certain subjectivity towards the good faith test which complies all too well with the English control system on unfair terms. The absence of bad faith or the existence of good faith might be an issue in negotiations between the OFT and suppliers in reaching amicable resolutions of disputes.

The temptation to revert back to common law standards is counterbalanced by the dominant role of the indicative list in Schedule 3 to the UTCCR 1994 as a yardstick to measure fairness in consumer contracts. In theory, the list is not a blacklist. No term will be considered unfair simply because it is listed therein. Fairness depends on an assessment of good faith, and all the particular facts of each case are taken into account.[373] The ECJ found no difficulty in understanding paragraph 1(q)[374] of the Annex to the Directive – the so-called jurisdiction clause – as prohibiting any contract term which excludes or hinders the consumer's right to take legal action.[375] However, the ECJ left room for divergent decisions by its 'so far as possible' formula. That is why the UK approach and the ECJ's approach seem to be on the same wavelength with regard to their line of arguments.[376]

Some of the terms listed in Schedule 3 to the UTCCR 1994 and in the Annex to the Directive, particularly those concerning 'hidden terms'[377] and 'general variation clauses',[378] are claimed to be of particular importance to the notion of good faith. Again, such an understanding can be viewed as an attempt to build a bridge between existing UK law and the novel elements of the UTCCR 1994 by combining substantive and procedural aspects of fairness. 'Hidden terms' refers to terms with which a party had no real opportunity of becoming acquainted before the conclusion of the contract.[379] For example, a consumer may sign

[372] R. Watson, 'Six Months On: Unfair Contract Terms at Work' (1995/1996) 12 *Fair Trading* 14.

[373] Office of Fair Trading, Briefing, July 1995, 4.

[374] A term may be considered unfair if it 'exclud[es] or hinder[s] the consumer's right to take legal action or exercise any other legal remedy, particularly by requiring the consumer to take disputes exclusively to arbitration not covered by legal provisions, unduly restricting the evidence available to him or imposing on him a burden of proof which, according to the applicable law, should lie with another party to the contract'.

[375] Stuyck, 'Judgment of 27 June 2000 Joined Cases C-240/98 to C-244/96', 719.

[376] For further details, see pp. 418–23 below.

[377] Schedule 3, para. 1(i), to the UTCCR 1994; para. 1(i) of the Annex to the Directive.

[378] Schedule 3, para. 1(j), to the UTCCR 1994; para. 1(j) of the Annex to the Directive.

[379] Office of Fair Trading, Briefing, July 1995, 6.

a document which on its face refers to a second document, which is therefore incorporated by reference into the contract but which the consumer has no opportunity to read. The terms in this second document are 'hidden'. A term that is badly or obscurely drafted does not fall within the rule because it does not purport to bind the consumer to a term the contents of which he is not aware of. The objection to obscurely drafted terms is based on a lack of good faith,[380] but is analogous to the rule on hidden terms. 'General variation clauses' enable the supplier to alter the terms of the contract unilaterally without a valid reason specified in the contract.[381] Existing UK legislation assumes this general variation clause is relevant and permissible mainly in the context of contracts for services. If such a variation clause is found in a contract for the supply of goods, it will be void under the Sale of Goods Act 1979 and the UCTA.[382] Under section 3 of the UCTA, any term which purports to entitle the supplier to render a contractual performance substantially different from that which was reasonably expected of him is void 'except in so far as it satisfies the requirement of reasonableness'.

The application of the good faith test by the Office of Fair Trading

In its first bulletin, published almost one year after assuming its responsibility for the control of standard contract terms, the OFT gave some examples of contract terms which comply with the requirement of good faith. Those suppliers who use plain, intelligible language, who disclose and explain the terms to consumers, or who trade according to benchmarks of good industry practice, including codes of practice, may be more confident that they are acting in good faith towards consumers.[383] While a clear and proper explanation of contract terms, done in advance of signing the contract, complies with the requirement of good faith, the use of small print on the back of the receipt may not, and usually does not, comply with the requirement of good faith.[384]

Terms considered unfair by the OFT and therefore not in accordance with the notion of good faith are listed below.[385] All of these terms can also be found in the indicative list in Schedule 3 to the UTCCR 1994,

[380] *Ibid.*, 6. [381] *Ibid.*, 6. [382] *Ibid.*, 6.
[383] Office of Fair Trading, Unfair Contract Terms, Bulletin No. 1, May 1996, 6, point 1.6.
[384] *Ibid.*, 8–9, point 1.17. [385] Terms cited in *ibid.*, 9, point 1.18.

and this clearly indicates that the OFT used the Schedule 3 list in order to determine unfairness:

(1) entire agreement clauses: these exclude from the contract anything said or promised by a salesman or agent of the company;
(2) hidden clauses, as noted above;
(3) penalty clauses: these penalise consumers, for example by permitting a company to retain deposits, with no counterbalancing penalties for the company if it does not comply with its obligations;
(4) exclusion clauses: particularly those excluding liability for every possible eventuality; and
(5) variation clauses.

In its first bulletin, the OFT devoted particular attention to 'entire agreement clauses'. Under common law, the situations covered by this type of clause would probably be dealt with using the concepts of misrepresentation, mistake or promissory estoppel, depending on the circumstances of the case. The OFT views the use of 'entire agreement clauses' as an indicator of a failure to comply with the requirement of good faith. However, it 'would . . . permit a trader to disregard a reasonable promise made on his behalf in good faith, such as a delivery date, when it becomes inconvenient'.[386] What is remarkable about the OFT's statement concerning entire agreement clauses is that, when examining whether a term should be regarded as unfair, the OFT emphasises the potential effect of the clause not the intention behind it.[387] The OFT does not consider the supplier's argument that he did not intend to use clauses in an abusive way to be a valid reason for permitting their use. Protection for the consumer cannot rely on a trader's good intentions.[388] This view is based on the words of Schedule 2 to the UTCCR 1999 which lists terms 'which have the object or effect of . . . '. The use of the words 'or effect' indicates that a term may be unfair even if it was not the 'object' or intention of the trader to abuse it. It seems fair to say that the OFT takes an objective approach to the term, and thus does not confine itself merely to the procedural control of unfair terms.[389] However, entire agreement clauses are not viewed as automatically unfair.[390] If the supplier respects all the criteria in

[386] *Ibid.*, 16, point 2.5. [387] *Ibid.*, 16, point 2.6. [388] *Ibid.*, 16, point 2.6.
[389] H. Collins, 'Unfair Contract Terms in the UK' (1996) 81 *Svensk Jurist Tidning* 1.
[390] Office of Fair Trading, Unfair Contract Terms, Bulletin No. 1, May 1996, 16, point 2.6.

Schedule 3 to the UTCCR 1999, the supplier may benefit from the fact that the list is merely *indicative*.[391] Good faith is seen as a means of correcting inflexibility in the terms of the contract. Entire agreement clauses create a certain inflexibility, and for this reason alone they may violate the notion of good faith. Entire agreement clauses effectively prevent a consumer from negotiating favourable changes to standard terms. If entire agreement clauses were considered invalid, then this would allow the consumer to negotiate more favourable terms, and this would, in turn, make it more likely that the contract would meet the requirement of good faith.[392] According to the OFT, entire agreement clauses are also objectionable because they purport to deprive the consumer of rights he or she may in fact validly rely on,[393] and this is incompatible with the requirement of good faith under the Schedule to the UTCCR.

In the case report section of the bulletin, the OFT illustrates how the criteria in the Schedules to the UTCCR are applied.[394] However, the OFT does not explain in detail why it considers various different clauses to be unfair. However, it is clear from the cases reported in the bulletins that the OFT pays particular attention to the question of plain and intelligible language and to whether or not the consumer had a chance to examine the standard contract terms before entering into the contract. If this has not been done, then the OFT will consider the clause to be unfair.[395] The plain and intelligible language criterion is the criterion the OFT most often uses to determine whether a term is unfair. In only a few cases has the general unfairness test set out in regulation 4 of the UTCCR 1994 been specifically referred to.[396]

By the time the second bulletin was published, in September 1996, the OFT had dealt with 873 cases. The second bulletin also mainly dealt with the requirement of plain and intelligible language as an element of good faith, and it is clear that this had become the OFT's favourite criterion in examining the unfairness of standard contract terms. Although the requirement of plain and intelligible language is specifically set out in regulation 6 of the UTCCR 1994 and regulation 7(1) of the UTCCR 1999, the OFT never expressly invokes either of

[391] *Ibid.*, 17, point 2.9. [392] *Ibid.*, 17, point 2.9. [393] *Ibid.*, 17, point 2.9.

[394] In this first bulletin, twenty-five cases were examined.

[395] For example, *Re Stena Line Ltd*, Office of Fair Trading, Unfair Contract Terms, Bulletin No. 1, May 1996, 28; and *Re Goodalls Caravans Ltd*, *ibid.*, 30 and 31.

[396] For example, *Re Goodalls Caravans Ltd*, *ibid.*, 33; and *Re Falkirk Sunbed, Solarium & Ladies Health Club*, *ibid.*, 37 and 39.

those regulations to justify its decisions.[397] As the OFT says, '[e]ven if the Regulations had contained no specific requirement about plain language, it would clearly have been difficult to maintain that unintelligible or ambiguous terms were not unfair if they had some potential for detriment for the consumer'.[398] The OFT's preference for using the requirement of plain and intelligible language may equally be explained by the fact that, under common law, in order to be enforceable, a term should be capable of being read and understood by the consumer.[399] Regulation 6 is linked in particular to Schedule 3, paragraph 1(i),[400] and, according to the OFT,[401] this indicates the scope of the general requirement of good faith. The OFT recognises that the use of legal jargon and other specialised terms that complicate the language of the contract are often used as a form of shorthand.[402] At the same time, the OFT emphasises the fact that 'brevity is not a specific requirement of the Regulations' and that intelligibility is more important than brevity.[403] The use of plain language, however, forms only part of the requirement of good faith.[404] In assessing good faith, the following criteria are also taken into account: the amount of time a consumer was given to study the terms of the contract; the availability and use, prior to the contract being agreed, of leaflets and brochures providing background information to the consumer; and the availability of a 'cooling-off' period after the consumer has signed the contract in which he or she may cancel the contract without incurring a penalty. Of course, explanatory leaflets and cooling-off periods can never be a substitute for the use of plain and intelligible language.[405] The requirement of plain and intelligible language applies even to core terms.[406] Core terms are those that define the main subject-matter of a contract and the price paid for it, and are usually exempted from the fairness

[397] Regulation 6 provides: 'A seller or supplier shall ensure that any written term of a contract is expressed in plain, intelligible language, and if there is a doubt about the meaning of a written term, the interpretation the most favourable to the consumer shall prevail.'

[398] Office of Fair Trading, Unfair Contract Terms, Bulletin No. 2, September 1996, 8, point 2.3.

[399] *Ibid.*, 8, point 2.3.

[400] '[I]rrevocably binding the consumer to terms with which he had no real opportunity of becoming acquainted before the conclusion of the contract.'

[401] Office of Fair Trading, Unfair Contract Terms, Bulletin No. 2, September 1996, 8, point 2.5.

[402] *Ibid.*, 10, point 2.15. [403] *Ibid.*, 10, point 2.15. [404] *Ibid.*, 12, point 2.21.

[405] *Ibid.*, 13, point 2.24. [406] *Ibid.*, 13, point 2.25.

test,[407] and therefore the fact that the plain and intelligible language requirement is applied to core terms demonstrates the importance of the plain and intelligible language requirement within the notion of good faith.

In the case report section of the second bulletin, the OFT again relied mainly on the indicative list in Schedule 3 to the UTCCR 1994 to determine the unfairness of a standard term. In some cases, the OFT emphasised that the plain and intelligible language requirement is an important part of the requirement of good faith.[408] The plain and intelligible language requirement was the principle invoked most often, by reference either to regulation 4 itself or to Schedule 3, paragraph 1(i). But the notions of a 'cooling-off' period, as well as 'imbalance' and 'bad bargain', were also used to determine that terms were unfair.[409]

In the OFT's third bulletin, published in March 1997, the notion of good faith was less evident. The concept is still crucial, even if it is not expressly referred to quite as often. Now, the OFT does not rely on the notion of good faith as such, but rather invokes its different components. This may be viewed as a typical English approach. The OFT prefers to refer to the notion of *fairness* rather than to the notion of good faith, even though the latter is part of the former.[410] It may therefore be assumed that the terms 'good faith' and 'fairness' refer to the same concept, that is, they are, at least for the OFT, synonymous. However, the OFT's opinion is not very clearly expressed on this point.

In the third bulletin, published in March 1997, the OFT relied substantially on Schedule 3 and its indicative list. In particular, the importance of paragraph 1(b) of Schedule 3, which identifies as potentially unfair those terms which inappropriately exclude or limit the supplier's liability for breach of contract, was stressed. The OFT also refers to other subsections of that paragraph, which together flesh out

[407] Regulation 3(2) provides: 'In so far as it is in plain, intelligible language, no assessment shall be made of the fairness of any term which (a) defines the main subject matter of the contract, or (b) concerns the adequacy of the price or remuneration, as against the goods or services sold or supplied.'

[408] For example, *Re AIG Europe (UK) Ltd*, Office of Fair Trading, Unfair Contract Terms, Bulletin No. 2, September 1996, 16; *Re Connoisseur Cars, ibid.*, 19; *Re David Lloyd Leisure plc, ibid.*, 22; and *Re First Parking Services Ltd, ibid.*, 23.

[409] For example, *Re Neville Johnson Offices Ltd, ibid.*, 27; *Re Buylow Ltd, ibid.*, 17; *Re The Guarantee Guild Ltd, ibid.*, 25.

[410] Regulation 4 (now regulation 5).

the requirement of good faith more precisely. The various different types of terms including the following:

(1) *No liability for unsatisfactory goods or services.* Terms excluding all liability for damage caused by the supplier or seller during their work are likely to be unfair, as they would cover damage which could have been avoided by the exercise of reasonable care.[411] The same is true with regard to terms excluding all liability for *consequential loss.*[412] 'Consequential loss' is a technical term which may mislead consumers into thinking that he has no claim for any loss consequent on a breach of contract by the supplier.[413] 'Consequential loss' in fact covers losses which are *unforeseeable.* Foreseeable loss is covered by law and cannot be excluded without the risk of the term being found to be unfair.
(2) *Restrictions on liability, etc.* Terms which provide that the supplier may impose a charge for remedying defects in products he has supplied are likely to be considered unfair. A business must by law supply goods that are not defective, whether or not it has manufactured them itself.[414] This does not affect the business's right to make charges for remedying defects which are the consumer's fault.[415]
(3) *Unreasonable time limits on claims.* Terms that exclude the supplier's liability for defective products and workmanship where these defects are not brought to the attention of the supplier within a stated period after performance of the contract is completed are potentially unfair.[416] The sanction imposed by such a term is inappropriate and, in some circumstances, illegal.[417]
(4) *Restriction on the right to set-off.* These terms purport to prevent the consumer withholding payment of any sum due to the seller or supplier by reason of any defects. The right of set-off is usually allowed under the law.[418] These terms are therefore potentially unfair.
(5) *Exclusion of liability for delay.* The OFT normally challenges clauses excluding liability for delay, however caused.[419] No objection is normally made, however, to a term which is restricted in scope to delays caused by factors beyond the seller or supplier's control.[420]

411 Office of Fair Trading, Unfair Contract Terms, Bulletin No. 3, March 1997, 8.
412 *Ibid.*, 8. 413 *Ibid.*, 8. 414 *Ibid.*, 9. 415 *Ibid.*, 9. 416 *Ibid.*, 9, point 2.10.
417 *Ibid.*, 10, point 2.12. 418 *Ibid.*, 10, point 2.13. 419 *Ibid.*, 11, point 2.17.
420 *Ibid.*, 11, point 2.17.

In the same bulletin, the OFT also referred again to 'entire agreement clauses'. It proposed alternatives that took into account both the interests of the consumer and those of the supplier, for example a clause that expresses the supplier's (but not the consumer's) intention that written terms should prevail.[421] The proposed wording reminds one of the common law 'parol evidence rule'. Indeed, the OFT confirms that such a term would reinforce the common law presumption in favour of written terms without purporting to make the term conclusive.[422] Another possibility would be a term which permits the consumer to ask for any changes to be put in writing.[423]

Perhaps even more important, and certainly more far-reaching, are the OFT's efforts to give clearer shape to the general fairness test under regulation 4 of the UTCCR 1994 and regulation 5 of the UTCCR 1999. It will be recalled that Schedule 3 to the UTCCR 1994 was an important indicator in determining good faith.[424] However, the OFT went further than simply reciting Schedule 3. It identified the types of terms which, though not listed in Schedule 3, are nevertheless questionable in light of the test of fairness.[425] Such terms include the following:[426]

(1) *Indemnification clauses.* These clauses impose a liability on the consumer which the supplier is better able to bear,[427] for example because he is better able to insure against it, or to control it, or both.[428] The OFT gave the example of a clause that makes the consumer responsible for any damage to materials etc., even when the consumer was not negligent.
(2) *Unfair enforcement clauses.* This type of term gives a company unduly wide powers to enforce its contractual rights.[429] The example given by the OFT was a clause allowing the company, in the event of a delay in payment by a consumer, to enter the consumer's property in order to repossess goods it had supplied. Such a clause creates an imbalance between the parties which would be contrary to the principle of good faith.
(3) *Signed statements.* Many contracts require the consumer to sign a statement to the effect that the consumer has read the contract

[421] *Ibid.*, 17, point 9.5. [422] *Ibid.*, 17, point 9.5. [423] *Ibid.*, 17, point 9.5.
[424] *Ibid.*, 18. [425] *Ibid.*, 18.
[426] It should be noted that, in subsequent Bulletins, the OFT added further categories of unfairness, and generalised the last-mentioned category to cover terms conferring an undue discretion on the supplier as regards performance of the contract.
[427] Office of Fair Trading, Unfair Contract Terms, Bulletin No. 3, March 1997, 18.
[428] *Ibid.*, 18. [429] *Ibid.*, 18.

and associated documents.[430] Such statements are a violation of the principle of fairness, and therefore are of no effect. The OFT instead proposed giving the consumer a warning that he should read the contract. Such a warning not only is likely to be considered fair in itself, but may serve to increase the likelihood of other terms being considered fair.[431]

(4) *Delivery/installation in consignments*. Such a term allows the supplier to deliver and/or install goods in as many or as few consignments as the supplier thinks fit. This creates an imbalance in the contract, which the OFT considers unfair.[432] According to the OFT, such matters as the time and method of delivery should be matters for individual agreement, not a standard term.

As time has passed, the OFT has demonstrated increasing confidence in handling the general fairness test by which the notion of good faith is applied to standard terms. The OFT seems to have a clearer idea of what should be considered as fair. But, reading the bulletins, one cannot escape the feeling that the OFT evaluates terms without reference to good faith. This is not to say that the OFT does not give reasons when it determines that a term is unfair. But it does emphasise the formal test of plain and intelligible language.

In December 1997, the OFT published its fourth bulletin. The bulletin summarised the work done and the results achieved by the OFT since it first started controlling standard terms. The bulletin did not, however, add anything that was substantially new. However, the OFT recapitulated the legislative background of its work. Thus, the OFT talked about its conception of the good faith test. According to the OFT, the requirement of good faith does not equate merely to an absence of bad faith, in the narrow English sense of dishonest or deceptive conduct in the way a term is likely to be used.[433] The OFT invoked the Directive as a means to 'make an overall evaluation of the different interests involved', having regard to certain factors set out in Schedule 2 to the UTCCR 1994.[434] To the OFT, the most important factors to be considered in this evaluation are, first, the extent of any inequality of bargaining power between supplier and consumer, and, secondly, whether, on an overall assessment of the contract and the surrounding circumstances, there is reason to believe that the trader will, if he

[430] *Ibid.*, 19, point 11.8. [431] *Ibid.*, 19, point 11.8. [432] *Ibid.*, 19, point 11.11.
[433] Office of Fair Trading, Unfair Contract Terms, Bulletin No. 4, December 1997, 23.
[434] *Ibid.*, 23.

continues to use the term, be dealing fairly and equitably with consumers, and be taking into account their legitimate interests.[435] The OFT considers this test to be a strict test. The OFT also sees the two elements of this test as cumulative. According to the OFT, where there is a substantial disparity between the relative positions of the parties, the fairness and equity of conduct in relation to a suspect term is all the more important.[436] Therefore, any potential abuse of economic power is likely to violate the requirement of good faith.[437] For the OFT, good faith will often 'turn on whether the trader's marketing practices, documentation, and administrative procedures enable consumers to know exactly what they are doing, and to pull back from commitment at any point until the whole picture is clear to them'.[438] One may wonder whether this is again more a formal criteria than a substantive point.

The fourth bulletin, published in December 1997, summarised the OFT's approach to and understanding of the notion of good faith. The fifth bulletin, published in October 1998, added nothing new to the OFT's understanding of 'good faith'. It used the same criteria as in previous bulletins. The OFT, it would appear, has developed its understanding of good faith and is sticking to it. This view is confirmed by the sixth bulletin, published in April 1999, in which, again, nothing new was added. The standard terms vary, but the elements of the notion of good faith employed by the OFT do not. The OFT, in its evaluation of the fairness of standard contract terms, uses Schedule 2 to the UTCCR 1994 as its principal guidance, and often justifies its decisions by reference to this Schedule. The requirement of plain and intelligible language is constantly cited.[439]

The seventh bulletin was published in July 1999. For the first time, a case of alleged unfair contract terms was pending before a court, *Director-General of Fair Trading* v. *First National Bank plc*.[440] Prior to this, all cases had been resolved through the acceptance of undertakings. However, the bulletin added nothing more to the definition of 'good faith'. Particular problems were seen in the home improvement industry[441] and the air travel industry.[442] The most common unfair

[435] *Ibid.*, 23. [436] *Ibid.*, 23. [437] *Ibid.*, 23. [438] *Ibid.*, 23.

[439] Cf. Office of Fair Trading, Unfair Contract Terms, Bulletin No. 6, April 1999, 8 and 9.

[440] In *Re First National Bank*; Office of Fair Trading, Unfair Contract Terms, Bulletin No. 7, July 1999, 4.

[441] *Ibid.*, 4.

[442] For example, cancellation of the remaining coupons if part of a ticket is unused because the customer has missed a flight; further examples are given at *ibid.*, 5.

terms in the reporting period, however, continued to be terms excluding or limiting liability for shortcomings in the quality of goods and/or services supplied.[443] As the OFT recognises, the promotion of plain language remains a priority.[444]

The eighth bulletin, published in December 1999, was the last bulletin covering cases brought under the UTCCR 1994. The UTCCR 1994 were revoked and replaced by the UTCCR 1999 on 1 October 1999.[445] Although the UTCCR 1999 are very similar to the UTCCR 1994, there was one important change, inasmuch as Schedule 2, dealing with the definition of 'good faith', was not re-enacted in the UTCCR 1999.[446] According to the OFT, the old Schedule 2 was dropped because it mainly embodied material from the recitals to the Directive, not from the substantive provisions of the Directive.[447] However, according to the OFT, 'this makes no practical difference, since regard can and indeed must still be had to the recitals in interpreting the 1999 Regulations'.[448] After the revocation of the old Schedule 2, it might have been expected that the OFT would change its method of reasoning and develop new criteria and, above all, make more use of the notion of good faith.

The ninth bulletin, published in August 2000, was the first to consider cases under the new UTCCR 1999. The tenth, eleventh and twelfth bulletins followed shortly thereafter. As before, the OFT relied mainly on the indicative list in Schedule 2 to the UTCCR 1999 (previously found in Schedule 3 to the UTCCR 1994), and on the provision concerning plain and intelligible language, in order to declare a term unfair. Even though the OFT has said that 'the reasons for considering terms unfair are generally indicated by reference to the nearest example of unfair terms given in Schedule 2 to the Regulations' and that 'fairness is assessed by reference to the test embodied in regulation 6 [former regulation 4], [and] not on the basis of establishing a correspondence with one of the types of term listed in the Schedule',[449] one is left with the feeling that the test of fairness is often done by reference to a combination of Schedule 3 and the plain and intelligible language provision. Very seldom are terms declared unfair without reference to either or both of these factors. The OFT is apparently convinced that the plain and intelligible language requirement is part of the

443 *Ibid.*, 6. 444 *Ibid.*, 6.
445 Office of Fair Trading, Unfair Contract Terms, Bulletin No. 8, December 1999, 3.
446 *Ibid.*, 3. 447 *Ibid.*, 3. 448 *Ibid.*, 3.
449 Office of Fair Trading, Bulletin No. 9, August 2000, 6; Bulletin No. 10, October 2000, 2; Bulletin No. 11, October 2000, 1; Bulletin No. 12, November 2000, 5.

unfairness test, as is shown, for example, by its comment, in the eleventh bulletin, on an indemnity term. The OFT invoked the plain and intelligible language provision to justify its decision that the term was unfair by declaring that the term was 'unclear about the scope of the financial guarantees required and caused imbalance in the parties' rights as terms had the effect of intimidating the guarantor'.[450] The general and often generous reference does not necessarily mean that the OFT is not aware of the differences between regulations 3, 4 and 6, but it shows a certain lack of rigour in the OFT's legal arguments. However, the OFT kept the definition of good faith in mind, even if, in its decisions, it did not expressly say so. In the introduction to its publication, *Guidance on Unfair Terms*, dated February 2001, the requirement of good faith is defined by the OFT as embodying

> a general principle of fair and open dealing. It does not simply mean that the term should not be used in a deceitful way. Suppliers are expected to respect consumers' legitimate interests in drafting contracts, as well as, negotiating and carrying them out.

In the *Guidance on Unfair Terms*, the OFT created a miscellaneous category of potentially unfair terms that would fail the test of fairness set out in regulation 5 to the UTCCR 1999 without falling obviously within any of the categories set out in Schedule 2. Schedule 2 is explicitly declared to be non-exhaustive, and therefore there was room for expanding the list of terms. These additional terms are similar to those listed in Schedule 2, but operate in a different way.[451]

The thirteenth bulletin was published in April 2001, covering 232 cases. It reported one case in which the OFT referred to the requirement of good faith in order to justify its decision that a term, which failed to draw to the consumer's attention the fact that there was a significant limit on the availability of the 'money back guarantee', an important feature of the service offered, was unfair. The fourteenth bulletin was published in May 2001, and covered 204 cases from October 2000 to December 2000. Mostly, the UTCCR 1999 were applied as a yardstick. In only one case was the criterion of good faith applied. In

450 Office of Fair Trading, Bulletin No. 11, October 2000, 26.

451 The list contains the following types of term: allowing a supplier to impose an unfair financial burden; transferring unfair risks to consumers; onerous enforcement clauses; excluding a consumer's right to assign; consumer declarations about contractual circumstances; excluding a consumer's non-contractual rights; and delivery at the supplier's discretion.

the general terms and conditions of occupation of a residential home, a clause providing that the operator of the home could retain the resident's furniture on the death of the resident unless otherwise agreed in writing at the time of admission was regarded as violating the principle of good faith.

The fifteenth bulletin (published in August 2001 and reporting 343 cases), the sixteenth bulletin (published in December 2001 and reporting 297 cases), the seventeenth bulletin (published in March 2002 and reporting 236 cases), the eighteenth bulletin (published in May 2002 and reporting 230 cases) and the nineteenth bulletin (published in August 2002 and reporting 252 cases) are all unremarkable and reflect the OFT's 'traditional approach'. The terms were generally all measured against the standards provided by Schedule 2 or regulation 7. The majority of the terms were revised, not deleted. The plain and intelligible language requirement, especially concerning the use of legal jargon, seems to be the most problematic one, closely followed by liability exclusion clauses. Although the OFT recognises the flaws in the standards in Schedule 2 and regulation 7, nevertheless it continues to apply them. In the introduction to every bulletin, the OFT reminds the reader that references to the two standards are made *for convenience only* and that fairness should be assessed by reference to the test set out in regulations 5 and 6 (which contain the criterion of good faith) and not on the basis of establishing a correspondence with one of the items listed in Schedule 2. Schedule 2 is non-exhaustive, and simply illustrates the types of term which may be considered unfair in light of all the circumstances. The application of the standards in Schedule 2 and regulation 7 has the advantages of being simple and able 'to illustrate the OFT's line on the fairness of different kinds of terms as concisely as possible'.

In November 2002, the twentieth bulletin was published.[452] The bulletin reported 228 cases. In some of these cases, the criterion of good faith was used to delete offending clauses from contracts (rather than, as heretofore, rewriting them). The following are examples of clauses which were deleted, as reported in the twentieth bulletin.

- A company rented out cottages for holidays. One of the clauses in the rental agreement stated that the security deposit paid by the holidaymaker would not be immediately refunded after the holiday had finished. The clause was deleted from the contract.

[452] At the time of writing, this was the most recent bulletin.

- A tour operator used the following clause in its contract: 'Any alterations to the booking within five weeks of the departure date would be treated as a cancellation and cancellation charges would be applied.' The clause was rewritten to state that changes to the booking would be subject to the payment of an administration charge of £5 and all costs incurred in making the alteration, and to include a warning that the costs of making changes to the booking would increase as the date of departure grew closer.
- A term in a contract used by a tour operator permitted the tour operator to terminate the contract unilaterally at its absolute discretion in the event that the behaviour of the holidaymaker proved unacceptable. This clause was deleted.
- A tour operator used a term in its contract which stated that any changes made to the booking within six weeks of the date of departure would be treated as a cancellation, and cancellation charges would therefore be applied. The term was revised to state that changes to the booking within six weeks of for date of departure would be subject to the payment of an administration charge of £15 per person and all costs necessarily incurred in making the changes. The term now also stated that no changes would be permitted within two weeks of the date of departure.

These and similar terms were either deleted or revised on the ground that they failed to meet the criterion of good faith. The OFT is demonstrating a considerable amount of commonsense in its approach to dealing with such terms, and, in the cases reported, it appears that the holiday industry is ready to accept changes or deletions to its standard terms of business.

Conclusion

Ten years after the UTCCR 1994 first came into force, the OFT is becoming increasingly confident in its application of the good faith criterion. At first, the formal aspects of the good faith test, such as the vocabulary and structure of the contract, seemed to predominate in the OFT's thinking. In time, the OFT transcended this purely formalistic approach. The notion of good faith is a general one that needs to be fleshed out with detail in order for it to be applied successfully. This remains true even in civil law countries where the notion of good faith has been in use as a general principle for much longer than in the UK. At first glance, the UK approach to good faith seems to be similar to that used in civil law countries. However, on closer inspection, a number of issues arise which are yet to be resolved.

The first such issue concerns the consistency of the approach developed and applied by the OFT to exercise good faith control. In theory, the OFT aims to draw a distinction between the requirement of plain and intelligible language under regulation 3(2) of the UTCCR 1994 and the fairness test under regulation 4 of the UTCCR 1994 (respectively, regulations 7 and 5 of the UTCCR 1999). Although the case reports in the bulletins do not provide sufficient details to make a full analysis, the details that have been provided tend to show that the OFT is not wholly meeting this intended aim. The OFT appears to conflate the two tests using the requirement of plain and intelligible language as a bridge to good faith. The advantage of such a policy lies in the fact that it can fill a gap in the legal sanctions for non-compliance. If a clause fails to meet the requirement of plain and intelligible language, this will lead to a violation of good faith, the legal consequence of which will be that the term is unfair. However, the disadvantage of such a policy is that the OFT has difficulty in giving a proper meaning to the substantive good faith test. The two distinct elements of the unfairness test, that is, that, first, there is a significant imbalance in the parties' rights and obligations arising under the contract, and, secondly, that that imbalance is contrary to good faith, are not really applied as such.

The second issue goes to the heart of the matter. There is a tendency for the OFT to perpetuate English legal traditions and culture, particularly as regards enforcement. The UTCCR 1994 and 1999 are understood as a development of the pre-existing common law techniques of incorporation and construction. This becomes most evident in the procedural aspect of the good faith test. There is much – perhaps too much – emphasis on the need to negotiate the contract 'in good faith', or by 'fair dealing' or by reference to similar concepts, the essential idea being that the supplier must bring the terms and their contents to the attention of the consumer. If the supplier does so, he will be considered to be dealing in good faith. In essence, such an application of the good faith test looks much more at the individual circumstances than at the standard situations under which contracts are imposed upon consumers. This is, to be sure, one of the major advantages (or shortcomings, depending on your perspective) of the English approach. English law looks at unfair terms and not at unfair *standard* terms. The UTCCR 1994 and 1999, though exercising formally binding control over standard terms, are applied as if they deal with contract terms. None of the case reports in the bulletins indicates that the legal quality of the contract term is fully investigated. There is no or little scrutiny devoted to the question of whether the contract terms have been individually negotiated or not – which ought to be a necessary prerequisite to the application of the UTCCR. Such an approach makes sense, at least in the eyes of German lawyers, if the control is focused on procedural transparency. One may therefore wonder whether there is a mutual relationship between the nature of the terms and the substance of control. Only standardised terms may be submitted to a substantive good faith test. However, it would be wrong to assume that the UK approach is restricted to guaranteeing procedural good faith. Rather, one should assume that the UK approach has developed a promising intermediate solution between a mere procedural test and a fully fledged substantive test. The key to such an understanding may be found in the background to and in the application of the indicative list. The list derives from the UCTA, with its policy of prohibiting clauses exempting or restricting liability. The limited application of the UCTA is due to its lack of an appropriate enforcement structure. The Directive and the UTCCR have succeeded in merging two different legal traditions – the common law which seeks to eliminate unfair terms altogether, and the civil law which seeks to provide for appropriate enforcement structures. In essence, what the OFT is mainly doing is applying the control standards of the UCTA as enshrined in the UTCCR.

Good faith before the UK courts: the European perspective

In substance, good faith has not yet been in issue in a case before the ECJ. However, two particular areas of dispute have come before the UK courts, which help to define those areas in which UK and EC law clash. The first area of dispute concerns enforcement, in particular, the issue of whether consumer organisations should have a right to take action. In the end, policy-making prevailed over decision-making in the courts. Whether consumer organisations will gain any tangible benefit from the new powers remains to be seen.[453] The second area of dispute comes nearer to the true and correct understanding of good faith. *Director-General of Fair Trading* v. *First National Bank plc*, as

[453] Howells, 'Good Faith in Consumer Contracting' in Brownsword, Hird and Howells (eds.), *Good Faith*, 91.

decided by the House of Lords, now provides a fuller insight into how English courts view the notion of good faith. All in all, it seems as if the OFT is very much bound to realise procedural good faith, although with the strong support of the House of Lords. Perhaps consumer organisations should take the lead in ensuring substantive good faith is implanted into UK contract law.

The failed reference to the ECJ: a pyrrhic victory for NGOs?

Given that the case was withdrawn before it was heard by the ECJ, and given that the Consumers' Association achieved their intended aim through political agreement with the UK government, why should it be necessary to reconstruct the case of *Secretary of State for Trade and Industry, ex parte the Consumers' Association*?[454] Everybody seems to be satisfied with this outcome: consumers, because the Consumers' Association can now bring cases to court; the Labour government, because it kept a promise; and the European Commission, because it feels its reading of the Directive has been at least indirectly confirmed. However, there are three reasons which justify a reconstruction of the case.

(1) At the strict legal level, there are lessons to be learnt by all sides about the use of poor legal reasoning, first by the Consumers' Association, who used political arguments rather than hard legal reasoning to support their case, secondly by the defendants, who wished to maintain the monopoly of the OFT in bringing cases before the courts, and thirdly by the High Court judge who saw a reference to the ECJ as the best way to avoid having to deal with a difficult case.
(2) At the legal-political level, there are lessons to be learnt about how the use of EC law can result in changes to national law. Such lessons will not be lost on any of the parties to the case or on the High Court itself. Such lessons will, of course, have been learnt before, but there is no harm in reinforcing the point.
(3) From a comparative perspective, the differences between the Sunday trading litigation, the equal treatment litigation and the good faith litigation before the ECJ are very revealing. Of the three cases, the Sunday trading litigation was the most co-ordinated and most well argued before the ECJ. The various equal treatment cases were

[454] Quotes given here are based on a transcript of the judgment.

> somewhat less well co-ordinated before the ECJ. The good faith litigation before the ECJ did not really get off the ground. The latter case was more political than legal in its presentation.

The background to the conflict in the good faith litigation is clear. The UK government, when implementing Directive 93/13/EEC into UK law by means of the UTCCR 1994, refused to grant consumers and their representative organisation *locus standi* to bring cases before the courts. Consumer organisations, in particular the Consumers' Association, argued that this was an incomplete implementation of, in particular, Article 7 of the Directive, and thus that the UK government acted *ultra vires* in denying consumer organisations legal standing. Although a genuine legal issue lay at the heart of the matter – that is, whether Article 7 had been fully transposed – it became more of a political issue. On the one hand, the UK government defended the traditional role of the OFT in representing consumer interests. On the other hand, consumer organisations believed they were better placed to represent consumer interests.[455]

Article 7(1) and (2) of Directive 93/13/EEC provides as follows:

1. Member States shall ensure that, in the interests of consumers and of competitors, adequate and effective means exist to prevent the continued use of unfair terms in contracts concluded with consumers by sellers or suppliers.
2. The means referred to in paragraph 1 shall include provisions whereby persons or organisations, having a legitimate interest under national law in protecting consumers, may take action according to the national law concerned before the courts or before competent administrative bodies for a decision as to whether contractual terms drawn up for general use are unfair, so that they can apply appropriate and effective means to prevent the continued use of such terms.

The applicants

The applicants were two non-governmental organisations representing the interests of consumers, that is, the Association for Consumer Research and the Consumers' Association. A third non-governmental organisation, the National Consumer Council, did not join the

[455] For a more in-depth analysis of the reasons behind the UK policy, see Teubner, 'Legal Irritants', 11.

litigation.[456] The first applicant is a registered charity and a company limited by guarantee, which was incorporated in 1957. The second applicant is a wholly owned subsidiary of the first applicant. It publishes the results of the research, product testing and investigations carried out by the first applicant, in a variety of magazines and books. The principal argument of the two applicants was that Article 7 of the Directive gives consumer organisations such as the applicants a right to take legal action under English law to obtain decisions from a court or tribunal as to whether contractual terms drawn up for general use are unfair. Therefore, the applicants sought judicial review of the government's decision not to implement this aspect of Article 7. Member States were supposed to implement the Directive by 31 December 1994, although the UTCCR 1994, intended to implement the Directive, came into force on 1 July 1995.

The applicants put forward three arguments in support of their case:

(1) the applicants claimed to have a legitimate interest under national law by virtue of Article 7(2) of the Directive;
(2) the applicants argued that the Member States were obliged under the Directive to give consumer organisations a right to commence legal action under English law; and
(3) the applicants argued that the fact that the OFT was the sole holder of such a right did not fully guarantee effective protection of consumers against unfair contract terms.

The applicants' legitimate interest under national law

The two applicants attempted to demonstrate that they legitimately represented consumers in the UK. In doing so, they relied on facts, not on legal arguments, and therefore their argument could not be linked directly to the wording of Article 7. To support their arguments, the applicants could point to the fact that they had represented consumer interests in the UK for decades. In particular, they could highlight their flagship publication, *Which?* magazine. *Which?* and its sister magazines are sold by subscription. Membership of the applicants is said to be spread throughout the UK, and in 1994 stood at 800,000 members. The applicants claimed to be actively involved in a large number of campaigns on consumer issues at national, European and international

[456] The National Consumer Council was not included in this research. Some remarks may be found in Howells and Weatherill, *Consumer Protection Law*, 499; and M. Whincup, *Consumer Legislation in the United Kingdom and the Republic of Ireland* (New York, 1980), 3.

level. Their activities included a broad involvement in the law-making process at the national and European levels. The applicants claimed to have responded, in 1994 alone, to 106 separate consultation documents issued by the government and statutory bodies on matters concerned with consumer protection.

The obligation under Article 7(2) to grant consumer organisations the right to take action

The principal, legally based challenge made by the applicants consisted in demonstrating that Article 7(2) imposes an obligation on the Member States to grant consumer organisations the right to take action. However, the applicants did not attempt to bolster their legal argument by attempting to establish a Europe-wide network of consumer organisations and consumer lawyers in order to make use of European and comparative legal reasoning. The applicants instead relied on a collection of documents said to show the 'true' purpose of Article 7 of the Directive,[457] as follows:

(1) Resolution (76)47 of the Committee of Ministers of the Council of Europe on unfair terms in consumer contracts and on appropriate methods of control demonstrates that, as early as 1976, the role of consumer groups in challenging unfair contract terms was recognised.
(2) In 1992, Commissioner Peter Sutherland and other members of the High-Level Group on the Operation of the Single Market reported to the Commission that there was a need for consumer groups to be given better rights of access to courts in order to promote the single market.
(3) On 15 December 1992, the Vice-President of the European Commission, Mr Christoffersen, informed the European Parliament that, 'under the Directive, Member States are required to ensure that adequate and effective means exist to prevent the continued use of unfair contract terms. These means must include provisions, for example, conceding to consumers organisations the right to take a case to court.'
(4) On 2 March 1993, the Council of the European Community noted that 'the Directive gives consumer associations the right to ask the courts or the relevant administrative bodies to remove from

[457] First Affidavit of S. McKechnie, Director of the Association for Consumer Research and Chief Executive Officer, in the Court of Appeal.

contracts unfair terms drawn up for general use or recommended by trade associations'.

(5) In May 1993, one of the senior Commission officials responsible for the Directive, Mário Tenreiro, stated:

> Member States are therefore free, in my view, to lay down criteria which associations must fulfil to be recognised as having a legitimate interest (in general) in protecting consumers, but they are then obliged to afford to any association which does fulfil these criteria the right to demand that the use of unfair terms must stop. By contrast to Directive 84/450 on misleading advertising where the question is more debatable, the present Directive thus clearly bestows a right of action on consumers' associations. The definition of the criteria for determining the 'right of action' of these associations has not, as in Directive 84/450, been left to the Member States to assess. The unfair terms Directive only entrusts to the Member States the definition of applicable criteria for determining 'criteria for action' of these associations (general criteria such as the number of members, a certain degree of activity in the sphere of consumer protection).

He added that Member States had the freedom to choose the forum in which these rights could be exercised, that is, courts or administrative bodies.

The applicants concluded by stating that, in some Member States, consumer organisations have for many years enjoyed a right of access to the courts to challenge unfair contract terms. Again, no survey was presented to support this statement, although it would have been easy to introduce such a comparative analysis. The applicants summed up their objective in bringing this litigation as follows:

> [We] are eager to have such a right because this is the only practical means of ensuring that unfair contract terms are not generally applied.

Such a statement should have been supported by evidence to the effect that the control of unfair terms in the UK was deficient, and that Article 7 of Directive 93/13/EEC provided sufficient ground to argue that adequate and effective means had to be provided to ensure that unfair contract terms were eliminated. There is considerable case law of the ECJ to provide a basis for effective legal protection, and such a basis may even be found in human rights law.[458] The applicants, however, failed to do this.

The alleged ineffectiveness of the OFT

The OFT is a governmental agency, and therefore a public body. The applicants claimed that Article 7 of the Directive did not permit Member States to confer an *exclusive* power on such a body to take legal action in respect of unfair terms, to the exclusion of private bodies representing consumer interest. This was said to be all the more so since the Directive was not solely concerned with protecting the interests of consumers. There is a considerable weight of legal reasoning behind such a statement, and one can only wonder at why the applicants did not make use of such legal reasoning.

The alleged ineffectiveness of the OFT in protecting the interests of consumers should have been a fertile ground of argument for the applicants. The first bulletin of the OFT was published in July 1995. The applicants should have presented a comprehensive analysis of the OFT's activities, as set out in the bulletin, in order to justify their claim that the OFT was ineffective at representing the interests of consumers. Instead, the applicants simply stated that the OFT was seeking to balance the interests of consumers against those of commerce. The object of the exercise of Article 7, namely, to eliminate unfair contract terms, was said not to be achievable by the OFT alone because the OFT has limited time and resources to devote to such a task. Further support for this view may have been found in the fact that commercial enterprises often did not view a threat of legal action by the OFT as a serious threat, and this therefore allowed them to maintain the use of unfair terms in their contracts.

The Department of Trade and Industry

The Department of Trade and Industry (DTI) rejected the applicants' arguments on all three grounds.[459] Interestingly, the DTI used legal arguments to reject the applicants' claim. However, the DTI's arguments themselves remained within the boundaries of a UK perspective. No reference was made to civil law regimes to reject the applicants' arguments. The argument was purely one of UK law *vis-à-vis* EC law, or

[458] This was already the case at the time the applicants went to court: see S. Weatherill and P. Beaumont, *EC Law* (3rd edn, London, 1999), 244.
[459] First Affidavit of D. Hellings for the DTI, 15 June 1995.

perhaps it may be better to describe it as a UK view of European law. However, even this limited approach was sufficient to reject the applicants' arguments, and this was made all the easier by the applicants' failure to use legal arguments based on European law.

The legitimacy of consumer associations

The then Minister for Small Firms and Consumer Affairs did not regard the Consumers' Association as having under UK law a legitimate interest in the protection of consumers.[460] For the Secretary of State, none of the matters mentioned by the applicants demonstrated that their legitimacy had been recognised under national law. Such legitimacy cannot be acquired merely by virtue of the historical fact that an organisation has sponsored Parliamentary Bills or has been consulted by the government on numerous occasions. In a lengthy statement, the DTI concluded that the reference in Article 7(2) of the Directive to 'having a legitimate interest under national law' must be understood as 'under national statute'. It is therefore for each Member State to determine under its own national law which organisations, if any, have sufficient legitimacy to represent consumer interests. The applicants should have foreseen this argument put forward by the DTI. European law sets minimum standards as regards the legitimacy of consumer organisations, which would have provided ample scope for the applicants to counter the DTI's argument.[461]

The Directive grants a discretion to the Member States

The principal argument used by the DTI, however, was that the Directive does not impose any *obligation* on the Member States to grant consumer organisations the right to take action. Rather, the Directive grants a *discretion* as to whether or not to grant consumer organisations the right to take action. The DTI's argument was that the obligation under Article 7(1) is qualified by the words 'adequate and effective', and these words import an element of discretion. It is therefore for the Member States to determine what is 'adequate and effective'. Article 7(2) of the Directive gives a definition of what the 'means' referred

[460] Letter from the Right Honourable the Earl Ferrers DL, Minister for Small Firms and Consumer Affairs, to Derrick Prentice, Assistant Director of the Consumers' Association, 6 January 1995.

[461] For a more in-depth analysis, see T. Pfeiffer, 'Richtlinie 93/13/EWG des Rates über mißbräuchliche Klauseln in Verbraucherverträgen' in E. Grabitz and M. Hilf, *Das Recht der Europäischen Union* (Munich, 1999), Art. 7, at 17–18.

to in Article 7(1) must include. Article 7(2) must also be subject to the same discretionary element; otherwise, the obligation under Article 7(2) would be wider in scope than the obligation in Article 7(1). Clear words would be necessary to remove the discretionary element in Article 7(1) from Article 7(2), for example, '*all* persons and organisations having a legitimate interest under national law'. However, no such words were used in the Directive. The DTI's argument here is very much in line with classical UK law-making.[462]

The policy statements by officials of the European Commission, etc. introduced as evidence by the applicants to support their case probably cannot be relied on as an aid to interpretation, and none of the statements is capable of overriding the plain meaning of Article 7(2). In relation to the first three such documents, as noted above, the Council submitted that it is established that statements made by officials, even formal statements made by the Council itself, and unofficial and informal interpretations of legislation, cannot be taken into account by the courts in interpreting EC law obligations. As authority for this principle, the Council referred to *Lemmerz-Werke* v. *High Authority*,[463] *Commission* v. *Italy*[464] and *Hauptzollamt Bremen-Freihafen* v. *Waren-Import-Gesellschaft Krohn & Co.*[465] The applicants could, however, have relied on *Grimaldi*[466] and *GB-INNO*[467] to counter this argument put forward by the Council.

The Office of Fair Trading as the sole and proper representative of the interests of consumers

The DTI argued that the OFT was the sole and proper representative of the interests of consumers in the UK. The Director-General of Fair Trading, the executive head of the Office of Fair Trading, is, in the DTI's view, a person having a legitimate interest under national law in protecting consumers, pursuant to the adoption of the Fair Trading Act 1973.[468] Prior to the adoption of the UTCCR 1994,

462 For a similar approach, see Coote, 'Statutes', 312.

463 Cases 53 and 54/63, [1963] ECR 239 at 247.

464 Case 38/69, *Commission* v. *Italy* [1970] ECR 47 at 57.

465 Case 74/69, *Hauptzollamt Bremen – Freihafen* v. *Waren-Import-Gesellschaft Krohn and Co.* [1970] ECR 451 at 459.

466 Case 322/88, *Grimaldi* v. *Fonds des maladies professionnelles* [1989] ECR 4407.

467 Case 362/88, *GB-INNO-BM NV* v. *Confederation du Commerce Luxembourgeoise Asbl* [1990] ECR I-667.

468 This is very much in line with the way English society organises law-enforcement: see Teubner, 'Legal Irritants', 11.

the Director-General did not have an interest under national law in protecting consumers specifically in respect of unfair contract terms. Conferring a right of action to protect consumers on the Director-General, but only on the Director-General, has a number of advantages from the point of view of complying with the Directive's requirement to provide adequate and effective means to prevent the continued use of unfair contract terms:[469]

(1) The Director-General has considerable experience in assessing the nature of complaints and, if necessary, is able to filter out those which are frivolous or vexatious.
(2) Any decision by the Director-General to bring or not to bring proceedings is subject to judicial review.
(3) The Director-General has the power to accept an undertaking in lieu of bringing formal proceedings, and he is experienced in monitoring such undertakings.
(4) The Director-General has a discretion, which is subject to judicial review, to disseminate certain information to persons likely to be affected by the UTCCR 1994 and 1999.

The Member States have a discretion as regards *who* is to enforce the Directive. In the UK's case, the Director-General is said to be the most appropriate person or institution to defend the interests of consumers. It does not matter that the Director-General has additional obligations to that of protecting the interests of consumers, and therefore that, in practice, the OFT seeks to balance the interests of consumers against those of commerce. There is no requirement in the Directive that the interest in protecting consumers must be an *exclusive* interest.

The reasoning of the High Court

The judgment of Hidden J in the High Court demonstrates the difficulties English courts face when dealing with EC law. One may wonder how the case, based as it was on such poor legal reasoning, managed to reach the High Court. As noted above, there were very few legal arguments brought forward by the applicants and the respondents to support their respective positions. Most of the arguments were policy statements rather than legal arguments. Almost no attempt was made

[469] First Affidavit of D. Hellings for the DTI, 15 June 1995.

to fit the case into the European legal context. It is no surprise therefore that the judge became rather irritated at this:

> It is as well if I were to remind myself that I am sitting as a judge in a national court and I am seeking to construe Community law, an exercise which must be conducted by reference not to principles of English law in relation to construction, but by reference to the principles of Community law. Mr Pannick and Mr Parker, in their conflicting submissions, are of course doing their best to assist the resolution of the conflict, but in doing so they are inevitably highlighting the difficulty and the complexity of the task.

Most of the judgment is devoted to fully presenting the position of the applicants and that of the DTI. Hidden J seems to feel lost in European law, in which the teleological (purposive) approach to interpretation of Community legislation is so strikingly close to policy statements.[470] He expresses his concern in the words of Lord Diplock and Bingham J. Lord Diplock, in *Hen & Derby* v. *Director of Public Prosecutions*, said:

> The European Court, in contrast to English courts, applies teleological rather than historical methods to the interpretation of the treaties and other Community legislation. It seeks to give effect to what it conceives to be the spirit rather than the letter of these treaties; sometimes, indeed, to an English judge it may seem to the exclusion of the latter.

In *Custom and Excise Commissioners* v. *ApS Samex*, Bingham J said:[471]

> The interpretation of Community instruments involves very often not the process familiar to common lawyers of laboriously extracting the meaning from words used but the more creative process of supplying flesh to a spare and loosely constructed skeleton. The choice between alternative submissions may turn not on purely legal considerations, but on a broader view of what the orderly development of the Community requires.

It was then only a short step to refer the case to the ECJ and to let the ECJ decide what exactly should be understood by Article 7(2) and whether or not Member States are obliged to grant consumer organisations a right to take action. Hidden J relied on *R.* v. *International Stock Exchange of the United Kingdom and the Republic of Ireland Ltd, ex*

470 Hidden J refers to Case 283/81, *CILFIT* v. *Ministry of Health* [1982] ECR 3415 at 3430.
471 [1983] 1 All ER 1042 at 1055.

parte Else (1982) Ltd,[472] in which Bingham MR set out the criteria to be applied when referring points of Community law to the ECJ:

> I understand the correct approach in principle of a national court (other than a final court of appeal) to be quite clear: If the facts have been found and the Community law issue is critical to the court's final decision the appropriate course is ordinarily to refer the issue to the Court of Justice unless the national court can with complete confidence resolve the issue itself. In considering whether it can with complete confidence resolve the issue itself, the national court must be fully mindful of the differences between national and Community legislation, of the pitfalls which face a national court venturing into what may be an unfamiliar field, of the need for uniform interpretation throughout the Community and of the great advantages enjoyed by the Court of Justice in construing Community instruments. If the national court has any real doubt, it should ordinarily refer.

The parties did not agree on whether the case should be referred to the ECJ. The applicants were happy for the case to be referred; the DTI were not. In the end, the judge decided to refer the case, with these words:

> In light of [the views of Bingham MR, as quoted above] in the circumstances of this case, I am satisfied that I should refer the question of Community law to the ECJ.

A poor case but a good win for the applicants

It would have been interesting if the ECJ had had the opportunity to decide the issue, mainly in order to see how the Advocate-General and the ECJ would have analysed the case. However, as we saw above, this was not to be. In 1997, a new government was elected in the UK, who agreed to amend the law to permit the Consumers' Association and various statutory bodies to take formal legal action in the courts on their own account.

Since then, EC law has considerably developed. If the case were argued now, one would start from the perspective that Member States are obliged under Article 153 (ex Article 129), in combination with the enforcement provisions of Directive 93/13/EEC, to provide for a right for consumer organisations to seek an injunction in the national courts.[473]

[472] [1993] QB 534 at 545.

[473] The argument is more fully developed in Reich and Micklitz, *Europäisches Verbraucherrecht*, 1160.

The question remains of how a badly prepared and poorly reasoned case managed to bring about a major change in UK policy. At the time the case was suspended, there was no indication at all as to whether the ECJ would decide in favour of the appellants. Contrary to the Sunday trading litigation, there was no pressure exerted by European law on UK politics. It may simply be that the new government did not want to lose a case before the ECJ so early in its life. However, a much more important reason would appear to be that there was a policy shift in UK enforcement strategies. Traditionally, compensation for market failure lay in the hands of public agencies. The OFT is certainly a key player in market regulation. In a broad sense, the use of unfair contract terms may have been regarded as an aspect of the free market that needed to be controlled. It seems as if the new Labour government may simply have found a low-cost solution to a complicated issue.

The Consumers' Association was therefore given *locus standi*. The Consumers' Association is, however, far from making good use of its new powers. This does not mean that the UTCCR 1999 are of no effect at all. Paradoxically, the introduction of a right for the Consumers' Association to seek an injunction in the courts has considerably strengthened the position of the OFT as a consumer-protection-oriented public authority. The OFT has to an unexpected degree become involved in the control of consumer matters. It remains to be seen whether this apparent shift will be an enduring one or a flash-in-the-pan.

To date, the OFT has succeeded in giving full effect only to procedural good faith and transparency. The realisation of substantive good faith will apparently depend on the Consumers' Association and its willingness to test the reach of its new power in the courts. If it refrains from using its new power, it will return to its former position of being a 'free-rider', relying on others (here, the OFT) to defend the interests of consumers in the courts.

The first case under the UTCCR 1994 before the English courts

Director-General of Fair Trading v. *First National Bank plc*[474] was the first case under the UTCCR 1994 to reach the courts.[475] The case

[474] [2002] 1 AC 481; [2001] 3 WLR 1297; [2002] 1 All ER 97.

[475] The presentation is taken from (1999) 9 *Consumer Policy Review* 198. For a more in-depth analysis of the background behind it, see S. Whittaker, 'Assessing the Fairness of Contract Terms' (2004) *Zeitschrift für Europäisches Privatrecht* 75 at 78–81.

concerned an application by the Director-General in March 1999 for an injunction against First National Bank plc, the largest independent grantor of consumer finance and provider of home improvement loans in the UK. The Director-General's application for an injunction was made under regulation 8(2) of the UTCCR 1994. The Director-General claimed an injunction restraining the bank from entering into or enforcing any loan agreement with a consumer which provided for contractual interest to accrue on any judgment obtained by the bank under that agreement, or which otherwise provided for interest to accrue on interest, on the ground that such a provision was contrary to the UTCCR 1994. The Director-General lost before the High Court, won before the Court of Appeal, but finally lost before the House of Lords.

The allegedly unfair clauses were in the bank's standard form loan agreement. By clauses 3 and 8 of the agreement, interest at a variable 'contractual rate' was payable on the amount of the principal outstanding, together with accrued unpaid interest existing at the date of any judgment obtained by the bank, during the period after judgment until payment. Clause 8 provided:

> Time is of the essence making all repayments to FNB [the bank] as they fall due. If any repayment instalment is unpaid for more than seven days after it becomes due, FNB may serve a notice on the consumer requiring payment before a specified date not less than seven days later. If the repayment instalment is not paid in full by that date, FNB will be entitled to demand payment of the balance on the customer's account and interest then outstanding together with all reasonable legal and other costs and expenses claimed or incurred by FNB in trying to obtain the repayment of the unpaid instalments or of such balance and interest. Interest shall be charged in accordance with condition 3, at the rate stated in Article D overleaf (subject to variation) until payment after as well as before any judgment (such obligation to be independent of and not to merge with the judgment).

Clause 3 provided:

> The rate of interest will be charged on a day-to-day basis on the outstanding balance and will be debited to the customer's account monthly in arrears. Payments made by the customer may be credited first to capital or interest outstanding under this agreement at the discretion of FNB . . .

Paragraph D of the agreement set out the monthly rate of interest (the contractual rate) which varied in accordance with the bank's base lending rate. The Director-General was concerned that borrowers consenting to judgment on terms as to payment over a period of time would find themselves faced with a substantial bill for interest on top of the balance.[476] Sometimes, the accrued interest was greater than the amount of the judgment debt. The Director-General argued that this was unfair under the UTCCR 1994 in that, 'contrary to the requirement of good faith, it caused a significant imbalance in the parties' rights and obligations to the detriment of the consumer'. The bank contended that the interest provision was a 'core' term of the loan agreement under regulation 3(2), in that it concerned 'the adequacy of the price or remuneration, as against the ... services ... supplied'. Clause 3 was not therefore subject to challenge under the UTCCR 1994.

The essence of the conflict

Two issues were at the heart of the case: first, whether or not the two clauses should be regarded as 'core terms'; and, secondly, if the terms were subject to control, whether they must be regarded as unfair under regulation 4 of the UTCCR 1994. All three courts (the High Court, the Court of Appeal and the House of Lords) found no difficulty in agreeing on a narrow meaning of 'core terms', but there was considerable disagreement on the *impact* – not so much on the substance – of the civil law concept of good faith in contrast to the common law concept of open and fair dealing. The High Court found the terms not to be unfair, as did the House of Lords. Only the Court of Appeal agreed with the OFT. One might therefore feel tempted to conclude that the good faith test, in the form of a substantive reasonableness test, has found its way into UK contract law.[477] However, it is submitted that the litigation concerned the interaction between the requirements laid down in statutory law and the freedom of contract. As the case progressed through the courts, the true nature of the litigation became clearer.

[476] The practical effect of this can be seen in one case, in which a borrower was ordered by the court to repay First National Bank a £5,000 debt over five years which in the event grew to a debt of over £14,000: see M. Dean, 'Defining Unfair Terms in Consumer Contracts – Crystal Ball Gazing? Director-General of Fair Trading v. First National Bank plc' (2002) 65 *Modern Law Review* 773, n. 3.

[477] This seems to be the reasoning of the Law Commissions' Joint Consultation Paper, 'Unfair Terms in Contracts', 46.

The High Court judgment

On 30 July 1999, Evans-Lombe J gave judgment in the High Court.[478] As regards clause 3, the Director-General seemed to have accepted that this particular clause could not be assessed as unfair because, being the provision which fixed the contractual rate of interest, it concerned 'the adequacy of the . . . remuneration as against the . . . services . . . supplied'.[479] Therefore, the first barrier for the Director-General to overcome was to bring clause 8 within the scope of the UTCCR 1994. Evans-Lombe J had no difficulty in rejecting counsel's attempts on behalf of the bank to argue that clause 8 must be understood as a core term within the meaning of regulation 3.

In considering procedural fairness *vis-à-vis* substantive fairness, the High Court took *Interfoto Picture Library Ltd* v. *Stiletto Visual Programmes Ltd*[480] as a starting-point, in which Bingham LJ equated 'good faith' with 'fair and open dealing':

> In many civil law systems, and perhaps in most legal systems outside the common law world, the law of obligations recognises and enforces an overriding principle that in making and carrying out contracts parties should act in good faith. This does not mean that they should not deceive each other, a principle which any legal system must recognise; its effect is perhaps most ably conveyed by such metaphorical colloquialisms as 'playing fair', 'coming clean' or 'putting one's cards face upwards on the table'. It is in essence a principle of fair and open dealing. In such a form it might, I think, be held on the facts of this case that the plaintiffs were under a duty in all fairness to draw the defendants' attention specifically to the high price payable if the transparencies were not returned in time and, in the 14 days had expired to point out to the defendants the high costs of continued failure to return them.

According to Evans-Lombe J, 'fair and open dealing' equates to procedural and substantive good faith. He explicitly recognised that substantive and procedural good faith have to be clearly distinguished. However, substantive good faith rather disappeared from view when the judge decided that the legislation was the ultimate determinant of unfairness. The same was true with regard to procedural fairness. While the judge recognised that 'it would plainly be better practice

[478] [2000] 1 WLR 98; [2000] 1 All ER 240.

[479] Regulation 3(2)(b).

[480] [1989] 1 QB 433 at 439.

if steps were taken, either in relevant documentation or by expressed communication, to draw the provisions of clause 8 to the attention of potential and actual borrowers before they enter into loan agreements with the bank or at the time when, having defaulted, they are considering making an offer to the bank of payment by instalments', he did not hold the missing *contractual* information to render the clause unfair.

The Court of Appeal

The Court of Appeal gave its decision on 3 February 2000.[481] It distinguished three elements of the fairness test: first, the absence of good faith; secondly, a significant imbalance in the parties' rights and obligations under the contract; and, thirdly, a detriment to the consumer. Like the High Court, the Court of Appeal emphasised the strong conceptual roots of good faith in civil law systems. However, the Court of Appeal began its analysis by referring to Bingham LJ's equation of 'good faith' with 'fair and open dealing' (as quoted above). The Court of Appeal also quoted Professor Beale's statement in his chapter in Beatson and Friedman's book,[482] in which he draws a distinction between the substantive and the procedural aspects of good faith. Although the court did not really discuss the different concepts and their potential implications, there seems to be an undertone in the judgment sympathetic to the academic understanding of good faith. The imbalance test is understood as substantially overlapping with the notion of good faith. The Court of Appeal discussed more fully than did the High Court the element of 'detriment to the consumer' in the UTCCR 1994 and what this concept refers to. To this end, the Court of Appeal asked whether the consumer is unfairly affected by clause 8. It seems as if the court was impressed by the willingness of counsel for the bank to accept that the relevant term 'could cause hardship'.[483] This concession seems to have facilitated the Court of Appeal's conclusion that there must be some merit in the arguments brought forward

[481] *Director-General of Fair Trading* v. *First National Bank plc* [2000] 2 All ER 759; comment by C. Mitchell, 'Unfair Terms in Consumer Contracts' (2000) 116 *Law Quarterly Review* 557.

[482] H. Beale, 'Legislative Control of Fairness: The Directive on Unfair Terms in Consumer Contracts' in J. Beatson and D. Friedman (eds.), *Good Faith and Fault in Contract Law* (Oxford, 1997), 231.

[483] *Director-General of Fair Trading* v. *First National Bank plc* [2000] 2 All ER 759 at 769, para. 33.

by the Director-General that consumers may suffer from unexpected disadvantages. Peter Gibson LJ said:[484]

> In our judgment the relevant term is unfair within the meaning of the regulation to the extent that it enables the bank to obtain judgment against a debtor under a regulated agreement and an instalment order under section 71 of the [County Courts Act 1984] without the court considering whether to make a time order, or, if it does and makes a time order, whether also to make an order under section 136 [of the Consumer Credit Act 1974] to reduce the contractual interest rate. The bank, with its strong bargaining position as against the relatively weak position of the consumer, has not adequately considered the consumer's interest in this respect. In our view the relevant term in that respect *does create unfair surprise*[485] and so does not satisfy the test of good faith; it does cause a significant imbalance in the rights and obligations of the parties by allowing the bank to obtain interest after judgment in circumstances when it would not obtain interest under the [County Courts Act 1984] and the [County Courts (Interest on Judgment Debts) Order 1991][486] and no specific benefit to compensate the borrower is provided, and it operates to the detriment of that consumer who has to pay the interest.

Here, the Court of Appeal addressed itself to the core issue of the litigation, that is, the freedom of contract versus statutory requirements. The crux of the Court of Appeal's argument seems to be 'unfair surprise'. Under German law, a clause which contains an 'unfair surprise' is a clause which breaches procedural as well as substantive good faith.[487] It remains procedural, as a possible unfair surprise can be overcome in individual litigation throughout appropriate means of information; it is substantive, as the unfair surprise at issue is one in preventive action where standard situations have to be assessed.

The House of Lords

The House of Lords was refreshingly clear in the way in which it defined 'core terms', but was less clear on the concept of fairness. Whereas Bingham LJ's understanding of good faith in the *Interfoto* case (as quoted above) focused on procedural fairness, Lord Steyn, by contrast, was in the present case much clearer in his attempt to leave the door open for substantive fairness tests. In essence, the whole judgment of the

[484] *Ibid.*, paras. 34 and 35. [485] Emphasis added. [486] SI 1991 No. 1184.
[487] For an identical reading, see Mitchell, 'Unfair Terms in Consumer Contracts', 557.

House of Lords focused on the interaction between the statutory requirements in the relevant consumer credit legislation and the residual freedoms of contract. The message is simple: issues which are left undetermined under the consumer credit legislation remain outside the good faith test. It is for the legislator and not for the courts to define standards of fairness outside those set out in statute. Seen thus, the judgment of the House of Lords is very much in line with mainstream UK legal thought.

On core terms, Lord Bingham came to the following conclusion:[488]

> In agreement with the judge [in the High Court] and the Court of Appeal, I do not accept the bank's submission on this issue. The regulations, as Professor Sir Guenter Treitel QC has aptly observed (*The Law of Contract*, 11th ed., 2003, pp. 271 et seq) 'are not intended to operate as a mechanism of quality or price control' and regulation 3(2) (shoudn't it be reg. 6(2) as referred to in the 11th ed.) is of 'crucial importance in recognising the parties' freedom of contract with respect to the essential features of their bargain' (*ibid.*, at p. 249). But there is an important 'distinction between the term or terms which express the substance of the bargain and "incidental" (if important) terms which surround them' (*Chitty on Contracts*, 28th ed., 1999, 'Unfair Terms in Consumer Contracts', p. 747, para. 15-025). The object of the regulations and the Directive is to protect consumers against the inclusion of unfair and prejudicial terms in standard-form contracts into which they enter, and that object would plainly be frustrated if regulation 3(2)(b) were so broadly interpreted as to cover any terms other than those falling squarely within it. In my opinion the term, as part of a provision prescribing the consequences of default, plainly does not fall within it. It does not concern the adequacy of the interest earned by the bank as its remuneration but is designed to ensure that the bank's entitlement to interest does not come to an end on the entry of judgment . . .

On procedural and substantial fairness, Lord Bingham made the following comment:

> The requirement of good faith in this context is one of fair and open dealing. Openness requires that the terms should be expressed fully, clearly and legibly, containing no concealed pitfalls or traps. Appropriate prominence should be given to terms which might operate disadvantageously to the customer. Fair dealing requires that a supplier

[488] Judgment, para. 12.

> should not, whether deliberately or unconsciously, *take advantage*[489] of the consumer's necessity, indigence, lack of experience, unfamiliarity with the subject-matter of the contract, weak bargaining position or any other factor listed in or analogous to those listed in Schedule 2 of the regulations. Good faith in this context is not an artificial or technical concept; nor, since Lord Mansfield was its champion, is it a concept wholly unfamiliar to UK lawyers. It looks to good standards of commercial morality and practice. Regulation 4(1) lays down a composite test, covering both the making and the substance of the contract, and must be applied bearing clearly in mind the objective which the regulations are designed to promote.

The key notion in the test is that of 'taking advantage'. This refers to a particular state of mind of the contracting party, in so far as it is strongly related to motives and intentions. Taking advantage is much nearer to procedural fairness than it is to substantive fairness. Directive 93/13/EEC refers to 'the legitimate expectations of consumers'.[490] The supplier cannot unilaterally define the consumer's expectations, nor can the consumer define his or her own expectations. Only 'legitimate' expectations are protected. Thus, the rights of suppliers and the rights of consumers need to be balanced.

Lord Steyn begins his judgment by referring to Bingham LJ's understanding of good faith in *Interfoto*, but then goes a decisive step further. He puts much more emphasis on the substantive aspect of the good faith test, a test which is unrelated to the subjective perspectives of the supplier:[491]

> Schedule 3 to the [UTCCR 1994] (which corresponds to the Annex to the Directive) is best regarded as a checklist of terms which must be regarded as potentially vulnerable. The examples given in Schedule 3 convincingly demonstrate that the argument of the bank that good faith is predominantly concerned with procedural defects in negotiating procedures cannot be sustained. Any purely procedural or even predominantly procedural interpretation of the requirement of good faith must be rejected.

[489] Emphasis added.

[490] Macdonald, 'Scope and Fairness' 763–9; for a more in-depth analysis of the background of legitimate expectations, see H.-W. Micklitz, 'Social Justice in European Private Law' (1999/2000) 19 *Yearbook of European Law* 167–88.

[491] Judgment, para. 36, as quoted by the Law Commissions' Joint Consultation Paper, 'Unfair Terms in Contracts', 46.

There is little disagreement among their Lordships about the interaction between statutory law and the freedom of contract. Lord Bingham sets the tone in clear and outspoken language. There can be no content control where the legislator has remained silent.[492] On substantive fairness, Lord Bingham stated:

> Should it then be said that the provisions of the [County Courts (Interest on Judgment Debts) Order 1991][493] render the term unfair, providing as [the 1991 Order] does for a continuing obligation to pay interest after judgment notwithstanding the payment of instalments by the borrower in accordance with a court order? It is, I think, pertinent that the [Consumer Credit Act 1974], which laid down a number of stipulations with which regulated agreements must comply, did not prohibit terms providing for post-judgment interest . . . The 1974 Act was passed to protect consumers and such a prohibition would no doubt have been enacted had it been recognised as a necessary or desirable form of protection.

On procedural fairness, Lord Bingham stated:

> I have no hesitation in accepting the proposition, inherent in the Director's submissions, that this situation is unacceptable. I have much greater difficulty in deciding whether the difficulties derive, as the Court of Appeal concluded, from the unfairness of the term or from the absence of procedural safeguards for the consumer at the stage of default. When the contract is made, default is a foreseeable contingency, not an expected outcome. It is not customary, even in consumer contracts, for notice to be given to the consumer of statutory reliefs open to him if he defaults. The [Consumer Credit Act 1974] does not require that notice of the effect of sections 129 and 136 be given.

Lord Steyn followed suit, although somewhat hesitantly:[494]

> Initially, I was inclined to uphold this policy argument [of the Director-General of Fair Trading]. On reflection, however, I have been persuaded that this argument cannot prevail in circumstances in which the legislature has neither expressly nor by necessary implication barred a stipulation that interest may continue to accrue after judgment until payment in full.

The arguments of the Law Lords underline the desirability of clarification by a higher authority, that is, the ECJ.

[492] Judgment, paras. 22 and 24. [493] SI 1991 No. 1184. [494] Judgment, para. 38.

Conceptual differences between the UK good faith test and Directive 93/13/EEC: a German perspective

There are at least three questions which need to be referred to, and answered by, the ECJ:

(1) UK law currently distinguishes between procedural and substantive good faith,[495] but the Directive itself does not make such a distinction. The ECJ needs to determine whether such a distinction is permitted by Article 3 of the Directive.

(2) UK law uses the notions of 'taking advantage' and 'legitimate expectations' as a means to control contract terms. The Directive does not refer to or define either of these concepts. Nevertheless, the concepts are very useful in determining fairness. This is all the more so since 'taking advantage' has a subjective, procedural aspect to it. The ECJ needs to determine whether the use of such concepts is permissible under the terms of the Directive.

(3) The relationship between the good faith test (as a means to limit contractual freedoms) and statutory regulations also needs to be considered by the ECJ. This is arguably the most important of the three issues, as it relates to the scope of application of the Directive. The House of Lords used a traditional common law approach to this issue, in that it limited content control to those areas in which the legislator – whether the national legislator under the UTCCR 1994 or the European legislator under the Annex to the Directive – has provided guidance.

A possible reference of the case to the ECJ was always present in the background during the course of the litigation. It is therefore no surprise that the House of Lords discussed this very possibility. However, the House of Lords eventually decided that no reference was necessary. It made lengthy statements in justification of this decision – something which all the supreme courts of the Member States are prone to do.[496] However, unusually, Lord Bingham's justification was rather on the short side, and unconvincing:[497]

> The test laid down by regulation 4(1), deriving as it does from Article 3(1) of the Directive, has understandably attracted much discussion in

[495] S. Whittaker, 'Assessing the Fairness of Contract Terms', 75 at 89–90.

[496] This the overall message from Dean, 'Defining Unfair Terms in Consumer Contracts', 773.

[497] Judgment, para. 17.

> academic and professional circles and helpful submissions were made to the House on it. It is plain from the recitals to the Directive that one of its objectives was partially to harmonise the law in this important field among all Member States of the European Union. The Member States have no common concept of fairness or good faith, and the Directive does not purport to state the law of any single Member State. It lays down a test to be applied, whatever their pre-existing law, by all Member States. If the meaning of the test were doubtful, or vulnerable to the possibility of differing interpretations in differing Member States, it might be desirable or necessary to seek a ruling from the ECJ on its interpretation. But the language used in expressing the test, so far as applicable in this case, is in my opinion clear and not reasonably capable of differing interpretations.

Substantive good faith is not yet a part of UK contract law. References from other Member States may therefore be necessary to clarify the content of the concept of good faith. Alternatively, consumer organisations in the UK may need to take the initiative. This is all the more necessary if the UK's understanding of the concept of good faith is to form a part of a truly European concept of good faith, including both procedural and substantial fairness. It may be that the most valuable contribution the UK could make would be to extend the concept of good faith to cover both individually negotiated terms and standard contract terms.

5

The limits of judicial activism and perspectives for legal politics

In 1995, Chalmers, after ten years' experience with the Single European Act, wrote:[1]

> The language of economic constitution has been more extensively articulated than that of civil and political freedoms. If this base were eroded very real dilemmas would be posed to the future jurisdiction and authority of the Court of Justice, and it might be that the integrationist cause will in future need strong legislators rather than strong judges.

If his reading is correct, the European legal order remains far removed from being the 'constitutional charter' the ECJ has read into the EC Treaty. In light of the findings from the three case studies in this book, I will argue that Europe more than ever needs strong judges to whom cases may be referred not only through the workings of market forces but also by competent public interest groups. However, unlike Lord Denning,[2] I do not believe that the shaping of the European legal order can be left in the hands of the judiciary alone. The case studies provide ample evidence of the wisdom of judges, both UK and European, and of how far the judiciary can go in pushing for greater rights and more effective remedies, thus amply demonstrating the benefits as well as the limits of judicial activism. UK and European judges do not behave like legislators; they are well aware of the role and function politics will and must play in the furtherance of the European project. Therefore, I am quite sceptical when political scientists claim that 'politics' has supremacy over 'law' in the quest to save the national social welfare state from the market-driven European legal order. These efforts lead

[1] D. Chalmers, 'The Single Market: From Prima Donna to Journeyman' in J. Shaw and G. More (eds.), *New Legal Dynamics of European Union* (Oxford, 1995), 55–72.

[2] 'You need have no fear. The judges in England have always in the past – and always will – be vigilant in guarding our freedoms. Someone must be trusted. Let it be the judges.' As quoted by J. Morgan, 'Law's British Empire' (2002) 22 *Oxford Journal of Legal Studies* 729 at 730.

one to question the legal authority (that is, the independence) of the judiciary, particularly of the ECJ. It will be the rule of law which is then at stake.

I will try to show in my concluding remarks that the preliminary reference procedure, enshrined in Article 234 (ex Article 177), constitutes the *principal democratic foundation* of the European legal order *if* three conditions are met:

(1) national and European courts must truly co-operate;
(2) public interest groups must turn themselves into professionalised legal players; and
(3) EU rights and remedies must be understood as *political* rights.

The first condition listed above implies that judicial co-operation, as it stands today, is in disorder. It does not matter whether the interaction is characterised as co-operation or discourse. What really matters is the incapacity of national courts and the ECJ to *mutually communicate*. This is the first finding resulting from the three case studies.

The second condition listed above starts from the premise that there is a striking difference between public interest groups and trade organisations in the degree to which these two groups are able to recognise and act on the opportunities presented by 'organised law-enforcement'. While trade organisations are usually sufficiently astute and well organised to raise issues of concern to them in the most appropriate and effective legal-political forum, public interest groups by contrast lack the necessary professional and communication skills to do the same. This is the second finding resulting from the three case studies.

The third condition listed above is certainly the most challenging one, as it necessitates a balance to be struck between the limits of judicial activism and legal politics. The case studies help to explain the link between market freedoms, social policies, the European private legal order and the ever growing legitimacy gap. The case studies show how judicial co-operation has led to the use of *political* rights and *political* remedies to overcome the legitimacy gap. This is the third finding resulting from the three case studies.

No Treaty amendment is necessary to re-establish an ideal-type judicial co-operation. Judicial co-operation must be redefined in order to transform national courts into true 'European courts' and to increase the capacity of the ECJ to engage in dialogue with the referring national court and the national legal community. Public interest groups will have to learn the language of European litigation. They will have to undergo a process of professionalisation which will enable them to correctly assess the opportunities presented by 'organised law-enforcement' and to avoid an 'instrumental overkill'. Understanding the right to enjoy market freedoms, the right to equal treatment and the right of consumers to access justice (*Zugangsgerechtigkeit*) and the corresponding remedies as *political* rights might contribute to closing the legitimacy gap. Thus, the European legal order can gradually develop, through a balanced judicial activism, from a market-driven legal order into a 'constitution' with a social outlook. However, such a European legal order will not replace the national legal orders; rather, it will supplement them in remedying deficiencies which result from nationally based politics. Therefore, the substance of the European legal order will clearly deviate from the present legal orders of the Member States, in that the European legal order will help to establish market freedoms, equal treatment and access to justice for consumers. However, the European legal order will not be able to meet the challenge to the social welfare paradigm, of providing for social justice in an enlarged (and even more non-homogeneous) European Community.[3]

Communication in disorder: judicial co-operation between national and European courts

The traditional view is that the co-operation between the national courts and the European courts has been a success. If the aim of the project is 'European integration', then co-operation between the courts may indeed be seen as a success. If, however, the focus is turned to the means by which European integration should – or should not – be achieved, then it is more difficult to discern successful co-operation. The reconstruction of the Sunday trading litigation, the equal treatment litigation and the good faith litigation provides a full insight into the ways in which the courts are working together, and the findings are much less encouraging.

The national and European courts *are* co-operating on some levels. However, even here, the way in which they communicate is in disorder. National courts are not behaving like true 'European courts'. They

[3] See more generally on limiting the reach of EU law as a strategy for enhancing the legitimacy of the European project, S. Weatherill, 'Competence Creep and Competence Control' (2004) 23 *Yearbook of European Law*, forthcoming.

use their steadily increasing powers to try to resolve national conflicts in European courts. The ECJ on the other hand has not been able to develop ground rules on co-operation between itself and the national courts. The 'forgotten' fourth dimension of the proportionality rule has remained underdeveloped. The Advocates-General have not been able to function as a translator between the two styles of communication, the vertical style of national problem-solving and the horizontal style of the construction of a European legal order. Disordered communication results in the ECJ making '*à la carte* decisions'. National courts fluctuate between over-fulfilment and rejection, and national parliaments, if they become involved, strive to find national solutions within the confines of European boundaries.

National courts are not behaving like 'European courts'

The steadily increasing power of the judiciary, and national conflict resolution

The steadily increasing power of the judiciary, or the 'judicialisation of politics', is paradigmatic for the development of modern democratic societies.[4] The phenomenon is a centenary process into which the preliminary reference procedure fits very well. However, peculiarities in the process may be discerned in each national legal order. Three such peculiarities are important for understanding the role and function of the UK courts in using EC law for national conflict resolution.

The first peculiarity of the UK legal order is the development of judicial review by the UK courts in order to exercise at least some control over politics.[5] A realisation of this is necessary in order to understand better the reasons why the UK courts faced difficulties in applying the proportionality rule after *Torfaen* to decide whether or not shops could open on Sundays.

The second peculiarity of the UK legal order results from the decision of the Conservative government in 1979 to terminate the dialogue and co-operation between the government, business and the trade unions which the previous Labour government had been so keen on.[6] Disputes which had been solved in Downing Street at a political level

[4] J. A. Griffith, *The Politics of the Judiciary* (Manchester, 1977).
[5] R. Thomas, 'Law and Politics' in I. Holliday, A. Gamble and G. Parry (eds.), *Fundamentals in British Politics* (Basingstoke, 1999), 142.
[6] P. Norton, *The British Polity* (4th edn, New York, 2000), 169 at 183.

were now shifted to the courts. Once the trade unions' faith in the newly introduced European social dialogue and the European collective bargaining process evaporated,[7] the courts were recognised as an appropriate substitute means of finding solutions to equal treatment disputes by using European law in the UK courts.

The third peculiarity of the UK legal order is the way in which control over unfair contract terms is exercised through governmental agencies, here the Office of Fair Trading.[8] Directive 93/13/EEC shifted control over unfair contract terms to the judiciary and away from the Office of Fair Trading. While the increased power of the national courts in general, and more particularly in light of the preliminary reference procedure, is self-evident,[9] the particular way in which the national courts have used and are using their increased power to resolve national conflicts with the help of European law remains unimaginative. It is here that the case studies provide a deeper insight. Therefore, the three particularities are interlinked and will have to be considered altogether.

The Sunday trading litigation was just one building block in the establishment of market freedoms under the common market and the internal market. It might be a paradox to conclude that the Sunday trading litigation increased the powers of the judiciary since neither the ECJ nor the House of Lords finally resolved the conflict. Nevertheless, the length of the litigation, the involvement of the courts and the down-to-earth subject-matter of the litigation all combined to make Euro-litigation popular. Since then, national courts have learnt the lesson that they have the power to challenge national legislation before the European courts. The borderline between legislative/executive

[7] M. Stratigaki, 'The European Union and the Equal Opportunities Process' in L. Hantrais (ed.), *Gendered Policies in Europe* (Basingstoke, 2000), 27 at 47; C. Howell, 'Unforgiven – British Trade Unionism in Crisis' in A. Martin, G. Ross *et al.* (eds.), *The Brave New World of European Labour* (Oxford, 1999), 26 at 48; J. McIlroy, 'Journey into Europe' in J. McIlroy (ed.), *Trade Unions in Britain Today* (2nd edn, Manchester, 1995), 313 at 319.

[8] G. Teubner, 'Legal Irritants: Good Faith in British Law or How Unifying Law Ends Up in New Divergences' (1998) 61 *Modern Law Review* 11 at 24, who emphasises, referring to D. Soskice, 'Divergent Production Regimes: Co-ordinated and Unco-ordinated Market Economies in the 1980s and 1990s' in H. Kitschelt, P. Lange, G. Marks and J. Stephens (eds.), *Continuity and Change in Contemporary Capitalism* (Cambridge, 1999), 271, that the co-ordination between the economic and other sectors is either market-driven or governmental-driven. Leaving conflict resolution to the Office of Fair Trading is in line with the traditional socio-economic context in Britain.

[9] See the analysis of M. Beloff, 'Towards a Supreme Court? The British Experience' (1990) 33 *The Irish Jurist* 1.

powers and the judiciary is being swept away by Euro-litigation, despite Hoffmann J's efforts in *Stoke-on-Trent* to settle the law, that is, to redefine the boundaries between the power of the judiciary and the power of the executive and the legislator. The proportionality rule goes further than the UK's judicial review in that the former grants national courts the power to strike down a regulatory decision, albeit only in individual cases. The lower courts remained confused by the message in *Torfaen*. They were at the time unwilling to exercise the power given to them by the ECJ, and instead preferred to follow Hoffmann J. Neither Hoffmann J nor the lower courts were looking beyond the boundaries of national law. They understood *Torfaen* as an inadequate reply to a national conflict insofar as the ECJ refused to spell out for the UK courts how to apply the proportionality rule. That is why the national courts pushed even harder and sought for an answer in the *Stoke-on-Trent* case. The ECJ's retreat signalled that the national conflict must and should be resolved by means of national law, largely outside EC law.

An even more far-reaching shift of competences took place in the field of social policy. The Single European Act and the particular policy of the Conservative government at that time boosted the shift away from the executive (and even the legislator) to the judiciary. The Single European Act helped to legitimise the European judiciary in its efforts to give shape to Directives 75/117/EEC and 76/207/EEC. The UK government, albeit unwittingly, forced trade unions and women's organisations to fight for equal treatment in the national courts and in the European courts. The outlook at that time for trade unions and women's organisations in their fight for equal treatment was promising for two reasons. First, in 1979, the European rules were more favourable to the enforcement of equal treatment than the national rules. Secondly, the UK's labour courts (the industrial tribunals and the Employment Appeal Tribunal), encouraged by the Equal Opportunities Commission, were willing to fill the gap left by a Conservative government that was characteristically unwilling to become involved in such social policy matters. Therefore, unintentionally, the Conservative government had opened the floodgates for Euro-litigation in equal treatment matters. The particular circumstances in the field of social policy between 1979 and 1997 under a Conservative government may explain why the UK courts bringing cases to the ECJ were looking entirely at the national level. The series of cases brought to the ECJ were meant to overcome deficiencies in the national equal treatment legislation.

Good faith litigation adds a further dimension to the competence shift, which derives from the legal form in which the conflict is presented to the courts. Equal treatment litigation was, at least technically, based on the claim of an individual employee against his or her employer (or former employer, or prospective employer). However, in reality, in some cases at least, the claim was a collective one, and the claim was also strategic in that the Equal Opportunities Commission chose the appropriate claimant for the particular issue.[10] Directive 93/13/EEC first led, by virtue of the UTCCR 1994, to a collective power being conferred on the Office of Fair Trading and, subsequently, by virtue of the UTCCR 1999, to a collective redress mechanism being conferred on the Consumers' Association. It is hard to predict to what extent these new forms of redress might enhance the power shift or whether its mere existence suffices to keep possible conflicts in the hands of the executive (that is, the Office of Fair Trading). The *First National Bank* case may be viewed as a message addressed to the Consumers' Association that the Office of Fair Trading is willing to use its powers and to bring cases to court in order to implement consumer protection. It remains to be seen whether *First National* is a one-off case or whether the Office of Fair Trading really has changed its enforcement strategy. The legal-political environment of the good faith litigation is not comparable to that of the equal treatment litigation. Directive 93/13/EEC is regarded as an alien element in UK law, imposed by Brussels. The UK legal community, the courts and academics, largely defend the existing enforcement structure, and prefer to use the existing scheme of limited judicial control over unfair contract terms. There is no pressure, directly or indirectly, from the UK government for judicial control over unfair contract terms. The UTCCR 1999, which granted legal standing to the Consumers' Association, was more an alibi than true governmental involvement. Therefore, it is no surprise that the House of Lords refused to refer *First National* to the ECJ. Keeping the litigation away from the ECJ allowed the House of Lords to shape a European understanding of good faith which fits well into the boundaries of the national law. While good faith is discussed all over Europe, and while there are a number of Member States whose courts are actively making use of the concept of good faith to eliminate

[10] Although this is not always obvious, it is sometimes strikingly clear: see Case C-408/92, *Smith* v. *Advel Systems Ltd* [1994] ECR I-4438, where five cases were selected out of seventy-six possible cases.

unfair contract terms, the House of Lords relied on UK law alone and on the opinions of a few UK academics in their reading of Directive 93/13/EEC to decide that no clarification of the European concept of good faith was needed. The House of Lords' decision seems guided much more by an intention to leave UK law unaffected by EC law than by an intention to resolve the national conflict by reference to EC law.

In sum, the common factor emerging from the three case studies is the theoretical increase of the judiciary's power which, *prima facie*, is used for national conflict resolution alone. However, a closer look reveals that, in reality, the true power of the judiciary, and the resolution of national conflicts, largely depended on the UK government's involvement. There is therefore a gap here between the theory and the practice. Whether or not the judiciary is able to make use of its power is related to the context of the dispute. The UK government's Shops Bill of 1986, which was intended to liberalise the opening hours of shops, was defeated in Parliament, and therefore the government was looking for another way to resolve the dispute. When therefore the Sunday traders invented the 'European defence', they could rely on the government's agreement to submit the dispute to the ECJ. Thus a failure by the national parliament led indirectly to Euro-litigation.

Quite the contrary was the case with equal treatment. This was not a social policy matter with which the government of the day wished to involve itself, and it was therefore left to the trade unions and women's organisations to take cases to the ECJ. There is therefore a second lesson to be learnt here. Once a government has decided that it was willing to let a particular matter be decided by the ECJ, it could not later reject the ECJ's decision if it did not like it. Thus, the government policy of not wishing to become involved in this particular social policy matter backfired when it was obliged to accept, however unwillingly, the decisions of the ECJ. It is an inherently contradictory stance on the one hand to accept the role of the European judiciary in the development of market freedoms, but on the other hand to deny the very same role of the European judiciary with regard to the realisation of equal treatment.

The attitude of the UK government to the good faith litigation fell somewhere between its willing involvement in the Sunday trading litigation and its antipathy to the equal treatment litigation. The government has now fully implemented Directive 93/13/EEC to everyone's satisfaction. However, the government is not involved to the same degree as the courts, as the latter make use of their newly established powers.

All in all, the effects of the power shift, already evident in the Sunday trading litigation, became even more evident in the later cases. The steadily growing power of the judiciary, particularly in the field of equal treatment litigation, has led, and will continue to lead, to profound changes in society.[11] Social change is already particularly evident in the field of equal treatment. However, such change is less evident in the field of private law. According to Teubner,[12] there is a strong correlation between a market-driven economy and the established power structures. The Office of Fair Trading was set up to exercise control not only over unfair terms but also over unfair marketing practices in general. Such a structure is characteristic of a market-driven economy. A shift in control away from the administrative control exercised by the Office of Fair Trading to the judicial control exercised by the courts, where such a shift is a result of an increasing use by the Office of Fair Trading, other statutory bodies and the Consumers' Association of their powers to seek an injunction, will have far-reaching consequences for the balance between a market-driven economy and the political control of unfair marketing practices. Therefore, Directive 93/13/EEC must be regarded as a 'legal irritant'. It is submitted that the findings of the case studies fit well into such an analysis. The least that is required is a strong governmental incentive to catalyse the competence shift in good faith litigation.

Recalcitrant lower courts

There is obviously a conflict between the lower courts and the higher courts as to the correct handling of the preliminary reference procedure. The higher courts, in the UK as elsewhere, tend to settle the law so as to prevent the lower courts from circumventing the authority of the higher courts. However, the lower courts are difficult to discipline. They have a natural tendency to try to resolve disputes without referring them to the higher courts. Contrary to Alter, I will argue that

[11] See Beloff, 'Towards a Supreme Court?', 1, for a historical constitutional perspective. See also S. Sedley, 'The Sound of Silence: Constitutional Law without a Constitution' (1994) 110 *Law Quarterly Review* 270 at 281 (though he makes no explicit reference the EC context). With regard to the attitude of the Thatcher government to referring social conflicts to the European courts, see N. Johnson, 'The Judicial Dimension in British Politics' (1998) 36 *Journal of Common Market Studies* 148 at 155. For a much more reluctant reading, see J. Golub, 'The Politics of Judicial Discretion: Rethinking the Interaction between National and the European Courts' (1996) 19 *West European Politics* 360.

[12] See note 8 above.

it is not competition between the lower courts and the higher courts, but a desire to reach a resolution of disputes, which is the driving force behind the preliminary references made by the lower courts.

The best (and certainly the most effective) means for the higher courts to stem the flow of references is for the higher courts to provide guidance on when to make references. The higher courts distrust the judicial activism of the lower courts.[13] As early as 1974, in *Bulmer* v. *Bollinger*,[14] Lord Denning provided guidelines to the lower courts on this matter. The criterion laid down in this case was whether the use of Community law was 'necessary for the decision'. *Bulmer* v. *Bollinger* was revisited by Bingham MR in *R.* v. *International Stock Exchange of the United Kingdom and the Republic of Ireland Ltd, ex parte Else (1982) Ltd.*[15] Under the guidance given by Bingham MR, three conditions had to be met before a reference could be made: first, the facts must be clear; secondly, Community law provisions had to be critical to the final outcome of the case; and, thirdly, the national court had to consider whether it could construe the Community law provisions involved with complete confidence, and only if it considered itself unable to do so could it make a reference. The second criterion, in particular, seems wider in scope than Lord Denning's guidance. There is obviously a difference between 'necessary for the decision' and 'critical to the final outcome'.[16] It seems as if the lower courts and the higher courts view these criteria in different ways. While the higher courts use a strict interpretation of the criteria, the lower courts tend to interpret the criteria in the context of the facts of the case, and therefore the application of the criteria may differ from case to case. If the lower courts feel the need to refer the case to the ECJ, they 'twist' (or 'interpret') Lord Denning's guidelines so as to make a reference possible. In

[13] On the whole, however, and with due regard to the three fields investigated here, there is no evidence that the lower courts refrain from referring cases to the ECJ because the higher courts disapprove of the lower courts sending cases directly to the ECJ and thus 'leapfrogging' the higher courts. See C. Lenz and G. Will, 'The Preliminary Ruling Procedure and the United Kingdom' (1996) 19 *Fordham International Law Journal* 844 at 859; and A. Burley and W. Mattli, 'Europe before the Court: A Political Theory of Legal Integration' (1993) 47 *International Organization* 41. For a contrary view, see Golub, 'The Politics of Judicial Discretion', 360 at 363.

[14] *H. P. Bulmer Ltd* v. *J. Bollinger SA (No. 2)* [1974] Ch 401; [1974] 3 WLR 202; [1974] 2 All ER 1226; [1974] 2 CMLR 91.

[15] R. v. *International Stock Exchange of the United Kingdom and the Republic of Ireland, ex parte Else (1982) Ltd* [1993] QB 534; [1993] 1 All ER 420; [1993] CMLR 677.

[16] L. Gormley, 'References for a Preliminary Ruling: Art. 234 from the United Kingdom Viewpoint' (2002) 66 RabelsZ 467–8.

view of the fact that the lower courts 'interpret' the criteria for making a reference in the context of the facts of each case, it is necessary to consider the application of the criteria in the context of our three case studies.

In the Sunday trading litigation, the situation before and after *Torfaen* has to be clearly distinguished. The lower courts were willing to accept the Sunday traders' 'European defence'. Quite a number of magistrates' courts were willing to refer the Sunday trading issue to the ECJ. It was the ECJ which chose *Torfaen* as the appropriate test case.[17] When *Torfaen* was decided and the case sent back to the national courts, the lower courts had difficulties in understanding the application of the proportionality principle. Judges in the lower courts had to decide on complicated EC law issues, and they had to do so under considerable pressure from the Sunday traders. The result was inconsistency between the decisions of the various national courts and, therefore, uncertainty in the correct application of the proportionality principle. This was the moment when Hoffmann J entered the scene. In *Stoke-on-Trent*, he used his considerable personal authority to attempt to settle the law and to remove the uncertainties and inconsistencies in the application of the law in the lower courts by providing guidance on the correct reading of EC law. It must be recalled that Hoffmann J was in a favourable position here, as there was no precedent to bind him. Therefore, he was free to develop his own approach. There is, however, an undertone of remonstration in his judgment in which he seeks to 'discipline' the lower courts for their handling of the Sunday trading litigation. He sets out his interpretation of the law, and warns the lower courts not to develop their own inconsistent interpretations of EC law nor if possible to make further references to the ECJ. Whether the lower courts were willing to obey Hoffmann J or not can no longer be determined. In *Stoke-on-Trent*, the ECJ restored the autonomy of the UK legislator. Therefore, there was no longer any scope for inconsistent applications of the proportionality principle.

The starting-point in the equal treatment litigation is different. As early as 1978, in *Shields* v. *E. Coomes Holdings Ltd*,[18] Lord Denning gave a comprehensive review of Community law.[19] This judgment may be

[17] See p. 53 above. [18] [1978] 1 WLR 1408; [1979] 1 All ER 456.

[19] C. Kilpatrick, 'Community or Communities of Courts in European Integration? Sex Equality Dialogues between UK Courts and the ECJ' (1998) 4 *European Law Journal* 121 at 136.

understood as a plea by Lord Denning for relevant cases to be referred to the ECJ. Such a reading fits in well with the overall political climate of the time, in which, in the employment field, the courts were increasingly seen as mediators of conflicts between employers and employees. However, the lower courts differed widely in their reaction to Lord Denning's plea. One might even conclude (though this may be rather overstretching the analysis) that the lower the court, the more likely it was to favour making references in equal treatment cases. If this was true, it may have been due to the fact that lay members of industrial tribunals and the Employment Appeal Tribunal[20] (the courts most often involved in the lower levels of equal treatment cases, most of which arose out of employment relationships) were more likely to favour making references to the ECJ, and were moreover able to force a reference by outvoting the legally qualified chairman of the tribunal. Industrial tribunals used EC law in *Smith*, *Johnston*, *P* v. *S* and *Grant* to circumvent the (possibly) contradictory opinions of the Employment Appeal Tribunal and the (definitely) contradictory opinions of the Conservative government to obtain a legal outcome which promoted equality of treatment and which more particularly widened the scope of application *sedes materiae* and *sedes personae*.[21] However, the issue of effective judicial protection was at stake, and this issue must be regarded principally as the domain of the Court of Appeal and the House of Lords, which have never lost their inclination to tell the lower courts how to define the scope of application of equal treatment correctly whenever the opportunity arose. In *Webb*, for example, the House of Lords demonstrated its clear concern to avoid decisions which deviated from those of the lower courts. There was no such need in the field of remedies, where the higher courts were heavily involved in providing women with appropriate remedies.

In good faith litigation, there were no successful references to the ECJ, either from the higher courts or from the lower courts. The higher courts apparently wish to ensure the consistency of UK contract law by avoiding inconsistent and/or contrary decisions by the lower courts on the legal standards to be applied. *George Mitchell (Chesterhall) Ltd*

[20] For example, in *Levez* v. *T. H. Jennings (Harlow Pools) Ltd* [1996] IRLR 499. See C. Kilpatrick, 'Gender Equality: A Fundamental Dialogue' in S. Sciarra (ed.), *Labour Law in the Courts: National Judges and the European Court of Justice* (Oxford, 2001), 31 at 50.

[21] See Table 3.2, p. 273 above; and K. J. Alter, 'The European Court's Political Power' (1996) 19 *Western European Politics* 458 at 466.

v. *Finney Lock Seeds Ltd*[22] is an example of this. The House of Lords claims the authority to define what the law is and to leave decisions regarding the facts to the lower courts. The House of Lords clearly stated that the decision as to whether a term is fair or not is one of fact which has to be decided at the level of the lower courts. The 'utmost respect' said to be shown by the higher courts for the decisions of the lower courts clearly indicates that the lower courts should stick to the facts and should not become involved in determining legal principles. The lower courts should apply the rules set out for them by the House of Lords. The same thinking lies behind the *First National Bank* case.[23] The House of Lords has provided the lower courts with guidance on the correct application of the good faith principle. However, there is a substantial difference between the UCTA and the UTCCR which might pave the way for the lower courts to escape the strictures of the House of Lords in order to bring cases to the ECJ under the UTCCR. The UCTA deals with unfair terms, the UTCCR with unfair *standard* terms. The clear-cut distinction between law and facts is not easily transferable to the EC level, although the ECJ has not yet decided on the legal nature of standard contract terms.[24]

In sum, the lower courts have shown a marked recalcitrance in the area of equal treatment litigation, but not in the other areas studied here. This is particularly the case in the good faith litigation, and this, it is suggested, is largely due to the fact that neither the OFT nor the Consumers' Association makes much use of their right to seek an injunction. Seeking an injunction, however, is the only way to involve the courts in this area, and thus to initiate a dialogue between the lower courts and the higher courts over the correct interpretation of the good faith principle.

The UK courts' legal pragmatism and their indifference to European integration

For a civil law lawyer, it is striking to see how relaxed the UK courts are when discussing and determining their relationship with the ECJ. The most appropriate German words to describe this would be *gelassen* and *Gelassenheit*, or, in English, respectively, 'calm', 'composed' or 'cool', and 'calmness', 'composure' or 'coolness'. From the judgments of the

22 [1983] 2 AC 803.

23 *Director-General of Fair Trading* v. *First National Bank plc* [2001] 3 WLR 1297; [2002] All ER 97.

24 See pp. 293–4 above.

courts as well as from interviews with the judges, one gets the impression that the overwhelming attitude of UK judges, whenever the question comes up as to whether a case should be referred to the ECJ, is 'let us seek advice in the ECJ'. This *pragmatic*[25] attitude is evident in all references, regardless of whether they are made by a judge sitting in the lowest court of the land or by a member of the House of Lords. Judges in the civil law system do not have the same attitude. The reason for this may be that UK judges do not have to defend the idea of a consistent legal order. They have been used to living with different legal orders for centuries, and they need not strive for consistency as an objective in itself, as is the case, for example, of private law in Germany.

A second characteristic of judges in the UK is their indifference to the project of European integration.[26] Most of the references do not demonstrate an 'involvement' in the project of European integration; rather, the references merely seek advice from the ECJ as to questions of Community law in order to resolve a particular national conflict. Maybe judges in the UK do not like to demonstrate too clearly that they are committed to European law. There is certainly a link between being 'cool' and at the same time being 'indifferent'. 'Indifference' more clearly expresses the conviction that the English legal system has survived more than one supranational legal project and that it has learnt to take the best out of 'alien' systems in order to improve the national system.

The ECJ's contribution: the neglected institutional (federal) dimension

The greater the co-operation between national and European courts, the greater its importance for the making and development of the European legal order, and the more indispensable it is to setting up an institutional framework for the courts to work together. National courts need to know their tasks and responsibilities, and the same is true for the European courts.[27] Strictly speaking, Article 234 (ex Article 177) does not contain rules concerning the way in which the national

[25] Lord Goff, 'The Future of the Common Law' (1997) 46 *International and Comparative Law Quarterly* 745 at 753.

[26] This is in line with Sciarra's findings in 'Integration Through Courts: Article 177 as a Pre-federal Device' in S. Sciarra (ed.), *Labour Law in the Courts: National Judges and the European Court of Justice* (Oxford, 2001), 1 at 23.

[27] The roles may be changing over time: see C. Barnard and E. Sharpston, 'The Changing Face of Article 177 References' (1997) 34 *Common Market Law Review* 1113.

and European courts should co-operate. The procedural details are instead set out in the Rules of Procedure of the ECJ. It is only since May 2000 that the ECJ has been able to request a clarification of referred questions from the referring court.[28] However, in none of the cases studied here has the ECJ made use of this new power.

While such requests for clarification will no doubt increase the level of co-operation between the national courts and the ECJ in the future, the reconstruction of the Sunday trading and equal treatment litigation demonstrates uncertainties on the part of the national courts *and* the ECJ. These uncertainties result from the expansion of the ECJ's jurisdiction into areas in which it necessarily comes into conflict with the jurisdiction of the national courts, where legal rules on 'co-operation' are lacking, and where there is a need to develop such rules on how to share or divide jurisdiction either *de lege lata* or *de lege ferenda*. The ECJ got caught in the dilemma of the weak institutional outlook of the European Community by its broad understanding of 'measures having equivalent effect' under Article 28 (ex Article 30) and 'equal pay without discrimination based on sex' under Article 141 (ex Article 119). The Sunday trading litigation and the equal treatment litigation both provide evidence of the interrelationship between expanding European jurisdiction and the lack of institutional rules on co-operation between national and European courts.

The conflict is one of 'law' and 'facts'.[29] Euro-litigation provides the opportunity for separating the conflict from its social and moral environment, and from equality and justice, and to present the case in a purely legal context.[30] The legal means to solve it is the proportionality rule.[31] The ECJ decides on the law and the national courts apply the law to the facts. So far, so good. Sunday trading demonstrates the difficulties on both sides of this divide. Equal treatment litigation may

[28] Art. 104(V) of the Rules of Procedure of the Court, OJ 2000 No. L122, 16 May 2000, 43.

[29] On the importance of facts in the English legal system, see G. Radbruch, *Der Geist des Englischen Rechts* (Göttingen, 1956), 8: 'Die Art des englischen Denkens, wie es inbesondere in Francis Bacon bahnweisenden Einfluß gewonnen hat, kann mit den Worten Empirismus und Induktion gekennzeichnet werden. Englischem Denken liegt es nicht, die Tatsachen mittels der Vernunft zu vergewaltigen, es sucht die Vernunft in den Dingen, Vernunft ist ihr "die Natur der Sache".'

[30] On the paradox of a formal autonomous conception of the law being the perfect instrument of politics, see M. Shapiro, 'Comparative Law and Comparative Politics' (1980) 53 *Southern California Law Review* 537 at 542; and M. Volcansek, 'Supranational Courts in a Political Context' in M. Volcansek (ed.), *Law Above Nations* (Gainesville, 1997), 1 at 11.

[31] Hoffmann, 'The Influence of the European Principle of Proportionality' in Ellis (ed.), *Principle of Proportionality*, 106 at 111, who draws a direct line from *Stoke-on-Trent*

be less spectacular, at least from a European perspective. The ECJ had placed indirect discrimination under Article 141. The national courts must decide if there is indirect discrimination based on the facts, and, in cases in which indirect discrimination is found to be present, whether it can be justified. *Enderby* and subsequent cases in the UK show that the courts struggle hard to apply these rules. The division of responsibilities – with the 'law' being decided by the ECJ, and the 'facts' being decided by the national courts – may lead to a paradoxical result. There is inevitably sometimes disappointment caused on the national level by the ECJ's judgments, and Alter interprets this as a deliberate strategy by the ECJ to avoid provoking conflicts between the law and politics.[32] If her analysis is correct, the division of tasks and responsibilities between the ECJ and the national courts, based on the distinction between 'law' and 'fact', is bound to fail. In equal treatment litigation, the story ended with the ECJ sounding the retreat, just as it did in the Sunday trading litigation.

It would be wrong to conclude that the ECJ did not realise the institutional implications of the co-operation between national and European courts. These implications were already evident in the Sunday trading litigation and were given clear shape in *Keck*. The legal debate in and around Sunday trading, even after *Keck*, still focuses too much on the substance of EC law, that is to say, on the pretended weaknesses of the concept of 'measures having equivalent effect' in getting to grips with Sunday trading-type litigation. Advocate-General van Gerven made great efforts in his Opinion in *Stoke-on-Trent* to develop ground rules for the urgently needed institutional framework in which co-operation between the national courts and the ECJ could be settled. The ECJ gave further hints on future co-operation in *Keck*.[33] No similar developments may be reported arising from equal treatment litigation, however.[34]

to *Enderby*, or from proportionality in Sunday trading to objective justifications in equal treatment litigation.

[32] With regard to supremacy, see K. J. Alter, 'The European Court's Political Power' (1996) 19 *Western European Politics* 458 at 473.

[33] Case C-267 and 268/91, *Keck and Mithouard* [1993] ECR I-6097.

[34] The transparency principle, as developed by Advocate-General Lenz in *Danfoss* and confirmed in *Enderby*, has the potential to serve as a starting-point for introducing an additional element into the co-operation mechanism. However, not even Advocate-General Lenz was prepared to dwell on that perspective; see R. Erhard-Jacqué, 'Der Beitrag des Generalanwaltes Carl Otto Lenz zur Rechtsprechung des EuGH auf dem Gebiet der Gleichbehandlung von Mann und Frau sowie soziale Sicherheit' (1999) ZEuS 533.

An analysis of the ECJ's failure to develop ground rules for co-operation requires a more in-depth analysis of the proportionality rule as a potential means of overcoming the legitimacy gap, and a more in-depth analysis of what lies behind the distinction between 'law' and 'fact'. The challenge will be met by reference to the three case studies.

The fourth dimension of the proportionality principle: no blueprint for judicial co-operation

Co-operation between national and European courts has a federal dimension, in which the boundaries of national and European jurisdiction have to be delimited. The federal dimension of the European Community, and more particularly of the national and European courts, is a highly sensitive issue in the UK. The federal dimension connotes the idea of the European Community becoming, or possibly already being, a sort of supranational state. The hypothesis defended here makes it plain that the European legal order as it stands today necessarily incorporates a federal dimension. Up until now, the implications of a federal legal order have been discussed with due regard to rights and remedies. However, it is difficult, maybe even impossible, to develop out of rights an institutional framework that gives shape to the federal dimension. The ECJ is moving back and forth between accepting the challenge itself and leaving it to the Member States as the true participants in the Rome Treaty. I will not speculate on where the ECJ will go in the future; I will merely try to show how the ECJ has used and uses the proportionality principle as a building block to extend the European legal order beyond the area of rights and remedies. Sunday trading is of paradigmatic importance for understanding the difficult situation that both the ECJ and the national courts have had to face as a result of their increased co-operation.

The English courts did not understand what the ECJ was saying in *Torfaen*.[35] Coming, as I do, from the Member State which is most familiar with (and possibly even 'invented') the proportionality principle,[36] I was struck by the difficulties the English courts faced in applying the judgment in *Torfaen*. From a German lawyer's perspective,[37] *Torfaen* is

[35] Case C-145/88, *Torfaen Borough Council* v. *B&Q plc* [1989] ECR 3851; [1990] CMLR 337.

[36] See Lord Goff, 'The Future of the Common Law', 745 at 747.

[37] See Hoffmann, 'The Influence of the European Principle' in Ellis (ed.), *Principle of Proportionality*, 106, who starts his analysis by pointing to the German background of the proportionality principle.

based on the classical concept of shared powers inherent in the proportionality rule: the ECJ decides that the Shops Act 1950 violates Article 28 (that is to say, European *law*); the national courts then decide on a case-by-case basis under what circumstances the provisions of the Act might be in compliance with Article 30 (that is to say, the *facts*). This is the classical (German?) idea of how the proportionality rule should work. The ECJ provides the criteria, and the national courts have to apply those criteria. However, the message did not get through. The English courts were unable to decipher the 'cryptic' message from the ECJ.

On the other hand, the ECJ and the Advocate-General did not envisage the difficulties the English courts would have in applying the proportionality test. This is evident from the way in which the ECJ handled the reference in *Torfaen*. The case had been decided by five judges. It was seen as a standard case in line with the ECJ's case law on measures having equivalent effect, although Sunday trading had never been the subject of a previous reference. The Advocate-General understood *Torfaen* as an opportunity merely to redraw the borderlines of Article 28 (ex Article 30). He therefore took *Torfaen* as a low-profile case, one which would be easy to resolve. He also underestimated the importance the Sunday traders had put on the 'European defence'. Possibly, both the ECJ and the Advocate-General might have thought that the best way to cool the heated emotions was to keep Sunday trading away from the ECJ and to let the national courts decide the issue of opening hours. By the time *Stoke-on-Trent* came to the ECJ, the ECJ had realised that 'they had made a mess' in *Torfaen*.[38] Hoffmann J's judgment in *Stoke-on-Trent* had highlighted the two limbs – separation of powers and supremacy – of the constitutional implications of the proportionality principle. This necessitated getting to grips with what is termed the 'federal or institutional dimension'. Therefore, the ECJ was well aware that *Stoke-on-Trent* was an opportunity for them and for the Advocate-General to delve more deeply into the matter. Van Gerven clarified the federal dimension of the proportionality rule. The ECJ decided the issue in a plenary session, with all thirteen judges sitting on the bench. Its views on the proportionality rule as a means of constructing a federal dimension are more akin to booting the ball as far away as possible rather than a sound legal analysis weighing the pros and cons of going one step further in shaping the European legal order.

[38] Interview with Stuart Isaacs QC on 24 July 1999.

Law and fact: the missing clarification of the substance of judicial co-operation

There are differences in the way the European courts and the English courts understand the proportionality rule. These differences are evident from the views of Advocate-General van Gerven and Hoffmann J,[39] who seem to disagree on whether the proportionality rule permits the judiciary to decide the issue of the legality of legislative acts. Van Gerven defends a well-settled principle of EC law underpinning the powers of the judiciary, while Hoffmann J refers to a basic principle of English law concerning the proper division of powers between the judiciary and the legislature. The conflict cannot be overcome merely by referring to the supremacy of EC law over English law. It is precisely the *institutional dimension* of the proportionality rule which is at stake here. Hoffmann J is right to raise the question of who should decide on what in a European legal order – that is, either, on the one hand, the national and the European courts jointly and/or the judiciary and the legislator jointly, or, on the other hand, the legislator – in clarifying the responsibilities of both the national and the European courts.[40]

The ECJ must get to grips with the federal dimension of the proportionality rule – sooner or later. In *Stoke-on-Trent*, van Gerven set out a model of how the division of tasks between the national courts and the ECJ could look. His model was based mainly on drawing a distinction between the *factual* and the *legal* implications of the proportionality rule. In essence, the model has three steps:

(1) the national court has to provide the ECJ with all the relevant facts of the case;
(2) the ECJ will then determine the legal criteria to be applied;
(3) the legal criteria must then be applied to the facts of the case by the national court.

However, even this model does not fully take into account the concerns of the English courts in the Sunday trading litigation. The model is too mechanical, in that there is no room for the national courts and the

[39] Hoffmann, 'Sense of Proportion', in Andenas and Jacobs (eds.), *European Law*, 149; Hoffmann, 'The Influence of the European Principle' in Ellis (ed.), *Principle of Proportionality*, 37.

[40] Although it seems as if Lord Hoffmann looks at the proportionality principle predominantly from the perspective of an English judge. He touches upon the institutional dimension but does not really develop it, not even in his (so far) last word on proportionality, Hoffmann, 'The Influence of the European Principle' in Ellis (ed.), *Principle of Proportionality*, 106.

ECJ to communicate during each of these three steps and if necessary to move the process back and forth between the three steps. In *Stoke-on-Trent*, van Gerven made the point that co-operation between national courts and the ECJ in a pending case might conflict with national procedural law.[41] In such circumstances, the next step, at least in theory, would be to test whether national procedural law has to comply with EC law, and, if so, how. Van Gerven did not go that far, probably because he did not want proportionality to become the central issue in the ECJ's judgment in *Stoke-on-Trent*. However, just as the European Commission did, he pushed the ECJ hard to decide the issue of proportionality. The ECJ did so. Its judgment did not, however, answer the fundamental concerns of the English courts. The English courts were right in asking what exactly were the criteria that the ECJ wanted them to apply after *Torfaen*. These questions are as yet unresolved, and it is worth reiterating them here:

(1) To what extent do exceptions affect the general objective of the legislation, particularly if the exceptions are inconsistent?
(2) Is legal unity in the application of proportionality an arguable point?

The ECJ did not provide a direct answer to these two questions, although an answer of sorts may be found by reading between the lines of the judgment. It seems as if the ECJ intended to isolate the general policy objective of the Shops Act, thus setting aside any possible exceptions in which conflicting objectives may be hidden. The ECJ favoured taking a hard look at each exception separately. Such a reading would be in line with the ECJ's case law on Article 28 (ex Article 30).[42] Legal unity seems to be a Community concern, but not legal unity in the Member States.[43] The ECJ 'killed the case' at the expense of the national courts' competence, and returned the issue of Sunday trading

41 Van Gerven is much clearer in his academic writing; see W. van Gerven, 'The Effect of Proportionality on the Actions of Member States of the European Community: National Viewpoints from Continental Europe' in E. Ellis (ed.), *The Principle of Proportionality* (Oxford, 1999), 37 at 58–63.

42 S. Weatherill, 'Recent Case Law Concerning the Free Movement of Goods: Mapping the Frontiers of Market Deregulation' (1999) 36 *Common Market Law Review* 51.

43 See in particular the implementation of *Enderby* by the UK courts in M. Connolly, 'How a European Court of Justice Decision on Equal Pay May Affect British Indirect Discrimination Law' (1996) 1 *Web Journal of Current Legal Issues*; more generally see E. Ellis, 'The Concept of Proportionality in European Sex Discrimination Law' in E. Ellis (ed.), *The Principle of Proportionality in Europe* (Oxford, 1999), 165 at 180, who recognises a 'disturbingly large and growing discretion' in the hands of the Member States' courts in the application of the proportionality principle.

to Parliament. What remains is the legal unity only of the European legal order. Co-operation would then require the ECJ to take a step back from bolder and more ambitious attempts to give shape to the federal dimension, that is to say, the question of how co-operation in the decision-making process should look. Read this way, co-operation requires avoiding overlapping jurisdictions in one and the same matter.

Different cases raise different issues. Sunday trading is certainly not the end of the proportionality rule in its incomplete *fourth* dimension – if I understand the institutional dimension as the one missing in van Gerven's co-operation scenario. The effect of the three-stage proportionality test – as it still stands today – cannot and should not be that national courts continue to refer the same issue to the ECJ until the ECJ is in possession of all the necessary *factual* information to take a firm legal decision in which it either confirms or denies the compliance of the national law with European law. It is overstating the matter to claim that the English courts wanted the ECJ to decide for itself the question of Sunday trading either by declaring the Shops Act disproportionate or by making van Gerven's three-stage process applicable. 'Cool indifference' again would be a better way of describing the English courts' second reference. The English courts were looking for an interpretation of Article 28 (ex Article 30) which would allow them to apply the national law correctly and to put an end to the Sunday trading saga. They wanted to decide a case rather than to decide broader legal principles. Only Hoffmann J showed a concern for the 'constitutional implications' of the proportionality rule. The national court's final decision in *Stoke-on-Trent* released the ECJ from taking any responsibility for deciding on the substance of the Sunday trading issue. It is not at all clear whether *Stoke-on-Trent* was the judgment the UK courts and the UK government expected to get. Although the outcome was widely expected, the institutional dimension of the proportionality rule fell by the wayside, even though, now more than ever, it needs answering.

Similar issues arose in the equal treatment litigation as to the correct division of powers between the national courts and the European courts in indirect discrimination cases. These issues arise from a consistent policy pursued by the ECJ. There is a direct link between *Stoke-on-Trent* and *Enderby*.[44] Both cases are at the heart of the matter of how and where to draw the correct line between the jurisdiction of

[44] Case C-127/92, *Enderby* v. *Frenchay Health Authority and Secretary of State for Health* [1993] ECR I-5535.

the national courts and that of the European courts. The legal backgrounds to the two cases are comparable. Just as in *Stoke-on-Trent*, the ECJ was not prepared in *Enderby* to give clearer shape to the issue of how both courts should co-operate. Van Gerven's three-stage approach simply failed. The national courts provided the ECJ with all the relevant facts, so that step one was fully satisfied. A study of the case demonstrates how deeply the ECJ had to immerse itself into the facts of the case. Here, the integration of indirect forms of discrimination into the scope of EC rules on equal treatment produces its full effects. These effects are considered to be ambiguous and even counter-productive. The ECJ has to face the result of its own case law. It is unable to satisfy the second stage of the three-stage process. The legal criteria which the ECJ set out on the basis of the facts did not help the national courts to apply the same criteria to the concrete facts of the case! There are two ways of reading *Enderby*, which are that the ECJ is either unwilling or is unable to provide the necessary guidance. *Stoke-on-Trent* and *Enderby* tacitly and effectively return the issue back to the national courts. If this is a correct analysis, then it seems that the ECJ is willing to accept legal diversity among the Member States, if not in the application then certainly in the effects of its own rulings. Whatever the ECJ intended, this is precisely the outcome of the indirect discrimination cases. The structural deficiencies in shaping institutional patterns out of substantive rules are obvious.

The ECJ has not yet had the opportunity to decide the issue of good faith. *Océano*[45] demonstrates that the ECJ still relies on the division between 'law' and 'facts':

> It follows that, where a jurisdiction clause is included, without being individually negotiated, in a contract between a consumer and a seller or supplier within the meaning of the Directive and where it confers exclusive jurisdiction on a court in the territorial jurisdiction of which the seller or supplier has his principal place of business, it must be regarded as unfair within the meaning of Article 3 of the Directive *in so far as it causes*, contrary to the requirement of good faith, a significant imbalance in the parties' rights and obligations arising under the contract to the detriment of the consumer.[46]

[45] Case C-240 to 244/96, *Oceano Grupo Editorial SA* v. *Quintero* [2000] ECR I-4941; and see J. Stuyck, 'Judgment of 27 June 2000, Joined Cases C-240/98 to C-244/96 Océano Grupo Editorial SA v. Rocio Murciano Quintero and Salvat Editore SA v. José M. Sánchez Alcón Prades, nyr' (2001) 36 *Common Market Law Review* 719.

[46] Case C-240 to 244/96, *Oceano Grupo Editorial SA* v. *Quintero* [2000] ECR I-4941, para. 27 (emphasis added).

The ECJ is not confirming the Advocate-General's view that the aim of the Directive is to remove a generally assumed imbalance between consumers and sellers. The aim is rather to exclude those clauses which are shown, *in concreto*, to cause a significant imbalance. By using the expression 'in so far as it causes', the ECJ is doing nothing more than applying Article 3(1) of Directive 93/13/EEC. The ECJ refers to the proportionality rule, and to the basic distinction between *law* and *facts*.[47] It would then be for the national courts to decide, in the case at hand, whether the Directive has been respected or not. Such a reading is consistent with the reluctance expressed in German legal doctrine to allow the ECJ to decide the issue of the fairness of particular contract terms. In theory, the ECJ would not exclude the possibility of doing so if, exceptionally, the national court had provided all the relevant facts to permit it to decide the case for itself. Such a reading would be more acceptable to common law, which is used to referring to the circumstances of the case; under German law, however, courts regularly submit standard terms to full content control. From a German perspective, if all the facts are presented to the ECJ, then the ECJ would have jurisdiction, just as the German Supreme Court would have jurisdiction in an analogous situation.[48] Should the ECJ follow the German example? The intensive look of the UK courts at the concrete circumstances behind the discriminated contract term might help to disclose the stereotyped arguments behind the good faith doctrine.[49]

The clash of two styles of communication: national vertical versus European horizontal

There is a second reason why the co-operation between national courts and the ECJ does not work, which is caused not by procedural deficiencies in dividing responsibilities between the two courts, but by the way in which the courts communicate. There is a structural difference in the style of communication: national courts look *vertically* at the ECJ to seek a resolution of their national conflicts; the ECJ replies

[47] Stuyck, 'Judgment of 27 June 2000', 719.

[48] For details, see W.-H. Roth, 'Generalklauseln im Europäischen Privatrecht' in J. Basedow, K. Hopt and H. Kötz (eds.), *Festschrift für Ulrich Drobnig* (Tübingen, 1998), 135; and M. Franzen, *Privatrechtsangleichung durch die Europäische Gemeinschaft* (Berlin, 1999), 556.

[49] M. Auer, 'Good Faith: A Semiotic Approach' (2002) 2 *European Review of Private Law* 279.

from a *horizontal* perspective. In theory, the Advocates-General could act as a catalyst between the national courts and the ECJ; in practice, the Advocates-General cannot fully meet this challenge, although they demonstrate a stronger commitment to the subject-matter of the conflict than does the ECJ. The clash of the two styles of communication is perhaps one of the major findings of the three case studies in this book, and its consequences need to be elaborated.

The Advocate-General: a catalyst between the national courts and the ECJ

Civil law systems tend to overstate the importance of the judgment of the ECJ as compared to that of the Advocate-General's conclusions, and therefore the Advocate-General's conclusions are often not taken into account at all. However, the European judiciary does not speak with one voice. Only the Advocate-General and the judges, when considered together, provide a complete picture of the judgment. The case studies provide ample evidence of the degree to which the conclusions of the Advocates-General make the ECJ's judgment comprehensible. Sometimes, the conclusions of the Advocates-General foreshadow the ECJ's judgments by a couple of years. By way of example, it suffices to reiterate the relationship between *Torfaen*, *Stoke-on-Trent* and *Keck*.

Advocates-General have a particular way of communicating. Just like English judges, they make personal statements, and thus express their own views. This may be the reason why UK judges are ready to listen to the Advocates-General. Sometimes, as was the case in the Sunday trading litigation, it is the tacit policy of the ECJ to assign the same Advocate-General to similar, subsequent cases. It therefore becomes possible to identify common characteristics and individualistic touches in an Advocate-General's Opinions in a series of cases. In the Sunday trading cases, it was Advocate-General van Gerven who wrote the conclusions in *Torfaen*, *Marchandise*, *Conforama* and *Stoke-on-Trent*. The situation is less clear-cut in the equal treatment litigation. The reconstruction of a large number of equal treatment cases over two decades necessarily covered the work of several Advocates-General.[50] In *Marshall I* and *Marshall II*, the Advocate-General was again van Gerven. His particular character may be found in his consistent effort to systematise the case law and to seek long-term solutions. One might

[50] On the involvement of Advocate-General Lenz in equal treatment litigation, see Erhard-Jacqué, 'Der Beitrag des Generalanwaltes Carl Otto Lenz', 533.

conclude that the Advocates-General are as a rule more 'committed' to the cases they deal with. This becomes clear in their language, as well as in the way they present the case. A striking though unusual example is that of the conclusions of Advocate-General Tesauro in *P* v. *S*, in which he strongly supported the appellant's claim for the equal treatment of transsexuals. He certainly went beyond the formalistic, legal language in which the Opinions of Advocates-General are usually couched, and showed a clear concern, even a partisanship, for the appellant.

Setting these rare emotional outbursts aside, what remains is a remarkable unity in the way in which the Advocates-General handle cases. They attempt to transpose a nationally based conflict into the European legal context. The real conflict has a *vertical* dimension, and appellants and even referring courts might feel tempted to use the ECJ as a court of last resort which the national courts expect to resolve a case which they themselves have been unable to do. The challenge for the Advocates-General is to transpose the case into a *horizontal* European perspective. They do this by embedding the nationally based conflict into the relevant European legal context. This is the reason why Advocates-General tend to reword the referred questions, so as to remove the national, vertical element and to set it in the context of established EC rules. Deficiencies in communication may, however, be discerned at both ends of the communication link, and in relation to both legal and factual elements.

The Advocates-General carefully analyse the national *legal* context of the case at issue, but do so mainly from a European perspective. This means that the Advocates-General are interested in the national legal background to the dispute only in so far as it is relevant to determining a response to the referred questions in a European legal context. From the perspective of a national lawyer, the Advocates-General's legal analyses of the national law appears rather slim. The Advocates-General attempt to analyse the national rules without referring to the national context in which those national rules operate. In such a situation, the nationally bound *facts* of the case are necessarily neglected. This is not a fault of the Advocates-General, but rather is caused by a conflict between the national courts seeking a resolution to a national conflict and the Advocates-General seeking to develop the European legal order. The result of this structural deficiency is that Advocates-General quite often do not grasp the far-reaching implications of the ECJ's judgments for the national legal order as regards both law and fact.[51] This is the clear conclusion which must be drawn from the reconstruction of the Sunday trading and equal treatment cases.

The ECJ's structural incapacity to communicate with the national courts and the national legal community

From the perspective of a civil law lawyer, the judgments of the ECJ are often rather short, and do not therefore fully reveal the degree to which the ECJ has considered the arguments of the parties or the reasons why national courts made their references. Civil law lawyers who focus on the judgment alone criticise the ECJ for its opaque and incomprehensible reasoning, while common law lawyers often have difficulty in understanding why the ECJ does not fully consider its own precedents. I think it is not so much the different institutional setting but rather the different perspective from which the ECJ argues which raises concern. The ECJ bases its decision on the ground prepared by the Advocate-General. The ECJ considers the problem from a *horizontal* perspective, that is, it considers the way in which the judgment fits into its own case law on similar matters. This is abundantly clear in *Torfaen*. The ECJ believed that it had decided the issue definitively, and must have been surprised by the confusion the judgment created in the English courts. The same type of problem arose in *Barber*. The ECJ failed to foresee the reaction of the Member States, who were unwilling to permit the ECJ to interfere to such a great extent with the social security systems of the Member States. The same was true in *Sanchez*,[52] though this was not a reference from the UK. The ECJ was attempting to establish a coherent European system of liability,[53] and *Sanchez* was just another step in that direction. If the *First National* case had been referred to the ECJ, it would have created similar reactions. There is therefore more to this than a simple unwillingness on the part of the ECJ to be more explicit about its reasoning or to use precedent.

[51] When *Torfaen* was decided, neither the Advocate-General nor the ECJ knew of the political background of the Sunday trading campaigners; interview with Advocate-General van Gerven on 14 October 1999.

[52] Case C-183/00, *González Sánchez* v. *Medicina Asturia* [2002] ECR I-3901.

[53] See W. van Gerven, 'Bridging the Unbridgeable – Community and National Tort Laws after Francovich and Brasserie' in H.-W. Micklitz and N. Reich (eds.), *Public Interest Litigation before European Courts* (Baden-Baden, 1996), 57.

The structural problem arises from the fact that the *vertical* perspective of the referring courts and the *horizontal* perspective of the ECJ do not fit well together. National courts seek advice from the ECJ on how to interpret their case in light of EC law. They devote time and energy to the wording of the referred questions. This is particularly true in the UK where legal counsel have a key role to play in the drafting of referred questions. In *Worringham*,[54] the questions to be referred were agreed between counsel for the parties after weeks of negotiation.[55] In response, the ECJ often makes apodictic statements about European law, but fails to reply to specific referred questions. Golub's[56] and Kilpatrick's[57] findings can easily be corroborated by reference to the reconstruction of the Sunday trading and equal treatment litigation. *Torfaen* is a classical case in which the UK courts hoped to receive a helpful and reasoned judgment; instead, what they got was a judgment which was incapable of being applied in the UK legal environment. In *Macarthys*, the Court of Appeal asked whether Article 141 (ex Article 119) and Directive 75/117/EEC permitted hypothetical comparisons to be made in equal pay cases; in *Jenkins*, the Employment Appeal Tribunal had asked whether it should follow the *Fletcher* approach developed by the Court of Appeal and not allow a commercial benefit to the employer to constitute a defence to an equal pay claim, or alternatively whether a disparate impact argument could be read into the Equal Pay Act 1970 on the basis of Community law.[58] These were important issues, and more examples could be cited. Just like the Advocates-General, the ECJ often takes advantage of its freedom to reword the questions (which may have already been reworded once by the Advocate-General) in order to be able to attribute an autonomous

[54] Case 69/80, *Worringham* v. *Lloyds Bank Ltd* [1981] ECR 767.

[55] Kilpatrick, 'Community or Communities of Courts in European Integration?', 121, at 135, referring to A. Lester, 'The Uncertain Trumpet, References to the Court of Justice from the United Kingdom: Equal Pay and Equal Treatment without Sex Discrimination' in H. G. Schermers *et al.* (eds.), *Article 177 EEC: Experience and Problems* (The Hague, 1987), 164 at 165.

[56] Golub, 'The Politics of Judicial Discretion', 360 at 379, referring to Toth, who observes that English courts and tribunals are (perhaps justifiably) disappointed with some of the preliminary rulings they received in the equal pay and equal treatment cases. His conclusion, however, of referring issues repeatedly until the ECJ is finally made aware of the existence of the real problem, is not the answer.

[57] Kilpatrick, 'Community or Communities of Courts in European Integration?', 121 at 138–9.

[58] See pp. 281–3 above.

interpretation to the legal term at issue. This autonomous interpretation shields the ECJ from a need to make a vertical reading of the case.[59] National courts must therefore often feel that the ECJ makes arbitrary use of the right to choose those elements of the references it sees fit for developing an autonomous European law.

The reactions of the national courts to these unsatisfactory judgments are varied. Kilpatrick[60] has identified three types of reaction: (1) same issue repetition; (2) same issue, same court repetition; and (3) persuasive repetition. Two of these three reactions can easily be identified in the Sunday trading and equal treatment litigation. First, same issue repetition can be identified in the Sunday trading and equal treatment cases, mainly with regard to the scope of application *sedes materiae* (for example, *Barber*). Secondly, persuasive repetition can be identified mainly in the field of judicial review. What really matters is the way in which the ECJ reacts to references on subject-matters which it thinks it has already clarified. The national courts wish the ECJ to change its style of communication, that is, to use a vertical rather than a horizontal perspective. Only such a shift would establish efficient and successful judicial co-operation, at least in the eyes of the national courts. However, the ECJ prefers to stick to its horizontal perspective, even if this does cause problems for the national courts. Therefore, Alter may be correct in perceiving a marked discrepancy between the promising possibilities of European law and its disappointing application in practice by the ECJ in order to achieve an acceptable balance between the European judiciary and Member State politics.[61] The ECJ has three options:

(1) it can determine that national law is incompatible with Community law obligations ('acceptance');
(2) it can determine that national law is fully compatible with Community law obligations ('rejection'); or
(3) it can determine that national law is compatible with Community law obligations, but nevertheless provide some means of remedying what it perceives as deficiencies in the national law ('compensation').

[59] For criticism, see M. Franzen, 'Der EuGH und das Bürgerliche Recht – dargestellt am Beispiel der EuGH-Urteile "Dietzinger" und "Draehmpaehl"' in M. E. Geis and D. Lorenz (eds.), *Staat, Kirche, Verwaltung: Festschrift für H. Maurer* (Munich, 2001), 889.
[60] Kilpatrick, 'Gender Equality' in Sciarra (ed.), *Labour Law in the Courts*, 31 at 47.
[61] Alter, 'The European Court's Political Power', 458 at 473.

Sunday trading comes under the first category. Here, the ECJ intended to 'kill the case'.[62] *Smith* and *Grant* fall into the second category. Here, the ECJ was unwilling to enforce pay equality, or to become involved in matters of distributive justice. Therefore, it resisted the pressure exerted on it and was unwilling to embrace more ambitious concepts of equal treatment. The third category is certainly the most challenging. Here, the ECJ closes one door but opens another. In the equal treatment litigation, the ECJ compensated for the deficiencies of its jurisprudence in indirect discrimination by putting more emphasis on judicial protection.

The deficiencies in the communication between the national courts and the ECJ could theoretically be overcome if the ECJ were willing and competent to utilise a particular form of impact assessment. However, the ECJ has no power, such as for example the German Constitutional Court has, to provide guidance on possible resolutions to the conflict. The ECJ cannot tell the UK courts how to implement the judgment, nor can it tell the national legislator how to bring national law into line with EC law. Nor is the ECJ in a position to monitor the final outcome of a case in the national courts in order to determine whether the final national judgment complies fully with the ECJ's judgment. As things stand, considerable effort is needed to determine whether and to what extent the judgment of the ECJ has been considered and followed.[63] One may wonder why the ECJ shows so little concern as to how judicial co-operation works in practice. There is a clear contradiction between the ECJ's standard formula to 'give full effect to Community law' and its apparent lack of interest in the final outcome of cases. The answer is simple: the ECJ has no legal power and no legitimate standing to monitor what happens in the Member States.

In sum, therefore, the ECJ may be well advised to stick to its horizontal perspective. If it were to become involved in a fully fledged vertical dialogue, it would have to neglect the Member States' thrust in the non-application of broad European principles. The result could well be then a political debate over the reach of the ECJ's jurisdiction. Therefore, there are limits to the degree to which the ECJ should extend its jurisdiction and engage in the vertical dialogue so favoured by the national courts. The inability of the ECJ to talk to the referring courts and the national community results largely from structural deficiencies in the institutional framework of the European Community.

[62] Lord Goff of Chieveley in an interview, 22 July 1999.

[63] Hakenberg, 'Vorabentscheidungsverfahren', 367, n. 28.

The effect of poor communication

It goes without saying that the clash between the national vertical and the European horizontal style of communication considerably affects the implementation of ECJ judgments in the Member States. Two possibilities have to be distinguished: either the national court can ignore or 'interpret' the judgment of the ECJ, and thereby effectively 'throw the case out'; or the ECJ's judgment requires that the national law be adapted to make it compatible with European law, which can only be done by the executive and/or the legislature. Equal treatment litigation seems to fall predominantly into the first category,[64] and Sunday trading into the second. The referring of conflicts to the European judiciary has adverse effects on the division of power in the Member States (though the particular effects differ from one Member State to another).

Implementation *à la carte*: strategies between over-fulfilment and rejection

The reconstruction of the Sunday trading and equal treatment litigation highlights three possible reactions to ECJ judgments by the national courts:

(1) over-fulfilment: the national courts apply European rules even though they are legally not obliged to do so;
(2) loyalty: the national courts strictly follow the advice of the ECJ; and
(3) rejection: the national courts refuse to implement the ECJ judgment.

'Over-fulfilment' stretches the reach of EC law beyond its boundaries. The legal effects of Europeanised national law outside secondary EC law are far from clear. There is growing academic discussion on the degree to which the over-implementation of the scope of Directives may be submitted to the jurisdiction of the ECJ.[65] The ECJ, contrary to its Advocates-General, is willing to extend the scope of application of EC law beyond its secondary law boundaries.[66] In such circumstances, the national legislator has taken an explicit decision to apply

[64] A striking example might be the final decision of the House of Lords in *Webb* v. *EMO Air Cargo (UK) Ltd* [1992] 4 All ER 929.

[65] B. Hess, 'Rechtsfragen des Vorabentscheidungsverfahrens' (2002) 66 RabelsZ 470 at 484–8.

[66] Case C-231/89, *Gmurzynska-Bscher* v. *Oberfinanzdirektion Köln* [1990] ECR I-4003, para. 15; Cases C-297/88 and 197/89, *Dzodzi* [1990] ECR I-3763; Case C-28/95, *Leur-Bloem* [1997] ECR I-4161; Case C-130/95, *Giloy* [1997] ECR I-4291; however,

the particular Directive to areas which in theory could remain outside the influence of secondary EC law. If the national courts take the same stance, in principle the same rules should apply. However, in the area of equal treatment and good faith, the UK legislator has lagged behind the requirements of EC law, and the UK courts have therefore had to struggle hard to bring national law into line with EC law via the preliminary reference procedure. The only case of over-fulfilment is *Webb*, in which the House of Lords gave horizontal direct effect to Directive 76/207/EEC.[67]

'Loyalty' seems to be the rule. One might therefore be tempted to conclude that the communication deficiencies between the national and the European courts should not be overstated. However, a closer look at the equal treatment and Sunday trading litigation shows that the situation is much more complicated than that. The UK courts were certainly loyal in that they were willing to accept the *supremacy* of EC law over national law. This holds true for both the Sunday trading litigation and the equal treatment litigation. This finding should be emphasised, as it allows us to fine-tune Alter's analysis of the link between the promise of European law and its disappointing application in practice by the ECJ. The supremacy of EC law is a well-established principle, even outside the area of European private law, because the Member States' courts, including the UK courts, were willing to follow suit. One may term such behaviour as 'delayed loyalty'. However, accepting the supremacy of EC law does not mean that the national courts are automatically willing to accept the substance of the ECJ's judgments. Loyalty is tied to conditions, for example the existence of clear-cut guidance from the ECJ (such as in *Macarthys* (hypothetical comparator[68]) and *Webb* (maternity protection in indefinite contracts)) or a pre-existing sensitivity to the legal issue (such as in *Foster* and *Marshall II* (the availability of appropriate remedies)).

for a different position, see Case C-346/93, *Kleinwort Benson* [1995] ECR I-615; and Case C-291/96, *Grado* [1997] ECR I-5531.

[67] *Webb* v. *EMO Air Cargo (UK) Ltd* [1995] 4 All ER 577. The House of Lords is not unique in its approach. Member State courts tend to do the same if they feel it appropriate; for the reasons behind this, see A. Stone, 'Constitutional Dialogues in the European Community' in Slaughter, Stone Sweet and Weiler, *The European Court*, 305 at 329.

[68] I do not share Kilpatrick's strong critique of the ECJ for not having discussed the issue of whether hypothetical comparators were necessary or not; see Kilpatrick, 'Community or Communities of Courts in European Integration?', 121 at 140. For me, such an expectation can be characterised as 'instrumental overkill'; see pp. 476–9 below.

The most difficult and certainly the most problematic category is 'rejection'. The reactions of the national courts in the Sunday trading litigation after *Torfaen* come close to a rejection of the ECJ's judgment. However, the UK courts must be given credit for attempting to apply an alien principle which challenged an Act of Parliament. Therefore, the classical case here is the ECJ's approach to indirect discrimination (part-time work) which started with *Jenkins* and ended with *Enderby*. *Jenkins* has been criticised as an extremely confusing judgment.[69] *Enderby* did not lead UK courts to a unified application of EC law.[70] The difficulty in the part-time work cases is one of 'law' and 'facts'. The ECJ can only provide the guidance requested if it digs deeper and deeper into the UK law, that is, if it takes a vertical perspective and starts a discourse with the national courts and defines the criteria to be used to distinguish unlawful from lawful indirect discrimination. This cannot be done without taking the facts of the case into account. The division of tasks between the national courts and the ECJ (that is, that the law is determined by the ECJ, and the facts by the national courts) will necessarily result in disagreement, and possibly disappointment to the national courts.

In sum, it should be reiterated that the ECJ is not a court of last resort for the claimants. The division of tasks between the ECJ and the national courts necessarily results in inconsistencies, be it overfulfilment or rejection. Two questions are still awaiting an answer: first, to what extent might national courts decline to use the preliminary reference procedure after having received unsatisfactory answers from the ECJ; and, secondly, whether and to what extent improved judicial co-operation might overcome the disintegrative effects of the different styles of communication.

European legal boundaries for the national parliament

The starting-point for the research differs as between the three fields under consideration here. In the Sunday trading cases, the conflict concerned whether the Shops Act 1950 complied with *primary* EC law; in

[69] Kilpatrick, 'Community or Communities of Courts in European Integration?', 121 at 139.

[70] With regard to the effects of *Enderby*, see Connolly, 'How a European Court of Justice Decision'; and, more generally, Ellis, 'The Concept of Proportionality' in Ellis (ed.), *The Principle of Proportionality*, 165 at 180, who claims to recognise a 'disturbingly large and growing discretion' in the hands of the Member States' courts in the application of the proportionality principle.

the equal treatment litigation and the good faith litigation, the conflict concerned whether the relevant provisions of UK law complied with *secondary* EC law. In the field of equal treatment, the UK legislator had enacted the Equal Pay Act 1970 and the Sex Discrimination Act 1975. The UK started from the premise that it had foreshadowed Directives 75/117/EEC and 76/207/EEC and in its pre-existing legislation thus there was no need to enact additional legislation (although academic writers and politicians had pointed to weaknesses and loopholes in the two Acts).[71] Therefore, to some extent the equal treatment litigation resulted from insufficient implementation of the two Directives. The first (and so far the only UK) reference[72] under Directive 93/13/EEC raised similar questions. However, the ECJ was denied the opportunity to decide the case when the new Labour government agreed to amend the law to satisfy the demands of the applicants. Both types of litigation (that is, litigation concerning the compliance of domestic law with *primary* EC law, and litigation concerning the compliance of domestic law with *secondary* EC law) demonstrate that it is often an onerous and lengthy process to bring UK legislation fully into compliance with EC standards. EC law does not define boundaries; rather, it gives a mandate to the UK legislator to take the necessary steps to enact new law if the present law cannot be made fully compliant with EC law merely by a process of 'European interpretation'.

Sunday trading is different. Whereas the ECJ emphasises the need to 'level up' the UK's equal treatment legislation, it was requested to 'level down' the freedoms granted under the Shops Act 1950. Therefore, Sunday trading is unique. The freedom to trade under Article 28 (ex Article 30) was used to challenge the legality of the Shops Act 1950. That is why one may refer to the paradigmatic nature of the Sunday trading legislation as a means of understanding the boundaries that European law can impose on national law-making. It must be recalled that the Member States are in principle free to decide whether to implement EC law in the form of primary (that is, Parliamentary Acts)

[71] F. G. Duina, 'Explaining Legal Implementation in the European Union' (1997) 25 *International Journal of the Sociology of Law* 155 at 162; and M. Stratigaki, 'The European Union and the Equal Opportunities Process' in L. Hantrais (ed.), *Gendered Policies in Europe* (Basingstoke, 2000), 27 at 29.

[72] Judgment of 28 February 1996, *R.* v. *Secretary of State for Trade and Industry, ex parte Consumers' Association and Which?*, High Court, unreported (available on Lexis). Quotes given here are based on a transcript of the judgment.

or secondary (that is, administrative regulations) legislation. Due to the peculiarities of the UK's Parliamentary system where time in Parliament is short, most secondary EC law is implemented by way of administrative regulations.[73] This was the case with the implementation of Directive 93/13/EEC into UK law, which was done by means of the UTCCR 1994. It seems to be a commonly held belief among commentators that there is a need to consolidate the UCTA and the UTCCR; however, the scarcity of Parliamentary time will probably mean that this will not be done in the near future.

The Sunday trading saga ended up in Parliament only after the ECJ had been willing to decide the issue of proportionality in *Stoke-on-Trent*.[74] The question of Sunday trading was, in the view of the English courts, most appropriately dealt with in Parliament, and the courts will therefore have been pleased to see the matter end up there. The outcome of the Sunday trading litigation may therefore be viewed as a belated confirmation of Hoffmann J's reasoning in *Stoke-on-Trent*.[75] Such a conclusion would neglect the fact that the power of Parliament depended on the scope and reach of Community law. In *Stoke-on-Trent*, the ECJ eventually decided that Article 28 (ex Article 30) was not applicable, but in deciding the issue of proportionality, it set out the criteria which Parliament had to consider in reforming the law. Any resolution of the Sunday trading saga had to weigh the concept of free trade against the protection and preservation of the special character of Sunday, or, to put it into EC language, to balance economic objectives against socio-political objectives. The ECJ explicitly recognised the preservation of the special character of Sunday as a legitimate objective which could be taken into account in any reform of the law. Therefore, the national legislator was required to weigh conflicting objectives. Objectives that are legitimate under EC law cannot be overridden. The Parliamentary defeat of the Shops Bill in 1986 resulted partly from the government's attempt to fully liberalise the opening hours of shops at the expense of socio-political considerations. European law does not permit free trade objectives to override to so great an extent legitimate socio-political objectives. The latter

[73] T. Daintith (ed.), *Implementing EC Law in the United Kingdom* (Chichester, 1995).

[74] Case C-169/91, *Stoke-on-Trent City Council* v. *B&Q plc* [1992] ECR 6635; [1993] 1 CMLR 426.

[75] *Stoke-on-Trent City Council* v. *B&Q plc* [1999] 3 CMLR 897, para. 44.

objectives had to be fully taken into account when Parliament finally reformed the Sunday trading legislation in the Sunday Trading Act 1994. Member States are not free to set any opening hours they wish: for example, European law set limits on the extent to which Member States may enact legislation which discriminates against imported goods.

Improvements in judicial co-operation

Legal doctrine has been considering for some time how judicial co-operation between national and European courts could be improved. Numerous proposals have been made, which can be divided into two categories: they are either bound to the higher court's perspective or they place emphasis on the broader theoretical context of reshaping judicial co-operation in a multi-level supranational legal order. As early as 1997, Barnard and Sharpston proposed granting the ECJ the power to request clarification of referred questions from the referring court.[76] The idea behind this was to allow the ECJ to make certain that it had fully understood the essential issue to which the national court was seeking an answer. The proposal was based on the assumption that the ECJ was able to determine what the essential issue was, an assumption which turned out to be misplaced. Barnard and Sharpston, in their article, referred to a proposal by Advocate-General Jacobs.[77] Jacobs proposed a regime under which the ECJ would no longer be obliged to give a ruling on each and every question referred. This proposal would tie in well with an apparent preparedness on the part of the English courts to introduce into Article 234 (ex Article 177) a procedure under which the ECJ could decide whether or not to accept the referral.[78] The European judges have developed a similar model to better deal with the steadily increasing number of referrals.[79] However, there remains little willingness on the part of the politicians to discuss the reorganisation of the European judicial system. It seems unrealistic therefore to expect a Treaty amendment to resolve the whole issue of judicial co-operation. Improvements will therefore need to be achieved little by little, and

[76] Barnard and Sharpston, 'The Changing Face of Article 177', 1113 at 1167.
[77] *Ibid.*, 1167.
[78] Lord Hoffmann was arguing for this, in an interview with the author on 9 June 1999.
[79] See 'Abschlußbericht der Reflexionsgruppe zur Reform der Europäischen Gerichte', Beilage T EuZW 2000.

with little fanfare. The modest amendment to the Rules of Procedure providing the ECJ with the right to request clarification fits perfectly into such a scenario.[80]

Top-down solutions tend to neglect the evident concern of national judges that their roles and responsibilities should be fully taken into consideration in any proposals to improve judicial co-operation. As EC law stands today, it will remain for the national judges to apply the EC rules, that is to say, to re-transform EC law as interpreted by the ECJ into the everyday realities out of which cases arise. The idea of integrating national courts more fully into a process of judicial co-operation has been justified by reference to the growing need for procedural rules in a multi-level legal order.[81] This would require that co-operation within preliminary reference proceedings should not only be understood from a vertical perspective, in which the national referring courts and the ECJ are intensifying their legal discourse, but also include the national courts of the other Member States, as well as the parties to the litigation, including public interest groups. Any such solution requires a definitive division of power within the newly shaped (joint) judiciary, and the interplay of 'law' and 'facts' – which is inherent in the preliminary reference procedure under Article 234 – would have to be reconsidered in order to clearly define under what circumstances the ECJ could act as a court of last resort.[82] I will not hide my desire for such a development in the judicial co-operation mechanism, which could eventually contribute to bridging the gap between the vertical national and the horizontal European perspective, but I realise that it will take time to achieve this.

There may be a medium-term solution to the current unsatisfactory preliminary reference procedure. No Treaty amendment would be required. Instead, the solution would be based on a regulatory mechanism which has been in existence for nearly twenty years, and which was successfully used as a means of enhancing co-operation between the administrative bodies of the Member States and the European Commission. The idea is simply to use the 'new approach to technical harmonisation and standards' as a blueprint for judicial

[80] Art. 104(V) of the Rules of Procedure of the Court, OJ 2000 No. L122, 16 May 2000, 43.

[81] Van Gerven, 'The Effect of Proportionality' in Ellis (ed.), *Principles of Proportionality*, 37 at 63, explicitly mentions the need for proceduralisation.

[82] It is a well-known phenomenon that, from time to time, the ECJ does indeed decide a case itself; with regard to equal treatment litigation, see Ellis, 'The Concept of Proportionality' in Ellis (ed.), *Principles of Proportionality*, 165.

co-operation.[83] It will be recalled that Decision 83/189/EEC[84] was the forerunner to the adoption of the famous 'White Paper on the new approach to technical harmonisation and standards' in 1985[85] and the comitology Directive 87/373/EEC in 1987.[86] These three documents have been amended several times, though without changing the ground rules for co-operation between the executives of the Member States, the Commission, private bodies and public interest groups in the field of technical regulation. The first step in the area of judicial co-operation would be to establish a network of information exchange between the national and the European courts; the second step would be to set up rules for co-operation, including, if possible, lawyers, academics, the parties and public interest groups. The idea is not, however, to propose a European Code on Procedural Law. The proposal is modest in that it intends to regulate only the field in which legislative incentives are needed, that is, in the fine-tuning of co-operation between the national courts and the European courts within the Article 234 procedure. This proposal may help to overcome the present deficiencies in the communication between the ECJ and the national courts as well as within the national legal community.[87]

Imbalances and incapacities in organised law-enforcement

The starting-point for private parties in fighting for their rights in the courts is different. Since Mancur Olson's[88] pioneering work on 'the logic of collective action', the interrelationship between special

[83] See my preliminary considerations, H.-W. Micklitz, 'Privatisation of Access to Justice in the European Legal Order' in T. Wilhelmsson and S. Hurri (eds.), *From Dissonance to Sense* (Aldershot, 1998), 505.

[84] Council Directive 83/189/EEC, as amended by Council Directive 88/182/EEC and by Council Directive 94/10/EC; see S. Weatherill, 'Compulsory Notification of Draft Technical Standards: The Contribution of Directive 83/189/EEC to the Management of the Internal Market' (1996) 16 *Yearbook of European Law* 129.

[85] OJ 1985 No. C136, 4 June 1985, 1.

[86] Council Decision of 13 July 1987 laying down the procedures for the exercise of implementing powers conferred on the Commission, OJ 1987 No. L197, 18 July 1987, 33 (now repealed). There is an ever-growing literature on comitology: see e.g. E. Vos, *Institutional Frameworks of Community Health and Safety Regulation, Committees, Agencies and Private Bodies* (Oxford, 1999); and C. Joerges and E. Vos (eds.), *EU Committees: Social Regulation, Law and Politics* (Oxford, 1999).

[87] M. Schwab, 'Der Dialog zwischen dem EuGH und nationalen Exegeten bei der Auslegung von Gemeinschaftsrecht und angeglichenem Recht' (2000) ZGR 446, who analyses the lack of communication between the ECJ and the national legal community in *Mediasafe* and *Marleasing*.

[88] M. Olson, *The Logic of Collective Action* (Cambridge, 1971).

interests and public interests (as diffuse interests)[89] and their different capacities to aggregate their interests are common ground. Under this concept, diffuse interests fall apart. They suffer from deficits in their aggregation, organisation and advocacy. Olson helps us to understand why consumer interests cannot be organised, or are much more difficult to organise, than the interests of Sunday traders and employees. However, the logic of collective action does not explain the potential differences between special interest and public (diffuse) interest groups in obtaining favourable rules relating to access to justice. So far, I have relied on substantive and procedural rights theory. In Weisbrod's[90] and Hirschman's[91] concept, a rights-based legal system has a natural bias in favour of property rights. Substantive and procedural rights theory explains why the holder of economic rights is better off in the European legal system than the holder of social rights. Both concepts, tied together, permit us to rank the three fields of research undertaken here. The Sunday traders are in the best position; they can easily aggregate their interests, translate them into economic rights and obtain access to the legal system. Employers and employees may engage in a collective bargaining process; however, they face many more difficulties in defending their *social* rights in the courts.[92] Consumers are to be found at the lower end of the three groups of litigants. They can neither aggregate their interests nor defend their rights.

My own interest in looking at organised law-enforcement differs somewhat from Olson on the one hand and from Weisbrod and Hirschman on the other. I take their analysis for granted; I accept imbalances in aggregating interests, and differences in bringing to bear economic and social rights. So far, my research confirms both theoretical concepts. For me, these findings are just the *outer* frame for effectively organising law-enforcement. The reconstruction of the three case studies allows us to take a more in-depth look at what goes on *inside*, or at how the outer frame is filled in by the litigants. This is exactly what Handler did, and this is where the emphasis in this book lies. Therefore, the guiding question in making a comparison between

[89] See N. Reich with the collaboration of D. Leahy, *Internal Market and Diffuse Interests: An Introduction to EC Trade Law* (Brussels, 1990).

[90] B. Weisbrod (ed.), *Public Interest Law – An Economic and Institutional Analysis* (Berkeley, 1978).

[91] A. O. Hirschman, *Exit, Voice and Loyalty* (Cambridge, 1970).

[92] S. Weatherill, 'Adressing Problems of Imbalanced Implementation in EC Law: Remedies in an Institutional Perspective' in C. Kilpatrick, T. Novitz and P. Skidmore (eds.), *The Future of Remedies* (Oxford and Portland, 2000), 87–116.

the three fields of research here is whether and under what circumstances private litigants, Sunday traders, women's organisations, trade unions, agencies and consumer organisations are making use of their rights and remedies.

The results are both discouraging and encouraging. The results are discouraging in that there is a strong relationship between the outer frame and the inner world, that is to say, imbalances in the rights-based legal order are reflected in the degree to which the parties are making use of their rights. However, viewed from a different perspective, the results are encouraging, in that there is a solution, provided the parties develop the necessary professional skills needed for effective and realistic law-enforcement. The argument will be developed in three steps. First, the use of EC law by the litigants will have to be compared; secondly, the professional and communication skills of the litigants will have to be analysed; and, thirdly, the impact of deficient professional and communication skills on organised law-enforcement will have to be looked at before possible solutions can be considered.

The instrumental exploitation of EC law

Appellants in Euro-litigation are united in their aim of using 'European law' as a means to an end. The Sunday traders deliberately instrumentalised European law in order to defeat the Shops Act 1950; the Equal Opportunities Commission used, and continues to use, European law to raise the standards of equal treatment in English law, and the Office of Fair Trading and/or the Consumers' Association may one day have recourse to European law to extend the boundaries of the UK concept of good faith.

The Sunday traders invented the idea of the 'European defence'. The Sunday trading litigation was ground-breaking in the way it used European law in the UK context. The word 'defence' suggests that the Sunday traders had to 'defend' a position granted to them under European law or – even more emphatically – that they had to 'defend' their economic freedom. The truth is that the Sunday traders 'exploited'[93] European law. They attacked national legislation using European law. Never before in the UK had litigants employed European law as a justification for disobeying national law.[94] The Sunday traders were eventually successful not before the ECJ but in the national

[93] Interview with Arthur Hugh Vaughan QC on 23 June 1999.
[94] Interview with Tony Askham, solicitor for the retailers, on 26 July 1999.

Parliament. The Shops Act 1950 was revoked by Parliament, and a new Act, the Sunday Trading Act 1994, was enacted, and was very much to their advantage. One might feel tempted to conclude that those who are able and willing to spend enough money on a campaign will ultimately achieve their objective.[95] Nobody knows how much money the Sunday traders spent over a period of nearly ten years on their campaign. In any event, their willingness to spend the money, and their publicly declared intention of using European law to force a change in the national law continues to affect the way in which European law is seen in the UK today.

The Equal Opportunities Commission was, and continues to be, behind most of the equal treatment litigation to reach the higher courts.[96] Usually, the Commission does not itself appear as an appellant but rather remains in the background and provides financial and legal support. The same is true where trade unions are involved. European law is not used as a 'defence' but rather as a means to 'claim' equality. The litigants supported by the Equal Opportunities Commission and trade unions do not defend freedoms; rather, their intention is to use European law as a means to obtain what they were not able to obtain under national law. EC law is used here to compensate for deficiencies in the national law. These litigants also use European law as a means of having the national law changed, this time not to increase freedoms but rather to eliminate sex discrimination and to establish equal treatment. There is though a hidden link to the Sunday trading litigation and the equal treatment litigation. Sunday trading had a legal-political dimension in the UK, and raised the overall awareness of European law in the public's mind. Since then, the potential power of European law has not gone unnoticed by lawyers and judges in the UK, and has been used in such diverse issues as the defence of fox-hunting[97] and as a means of claiming equal treatment for homosexuals.[98] As in the Sunday trading litigation, the success or failure of the 'European claim for equality' did not depend on the law alone but on, among other things, the resources available to the litigants. One may wonder whether European law would have ever played such an important role in equal treatment litigation had it not been for the Equal Opportunities

[95] *Ibid.*
[96] See Lord Slynn of Hadley, as quoted in Lenz and Will, 'The Preliminary Ruling Procedure', 844 at 861.
[97] The question was raised by Stuart Isaacs QC in an interview on 24 July 1999.
[98] See Case C-13/94, *P* v. *S and Cornwall County Council* [1996] ECR I-2145; and Case C-249/96, *Grant* v. *South West Trains Ltd* [1998] ECR I-623.

Commission, with its (limited but still substantial) financial and legal resources. Therefore, it may be too harsh a judgment to blame the Sunday traders for having 'exploited' European law. The pejorative undertone is misleading. It is accepted that it is the task of lawyers, in each and every case, to argue for an interpretation of the law most favourable to their clients. If EC law is exploited in Euro-litigation, then the Equal Opportunities Commission does not differ from the Sunday traders. They both use and instrumentalise European law in the same way, though to different ends.

For the time being there is no Euro-litigation in the UK that has measured the common law understanding of fairness in contract law against the notion of good faith under Directive 93/13/EEC. However, the one case which was referred to the ECJ, though it was withdrawn before it was formally heard,[99] underlines the potential power of European law to shape judicial protection in contract law. The reference would have allowed the ECJ to decide the question of whether consumer organisations must be given standing under Directive 93/13/EEC. To that extent, the intended use of EC law was clearly instrumental. The situation was different in the *First National Bank* case. While the discrepancies between the 'narrow' procedural English understanding of good faith and the 'broader' substantive European understanding are striking,[100] the Office of Fair Trading did not really make use of EC law to support its case. Its concern was much more to test the newly introduced concept of good faith in the banking sector than to instrumentalise the Directive to break down barriers in the application of good faith in the UK courts. The reason for this may be that good faith is alien to the UK legal system and therefore the Office of Fair Trading had difficulty in determining the correct understanding of the principle. The *First National Bank* case was therefore a test case which could be used to explore the meaning of good faith rather than resorting to EC law.

In summary, therefore, it can be seen that 'exploitation' is a common characteristic of all Euro-litigation, whoever might be behind it or whatever might be the objective – whether economic freedoms, equality between men and women, or justice for consumers. However,

[99] Judgment of 28 February 1996, *R.* v. *Secretary of State for Trade and Industry, ex parte Consumers' Association and Which?*, High Court, unreported (available on Lexis). Quotes given here are based on a transcript of the judgment.

[100] See pp. 370–6 above.

the potential power of the 'European defence' has not yet (apparently) come to the attention of the Office of Fair Trading.

The professional and communication skills of the litigants

Transforming a factual national policy issue into a European legal issue

The issues lying behind the litigation under study here are both real and complex: whether shops may open or close on Sundays: whether women are discriminated against; whether consumers may benefit from or suffer detriment from exclusion and limitation clauses. These are all matters of *fact*. These factual situations will be well known to many citizens of the UK, whether they are traders, consumers or employees.

This is not to say that the Sunday trading litigation has had no effect at all on Europe as a whole. However, the potential impact of the liberalisation of Sunday trading in the UK on the internal market and on the citizens of the other Member States is difficult to measure. An impact may be discernible over time, but presently it is still predominantly seen as a national issue affecting only one Member State. However, the Sunday trading litigation in the UK has contributed to keeping the shops open on Sundays all over Europe, or at least to making it easier for traders to fall within exemptions to a general prohibition and thus permitting them to open on Sundays.[101]

Equal treatment litigation, at least in theory, affects women all over Europe. However, the reality of equal treatment litigation is disillusioning. The reason for this is not only that the labour laws of the various Member States differ substantially from one to another, but also that there is still no true Europe-wide concern regarding the issues raised in the UK. The Equal Opportunities Commission was not therefore able to co-operate with trade unions and women's organisations outside the UK to establish a broader political and legal basis for their arguments.

[101] This seems to be the German policy. In theory, opening a shop on Sundays is still prohibited. However, local authorities use every pretext to circumvent the German *Ladenschlußgesetz*, by giving an extremely wide interpretation to exemptions. No one has the power to challenge this policy. Both traders and consumers are happy with this situation, and trade unions are no longer in a position to effectively challenge this policy.

All national cases which reach the European courts will have a *factual* basis set in a *national* context. Nevertheless, once the case reaches the European courts, it will become set in a European *legal* environment. At the European level, the case will be entirely dominated by European *law*, by the European *legal* system and by the European *legal* order. The national factual problem will have been transformed into a purely legal form, divorced from the moral implications inherent to the national legal order. Although the case will, by virtue of Article 234 (ex Article 177), retain a link to the national level, nevertheless this link is a rather tenuous one.[102] The Sunday traders and the equal treatment litigants had to transform a factual, national, socio-economic issue into a European *legal* issue.[103] Quite often, the challenge is not one of law and facts alone. Organised law-enforcement strategies are governed by more or less politically determined considerations. The Sunday traders intended to keep the shops open and to strike down the Shops Act 1950. The equal treatment litigants used EC law to substitute for the lack of interest of the UK government in the issue. Consumer litigants put pressure on the UK government to change the UTCCR 1994 in order to obtain legal standing in the courts. The three case studies provide a definite answer to the question of the degree to which the litigants succeeded in transforming factual national policy into a European legal problem. The litigants are more successful the more they are willing and able to transform their factual, national issue into the horizontal European legal environment. Undoubtedly, the Sunday traders did best here. By contrast, the equal treatment and consumer litigants were too focused on national problem-solving.

The so-called 'European defence' in the Sunday trading litigation was in substance a political defence. The object was abundantly clear. The Sunday traders intended to keep their shops open. Litigation, if initiated on a broad basis and with strong support from a whole sector of commerce, will always have a political dimension. Arthur Hugh Vaughan QC, the barrister representing B&Q, succeeded in harnessing

[102] I. Maher, 'Community Law in the National Legal Order' (1998) 36 *Journal of Common Market Studies* 237 at 245, where she refers to the situation where English courts are unable to apply the ECJ's decision in *Torfaen*.

[103] For the very same conclusion with regard to Sunday trading litigation, see M. Maduro, 'Europe and the Constitution: What If This Is As Good As It Gets?' in J. H. H. Weiler and M. Wind (eds.), *European Constitutionalism Beyond the State* (Cambridge, 2003), 74; van Gerven, 'The Effect of Proportionality' in Ellis (ed.), *The Principle of Proportionality*, 37 at 40 and 41.

this political dimension as part of his legal strategy, thereby avoiding allegations of misusing the law. What is more, the Sunday traders, with all the legal resources at their disposal, managed to transform a true national conflict into the European legal environment. The debates in *Torfaen* and *Stoke-on-Trent* turned on the scope and application of Article 28 (ex Article 30), and on the meaning given to it by the ECJ and its Advocates-General.

The call for 'justice' in the ECJ to compensate for 'injustice' in UK governmental policy is strikingly political in substance. The equal treatment litigants, like their counterparts in the Sunday trading litigation, overcame the first hurdle easily. Well advised by competent counsel, they took the utmost advantage of EC law to close the gaps in the national equal treatment legislation. Euro-litigation reveals the limits of the UK understanding of how national legislation must be interpreted, and how the UK conception of law often leads to unexpected results.[104] When a national, factual issue is set into its European legal context, it often becomes immediately evident that the national legislation falls short of the standards required by EC law. However, the equal treatment litigants did not wholly manage to transform their national, factual issue into the European legal context, and thus they failed to focus wholly on the European legal dimension. The litigants pushed hard to have their national conflict resolved in the ECJ, but overlooked the fact that any such solution found in the ECJ would have to fit into twenty-five legal orders and not just into the UK legal order alone. Thus, the equal treatment litigants failed to fully utilise the potential of EC law.

The first (and so far the only) UK litigation under Directive 93/13/EEC had an ambiguous outcome. The legal reasoning of the Consumers' Association is certainly substandard. The arguments of the appellants were poorly presented, and the counter-arguments of the respondents were only slightly better. However, the litigants managed largely to avoid using national law in their arguments (albeit there was no national law that could be used). In the High Court, the appellants presented policy arguments as legal arguments. Under these circumstances, it is all the more startling that the High Court managed to refer the case to the ECJ. Strictly speaking, the High Court should have requested the appellants to present better legal arguments in order to justify a referral. Hidden J's decision to refer the case to

[104] Most strikingly, Case C-185/97, *Coote* v. *Granada Hospitality Ltd* [1998] ECR I-5199.

the ECJ may to a large extent be due to his uncertainty in handling the case. This would explain why the High Court was willing to take policy arguments as legal arguments.

In summary, there are a number of lessons which can be learnt from the litigation which has been studied here. First, the underlying issue behind the litigation needs to be resolved on a national level, whether by the legislature or by the courts.[105] The ECJ can do no more than provide guidance to the parties on the correct interpretation of EC law. Secondly, the litigants must present their case in a way which allows the ECJ to determine the issues from its horizontal perspective but which nevertheless provides the litigants with a satisfactory answer to the national, factual issue. This hinges crucially on the ability of counsel to carefully and correctly draft the questions to be referred. The extent to which counsel can do this is often directly reflected in the utility of the judgment of the ECJ. Counsel often try to pin the ECJ down to answering national policy questions. It goes without saying that the ECJ is unable to do this. That is why it does not make sense to refer the same national problem again and again to the ECJ.[106]

Shaping national consensus as a pre-condition to referring conflicts from the national level to the EC level

Consensus here means consensus on referring the conflict, not consensus on the subject-matter of the conflict. This form of consensus-building lies in the hands of the litigants. They must ensure that ideally all those directly and indirectly concerned agree to refer the case from the national courts to the European courts. This includes not only the parties and all those experts behind the parties, but also the national judiciary and the national government. The greater the consensus, the easier it is to transform the national political conflict into a legal horizontal European environment. In our case studies, there are considerable differences in the degree to which the litigants managed to

[105] This is different from neo-realist or intergovernmental explanations of the role of the national courts in European integration. The latter explains the approach of national courts to Community law in terms of national interest with regard to the different policies of European integration; see K. Alter, 'Explaining National Court Acceptance of European Court Jurisprudence: A Critical Evaluation of Theories of Legal Integration' in A. Slaughter, A. Stone Sweet and J. H. H. Weiler (eds.), *The European Court and National Courts - Doctrine and Jurisprudence: Legal Change in Its Social Context* (Oxford, 1997), 227 at 234–8.

[106] See the references in note 55 above.

achieve this consensus. Not everyone who should have been involved in the process of consensus-building was in fact involved.[107] Here, *locus standi* fills an important gap.

The Sunday traders benefited from the most favourable starting-point. The referral of the issue of Sunday opening hours from the national to the European level, more precisely the transformation of a national, factual problem into the European legal environment, was considerably facilitated by the widespread consensus in UK society that law reform was needed and would come sooner or later.[108] The Sunday traders did not, however, try to come to an agreement with the 'Keep Sunday Special Campaign' (KSSC) that the best way to resolve the conflict would be to refer it to the ECJ. It seems as if the Sunday traders regarded the KSSC as a *quantité negligible*. The KSSC evidently did not realise the strategic importance of the Euro-litigation. The KSSC was obviously unable to foresee the possible consequences of referring the case from the national to the European level. When it became clear to the KSSC that its campaign on the national level had failed, it should have made an effort to get its arguments heard by the ECJ. However, the KSSC chose not to seek *locus standi* in the national courts, which is a prerequisite for getting access to the ECJ. Thus, the KSSC deliberately excluded itself from the Euro-litigation.[109] They simply lost track. The KSSC's arguments therefore had in effect to be presented by other players. Their arguments dealt mainly with the social and moral dimension of Sunday trading, and these issues were therefore not put to the ECJ as strongly as they otherwise would have been had the KSSC been able to speak for itself. 'Free-riding' therefore turned out to be the wrong strategy. The relationship between shopping on Sunday and the religious background of the original decision did not play a role at the European level.[110] Advocate-General van Gerven alone tried to build a legal argument out of the moral dimension of Sunday trading.

[107] Van Gerven, 'The Effect of Proportionality' in Ellis (ed.), *The Principle of Proportionality*, 37 at 63; more generally see H. Garding, 'Litigation by Public-Interest Groups in European Law' (1996) 39 *German Yearbook of International Law* 361.

[108] Interview with Stuart Isaacs QC on 24 July 1999.

[109] Possibly its success in Parliament led to a misconception of Euro-litigation; see F. Brown, 'The Defeat of the Shops Bill, 1986' in M. Rush (ed.), *Parliament and Pressure Politics* (Oxford, 1990), 213.

[110] E. Schalla, *Das Sonntagsverkaufsverbot in England und Wales, Unter Berücksichtigung Europäischen und Deutschen Rechts* (Cologne, 1994), 3, who gives an historical overview on Sunday trading regulation.

The starting-point for equal treatment litigation is again different. It is unlikely that any of the Member States would wish to see equal treatment issues being decided by the ECJ, and this includes the UK (even though there may have been a certain preparedness, or even support, at least under the Thatcher government, to accept a shift of conflict resolution from the national executive to the national judiciary).[111] Consensus regarding equal treatment litigation was mainly confined to the Equal Opportunity Commission, the trade unions, occasionally employers and often the national judiciary. The Equal Opportunities Commission was not usually involved in the litigation before the European courts, but it provided input at an early stage and thus demonstrated that European law could be used to overcome the narrow boundaries of national law. The fact that the Equal Opportunities Commission did not participate in its own right as a party to the proceedings before the ECJ does not appear to have harmed the resolution of equal treatment issues. Nevertheless, a greater involvement in formal proceedings before the European courts would undoubtedly contribute to a sharpening of the Equal Opportunities Commission's awareness of the cross-border dimension of equal treatment issues, or, to put it another way, to its awareness of equal treatment issues in all the Member States, not just the UK.

Good faith litigation raises similar issues in consensus-building. One may wonder whether good faith, with all its social and moral implications (implied at least in continental Europe),[112] could stand up in the European courts for the time being. In *R.* v. *Secretary of State for Trade and Industry, ex parte Consumers' Association*, there was consensus between the parties to the conflict and the High Court to seek a resolution to the conflict in the ECJ. The case did not involve good faith as such; rather, the conflict concerned *locus standi*, an issue which, as the Sunday trading litigation demonstrated, is essential to consensus-building. The *First National Bank* case could have become the first

[111] Johnson, 'The Judicial Dimension', 148 at 155; Lenz and Will, 'The Preliminary Ruling Procedure', 844 at 861, underlines the high number of references in equal treatment litigation.

[112] For a German legal perspective, see U. Reifner, 'Good Faith: Interpretation or Limitation of Contracts? The Power of German Judges in Financial Services Law' in R. Brownsword, N. Hird and G. Howells (eds.), *Good Faith in Contract: Concept and Context* (Aldershot, 1999), 269 at 271, referring to R. Samek, 'The Objective Theory of Contract and the Rule in L'Estrange v. Graucob' (1974) 52 *Canadian Bar Review* 351; for the contrary view in the common law, see Radbruch, *Der Geist des Englischen Rechts*, 13 and 15.

case in this area to reach the ECJ; however, consensus-building failed in this case. The parties to the conflict, and even academic commentators commenting on the case, demonstrated a certain preparedness to refer the case to the ECJ, but the courts were not prepared to recognise the ECJ as the most appropriate forum for deciding issues of good faith, although an alternative reason might have been the perception that a reference to the ECJ would have permitted the ECJ only to make a formal response to the referred questions, and thus would not have permitted the ECJ to take into consideration the socio-economic background to the dispute.[113] Consensus-building in good faith litigation is still at an early stage.

Bringing together a 'European elite' to make European law effective

There is ample evidence that, in order to make organised law-enforcement a success, one needs to bring together what may be termed a 'European elite' composed of lawyers, judges, counsel and academics to prepare the groundwork for Euro-litigation.[114] The true challenge for litigants is therefore to bring this European elite together, to focus their interest on the relevant policy issues and to initiate a legal discourse on the European law implications. Only such a European elite can guarantee a successful transformation of national politics into European law and a broad consensus for seeking advice on national legal issues in European law. The Sunday traders succeeded brilliantly in establishing such an elite: the equal treatment litigants succeeded in doing so only to a limited extent; the good faith litigants failed entirely to do so. So much is obvious. What we really need to determine are the factors which contribute to building such an elite. It seems as if elite-building is dependent on the subject-matter, on the available skills of the litigants to manage elite-building and on the degree to which all parties concerned are legally entitled to join the litigation.

[113] Teubner, 'Legal Irritants', 24–6.

[114] As far as Sunday trading in particular is concerned, see R. Rawlings, 'The Euro-Law Game: Some Deductions from a Saga' (1993) 20 *Journal of Law and Society* 309; with regard to equal treatment litigation, see Kilpatrick, 'Community or Communities of Courts in European Integration?', 121; Kilpatrick, 'Gender Equality' in Sciarra (ed.), *Labour Law in the Courts*, 31; for a critical view on the 'undemocratic' nature of elite-building, see Morgan, 'Law's British Empire', 729 at 730, 737, 740 and 741. However, elite-building happens in other areas of law and policy, but the transnational context of EU law, juxtaposed with 200 years of determinedly nationalistic jurisprudence, makes it particularly interesting in the EU context.

Those who have participated in Euro litigation form a close-knit and relatively small group of people regardless of the particular subject-matter of the litigation. Euro-litigation starts at the national level; here, the full case is considered in its factual and legal dimensions. The number of persons involved in this group is greater at the national level, as fact-finding typically involves non-lawyers (for example, expert witnesses) as well as lawyers. At the European level, lawyers and academics work in strict privacy. They alone participate in the legal proceedings before the ECJ. The length of the litigation in the Sunday trading saga, lasting for more than a decade and involving, as it did, a second reference by the House of Lords to the ECJ, is of paradigm importance in understanding the process of elite-building. That is why the words of Hoffmann J in *Stoke-on-Trent* reach far beyond the particular subject of Sunday trading:

> Since *Torfaen* there have been numerous prosecutions for Sunday trading in magistrates' courts and Crown Courts. In many of these, evidence has been led on the question of proportionality. A troupe of experts has toured the country giving their views over periods of several days and as a result some courts have convicted and others have acquitted. If the question depends simply on the oral evidence leading to trial even a decision of the House of Lords on appeal of these cases need not settle the matter. The prosecution will fail if the local authority's travelling expert fails to turn up, or if his evidence is different.[115]

Hoffmann J alluded to experts trained by the DIY stores to provide evidence that Sunday trading affects cross-border trade in the European market. The lawyers who represented the parties were always the same, and they too formed part of the 'troupe of experts' touring the country. Over time, the solicitors, barristers, experts and other witnesses developed a close relationship with each other as they appeared before the various courts around the country. When Stuart Isaacs QC, counsel for the local authorities, examined one of the witnesses in *Stoke-on-Trent*, the witness replied by asking, in a friendly manner, whether the issue wasn't one that they had already discussed at length in an earlier trial elsewhere. Hoffmann J interrupted this pleasant conversation between the barrister and the expert witness by saying: 'It looks as if I have come late to the party.'[116] This exchange of banter highlights how

[115] [1999] 3 CMLR 897, para. 36.
[116] Interview with Stuart Isaacs QC on 24 July 1999.

close the relationship was between those involved in the case, even when acting for opposing parties. However, Hoffmann J was wrong in assuming that he had come late to the party. He quickly managed to bring himself up to speed, and thus became a member of the group. The 'troupe of experts' is therefore not limited to economists and sociologists. The metaphor can easily be used for all those, including the judges, who participated in the Sunday trading litigation or in any other Euro-litigation, in particular the equal treatment litigation.[117]

The troupe of experts, which was substantial in number on the national level, was confined to lawyers at the European level. In principle, factual evidence is not heard in the ECJ, and therefore no expert witnesses (such as economists and sociologists) or witnesses of fact are required. The 'troupe of experts' is therefore now composed only of the barristers and their teams, of academics and of judges (of the national courts and the ECJ, including the Advocate-General). It can safely be concluded therefore that a relatively small number of lawyers have settled the law not only in Sunday trading but also in equal treatment litigation. This group of people represents the elite of European lawyers. The barristers are all specialists in European law, and know each other well.[118] The national judges who have delivered judgments in the Sunday trading litigation have enjoyed remarkable careers. This is particularly true of Hoffmann J. The bare statistics of the Sunday trading litigation readily demonstrate that even the notion of a 'handful' of lawyers may be an exaggeration, such was their small number. The situation is less evident in the equal treatment litigation, due to the greater length of time over which the cases were spread (two decades), and the more varied subject-matter of the cases. Nevertheless, it is clear that such a small number of highly qualified European lawyers will be bound together with both formal and informal ties the strength of which and the effect of which are difficult to evaluate. The outcome is the emergence of a team spirit.

In the Sunday trading litigation, there was one notable absence from the European elite. This was the 'Keep Sunday Special Campaign'. The KSSC missed the opportunity to join the inner circle of those who make European law. The KSSC simply failed to build up the necessary

[117] With regard to equal treatment, see J. Mummery, 'The Community Law Impact in Employment Cases' in M. Andenas and F. Jacobs (eds.), *European Community Law in the English Courts* (Oxford, 1998), 191 at 193.

[118] This is due largely to the way in which barristers are organised in the UK.

expertise which was a prerequisite to joining this elite. In the equal treatment litigation, the Equal Opportunities Commission was not formally represented in the elite group of lawyers, because it chooses not to appear as an appellant before the ECJ. There may be tactical reasons for this. However, the effect of this is that the Equal Opportunities Commission excludes itself from the European elite.

Good faith litigation is different. There are no cases which would have required the setting up of a European elite. There are nevertheless lessons to be learnt from *R.* v. *Secretary of State for Trade and Industry, ex parte Consumers' Association* and from the *First National Bank* case. The respective appellants, the Consumers' Association and the Office of Fair Trading, muddled through the cases on their own. There were, to be sure, lawyers and academics involved in the two cases. However, there was no *policy* established by the appellants to bring the expertise together to focus on the issues of, respectively, the *locus standi* of consumer organisations and good faith. The appellants in both cases were willing to do their best to fight for the interests of consumers, but the arguments sounded 'home-made' and even to an extent unprofessional. The question remains of why the parties to the case did not take advantage of the available expertise in good faith litigation outside the UK legal borders.

The impact on organised litigants

Success requires an all-embracing strategy

Table 5.1 demonstrates the factors governing the establishment of a successful strategy in European litigation. The general idea is to draw a distinction between the impact on law and politics on the one hand, and national and European strategies on the other. Those who might make use of the law to implement policy objectives will have to make

Table 5.1 *The factors governing the establishment of a successful strategy in European litigation*

Impact/strategy	National	European
Law/judiciary	Litigation	Litigation
Policy/legislator-executive	Lobbying	Lobbying

a choice between litigation strategies and legal-political strategies. Litigation strategies will necessarily lead you to the courts. One then needs to decide where the litigation is best placed, at the national and/or at the European level. Legal-political strategies will rely on the legislator or on the executive. One then needs to decide on the correct lobbying strategies at the national and/or the European level. The most successful strategy is one that encompasses both law and politics, national and European.

The Sunday traders had the best strategy. From the outset, they did not rely solely on either litigation or legal-political strategies. They pursued *both* strategies, instituting legal proceedings all over the country at the national and the European level and lobbying Parliament on a reform of the Shops Act 1950. In the UK, lobbying Parliament is very much the exception to the rule. The Sunday traders, however, managed to obtain access to Parliament, although initially they had failed to do this.[119] In the end, though, their only real missed opportunity was their failure to lobby the *European* legislator. The 'Keep Sunday Special Campaign' relied entirely on lobbying the national Parliament, and avoided the courts altogether. This turned out to be a major mistake.

The Equal treatment litigants chose litigation as a strategy only after legal-political strategies had failed at the national and European levels (at the national level due to the UK government's lack of interest in the matter at that time, and at the European level because the conciliation strategies introduced in the Single European Act turned out to be a failure).[120] Litigation in the national and European courts is able in some cases to compensate for failings on the political level. The equal treatment litigants therefore chose an either/or strategy, that is, either seeking a resolution through the courts or seeking a resolution through the legislator/executive.

The position of the good faith litigants was similar to that of the equal treatment litigants in their preparedness to select either the courts or the legislator/executive as the appropriate forum for seeking a resolution. However, the good faith litigants failed to match the equal treatment litigants inasmuch as the former did not systematically exploit the full potential of European litigation. Their strategy remained focused on national litigation.

[119] See Norton, *British Policy*, 189.
[120] McIlroy, 'Journey into Europe' in McIlroy (ed.), *Trade Unions*, 13.

Therefore, success in implementing national policies through European law largely depends on an all-embracing strategy. You need both to use the courts, and to lobby the legislator. Where there is no such strategy, failure is a near certainty.

Failure is caused by instrumental overkill

Each strategy has its limits. Even an all-embracing strategy might in the event fail. In the three cases studied here, the Sunday traders succeeded due to their flexibility in shifting the issue back and forth between law and politics and to some extent also between the national and the European levels. Such flexibility was lacking in the equal treatment litigation. Once women's organisations and trade unions had latched on to Euro-litigation as a strategic means of achieving their goal, they over-estimated the potential of litigation. This unwarranted belief in the potential of Euro-litigation inevitably resulted in frustration and disappointment on the part of the litigants. Disappointment may take many forms. The trade unions had set their hopes on Jacques Delors' conciliation strategies,[121] and women's organisations on the ECJ to implement 'justice' and not just 'equality of opportunity'.[122] Thus, a study of the equal treatment litigation allows us to define the conditions for an instrumental overkill of Euro-litigation:

(1) There is a shift away from resolving issues through politics (for example, by lobbying Parliament) towards resolving issues in the national and European courts.
(2) There is a focus on resolving national conflicts by way of European litigation, thus neglecting the horizontal dimension of Euro-litigation.
(3) There is no attempt made to develop a coherent strategy of referring successive and related cases to the ECJ so as to transform national issues into the European legal environment, nor of building a consensus among the legal community, both at the national level and at the European level, for referring cases to the ECJ. Nor is it perceived that there is a need to establish a 'European elite' to support the Euro-litigation.

[121] B. Bagilhole and P. Byrne, 'From Hard to Soft Law and from Equality to Reconciliation in the United Kingdom' in L. Hantrais (ed.), *Gendered Policies in Europe* (Basingstoke, 2000), 124; Stratigaki, 'The European Union' in Hantrais (ed.), *Gendered Policies*, 27.
[122] *Ibid.*

(4) There is a belief on the part of the judiciary that it alone is able to ensure equal treatment.[123]
(5) There is a tendency to stay away from Euro-litigation in order to shift the issue back to national politics.[124]

More professionalism is required

Professions are historically differentiated. Only five professions (priests, lawyers, medical doctors, scientists in general and artists) face an occupational field in which individuals or social aggregates suffer conflicts because they have lost their autonomy to act and decide competently. The reconstruction of autonomy and competence is the objective of those professions which sociology categorises as 'professionalised occupations' – it would be more correct to even speak of 'professionalised professions'. The core phenomenon of professionalised intervention is a striving for truth (the truth of the case, including the application of all professional knowledge available), the provision of a means of professional therapy, and an attempt to reach a consensus that an individually shaped autonomy must be regained. To achieve this, the professionalised actors must hermeneutically understand the case-bound deficiencies in the 'language of the case' by taking the role of the other (the client), then checking all the stocks of knowledge and rules which could be applicable to that specific case in order to resolve the conflict. In a close-up view, rules and knowledge never meet the singular case, and therefore the new knowledge has to be imported into the realm of professional theory. This is especially true in the field of judicial conflict resolution, in which the lay-persons involved suffer from a lack of knowledge and skills, and thus their personal autonomy in resolving the conflict is considerably reduced. The professionalised lawyer intervenes as a proxy for his or her client. Intervention by proxy here refers both to (1) establishing the factual basis of the case, and of the client's motives and interests in bringing the case, and (2) establishing how the case may be transformed into, and resolved by, a judicial process.

There will often be a mismatch between what a client wants and what the law can give him, particularly, as is usually the case, where there

[123] See Lord Denning, as quoted by Morgan, 'Law's British Empire', 729 at 730.
[124] M. Threlfall, 'Taking Stock and Looking Ahead' in Hantrais (ed.), *Gendered Policies*, 180 at 200, arguing that the next forum for action is primarily the domestic arena.

is more than one party to the case. A resolution to the case will need to be found which is able to reconcile, as far as possible, the claims of both the individuals involved and society as a whole (the latter's interests being expressed through law). The professionalised lawyer, in acting as a proxy for his client and in acting his part in the judicial process, will need to reconcile the contradictions inherent in these two roles. Where opposing parties instruct professionalised lawyers to act as their proxies, the lawyers will often be able to reach a consensus regarding a resolution of the conflict, and, by so doing, will restore a measure of personal autonomy to their respective clients. However, in our case studies, the degree to which the claimants were able to make use of such professionalised lawyers varied considerably.

The Sunday traders were the only litigants who met the challenge of fully using the potential of European law. It is true that the Sunday traders had in effect almost unlimited resources at their disposal, and this allowed them to engage the best lawyers in order to transform a national policy issue into the European legal environment, to develop an all-embracing strategy and to get its 'troupe of experts' travelling the length and breadth of the country giving evidence. However, while there was an undeniable difference in the resources available to the Sunday traders and those available to public interest groups such as the 'Keep Sunday Special Campaign', women's organisations, trade unions, the Equal Opportunities Commission and the Consumers' Association, it was not financial resources alone which made the difference. A properly constructed and professional litigation strategy could overcome most of the difficulties inherent in Euro-litigation. Public interest groups could have managed, as the Sunday traders did, to transform a national policy issue into the European legal environment. Such an approach requires public interest groups to look beyond the national context of the issue and to transform it onto a horizontal transnational perspective. They would need to develop a firm base in their home state from which to launch a Euro-litigation campaign. Last but not least, public interest groups have the potential to bring together a European elite in order to defend their interests in the courts.

The major deficiency evident in the strategies of the public interest groups is their focus on the *national* aspect of the issue. By focusing on the national issue, they overstretch the boundaries of the judge-made EC law. Public interest groups need to broaden their perspective; stated more precisely, they must develop an understanding of the *horizontal character* of the European legal order. Such a shift in perspective opens up new opportunities for transnational co-operation with public interest groups from other Member States. Here, contrary to the position of commercial litigants such as the Sunday traders, public interest litigants are in a favourable position.

Judicial strategies to overcome the boundaries of legal-political legitimacy in Euro-litigation

The hypothesis and the means: the scope of the European legal order, and subjective rights and remedies

The general hypothesis advanced here is that the ECJ has listened well to the conflicting signals it has received. It is aware of the fragile legitimacy of a judge-made European legal order, and therefore has developed three different strategies: (1) focusing on the content of the European legal order, (2) stressing the fundamental role and importance of subjective rights, and (3) insisting on the availability of remedies to enforce EU rights. These strategies will have to be considered in more detail before they can be used as a yardstick to evaluate the ECJ's success or failure in the Sunday trading, equal treatment and good faith litigation.

Delimiting the scope of the European legal order

The strongest attack to date on the judge-made European legal order by the Member States followed the ECJ's judgment in *Barber*. *Barber* was the turning point in the ECJ's ambitions to shape a judge-made European legal order. I discern a straightforward link between *Barber* (1990), *Keck* (1993), *Smith* v. *Advel Systems* (1994) and *Grant* (1998). Putting these decisions into their widest context demonstrates that a judge-made European legal order is not without limits, whether in the degree to which private litigants may use market freedoms to strike down purely national administrative-economic laws (*Keck*), or in the degree to which public interest litigants may refer to equal treatment principles to implement 'justice'. Thus the first judicial strategy for overcoming the fragile legitimacy of a judge-made European legal order is therefore to *limit the content of the European legal order.*

EU rights as political rights

The European legal order, even in its most developed form, is based on *rights*. The ECJ tries to compensate for weaknesses in the institutional (constitutional) framework through a recognition of *subjective*, enforceable rights.[125] Understanding subjective rights as *political* rights may contribute to increasing the legitimacy of the European legal order. Subjective rights are to be treated as political rights for three reasons:

(1) Subjective rights grant the right-holder the power to take legal action against his or her Member State, or even to directly enforce the right against the contracting party, if there is one.
(2) The subjective rights of one litigant need to be balanced against the subjective rights of other litigants.
(3) Subjective rights have a transnational dimension, in that the balancing process must be carried out in the context of the internal market, that is, in the context of the European (Economic) Constitution.

The first category is taken from Joerges (i.e. proceduralisation), the second is based on Reich (EU rights as citizen rights), and the third turns Maduro's and Menon and Weatherill's analyses of the ECJ's decisions on trade law encompassing out-of-state trading interests and in-state consumer interests into a general rights-based principle. This needs some explanation. Joerges puts the emphasis on EU rights as a means to strike down national legal rules or to raise substandard national legislation to EU standards in a supranational court. The concept of EU rights as political rights is not bound to negative rights: it is equally applicable to positive rights. Reich underlines the transformation process of EU rights into citizen rights. Such an understanding starts from a twofold premise: that subjective rights are made available by the ECJ and that conflicting values enshrined in subjective rights can be balanced out through litigation. Maduro and Menon and Weatherill focus on the particular transnational dimension in EU litigation which permits an integration of both in-state and out-of-state 'interests'. There is a world of difference between rights and interests. Reich's reading of this part of the European Constitution offers opportunities to dwell on the notion of rights in their transnational dimension.

[125] N. Reich, *Bürgerrechte in der Europäischen Union: Subjektive Rechte von Unionsangehörigen und Drittstaatsangehörigen unter besonderer Berücksichtigung der Rechtslage nach der Rechtsprechung des EuGH und dem Vertrag von Amsterdam* (Baden-Baden, 1999).

EU rights and EU remedies

The European legal order is built on a distinction between *rights* and *remedies*. It is for the European legal order, that is, the ECJ, to define the scope of European subjective *rights*, and for the Member States to provide for the appropriate *remedies*. While the ECJ defends the division of competences between the two legal orders, it is quietly shaping a true European set of remedies.[126] The hypothesis is that European remedies are essential to enforce European rights. Otherwise, the legitimacy of the European legal order cannot be maintained. EU remedies are equally *political* remedies, for three reasons:

(1) They challenge the often illusory nature of national remedies, thereby making considerable inroads into the national procedural law in order to create effective judicial protection.
(2) They guarantee that negative and positive rights, as far as they are granted under EC law, do not remain merely theoretical rights, but become rights which may be enforced in the real world.
(3) They have an inherent transnational dimension in that the remedies are able to fill gaps which result from the fact that national rights are confined in their application to national territories.

These three reasons follow the joint approach of Menon and Weatherill, Joerges, and Reich, who all justify the characterisation of subjective EU rights as political rights. Rights and remedies are inherently interlinked: rights are doomed to failure if there are no appropriate remedies with which to enforce them. It is for this reason that the ECJ has made great efforts to establish EU remedies. Ineffective national remedies undermine the European legal order. Effective EU remedies on the other hand allow for a fuller implementation of EU market freedoms and EU social policies even in cross-border conflicts. EU citizens, as the true holders of these rights and remedies, are in a much better position to enforce EC law beyond the national borders than are public agencies. Thus it is that EC law as a whole, and not just the ECJ, relies very much on private organisations and individuals to enforce the rights in transnational conflicts through appropriate

[126] Here, I rely on paras. 29–32 in N. Reich and H.-W. Micklitz (eds.), *Europäisches Verbraucherrecht* (4th edn, Baden-Baden, 2003), where I have analysed the interplay between rights and remedies in various fields including that of consumer protection.

EU remedies. Directive 98/27/EC on injunctions fits well into such a perspective.[127]

Delimiting the content of the European legal order

The European Community 'suffers' from a lack of deeply rooted values that reach beyond market freedoms. This 'deficiency' becomes clear in equal treatment litigation where the ECJ has avoided the need to make value-judgments by introducing procedural elements into the notion of equality. If this reading is correct, it will be difficult for the ECJ to use good faith litigation as a means of introducing elements of justice into the emerging European private legal order.

The Sunday trading litigation exposed the cracks in EC trade law

The Sunday trading litigation is unique in its use of EC law as a means to enlarge economic freedoms, and by doing so has greatly influenced the European legal order. The Sunday trading litigation constituted the beginning of the end of the ECJ's preparedness to set aside national legislation which impeded free trade within the European Community. Sunday trading was the 'subterranean crack' that permitted *Keck*.[128] Whatever the correct reading of *Keck* might be, the decision in *Stoke-on-Trent* had by then demonstrated a clear shift in the ECJ's policy. As the Member States were apparently unwilling to take the initiative to remove outdated economic-administrative laws and regulations from their statute books in the aftermath of *Cassis de Dijon*, traders were forced to use EU trade law to enlarge the market freedoms. The biggest challenge the traders had to meet was to close the gap left open to Member States which allowed them to justify the imposition of trade restrictions under the 'mandatory requirements doctrine'. This strategy turned out to be successful as long as the Member States were prepared – explicitly or implicitly – to accept the ECJ as the legitimate organ to take action on a supranational level. The more EU trade law

[127] Although one may wonder to what extent the most recently adopted Regulation on Enforcement Co-operation will shift control back to agencies. The Regulation was adopted on 7 October 2004, but has not yet been published in the *Official Journal*.

[128] J. H. H. Weiler, 'The Constitution of the Common Market Place: Text and Context in the Evolution of the Free Movement of Goods' in P. Craig and G. de Búrca, *The Evolution of EU Law* (Oxford, 1999), 369.

clashed with national policies and traditions, the more fragile did the acceptance of the ECJ's legitimacy become. Member States were not prepared, however, to give the ECJ an entirely free hand, even if they agreed with its policy of negative integration.

Sunday trading is an excellent example of this. While the majority of citizens in the UK were happy to accept Sunday trading, they (and the citizens of the other Member States) would not have been willing to permit the ECJ to decide on matters rooted in Christian values. Therefore, the ECJ acted wisely in not entering into a debate over the ability of the Member States to set limits to market freedoms by reference to 'social values', instead deciding the issue by reference to Article 28 (ex Article 30). That is why the Sunday trading case could be considered both to be and not to be a landmark case, in that, whereas it constituted a major step in the public awareness of EC law in the UK, it simultaneously foreshadowed a substantive change in the ECJ's concept of the European legal order. From then on, the reach and scope of the market freedoms were restricted. I would go so far as to state that, in *Stoke-on-Trent*, the ECJ began to interpret the European legal order for the first time as a genuine, supranational legal order whose rules are not meant to substitute for the equivalent national market orders, but rather to apply only where national market restrictions *affect* transnational trade. There is therefore a link between *Stoke-on-Trent*, *Keck* and *Tobacco*.[129] If the Member States intend to extend the scope of the European legal order beyond these boundaries, additional measures, even Treaty amendments, may be necessary. So far, the ECJ has delegated the power to the Member States. The demarcation line between law and politics is thus maintained.

The EC law on equal treatment is restricted to 'equality of opportunity'

In the heyday of the equal treatment litigation, the appellants, the Equal Opportunities Commission and legal doctrine all seemed to believe that the ECJ could provide the answers to those questions that the English legal-political system was not willing to give. We soon learnt that EC law might *help* to establish equality between men and women, and even between men/women and transsexuals, but EC law would not go beyond equality and strive for social justice. Thus,

[129] Judgment of 5 October 2000, Case C-376/98, *Germany* v. *Parliament and Council* (*Tobacco*) [2000] ECR I-8419.

equal treatment, in the EC context, is nothing more than 'equality of opportunity'.[130]

On three occasions, the Equal Opportunities Commission initiated proceedings in an attempt to stretch EC law beyond the notion of 'equality of opportunity'. The first such occasion was the EOC's attempt to use the *Barber*[131] judgment to raise the standards of equal treatment to the highest possible level.[132] However, this attempt failed after the ECJ's judgment in *Smith* v. *Advel Systems*. The second such occasion was the EOC's efforts to bring not only transsexuals (in *P* v. *S*[133]) but also homosexuals (in *Grant*[134]) within the notion of equal treatment. The third such occasion was *Enderby*, which focused on indirect discrimination. However, the ECJ refused to raise the standards of protection beyond formal equality. Although this was already evident from *Smith* v. *Advel Systems* and *Grant*, *Enderby* nevertheless demonstrated the ECJ's unwillingness to outlaw each and every form of indirect discrimination.

Again, we can see how the ECJ took steps to delimit the scope of the European legal order. The ECJ draws a clear demarcation line between the reach of EC law and that of national law, and between law and politics. EC law is meant to establish equality, not social justice. The latter remains in the hands of the Member States. The ECJ thereby avoids becoming entangled in complicated and highly controversial social issues. For example, the equal treatment of homosexuals, which was at stake in *Grant*, is understood as an extension of the socialist liberation ideology which sees divisions in society as an essential component of the operation of capitalism.[135] Such deeply rooted conflicts, regarding which there is no consensus within society, ought not to be decided by the ECJ on the basis solely of the economic implications of equal treatment.

The question remains to what extent the elimination of direct and indirect discrimination fits into such a scenario. Direct discrimination is prohibited by EC law. The internal market has to remain free of such obvious forms of discrimination. But does this mean that EC law is

[130] Mummery, 'The Community Law Impact' in Andenas and Jacobs (eds.), *European Community Law*, 191 at 198.

[131] Case C-262/88, *Barber* v. *Guardian Royal Exchange* [1990] ECR I-1889.

[132] Case C-408/92, *Smith* v. *Advel Systems Ltd* [1994] ECR I-4435.

[133] Case C-13/94, *P* v. *S and Cornwall County Council* [1996] ECR I-2143.

[134] Case C-249/96, *Grant* v. *South West Trains Ltd* [1998] ECR I-621.

[135] Morgan, 'Law's British Empire', 729 at 743, nn. 33 and 34.

interfering in matters of social justice? I suggest not. What the ECJ is really doing here is defining the conditions under which, for example, pregnant women may re-enter the labour market. The situation is even clearer in indirect discrimination. Here, the ECJ avoids deciding the issue of when indirect discrimination occurs, leaving this decision instead to the national courts. One may speculate as to under what circumstances, if any, the ECJ would go beyond formal equality of opportunity. The least that can be said is that additional regulatory steps would be required at the EU level to legitimise any such action taken by the ECJ.

EC private law and access to justice: the outlook for the future

In the absence of any ECJ decisions on good faith, I would like to put forward the hypothesis that, in the future, good faith in consumer contract law will be bound to *procedural good faith*.[136] The elimination of unfair contract terms cannot be regarded as a matter of social justice. This is the lesson to be learnt from the equal treatment litigation.

Procedural good faith would bring with it a *parity between consumers and suppliers in concluding contracts*. English contract law can contribute to a comprehensive understanding of procedural good faith, in contrast to substantive good faith. Procedural good faith would also cover incorporation and construction. It remains to be seen whether the ECJ is willing to develop such a comprehensive understanding of the concept of good faith which reaches beyond the scope of the Directive. The English experience provides a strong incentive for extending the scope of the Directive in order to integrate procedural good faith. Such an understanding also fits well with the ECJ's preparedness to consider the individual circumstances of each case, even if the contract at issue contains a term which is in principle outlawed under the indicative list. Just like the English courts, the ECJ seems to put less emphasis on the question of whether the term in question has been individually negotiated or is part of standard business terms and conditions.

The indicative list in the Annex to the Directive provides a minimum level of protection, at least with regard to *standard* terms where the

[136] See pp. 413–23 above. Such a reading might be confirmed by the most recent judgment, Judgment of 1 April 2004, Case C-237/02, *Freiburger Kommunalbauten GmbH Baugesellschaft & Co. KG* v. *Ludger Hofstetter et Ulrike Hofstetter* [2004] 2 CMLR 13.

individual circumstances are largely set aside. Thus, the indicative list establishes an agreed level of substantive good faith throughout the European Community. It should be recalled that, in *Océano*,[137] the ECJ emphasised that the terms in the indicative list cannot be regarded as void *per se*: the individual circumstances of the case still need to be taken into account by the national court. This is precisely *good faith in context*![138] Such an interpretation fits well with the established case law of the ECJ on indirect discrimination. Similarly, it is well grounded in Article 4 of the Directive. In light of the case law on indirect discrimination, the 'in so far as it causes' argument[139] may invite suppliers to rely on economic justifications to support their right to use terms included in the indicative list. If this reading is correct, terms included in the indicative list cannot be understood as a matter of social justice. The final decision would again be put in the hands of the Member States' courts. They are best placed to decide questions of fact.

Sooner or later, the ECJ will have to face the challenge of deciding on the issue of substantive good faith. This would require the ECJ to cross the boundaries of formal equality or parity, and develop its own conception of (consumer) contracts[140] and thus become involved in matters of social justice. Where no standards exist at all, good faith can only be determined by a European concept which takes into account

[137] Judgment of 27 June 2000, Joined Cases C-240 to 244/96, *Océano Grupo Editorial SA* v. *Rocio Murciano Quintero* and *Salvat Editore SA* v. *José M. Sánchez Alcón Prades* [2000] ECR I-4941; and the comment by J. Stuyck, 'Judgment of 27 June 2000' (2001) 38 *Common Market Law Review* 719.

[138] See R. Brownsword, G. Howells and T. Wilhelmsson, 'Between Market and Welfare: Some Reflections on Article 3 of the EC Directive on Unfair Terms in Consumer Contracts' in C. Willett (ed.), *Aspects of Fairness in Contract* (London, 1996), 25; C. Willett, 'Good Faith and Consumer Contract Terms' in R. Brownsword, N. Hird and G. Howells (eds.), *Good Faith in Contract – Concept and Context* (Aldershot, 1998), 67; M. Bridge, 'Good Faith in Commercial Contracts' in R. Brownsword, N. Hird and G. Howells (eds.), *Good Faith in Contract – Concept and Context* (Aldershot, 1998), 139; and Teubner, 'Legal Irritants', 11.

[139] The ECJ did not confirm the Advocate-General's view that the aim of the Directive is to remove more generally assumed imbalances between consumers and sellers. The aim rather is to exclude those clauses which are shown, *in concreto*, to cause a significant imbalance; see Art. 3(1) of the Directive and para. 24 of the Judgment: '. . . in so far as it causes . . . .'

[140] S. Whittaker, 'Unfair Contract Terms, Public Services and the Construction of a European Conception of Contract' (2000) 116 *Law Quarterly Review* 95.

the lack of societal values and the 'rights rhetoric'. I have suggested elsewhere that the concept of legitimate expectations might contribute to giving shape to substantive good faith in the European legal order.[141] Legitimate expectations fit well into the rights rhetoric of the ECJ and more broadly of the European legal order. Seen thus, contractual rights have a human rights dimension.[142] The findings of the three case studies imply that matters of justice cannot and should not be decided by the ECJ alone. The European legal order leaves room for the development of new concepts of social justice, that is, where the European Community might be competent to shape only the outer limits of the concept of good faith, and where the national courts will decide on individual or collective justice.

Such a reading is very much in line with English law. The English legal system does not like the idea of broad general legal principles that courts must refer to in order to ground their judgments.[143] Instead, the courts rely on their analysis of the facts at issue. It is here that EC law fits in, although in doing so it changes the outlook from objective standards in the application of the law to a more subjective rights-oriented approach.[144] However, such a scenario is ten years into the future. For the time being, it will be challenging enough simply to implement the requirements of the indicative list Community-wide and to agree on a genuine European concept of good faith.

141 H.-W. Micklitz, 'Social Justice in European Private Law' (1999/2000) 19 *Yearbook of European Law* 167.

142 R. Brownsword, 'Review of A. D. Forte (ed.), Good Faith in Contract and Property Law (Oxford, 1999)' (2000) 63 *Modern Law Review* 940; T. Wilhelmsson, 'Is There a European Consumer Law – And Should There Be One?' in Centro di studi e richerche di diritto comparato e straneiro, *Saggi, Conferenze et Seminari* (Rome, 2000), 41.

143 Bridge, 'Good Faith in Commercial Contracts' in Brownsword, Hird and Howells (eds.), *Good Faith in Contract*, 139 at 143; E. McKendrick, 'Good Faith: A Matter of Principle?' in A. D. Forte (ed.), *Good Faith in Contract and Property Law* (Oxford, 1999), 39; and H. MacQueen, 'Good Faith: An Undisclosed Principle?' in A. D. Forte (ed.), *Good Faith in Contract and Property Law* (Oxford, 1999), 5. English legal philosophers such as Treitel and Raz are quite hostile to the idea of accepting good faith as a general principle for the very reasons Reifner points out: see Reifner, 'Good Faith' in Brownsword, Hird and Howells (eds.), *Good Faith in Contract*, 269.

144 With regard to market freedoms and the subjectivisation of the *Wednesbury* doctrine through the EC proportionality rule, see C. Barnard and I. Hare, 'Police Discretion and the Rule of Law: Economic Community Rights Versus Civil Rights' (2000) 63 *Modern Law Review* 581; with regard to the subjectivisation of the UK reasonableness test through EC good faith regulation, see R. Bradgate, 'Unreasonable Standard Terms' (1997) 60 *Modern Law Review* 582 and Whittaker, 'Unfair Contract Terms', 95.

The mutual relationship between UK and EC law

The more EC law intervenes into national law, the more national Euro-litigation becomes. It is therefore no surprise that dialogue between the two legal systems increases with the degree of such intervention. In essence, UK law might contribute, or has contributed, at all three levels (trade law, the law on equal treatment and private law) to defining the outer limits of EC law. The findings from the three case studies invite more in-depth speculation on the role of the UK within the European Union. UK Euro-litigation, particularly in its coming together of national courts and the ECJ, and of the UK legal system and the European legal system, reflects a widespread reluctance within the UK for further European integration, and all the more so for the establishment of a supranational state.

The UK is not the only Member State to make use of the Article 234 (ex Article 177) reference procedure for the purposes of conflict resolution. The steadily narrowing perspective of Euro-litigation, and its ever stronger national bias in equal treatment and good faith litigation, may be outweighed by making national litigation more 'European' by integrating the other national legal orders and their responses to conflicts into Euro-litigation. The integration of comparative law and comparative legal practice into Euro-litigation[145] not only might lead to new insights into old struggles over freedoms, equality and justice, but might also help to increase the legitimacy of the judge-made European legal order.

EC rights as political rights in the making of the European legal order

The inherently political nature of EC rights must be analysed in accordance with its three dimensions: (1) the subjective right to challenge the UK government or UK employers in the courts; (2) an open-textured, rights-based mechanism for implanting social values in an endless chain of EU litigattion; and (3) a subjective right which includes a particular transnational dimension which takes account of extraterritorial interests.

The right to market freedoms

In the Sunday trading litigation, the Sunday traders invoked their *putative right* under Article 28 (ex Article 30) to open their shops on

[145] See R. Michaels, 'Im Westen nichts Neues?' (2002) 66 RabelsZ 97 at 104.

Sunday. They challenged the UK government in the ECJ to justify the compatibility with Community law of the Shops Act 1950 which limited these freedoms. The need for market freedoms in a market-based society is beyond any doubt. There may be disagreement over the reach of the market freedoms, and there may be disagreement on who is to oversee the establishment and completion of the market freedoms (whether the Community or the Member States), but the principle as such, and the value-judgments inherent in it, are recognised throughout the Community. Legal and economic theories derive their legitimacy and even their legality from the 'economic constitution of the European Community'.[146] Therefore, the Sunday traders' claim forced the UK government to implement a strategy to safeguard the UK's interests in the Euro-litigation. The ECJ decided in *Torfaen* and confirmed in *Stoke-on-Trent* that the Sunday traders may have such a right, at least in principle. This conclusion was based on the then prevalent interpretation of 'measures having equivalent effect'.

The right to economic freedoms stood opposed to employment protection and the preservation of the special (Christian) character of Sundays. In a traditional reading of Article 28 (ex Article 30), the ECJ appears as the guardian of the *interests* of the Member States, here the UK. However, it is possible to understand Article 28 (ex Article 30) as granting the Member States a legal 'right' to defend the interests of the UK public, possibly even as a European-based responsibility.[147] Such a reading entails two further questions: (1) who is the true holder of such a right, the state and/or public interest groups; and (2) what might be the content of such a right? It should be recalled that the legal standing of the 'Keep Sunday Special Campaign' under EC law was very doubtful; however, the KSSC did not even attempt to seek standing in the national courts, and therefore, in the event, the UK government appeared as the sole holder of the right before the ECJ. The content of such a right is again unclear, that is, the content of the social policies

[146] M. Streit and W. Mussler, 'The Economic Constitution of the European Community – From "Rome" to "Maastricht"' (1994) 5 *Constitutional Political Economy* 319; J. Basedow, *Von der deutschen zur europäischen Wirtschaftsverfassung* (Tübingen, 1992); for an American perspective, see D. Gerber, 'Constitutionalizing the Economy: German Neo-liberalism, Competition Law and the "New" Europe' (1994) 42 *American Journal of Comparative Law* 25; and Chalmers, 'The Single Market' in Shaw and More (eds.), *New Legal Dynamics*, 55.

[147] It will need to be considered, at least in theory, whether the Member States have a responsibility to ensure the sanctity of the Sabbath. On the notion of rights versus responsibilities, see H.-W. Micklitz, 'Social Justice', 167.

which may be recognised as legitimate, as well as the question of whether these rights should be vested in the hands of the Member States or the European Community. In the Sunday trading litigation, the issue of employment protection in *Conforama* and *Marchandise*[148] and the issue of the preservation of the special character of Sundays in *Stoke-on-Trent*,[149] were to be decided in the legal arena. From the perspective of the economic constitution of Europe, this requires a decision as to the degree to which social policies fit into the idea of a market-based society, and on whether the guardian of the social policies should be the European Community or the Member States. The ECJ indicated in *Stoke-on-Trent*, and confirmed in *Keck*,[150] that joint policy decisions by the European Community and the Member States are needed to give the Community a clearer institutional outlook.[151]

The extraterritorial dimension of the right to market freedoms has remained largely outside the Sunday trading conflict. The Sunday traders prepared statistics to provide evidence that the Shops Act 1950 affected intra-Community. These statistics, as well as the experts presenting them, constituted a substantial part of the evidence presented to the UK courts, and, though to a much lesser degree, to the ECJ. Contrary to what happened in *Keck* and *Tobacco*, the ECJ was not really willing to take account of any effect on intra-Community trade, possibly because the statistics were rather weak or possibly because the alleged effect was far from being evident. The transnational dimension of employment protection and of the preservation of the special character of Sunday played no role at all in the arguments before the ECJ. None of the parties made a survey of the rules in the other Member States in order to develop arguments in support of their case. If any of the parties had put forward such evidence, the ECJ would have been in an even more difficult situation. I conclude therefore that there is no consensus on the true nature of Sunday among the Member States.

148 Case C-312/89, *Union Departmentale des Syndicats CGT de l'Aisne* v. *Sidef Conforama* [1991] ECR 997; Case C-332/89, *Ministère Public* v. *Marchandise* [1991] ECR 1027; and C. Wallace, 'European Integration and Legal Culture: Indirect Sex Discrimination in the French Legal System' (1999) 19 *Legal Studies* 397 at 401, where she refers to the French *Cour de Cassation*, which has used the very same arguments in Sunday trading cases.

149 Case C-169/91, *Stoke-on-Trent City Council* v. *B&Q plc* [1992] ECR 6635; [1993] 1 CMLR 426.

150 Case C-267 and 268/91, *Keck and Mithouard* [1993] ECR I-6097.

151 See H.-W. Micklitz, 'Das Keck-Urteil des EuGH – Vom Binnenmarkt zurück zum Freihandel?' (1994) IStR 86–92.

This is particular true with regard to the religious character of Sunday. The dispute over the wearing of headscarves in some Member States as well as over the preamble to the proposed European Constitution indicates how difficult it will be to reach agreement over the role and function of religion in the European Community.[152]

The right to equal treatment

Slowly but surely, the European Community has developed its own social policies, including an equal treatment policy. Article 141 (ex Article 119) and Directives 75/117/EEC and 76/207/EEC provide a *subjective right* to equal treatment as a constitutional principle.[153] Such a right to equal treatment may be invoked before the ECJ in order to challenge substandard national legislation. The right to equal treatment is a positive right under which the holders can claim true equal treatment between men and women. Here, the state appears not as the party restricting freedoms but as the party granting protection. The original Directives on equal treatment did not, however, provide for *collective* rights to take action in the field of equal treatment.[154] This gap was instead filled by the House of Lords when it granted the Equal Opportunities Commission *locus standi* in equal treatment matters.[155]

It is not the state as such which is under attack in equal treatment litigation, but rather the state as an employer. This is due to the early policy of the ECJ to grant *vertical* direct effect to Article 141 (ex Article 119) and the two Directives. The consequence of this was that private employers and other private parties were mere bystanders to the litigation, although they were of course well aware that any decision by the ECJ could easily affect them. The effect of restricting Article

[152] J. H. H. Weiler, *Ein christliches Europa, Erkundungsgänge* (Salzburg and Munich, 2004).

[153] G. More, 'The Principle of Equal Treatment: From Market Unifier to Fundamental Right?' in P. Craig and G. de Búrca (eds.), *The Evolution of EU Law* (Oxford, 1999), 517.

[154] See, however, the newly introduced collective rights in Art. 7(2) of Directive 2000/43/EC implementing the principle of equal treatment between persons irrespective of racial or ethnic origin; Art. 9(2) of Directive 2000/78/EC establishing a general framework for equal treatment in employment and occupation; and Art. 6(3) of Directive 2002/73/EC amending Directive 76/207/EEC on the implementation of the principle of equal treatment for men and women as regards access to employment, vocational training and promotion, and working conditions.

[155] As to the importance of the House of Lords' judgment, see Mummery, 'The Community Law Impact' in Andenas and Jacobs (eds.), *European Community Law*, 191 at 193 and 194.

141 (ex Article 119) to its vertical direct effect had counterproductive effects in Euro-litigation. Those who were most affected by unequal treatment were effectively excluded from the judicial discourse. It was only in recent times, when the ECJ changed its policy on direct effect and permitted a horizontal direct effect to Article 141 (ex Article 119) that these hitherto excluded litigants were able to take advantage of Article 141 (ex Article 119) to enforce equal pay against their private employers. *Barber* is a perfect example of such a strategy.[156] However, as the ECJ continues to deny horizontal direct effect to Directives, the enforcement of the right to equal treatment is hampered because the ability to enforce the right is very much dependent on to whom it is addressed. While the horizontal direct effect of Directives would increase the legitimacy of the judge-made legal order and negate Scharpf's argument that the EU is a purely market-based entity, it would at the same time provoke new conflicts between the ECJ and the Member States.

Equal treatment litigation is essentially a conflict over rights. The rights of employers to define the content of employment contracts are opposed to the rights of employees to equal treatment. In balancing these conflicting rights, the ECJ must weigh social rights (social policies) against the rights of the Member States to decide to what extent they should be bound by the EC rules on equal treatment. Contrary to the position in the Sunday trading litigation, the ECJ was not asked to reduce market freedoms but rather to positively shape the level of protection granted to Member State citizens.

Freedom appears in two different forms. First, in private law relations, it is a *market* freedom, which is based on the private autonomy of private parties. Secondly, in public law relations, freedom may have a *political* dimension (as in *Johnston*[157]), or alternatively it may be the *economic* freedom to determine where and how to spend one's money (as in *Barber*[158]). Employers rely on these freedoms to justify unequal treatment. The ECJ is in a delicate position when it weighs

[156] See van Gerven in Case C-262/88, *Barber* v. *Guardian Royal Exchange* [1990] ECR I-1889.

[157] Case 222/84, *Johnston* v. *Chief Constable of the Royal Ulster Constabulary* [1986] ECR 1651.

[158] See Case C-262/88, *Barber* v. *Guardian Royal Exchange* [1990] ECR I-1889; for its follow-up in the courts and in practice, see G. Moffat and L. Luckhaus, 'Occupational Pension Schemes, Equality and Europe: A Decade of Change' (1998) 20 *Journal of Social Welfare and Family Law* 1.

social rights/policies against economic/political freedoms, a process which necessarily involves deciding who will pay for the extra costs involved in equal treatment. The legal question then becomes to what extent 'economic reasons' may be used as a justification for unequal treatment in private law and/or in public law relations. In theory, respondents may not rely on economic justifications in equal treatment litigation. In practice, the ECJ indirectly takes into account economic justifications when deciding issues of equal treatment. This is abundantly clear from *Barber*,[159] in which the ECJ denied retrospective effect to its judgment; it is likewise clear from *Smith* v. *Advel Systems*[160] and *Grant*,[161] in which the costs of equal treatment were held to be a relevant factor. Restricting equal treatment to what Member States and private employers can afford means that EC law is not succeeding in raising the standard of equal treatment to the highest possible level.[162] The Member States and the Community will need to take a policy decision on the role and function of social rights within the economic constitution of Europe – if they want to do so.[163]

There is no transnational dimension to the right to equal treatment, judging by the evidence available. This is due to the fact that equal treatment litigants are bringing *national* problems before the ECJ. In theory, part of the task of the ECJ is to establish the relationship between the various national legal orders of the Member States and the European legal order. In practice, however, if such attempts are made by the ECJ, this is not apparent from its judgments.[164] The need to do this will increase as market freedoms touch more and more upon social rights generally (not just those concerned with equal treatment). *Centros*,[165] *Überseering*[166] and *Inspire Art*[167] have already brought the

[159] Case C-262/88, *Barber* v. *Guardian Royal Exchange* [1990] ECR I-1889.
[160] Case C-408/92, *Smith* v. *Advel Systems Ltd* [1994] ECR I-4435.
[161] Case C-249/96, *Grant* v. *South West Trains Ltd* [1998] ECR I-623.
[162] These limits would have to be overcome even if equal treatment is understood as a broad constitutional principle; see More, 'The Principle of Equal Treatment' in Craig and de Búrca, *Evolution of EU Law*, 517.
[163] H.-W. Micklitz and S. Weatherill, *European Economic Law* (Aldershot, 1997); and More, 'The Principle of Equal Treatment' in Craig and de Búrca, *Evolution of EU Law*, 517 at 519.
[164] It is well known that the ECJ often makes comparisons of the national legal orders of the Member States. Sometimes, the conclusions of the Advocates-General contain a comparative element.
[165] Judgment of 9 March 1993, Case 212/97, *Centros* [1999] ECR I-1459.
[166] Judgment of 5 November 2002, Case 208/00, *Überseering* [2002] ECR I-9919.
[167] Judgment of 30 September 2003, Case C-167/01, *Inspire Art* [2003] ECR I-10155.

relationship between the freedom of establishment and the Member States' co-determination laws into the European legal arena.

The right of access to justice for consumers

The starting-point in respect of good faith litigation is similar to that in the equal treatment litigation. The first point is the question of whether individual consumers benefit from *subjective* directly enforceable rights in private law relations. There is no equivalent to Article 141 (ex Article 119) for consumers. The newly introduced Article 153 (ex Article 129) has not (yet) been granted direct effect. One eminent legal commentator has raised the question of whether the right to information may be granted direct effect at least in combination with Directives that give shape to the right to information.[168] Such a reading of Article 153 (ex Article 129) opens up a new perspective not only in consumer law but more particularly in good faith litigation. Thus, consumer rights, if any, have to be based on Directive 93/13/EEC. Legal-judicial imagination is required to define the possible content of such consumer rights. While the ECJ has not yet been active in this area, legal doctrine is already advocating an individual and enforceable right to challenge the *transparency* of contract terms.[169]

During the course of good faith litigation, a supplier will oppose his or her right to private autonomy (based on market freedoms[170]) against individual or collective consumer rights. In coming to its decision, a court will therefore need to strike the right balance between the consumer's and the supplier's rights. This is common ground in Euro-litigation. The Annex to the Directive provides guidance on the content of consumer contracts. The terms included in the Annex are not, in principle, available to the parties. It is tempting to link the consumer's right to conclude a contract on the basis of transparent terms with the indicative list. The consumer would then have a 'right' to a contract which contains no such terms as are included in the Annex.

Beyond this individual right, Directive 93/13/EEC establishes the *collective* right for state enforcement agencies and/or consumer

[168] N. Reich, 'Verbraucherrecht und Verbraucherschutz im Vertrag von Amsterdam' (1999) 14 VuR 3 at 7.

[169] T. Pfeiffer, 'Richtlinie 93/13/EWG des Rates über mißbräuchliche Klauseln in Verbraucherverträgen' in E. Grabitz and M. Hilf (eds.), *Das Recht der Europäischen Union* (Munich, 1999), Art. 5, at 33.

[170] P.-C. Müller-Graff (ed.), *Gemeinsames Privatrecht in der Europäischen Gemeinschaft* (Baden-Baden, 1999).

organisations to take action in the national courts to eliminate standard terms which do not comply with the indicative list in the Annex or which are contrary to good faith. The Labour government amended the UTCCR so as to grant legal standing to the Consumers' Association. However, it was the Office of Fair Trading that initiated proceedings in *Director-General of Fair Trading* v. *First National Bank plc.*[171] Although there is no direct link between the new powers granted to the Consumers' Association and the recent 'judicial activism' of the Office of Fair Trading, it may nevertheless be suggested that the Office of Fair Trading is not willing to leave the floor to consumer organisations. Whether this is the case or not, the ground is better prepared for future Euro-litigation in this area. There is now not one but two organisations which may in the long run play a similar role to that of the Equal Opportunities Commission.

The *addressee* of these individual and collective rights is first and foremost the private supplier. The Directive does not address 'emanations of the state'. These latter bodies are exempted from the scope of application of the Directive, although it is here that unfair contract terms are most often encountered. At first sight, this raises the possibility of extending the scope of application of the Directive[172] to 'emanations of the state': just as the Equal Opportunities Commission took cases first against public employers (using *vertical* direct effect) and later extended this to private employers, so the same may be done with respect to the scope of application of the Directive, albeit in reverse order. The private employer is the primary addressee of the Directive, although the Directive has no *horizontal* direct effect in private law relations. Vertical direct effect, so effectively used in equal treatment litigation, will not permit this to be done in good faith litigation.

Table 5.2 demonstrates that it is impossible to combine individual/collective rights under Directive 93/13/EEC with its vertical direct effect, that is, to combine the challenge of the subject-matter – national unfair terms legislation before the ECJ – with the state as the potential addressee of the Directive – as a public company. This means that, in

171 [2000] 2 All ER 759.

172 P. Rott and B. Butters, 'Öffentliche Dienstleistungen und Vertragsgerechtigkeit im Lichte des Gemein-schaftsrechts' (1999) 14 VuR 75 at 107. See also Whittaker, 'Unfair Contract Terms', 95, who refers to the same study which formed the background to Rott and Butters' study.

Table 5.2 *The relationship between vertical direct effect and horizontal direct effect, and the addressee in equal treatment and good faith litigation*

	Vertical direct effect	Horizontal direct effect
Addressee in equal treatment	Public employers (+)[a]	(–) but Art. 141 as a way out
Addressee in good faith	Private companies (–)	(–) no way out (Art. 153 as an option)
	Public companies (?)	

[a] + means 'yes'; – means 'no'.

each and every good faith litigation, the national private legal order as such is at stake.

While the transnational dimension in good faith litigation is evident, the ECJ has so far refrained from taking national private legal orders into account. All that the ECJ did in *Commission* v. *Netherlands* was to invoke the transnational right of the consumer to be informed of his or her rights. The impact of Directive 98/27/EC on injunctions is not yet clear, although it paves the way for bringing together different legal orders in Euro-litigation.

The 'rights rhetoric' and the English legal system

The 'rights rhetoric' requires the existence of rights, a definition of the holder of the rights and an addressee of the rights. English law, and the conclusions which can be drawn from the three case studies, demonstrate the potential of the rights rhetoric to determine the correct holder of the rights and (most of all) the correct addressee of the rights. The *lack* of European societal values (*einer objektiven Ordnung*) is obvious. In the light of the foregoing analysis, this lack may become a strength. The EC rights rhetoric constitutes a sound compromise in the further development of a European legal order, in which societal values have to be developed out of subjective rights. The rights rhetoric allows English law to avoid debates over broad and alien principles and to engage in the battle of rights. English law is very close to accepting that change.

English law is unable to help in this respect where European law has established contrary boundaries. The denial of horizontal direct effect prevents the European legal order from establishing binding social standards in private law relations. One may wonder whether the ECJ would overstep its self-imposed boundaries if it were to take the duties resulting from secondary Community law into consideration. *Barber* has established the right to equal pay, even in horizontal relations; at the same time, the new beneficiaries of those rights also had to accept the effects of their claim – that is, that the extra costs of equal treatment are now shared by men and women alike.

EU remedies in the European legal order

EU remedies are needed to give effect to EU rights. This finding will be developed out of the threefold premise that national remedies do not suffice to guarantee effective judicial protection, and therefore genuine EU remedies need to be developed to implement EC law not only within the Member States, but also in transnational conflicts. The three case studies highlight a remarkable difference: in the Sunday trading litigation (a litigation based on EU trade law), the remedies were developed out of provisions of the Treaty, whereas, in the equal treatment and good faith litigation, the remedies were based on secondary Community law.

Remedies in the Sunday trading litigation: interim relief and state liability

The Sunday trading litigation demonstrates to what degree the outcome of the case was linked to the availability of European remedies.[173] The Sunday traders may well have lost their case had the local authorities been able to take out injunctions, force the shops to close, and transfer the burden of the potential liability claims onto the national government. The *Francovich* doctrine, however, was not yet fully developed, and therefore this was not possible. The issue here was whether and to what extent the local authorities had to give cross-undertakings in damages under UK law. Both the Sunday traders and the local authorities referred to EU remedies to support their positions. A fully fledged EU remedy on state liability would have considerably increased the room for manoeuvre of the local authorities. If the local authorities had been released from the risk of legal liability and had obtained

[173] For a discussion of the importance of cross-undertakings in damage, see pp. 79–83 above.

injunctions forcing the shops to close, the Sunday traders would have sought interim relief from the ECJ in order to protect their putative right to trade on Sunday. This situation amply demonstrates that EU remedies largely determined the outcome of the whole conflict.

The Sunday trading litigation had no transnational element which necessitated the use of EU remedies. Such a situation could have arisen if the Sunday traders had been able to claim that other Member States permitted more liberal opening hours, or that other Member States, although they prohibited Sunday opening in theory, in practice did not apply the law. The latter argument came up in *Hedley Lomas.*[174]

Remedies in equal treatment litigation: sanctions

The equal treatment litigation seems to confirm the need for European remedies to enforce European rights on equal treatment. The ECJ rigorously implements those rules over which it claims sole jurisdiction. As the Member States had shown a certain reluctance to enforce the EC rules on equal treatment, the ECJ took advantage of the widely drafted terms of Article 6 of Directive 76/207/EEC to 'Europeanise' judicial protection and to force the Member States to provide adequate *sanctions.*[175] Initially, in 1986 that meant that the ECJ relied on the Member States to provide appropriate remedies to sanction violations of the equal treatment doctrine. That is why the ECJ denied direct effect to the second limb (the obligation to impose sanctions) of Article 6 in *von Colson*[176] and later in *Johnston.*[177] When it became apparent that national remedies were not working, the ECJ changed its policy and conceded direct effect to the second limb of Article 6 in *Marshall II.*[178] The very same logic lies behind *Coote*[179] and *Levez.*[180]

It is fair to conclude that EU remedies greatly affected the equal treatment litigation at both the Member State and the EU levels. Without

[174] Case C-5/94, *R.* v. *Ministry of Agriculture, Fisheries and Food, ex parte Hedley Lomas (Ireland) Ltd* [1996] ECR I-2553; [1996] 2 CMLR 391.

[175] Kilpatrick, 'Community or Communities of Courts in European Integration?', 121 at 136.

[176] Case 14/83, *Von Colson and Kamann* v. *Land Nordrhein-Westfalen* [1984] ECR 1891 at 1908; and see J. Shaw, 'European Community Judicial Method: Its Application to Sex Discrimination' (1990) 19 *Industrial Law Journal* 228 at 234, n. 33.

[177] Case 222/84, *Johnston* v. *Chief Constable of the Royal Ulster Constabulary* [1986] ECR 1651.

[178] Case C-271/91, *Marshall* v. *Southampton and South West Hampshire Area Health Authority (Marshall II)* [1993] ECR I-4367.

[179] Case C-185/97, *Coote* v. *Granada Hospitality Ltd* [1998] ECR I-5199.

[180] Case C-326/96, *Levez* v. *T. H. Jennings (Harlow Pools) Ltd* [1998] ECR I-7835; [1999] All ER (EC) 1.

the courage of the ECJ, the equal treatment litigants would have had to rely on ineffective national remedies. Again, the transnational dimension is missing in the cases studied here, even though it is essential that EU labour law be made compatible with the national legal orders. Therefore, the question did not arise of whether EU remedies were needed to fill a gap in the Member States' national legal orders. The newly introduced right to collective action in equal treatment litigation, if combined with Directive 98/27/EC on injunctions, might set new incentives.

Remedies in good faith litigation: sanctions and injunctions

Legal doctrine has devoted little attention to the potential of subjective rights in private law matters. There is a certain preparedness to discuss the criteria under which Articles in private law Directives may be understood as granting rights to consumers. Legal doctrine has even greater difficulties in developing *remedies* to give effect to these rights. If we suppose for the purposes of argument that there exists an *individual* right to a transparent contract, what are the consequences if such a right is not respected? Is the contract void, and should the consumer have a right to compensation and, if so, for what? Article 7(1) of Directive 93/13/EEC uses the standard formula of EC private law.[181] Member States are obliged to ensure that 'adequate and effective means exist' to protect consumers against unfair contract terms. Bearing in mind the experience with Articles 5 and 6 of Directive 76/207/EEC, one may wonder what the ECJ will read into Article 7 of Directive 93/13/EEC. The key question will be what 'adequate and effective means' requires. Experience in equal treatment litigation shows that the ECJ might put pressure on the Member States to ensure at least that the blacklisted terms in the indicative list are eliminated.

Collective rights and collective redress raised much more concern, particularly in the UK. Article 7(2)[182] compelled the UK to grant powers to the Office of Fair Trading under the UTCCR 1994, and later also

[181] Art. 7(1) provides: 'Member States shall ensure that, in the interests of consumers and of competitors, adequate and effective means exist to prevent the continued use of unfair terms in contracts concluded with consumers by sellers or suppliers.'

[182] Art. 7(2) provides: 'The means referred to in paragraph 1 shall include provisions whereby persons or organizations, having a legitimate interest under national law in protecting consumers, may take action according to the national law concerned before the courts or before competent administrative bodies for a decision as to whether contractual terms drawn up for general use are unfair, so that they can apply appropriate and effective means to prevent the continued use of such terms.'

to consumer organisations under the UTCCR 1999. So far, the Member States have tended to view the appropriate remedy as an *injunction*. This is the same logic that produced Directive 98/27/EC. However, *Cofidis*[183] allows for a broader understanding of the remedies required under Directive 93/13/EEC. It seems therefore that the ECJ may be willing to develop a right to compensation out of Article 7(2).[184]

National remedies and EU remedies in tandem?

A European legal order based on rights cannot exist without European remedies. The ECJ has made clear that it pays more than mere lip-service to the doctrine of effective legal protection. The enforceability of EU rights, be they individual or collective rights, is high on the ECJ's agenda. The rather basic EU remedies provided in the equal treatment and the good faith Directives serve the ECJ as a sufficient basis to shape European remedies in these areas. The ECJ applies a step-by-step approach. It only intervenes where national remedies prove ineffective. While the ECJ does not seek to undermine the Member States' competence in providing appropriate remedies, in reality it *is* shaping EU remedies for EU rights. Member State remedies, however, subsist only in a national context.

The effects of the three strategies on the legitimacy gap

As I said in my introductory remarks, this book does not claim to provide answers to all the questions it raises. Instead, I want to demonstrate the potential of judicial co-operation if it is done correctly. Nevertheless, the question remains of whether the strategies the ECJ has developed are sufficient to close the legitimacy gap or whether politics will continue to blame the judge-made legal order for burying the Western-style social welfare state. The latter would undermine the ECJ's authority. Readers may criticise my analysis for being naive in overstating the undemocratic power of judges.[185] Three final remarks with regard to the three strategies[186] under review will indicate the

[183] Case C-473/00, *Cofidis SA* v. *Fredout* [2002] ECR I-875.

[184] P. Rott, 'Effektiver Rechtsschutz vor missbräuchlichen AGB – Zum Cofidis-Urteil des EuGH' (2003) EuZW 10–14.

[185] See Morgan, 'Law's British Empire', 729 at 744.

[186] The three strategies are: (1) delimiting the scope of the European legal order; (2) transforming the subjective rights of market citizens into the political rights of Union citizens; and (3) developing European remedies to enforce European rights.

further potential of the politics of judicial co-operation to overcome legitimacy gaps or even to produce new legitimacy gaps.

First, delimiting the European legal order raises the function and role of the national legal order in the realisation of market freedoms, equality and justice. Since *Cassis de Dijon*, the ECJ's use of European law has greatly contributed to modernising the national legal orders. This is particularly true with regard to market freedoms. The ECJ pushed the Member States to overhaul their systems of national administrative-economic law and regulation, sometimes dating back to the first half of the twentieth century. When the ECJ sounded the retreat in *Keck*, Member States tended to fall back into *agony*. Politics prevailed over law to the detriment of the market freedoms. Confining the European legal order to the right to equality or to access to justice leads to the simultaneous development of a market-based supranational legal order and a social-policy-based national legal order. The balance between these two legal orders, however, remains fragile. The present turmoil in the Member States on the remodelling of the social welfare state can be seen as a confirmation of the ECJ's policy of keeping matters of material justice outside the European legal order and relying on procedural justice. However, if the social welfare state is reconstructed on the basis of the social values inherent in the European legal order, the European Union will become – or remains – the scapegoat for accusations that it has undermined the social welfare state. The power of the judiciary to balance the conflicting interests of the EU and the Member States is obviously limited.

Secondly, the rights rhetoric, which is so characteristic of the European legal order, has the potential to provoke further judicial activism. The EU has only just started to transform market citizens into European citizens and endow them with appropriate and effective rights. Shaping effective rights, even in the relatively narrow fields of equal treatment and good faith, is still in its infancy.[187] The more the ECJ uses rights to build a European legal order beyond market freedoms, the more it will need to take into account the reverse side of rights – duties.[188] The ECJ has not so far made use of the notion of duties as a means to shape the European legal order. Building duties into the

[187] Reich, *Bürgerrechte in der Europäischen Union*; see, in particular, N. Reich in collaboration with S. Harbacevica, 'Citizenship and Family on Trial: A Fairly Optimistic Overview of Recent Court Practices with Regard to Free Movement of Trade or Persons' (2003) 40 *Common Market Law Review* 615–38.

[188] Morgan, 'Law's British Empire', 729 at 732.

European legal order would increase the legitimacy of a judge-made legal order – and might even contribute to shaping European social values. The question is as simple as it is difficult to answer: what are the legal consequences if EU citizens do not invoke the rights granted to them by the Treaty and by the ECJ? The equal treatment litigation and the good faith litigation are no more than the start of a long debate on this issue.

Thirdly, a further challenge to the fragile relationship between the European legal order and the Member States' legal orders – and for law and politics – results from the development of European remedies. While EU remedies are necessary for the implementation of EU rights – and possibly also EU duties – EU remedies challenge the sovereignty of the Member States, legally speaking, in a field in which the EU either has no competence or has only a very weak competence. The transnational dimension of European remedies will soon become apparent. The number of *Hedley Lomas* types of conflict will increase in the years to come, and it remains to be seen whether the ECJ will manage to defend the monopoly of the European Commission to control law-enforcement in the Member States. The transnational dimension of remedies may point in a different direction. *European* remedies are urgently needed not only by the Commission but also by private litigants to enforce EC law with regard to market freedoms and access to equality and justice. There is more at stake here than the Europe-wide enforcement of EU minimum standards. At the heart of the conflict is the rule of law. If the Member States accept substantial disparities in enforcement, particularly in an enlarged European Union, then the role and rule of European law will be in jeopardy. European remedies are just one means to close that gap.

BIBLIOGRAPHY

Abanulo, A., 'Equal Pay for Work Equal Value: The "Result-Oriented" Approach that Never Was' (1999) 28 *Industrial Law Journal* 365

Adams, J. and Brownsword, R., 'The Unfair Contract Terms Act: A Decade of Discretion' (1988) 104 *Law Quarterly Review* 94

Alter, K. J., 'The European Court's Political Power' (1996) 19 *Western European Politics* 458

'Explaining National Court Acceptance of European Court Jurisprudence: A Critical Evaluation of Theories of Legal Integration' in Slaughter, A., Stone Sweet, A. and Weiler, J. (eds.), *The European Court and National Courts – Doctrine and Jurisprudence: Legal Change in Its Social Context* (Oxford, 1998), 227

Andenas, M. and Jacobs, F., *European Community Law in the English Courts* (Oxford, 1998)

Armstrong, K., 'Legal Integration: Theorizing the Legal Dimension of European Integration' (1998) 36 *Journal of Common Market Studies* 155

Arnull, A., 'Social Policy: The Beat Goes On' (1987) 12 *European Law Review* 56

'What Shall We Do on Sunday?' (1991) 16 *European Law Review* 112

'Current Survey: Anyone for Tripe?' (1993) 18 *European Law Review* 314

'Owning up to Fallibility: Precedent and the Court of Justice' (1993) 30 *Common Market Law Review* 247

Askham, T., Burke, T. and Ramsden, D. (eds.), *Current EC Legal Development Series: EC Sunday Trading Rules* (London, 1990)

Auer, M., 'Good Faith: A Semiotic Approach' (2002) 2 *European Review of Private Law* 279

Bagilhole, B. and Byrne P., 'From Hard to Soft Law and from Equality to Reconciliation in the United Kingdom' in Hantrais, L. (ed.), *Gendered Policies in Europe: Reconciling Employment and Family Life* (Basingstoke, 2000), 124

Barnard, C., 'Sunday Trading: A Drama in Five Acts' (1994) 57 *Modern Law Review* 449

'A European Litigation Strategy: The Case of the Equal Opportunities Commission' in Shaw, J. and More, G., *New Legal Dynamics of the European Union* (Oxford, 1995), 253

'Equal Treatment' in O'Leary, S. and Dashwood, A. (eds.), *The Principle of Equal Treatment in the EC Law* (London, 1997), 59

'The Principle of Equality in the Community Context: P, Grant, Kalanke und Marschall: Four Uneasy Bedfellows?' (1998) 57 *Cambridge Law Journal* 352

Barnard, C. and Hare, I., 'Police Discretion and the Rule of Law: Economic Community Rights versus Civil Rights' (2000) 63 *Modern Law Review* 581

Barnard, C. and Hepple, B., 'Indirect Discrimination: Interpreting Seymour-Smith' (1999) 58 *Cambridge Law Journal* 399

Barnard, C. and Sharpston, E., 'The Changing Face of Article 177 References' (1997) 34 *Common Market Law Review* 1113

Basedow, J., *Von der deutschen zur europäischen Wirtschaftsverfassung* (Tübingen, 1992)

'A Common Contract Law for the Common Market' (1997) 33 *Common Market Law Review* 1169

'Gestaltung rechtsgeschäftlicher Schuldverhältnisse' in *Münchener Kommentar zum Bürgerlichen Gesetzbuch*, vol. 2a, *Schuldrecht Allgemeiner Teil*, §§ 241–432 (4th edn, Munich, 2003), 1057

Beale, H., 'Penalties in Termination Provisions: Review of Recent Cases Including Building and Hire Purchase Contracts' (1988) 104 *Law Quarterly Review* 355

'Legislative Control of Fairness: The Directive on Unfair Terms in Consumer Contracts' in Beatson, J. and Friedman, D. (eds.), *Good Faith and Fault in Contract Law* (Oxford, 1997), 231

Beatson, J., *Anson's Law of Contract* (28th edn, Oxford, 2002)

Beatson, J. and Friedman, D. (eds.), *Good Faith and Fault in Contract Law* (Oxford, 1997)

Bell, M. and Waddington, L., 'Reflecting on Inequalities in European Equality Law' (2003) 28 *European Law Review* 349

Beloff, M., 'Towards a Supreme Court? The British Experience' (1990) 33 *Irish Jurist* 1

Boch, C., 'Case Note on Case C-32/93, Webb v. EMO Air Cargo (UK) Ltd [1994] ECR I-3567 in the House of Lords [1995] 1 WLR 1454' (1996) 33 *Common Market Law Review* 547

Bowers, J. and Moran, E., 'Justification in Direct Sex Discrimination Law: Breaking the Taboo' (2002) 31 *Industrial Law Journal* 307

Bradgate, R., 'Unreasonable Standard Terms' (1997) 60 *Modern Law Review* 582

Bragg, R., 'Implementation of the EC Directive on Unfair Contract Terms in Consumer Contracts: The Department of Trade and Industry Consultation Document' (1994) 53 *Cambridge Law Journal* 29

Bridge, M., *The Sale of Goods* (Oxford, 1998)

'Good Faith in Commercial Contracts' in Brownsword, R., Hird, N. and Howells, G. (eds.), *Good Faith in Contract: Concept and Context* (Aldershot, 1998), 139

Bright, S., 'Legal Studies – Winning the Battle Against Unfair Contract Terms' (2000) 20 *Journal of the Society of Public Teachers of Law* 331

Brown, F., 'The Defeat of the Shops Bill, 1986' in Rush, M. (ed.), *Parliament and Pressure Politics* (Oxford, 1990), 213

Brownsword, R., 'Review of Forte, A. D. (ed.), Good Faith in Contract and Property Law (Oxford, 1999)' (2000) 63 *Modern Law Review* 940

'Individualism, Co-operativism and an Ethic for European Contract Law' (2002) 64 *Modern Law Review* 628

Brownsword, R., Hird, N. and Howells, G. (eds.), *Good Faith in Contract: Concept and Context* (Aldershot, 1998)

Brownsword, R., Howells, G. and Wilhelmsson, T., 'Between Market and Welfare: Some Reflections on Article 3 of the EC Directive on Unfair Terms in Consumer Contracts' in Willett, C. (ed.), *Aspects of Fairness in Contract* (London, 1996), 25

Brunetta d'Usseaux, F., 'Formal and Substantive Aspects of the Transparency Principle in European Private Law' (1997) 5 *Consumer Law Journal* 231

de Búrca, G., 'Giving Effect to European Community Directives' (1992) 55 *Modern Law Review* 215

'The Principle of Proportionality and Its Application in EC Law' (1993) 13 *Yearbook of European Law* 105

Burley, A.-M. and Mattli, W., 'Europe before the Court: A Political Theory of Legal integration' (1993) 1 *International Organization* 41

Burroughs, E., 'The Seller Is Not Liable for ...' (1995) 145 *New Law Journal* 1368

Burrows, N., 'Maternity Rights in Europe – An Embryonic Legal Regime' (1991) 11 *Yearbook of European Law* 273

Campbell, A. and Lardy, H., 'Discrimination against Transsexuals in Employment' (1996) 21 *European Law Review* 412

Cassese, A., Clapham, A. and Weiler, J. (eds.), *Human Rights and the European Community: A Critical Overview* (vol. I), *Human Rights and the European Community: Methods of Protection* (vol. II), *Human Rights and the European Community* (vol. III), (Baden-Baden, 1991)

Chalmers, D., 'The Single Market: From Prima Donna to Journeyman' in Shaw, J. and More, G. (eds.), *New Legal Dynamics of the European Union* (Oxford, 1995), 55

Collins, H., 'CCT, Equal Pay and Market Forces' (1994) 23 *Industrial Law Journal* 341

'Good Faith in European Contract Law' (1994) 14 *Oxford Journal of Legal Studies* 229

'European Private Law and the Cultural Identity of States' (1995) 3 *European Review of Private Law* 353

'Unfair Contracts Terms in the UK' (1996) 81 *Svensk Jurist Tidning* 1

Connolly, M., 'How a European Court of Justice Decision on Equal Pay May Affect British Indirect Discrimination Law' (1996) 1 *Web Journal of Current Legal Issues* 1

Connor, T., 'Community Discrimination Law: No Right to Equal Treatment in Employment in Respect of Same Sex Partner' (1998) 23 *European Law Review* 378

Coote, B., 'Statutes, Unfair Contract Terms Act 1977' (1978) 41 *Modern Law Review* 312

Craig, P., *Administrative Law* (5th edn, London, 2003)

Craig, P. and de Búrca, G. (eds.), *EU Law: Text, Cases and Materials* (3rd edn, Oxford, 1998)

(eds.), *The Evolution of EU Law* (Oxford, 1999)

Curtin, D., 'Scalping the Community Legislator: Occupational Pensions and "Barber"' (1990) 27 *Common Market Law Review* 475

Daintith, T. (ed.), *Implementing EC Law in the United Kingdom* (Chichester, 1995)

Dauses, M. A., *Das Vorabentscheidungsverfahren nach Artikel 177 EG-Vertrag* (2nd edn, Munich, 1995)

Dean, M., 'Unfair Contract Terms: The European Approach' (1993) 56 *Modern Law Review* 581

'Consolidation or Confusion? – The EC Directive on Unfair Contract Terms' (1995) 145 *New Law Journal* 28

'Defining Unfair Terms in Consumer Contracts – Crystal Ball Gazing? Director-General of Fair Trading v. First National Bank plc' (2002) 65 *Modern Law Review* 773

Diamond, P., 'The Shops Act and the EEC Treaty' (1989) 153 *Justice of the Peace* 51

'Sunday Trading and the Sovereignty of Parliament' (1990) 7 *Trading Law* 216

'Dishonourable Defences: The Use of Injunctions and the EEC Treaty – Case Study of the Shops Act 1950' (1991) 54 *Modern Law Review* 72

Dicey, A., *Introduction to the Study of the Law of the Constitution* (10th edn, London, 1959)

Docksey, C., 'The Principles of Equality between Women and Men as a Fundamental Right under Community Law' (1991) 20 *Industrial Law Journal* 258

Duina, F., 'Explaining Legal Implementation in the European Union' (1997) 25 *International Journal of the Sociology of Law* 155

Ellis, E., 'Can Public Safety Provide an Excuse for Sex Discrimination?' (1986) 102 *Law Quarterly Review* 496

'Discrimination on the Ground of Pregnancy in EEC Law' (1991) *Public Law* 159

'Case Note on Case C-127/92, Enderby v. Frenchay Health Authority and the Secretary of State for Health, Judgment of 27 October 1993, not yet reported' (1994) 31 *Common Market Law Review* 387

(ed.), *The Principle of Proportionality in Europe* (Oxford, 1999)

'The Concept of Proportionality in European Sex Discrimination Law' in Ellis, E. (ed.), *The Principle of Proportionality in Europe* (Oxford, 1999), 165

Erhard-Jacqué, R., 'Der Beitrag des Generalanwalts Carl Otto Lenz zur Rechtsprechung des EuGH auf dem Gebiet der Gleichbehandlung von Mann und Frau sowie soziale Sicherheit' (1999) ZEuS 533

Fenwick, H., 'Indirect Discrimination in Equal Pay Claims: Backward Steps in the European Court of Justice?' (1995) 1 *European Public Law* 331

Flynn, L., 'Case Note on C-13/94, P v. S and Cornwall Country Council' (1997) 34 *Common Market Law Review* 367

Forte, A. D. (ed.), *Good Faith in Contract and Property Law* (Oxford, 1999)

Franzen, M., *Privatrechtsangleichung durch die Europäische Gemeinschaft* (Berlin, 1999)

'Der EuGH und das Bürgerliche Recht – dargestellt am Beispiel der EuGH-Urteile "Dietzinger" und "Draehmpaehl"' in Geis, M.-E. and Lorenz, D. (eds.), *Staat, Kirche, Verwaltung: Festschrift für H. Maurer* (Munich, 2001), 889

Fredman, S., 'European Community Discrimination Law: A Critique' (1992) 21 *Industrial Law Journal* 119

'Equal Pay and Justification' (1994) 23 *Industrial Law Journal* 37

'The Poverty of Equality: Pensions and the ECJ' (1996) 25 *Industrial Law Journal* 91

Galanter, M., 'Why the "Haves" Come Out Ahead: Speculations on the Limits of Legal Change' (1974) 9 *Law and Society Review* 95

Garding, H., 'Litigation by Public-Interest Groups in European Law' (1996) 39 *German Yearbook of International Law* 361

Gerber, D., 'Constitutionalizing the Economy: German Neo-liberalism, Competition Law and the "New" Europe' (1994) 42 *American Journal of Comparative Law* 25

Gerstenberg, O., 'The New Europe: Part of the Problem – Or Part of the Solution to the Problem' (2002) 22 *Oxford Journal of Legal Studies* 565

van Gerven, W., 'Bridging the Unbridgeable – Community and National Tort Laws after Francovich and Brasserie' in Micklitz, H.-W. and Reich, N. (eds.), *Public Interest Litigation before European Courts* (Baden-Baden, 1996), 57

'Bridging the Unbridgeable – Community and National Tort Laws after Francovich and Brasserie' (1996) 45 *International and Comparative Law Quarterly* 507

'The Effect of Proportionality on the Actions of Member States of the European Community: National Viewpoints from Continental Europe' in Ellis, E. (ed.), *The Principle of Proportionality* (Oxford, 1999), 37

Lord Goff, 'The Future of the Common Law' (1997) 46 *International and Comparative Law Quarterly* 745

Gold, S., 'District Judge Stephen Gold Explains This and That in the Civil Way' (1999) 149 *New Law Journal* No. 6909, 1556; (1999) 149 *New Law Journal* No. 6910, 1589

Golub, J., 'The Politics of Judicial Discretion: Rethinking the Interaction between National and the European Courts' (1996) 19 *Western European Politics* 360

Goode, R., 'Insularity or Leadership? The Role of the United Kingdom in the Harmonisation of Commercial Law' (2001) 50 *International and Comparative Law Quarterly* 751

Gormley, L., 'Case Study of Torfaen Borough Council v. B&Q plc' (1990) 27 *Common Market Law Review* 141

'References for a Preliminary Ruling: Article 234 from the United Kingdom Viewpoint' (2002) 66 RabelsZ 459

Grabitz, E. and Hilf, M., *Das Recht der Europäischen Union: Kommentar* (Munich, 1999)

C. Greenwood, 'European Community Law' (1991) *All England Annual Review* 141

Griffith, J. A., *The Politics of the Judiciary* (Manchester, 1977)

Grotius, H., *De Jure Belli ac Pacis* (Lugduni, Batavorum, 1919)

Grundmann, S., *Europäisches Schuldvertragsrecht* (Berlin, 1999)

Grundmann, S. and Stuyck, J. (eds.), *An Academic Green Paper on European Contract Law* (London, 2002)

Guest, A. (ed.), *Benjamin's Sale of Goods* (5th edn, London, 1997)

Gurowich, P., 'Comment' in Micklitz, H.-W., 'Obligation of Clarity and Favourable Interpretation to the Consumer (Art. 5)' in European Commission (ed.), *The 'Unfair Terms Directive', Five Years On – Evaluation and Analysis* (Brussels Conference, 1–3 July 1999) (2000), 147

Hakenberg, W., 'Vorabentscheidungsverfahren und europäisches Privatrecht – Erfahrungen aus europäischer Sicht' (2002) 66 RabelsZ 367

Harlow, C. and Rawlings, R. (eds.), *Pressure through Law* (London, 1992)

Hervey, T., 'Justification for Indirect Sex Discrimination in Employment: European Community and United Kingdom Law Compared' (1991) 40 *International and Comparative Law Quarterly* 807

Hess, B., 'Rechtsfragen des Vorabentscheidungsverfahrens' (2002) 66 RabelsZ 470

Hirsch, G., 'Europäischer Gerichtshof und Bundesverfassungsgericht-Kooperation oder Konfrontation' (1996) NJW 2457

Hirschman, A. O., *Exit, Voice and Loyalty* (Cambridge, 1970)

Hoffmann, A., 'Sense of Proportion' in Andenas, M. and Jacobs, F. (eds.), *European Law in the English Courts* (Oxford, 1998), 149

'The Influence of the European Principle of Proportionality upon UK Law' in Ellis, E. (ed.), *The Principle of Proportionality* (Oxford, 1999), 106

Hoffmann, D., 'Consommation – Publicité et protection des consommateurs en droit communautaire' (1987) 46 Fasc. 905

Hondius, E., 'Unfair Contract Terms: Towards a European Law' (1997) 2 *European Review of Private Law* 121

Honeyball, S. and Shaw, J., 'Social Policy: Sex, Law and the Retiring Man' (1991) 16 *European Law Review* 47

Howell, C., 'Unforgiven – British Trade Unionism in Crisis' in Martin, A. *et al.* (eds.), *The Brave New World of European Labor* (Oxford, 1999), 26

Howells, G., 'Good Faith in Consumer Contracting' in Brownsword, R., Hird, N. and Howells, G. (eds.), *Good Faith in Contract: Concept and Context* (Aldershot, 1998), 91

Howells, G. and Weatherill, S., *Consumer Protection Law* (Aldershot, 1995)

Jarvis, M., 'The Sunday Trading Episode: In Defence of the Euro-Defence' (1995) 44 *International and Comparative Law Quarterly* 451

Joerges, C., 'Wettbewerbsschutz und Vertragsgerechtigkeit in den Beziehungen zwischen Automobilherstellern und -händlern: Über die Aufgaben richterlicher Rechtspolitik in "Relationierungsverträgen"' in Broda, C., Deutsch, E., Schreiber, H.-L. and Vogel, H.-J. (eds.), *Festschrift für Rudolf Wassermann* (Neuwied, 1985), 697

'Legitimationsprobleme des europäischen Wirtschaftsrechts und der Vertrag von Maastricht' in Brüggemeier, G. (ed.), *Verfassungen für ein ziviles Europa* (Baden-Baden, 1993), 91

'Die Europäisierung des Privatrechts als Rationalisierungsprozess und als Streit der Disziplinen – Eine Analyse der Richtlinie über missbräuchliche Klauseln in Verbraucherverträgen' (1995) ZEuP 181

'The Europeanisation of Private Law as a Rationalisation Process and as a Contest of Legal Disciplines – An Analysis of the Directive on Unfair Contract Terms in Consumer Contracts' (1995) 3 *European Review of Private Law* 175

'Legislative Folgen legislativer Harmonisierung: ein komplexes Problem und ein unscheinbares Exempel' in Schulte-Nölke, H. and Schulze, R. (eds.), *Europäische Rechtsangleichung und nationale Privatrechte* (Baden-Baden, 1999), 205

'Deliberative Supranationalism – Two Defences' (2002) 8 *European Law Journal* 133

'Europäisierung als Prozess: Notizen zur Debatte um die Kodifizierung des Europäischen Privatrechts', Beitrag zur Berliner Tagung der Deutsch-Französischen Juristenvereinigung, 9–11 October 2003 (manuscript)

'On the Legitimacy of Europeanising Private Law: Consideration on a Justice-Making Law for the EU Multi-Level System' (2003) 7:3 *Electronic Journal of Comparative Law*

'Zur Legitimität der Europäisierung des Privatrechts, Überlegungen zu einem Recht-Fertigungs-Recht für das Mehrebenensystem der EU' in Joerges, C. and Teubner, G. (eds.), *Rechtsverfassungsrecht – Recht-Fertigung zwischen Privatrechtsdogmatik und Gesellschaftstheorie*, Internationale Studien zur Privatrechtstheorie Bd 4 (Baden-Baden, 2003), 183

Joerges, C. and Vos, E. (eds.), *EU Committees: Social Regulation, Law and Politics* (Oxford, 1999)

Johnson, N., 'The Judicial Dimension in British Politics' (1998) 21 *Western European Politics* 148

Jowell, J. and Oliver, D. (eds.), *New Directions in Judicial Review* (London, 1988)

Jowell, J. and Lester, A., 'Proportionality: Neither Novel nor Dangerous' in Jowell, J. and Oliver, D. (eds.), *New Directions in Judicial Review* (London, 1988), 51

Kaye, T., 'Surveying the Scene: A Valuer's Duty of Care' (1989) 52 *Modern Law Review* 841

'Implementing an EC Directive on Unfair Terms' (1995) 3 *Web Journal of Current Legal Issues* 1

Kentridge, J., 'Direct and indirect Discrimination after Enderby' (1994) *Public Law* 198

Kilpatrick, C., 'Community or Communities of Courts in European Integration? Sex Equality Dialogues between UK Courts and the ECJ' (1998) 4 *European Law Journal* 121

'Gender Equality: A Fundamental Dialogue' in Sciarra, S. (ed.), *Labour Law in the Courts: National Judges and the European Court of Justice* (Oxford, 2001), 31

Novitz, T. and Skidmore, P., *The Future of Remedies in Europe* (Oxford, 2000)

Koopmans, T., 'The Technique of the Preliminary Question – A View from the Court of Justice' in Schermers, H. *et al.* (eds.), *Article 177: Experiences and Problems* (The Hague, 1987), 327

'The Birth of European Law at the Cross Roads of Legal Traditions' (1991) 39 *American Journal of Comparative Law* 493

Krimphove, D., *Europäisches Arbeitsrecht* (2nd edn, Munich, 2001)

Lairg, Q., 'Judges and Decision-Makers: The Theory and Practice of Wednesbury Review' (1996) *Public Law* 59

Law Commission [of England and Wales], Consultation Paper No 166, and the Scottish Law Commission, Discussion Paper No 119, 'Unfair Terms in Contracts: A Joint Consultation Paper' (London, 2002)

Lawson, R., 'The Unfair Contract Terms Act: A Progress Report' (1981) 131 *New Law Journal* 933

Leff, A., 'Unconscionability and the Code – The Emperor's New Clause' (1967) 115 *University of Pennsylvania Law Review* 485

Legrand, P., 'European Legal Systems Are Not Converging' (1996) 45 *International and Comparative Law Quarterly* 52

Lenz, C. and Will, G., 'The Preliminary Ruling Procedure and the United Kingdom' (1996) 19 *Fordham International Law Journal* 844

Lester, A., 'The Uncertain Trumpet: References to the Court of Justice from the United Kingdom: Equal Pay and Equal Treatment without Sex Discrimination' in Schermers, H. G. *et al.* (eds.), *Article 177 EEC: Experience and Problems* (The Hague, 1987), 164

Levitski, J., 'The Europeanization of British Style' (1994) 42 *American Journal of Comparative Law* 347

Macdonald, E., 'Scope and Fairness of the Unfair Terms in Consumer Contracts Regulations: Director-General of Fair Trading v. First National Bank' (2002) 65 *Modern Law Review* 763

MacQueen, H., 'Good Faith in the Scots Law of Contract: An Undisclosed Principle' in Forte, A. (ed.), *Good Faith in Contract and Property* (Oxford, 1999), 2

Maduro, M., *We the Court: The European Court of Justice and the European Economic Constitution* (Oxford, 1998)

'Never on a Sunday – What Has (EU) Law Got To Do with It' in Sciarra, S. (ed.), *Labour Law in the Courts: National Judges and the European Court of Justice* (Oxford, 2001) 273

'Europe and the Constitution: What If This Is As Good As It Gets?' in Weiler, J. H. and Wind, M. (eds.), *Rethinking European Constitutionalism* (Cambridge, 2003), 74

Maggs, C., 'Consumer Concerns – There Is Room for Improvement to the Unfair Terms in Consumer Contracts Regulations, Coming into Force in July' (1995) *Law Society Gazette* 24

Maher, I., 'Community Law in the National Legal Order' (1998) 36 *Journal of Common Market Studies* 237

Mancini, G. F. and Keeling, D. T., 'Democracy and the European Court of Justice' (1994) 175 *Modern Law Review* 175

Mancini, G. F. and Keeling, D. T., 'Language, Culture and Politics in the Life of the European Court of Justice' (1995) 1 *Columbia Journal of European Law* 397

Markesinis, B. S., 'Learning from Europe and Learning in Europe' in Markesinis, B. S. (ed.), *The Gradual Convergence: Foreign Ideas, Foreign Influences and English Law on the Eve of the 21st Century* (Oxford, 1994), 1

Mattli, W. and Slaughter, A.-M., 'Constructing the European Community Legal System from the Ground Up: The Role of Individual Litigants and National Courts' (Robert Schuman Centre, European University Institute, 1996), 56

McCrudden, C., 'The Effectiveness of European Equality Law: National Mechanisms for Enforcing Gender Equality Law in the Light of European Requirements' (1993) 13 *Oxford Journal of Legal Studies* 320

McIlroy, J., 'Journey into Europe' in McIlroy, J. (ed.), *Trade Unions in Britain Today* (2nd edn, Manchester, 1995)

McKendrick, E., 'Good Faith: A Matter of Principle?' in Forte, A. (ed.), *Good Faith in Contract and Property Law* (Oxford, 1999), 39

Menon, A. and Weatherill, S., 'Legitimacy, Accountability, and Delegation in the European Union' in Arnull, A. and Wincott, D. (eds.), *Accountability and Legitimacy in the European Union* (Oxford, 2002), 113

Michaels, R., 'Im Westen nichts Neues?' (2002) 66 RabelsZ 97

Micklitz, H.-W., 'Consumer Rights' in Cassese, A., Clapham, A. and Weiler, J. H. (eds.), *European Union – The Human Rights Challenge, Human Rights and the European Community: The Substantive Law* (Florence, 1991), 53

'Organisierte Rechtsdurchsetzung im Binnenmarkt' (1992) KritV 172

'Das Keck-Urteil des EuGH – Vom Binnenmarkt zurück zum Freihandel?' (1994) IStR 86

'Privatisation of Access to Justice in the European Legal Order' in Wilhelmsson, T. and Hurri, S. (eds.), *From Dissonance to Sense* (Aldershot, 1998), 505

'Social Justice in European Private Law' (1999/2000) 19 *Yearbook of European Law* 167

'Obligation of Clarity and Favourable Interpretation to the Consumer (Art. 5)' in European Commission (ed.), *The 'Unfair Terms Directive', Five Years On – Evaluation and Analysis* (Brussels Conference, 1–3 July 1999) (2000), 147

Micklitz, H.-W. and Reich, N. (eds.), *Public Interest Litigation before European Courts* (Baden-Baden, 1996)

Micklitz, H.-W., Roethe, T. and Weatherill, S., *Federalism and Responsibility* (London, 1994)

Micklitz, H.-W. and Weatherill, S., *European Economic Law* (Aldershot, 1997)

Miller, C., Harvey, B. and Parry, D., *Consumer and Trading Law: Text, Cases and Materials* (Oxford, 1998)

Mitchell, C., 'Unfair Terms in Consumer Contracts' (2000) 116 *Law Quarterly Review* 557

Moffat, G. and Luckhaus, L., 'Occupational Pension Schemes, Equality and Europe: A Decade of Change' (1998) 20 *Journal of Social Welfare and Family Law* 1

Moore, S., 'Sex, Pregnancy and Dismissal' (1994) 19 *European Law Review* 653

'"Justice Doesn't Mean a Free Lunch": The Application of the Principles of Equal Pay to Occupational Pension Schemes' (1995) 20 *European Law Review* 159

More, G., 'The Principle of Equal Treatment: From Market Unifier to Fundamental Right?' in Craig, P. and de Búrca, G. (eds.), *The Evolution of EU Law* (Oxford, 1999), 517

Morgan, J., 'Law's British Empire' (2002) 22 *Oxford Journal of Legal Studies* 729

Morris, P., 'Sex Discrimination, Public Order and the European Court' (1987) *Public Law* 334

Mortelmans, K., 'Article 30 of the EEC Treaty and Legislation Relating to Market Circumstances: Time to Consider a New Definition?' (1991) 28 *Common Market Law Review* 115

Müller-Graff, P.-C. (ed.), *Gemeinsames Privatrecht in der Europäischen Gemeinschaft* (Baden-Baden, 1999)

Lord Mummery, 'The Community Law Impact on Employment Cases' in Andenas, M. and Jacobs, F. (eds.), *European Community Law in the English Courts* (Oxford, 1998), 191

Napier, B., 'Proving Equal Value – The European Court Lends a Hand' (1993) 19 *New Law Journal* 1648

Niglia, L., 'The Non-Europeanisation of Private Law' (2001) 4 *European Review of Private Law* 575

Norton, P., *The British Policy* (4th edn, New York, 2000)

Oliver, P., 'Sunday Trading and Article 30 of the Treaty of Rome' (1991) 20 *Industrial Law Journal* 298

Free Movement of Goods in the EC (3rd edn, London, 1996)

Olson, M., *The Logic of Collective Action* (Cambridge, 1971)

Palmer, N., 'Exclusions of Liability under Non-Contractual Bailments and Unfair Contract Terms Act – II' (1978) 128 *New Law Journal* 915

'Clarifying the Unfair Contract Terms Act' (1986) 7 *Business Law Review* 57

Palmer, N. and Yates, D., 'The Future of the Unfair Contract Terms Act 1977' (1981) 40 *Cambridge Law Journal* 108

Petersmann, E.-U., 'Constitutionalism and International Organizations' (1997) 17 *Northwestern Journal of International Law and Business* 398

Pfeiffer, T., 'Richtlinie 93/13/EWG des Rates über mißbräuchliche Klauseln in Verbraucherverträgen' in Grabitz, E. and Hilf, M. (eds.), *Das Recht der Europäischen Union* (Munich, 1999), 1

Pflug, H.-J., *Kontrakt und Status im Recht der Allgemeinen Geschäftsbedingungen* (Munich, 1986)

Radbruch, G., *Der Geist des Englischen Rechts* (Göttingen, 1956)

Rawlings, R., 'The Eurolaw Game: Some Deductions from a Saga' (1993) 20 *Journal of Law and Society* 309

Rawls, J., *Justice as Fairness* (Cambridge, 2001)

Reich, N., 'Rechtsprobleme grenzüberschreitender irreführender Werbung im Binnenmarkt' (1992) 56 RabelsZ 444

'The November Revolution of the European Court: Keck, Meng and Audi Revisited' (1994) 31 *Common Market Law Review* 459

'A European Constitution for Citizens – Reflections on the Rethinking of Union and European Law' (1997) 3 *European Law Journal* 131

Bürgerrechte in der Europäischen Union: Subjektive Rechte von Unionsangehörigen und Drittstaatsangehörigen unter besonderer Berücksichtigung der Rechtslage nach der Rechtsprechung des EuGH und dem Vertrag von Amsterdam (Baden-Baden, 1999)

'Verbraucherpolitik und Verbraucherschutz im Vertrag von Amsterdam' (1999) 14 VuR 3

Reich, N. and Micklitz, H.-W., *Europäisches Verbraucherrecht* (4th edn, Baden-Baden, 2003)

Reich, N., with the collaboration of Harbacevica, S., 'Citizenship and Family on Trial: A Fairly Optimistic Overview of Recent Court Practices with Regard to Free Movement of Trade of Persons' (2003) 40 *Common Market Law Review* 615

Reich, N., with the collaboration of Leahy, D., *Internal Market and Diffuse Interests: An Introduction to EC Trade Law* (Brussels, 1990)

Reifner, U., 'Good Faith: Interpretation or Limitation of Contracts? The Power of German Judges in Financial Services Law' in Brownsword, R., Hird, N. and Howells, G. (eds.), *Good Faith in Contract: Concept and Context* (Aldershot, 1998), 269

Reynolds, F., 'The Unfair Contract Terms Act 1977' (1978) *Lloyd's Maritime and Commercial Law Quarterly Review* 201

'Unfair Contract Terms' (1994) 110 *Law Quarterly Review* 1

'Classification of Statements' in Guest, A. (ed.), *Benjamin's Sale of Goods* (5th edn, London, 1997), paras. 10-001 to 10-039

Robert, G., 'Commercial Contracts and the Commercial Court' (1984) 100 *Law Quarterly Review* 382

Rostow, E. V., 'The Democratic Character of Judicial Review' (1952) 66 *Harvard Law Review* 193

Roth, W.-H., 'Generalklauseln im Europäischen Privatrecht' in Basedow, J., Hopt, K. and Kötz, H. (eds.), *Festschrift für Ulrich Drobnig* (Tübingen, 1998), 135

Rott, P., 'Injunctions for the Protection of Consumers' Interests after the Implementation of Directive 98/27/EC into German and English Law' (2001) 24 *Journal of Consumer Policy* 401

'Effektiver Rechtsschutz vor missbräuchlichen AGB – Zum Cofidis-Urteil des EuGH' (2003) 14 EuZW 5

Rott, P. and Butters, B., 'Öffentliche Dienstleistungen und Vertragsgerechtigkeit im Lichte des Gemeinschaftsrechts' (1999) 3 VuR 75

Samek, R., 'The Objective Theory of Contract and the Rule in L'Estrange v. Graucob' (1974) 52 *Canadian Bar Review* 351

Schalla, E., *Das Sonntagsverkaufsverbot in England und Wales: unter Berücksichtigung europäischen und deutschen Rechts* (Cologne, 1995)

Scharpf, F. W., *Governing in Europe: Effective and Democratic?* (Oxford, 1999)

Schiek, D., 'Diskriminierung wegen "Rasse" oder "ethnischer Herkunft" – Probleme bei der Umsetzung der Richtlinie 2000/43/EG im Arbeitsrecht' (2003) 2 AuR 44

Schwab, M., 'Der Dialog zwischen dem EuGH und nationalen Exegeten bei der Auslegung von Gemeinschaftsrecht und angeglichenem Recht' (2000) 3 ZGR 446

Sciarra, S., 'Dynamic Integration of National and Community Sources: The Case of Night-Work for Women' in Hervey, T. K. and O'Keeffe, D. (eds.), *Sex Equality Law in the European Union* (Chichester, 1996), 99

'Integration Through Courts: Article 177 as a Pre-Federal Device' in Sciarra, S. (ed.), *Labour Law in the Courts: National Judges and the European Court of Justice* (Oxford, 2001), 1

'Job Centre: An Illustrative Example of Strategic Litigation' in Sciarra, S. (ed.), *Labour Law in the Courts: National Judges and the European Court of Justice* (Oxford, 2001), 241

Sealy, L., 'Unfair Contract Terms Act 1977' (1978) 37 *Cambridge Law Journal* 15

Sedley, S., 'The Sound of Silence: Constitutional Law without a Constitution' (1994) 110 *Law Quarterly Review* 270

Shapiro, M., 'Comparative Law and Comparative Politics' (1980) 53 *Southern California Law Review* 537

Shaw, J., 'European Community Judicial Method: Its Application to Sex Discrimination' (1990) 19 *Industrial Law Journal* 228

Shrubsall, V., 'Protective Practices and the Equal Treatment Directive' (1987) 16 *Industrial Law Journal* 118

Skidmore, P., 'Can Transsexuals Suffer Sex Discrimination?' (1997) 19 *Journal of Social Welfare and Family Law* 105

'Sex, Gender and Comparators in Employment Discrimination' (1997) 26 *Industrial Law Journal* 51

Slaughter, A.-M., Stone Sweet, A. and Weiler, J. H. (eds.), *The European Court and National Courts Doctrine and Jurisprudence: Legal Change in Its Social Context* (Oxford, 1997)

Smith, L., 'Fischereipolitik, EG-Recht und britische Justiz' (1992) EuZW 308

Sobich, P., 'Verfahrensrechtliche Kontrolle "unfairer" AGB in Großbritannien: The Unfair Terms in Consumer Contracts Regulations 1994' (1998) 9 RIW 684

Soskice, D., 'Divergent Production Regimes: Co-ordinated and Unco-ordinated Market Economies in the 1980s and 1990s' in Kitschelt, H., Lange, P., Marks, G. and Stephens, J. (eds.), *Continuity and Change in Contemporary Capitalism* (Cambridge, 1999), 271

Steiner, J., 'Drawing the Line: Uses and Abuses of Article 30 EEC' (1992) 29 *Common Market Law Review* 749

Steiner, J. and Woods, L., *Textbook on EC Law* (5th edn, London, 1996)

Steyn, J., 'The Role of Good Faith and Fair Dealing in Contract Law: A Hair-Shirt Philosophy?' (1991) *Denning Law Journal* 131

'Contract Law: Fulfilling the Reasonable Expectations of Honest Men' (1997) 113 *Law Quarterly Review* 433

Stone Sweet, A., 'Constitutional Dialogues in the European Community' in Slaughter, A.-M., Stone Sweet, A. and Weiler, J. H. (eds.), *The European Court and National Courts – Doctrine and Jurisprudence: Legal Change in Its Social Context* (Oxford, 1998), 303

Stone Sweet, A. and Brunell, T. L., 'The European Court and the National Courts: A Statistical Analysis of Preliminary References' (1998) 92 *American Political Science Review* 63

Stone Sweet, A., Brunell, T. L. and Sandholtz, W., 'European Integration and Supranational Governance' (1997) 4 *Journal of European Public Policy* 297

Stone Sweet, A. and Sandholtz, W. (eds.), *European Integration and Supranational Governance* (Oxford, 1998)

Storme, M., 'Harmonisation of the Law on (Substantive) Validity of Contracts (Illegality and Immorality)' in Basedow, J., Hopt, K. and Kötz, H. (eds.), *Festschrift für Ulrich Drobnig* (Tübingen, 1998), 195

Stott, D., 'What Price Certainty?' (2002) 3 *European Law Review* 351

Stratigaki, M., 'The European Union and the Equal Opportunities Process' in Hantrais, L. (ed.), *Gendered Policies in Europe* (Basingstoke, 2000), 27

Streit, M. and Mussler, W., 'The Economic Constitution of the European Community – From "Rome" to "Maastricht"' (1994) 5 *Constitutional Political Economy* 319

Stuyck, J., 'Patterns of Justice in the European Constitutional Charter. Minimum Harmonization in the Field of Consumer Law' in Krämer, L., Micklitz, H.-W. and Tonner, K. (eds.), *Law and Diffuse Interests in the European Legal Order: Liber Amicorum Norbert Reich* (Baden-Baden, 1997), 279

'Judgment 27 June 2000, Joined Cases C-240/98 to C-244/96 Océano Grupo Editorial SA v. Rocio Murciano Quintero and Salvat Editore SA v. José M. Sànchez Alcón Prades *et al.*, nyr' (2001) 38 *Common Market Law Review* 719

Szyszczak, E., '"The Status To Be Accorded to Motherhood": Case C-32/93 Webb v. EMO Air Cargo (UK) Ltd' (1995) 58 *Modern Law Review* 860

'Positive Action after Kalanke' (1996) 59 *Modern Law Review* 876

Teubner, G., 'Legal Irritants: Good Faith in British Law or How Unifying Law Ends Up in New Divergences' (1998) 61 *Modern Law Review* 11

Thomas, R., 'Law and Politics' in Holliday, I., Gamble, A. and Parry, G. (eds.), *Fundamentals in British Politics* (Basingstoke, 1999), 142

Threlfall, M., 'Taking Stock and Looking Ahead' in Hantrais, L. (ed.), *Gendered Policies in Europe* (Basingstoke, 2000), 180

Tonner, K., 'Die Rolle des Verbraucherrechts bei der Entwicklung eines europäischen Zivilrechts' (1996) JZ 533

Treitel, G., *The Law of Contract* (11th edn, London, 2003)

Volcansek, M., 'Supranational Courts in a Political Context' in Volcansek, M. (ed.), *Law above Nations* (Gainesville, 1997), 1

Vos, E., *Institutional Frameworks of Community Health and Safety Regulation, Committees, Agencies and Private Bodies* (Oxford, 1999)

Wagner, C. and Althen, R., 'Umsetzung der Richtlinie des Rates über mißbräuchliche Klauseln in Verbraucherverträgen im Vereinigten Königreich' (1995) 3 RIW 546

Wallace, C., 'European Integration and Legal Culture: Indirect Sex Discrimination in the French Legal System' (1999) 19 *Legal Studies* 397

'Community Sex Discrimination in National Courts: A Legal Cultural Comparison' in Shaw, J. (ed.), *Social Policy in an Evolving EU* (Oxford, 2000)

Watson, R., 'Six Months On: Unfair Contract Terms at Work' (1995/6) 12 *Fair Trading* 14

Watts, P., 'Consumer Concern – The New Regulations on Unfair Terms in Consumer Contracts Are Disappointingly Unclear in Their Drafting and Scope' (1995) *Law Society Guardian Gazette* 14

Weatherill, S., 'Compulsory Notification of Draft Technical Standards: The Contribution of Directive 83/189/EEC to the Management of the Internal Market' (1996) 16 *Yearbook of European Law* 129

'Recent Case Law Concerning the Free Movement of Goods: Mapping the Frontiers of Market Deregulation' (1999) 36 *Common Market Law Review* 51

'Addressing Problems of Imbalanced Implementation in EC Law: Remedies in an Institutional Perspective' in Kilpatrick, C., Novitz, T. and Skidmore, P. (eds.), *The Future of Remedies* (Oxford and Portland, 2000), 87

'Pre-emption, Harmonization and the Distribution of Competences to Regulate the Internal Market' in Barnard, S. and Scott, J., *The Law of the Single European Market* (Oxford, 2002), 42

'Competence Creep and Competence Control' (2004) 23 *Yearbook of European Law*, forthcoming

Weatherill, S. and Beaumont, P., *EU Law* (3rd edn, London, 1999)

Weiler, J. H., 'The Transformation of Europe' (1991) 100 *Yale Law Journal* 2403

'Journey to an Unknown Destination: A Retrospective and Prospective of the European Court of Justice in the Arena of Political Integration' (1993) 31 *Journal of Common Market Studies* 417

'The European Court of Justice and Its Interlocutors' (1994) 26 *Comparative Political Studies* 510

'The Constitution of the Common Market Place: Text and Context in the Evolution of the Free Movement of Goods' in Craig, P. and de Búrca, G., *The Evolution of EU Law* (London, 1999), 349

Ein christliches Europa, Erkundungsgänge (Salzburg and Munich, 2004)

Weiler, J. H., Haltern, U. R. and Meyer, F. C., 'European Democracy and Its Critique' (1995) 18 *Western European Politics* 4

Weisbrod, B (ed.), *Public Interest Law – An Economic and Institutional Analysis* (Berkeley, 1978)

Whincup, M., *Consumer Legislation in the United Kingdom and the Republic of Ireland* (New York, 1980)

White, E., 'In Search of the Limits of Article 30 of the EEC Treaty' (1989) 26 *Common Market Law Review* 235

Whittaker, S., 'Unfair Contract Terms, Public Services and the Construction of a European Conception of Contract' (2000) 116 *Law Quarterly Review* 95

'Judicial Interventionism and Consumer Contracts' (2001) 117 *Law Quarterly Review* 215

'Assessing the Fairness of Contract Terms' (2004) *Zeitschrift für Europäisches Privatrecht* 75

Whittaker, S. and Zimmermann, R., 'Good Faith in European Contract Law: Surveying the Legal Landscape' in Zimmermann, R. and Whittaker, S. (eds.), *Good Faith in European Contract Law* (Cambridge, 2000), 7

Whittle, R. and Bell, M., 'Between Social Policy and Union Citizenship: The Framework Directive on Equal Treatment in Employment' (2002) 27 *European Law Review* 677

Wieacker, F., 'Foundation of European Legal Cultures' (1990) 38 *American Journal of Comparative Law* 1

Wilhelmsson, T., 'Public Interest Litigation on Unfair Terms' in Micklitz, H.-W. and Reich, N. (eds.), *Public Interest Litigation before European Courts* (Baden-Baden, 1996), 385

'Is There a European Consumer Law – And Should There Be One?' (Centro di studi e richerche di diritto comparato e straneiro, Saggi, Conferenze et Seminari) (Rome, 2000), 41

Wilkinson, H., 'Unfair Contract Terms – Hydra-Headed Monsters' (1999) 149 *New Law Journal* 773

Willett, C. (ed.), *Aspects of Fairness in Contract* (London, 1996)

'From Reindeers to Confident Consumers: UK Consumer Bodies and the Unfair Terms Directive' in Micklitz, H.-W. and Reich, N. (eds.), *Public Interest Litigation before European Courts* (Baden-Baden, 1996), 403

'The Directive on Unfair Terms in Consumer Contracts and Its Implementation in the United Kingdom' (1997) 2 *European Review of Private Law* 223

'Good Faith and Consumer Contract Terms' in Brownsword, R., Hird, N. and Howells, G. (eds.), *Good Faith in Contract: Concept and Context* (Aldershot, 1998), 67

Wintemute, R., 'When Is Pregnancy Discrimination Indirect Sex Discrimination?' (1998) 27 *Industrial Law Journal* 23

Wynn, M., 'Equal Pay and Gender Segregation' (1994) 110 *Law Quarterly Review* 556

'Pregnancy Discrimination: Equality, Protection or Reconciliation' (1999) 62 *Modern Law Review* 435

INDEX